*Modern Greece*

**Recent Titles in Understanding Modern Nations**

Modern China
*Xiaobing Li*

Modern Spain
*Enrique Ávila López*

Modern Mexico
*James D. Huck Jr.*

Modern India
*John McLeod*

Modern Saudi Arabia
*Valerie Anishchenkova*

Modern Brazil
*Javier A. Galván*

# *MODERN GREECE*

**Elaine Thomopoulos, Editor**

Understanding Modern Nations

BLOOMSBURY ACADEMIC
NEW YORK • LONDON • OXFORD • NEW DELHI • SYDNEY

BLOOMSBURY ACADEMIC
Bloomsbury Publishing Inc
1385 Broadway, New York, NY 10018, USA
50 Bedford Square, London, WC1B 3DP, UK
29 Earlsfort Terrace, Dublin 2, Ireland

BLOOMSBURY, BLOOMSBURY ACADEMIC and the Diana logo
are trademarks of Bloomsbury Publishing Plc

First published in the United States of America by ABC-CLIO 2022
Paperback edition published by Bloomsbury Academic 2025

Copyright © Bloomsbury Publishing Inc, 2025

COVER PHOTOS: Acropolis, Athens, Greece. (Sven Hansche/Dreamstime);
Santorini, Village of Fira. (JOHN KELLERMAN/Alamy Stock Photo);
Greek Presidential Guard. (Stephen Hogg/Alamy Stock Photo); Crete Island, Greece.
(Smallredgirl/Dreamstime)

All rights reserved. No part of this publication may be reproduced or
transmitted in any form or by any means, electronic or mechanical,
including photocopying, recording, or any information storage or retrieval
system, without prior permission in writing from the publishers.

Bloomsbury Publishing Inc does not have any control over, or responsibility for,
any third-party websites referred to or in this book. All internet addresses given
in this book were correct at the time of going to press. The author and publisher
regret any inconvenience caused if addresses have changed or sites have
ceased to exist, but can accept no responsibility for any such changes.

Library of Congress Cataloging-in-Publication Data
Names: Thomopoulos, Elaine Cotsirilos, editor.
Title: Modern Greece / Elaine Thomopoulos, editor.
Description: Santa Barbara, California : ABC-CLIO, an imprint of ABC-CLIO,
LLC, [2022] | Series: Understanding modern nations | Includes bibliographical
references and index.
Identifiers: LCCN 2021023090 (print) | LCCN 2021023091 (ebook) |
ISBN 9781440854910 (print) | ISBN 9781440854927 (ebook)
Subjects: LCSH: Greece—History—20th century—Encyclopedias. | Greece—
History—21st century—Encyclopedias.
Classification: LCC DF833 .M63 2022 (print) | LCC DF833 (ebook) |
DDC 949.507/603—dc23
LC record available at https://lccn.loc.gov/2021023090
LC ebook record available at https://lccn.loc.gov/2021023091

ISBN: HB: 978-1-4408-5491-0
PB: 979-8-7651-4110-6
ePDF: 978-1-4408-5492-7
eBook: 979-8-2161-1856-5

Series: Understanding Modern Nation

To find out more about our authors and books visit www.bloomsbury.com
and sign up for our newsletters.

# Contents

# Series Foreword

We live in an evolving world, a world that is becoming increasingly globalized by the minute. Cultures collide and blend, leading to new customs and practices that exist alongside long-standing traditions. Advancing technologies connect lives across the globe, affecting those from densely populated urban areas to those who dwell in the most remote locations in the world. Governments are changing, leading to war and violence but also to new opportunities for those who have been oppressed. The *Understanding Modern Nations* series seeks to answer questions about cultures, societies, and customs in various countries around the world.

*Understanding Modern Nations* is geared toward readers wanting to expand their knowledge of the world, ideal for high school students researching specific countries, undergraduates preparing for studies abroad, and general readers interested in learning more about the world around them. Each volume in the series focuses on a single country, with coverage on Africa, the Americas, Asia and the Pacific, and Europe.

Each country volume contains 16 chapters focusing on various aspects of culture and society in each country. The chapters begin with an Overview, which is followed by short entries on key topics, concepts, ideas, and biographies pertaining to the chapter's theme. In a way, these volumes serve as "thematic encyclopedias," with entries organized for the reader's benefit. Following a general Preface and Introduction, each volume contains chapters on the following themes:

- Geography
- History
- Government and Politics
- Economy
- Religion and Thought
- Social Classes and Ethnicity
- Gender, Marriage, and Sexuality
- Education
- Language
- Etiquette
- Literature and Drama
- Art and Architecture

- Music and Dance
- Food
- Leisure and Sports
- Media and Popular Culture

Each entry concludes with a list of cross references and Further Readings, pointing readers to additional print and electronic resources that might prove useful.

Following the chapters are appendices, including "A Day in the Life" feature, which depicts "typical" days in the lives of people living in that country, from students to farmers to factory workers to stay-at-home and working mothers. A Glossary, Facts and Figures section, and Holidays chart round out the appendices. Volumes include a Selected Bibliography, as well as sidebars that are scattered throughout the text.

The volumes in the *Understanding Modern Nations* series are not intended to be comprehensive compendiums about every nation of the world, but instead are meant to serve as introductory texts for readers, examining key topics from major countries studied in the high school curriculum as well as important transitioning countries that make headlines daily. It is our hope that readers will gain an understanding and appreciation for cultures and histories outside of their own.

# PREFACE

"You are Greek? There are modern Greeks today?" My sister Pauline was asked these questions by a fellow student at North Texas University. This was decades ago, but even today, many Americans know about the ancient Greeks and their contribution to Western civilization but are clueless about the Greeks of today. They have been taught about the beginning of democratic governance, the artistic and architectural achievements such as the Parthenon, and the contributions of Socrates, Pythagoras, and Aristotle. They remember the Greek myths they learned in school and that the New Testament was written in Greek. They know about the Greece of ancient times, but they know little about the Greece of modern times. This book bridges that gap and brings the reader an up-to-date story of Greece, with an exploration of various themes found throughout the book, including the influence of ancient Greece on the Greece of today, the diverse people of Greece, and the interaction and influence of foreign powers, including the United States.

In this thematic encyclopedia about contemporary Greece, distinguished scholars explore Greece's rich history, culture, and traditions, as well as the economic woes, influx of refugees, and social justice issues now facing Greece. This fascinating book for students, teachers, tourists, and the general public is organized into the following topics: geography; history; government and politics; economy; religion and thought; social classes and ethnicity; gender, marriage, and sexuality; education; language; etiquette; literature and drama; art and architecture; music and dance; food; leisure and sports; and media and popular culture. Each chapter is followed by entries that focus on particular topics within these broad categories.

The easy-to-read chapters, as well as a timeline, thirty-one photographs, tables, sidebars, maps, and an index, enable a reader to gain a comprehensive understanding of Greece. Of particular interest is the "Day in the Life" section that captures the activities of a high school student, a farmer in a small island village, a retired couple struggling on a limited income, and a bank employee in Athens who has seen her income reduced by 15 percent because of the austerity measures that the government has imposed. The advantage of this thematic encyclopedia is that the readers can focus on a particular topic, since each entry can be read and understood without reading the book in its entirety.

The volume has sixteen chapters. Chapter 1, "Geography," describes Greece's topology—its mountains, seashore, and farmland, as well as climate, which in the summer lures sun worshippers to its beaches but in winter delights skiers with abundant snow. Entries in the chapter cover its various regions and major cities and its delightful national parks and protected areas. They also describe its abundant wildlife and vegetation and the effects of pollution and erosion.

Chapter 2, "History," gives an overview of the history from ancient times to the present. By profiling the biographies of twenty-two people, the reader becomes aware of the diverse personalities that shaped the nation. A timeline puts the whole of Greek history in perspective.

Chapter 3, "Government and Politics," traces the metamorphosis of Greece politics after the fall of the junta, a military dictatorship, in 1974. It presents Greece's return to democracy, its system of government, and the basic rights awarded to the populace. Entries describe the corruption rampant in Greece, its foreign policy, and the political arena. The latter includes the emergence of the ultranationalist party Golden Dawn and the radical left party SYZIRA that governed the country from 2015 to 2019.

Chapter 4, "Economy," describes the present economic crisis and its origins, the austerity measures imposed on the people, and Greece's industries, including agriculture, shipping, and tourism.

Chapter 5, "Religion and Thought," covers the Greek Orthodox religion, with which about 90 percent of the people living in Greece identify, as well as other minority religions. The relationship of church and state and freedom of religion is also discussed, as well as the fascinating belief in the "evil eye."

Chapter 6, "Social Classes and Ethnicity," highlights the diversity within Greece and addresses a new phenomenon: the arrival of immigrants and refugees who are changing the character of the country.

Chapter 7, "Gender, Marriage, and Sexuality," outlines the changing role of women and the family, as well as the struggles of the LGBT community to gain acceptance.

Chapter 8, "Education," takes a thorough look at the educational system from preschool to graduate school, including efforts to make education available to refugee children, special needs children, and adults who did not complete high school.

Chapter 9, "Language," outlines not only the Greek language but also minority and disappearing languages and describes gestures, including those to avoid.

Chapter 10, "Etiquette," explains Greek concepts such as *philotimo*, living according to a code of honor that includes kindness and helping others, and *philoxenia*, welcoming of strangers. It examines proper etiquette during everyday life or at special occasions such as weddings or baptisms. The Greeks have a long tradition of expressing their struggles and triumphs through literature and drama.

Chapter 11, "Literature and Drama," profiles ancient bards such as Homer and also modern authors such as the Nobel Prize–winning literary giants Odysseas Elytis and George Seferis.

Chapter 12, "Art and Architecture," reviews the art and architecture that can been seen in Greece today, including the iconic Parthenon of ancient Greece, the numerous neoclassical buildings that were built during the reign of the first king of Greece in the nineteenth century, traditional arts like embroidery and metalworking, and contemporary art and architecture.

Chapter 13, "Music and Dance," vivaciously brings to light the variety of musical expressions that have developed in Greece, including the centuries-old Byzantine Greek Orthodox Church music; contemporary classical music in the Western tradition, *rebetiko*, which some have compared to the African American blues, as well as the many different types of traditional folk music and dance.

Chapter 14, "Food," which explores the origin of Greek cuisine dating back to ancient Greece, is one of the most delightful chapters. It also presents contemporary food culture and regional variations.

Chapter 15, "Leisure and Sports," brings readers a picture of how Greeks have fun, whether it is enjoying soccer or basketball, hanging out with family or friends in outdoor cafés or the bars, or taking a leisurely vacation by the sea.

Chapter 16, "Media and Popular Culture," explores how print media, television, film, and social media influence the lives of the Greek people, as well as the changes in media that have occurred as a result of the recent financial crisis. For example, the lack of funding for films has resulted in low-budget films and collaboration with other European and international producers.

*Modern Greece* has been a labor of love for me. Especially gratifying was the privilege I had in working with the writers of this book, an amazing group of scholars. They include Alexander Billinis, Nikos Christofis, Beatriz Badikian-Gartler, Angelyn Balodimas-Bartolomei, Harriette Condes-Zervakis, Kosta Dalageorgas, Alexander Fatouros, Georgia Giannakopoulou, Susanna M. Hoffman, Marianthe Karanikas, Katherine Kalaidis, Aphrodite Matsakis, Daphne Nicolitsas, Nick Poulakis, Anna Poupou, John Psiharis, Evaggelos Vallianatos, Angeliki Varela, and Theodore G. Zervas. I could have not completed the book without their excellent research and writing skills.

Two of the contributors, Alexander Fatouros and Anna Poupou, also provided photographs. These beautiful pictures and those by Susan Goldman, Irene Loutzaki, Andreas Theoktistou, and John Vlahakis added a welcome dimension to the book. As they say, a picture is worth a thousand words.

I especially appreciate the valuable assistance given to me or to the other contributors by Georgios Anagnostou, George Athemeliotis, Paris Papamichas Chronakis, Litsa Dalageorgas, George Dervis, Thomas Gallant, Nancy Cronkite, Zoi Kavvadas, Rev. Paul Martin, Pauline Nugent, Alexander Rassogianis, John Rassogianis, Jeanne Shuler, Mathieu Sussman, and Angeliki Tsiotinou. Some read the book in whole or in part and made insightful suggestions. Others helped by doing research or providing bibliographic references.

Computer skills are crucial to writing a modern-day book. I learned the intricacies of the computer through the tutoring of my computer gurus: Brian Jackson of the Lincoln Township Library, Stevensville, Michigan, and Ralph Rumph of the St. Joseph and Lincoln Township Senior Center, St. Joseph, Michigan.

The writing groups that have given me excellent guidance include Isabel Jackson's Group at the Box Factory for the Arts in St. Joseph Michigan; the Westmont Library

Group in Westmont, Illinois; and Richard Blake's group, which met at the Bridgman Library in Bridgman, Michigan. Also thanks to Anne Vandermolen and April Satanek, who met with me monthly at our writer's group at the Lincoln Township Library in Stevensville, Michigan. I also am grateful to Denise Malevitis from the Bridgman Library, who helped me locate books through the interlibrary loan system.

I could not have completed the book without Kaitlin Ciarmiello, senior acquisitions editor at ABC-CLIO. I had worked with her on my other book, *History of Greece*, and was thrilled to be the recipient of her expert and patient guidance once again. I also thank Erin Ryan, specialist, editorial operations, from ABC-CLIO and the editorial team at Amnet Systems for their help in bringing the book to fruition.

I owe a lot of credit to my family for supporting me in this endeavor, and especially to my late husband and best friend, Nick. He encouraged me to take on this ambitious project, and in the early stages of the book, even when he became gravely ill, he supported me wholeheartedly. In spirit, he has been with me every step of the way. I dedicate the book to him.

# INTRODUCTION

Greece seems like a paradise of sun, sand, and sea, with fun-loving and friendly people. It is all that and much more. Its population has a high literacy rate and high life expectancy. Greece is an independent and democratic nation of proud men and women who like to see themselves as independent. In reality, they look to a history that has been much influenced by foreign nations.

First there were the Great Powers—Britain, Russia, and France—who helped Greece win their war of independence from four hundred years of Ottoman rule. They financed loans, supplied armed forces, and, in 1828, helped defeat the combined naval forces of the Ottomans and Egyptians at the Battle of Navarino. The War of Independence ended in 1829, with the evacuation of the Ottomans and the Egyptians. In 1830, the Great Powers signed the London Protocol, which recognized Greece as an independent nation. In 1832, the Great Powers negotiated with the Ottoman Empire regarding Greece's borders in the Treaty of Constantinople. They also selected a king who was not a Greek but a Bavarian—King Otto. Since the king was only seventeen, three Bavarian regents controlled Greece until he came of age in 1835. The Great Powers had a great influence on Greece in the nineteenth and twentieth centuries.

During World War II, from 1941 to 1944, the Axis powers of Germany, Bulgaria, and Italy occupied the country. The Italians left in 1943. The Axis occupation forces brutalized and killed Greek citizens, including most of the Jewish population, and destroyed towns and villages.

Foreign powers continue to have an influence on the Greece of the twenty-first century. One of those powers is the United States. Since the birth of modern Greece, the United States and Greece have forged a close relationship. Sometimes mutual respect and love prevail; other times the relationship sours. However, throughout the years, they have stood by each other.

When the Greeks declared their independence from the Ottoman Empire in 1821, the United States remained neutral and did not give financial assistance. However, American educational institutions and churches raised money for the cause by conducting lectures, theatrical performances, and dances. An African American group sent money they had gathered through an elegant ball held in New York City. Moreover, courageous American men, moved by the David and Goliath struggle, put their lives on the line by fighting in the Greek War of Independence.

Greek immigrants to America helped strengthen the bond between the United States and Greece. In Greece today, it is hard to find a Greek who does not have relatives in America or whose grandfather or great-grandfather had not immigrated to or worked in the United States. According to the U.S. Department of State 2010 Census, over 1.3 million people in the United States claimed Greek ancestry. In 2006, according to the Department of State, as many as 90,000 U.S. citizens resided in Greece.

The immigrants came in two waves: at the turn of the twentieth century and then again after World War II. Between 1890 and 1917, about 450,000 Greeks, including those from Asia Minor, immigrated to the United States. From 1918 to 1924, an additional 70,000 came. In 1924, the restrictive immigration policies of the United States essentially closed the door to Greek immigrants until after World War II. From 1945 to 1965, about 75,000 came to the United States, and from 1966 to 1979, about 160,000 arrived.

The first wave of immigrants consisted primarily of young Greek males who came to work in the railroads, factories, and mines of America and return home with money in their pockets. About 30–50 percent did return to Greece. Those who made their home in the United States continued to support family left behind in Greece. The strong family ties between Greeks on both sides of the Atlantic further strengthened the affinity between Greece and the United States. The Greek Americans have provided financial aid to relatives in Greece and humanitarian assistance to the country and have lobbied the U.S. government in regard to foreign affairs. The nation of Greece, in turn, has provided teachers for the Greek-language schools in the United States and promoted Greek culture.

The United States and Greece were allies in World War I, World War II, and the Korean War. Greece also sent naval vessels during the Persian Gulf War and supported the NATO peacekeeping effort in Kosovo. Greece had become a member of NATO in 1952.

As another example of solidarity, in 1953, the Greek government entered into an agreement with the United States that allowed the operation of military facilities on its soil. The United States set up four facilities, but in the 1990s, three were disbanded. One remains at Souda Bay in Crete; it was first established in 1969.

Although the Greek nation fought on the side of the Allies in World War I, and many Greek immigrants served in the U.S. Armed Forces, the early immigrants continued to face vitriolic prejudice from the general community and in particular from the Ku Klux Klan. They were called "dirty Greeks" or "goddamn Greeks." To combat this prejudice, the American Hellenic Educational Progressive Association (AHEPA), a fraternal association, was founded in 1922.

The prejudicial feeling of Americans toward Greeks changed dramatically after World War II. In the autumn of 1940, the Greeks demonstrated their heroism by pushing the Italian army, which had invaded Greece at the Albanian border, out of the Pindus Mountains of Greece and into Albania. That was the first victory in Europe against the Axis during World War II. Throughout the United States, newspapers articles and political cartoons celebrated the courage of the Greeks.

Unfortunately, Greece could not defeat the Germans who invaded in the spring of 1941. Destruction and famine resulted from the Axis occupation of Greece, which lasted until 1944. The Greek War Relief Association, organized by Greek Americans, saved millions of Greeks from starvation. Famous movie stars, including Judy Garland and Frank Sinatra, as well as the general populace supported the war relief effort.

Shortly after liberation of mainland Greece in 1944, Greece became involved in a brutal civil war fought between Greek government troops and the Communist-controlled Democratic Army of Greece. U.S. military aid, as well as military advisors, helped in the defeat of the Communists in 1949.

The generosity of the United States through the Truman Doctrine, as well as the subsequent Marshall Plan, gave more than military aid. It provided food and medical assistance to the people of Greece, enabled the restoration of harbors, opened the Corinth Canal, and built roads. Farming was helped by importing farm machinery, seeds, and fertilizers.

To express their appreciation of Harry S. Truman, the Greek fraternal organization AHEPA erected a statue of the president who was behind the Truman Doctrine and the Marshall Plan. Since its installation in Athens in 1963, the twelve-foot, three-ton statue has been defaced or torn down at least four times. Those to the left of the political spectrum have thus expressed their lingering hatred of the United States, whom they see as an imperialistic power meddling in their country's affairs. They see the involvement of the United States in the civil war and afterward in the Marshall Plan as being problematic. They also are critical of the support the United States gave to the dictatorship of the junta, three colonels who had toppled the government's democratic system in a bloodless coup in 1967 and governed the country until 1974.

After World War II and the Greek Civil War, the United States once again became a destination for Greeks dreaming of a better life. Despite the beginning of recovery that the Marshall Plan jump-started, things continued to be difficult in the 1950s, 1960s, and 1970s. Greece could not sustain itself, and its citizens started to emigrate. In contrast to the first wave of immigrants, those who came in the second wave often came as family units. These newer immigrants to the United States revitalized the Greek American institutions and strengthened the link between Greece and America.

From 1967 to 1974, many Greeks left their country because of the repressive government of the junta. The rule of the junta caused many Greeks to condemn the United States, since they believed that the CIA supported the coup. As yet, there has not been substantial proof to back up this accusation.

Although they may not have backed the coup, the United States, especially the Nixon administration, did support the dictatorship of the junta after it assumed power. President Bill Clinton felt that the United States erred in its support of the junta. As reported by Terence Hunt, Associated Press, in the *Topeka Capital Journal* on November 21, 1999, Clinton, during his visit to Athens, said, "When the Junta took over in 1967 here, the US allowed its interests in prosecuting the Cold War to prevail over its interest, I should say its obligation, to support democracy, which was, after all, the cause for which we fought the Cold War. It is important that we acknowledge that."

He issued his statement a few days after a violent demonstration on November 17, 1999. The demonstrators smashed stores and banks and set fires. About ten thousand of them protested U.S. policy in Kosovo and Bosnia and the bombing of Yugoslavia, which hurt Greece's long-standing allies, the Serbians.

The Greeks have also objected that the United States did nothing to deter the Turkish invasion of Cyprus in 1974. They were incensed when they discovered that Turkey had illegally used American-supplied arms in violation of U.S. laws and agreements. A lobbying effort by the Greek American community helped bring about an arms embargo on Turkey, which started in February 1975 and lasted until October 1978.

Beginning in 2008, Greece became involved in a financial crisis that threatened bankruptcy and possible withdrawal from the European Union (EU). During the early years of the crisis, the stock market in the United States went up and down depending on what was happening in Greece. The media portrayed the Greeks as the "bad guys" who were financially irresponsible, and the public opinion of Americans toward Greece suffered. Greece had begun on the road to recovery, and public opinion is now more favorable.

Despite problems that have developed in their relationship from time to time, the governments of Greece and United States continue to maintain their friendship. When U.S. secretary of state Hillary Clinton met with Greek foreign minister Stavros Lambrinidis at the State Department, they both emphasized the strong mutual relationship between their countries. Clinton said, "Greece is a long standing ally of the US. In ways large and small, life in our country is enriched by the energy and contributions of our many Greek-Americans. And abroad Greece and the US share common goals for stability and prosperity in Southeastern Europe, North Africa and the Middle East. US looks forward to broadening deepening and strengthening this already very vital relationship" (*Greek Reporter* 2011).

During the meeting, Lambrinidis said, "Greece and the US do know of difficulties. We have been together, stood by each other during difficult wars, and we are standing by each other today, as well . . . " (*Greek Reporter* 2011).

Greece has been a strong ally throughout the years. President Donald Trump praised Greece as one of the countries of NATO to put 2 percent of their GDP into defense, while criticizing other countries for not doing their fair share. Greece has a strategic location, at the crossroads of three continents (Europe, Asia, and Africa), and is important to U.S. interests, a reason the United States maintains a naval base in Crete.

The relationship Greece has to the EU, like that of the United States, has sometimes been close yet at other times seen by the Greeks as problematic.

Greece was anxious to become part of the EU. Benefits included no additional tariffs on goods traded with other EU member states and the ability of EU citizens and capital to move freely across borders. The latter made it easier for Greeks to attend school or obtain employment in other member states and for others in the EU to travel to Greece. By getting together as a group, the EU has also negotiated better trade policies with other non-EU countries. The EU helped finance infrastructure, such as road and telecommunication networks, and promoted environmental, human rights, and anti-corruption policies, which the Greek government has integrated into its constitution and laws.

Since 2010, however, Greece has had a touchy relationship with the EU, although as witnessed by the Eurobarometer surveys, the public sentiment is in favor of its continuing to be a member of the EU. The European Commission, the European Central Bank, and the International Monetary Fund (known as the Troika) had negotiated loans to Greece when it was on the brink of bankruptcy but at a rate that Greece has found hard to pay off. Another downside to EU membership is the loss of control over fiscal policy (its inability to devaluate its own currency and/or control interest rates). Many Greeks, recalling the German occupation during World War II, resent the power Germany, represented by German chancellor Angela Merkel, had over them. Also, there is a debate as to whether or not all the austerity restrictions placed on the Greeks as a condition of obtaining the loan packages have actually harmed rather than helped the economy. Greece also felt abandoned by the EU after neighboring countries closed their borders to refugees and immigrants in 2015, with tens of thousands of them becoming stranded in Greece. The EU did not give Greece adequate resources to take care of them, nor would other wealthier EU countries accept them.

Greece has had a centuries-old contentious relationship with its neighbor Turkey. It has been a thorn in the side of Greece, a thorn that has never been removed. The Greeks remember the four hundred years of Ottoman occupation, the genocide of Greeks of Asia Minor and Pontos at the hands of the Ottoman Turks during the early part of the twentieth century, the pogrom against the Greeks in Istanbul in 1955, and the occupation of the northern part of the nation of Cyprus with the subsequent displacement of the Greek Cypriots. At present, Greece is objecting to Turkey's violation of its airspace, at times pursuing Turkish fighter jets with their own fighter jets. Turkey has also indicated its intention to drill for oil in Greek waters. One reason that Greece spends as much as it does on its armed forces and continues to have a draft is that it fears a war with Turkey.

Greece has also had its difficulties with its neighbor to the north, the nation now known as the Republic of North Macedonia, formerly known as the Former Yugoslav Republic of Macedonia (FYROM). They disagreed on whether or not the newly created nation had the right to use "Macedonia" in its name, the same name that is used by a neighboring Greek province. Greece resented FYROM laying claim to their great leader Alexander the Great, who spread the Greek language and culture throughout the Middle East and as far as India, and usurping their symbol, the Star of Vergina, on its flag. Most important, they feared FYROM would lay claim to Greek territory. The decades-long debate was recently resolved in 2019 by the SYRIZA government and its counterpart in FYROM when they came to an historic agreement on a new name, Republic of North Macedonia.

China is one of the more recent foreign powers to have an influence on Greece. In 2016, COSCO, a Chinese shipping company, bought a majority stake in the port of Pireaus, which is located at a strategic point between Europe and Asia. In 2018, Greece joined China's Belt and Road Initiative, and in 2019, China unveiled plans to invest 600 million dollars more to further develop Pireaus. It seems good economically, but some wonder about the "hidden costs," for example, turning a blind eye to China's human rights violations or the potential China has to use the transportation centers that are part of the Belt and Road Initiative for military purposes. They wonder how further foreign investment and intervention will change the character of the Greeks.

Immigration of foreigners to Greece is another factor that has had a profound influence on Greece. According to the 2011 census, more than 8 percent of the resident population had citizenship in another country. This is a significant change from the time during the 1950s through the 1980s when Greeks were leaving their country, and there were few emigrants. The emigrants started coming to Greece in the 1990s after the breakup of the USSR. They included Albanians, Bulgarians, and Eastern Europeans who sought a better way of life in Greece. In the past decade, millions of refugees and migrants have also arrived from the Middle East and Africa, fleeing their homes to escape wars and poverty. Since 2015, Greece stopped being a transit point for them on their way to other parts of Europe. Tens of thousands became stranded in Greece after its neighbors closed their borders, at a time when Greece was in the midst of a financial crisis. Many are still detained in squalid refugee camps as they wait for a decision on whether or not they will be granted asylum.

On the basketball court in Athens's Sepolia district, where world-famous basketball player Giannis Antetokounmpo first played, Greek street artist Same84 painted a mega mural of his likeness. Antetokounmpo, whose parents were born in Nigeria and immigrated to Greece, has been warmly accepted by most Greeks. Antetokounmpo plays for the Milwaukee Bucks and earned the NBA's most valuable player award in June 2019. (Photo by Anna Poupou)

Greece has had to cope with refugees before. About a million and a half came from Asia Minor and Pontos during the exchange of population between Greece and Turkey that was negotiated in 1923. Included in this exchange were those who left their countries before October 18, 1912. The exchange of populations included many Greeks who had fled Turkey to come to Greece during the atrocities of the Greco-Turkish War from 1919 to 1922. Though Greek ethnically, they were vastly different from the native-born Greeks. Some did not even speak Greek or spoke a Greek language called Pontian that could not be understood by the native Greeks. They faced prejudice from the native-born Greeks when they first arrived but were recognized as citizens. After several generations, they became integrated into the fabric of the community.

Most of the refugees/migrants who have come to Greece more recently are not Greek by ethnicity, with the exception of ethnic Greeks that came from countries like Albania or Russia in the 1990s and early 2000s. Neither are they Greek Orthodox, the prevailing religion. Greece, like other European countries, is becoming more diverse and is facing an identity crisis as to who is "Greek." Since 2015, the Greek government has made it easier for those who do not have Greek ethnicity to become citizens, but many ethnic Greeks are slow to accept those without Greek DNA as fellow Greeks. An exception to this is basketball player Giannis Antetokounmpo, whose parents immigrated from Nigeria and who most Greeks recognize with pride as one of their own.

**See also:** Chapter 15: Sidebar: Giannis Antetokounmpo, World-Famous Basketball Superstar.

**Further Reading**

Gazi, Effi. 2005. "Constructing the National Majority and Ethnic/Religious Minorities in Greece." In *Statehood beyond Ethnicity: Minor States in Northern and Eastern Europe, 1600–2000*, edited by Linas Eriksonas and Leos Müller, 303–317. Brussels: Peter Lang.

Moskos, Peter C., and Charles C. Moskos. 2017. *Greek Americans: Struggle and Success*, 3rd edition. New York: Routledge.

Thomopoulos, Elaine. 2012. "Grenemies: Exploring the Love-Hate Relationship between the US and Greece." *GreekCircle* 11, no. 3 (Spring/Summer): 30–31. Portions of the introduction are from this article.

Toli, Fani. 2011. "Strong Bilateral Relationships between Greece and USA." *Greek Reporter*, October 28, 2011. Accessed April 14, 2020. https://usa.greekreporter.com/2011/10/28/strong-bilateral-relationships-between-greece-and-usa/.

# GREECE

BULGARIA
REPUBLIC OF NORTH MACEDONIA
TURKEY
ALBANIA
Alexandroupolis
Kavala
Thessaloniki
Sea of Marmara
Mount Olympus
Limnos
Ioannina
Larrisa
Corfu
Igoumenitsa
Volos
Lesbos
Aegean Sea
Lefkada
TURKEY
Chalkida
Chios
Kefalonia
Patras
Elefsis
Piraeus
ATHENS
Samos
Zakynthos
Tripoli
Laurion
Ionian Sea
Sparta
Naxos
Kos
N
Rhodes
Sea of Crete
Mediterranean Sea
Irakleion
Crete
0 75 150 km
0 75 150 mi
20°
22°
24°
26°
28°

CHAPTER 1

# GEOGRAPHY

## OVERVIEW

Greece is a mountainous country located in the southernmost part of the Balkan Peninsula in Southeastern Europe. It shares land borders with Albania, the Republic of North Macedonia, and Bulgaria in the north, and Turkey in the east. Italy lies to the west across the narrow Ionian Sea.

Both the mainland and its over two thousand islands are generally mountainous and rocky, with narrow valleys intensively farmed and home to most of its inhabitants.

Most of Greece borders the sea, and when adding more than two thousand islands, Greece has one of the world's largest coastlines, notwithstanding the country's small land area of 50,944 square miles.

The sea and its proximity are a constant fact of Greek geography and life. No wonder that Greece owns the world's largest merchant fleet, and from prehistoric times Greeks have been intrepid seafarers. The presence of the sea and the general poverty of the land have made shipping an option from time immemorial, and they also account for Greece's high emigration rates since ancient times.

Mountains dominate the Greek landscape. Several of them rise to a height of over 7,000 feet, and these are located throughout the country, including the islands, particularly Crete. The highest mountain in Greece is Mount Olympus, at 9,575 feet elevation. Its height inspired the ancient Greeks to consider it the home of their god. The main mountain range in Greece, the Pindus Mountain Range, is a continuation of the Dinaric Alps further north in the Balkans. It runs along the spine of the Greek peninsula on a north-south axis. These mountains extend through the Peloponnesus. The Rhodope Mountains, a lower range, run on an east-west axis. They form part of the frontier between Greece and Bulgaria.

Several plains of various sizes form the exception to the geographic rule of mountains and craggy peninsulas that make up Greece. Greece has two major plains, intensively cultivated, in Macedonia and Thessaly. Soil erosion is a perennial problem in the plains, due to their being farmed for thousands of years.

In contrast to rivers in the countries to Greece's north, Greek rivers are not navigable by commercial craft. Most rivers in the south of the country are small creeks, which often dry up for several months of the year. Only in the north of the country are there substantial rivers, the majority with sources in countries to Greece's north,

The road from Kalamata to the town of Karadamyli in Mani has splendid scenery, with views of the mountains, trees, and seashore. About 80 percent of Greece is mountainous. Forests cover 25 percent of Greece, and the coastline is 9,333.61 miles long. (Photo by John Vlahakis)

specifically Albania, North Macedonia, and Bulgaria. The major Greek rivers are Nestos, Strymon, Aliakmon, Aoos, and Evros, part of which forms Greece's border with Turkey.

As a mountainous country with plateaus and valleys, Greece has several lakes, again, most commonly, in the more verdant north. There are also several big brackish lagoons with large fisheries and salt collection industries. Several marshy lakes, most notably near the cities of Thessaloniki and Thebes, have been largely drained and converted to highly productive farmland. There are also quite a few artificial lakes of various sizes used as reservoirs.

Greece is divided into thirteen administrative divisions, or *peripheries* in Greek. They include Attica, Central Greece, Central Macedonia, Crete, Eastern Macedonia and Thrace, Peloponnesus, North Aegean, South Aegean, Western Greece, Ionian Islands, Epirus, Thessaly, and Western Macedonia. These peripheries do not necessarily conform to the historical or geographic provinces of the past. For example, part of Peloponnesus belongs to the Western Greece or Attica periphery. Aside from Mount Athos, a monastic republic in Greece's northern province of Macedonia, there are no autonomous regions in Greece.

Greece became formally independent in 1830, and the country was a fraction of the size and population it is now. It grew to its current geographic size by increments, usually after wars or diplomatic action.

Most of Greece conforms to what is called the Mediterranean climate, with hot, dry summers and cool, rainy winters. Given the ubiquitous high mountain ranges throughout the country and its islands, microclimates based on altitudes are numerous, and the climate in the extreme interior north bordering North Macedonia, Albania, and Bulgaria is also more typical of the continental climate of the interior Balkans. The general Mediterranean climate enables Greece to be a top global producer of Mediterranean products such as citrus fruits and olive oil.

Greece had a population of 10,815,197 according to the 2011 census. In 2017, the estimated population was 10,768,477, and in 2018, it was 10,761,523. Males accounted for 49 percent and females 51 percent in the 2011 census. In 2011, the resident population who claimed Greek citizenship was 91.6 percent. The largest share of foreign citizens residing in Greece were from Albania (52.7 percent, 480,851), followed by Bulgaria (8.3 percent, 75,917), Romania (5.1 percent, 46,524), Pakistan (3.7 percent, 34,178), Georgia (3.0 percent, 27,407), Ukraine (1.9 percent, 17,008), United Kingdom (1.7 percent, 15,388), Cyprus (1.6 percent, 14,448), Poland (1.6 percent, 14,145), Germany (1.2 percent, 10,782), Egypt (1.1 percent, 10,455), Moldovia (1.1 percent, 10,391), and the Philippines (1.1 percent, 9,807). Other countries accounted for 11.9 percent of foreign citizens residing in Greece.

The population has decreased in the past few years due to the large-scale emigration of working-age Greeks, primarily to other European Union countries. The net population loss in 2017 was 0.06 percent, and this has continued over many years. At the same time, Greece's already low birth rate has fallen further. It was at 8.4 births/1,000 population. Greeks have one of the world's highest life expectancy rates, 78.3 years for males and 83.6 for females, according to the World Health Organization statistics for 2017. Unfortunately, the economic crisis since 2009 has impacted the health of Greeks, with the death rate steadily rising.

While Greece is poorer than many other Western countries, its demographics largely reflect those of a mature Western economy: falling birth rates and a relatively high number of immigrants. The country received hundreds of thousands of immigrants, legal or undocumented, following the breakup of Eastern Europe's Communist regimes in the 1990s and the collapse of the Albanian economy. The Albanians and Bulgarians were the largest groups of immigrants, many of whom have assimilated and settled in Greece, often intermarrying with locals. In the past ten years, refugees and immigrants escaping war and poverty have come from the Middle East, Africa, and Asia. They are having a harder time assimilating, and many of them are trying to travel to more prosperous European countries to find work or join family. Tens of thousands became stranded in Greece after bordering European countries closed their borders.

According to the 2011 census, the Greek population is 79 percent urban and 21 percent rural, with a larger percentage of the population (approximately 12 percent) engaged in farming than is typical of Western—but not Eastern—Europe. According to the United Nations 2019 Human Development Index Report, when compared to countries around the world, Greece has an extremely high Human Development Index (HDI), a rating factoring in educational levels, life expectancy, and income. It ranked 32 out of 189 countries.

Greece is remarkably homogeneous, with over 90 percent of the population ethnically Greek and Orthodox Christian. The large-scale immigration in the past quarter century has had its impact, but the country remains ethnically and religiously cohesive. Greece does have some ethnic and religious minorities, aside from the officially recognized Muslim minority of Thrace. The largest ethnic group is the Albanians. Thousands came in the 1990s after the split-up of the Soviet Union and the collapse of the Albanian economy. More recent immigrants include refugees from war-torn Syria, Iraq, and Afghanistan, as well as economic immigrants from the Balkans, Asia, and Africa. There are also small Jewish and Catholic religious minorities who have been in Greece for centuries. The Catholic minorities can be found on the Aegean Islands of Tinos, Syros, and Naxos, while the Jews, who number about five thousand, are located mainly in Athens and Thessaloniki. Other groups include the Arvanites, who reside in Attica Province, the islands of Evia, Hydra, Spetses, and the eastern Peloponnesus, and Vlachs, who reside in parts of Macedonia and Thessaly, specifically Metsovo. These two groups identify themselves as being of Greek descent. Some of them continue to speak the languages of Arvanitika (an Albanian dialect) and Vlach (a Romanian dialect).

Greece does not compile statistics on ethnolinguistic minorities, other than for the officially recognized Muslim religious minority, so estimates are hard to determine.

*Alexander Billinis*

**Further Reading**

*Central Intelligence Agency World Factbook 2019–2020.* Accessed March 1, 2021. https://www.cia.gov/library/publications/the-world-factbook/geos/gr.html.

Hellenic National Meteorological Service. "Climate Atlas of Greece 1971–2000" (in Greek). Accessed March 15, 2020. https://web.archive.org/web/20170921184739/http://www.hnms.gr:80/hnms/greek/pdf/Climate_Atlas_Of_Greece.pdf.

Hellenic Republic, Hellenic Statistical Authority. 2014. "Population and Housing Census 2011." Piraeus, September 12, 2014. Accessed March 1, 2021. https://www.statistics.gr/documents/20181/1215267/A1602_SAM01_DT_DC_00_2011_03_F_EN.pdf/cb10bb9f-6413-4129-b847-f1def334e05e.

Hellenic Republic, Hellenic Statistical Authority. "Greece in Figures. October to December 2019." Accessed March 1, 2021. https://www.statistics.gr/documents/20181/1515741/GreeceInFigures_2019Q4_EN.pdf.pdf/d0149260-0983-9d80-e5c1-4368dc87fda3.

Higgins, Michael Denis, and Reynold Higgins. 1996. *A Geological Companion to Greece and the Aegean.* Ithaca, NY: Cornell University Press.

*Human Development Report 2019.* New York: United Nations Development Program. Accessed March 1, 2020. http://hdr.undp.org/sites/default/files/hdr2019.pdf.

Index Mundi. 2019. "Greece Demographics Profile." Last updated December 7, 2019. Accessed February 21, 2020. https://www.indexmundi.com/greece/demographics_profile.html.

## Aegean Islands

The Aegean Basin contains nearly two thousand islands of various sizes, the vast majority of which are tiny, uninhabited islets. They range from Crete, the fourth largest island in the Mediterranean, to rocks the size of a house. The islands vary greatly according to climatic, topographic, and historical factors, and it is best to divide the islands into more discreet sections to account for their differences.

## CRETE

Crete is the largest Greek island and the fourth largest in the Mediterranean with a landmass of 3,206 square miles and a population of over six hundred thousand. The island, with its distinct dialect and unique culture, is both very different from other parts of Greece and, at the same time, passionately Greek.

Crete is a study in contrasts, with several high snowcapped mountains looking down on extremely narrow and fertile plains. It is one of the few Greek islands with agricultural bounty, as its well-watered plains produce fruits, grains, and wines, along with the ubiquitous olive oil. Its three principal cities are Iraklion, Rethymnon, and Chania.

Crete was the center of the Minoan culture (2500–1450 BCE), one of the oldest civilizations in Europe, which greatly influenced that of mainland Greece. It spent nearly half a millennium under Venetian rule, from 1204 to 1669 CE. Its culture and architecture reflect not only its Greek and Byzantine foundations but also that of its occupiers: the Venetians, Arabs, and Ottomans. Cretans fought in the Greek War of Independence in 1821 to free themselves from the Ottomans but were unable to unite their island with the emerging Greek state. Union with Greece was the constant goal of the Cretans, who revolted with regularity against Turkish rule until succeeding in gaining a form of autonomy in 1897. Formal union with Greece occurred after the First Balkan War of 1912 on December 1, 1913.

## THE SARONIC ISLANDS AND THE CYCLADES ISLANDS

The Saronic Islands and the Cyclades Islands of the south-central Aegean are generally smaller in size and vary considerably in size, population, history, and fertility of the land.

The Saronic Islands are four principal islands of the Saronic Gulf, south and east of Athens, as well as several smaller satellite islands. The four islands are Aegina, Poros, Hydra, and Spetses. All are popular day-trip destinations from Athens and possess a typical Mediterranean climate. Aegina, Poros, and Spetses are quite verdant, while Hydra, in spite of the name connoting water, is arid. All four islands, most particularly Hydra, have traditional island architecture. The islands played key roles in the Greek War of Independence. This is particularly true of Hydra and Spetses, which were wealthy shipping islands at the time of the war. The ships from these two islands formed the bulk of the Greek fleet.

East of the Saronic Islands are the Cyclades Islands, whose name derives from the Greek word *kyklos* (circle), as these islands form a circle around the island of Delos, which was sacred to the Cult of Apollo in classical Greece. The Cyclades Islands are generally the peaks of submerged mountains, with varying degrees of fertility, and all having a Mediterranean climate moderated by strong breezes. Mykonos and Santorini, islands well known to tourists, are both in the Cyclades, and the beautiful vistas of volcanic Santorini and the charming whitewashed houses and windmills of Mykonos are iconic symbols of Greece the world over.

Both the Saronic and Cyclades Islands became part of Greece at the time of independence. The islands played key roles in the struggle and the establishment of the newly emerged independent Greece.

## EASTERN AEGEAN ISLANDS

East and north of the Cyclades are the Eastern Aegean Islands, many of which are just a few kilometers from the Turkish mainland. The principal islands are Thasos, Samothrace, Limnos, Lesvos, Chios, Psara, Ikaria, and Samos.

The islands vary considerably in size, population, and development. The two northernmost, Thasos and Samothrace, are thickly wooded, and the latter has high and forbidding mountains. Limnos, Lesvos, Chios, and Samos are large islands with diverse economies, historical, and maritime traditions, and often large diasporas abroad. The islands' proximity to the Turkish mainland also reflects long-standing ties with Asia Minor, which were severed when these islands were liberated by the Greek navy in 1912 and, more definitively, when the Greek population was evicted from Asia Minor in 1923 because of the population exchange between the Greek Orthodox Christians in Asia Minor and Muslims in Greece.

## DODECANESE ISLANDS

Derived from the Greek word *dodeka* (twelve), the Dodecanese Islands in the southeastern Aegean consist of fifteen principal islands and many smaller islands. The principal islands include Rhodes, the largest, and Agathonisi, Astypalaia, Chalki, Kalymnos, Karpathos, Kasos, Kos, Leipsoi, Leros, Nisyros, Patmos, Symi, Tilos, and Kastellorizo. Rhodes has long dominated the group, both in history and administratively. The islands' historical sites, from antiquity, that is, the Byzantine, Crusader, and Ottoman eras, to the present, attract many tourists. The Medieval City of Rhodes has been designated by the UNESCO as a World Heritage Site.

The Dodecanese Islands were captured by the Italians from the Turks in the Italo-Turkish War of 1911, and Greece gained formal possession of the islands after World War II, in 1947.

*Alexander Billinis*

**See also:** Chapter 2: Overview.

**Further Reading**

Higgins, Michael Denis. 2008. *Geology of the Greek Islands*. Berkeley: University of California Press.

Higgins, Michael Denis, and Reynold Higgins. 1996. *A Geological Companion to Greece and the Aegean.* Ithaca, NY: Cornell University Press.

Louis, Diana Farr. 2009. *The Secret of the Greek Islands.* New York: Petro Books.

## Athens/Piraeus and Attica Province

Attica Province contains the cities of Athens and Piraeus as well as the greater metropolitan area. Athens has a population of 664,046, and Piraeus a population of 163,688, according to the 2011 census. The province is the most populated area of Greece, with 3.8 million people. The actual population is larger as many residents are registered in other areas of Greece, and it does not accurately reflect the large legal and undocumented migrant population. The province contains about 40 percent of Greece's population and economic output. It has a Mediterranean climate, and its valleys and plains are largely arid. Wooded hills and mountains within and around Athens often fall victim to fires, due to either the dry climate in summer or arsonists seeking to free land for development, as a growing Athens consumes more foothills.

Athens became Greece's capital in 1834, chosen in part for its classical Greek associations, most particularly the constant inspiration of the Parthenon seen high on the Acropolis. From a tiny village in 1834, the city grew as the Greek state developed and expanded, most notably with the onset of industrialization in the late 1800s and, more specifically, after the Asia Minor Catastrophe in the early 1920s, following World War I, when Greece absorbed nearly 1.5 million refugees, primarily Greeks, from Turkey, Bulgaria, and the Soviet Union. Several hundred thousand arrived in Athens and the port of Piraeus. Dislocations from the Greek Civil War of 1946–1949 and the further growth of the Greek economy postwar brought nearly 40 percent of the Greek population to Attica. The province serves as the main transport, air, and maritime hub for the country. Athens is a key tourism site, where ancient Greek, Roman, and Byzantine ruins provide inspiration.

Piraeus is one of the largest ports in the Mediterranean, serving as the headquarters for several Greek shipping companies. It has been Athens's port from ancient times, and during the Classical period of Athenian greatness, Piraeus was connected to Athens by a walled corridor, remains of which are sometimes visible in the urban sprawl. Now the two cities are joined as one conurbation, and nearby Eleusina, a key industrial and shipping center, constitutes a single urban metropolis.

Not far from the sprawl of Athens are excellent beaches to the south and east of the city, the so-called Athenian Riviera, which goes down to the ruins of the Temple of Poseidon at Cape Sounion, the southernmost part of Attica Province.

In the north of Athens, there are beautiful mountains, including nearby Pendeli, the source of the Parthenon's dazzling white marble, and Parnitha, a mountain reached by either tram or automobile, with a hilltop casino overlooking most of Attica.

*Alexander Billinis*

The Acropolis Metro station, with a reproduction of sculptures found on the pediment of the Parthenon. This beautiful station also contains ancient relics that were excavated when building the station. The Athens Metro, the rapid-transit subway system that was initiated in 2000, has been an effective solution to the pollution, parking, and traffic problems of Athens and surrounding areas. (Photo by Elaine Thomopoulos)

**See also:** Chapter 2: Overview. Chapter 4: Privatization of Transportation. Chapter 6: Overview.

**Further Reading**

Balodimas-Bartolomei, Angelyn. 2009. *Footsteps through Athina: A Traveler's Guide to Greece.* Park Ridge, IL: Palo Albums.

Higgins, Michael Denis, and Reynold Higgins. 1996. *A Geological Companion to Greece and the Aegean.* Ithaca, NY: Cornell University Press.

## Epirus

Similar to Macedonia and Thrace, Epirus is Greece's northern historic province and its own periphery; it has a population of 337,000. It is bordered on the west by the Ionian Sea, which generally has a more humid climate than the Aegean Sea. Along the coastline a Mediterranean climate prevails, but inland climate is continental, characterized by high mountains, deep river gorges, and the occasional plains. The Vikos Gorge, three thousand feet deep in some places, is one of the world's deepest canyons.

Animal husbandry was a key traditional agricultural activity, though the region was particularly industrious in craft making. As elsewhere in mountainous Greek areas, a large portion of the population has emigrated, either seasonally or permanently.

Epirus's largest city is Ioannina (Yannina), one of the most picturesque in Greece. The town's architecture and winding hills boast considerable Ottoman and Byzantine influences, and reminders of the Ottoman past in edifices are all too frequent. It has a very pretty lake, Lake Pamvotida, with an island fortress, recalling an era when this was the capital of Ali Pasha's domain, a semi-independent entity in the Ottoman Empire run by an Albanian Muslim pasha who, despite his cruelty, was a great patron of the arts.

In Greek Epirus, in addition to Greek speakers, there is a population of Vlachs, a linguistic minority who speaks a dialect of Romanian as well as Greek. Vlachs are Orthodox Christian and nearly always identify themselves as Greek. Greece added the Arta area of Epirus after the First Balkan War in 1912. The rest of Epirus was liberated by the Greek Armed Forces in the Second Balkan War of 1913.

As with Macedonia and Thrace, the traditional geographic and historic area of Epirus extends beyond the border of Greece, into neighboring Albania directly to the north. In what Greeks call "Northern Epirus" (which is known to the Albanians as southern Albania), there is a considerable Greek population.

*Alexander Billinis*

**See also:** Chapter 2: Overview. Chapter 9: Dialects and Minority Languages.

**Further Reading**

Sakellariou, M. B. 1997. *Epirus: 4000 Years of Greek History and Civilization.* Athens: Ekdotike Athenon.

## Erosion

With more than 9,320 miles of coastline, 60 percent mainland and 40 percent islands, Greece has experienced a high degree of coastal erosion. In fact, nearly one-third of the Hellenic coastline has eroded over the past thirty years. The four types of coasts found in Greece are hard rock coasts (44 percent), soft rock or conglomerate cliff coasts with pocket beaches (14 percent), beach zones (36 percent), and mud coasts (6 percent).

In 2018, two university studies warned of extensive coastal erosion in several areas of Greece. The first study, conducted by the University of Athens, found that roughly a nine-mile stretch of the coast near Corinth lost an average of seven inches annually. In some areas, up to twenty-seven inches have been lost. These alarming losses are threatening residents' properties and livelihoods. This extreme level of erosion began in 1987 and is visible to the naked eye. The coastal properties most in danger were developed over decades with little planning or government oversight in an era when erosion was not a concern.

The second study, by the University of the Aegean, found that as a result of coastal erosion, beaches on six islands will have lost at least 50 percent of their surface areas by 2050. They anticipate "economic death" for the following cities: Kamari on Santorini, Eresos and Tsamakia on Lesvos, Kataraktis and Aghia Ermioni on Chios, Masouri on Kalymnos, as well as parts of Halki and Agathonisi.

Soil erosion resulting from unsustainable agricultural practices, overgrazing, deforestation, wildfires, wind patterns, road construction, and other causes is also a concern. The Mediterranean region, populated by humans for thousands of years, is considered by many to be the area most impacted by humans; it is a challenge to address the effects of centuries of past land use and mismanagement. The mountainous terrains of Greece present unique challenges to the nation, since soil and sediment are washed to lowland areas or the sea by rain waters. Deforestation, a result of wildfires, clearing of forests, and overgrazing, contributes to the severity of the problem. To reduce the impact of increased soil erosion, Greece has initiated reforestation efforts and has implemented measures to prevent and suppress wildfires.

It is expected that the rate of erosion will increase, as the impact of global warming, in particular rising sea levels, increases. As a nation of coastlines and islands, Greece is especially vulnerable to erosion. It is working to update its coastal planning, land management, and zoning laws to address this new reality.

*John Psiharis*

**See also:** Chapter 1: Pollution of the Air; Pollution of the Water.

**Further Reading**

Climate Change Post. 2019. "Greece: Coastal Erosion Greece." Last updated April 2, 2019. Centre for Climate Adaptation. Accessed April 1, 2021. https://www.climatechangepost.com/greece/coastal-erosion/.

Lialios, Giorgos. 2018. "Coastal Erosion Severe in Parts of Greece." *ekathimerini*, November 2, 2018. Accessed April 1, 2021. http://www.ekathimerini.com/225719/article/ekathimerini/news/coastal-erosion-severe-in-parts-of-greece.

## Flora, Fauna, and Natural Resources

Despite the country's small size, Greece has considerable biodiversity. This is due to its mountainous interior, which creates multitudes of microclimates, as well as the vast, jagged coastline, which fosters a dizzying variety of marine life, in spite of overfishing and considerable aquatic pollution.

Greece has over 6,900 species of vascular plants, of which 1,300 are endemic to the country. Forests cover about 30 percent of the country. At a crossroads of Balkan, Anatolian, and Mediterranean flora, it is not surprising that Greece possesses such diversity. Greece's various elevations and climates also contribute to the diversity.

At lower elevations, from sea level to fifteen hundred feet, there are olive and citrus groves and poplar, plane, oak, and cypress trees. From fifteen hundred to thirty-five

Olive trees can be found throughout Greece. Greece ranks third in production of olive oil, after Spain and Italy, and is the top exporter of the highest quality extra virgin olive oil. The olive tree can live, on average, for 300 to 600 years. A tree in Chania, Crete, is reported to be 2,000 to 4,000 years old. (Photo by Elaine Thomopoulos)

hundred feet, forests of oak, chestnut, and pine grow. Plane and cypress trees can also be found in Greece, especially in lower altitudes. In the summer, many parts of Greece become very dry and prone to fires, which erupt nearly every summer. The dry pines and shrubbery provide perfect kindling for flames.

The agricultural products of Greece include wheat, corn, rice, barley, sugar beets, olives, tomatoes, potatoes, grapes, melons, citrus fruits, apples, figs, dates, almonds, pomegranates, tobacco, and cotton.

Greek fauna is also incredibly diverse, a result of the country's varied terrain and the millennia-long admixture of European, Asian, and African species. Greece hosts bears, wild cats, wolves, deer, squirrels, foxes, hares, porcupines, boar, and a rare species of wild goat, the ibex, which clings to the steep hills of Crete. All told, there are 116 mammal species, of which 57 belong to endangered species categories. Greece is a key north-south stopover for birds. It has over 422 species, about two-thirds of which are migratory birds. Indigenous birds include the owl, pelican, pheasant, partridge, woodcock, and nightingale. In the Dadia-Lefkimmi-Soufli Forest of northern Greece, near Alexandroupolis, 36 of the 38 predatory birds of Europe have been sighted. They include the rare imperial eagle, the lesser spotted eagle, and the black and griffon vultures. As it is situated at the crossroads of Europe, Asia, and Africa, the forest has become one of the two main bird migration routes in Europe.

With its huge coastline and protected bays and lagoons, Greece has a very large—and environmentally stressed—aquatic biodiversity. About 246 species of marine life have been identified, including squid, octopus, starfish, jellyfish, lobster, sea urchin, red mullet, shrimp, crab, oyster, mussel, and cockle. Aside from a large variety of commercially harvested fish and shellfish, there are the Mediterranean monk seals common in the northern Aegean and the loggerhead sea turtles (*Caretta caretta*) found in Crete and the Ionian Islands. There are also playful dolphins, friends of the Greek mariner since Minoan times, as well as whales and porpoises.

The *Caretta caretta* turtles are protected as an endangered species. They always return to the same beach to lay their eggs. Their offspring hatch at night and follow the brightest light to the ocean's edge. At night on the coastlines where they make their nests, natives and tourists follow a lights-out policy. "Keep Out" signs posted on short plastic fences keep out humans and predators but allow the newly hatched turtles to head for the sea. Two organizations that strive to help them are ARCHELON and MEDASSET.

This specially designed cage can be found on the beaches of Zakynthos. It protects the turtle's nest from tourists and predators but allows the endangered *Caretta caretta* baby turtles, which hatch from eggs buried in the sand, to emerge and rush toward the sea. (Photo by Elaine Thomopoulos)

Greece has fifty-nine species of reptiles and eighteen species of amphibians. They include the tree frog, Turkish gecko, wall gecko, fire salamander, sand viper, lizard elapi, lizard snake, ladder snake, and Greek tortoise. It also boasts one of Europe's largest fish farming industries, a key export area and necessary for the Greeks' huge consumption of fish products.

Greece has a variety of mineral resources. Bauxite, which is used to produce aluminum, is the most significant one. Bauxite deposits are found in central Greece within the Parnassos-Ghiona geotectonic zone and on the island of Evia. Greece is among the top three producers of bauxite in the world. There are also deposits of aluminum, nickel, magnesite, bentonite clay, and marble. Greece exported 11.4 percent of the world's marble in 2017. It was among the top ten producers of bentonite in the world and the only producer of huntite-hydromagnesite, a rare mineral added as a fire retardant to plastic.

*Alexander Billinis and Elaine Thomopoulos*

**See also:** Chapter 1: Protected Areas and UNESCO Monuments of World Heritage. Chapter 4: Agriculture.

**Further Reading**

Gibbons, Bob. 2003. *Travellers Nature Guides: Greece.* Oxford: Oxford University Press.

Kiprop, Joseph. 2019. "What Are the Major Natural Resources of Greece?" WorldAtlas, August 14, 2019. Accessed April 1, 2021. worldatlas.com/articles/what-are-the-major-natural-resources-of-greece.html.

Mining Greece. n.d. Accessed May 1, 2021. https://www.miningreece.com/mining-greece/investing-in-greece/investing-in-greek-mineral-wealth/.

Parnitha National Park. 2006. "National Parks." Prefecture of Attica, Forest Service of Parintha. Accessed April 1, 2021. http://www.parnitha-np.gr/national_parks.htm.

Strid, Arne, and Kit Tan, eds. 1991. *Mountain Flora of Greece.* Vol. 2. Edinburgh: University Press.

## Ionian Islands

On the west side of the Greek mainland, across from Italy, are the Ionian Islands, also known in Greek as the *Eftanisia* (the seven islands). The principal Ionian islands from north to south are Corfu (Kerkyra), Paxi, Lefkada, Ithaka, Cephalonia, Zakynthos, and Kythira. The islands' beautiful beaches make them popular tourist destinations. The Ionian Islands have a more humid climate than most of the Aegean Islands, with the result that these islands tend to be more verdant, another thing that makes them attractive to tourists.

In 1953, a major earthquake, with a surface wave magnitude of 7.2, hit the islands of Kefalonia and Zakynthos. Most of the buildings on these two islands were leveled. Thereafter, the government instituted strict building codes, which has prevented further damage by subsequent earthquakes. Many of the buildings that were destroyed had been built when the islanders were under Venetian rule, over two hundred years earlier.

The Ionian Islands' culture, architecture, and dialects clearly reflect the influence of the Venetians. Like the rest of Greece, ruins and legacies from many eras abound, but the majority of the architecture reflects Venetian styles. They would hardly be out of place in Italy or along the Croatian Adriatic coast. Despite the centuries of Italian rule, the local Greeks were passionately Greek and Orthodox; there was only a very small group that converted to Catholicism, and often Venetians living there were Hellenized. Greece's first governor, Count Ioannis Kapodistrias, was born of a Hellenized Venetian family in Corfu.

The Ionian Islands passed from Venetian to French rule in 1797 and briefly to a joint Russian-Ottoman Protectorate and again to French control until the British evicted the French in 1814. They were not under the rule of the Ottoman Empire, with the exception of a few years for Zakynthos and nearly two hundred years for Lefkada. The Ionian Islands had an elected assembly, and British rule generally improved infrastructure and living standards. These islands served as a base from which Greek revolutionaries plotted to overthrow Turkish rule. Once Greece became independent, the Ionian islanders agitated for union with Greece, which Britain granted in 1864.

*Alexander Billinis*

**See also:** Chapter 2: Overview.

**Further Reading**

Higgins, Michael Denis. 2008. *Geology of the Greek Islands.* Berkeley: University of California Press.

Louis, Diana Farr. 2009. *The Secret of the Greek Islands.* New York: Petro Books.

Potts, Jim. 2010. *The Ionian Islands and Epirus: A Cultural History.* Oxford: Oxford University Press.

Simmonds, Jane, et al., eds. 2011. *The Greek Islands.* London: Dorling Kindersley Limited.

## Macedonia and Thrace

### MACEDONIA

Macedonia is a province of Greece divided up into three prefectures (*peripheries*). It includes the autonomous Monastic Community of Mount Athos. Historically, it was part of a larger geographical region that included not only Greece but also a part of southwestern Bulgaria and the Republic of North Macedonia. Macedonia's climate varies, from Mediterranean along the coastline, to Alpine and Continental, particularly in its western, inland areas. Greece's highest peak, Mount Olympus, is in southwestern Macedonia, and in classical Greece this series of mountains was known as the "Home of the Gods."

Though generally Mediterranean in climate, Macedonia is lusher in vegetation than southern Greece. Several rivers flow through Macedonia into the Aegean Sea, notably the Axios or Vardar River, the Aliakmon River, and the Nestos River, which forms the traditional border between Macedonia and Thrace provinces.

Greece's second-largest city, Thessaloniki (Salonika), with over one million people in its metropolitan area, is one of the most historic cities in Europe. Founded by the ancient Greek kings of Macedonia, the city remained a key port and cultural hub during the Roman Empire and was the Byzantine Empire's second-largest city. Its commerce and culture were second only to those of Constantinople (modern-day Istanbul). In the ninth century, two brothers from Thessaloniki, Cyril and Methodius, brought the Cyrillic alphabet and the Orthodox Christian religion to the Slavic peoples to the north of the city. The city's port remains a key transport center not just for Greece but also for the Balkan Peninsula and beyond.

Macedonia is the home of Alexander the Great, and the local flag of the province displays the Golden Sunburst of this ancient Greek kingdom on a blue background. Ancient cities such as Pella, Alexander the Great's birthplace, and the city of Philippi in eastern Macedonia are key tourist attractions, as are the beaches along the Aegean coastline, particularly the Halkidiki Peninsula due east of Thessaloniki.

Macedonia was liberated by the Greek army in the First and Second Balkan Wars of 1912 and 1913. The province received hundreds of thousands of Greeks expelled from Turkey, Bulgaria, and Russia, which gives it a very diverse mosaic of Greek regional cultures. It reflects cultural influences from Turkey, Bulgaria, Serbia, Republic of North Macedonia, and Sephardic Jewry.

## THRACE

Thrace, Greece's northeasternmost province, borders Bulgaria and Turkey. It is to the east of the Greek province of Macedonia. While the climate is Mediterranean along the coast, in the mountainous interior it quickly changes to continental. A continental climate is one that is relatively dry but with hot summers and cold winters. In Thrace, about 30 percent of the population is Muslim, including Turks, Bulgarian-speaking Muslims (known in the region as Pomaks), and Muslim Roma. This is Greece's largest religious minority and the only part of the country with a significant non-Orthodox and nonethnic Greek population. Thrace's principal cities, Xanthi and Komotini, are a fascinating blend of Orthodox and Muslim cultures. Like Macedonia, the original geographical area was divided into separate countries. Thrace as a geographical entity includes northern (Bulgarian) Thrace, eastern (Turkish) Thrace, and western (Greek) Thrace. Greek Thrace, also known as "Western Thrace," formally became part of Greece in 1923 with the Treaty of Lausanne, which was negotiated after the Greek-Turkish War.

Thrace is famous for its natural beauty, including the Rhodope Mountains with its Muslim villages on high, the intensely cultivated tobacco fields, its wild rushing rivers, and the deltas of the Evros River, which host millions of migratory birds each spring.

Thrace is also well known for its handicrafts. These include silk making, an industry unbroken since Byzantine times, concentrated particularly in the town of Soufli. The province is undeveloped, other than for the handicraft industry, tourism, agriculture, and the military. A large portion of Greece's military is stationed here because of its proximity to Turkey.

*Alexander Billinis*

**See also:** Chapter 5: Sidebar: Mount Athos: Oldest-Surviving Monastic Community Is Home to Two Thousand Monks. Chapter 6: Muslim Religious Minority of Western Thrace.

**Further Reading**

Fly Me to the Moon Travel. "Soufli Silk Road." Accessed August 21, 2020. https://flymetothemoontravel.com/soufliilk-trade/.

Sakellariou, Michael. 1983. *Macedonia: 4000 Years of Greek History and Civilization.* Athens: Ekotike Athinon.

## National Parks

The Greek National Parks System consists of twenty-two designated parks located throughout mainland Greece and the islands. In addition, there are designated special protection areas for wildlife, birds, wetlands, and aesthetic forests. A "preserved natural monuments" designation is granted to areas of aesthetic, historical, and cultural value, as well as to areas of great ecological, paleontological, or geomorphologic interest.

National parks preserve and protect an array of flora and fauna, geological formations, and underground aquatics. Most national parks include forests and prohibit hunting, grazing, logging, uprooting plants, cutting down trees, settlements, industry, or any other activities that could be detrimental to the serene state of the parks. They consist of an area that is designated for absolute protection, often referred to as the core, surrounded by a buffer zone meant to enclose and protect the inner cores of the parks. In the buffer zones, there can be found traditional subsistence agriculture and visitors' facilities.

In 1938, Mount Olympus became Greece's first national park after Prime Minister Ioannis Metaxas created a national parks system. The 193-square-mile region has since been declared one of "The Most Important Bird Areas of the European Community." Later that year, Mount Parnassos received a National Park designation. Mount Parnitha, north of Athens, was established in 1961 and Samaria's Gorge and Mount Ainos in 1962. Mount Pindos (Valia-Calda) and Mount Oiti were designated National Parks in 1966, Vikos Gorge-Aoos River in 1973, and the Prespes Lakes in Northern Macedonia and Sounion in Attica in 1974.

Since 1992, additional areas were granted "national park" status. They include:

- Northern Sporades National Marine Park in the Aegean Sea in 1992, which includes the terrestrial and marine areas of the Northern Sporades Archipelago, as they provide refuge for the monk seal (*Monachus monachus*),
- National Marine Park of Zakynthos in the Ionian Sea in 1999, for the protection of the sea turtle *Caretta caretta*,
- National Park of Schoinias in 2003 for the protection of the Schinias wetland and the pine (*Pinus pinea*) forest,
- Dadia-Lefkimmi-Soufli Forest, for the protection of the birds of prey that live there,
- North Pindos,
- Lake Karla,
- Mesolonghi Lagoon,

- Axios-Aliakmonas-Gallikos-Loudias-Kaloxori Lagoon,
- Kastoria Lake,
- Psalidi area in Kos Island in the Aegean Sea,
- Lake Kerkini,
- Evros Delta, and
- Amvrakikos Gulf.

*John Psiharis*

**See also:** Chapter 1: Flora, Fauna, and Natural Resources; Protected Areas and UNESCO Monuments of World Heritage.

**Further Reading**

Parnitha National Park. 2006. "National Parks." Prefecture of Attica, Forest Service of Parintha. Accessed April 1, 2021. http://www.parnitha-np.gr/national_parks.htm.

Travel Triangle. "National Parks in Greece: 9 Places to Experience the Best of Greek Beauty and Wilderness." Accessed March 9, 2019. https://traveltriangle.com/blog/national-parks-in-greece.

## Peloponnesus

The Peloponnesus is the southernmost peninsula of Greece, of the Balkan Peninsula, and of mainland Europe. Technically, the Peloponnesus, Greek for "the island of Pelops," is an island. It was connected to the Greek mainland by a narrow isthmus about six miles across, which was cut into a canal in the late 1800s by a Greek-French consortium. The Corinth Canal cuts through the Isthmus of Corinth to connect the Gulf of Corinth with the Saronic Gulf in the Aegean Sea. Because of its narrow dimension, it does not accommodate modern ocean freighters.

Like most of Greece, the Peloponnesus is largely mountainous, and until recently travel in the interior was difficult, with poor roads over steep mountains and gorges. In the past three decades, EU-funded motorways have opened up the peninsula to transportation. The largely mountainous peninsula has two key plains: one in the east, around the towns of Argos and Nafplion, and the other in the southeast, in the Eurotas River Valley near Sparta. Both locations are intensely cultivated with typical Mediterranean products such as citrus fruits and olives. Much of the interior is mountainous, alternatively wooded or rocky, and often the mountains go straight into the sea. Animal husbandry is a common pursuit in the interior.

The generally forbidding geography has resulted in a large outflow of Peloponnesians to Athens or abroad. They form a very large portion of the Greek diaspora, particularly in the United States.

Patras and the Nafplion-Argos area are the largest cities, and both are ports. Patras is a key manufacturing center and a hub for trade with Italy, always one of Greece's largest trading partners.

In spite of its forbidding geography, the Peloponnesus is home to some of Greece's most historically significant sites. They include Olympia, site of the ancient Olympic Games, which have inspired their modern counterpart; the Mycenean ruins around Napflion; and the city of Sparta. These ancient wonders continue to be emblazoned on the Western consciousness, as do the Byzantine wonders of Mystra and Monemvasia and the Venetian fortresses dotting the landscape. Most notable of the latter is the delightful Italianate city of Nafplion, which was Greece's first capital after her liberation from the Turks in 1830.

*Alexander Billinis*

**See also:** Chapter 1: Overview.

**Further Reading**

Higgins, Michael Denis, and Reynold Higgins. 1996. *A Geological Companion to Greece and the Aegean*. Ithaca, NY: Cornell University Press.

## Pollution of the Air

Greece, like its European neighbors, has experienced declining air quality, especially in urban areas, largely due to the economic crisis. This is a recent reversal from two decades of efforts that yielded significant improvement.

Among the reasons for the increase in air pollution were the government's lifting of long-standing bans on diesel cars in the cities of Athens and Thessaloniki and the lowering of diesel fuel taxes. These actions were meant to help transporters and citizens struggling during the economic crisis. The policies had helped Greece reduce nitrogen dioxide emissions by half between 1996 and 2006, in comparison to other European countries that lacked meaningful improvements on this metric.

The tripling of the cost of heating gas during the economic crisis, which forced many to burn wood in fireplaces and wood-burning stoves, also contributed to the declining air quality. In 2013, winter particle pollution had increased 30 percent in Thessaloniki. Scientists found that much of the wood being burnt was tainted with lead, arsenic, cadmium, and other chemicals, releasing those compounds into the air. This was a result of people burning painted or treated wood, and even their rubbish, to stay warm.

According to the "European Environment Agency 2019 Fact Sheet on Air Pollution in Greece," the percentage of urban population subjected to ozone concentrations that were above acceptable European Union (EU) standards showed a drastic change: from 47.9 percent in 2014 to 96.8 percent in 2017.

A 2017 study found that in 2015, 8 percent of deaths in Greece were attributed to pollution. Of about 122,000 deaths that year, 7,216 were related to air pollution, 257 to water pollution, and 1,422 to polluted workplaces.

In 2018, Athens announced its intention to ban all diesel vehicles from the city center beginning in 2025. In January 2019, the European Commission issued a formal notice to Greece, warning of increasing air pollution levels and the urgent need to take action. The commission noted Greece's violation of European legislation setting limits for air pollutants. In Athens, the report found that nitrogen dioxide had been above established limits since 2010 and cited a failure to monitor air pollution in the northern port city of Thessaloniki.

*John Psiharis*

**See also:** Chapter 4: Energy.

**Further Reading**

"Brussels Warns Greece to Reduce Athens Pollution Levels." *Ekathimerini*. January 24, 2019. Accessed February 17, 2019. http://www.ekathimerini.com/236962/article/ekathimerini/news/brussels-warns-greece-to-reduce-athens-pollution-levels.

European Environment Agency. 2019. "Greece – Air Pollution Fact Sheet." Accessed February 16, 2020. https://www.eea.europa.eu/themes/air/country-fact-sheets/2019-country-fact-sheets/greece.

Fuller, Gary. 2016. "Air Quality Worsens in Greece as Recession Bites." *The Guardian*. October 30, 2016. Accessed February 15.2020. https://www.theguardian.com/environment/2016/oct/30/air-quality-worsens-greece-recession-bites-world-pollutionwatch.

Hartley, Gary. 2018. "Athens Is Trying to Cut Fumes from Its Roads and Smoke from Its Bars." City Metric. March 12, 2018. Accessed February 16. 2020. https://www.citymetric.com/horizons/athens-trying-cut-fumes-its-roads-and-smoke-its-bars-3738.

Logothetis, Georgia. 2017. "Pollution Kills 1 in 12 Greeks. Time for a Massive Cleanup Act." Hellenic Leaders. October 31, 2017. Accessed February 15, 2020. https://medium.com/@HellenicLeaders/pollution-kills-1-in-12-greeks-time-for-a-massive-clean-up-act-c2d078d1c6b6.

## Pollution of the Water

Water pollution is at high levels in Greece, as it is in many parts of the industrialized world. Nitrate and phosphate pollution in rivers, lakes, and wetlands is evident. In Greece, the majority of water pollution is attributed to livestock farming, industrial pollutants, sewage, and agricultural chemicals such as fertilizers and pesticides.

Water pollution levels in Greece's thirty natural and twelve artificial lakes vary. Surface freshwater in the Pindus region and throughout Epirus (northwest Greece) is considered very clean. Some lakes, such as Vestonis, Vegoritis, Ag. Vasilios (Koronia), Doirani, Kastoria, and Pamvotis, are experiencing higher levels of pollution resulting from fertilizers, pesticides, heavy metals, organic matter, and untreated sewage. The Gulf of Saronikos, which contains 50 percent of Greece's industrial facilities, is one of the most polluted areas in the nation.

The safety of drinking water varies throughout Greece. Water testing in nine regions occurs on a regular basis. These were among the findings: Attica prefecture proved to have good quality water, while the Cyclades Islands were about the worse due mainly to limited water resources. In general, mainland water supplies are considered to be better than those of many of the islands. Tests of the Athens's water supply for thirteen heavy metals and metalloids showed values below the regulated levels; however, testing in two of the fifty-two villages in Thessaloniki prefecture revealed higher than permitted levels of nitrates.

Greece has not aggressively addressed the water pollution crisis and actually made it worse by easing environmental rules during the economic crisis. In 2019, the European Commission asked the EU's highest court to fine Greece for its failure to protect its waters from agricultural nitrate contamination. It asked the court to impose daily fines of 2,600 euros dating back to 2015, when the EU Court of Justice ruled that Greece had not complied with terms of an agreement to designate Nitrate Vulnerable Zones. Since then, Greece has designated twelve such zones but has not implemented any action plans on them. The commission also requested that the fine for noncompliance be increased tenfold to 23,700 euros if Greece did not comply by the next court ruling.

A bright spot in terms of water quality is the bathing waters. There are over two thousand monitoring points, and twenty-five thousand samples have been collected. Since 2001, Greece has met mandatory water standards 98 percent of the time.

*John Psiharis*

**See also:** Chapter 4: Agriculture.

**Further Reading**

McCann, Eileen Wray. 2019. "Water Quality Concerns in Greece." Circle of Blue, March 11, 2019 Accessed February 24, 2020. https://www.circleofblue.org/2019/world/water-quality-concerns-in-greece/.

Nations Encyclopedia. 2009. "Greece – Environment." Accessed February 23, 2020. https://www.nationsencyclopedia.com/Europe/Greece-ENVIRONMENT.html.

Nguyen, Long Vu. n.d. "Three Environmental Issues of Greece." University of California – Irvine. Accessed February 24, 2020. https://www.ics.uci.edu/~wmt/courses/ICS5_W13/Greece.html.

Valavanidis, Athanasios, and Thomas Vlachogianni. 2011. "The Most Important and Urgent Environmental Problems in Greece in the Last Decade (2000–2010)." Department of Chemistry, University of Athens, March 18, 2011. Accessed February 24, 2020. http://195.134.76.37/scinews/Reports/Rep_Env_problems2000-10.htm.

## Population Decline

Greece has a population of approximately eleven million. Within the past decade, it has witnessed a subtle decline in population. As the population rate continues to fall, several sources emphasize the seriousness of this decrease and insist that the country is in a struggle for survival. Although the crippling economic crisis can be blamed for many devastating social and health consequences, population challenges existed well before the economic collapse and even added to the financial situation. However, during the years of the financial crisis, which began in 2008, the challenges became exacerbated.

One of Greece's greatest challenges is that it is aging faster than many other countries in Europe, with 21.4 percent of its population over sixty-five years of age. Only Japan and Italy have surpassed Greece with a higher percentage of elderly citizenry. Although the country has had one of the highest, steadily increasing rates of life expectancy in Europe for over fifty years, the World Health Organization states that since 2011, it has been outstripped by other EU countries. While it stands at about seventy-eight years for men and eighty-three years for women, Greece's elders have been confronting many more obstacles than their European counterparts. Cuts on health-care systems and pensions have made life for the Greek elderly one of constant misery, leading to a rise in mental illness and chronic diseases.

In 2014, the Global Age Watch Index, which assesses the social and economic well-being of the older population in ninety-six countries around the world, ranked Greece at seventy-nine, making it the lowest ranked country in western Europe. Based on four criteria—income, health, capabilities, and enabling environments—the study demonstrated that unemployment, low educational attainment, and dissatisfaction with transport, safety, and civic freedom were stifling the elderly in Greece. It also showed that Greek elderly had the worst quality of life in Europe. Much of the disenchantment can be attributed to the effects of the austerity measures that Greece had to implement. These measures were imposed by the Troika (the European Commission, the European Central Bank, and the International Monetary Fund), starting in 2010, so that Greece could obtain loans to help it through its economic crisis. Pensioners suffered, since their pensions were reduced by up to 50 percent, with more reductions expected to take place in the upcoming years. To date, the Greek pension system is looked upon as one of the weakest in the world. Being a major burden on the economy, it has been blamed for contributing to the Greek crisis as nearly a quarter of Greece's eleven million people are retired. Until now, about 75 percent of Greek pensioners could retire before age sixty-one and often as early as forty-five. However, the austerity measures have changed this, bringing the new age of retirement to sixty-seven years.

Greece has also seen a high unemployment rate, which dramatically surged since the crisis and hit an all-time high of 28 percent in 2013. This has resulted in 57 percent of young people between the ages of eighteen and thirty-four living at their parents' home longer than in other European countries. Many of the elderly have been forced to support their grown children on their small pension incomes. Due to such conditions, young people are marrying later in life while birth rates are declining among married Greeks who are putting off having children that they simply cannot afford.

Since 1980, there has been a steady decline in the number of recorded births, averaging at 8.4 births/1,000 population in 2017. According to the *CIA World Factbook* and the Hellenic Statistical Authority (ELSTAT), the number of births in 2014 hit an all-time low, with the number of deaths exceeding those of birth by over 2 percent. ELSTAT's data shows that only in Crete and in the southern Aegean region are birth rates higher than death rates. The data also shows that the average age for Greek women to have children is thirty-one with the number of births to unmarried women remaining quite low when compared with other European countries. There have been a growing number of pregnant refugees and migrants giving birth in refugee camps or nearby hospitals. The World Population Review notes that there is also an increase in uninsured migrant mothers living outside the camps who after giving birth flee the hospitals at night with their unregistered babies as they are unable to pay the delivery cost of about $600–$1,200.

Migration brought on by the economic crisis has also contributed to the shrinking Greek population. Since 2008, over 450,000 young Greek professionals and graduates have left the country, seeking employment and a more secure future abroad. Countries such as Germany, the United Kingdom, Australia, and the Emirates are benefiting, while Greece is suffering from its worse brain drain in history. It is losing its best, talented professionals in medicine, education, computer technology, and engineering. The huge loss of human capital will have significant long-term implications for Greece's economic growth potential and its competitiveness throughout the next decade as it tries to recuperate from years of recession. Whereas many believe that Greece is on the road to recovery, the outlook for a demographic evolution of the Greek population is negative with experts predicting that the numbers will continue to decrease as the number of elderly citizens increases and low birth rates remain the trend.

*Angelyn Balodimas-Bartolomei*

**See also:** Chapter 4: Overview.

**Further Reading**

Central Intelligence Agency. *World Factbook*. Washington, DC: Central Intelligence Agency. Last Updated: April 15, 2021. Accessed April 16, 2021. https://www.cia.gov/the-world-factbook/countries/greece/.

Global Age Watch. 2015. "Age Watch Report Card. 79th Greece." Accessed May 12, 2018. https://www.helpage.org/global-agewatch/population-ageing-data/country-ageing-data/.

Hellenic Statistical Authority. "Births 2016." Accessed May 12, 2018. https://www.statistics.gr/en/statistics/-/publication/SPO03/2016.

World Atlas. 2018. "World Facts. Countries with the Largest Aging Population in the World." Accessed May 12, 2018. https://www.worldatlas.com/articles/countries-with-the-largest-aging-population-in-the world.html.

World Population Review. Accessed May 12, 2018. http://worldpopulationreview.com/countries/greece-population/.

## Protected Areas and UNESCO Monuments of World Heritage

According to the definition given by the International Union for the Conservation of Nature and Natural Resources (IUCN), the term protected area refers to: "An area of land and/or sea especially dedicated to the protection and maintenance of biological diversity, and of natural and associated cultural resources, and managed through legal or other effective means (Parnitha National Park 2006)."

In Greece, different protected areas have been established. Most of these are included in NATURA 2000, a European Network of Protected Areas. This network is based on two European Directives, the 92/43/EEC Directive for the protection of habitats and the 79/409/EEC Directive for the protection of birds.

Categories of protected areas in Greece are Aesthetic Forests, Preserved Natural Monuments, Ramsar Wetlands, Wildlife Refuges, Game Breeding Stations, Biogenetic Reserves, Biosphere Reserves, World Heritage Areas, Absolute Nature Reserve Areas, and European Diploma Areas.

Aesthetic forests are wooded areas or natural landscapes of special aesthetic, ecological, and tourist value, whose flora, fauna, and singular natural beauty must be protected. They are often part of the peripheral (buffer) zones of national parks. There are nineteen aesthetic forests in Greece with a total area of 81,815 acres.

Preserved natural monuments include individual trees or clumps of trees of outstanding botanical, paleontological, aesthetic, historic, and cultural value, as well as areas of great ecological, paleontological, or geomorphologic interest. There are fifty-one preserved natural monuments in Greece that cover an area of 41,612 acres.

Ramsar wetlands of international importance are defined by the International Convention of Ramsar, Iran (1971), of which Greece is a signatory. There are 146 contracting parties in this convention, with 1,462 wetlands, covering 309,870,148 acres. Ten of these are on Greek soil.

The 580 wildlife refuges in Greece cover 2,125,106 acres. These areas meet the basic needs of wild animals, such as food, water, and privacy. Local hunting prohibitions, game breeding stations, and controlled hunting areas can be established in order to "protect and save the country's natural environment" and "preserve, develop and exploit the game wealth of our country." These areas constitute a network of protected areas, where the laws for hunting play an important role in the preservation of wild fauna. The number of refuges and hunting prohibitions, as well as the changes in boundaries and sizes of these areas, are set each year. Additionally, there are twenty-one game breeding stations covering 2,937 acres and seven controlled hunting areas covering 268,956 acres.

In accordance with the 1979 European Union Directive 79/409/EEC, addressing preservation of wild birds, each member of the European Union is obliged to "preserve not only wild birds' populations, but also sufficient size and diversity of their biotopes, in order to achieve their protection." Greece has 113 of the special protection areas that were created for the preservation of certain species.

In accordance with the United Nations's Human and Biosphere program, two areas were designated Biosphere Reserves: Samaria Gorge and Olympus National Park. The reserves are recognized as important biodiverse ecosystems that need to be preserved through sustainable development and education, research, monitoring, and training.

The European Council declared sixteen areas in Greece as biogenetic reserves. They are defined as protected areas characterized by one or more typical, unique, endangered, or rare habitats, biocenoses, or ecosystems.

Mikro and Megalo Seitani in Samos, where the monk seals can be found, and Dystos Wetlands in Evvia are absolute nature reserves, and Cretan White Mountains National Park (Samaria) received the European Diploma of the Council of Europe. The Council of Europe awards these certificates in order to protect areas of exceptional European conservational interest. The council is not affiliated with the EU and is a different organization than the European Council.

The seventeen areas in Greece that have been declared monuments of world heritage by the UNESCO are:

- Meteora,
- Mount Athos,
- Temple of Apollo Epicurus at Vassae,
- Sanctuary of Asclepios at Epidaurus,
- Pythagorean and Heraion of Samos,
- Palaeochristian and Byzantine Monuments of Thessaloniki,
- Old Town of Corfu,
- Monasteries of Daphni, Osios Loukas, and Nea Moni of Chios,
- Medieval City of Rhodes,
- Monastery of Saint John "the Theologian" and the Cave of the Apocalypse on the island of Patmos,
- Delos Island,
- Mycenae and Tiryn,
- Olympia,
- Mystras,
- Delphi,
- Aigai (Vergina), and
- Acropolis of Athens.

Annually, visitors from throughout the nation and around the world descend on this network of parks and protected areas for recreation and relaxation, including camping, mountain climbing, rafting, and hiking. They study the environment and the biodiversity within it or simply bask in the magnificence and serenity of their surroundings.

*John Psiharis*

**See also:** Chapter 1: Flora, Fauna, and Natural Resources. Chapter 5: Sidebar: Mount Athos: Oldest-Surviving Monastic Community Is Home to Two Thousand Monks.

**Further Reading**

Parnitha National Park. 2006. "National Parks." Prefecture of Attica, Forest Service of Paritha. Accessed March 6, 2019. http://www.parnitha-np.gr/national_parks.htm.

Travel Triangle. "National Parks in Greece: 9 Places to Experience the Best of Greek Beauty and Wilderness." Accessed March 9, 2019. https://traveltriangle.com/blog/national-parks-in-greece.

Valavanidis, Athanasios. 2017. "Natural Forests and Natural Parks in Greece. Aesthetically Attractive and Fragile. Impact of Environmental Pollution, Deforestation, Overgrazing, Soil Erosion and Forest Fires." Accessed April 22, 2021. https://www.researchgate.net/profile/Athanasios-Valavanidis/publication/315051010_Natural_Forests_and_Natural_Parks_in_Greece_Aesthetically_Attractive_and_Fragile_Impact_of_Environmental_Pollution_Deforestation_Overgrazing_Soil_Erosion_and_Forest_Fires/links/58c96fc9aca27286b3af9476/Natural-Forests-and-Natural-Parks-in-Greece-Aesthetically-Attractive-and-Fragile-Impact-of-Environmental-Pollution-Deforestation-Overgrazing-Soil-Erosion-and-Forest-Fires.pdf.

## Thessaly and Central Greece

### THESSALY

Thessaly is Greece's breadbasket. Much of the province is a well-watered and fertile plain producing a large proportion of the country's cereals. Thessaly has a population of 733,000. Flanked by Macedonia to the north, Epirus to the west, and Central Greece to the south, it is open to the Aegean on the east. Volos, one of Greece's largest ports and industrial centers, is on Thessaly's coast. Its port is the third major commercial port in Greece. The province has several other large market towns, including Larissa, Thessaly's capital, and Trikala, its largest city.

Thessaly generally has a Mediterranean climate, though its western and northern areas, which are mountainous, have a climate both continental and at times alpine. It has fewer sites from the Classical Era, though its Byzantine monuments, most particularly the monasteries of Meteora, perched on high rock formations, draw both pilgrims and tourists.

Thessaly was annexed to Greece in 1881.

### CENTRAL GREECE

Central Greece, also called *Rumeli*, is located south of Thessaly. The area is roughly the geographic center of the Greek state, hence the name. Central Greece is made up of two peripheries and runs west to east from the Ionian Sea to the Aegean Sea. It includes Evia, which is technically an island but separated from the mainland at its narrowest point by a strait only 40 meters (130 feet) wide. The island has a fertile, verdant north, a mountainous center, and a relatively arid south. Aside from the mountains, the climate is typical Mediterranean.

The adjoining mainland is generally quite fertile, much of the plains having been part of Lake Kopais, a marshy area drained for agriculture in the 1880s. This includes the city of Thebes, a key local administrative center. Due west of Thebes, the mountains rise toward Mount Parnassus, one of Greece's highest mountains and a thriving winter sports center. As in other mountainous areas of Greece, animal husbandry has been the norm. Local towns, such as Livadia, which are set in an area of deep gorges and forests, are renowned for their grilled meats.

In the shadow of Mount Parnassus are the ruins of Delphi, one of the most important sites of classical Greece, set in a stunning panorama. The wall of Parnassus rises to the north, and hundreds of meters below lies the Gulf of Corinth, reminding the traveler that, as in most of Greece, the sea is never far away.

The mountains continue west of Parnassus toward the Ionian Sea, with several important towns along the Gulf of Corinth, such as Galaxidi, Nafpaktos, and Messonlongi, the site of a key battle in Greece's War of Independence. Away from the coast, the forbidding mountains were known in the Ottoman Era as the *Agrafa* (literally, "unwritten")—unregistered areas essentially outside the control of any central authority. The area remains sparsely populated until further north, at the town of Arta, where Epirus meets Central Greece.

*Alexander Billinis*

**See also:** Chapter 5: Monasteries and Nunneries.

**Further Reading**

Higgins, Michael Denis, and Reynold Higgins. 1996. *A Geological Companion to Greece and the Aegean*. Ithaca, NY: Cornell University Press.

Provatakis, M. 2006. *Meteora: History of the Monasteries and Monasticism*. Athens: Michalis Toumbis.

CHAPTER 2

# HISTORY

## OVERVIEW

Greece's history is a story of tragedies and triumphs, of death and destruction, but also of renewal and hope. Greece's story begins in the Stone Age, from 11000 to 3000 BCE, when early man started raising crops and crafting tools of stone. From 3000 to 2000 BCE, a Bronze Age civilization was established on the Cycladic Islands of the Aegean. Their art, consisting of primitive flat-looking figurines, can be seen in museums such as the Museum of Cycladic Art in Athens.

From 2500 to 1450, a flowering of civilization occurred on the island of Crete in the Aegean Sea. The people, who were called Minoans, used an early system of writing called Linear A (still undeciphered) and built palaces. The early palaces were destroyed by an earthquake or a series of earthquakes but were rebuilt. A tour of the Palace of Knossos shows beautifully decorated frescoes as well as practical indoor plumbing. The Aegean island of Thera (Santorini) also suffered destruction due to earthquakes. Here, archaeologists discovered the ancient town of Akrotiri.

From about 1600 to 1100, another ancient people called the Mycenaeans occupied Southern Greece, Athens, Thebes, Tiryns, as well as Crete. They used a writing system called Linear B, with which they recorded economic transactions as early as 1450. The Mycenaeans built fortifications, still in existence today, which were so massive that they were thought to be built by mythological giants called Cyclops. Inexplicably, from 1200 to 900, the Mycenaean civilization declined so much that evidence of their writing disappeared. From 1000 to 650, there was a renewal, with city-states such as Athens and Sparta developing. The city-states established colonies in central coastal Asia Minor, as well as in Spain, Italy, Africa, and along the shores of the Black Sea. Each city-state developed its own unique culture, and each one governed itself independently. From 900 to 800 BCE, writing again made its appearance, but in an entirely different format.

In 776 BCE, the first Olympic Games were held in honor of Zeus, the supreme god of the Greeks, in Olympia, Greece. The games brought the various city-states together every four years until the beginning of the fifth century BCE. There were also the Panathenaic games celebrating the Goddess Athena. They continued every four years into the third century BCE.

From 492 to 449 BCE, the Greeks fought the Persians, who extended their domination over Greek territories throughout Asia Minor. In 490, the Greeks defeated the

Persians in the Battle of Marathon. According to legend, Pheidippides ran about twenty-six miles to deliver the message, "We are victorious," and then he collapsed and died. We now run the marathon to commemorate this event. The war continued when the Persians invaded again in 480. A peace treaty between Athens and Persia was signed in 449.

Beginning in 461, Athens, under the leadership of Pericles, established a democratic government, where each male citizen had a vote. During his rule, which lasted until his death due to the plague in 430, Athens excelled in literature and the arts, and the Parthenon, dedicated to the Goddess Athena, was built. From 395 to 345, another long-term war was fought between Athens and its allies and Sparta and its allies. When Athens surrendered to Sparta in 404, thirty tyrants ruled Athens. Within a year, however, democracy was restored.

The reign of Alexander the Great (356–323 BCE) began in 336 after the assassination of his father, King Philip II (382–336), who had defeated Athens a few years before his death and had united all the city-states except Sparta. Alexander expanded his domain into a vast territory that included North Africa and Afghanistan. When he died at age thirty-three, his empire collapsed and was divided among his generals. One of the remaining parts of Alexander's empire was the Ptolemaic dynasty of Empress Cleopatra, who married Mark Antony of Rome. After the fleet of Cleopatra and Mark Antony was defeated in 31 CE at the Battle of Actium, Rome became a formidable power, taking control over Greece.

Between 49 and 51 CE, Saint Paul introduced Christianity into Greece. However, it was not until 389 that Emperor Theodosius established Christianity as the official religion of the Roman Empire. In 395, the Roman Empire was permanently divided into the Western and Eastern Empires. In 476, the Western Roman Empire collapsed. The Eastern Empire (now known as the Byzantine Empire) continued and flourished, with Greek being spoken throughout the empire, which extended to North Africa, Italy, and Southern Spain.

In 1054, the Christian church separated into two separate entities, now known as the Roman Catholic and Eastern Orthodox Churches. The Fourth Crusade in 1204, organized by the Roman Catholics to combat the Muslims, instead sacked the Eastern Orthodox city of Constantinople (present-day Istanbul). In 1261, Constantine Paleologos recaptured Constantinople and resurrected the Byzantine Empire, although it was smaller than it had previously been.

In 1453, another tragedy unfolded. The Ottoman Turks captured Constantinople, and thus began four hundred years of Ottoman rule over the Greeks. Greece declared its independence from Ottoman oppression in 1821. The last battle of the War of Independence from Ottoman rule was fought in 1829. The nation-state was recognized as an independent nation by the Great Powers of England, France, and Russia in the London Protocol of 1830. Its borders were not defined until 1832 in the Constantinople Protocol, which was signed by the Great Powers and the Ottoman Empire. In the same year, the Great Powers selected King Otto of Bavaria as Greece's first monarch. He assumed power in 1833. The Greeks called their new nation Hellas. Athens became the capital of Greece, and the first Greek university, which is still functioning today, was built in Athens in 1837.

Greece, in 1832, had only a third of the territory of what it has now. The timeline for addition of territory follows:

- In 1864, the islands of Corfu, Paxi, Lefkada, Ithaka, Kefalonia, Zakynthos, and Kythera were peacefully ceded by Britain.

**GREEK TERRITORIAL GAINS 1832–1948**

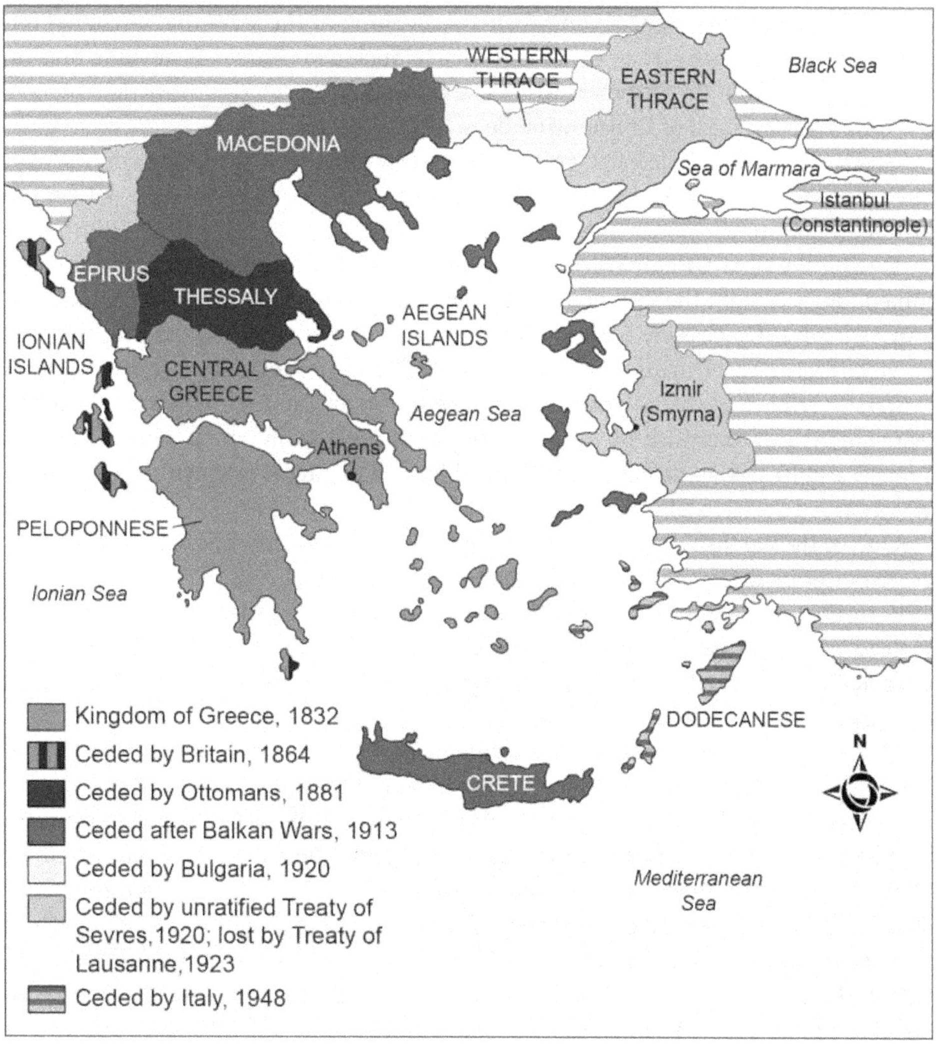

- In 1881, the Ottoman Empire ceded most of Thessaly, in Central Greece, and the region of Arta in Epirus, in northwestern Greece.
- In 1913, following Greece's victories in the Second Balkan War, the Ottoman Empire ceded the region of Macedonia, the rest of present-day Epirus, as well as the large Aegean island of Crete and some of the other smaller Aegean Islands.
- In 1919, following World War I, the Treaty of Neuilly awarded Western Thrace to Greece.
- In 1947, following World War II, Greece annexed the Dodecanese Islands in the Aegean Sea, the last territories to be added to Greece. They had been under the rule of Italy from 1911 to 1943, the Germans from 1943 to 1945, and the British since 1945.

Modern Greece has had more than its share of wars. After the War of Independence, rival factions fought among themselves. Some of the wars that occurred following Greece's declaration of independence included wars whose aim was to recapture land from the Ottoman Turks that they felt had been rightfully theirs before the Ottoman conquest of Constantinople in 1453.

Greece was soundly defeated in the Thirty-Day War with the Ottoman Turks in 1897. The one concession was that Crete became an autonomous state within the Ottoman Empire.

During the First Balkan War of 1912, Greece, Serbia, Montenegro, and Romania joined forces to fight the Ottomans and emerged victorious. During the Second Balkan War of 1913, Greece, Serbia, Montenegro, and Romania fought Bulgaria and emerged victorious. During World War I, in 1917, Greece declared war on the Central Powers (Germany, Austria-Hungary, and the Ottoman Empire). However, its forces were not mobilized until 1918. Because Greece assisted the Entente (United Kingdom, France, and Russia) in defeating the Central Powers during World War I, the country was awarded Western Thrace.

One of the earthshaking events in Greece during the early part of the twentieth century was its defeat at the hands of the Ottoman Turks during the war fought from 1919 to 1922. Greece had fought with the dream of adding territory; what happened instead is called the "Great Catastrophe" by the Greeks. After the Greek troops departed, a fire started by the Turks in Smyrna, now known as Izmir, killed thousands of Greeks and Armenians.

The genocide of the Greeks by the Ottoman Turks had started as early as 1912, but the former still had a huge presence in Asia Minor at the start of the war. During the war years, they had fled, fearing death. After the war, in 1923, Greek prime minister Eleftherios Venizelos helped negotiate an exchange of population between the Greek Orthodox living in Turkey and the Muslims living in Greece. The Greeks from Constantinople, as well as the Muslims from Western Thrace in Greece, were exempt from this population exchange. In fact, most of the Greeks had left before the 1923 population exchange to escape death and destruction. According to the agreement, those Greek Orthodox and Muslims who had left before October 18, 2012, were counted as part of the population exchange.

Two Greek evzones guard the Tomb of the Unknown Soldier, which was dedicated in 1932 to soldiers who perished in Greece's many wars. The evzones, members of an elite presidential guard that keeps watch over the tomb and presidential mansion in Athens, wear a distinct uniform that includes the kilt-like foustanella. General Theodoros Kolokotronis, a hero in the War of Independence, is said to have worn a foustanella with four hundred pleats, one for each year that Greece was under Ottoman domination until their declaration of independence in 1821. (Photo by Elaine Thomopoulos)

More than a million and a half refugees poured into Greece from Turkey, Bulgaria, and the Soviet Union between 1920 and 1928. Since Greece was a country of only a few million, it had a difficult time absorbing them. There was widespread prejudice of the native-born Greeks toward these Greeks from Asia Minor. The Greeks from Asia Minor, as well as those Greeks who arrived after the Turkish pogrom against the Greeks residing in Constantinople in 1955 and the Pontian Greeks that immigrated into the country after the breakup of the Soviet Union in 1991, are now integrated into the fabric of the nation.

The Great Depression hit Greece hard, and bankruptcy was declared in 1932. It suffered even greater hardship with loss of life and destruction of villages during World War II. When on October 28, 1940, Prime Minister Ioannis Metaxas said no to Mussolini's demand to allow Italian troops into Greece, the Italian troops invaded Greece from the Albanian border. In the first victory against the Fascists in World War II, the Greek army drove the Italian army back into Albania. However, Greece

Greek and Armenian refugee children from Anatolia stand outside of a one-story barrack near Athens, Greece, in 1923, the year Greece and Turkey participated in a mandatory exchange of populations. Most of the refugees in Turkey had already left before the exchange. Greece resettled more than a million refugees from 1912 to 1928. (Library of Congress)

succumbed to the Germans in the spring of 1941. During World War II, from 1941 to 1944, the Axis forces of Germany, Bulgaria, and Italy occupied Greece. The celebration of the liberation of mainland Greece and the Ionian Islands from Axis forces in 1944 was short lived.

From 1946 to 1949, brother fought brother in a civil war between government forces and a rival government set up by the Communists. The Communists, who were defeated during the Greek Civil War, fled for their lives into Communist-held lands and were not accepted back into Greece until 1974, when the military dictatorship was overthrown.

Although Greece has been organized as a democracy since 1843, when a new constitution was granted by King Otto, not all of its leaders have been democratically elected, and some have assumed power after coups. There have been eleven successful coups since 1832. The last one was the bloodless coup by three colonels in the Greek army. The dictatorial rule of the colonels lasted from 1967 to 1974. They took control of the press, burned books, and imprisoned suspected Communists on remote islands.

In 1974, Greece sent troops to the independent nation of Cyprus to support a coup by nationalistic Greek Cypriots who wanted union with Greece. Turkish troops then invaded the island and occupied its northern part, driving out the Greeks who resided there. The Turks tried to establish an independent nation in northern Cyprus, but that nation is only recognized by Turkey and Nakhichevan Autonomous Republic.

Throughout the years, Greece has struggled with the question of whether or not to have a king. Finally, in 1973, a referendum conducted by the junta voted against having a monarchy. A second referendum in 1974, after democracy returned to Greece, confirmed that decision.

Many changes occurred in the years that followed the end of the junta and the return to democracy. Laws passed in the 1980s recognized civil marriage, abolished the dowry tradition, made it possible for a woman to keep her mainden name after marriage, facilitated mutual consent and no-fault divorce, and legalized abortion. In 2001, Parliament passed a law eliminating "religion" on the nation's identity card. This occurred despite the opposition of the Greek Orthodox Church and tens of thousands of Greeks demonstrating against it.

In 1981, Greece became a member of the European Union (EU), although the euro was not used as currency until 2002. In the late 1980s, after the breakup of the Soviet Union, ethnic Greeks from Georgia, Kazakhstan, Russia, and Armenia immigrated to Greece. By 2000, two hundred thousand had arrived. In the 1990s, immigrants also arrived from Albania, following the collapse of the economy there.

In 2004, Greece celebrated. They had hosted the very successful Olympic Games, and the economy looked good. However, the good mood of the Greeks did not last long. By 2008, Greece experienced the effects of the worldwide recession. Young people, many of whom were college graduates, had an especially difficult time finding jobs.

The frustration of the youth erupted in riots during December 2008 and January 2009, following the death of a fifteen-year-old student who was shot by a policeman. In 2009, the economic condition of Greece became even worse, and the government asked the EU and the International Monetary Fund for loans. Memoranda of understanding (MoUs) outlined the obligations that were imposed upon Greece by what was called the Troika (the European Commission, the European Central Bank, and the International Monetary Fund) in order to receive the loans. The reforms that the Troika insisted upon included cutting the wages and benefits of government workers and retirees and raising taxes. This led to demonstrations of tens of thousands and strikes that shut down transportation and crucial government services. These demonstrations, which included clashes with police, Molotov cocktails, and tear gas, continued for the duration of the crisis, which as of 2020 had not been fully resolved. By 2019, Greece had achieved a better economic position. However, in 2020, the COVID-19 pandemic destabilized Greece's economy.

The economic crisis that Greece faced in late 2009, which continued through 2020, had started about ten years earlier. Records submitted before Greece's admission to the Eurozone (the EU countries using the euro as common currency), as well as afterward, did not present the true picture of its economic condition. The Eurozone (also referred to as the Euro Area) requires that countries fulfill certain membership criteria, including a budget deficit that does not exceed 3 percent of the gross domestic product (GDP) and a public debt limited to 60 percent of the GDP. Greece had left out certain expenses on the documentation it had submitted. Also, a derivatives deal that Goldman-Sachs first put in place in 2001 masked the true nature of Greece's deficit.

As interest rates were low and the economy seemed stable, the Greek government had taken out loans. Government spending on infrastructure and defense soared, and during the ten years before the financial crash, public wages doubled. The Greeks also took out loans or used their credit cards to purchase property and consumer goods. The economic health of Greece suffered, with much debt and not enough income to pay it back. Because Greece was tied into regulations of the EU, they could not change interest rates or print money to regulate the economy. Corruption also contributed to the financial crisis. This included paying bribes for obtaining licenses or building permits. Other examples of corruption included payment of government jobs for votes, which led to an inflated government bureaucracy, and widespread tax evasion. In September 2011, the government named six thousand firms that owed a total of 59 billion dollars.

The Greek government, over several administrations, tried to overhaul the tax collection mechanism and fight tax cheats. They also privatized several industries, including fourteen regional airports and the port of Piraeus.

Alexis Tsipras, of the radical left SYRIZA Party, had been prime minister from January 2015 to July 2019, except from August 20 to September 20, 2015, when he resigned to call a snap election because he lost the support of some of the MPs from his party. They had been opposed to his support of an 86 billion euro (95 billion dollars) bailout from the Troika. In July 2019, another election was held, with Kyriakos Mitsotakis of the New Democracy Party becoming prime minister. The Mitsotakis government in 2020 has had to deal with the COVID-19 pandemic and a worsening economy because of the pandemic.

*Elaine Thomopoulos*

**Further Reading**

Beaton, Roderick. 2019. *Greece: Biography of a Modern Nation.* Chicago, IL: University of Chicago Press.

Gallant, Thomas W. 2015. *The Edinburgh History of the Greeks, 1768 to 1913. The Long Nineteenth Century.* Edinburgh: Edinburgh University Press.

Gallant, Thomas W. 2016. *Modern Greece: From the War of Independence to the Present*, 2nd edition. London and New York: Bloomsbury Academic.

Leontis, Artemis. 2009. *Culture and Customs of Greece.* Westport, CT: Greenwood Press.

Thomopoulos, Elaine. 2012. *The History of Greece*: Santa Barbara, CA: Greenwood, an imprint of ABC-CLIO.

## TIMELINE

| | |
|---|---|
| 11000–3000 BCE | Stone Age settlements. They use stone tools and begin raising crops. |
| c. 3000–1100 | Bronze Age civilization in the Cycladic Islands of the Aegean Sea. |
| c. 2500–1450 | Minoan Bronze Age civilization on Crete and nearby islands. They use an as yet undeciphered writing system called Linear A, trade with people throughout the Middle East and Europe, and build palaces with indoor plumbing and murals. |
| c. 2000 | Minoan palaces are built on Knossos and other places in Crete. |

| | |
|---|---|
| 1700 | Palaces on Crete are destroyed by an earthquake or series of earthquakes but rebuilt. |
| 1600 (+/- 50 years) | Volcanic eruption on the Aegean island of Thera (Santorini). |
| c. 1600–1100 | Mycenaeans establish themselves in Peloponnesus, Athens, Thebes, Tiryns, and Crete. They use a writing system called Linear B to record economic transactions. |
| c. 1200–900 | Mycenaean civilization declines and evidence of writing disappears. |
| 1000–650 | Colonies are established first in central coastal Asia Minor in an area referred to as Ionia and then Spain, Italy, Africa, and along the shores of the Black Sea. |
| 900–800 | City-states develop, and writing is used again, although in different form. |
| c. 850 | Homer writes *The Iliad* and *The Odyssey* about the Trojan War and the ten-year journey of Odysseus home. Exact date and whether Homer is the true author is not known. |
| 776 | Olympic Games are first held in honor of god Zeus. They continue every four years until the beginning of the fifth century CE. |
| 725 | Spartans conquer Messenians and make them their slaves. |
| 640 | Messenians unsuccessfully rebel against the Spartans, alerting their masters to this danger. Spartans turn themselves into a military state that values strength, prowess, and endurance in men and women. |
| 621 | In Athens, Draco introduces a harsh law code, where even minor infractions are punishable by death. |
| 566 | Panathenaic games are held in honor of goddess Athena. They continue every four years into the third century CE and include not only athletic competitions but even religious and cultural events. |
| 546 | Persians extend their domination over Greek territories throughout Asia Minor. |
| 530 | Mathematician and philosopher Pythagoras of Samos establishes a school in the Greek colony of Cronos (in present-day Calabria, Italy). He is credited with developing what is now known as the Pythagorean theorem. |
| 507 | Cleisthenes's constitution grants equal rights to male citizens of Athens. |
| 490 | Greeks defeat Persians at the Battle of Marathon. According to a legend, Pheidippides runs about twenty-six miles and dies after delivering the message "We are victorious." |
| 480 | Persians defeat Spartans, under the command of the warrior-king Leonidas, at Thermopylae; Leonidas and his three hundred Spartan warriors are killed defending a mountain pass. The Persians set fire to Athens and occupy the city. |
| 480 | The Greek naval fleet, a coalition of city-states under the command of Themistocles, defeat outnumbered King Xerxes's Persian fleet at Salamis. |
| 479 | Greeks defeat Persians at the land battle near the city of Plataea. |
| 478 | Delian League, alliance of Athens and other city-states, founded to defend against Persian invasion. Treasury located on island of Delos. |

| | |
|---|---|
| 468 | Sophocles wins first prize in the Dionysia theatre competition in Athens, beating the established playwright Aeschylus. |
| 464 | Earthquake destroys part of Sparta and causes the death of thousands. |
| 460–445 | First Peloponnesian War between Sparta and its allies and Athens and its allies. |
| 461–430 | Pericles establishes democracy in Athens. There is blossoming of philosophy, sciences, and the arts. |
| 447 | Construction of Parthenon, dedicated to the goddess Athena, begins under the direction of sculptor and architect Phidias. The architects are Ictinus and Callicrates, and it is built upon the ruins of an older temple destroyed by the Persians. |
| 438 | Phidias is accused of stealing gold, but the charge is never proven. |
| c. 438 | Parthenon completed, although the work on decoration continues. |
| 431–404 | Later Peloponnesian War between Sparta and its allies and Athens and its allies. |
| 430–429 | Pericles, his wife, and two sons die because of the plague. One-third or more of those living in overcrowded Athens perish, and the city-state is weakened. |
| 404 | Athens surrenders to Sparta. Thirty tyrants rule Athens. |
| 403 | Democracy is restored in Athens. |
| 399 | Philosopher Socrates is condemned to death for impiety and destroying the morals of minors. He encouraged his pupils to think critically by asking them a series of questions. |
| 395–345 | Warfare between rival Greek city-states. |
| 387 | Plato founds the Academy in Athens. |
| 371 | Thebes defeats Sparta at Leuctra and becomes leading power. |
| 338 | Philip of Macedonia defeats Athens and its allies at Battle of Chaeronea. |
| 336–323 | Alexander the Great's reign begins after the assassination of his father, Philip of Macedon. He establishes an empire reaching to North Africa, India, and Afghanistan. With his death at age thirty-three, his empire collapses. |
| 335 | Philosopher and scientist Aristotle establishes Lyceum in Athens. |
| 281–275 | Pyrrhus of Epirus leads the Greeks in a series of battles between Greeks and Romans. |
| 212 | Romans sack Syracuse (in present-day Italy). Roman soldier kills philosopher and scientist Archimedes. |
| 146 | Macedonia becomes Roman province. |
| 86 | Roman general and statesman Sulla sacks Athens. |
| 31 | Rome defeats the combined forces of Mark Anthony and Cleopatra. The Ptolemaic dynasty of Empress Cleopatra of Egypt ends. |
| 49–51 CE | Saint Paul introduces Christianity to Greece. |
| 49–128 | Romans construct buildings and monuments in Athens, which becomes a center of education. |
| 285 | Roman Empire permanently divided into Eastern and Western Empires. |

| | |
|---|---|
| 313 | Edict of Milan's toleration of Christianity and other religions is put into effect by Emperors Constantine (who controls the Western Roman Empire) and Licinius (who controls the Eastern Roman Empire). Also orders restitution of confiscated Christian property. |
| 330 | Constantine assumes sole rule of Roman Empire and establishes capital in Byzantium (renamed Constantinople and now named Istanbul). |
| 380 | Emperor Theodosius establishes Christianity as the official religion of the Roman Empire. |
| 476 | Western Roman Empire collapses. Eastern Empire (Byzantine Empire) continues. |
| 533–554 | Byzantine Empire extends to North Africa, Italy, and Southern Spain. |
| 537 | Hagia Sophia Church in Constantinople rebuilt after the Nika riots. |
| c. 650 | Slavs invade Greece. |
| 726 | Emperor Leo III bans the use of icons. |
| 843 | Empress Theodora restores the use of icons. |
| 996 | Basil II reconquers Greece from the Bulgars. |
| 1054 | Schism between Roman Catholic and Eastern Orthodox churches. |
| 1204 | Fourth Crusade, initiated by Pope Innocent III, sacks Constantinople, capital of the Byzantine Empire. Venetians take possession of Corfu. |
| 1204–1669 | Venetians occupy Crete and remain until the Ottomans take possession. |
| 1259–1261 | Alexios Strategopoulos, general under Paleologos Michael VI, captures Constantinople. Paleologos resurrects Byzantine Empire, although it is smaller. |
| 1393 | Venetians take possession of the Ionian island of Kythira. |
| 1430 | Ottomans take possession of Thessaloniki. |
| 1453 | Ottomans take possession of Constantinople. |
| 1460 | Ottomans take possession of the Peloponnesus. |
| 1479–1684 | Ottomans rule the island of Lefkada. |
| 1482–1483 | Venetians take possession of the Ionian islands of Zakynthos, Cephalonia, and Ithaka. |
| 1669 | Ottomans take possession of Crete. |
| 1687 | Venetian cannonball hits the Parthenon, causing extensive damage. |
| 1688–1715 | Venetians take possession of the Peloponnesus, and rule it until it is recaptured by the Ottomans. |
| 1798 | Rigas Feraios, advocate of revolution against the Ottomans and author of the battle hymn "Therios," is executed by the Ottomans. |
| 1801–1812 | Lord Elgin removes about half of the surviving sculptures of the Parthenon, as well as sculptures from the Propylaea and Erechtheum, and transports them to Britain, where they are later put on display at the British Museum, where they are today. |
| 1803 | The women of the village of Souli in Epirus jump from the mountainside along with their young children, rather than being taken captive by local ruler Ali Pasha's Albanian Muslim troops. |
| 1814 | Secret society, Philiki Eteria, plans overthrow of Ottoman rule. Three merchants, Nikolaos Skoufa, Athanasios Tsakaloff, and Emmanuel Xanthos, meet in Odessa to form the society. |

| | |
|---|---|
| 1815 | United States of the Ionian Islands established under British protectorate. |
| 1821 | February. Alexander Ypsilantis and his army unsuccessfully combat the Ottomans in Moldavia and Wallachia. |
| 1821–1832 | War of Independence from Ottoman rule. |
| 1821 | Greeks defeat Ottomans in Battles of Gravia and Tripolitsa (Tripoli). |
| 1822 | Ottomans massacre Greeks on the island of Chios. One hundred thousand perish. |
| 1823 | Dionysios Solomos writes the poem "Hymn to Liberty," which becomes the national anthem. Nafplion becomes capital of revolutionary government. |
| 1824 | The renowned English poet Lord Byron arrives in Greece to fight in the War of Independence. He dies in Greece, probably of sepsis, a few months after his arrival. |
| 1825 | Egyptians join the Ottomans in fighting Greece and land ten thousand troops in the Peloponnesus. Ottoman/Egyptian victories follow. |
| 1827 | French/British/Russian fleet defeats Ottoman/Egyptian fleet in Bay of Navarino. |
| 1827 | Ioannis Capodistrias becomes first president. |
| 1830 | Britain, France, and Russia sign the London Protocol, which recognizes Greece as an independent nation. |
| 1831 | Capodistrias is assassinated by Konstantinos and Georgios Mavromichalis, brother and son of Petrobey Mavromichalis, a rival he had imprisoned. |
| 1832 | Treaty of Constantinople, which is signed by France, Britain, Russia, and the Ottoman Empire, defines the borders of the new nation-state of Greece and sets up the conditions for a monarchy. |
| 1833 | Prince Otto of Bavaria, who is seventeen, becomes king. Three Bavarian regents govern Greece until he turns twenty in 1835. Greek Orthodox Church declares itself autocephalous, no longer controlled by the Patriarchate in Constantinople. |
| 1834 | Capital is transferred from Nafplion to Athens, which along with the surrounding area has a population of 12,000. |
| 1837 | University of Athens built. |
| 1843 | After revolt by populace, King Otto grants new constitution. |
| 1844 | Constitution sets up a democratic parliament, reducing king's power. |
| 1847 | Don Pacifico, former Portuguese consul general to Athens and a British subject, claims an anti-Semitic mob vandalized his home in Athens, and Greek authorities did nothing to protect or compensate him. |
| 1850 | British Royal Navy blockades port of Piraeus, because of the failure of Greece to compensate British citizen Don Pacifico for the destruction of his home by vandals. Patriarchate in Constantinople recognizes the Church of Greece as autocephalous. |
| 1853–1856 | War is fought on the Crimean Peninsula between the Russians and the British, French, and Ottoman Turkish. During the war, King Otto encourages Greek troops to cross over the border to Thessaly (Ottoman territory) to support Russia. |

| | |
|---|---|
| 1853 | British Royal Navy again blockades Greece to prevent the nation from attacking the Ottoman Empire during the Crimean War. |
| 1854–1857 | French and English occupy the port of Piraeus to make sure Greece remains neutral during the Crimean War. |
| 1862 | King Otto is forced from the throne by an army-backed revolt. |
| 1863 | Prince George of Denmark becomes king of Greece. |
| 1864 | Britain peacefully hands over the Ionian islands of Corfu, Paxi, Lefkada, Ithaka, Kefalonia, Zakynthos, and Kythera. |
| 1864 | New constitution abolishes the senate, which had been appointed by king. The one-chambered Parliament members are elected by male citizens over the age of twenty-five. |
| 1866–1869 | Crete unsuccessfully revolts against the Ottoman Empire, This was one of a series of revolts in the nineteenth century. |
| 1870 | Seven brigands are executed for killing five European travelers. |
| 1870 | In northwestern Turkey, German archaeologist Heinrich Schliemann excavates what he believes to be ancient Troy, site of the Trojan War mentioned in Homer's *Iliad* and *Odyssey.* |
| 1875 | King George accepts the *dedilomeni* principle, whereas the monarchy calls upon the party leader with declared support of a majority in Parliament to form a government. |
| 1881 | Ottoman Empire cedes most of Thessaly and part of Epirus to Greece. |
| 1893 | Corinth Canal, which cuts through the Isthmus of Corinth to connect the Aegean Sea with the Ionian Sea, is completed. Prime Minister Chariklaos Trikoupis declares Greece bankrupt. |
| 1896 | Frenchman Pierre de Coubertin and Greek native Demetrios Vikelas organize the first modern Olympics, which are held in Athens. Spiridon Louis wins the marathon. |
| 1897 | Thirty-Day War, between Greece and the Ottoman Empire, with the Ottomans emerging victorious. Crete proclaimed autonomous Cretan state. |
| 1897–1924 | Five hundred thousand emigrate to America. |
| 1901, 1903 | Use of demotic (vernacular) Greek in Bible and play *Aeschylus* causes riots. |
| 1903 | Most of the Palace of Knossos at Crete is excavated by Sir Arthur Evans, British amateur archaeologist. |
| 1903–1908 | Greeks and Bulgarians clash in Macedonia, a territory then ruled by the Ottoman Empire. |
| 1905 | Prime Minister Theodoros Deliyiannis assassinated. |
| 1909 | Military coup at Goudi, Athens. Eleftherios Venizelos leads new government. |
| 1912 | Greece, Serbia, Bulgaria, and Montenegro fight the Ottoman Empire and win First Balkan War. |
| 1913 | March. King Constantine becomes king after his father, King George, is assassinated. |
| 1913 | June–July. Greece, Serbia, Montenegro, Romania, and Ottoman Empire fight Bulgaria in Second Balkan War. Greece adds Macedonia, Crete, and some of the other Aegean Islands to her territory. |

| | |
|---|---|
| 1914 | Great Britain annexes Cyprus. |
| 1915 | Eleftherios Venizelos resigns twice as prime minister over disagreement with King Constantine's refusal to support the Entente (United Kingdom, France, and Russia) against the Central Powers (Austria-Hungary, Germany, and Italy) in World War I. |
| 1916 | Venizelos becomes president of a rival government based in Thessaloniki that is set up to govern northern Greece, Crete, and other Greek islands. |
| 1917 | King Constantine is forced to leave. His son, Alexander, becomes king. Greece, now united under the leadership of Venizelos, declares war on the Central Powers, joining the Entente (United Kingdom, France, and Russia) during World War I. Fire rages in Thessaloniki, the second-largest city in Greece, leaving more than seventy thousand homeless, two-thirds of whom were Jewish. |
| 1918 | Greece mobilizes its armed forces during World War I and assists Entente in defeating Central Powers (Austria-Hungary, Germany, and Italy) and the Ottoman Empire. |
| 1919 | After World War I, Treaty of Neuilly awards Western Thrace to Greece. Voluntary exchange of populations takes place between Greeks living in Bulgaria and Bulgarians living in Greece. |
| 1919–1922 | Greece goes to war with Turkey to redeem lands in Asia Minor but is defeated. |
| 1919–1928 | About 1.2 million Greek Orthodox relocate from Turkey to Greece, and about 450,000 Muslims from Greece to Turkey. |
| 1920 | August. Treaty of Sevres provides for a Greek presence in eastern Thrace and on the Anatolian west coast, as well as islands of Imbros and Tenedos. |
| 1920 | October. King Alexander dies of infection from a monkey bite. December plebiscite results in the return of King Constantine. |
| 1921 | Greek army advances on Ankara in Turkey but is stopped by Turkish forces at Battle of Sakarya River. |
| 1922 | August/September. Greece loses war with Turkey. About thirty thousand Greeks and Armenians perish in the burning of Smyrna. About two hundred thousand refugees evacuated from Turkey to Greece. Greece loses claim to territory gained in Treaty of Sevres. |
| 1922 | September. Colonel Nikolaos Plastiras launches coup, and the Revolutionary Committee forces King Constantine to abdicate. His son, George II, succeeds him. |
| 1922 | November. Nine Greeks brought to trial for their role in the military disaster in Turkey, with six executed. |
| 1923 | Convention of Lausanne mandates the relocation of Greek Orthodox from Turkey to Greece and Muslims from Greece to Turkey. Treaty of Lausanne reverses territorial claims gained in Treaty of Sevres. The Gregorian calendar is adopted. |
| 1923 | Following a boundary dispute and the murder of an Italian general and three soldiers by unknown assailants within the Greek border, Benito Mussolini orders the bombardment and occupation of Corfu. Italy leaves after a month. |

| | |
|---|---|
| 1924 | Plebiscite abolishes monarchy. |
| 1928 | Venizelos resumes leadership of Greece. |
| 1932 | Greece declares bankruptcy. Venizelos resigns. |
| 1935 | Plebiscite restores monarchy. King George II returns as king. |
| 1936–1941 | Ioannis Metaxas appointed prime minister of Greece and assumes dictatorial powers. He creates EON, a national youth organization. |
| 1940 | August. Greek warship torpedoed by Italian submarine. |
| 1940 | October–December. Metaxas says no to Italy's demand to enter Greece. Italy invades Greece. Greek forces defeat the Italians in the Pindos Mountains of Greece and advance into Albania. |
| 1941 | January. Metaxas dies of infection. |
| 1941 | April. Axis forces of Germany and Italy invade Greece through Bulgaria, with Axis forces emerging victorious. |
| 1941 | May–June. German air force and paratroopers invade Crete, with Germany emerging victorious. |
| 1941–1944 | Axis powers occupy Greece. Italy departs in 1943. |
| 1941–1942 | Famine occurring during the entire occupation is especially severe during the early years of the occupation, with 250,000–500,000 dying. |
| 1942 | Archbishop Damianos and other prominent leaders write letter asking Germans to stop persecution of the Jews of Thessaloniki. |
| 1943 | Italy surrenders, and their occupation forces leave Greece. German and Bulgarian occupation forces remain. |
| 1943 | World War II Greek resistance groups the National Liberation Front (EAM) and the Greek People's Liberation Army (ELAS) fight each other. |
| 1944 | March. Communists establish rival government, Political Committee of National Liberation. |
| 1944 | November. Liberation from Axis forces. |
| 1944–1945 | December–January. Communist and government troops fight in the streets of Athens for six weeks. About eleven thousand die. |
| 1945 | After the termination of the war, only ten thousand of the seventy-two thousand Greek Jews who resided in Greece return. Nearly sixty thousand perished in concentration camps. |
| 1946 | Following a plebiscite, King George II is reinstated. He returns to find the palace looted and the country in shambles because of the war. |
| 1946–1949 | Civil war erupts between government troops and Communist-led Democratic Army, with government troops emerging victorious. |
| 1947–1949 | Hundreds of U.S. Liberty ships are sold to a group of Greek shipowners, which starts their rise to the top of the shipping industry. |
| 1947 | President Truman asks the U.S. Congress to give aid to Greece. King George II dies and his brother Paul becomes king. |
| 1948 | Dodecanese Islands are annexed. They have been under the rule of Italy from 1911 to 1943, the Germans from 1943 to 1945, and the British since 1945. |
| 1948 | Inflation is on the rise and one-third of population is destitute. |
| 1948–1949 | Greek children numbering twenty-two to twenty-eight thousand are transported by Greek Communists to Communist countries. |

| | |
|---|---|
| 1948–1951 | Through the U.S. Marshall Plan, Greece receives aid to rebuild after the devastation of World War II. |
| 1950–1974 | At least a million Greeks emigrate, mainly to Germany, Australia, United States, and Canada. |
| 1952 | Women's suffrage granted. Greece becomes member of NATO. |
| 1952–1957 | The regulations instituted in Egypt, including land redistribution and nationalization of foreign-owned banks, insurance, and manufacturing companies, forces most of the Greek community to leave. Many repatriate to Greece. |
| 1953 | Earthquakes hit islands of Kefalonia and Zakynthos. |
| 1955 | September 6 and 7. Pogrom against Istanbul's Greek and Armenian communities by the Turkish government. |
| 1963 | George Seferis wins Nobel Prize for literature. Prime Minister Constantinos Karamanlis resigns. |
| 1964 | King Paul dies, and his son Constantine becomes King Constantine II. |
| 1965 | King Constantine II and Prime Minister Georgios Papandreou disagree about control of armed forces. Papandreou resigns. |
| 1967–1974 | Colonels George Papadopoulos and Nikolaos Makarezos, and Brigadier General Stylianos Pattakos (referred to as the junta) govern Greece after bloodless coup. King Constantine goes into exile. |
| 1968 | Alexandros Panagoulis plants a bomb, planning to blow up Papadopoulos's car. Georgios Papandreou's funeral becomes a demonstration against the junta. |
| 1969–1980 | About 160,000 Greeks immigrate to the United States. |
| 1970s | Greek shipping industry becomes number one in the world. It is dominated by tycoons like Aristotle Onassis, Stavros Niarchos, and John Latsis, who ship bulk cargo throughout the world. |
| 1973 | Protest at Athens Polytechnical University against rule of the junta results in loss of lives. Monarchy abolished. |
| 1974 | Turkey invades Cyprus in response to Greece's involvement in a coup attempt against Cypriot president Archbishop Makarios. In Greece, democracy is restored. Civilian government of Karamanlis legalizes the Communist Party. |
| 1975 | Constantine Karamanlis heads interim government. King Constantine goes into exile after a referendum to abolish the monarchy. |
| 1975 | New constitution establishes Republican democracy. Karamanlis of New Democracy (ND) party becomes prime minister. |
| 1976 | Manolis Andronikos and other archaeologists unearth the burial site of the kings of Macedon, including the tomb of Philip II, father of Alexander the Great, at Vergina, Greece. |
| 1976 | *Dimotiki* (the language used by everyday people) becomes the official language of Greece, replacing *katharevousa* (a formal language based on ancient Greek and free of foreign words). |
| 1980 | Odysseus Elytis wins Nobel Prize for Literature. |

| | |
|---|---|
| 1981 | Greece joins European Economic Community. Panhellenic Socialist Movement (PASOK) wins election, with Andreas Papandreou becoming prime minister. |
| 1982–1983 | Revision of civil code changes family law, including abolition of dowry, reforms regarding women's rights within marriage, and recognition of civil marriages. |
| 1983 | Turkish Federated State of Northern Cyprus established but recognized only by Turkey and the Nakhichevan Autonomous Republic. |
| 1988 | Prime Minister Andreas Papandreou's orders that Turkish ship *Sismik-I* be sunk if it enters Greek waters brings Greece and Turkey to brink of war. |
| 1988 | Greece's and Turkey's leaders meet in Davos, Switzerland, to try to resolve differences. |
| 1989 | Greeks start arriving from former Soviet Union, including Georgia, Kazakhstan, Russia, and Armenia. By 2000, two hundred thousand have arrived. |
| 1990 | Konstantinos Mitsotakis's ND party forms government, with him as prime minister. Karamanlis becomes president. |
| 1993 | Andreas Papandreou's PASOK party returns to power. |
| 1996 | Territorial dispute between Greece and Turkey over Imia/Kardak (two deserted islands in Aegean Sea) brings Greece and Turkey to brink of war. U.S. president Bill Clinton intervenes. |
| 1990s | Greece expels thousands of undocumented Albanian immigrants. |
| 1999 | February. Rift between Turkey and Greece occurs when Öcalan, leader of Kurdish separatist movement PKK, enters Greece and then is housed at Greek embassy in Nairobi, Kenya. |
| 1999 | Earthquake hits first Turkey and then Greece, with outpouring of aid from each country. |
| 2000 | Two lines of the Athens Metro open. Many archaeological finds are discovered during excavation, some of which are put on display in metro stations. |
| 2001 | Religious affiliation omitted from mandatory Greek identification card, despite protests by the Greek Orthodox Church and thousands of Greeks. |
| 2001 | Greece joins Economic and Monetary Union of the European Union. |
| 2002 | Euro replaces drachma. |
| 2004 | ND wins elections. Costas Karamanlis becomes prime minister. Athens hosts Summer Olympics. |
| 2008–2009 | Three thousand forest fires burn in several areas but mainly the Peloponnesus and southern Evia. |
| 2008 | In December 2008 and January 2009, riots follow death of a fifteen-year-old student who was shot by a police officer in the Exarhia neighborhood of Athens. |
| 2009 | Forest fires lasting four days affect area northeast of Athens. PASOK party wins election; Georgios Papandreou become prime minister. Acropolis Museum opens to the public. |

| | |
|---|---|
| 2009–2019 | Greece experiences an economic crisis, and in 2010 enters into the first of three Memoranda of Understanding with the Troika (the International Monetary Fund, the European Central Bank, and the European Commission) in order to get loans to weather the crisis. Strikes and demonstrations erupt against the government's austerity measures, such as cutting wages of government workers and reduced pensions, instituted as conditions for obtaining the loans. |
| 2012 | Antonis Samaras of ND Party becomes prime minister. |
| 2015 | Alexis Tsipras of the radical left party SYRIZA becomes prime minister. Parliament passes Cohabitation Pact giving almost same rights as marriage to couples regardless of their sex. |
| 2018 | More than ninety people perish in wildfires near Athens. |
| 2019 | ND party wins elections. Kyriakos Mitsotakis becomes prime minister. |
| 2020 | The COVID-19 virus hits Greece. A Greek court determines that the political party Golden Dawn is a criminal organization, and delivers fifty-seven guilty verdicts to members and associates. |

## Alexander the Great (356–323 BCE)

Alexander the Great, who had been tutored by the renowned philosopher and scientist Aristotle, became king of Macedonia at the age of twenty, upon the assassination of his father, King Philip II of Macedon. Alexander developed his skill as a commander of soldiers in his teens. When he was eighteen, he took charge of the Companion Cavalry and helped his father defeat the Athenian and Theban armies at Chaeronea. Philip had united all the city-states except Sparta into the League of Corinth. After his father died, Alexander, a brilliant tactician, extended the empire. He acted with cunning, force, and sometimes brutality. In 335 BCE, when Thebes threatened its independence, he quashed the rebellion and had its inhabitants slaughtered or sold into slavery. The Greek Council decided to raze Thebes, a decision Alexander implemented. He ordered that the whole of the city be razed, except for the house of the poet he revered, Pindar, and the temples. Athens quickly came into line. Alexander went after Greece's ancient enemy, Persia, and defeated the army of Darius III. He went on to take over the entire Persian Empire. Alexander, while tolerating local religious and cultural practices, also introduced his empire to Hellenic ideals and language. After the conquest of the Persian Empire, Alexander turned to India. He and his army successfully outmaneuvered King Porus, whose army greatly outnumbered Alexander's army. He had intended to forge ahead and invade Arabia, but death awaited him instead. He rapidly succumbed to an unknown illness (probably malaria), dying in 323 BCE, a young man of thirty-three. He left no heirs, since both his young son and his half-brother had been murdered. With no plans for successors, the empire fell apart. In India, their rulers took over.

Alexander's generals divided what was left, with Deleucus seizing most of Persia and Ptolemy establishing the dynasty of the Ptolemies in Egypt. Cleopatra was the last ruler of the Ptolemaic dynasty.

*Elaine Thomopoulos*

**See also:** Chapter 9: The Greek Language.

**Further Reading**

Green, Peter. 2007. *Alexander the Great and the Hellenistic Age*. London: Phoenix.

McCarty, Nick. 2004. *Alexander the Great*. Camberwell, VIC: Penguin.

## Archimedes (c. 287–212 BCE)

Archimedes, who was born in the Greek colony of Syracuse, Italy, used mathematical concepts to investigate the world. His groundbreaking work in mathematics, astronomy, physics, and engineering set the foundation for science as we know it today. He discovered a method for approximating the value of pi and developed formulas for finding areas and volumes of spheres and cylinders. Farmers continue to use an irrigation method he had initially developed to prevent a ship from flooding. Shaped like a large screw, it drew water out of the ship. Farmers use it to draw water from rivers to their fields. His experiments with the lever resulted in his statement of the law of simple machines. The game he developed, "Stomachion," was the earliest evidence of the science of combinatorics, a precursor of statistics. It challenged its players to figure out how many ways fourteen geometric diagrams could be arranged to make a square. It was called "Stomachion" because it was such a difficult game that it triggered a bellyache. When Hieron II, the king of Syracuse, challenged him to single-handedly drag a barge out of the water, he did so with a compound pulley. He also determined whether the king's new crown was made of pure gold by using the law of buoyancy. He supposedly discovered this by noticing how his body displaced the water in the tub while he was bathing. The legend is that he ran naked out to the street, shouting, "Eureka!" ("I have found it!"). He used his engineering and scientific skills for the construction of powerful weapons in order to defend Syracuse against Roman aggression. Thanks to the ingenuity of Archimedes, Syracuse was invulnerable for two years. The Romans broke through in 212 BCE. In the midst of looting and carnage, Archimedes was killed by a Roman soldier.

*Elaine Thomopoulos*

**See also:** Chapter 2: Overview.

**Further Reading**

Geymonat, Mario. 2010. *The Great Archimedes*. Waco, TX: Baylor University Press.

Gow, Mary. 2005. *Archimedes: Mathematical Genius of the Ancient World*. New York: Enslow Publishers, Inc.

Heath, T. L. 1897. *The Works of Archimedes*. London: C. J. Clay and Sons.

Paipetis, Stephanos, and Marco Ceccarelli, eds. 2010. *The Genius of Archimedes*. New York: Springer Publishing.

## Bouboulina, Laskarina (1771–1825)

Laskarina Bouboulina was a naval commander revered for her leadership and generosity during the Greek War of Independence against the Ottomans. She demonstrated courage and determination, following in the footsteps of her father, Stavrianos Pinotsis, who had participated in the 1769–1770 Orlov Rebellion against the Ottomans. Bouboulina's mother Skevo gave birth to her in a Constantinople prison, while she was visiting her husband. Following his death, mother and baby went to Hydra, the birthplace of Stavrianos and Skevo. Four years later, when her mother remarried, they settled in Spetses.

By the time Bouboulina became involved in the revolution, she had been widowed twice and had seven children. Her second husband, Demetrios Bouboulis, died when she was forty. Bouboulina expanded her husband's successful trading business by having more ships built. This included the *Agamemnon*, one of the largest ships used during the War of Independence. She bribed the Ottoman official who had come to inspect the *Agamemnon*, which she had built in 1820 as a warship.

On March 13, 1821, days before the official beginning of the Greek War of Independence, Bouboulina raised a revolutionary flag of her own design in Spetses. On April 3, the island of Spetses revolted, followed shortly by Hydra and Psara. Bouboulina used her ships, skill, and money to combat the Ottomans in the War of Independence.

Bouboulina's ships participated in blockades and battles at Nafplion, Monemvasia, and Navarino (Pylos). She not only furnished ships for the War of Independence but also commanded them herself. She also equipped sailors and soldiers from Spetses with food, weapons, and ammunition during the first two years of the war and made the ultimate sacrifice when her eldest son died in the war.

Bouboulina was in Tripolitsa, where she had supplied a contingent of soldiers, when the revolutionaries under General Theodoros Kolokotronis captured the city. He became her friend, and later their children, Eleni Bouboulina and Panos Kolokotronis, married.

In 1825, her life came to a tragic end when an unknown assailant shot her in the forehead as she stood on the balcony of her home. This occurred after her son had eloped with one of the daughters of the Koutsis family. After her death, Russia conferred on her the honorary rank of Admiral of the Navy. On the island of Spetses, Bouboulina's family maintains a museum dedicated to her. Throughout Greece, streets are named after her, and songs commemorate this brave woman who contributed so much so that Greece could become independent.

*Elaine Thomopoulos*

**See also:** Chapter 2: Kolokotronis, Theodoros

**Further Reading**

Angelomatis-Tsougarakis, Helen. 2008. "Women in the Greek War of Independence." In *Networks of Power in Modern Greece*, edited by Mark Mazower. New York: Columbia University Press.

Demertzis-Bouboulis, Philip. 2001. *Laskarina Bouboulina*. Spetses: Bouboulina Museum.

## Callas, Maria (1923–1977)

Opera diva Maria Callas, who was born in New York City to Greek émigrés, was world renowned. With the passion she brought to her roles, her stunning beauty, and the splendor and range of her bel canto voice, she could move her audience to tears. She sang major roles in more than forty different operas and had hundreds of performances throughout Europe and America. The operas included *LaTraviata*, *Medea*, *Norma*, *Lucia di Lammermoor*, and *Aida*.

Callas's parents married in Greece, but after their first-born son died in Greece, they immigrated to New York. Her father, a pharmacist, changed his young family's name from Kalogeropoulos to Callas when Maria was a baby. Maria's life, like the operas she starred in, had tragic overtones. Her parents fought constantly during her early childhood. They separated when she was thirteen, and her mother moved to Athens with Maria and her sister.

At the age of fourteen, Maria enrolled in the respected National Conservatoire of Greece. She lived through the occupation by the Germans at a time when people were dying by the thousands in the streets of Athens from the famine of the early 1940s. In 1941, she made her opera debut by singing a minor role in the opera Boccaccio at the Royal Opera of Athens.

In 1945, she returned to the United States to reunite with her father. She also hoped to further her operatic career in the United States, but that did not happen.

Instead, she found fame and fortune in Italy after making her 1947 debut in Verona. In 1924, she married Giovanni Battista Meneghini, a wealthy industrialist who loved opera. With him as her manager, her operatic career soared. But she was dissatisfied about the weight she had gained. By 1954, she lost about eighty pounds, transforming herself so that she looked like a Greek goddess.

In 1959, she met Greek shipping magnate Aristotle Onassis, one of the wealthiest men in the world, and they had an affair that lasted through the 1960s. Both were married when they first met. Onassis and his wife divorced, and Callas's husband would not give her a divorce. She became a Greek citizen in 1966. According to the Greek Orthodox Church, since Callas was not officially married in the church, her marriage was not recognized. She was free to marry Onassis, but he did not want to get married. Nevertheless, Callas devoted herself to him, forgoing her career. She sang in only a few performances during her affair with Onassis, and her voice deteriorated.

Onassis's marriage to Jacqueline Kennedy in 1969 devastated Callas. She recovered from that blow enough to teach a series of master classes at the Juilliard School in New York from October 1971 to March 1972.

Callas was heartbroken when Onassis died in 1975. She died, reportedly of a heart attack, two years later. Her ashes were scattered over the sea of the Aegean by Greece's minister of culture.

*Elaine Thomopoulos*

**See also:** Chapter 2: Onassis, Aristotle Socrates.

**Further Reading**

Gage, Nicholas. 2001. *Greek Fire: The Story of Maria Callas and Aristotle Onassis.* New York: Alred A. Knoft.

Petsalis-Diomidis, Nicholas. 2001. *The Unknown Callas: The Greek Years.* Portland, OR: Amadeus Press.

Stassinopoulos, Arianna. 1981. *Maria Callas: The Woman behind the Legend.* New York: Ballantine Books.

## Damaskinos Papandreou, Archbishop (1890–1949)

Archbishop Damaskinos Papandreou saved thousands of Greek Jews from death during the Nazi occupation in World War II. He was born Dimitrious Papandreou in Dorvitsa, Greece. He excelled in his studies of both theology and law at the University of Athens, became an ordained priest of the Greek Orthodox Church in 1918, and was assigned an abbot of the Petraki and Penteli monasteries. In his role as a mediator, he brought peace to rival factions of Greek, Serbian, and Bulgarian monks. In 1922, he was appointed bishop of Corinth. In the early 1930s, he traveled to the United States at the request of the ecumenical patriarch. There, he helped organize the Greek Orthodox Archdiocese of America.

From 1941 to 1949, he was archbishop of Athens and all Greece. In 1943, Damaskinos became deeply troubled by the deportation of the Jews of Greece by the Nazis. He sent a letter, signed by him and twenty-eight other prominent citizens, to the collaborationist president of Greece, K. Logothetopoulos, protesting the treatment of the Greek Jews. An excerpt follows: "In our national consciousness, all the children of Mother Greece are an inseparable unity: they are equal members of the national body irrespective of religion. . . . Our holy religion does not recognize superior or inferior qualities based on race or religion, as it is stated: 'There is neither Jew nor Greek' (Gal. 3:28) and thus condemns any attempt to discriminate or create racial or religious differences. Our common fate both in days of glory and in periods of national misfortune forged inseparable bonds between all Greek citizens, without exemption, irrespective of race" ("Archbishop Damaskinos and Greek Intellectuals Protest Persecution of Greek Jewry").

According to the International Raoul Wallenberg Foundation, no document similar to this one, which protests against the actions of the Nazis, has been discovered. When the Nazi general Jürgen Stroop, an S.S. officer, found out about the letter, he threatened to shoot the archbishop. Damaskinos, a brave man, told his Nazi oppressor, "According to the traditions of the Greek Orthodox Church, our prelates are hanged, not shot. Please respect our traditions" (Burns n.d.).

The Nazis paid no attention to the letter and continued the deportations. Damaskinos did everything he could to help the Jews. He spoke to Angelos Evert, the police chief of Athens, and together they saved thousands of Jews by issuing fake baptismal certificates and false identifications.

The archbishop told monasteries and convents in Athens to shelter Jews and urged his priests to ask their congregations to hide the Jews in their homes. More than 250 Jewish children were hidden by Orthodox clergy alone. Despite their efforts, over 60,000 of the 70,000 Jews of Greece perished.

Damaskinos also served as regent of Greece from 1944, when the German forces departed, until 1946, when King George II returned to Greece. He continued as archbishop during the civil war between government troops and Communists, urging, without success, for a cessation of the hostilities. He died while serving as archbishop in March 1949, a few months before the civil war ended.

*Elaine Thomopoulos*

**See also:** Chapter 11: Sikelianos, Angelos.

**Further Reading**

"Archbishop Damaskinos and Greek Intellectuals Protest Persecution of Greek Jewry." Jewish Virtual Library. Accessed January 24, 2018. https://www.jewishvirtuallibrary.org/archbishop-damaskinos-and-greek-intellectuals-protest-persecution-of-greek-jewry.

Burns, Margie. n.d. "Archbishop Damaskinos." The International Raoul Wallenberg Foundation. Accessed January 24, 2018. http://www.raoulwallenberg.net/es/generales/archbishop-damaskinos/.

## George I, King (1845–1913)

George Christian William of the House of Gluecksburg was selected to be king in 1862. The seventeen-year-old, who was Danish, replaced King Otto, who was forced to leave. King George served for nearly fifty years, until his assassination in 1913. The title of King George was King of the Hellenes, rather than King of Greece, as it had been for King Otto. This new title implied that his responsibility did not stop with the newly declared nation but extended to the millions of Greeks who resided outside of Greece. It foreshadowed what was to dominate the beginning of the twentieth century—the *Megali Idea* (the Great Vision). This Great Vision of reclaiming lost lands, which were inhabited mostly by those of Greek descent, had been instilled in the psyche of the Greeks since the start of the nation. In January 1844, Prime Minister Ioannis Kolettis spoke to the National Assembly: "The Kingdom of Greece is not Greece. It constitutes only one part, the smallest and the poorest. . . . A Greek is not only a man who lives within the Kingdom, but also one who lives in Ioannina, Serres, Adrianople, Constantinople, Smyrna, Trebizon, Crete, in Samos, and in any land associated with Greek history and the Greek race. . . . . There are two great centers of Hellenism. Athens is the capital of the Kingdom. Constantinople is the great capital, the dream and hope of all Greeks" (Clogg, 1986, 6).

From 1864 to 1913, Greece obtained the Ionian Islands (given peacefully by Britain in 1864), as well as Thessaly and part of Epirus (following the Russian-Turkish War). During King George's reign, Greece's armed forces fought in the First and Second Balkan Wars. A few months after his death, the Greeks emerged victorious in the Second Balkan War. They added southern Epirus, Macedonia, Crete, and some of the other Aegean Islands to their country. Another major accomplishment during the reign of King George was the adoption of a new constitution in 1864. The senate was abolished (it had previously been appointed by the king), and a one-chambered *vouli* (legislature) came into effect. Members of the *vouli* were elected by male citizens who were twenty-five years of age and older. King George's rule came to an end when he was assassinated while on a visit to the city of Thessaloniki, a city that had been newly liberated from Ottoman rule. He was succeeded by his son Constantine. Subsequent kings were Constantine's three sons (George II, Alexander, and Paul) and Paul's son, Constantine II.

*Elaine Thomopoulos*

**See also:** Chapter 2: Overview.

**Further Reading**

Christmas, Walter. 1914. *The Life of King George of Greece.* Translated by A. G. Chater. New York: McBride, Nast, and Company. Accessed March 1, 2021. https://archive.org/details/kinggeorgeofgree00chririch.

Clogg, Richard. 1986. *A Short History of Modern Greece*, 2nd ed. Cambridge: Cambridge University Press.

Van der Kiste, John. 1994. *Kings of the Hellenes.* Stroud, UK: Sutton.

## Hippocrates (c. 460–377 BCE)

Hippocrates was born in the Greek island of Cos during the time of Pericles and the classical age of Greece. Soranus, a second-century biographer, reported that

Hippocrates learned medicine from his father and grandfather, and he in turn taught three of his sons the profession. Hippocrates is known as the Father of Medicine, and many of the teachings and quotations ascribed to him are from the *Corpus Hippocrates*. This collection of about sixty ancient Greek medical works contains a wealth of medical information, some of it contradictory, as well as rules of ethical behavior for a physician.

We do not know for sure if Hippocrates himself wrote any of the *Corpus*. Some of the authors were doctors who practiced during the classical age of Greece, but others practiced centuries later.

At the time Hippocrates started practicing medicine, some doctors thought that vengeful gods caused diseases, but the *Corpus Hippocrates* debunked this radical belief. Hippocratic physicians believed that environmental factors, diet, and habits of daily living caused disease. He is thought to have advised patients to eat healthy, get plenty of rest, have clean surroundings, and take walks. He is also said to have stressed the importance of recording observations, such as complexion, pulse, fever, pains, movement, and bodily excretions.

Hippocrates and his followers thought that disease was caused by the imbalance in the four humors of the body—blood, phlegm, black bile, and yellow bile (or sometimes serum)—and therefore the physician could advise a correction. For example, if there was too much phlegm, citrus fruit was prescribed.

Although the professional code that doctors follow today is different than the one put forth in the *Corpus*, it emphasizes several of the same tenets, including that the physician should do no harm, not administer poison, not have sexual relations with a patient, and keep the confidentiality of the patient. The command "Do no harm" is embodied in the Hippocratic Oath that many modern physicians subscribe to when graduating medical school.

*Elaine Thomopoulos*

**See also:** Chapter 2: Overview; Pericles.

**Further Reading**

Adams, Francis, trans. (1891) 1994. *Works by Hippocrates*. The Internet Classics Archive: Daniel C. Stevenson, Web Atomics © 1994–2000. Accessed April 19, 2021. http://classics.mit.edu/Browse/browse-Hippocrates.html.

Smith, Wesley D. 2002. *The Hippocratic Tradition*. First published by Cornell University Press in 1979. Accessed March 1, 2021. http://www.biusante.parisdescartes.fr/ressources/pdf/medicina-hippo2.pdf.

## Kapodistrias, Count Ioannis (1776–1831)

Ioannis Kapodistrias served as first president of Greece from 1828 to 1831, when he was assassinated. He was born in the Ionian island of Corfu and studied medicine in

Padua, Italy. He returned to Corfu where he practiced medicine and became active politically. He served as secretary of state during the Russian protectorate over the Ionian Islands and also served as a member of the Russian delegation at the Congress of Vienna. He became joint foreign minister, with Count Nesselrode, to Tsar Alexander I. In this role, he dealt with matters regarding the Near East. When asked to take over the leadership of the Philiki Eteria, a secret revolutionary society founded in Odessa in 1814 to plan the Greek revolution against the Ottomans, he refused. He believed the plan to be unrealistic. In 1822, after the revolt broke out, he resigned from the tsar's service and went to Geneva, where he put his efforts toward the Greek cause. He became the president of Greece in 1828. Kapodistrias introduced the first Greek currency and also instituted one of the first modern quarantine systems, which helped control epidemics such as typhoid fever, cholera, and dysentery. In 1831, Kapodistrias imprisoned revolutionary war hero and rival Petrobey Mavromichalis, the leader of a powerful clan based in the Mani region in southern Greece. Petrobey's brother Konstantin and son Georgios assassinated Kapodistrias in Nafplion, the capital, on the steps of Saint Spyridon Church.

*Elaine Thomopoulos*

**See also:** Chapter 2: Mavrogenous, Manto.

**Further Reading**

Brewer, David. 2003. *The Greek War of Independence.* Woodstock, NY: Overlook Press.

Woodhouse, Christopher Montague. 1973. *Capodistria: The Founder of Greek Independence.* Oxford: Oxford University Press.

## Karamanlis, Konstantinos (1907–1998)

Konstantinos Karamanlis served his country in the public service sector for almost fifty years. He was selected as a member of Parliament twelve times and was the prime minister from 1955 to 1963 and 1974 to 1980. Karamanlis was also twice elected president, from 1980 to 1985 and 1990 to 1995. He was born in the village of Proti, Macedonia. This was before that region became part of Greece in 1913, following the Second Balkan War. After spending his childhood in Macedonia, Karamanlis went to Athens to attain his degree in law. He was first elected member of Parliament in 1936, thus starting his long career as a politician. After he lost the 1963 election, he left for Paris, where he lived for eleven years. This self-imposed exile included the years of the repressive rule of the junta, which had taken over Greece in a military coup in 1967. When the junta fell in 1974, he was asked to return to establish a government of national unity. His supporters shouted "*Erhetai. Erhetai*" ("He is coming. He is coming") during celebrations throughout Greece. Fearing a new coup or assassination, he slept aboard a yacht, guarded by a naval destroyer, for three weeks. When he returned, Karamanlis established the New Democracy Party. After the Greek people voted to abolish the monarchy in 1974, Greece became a republic. In the same year, he legalized the Communist Party. Reforms regarding civil liberties and the role of women became part of the 1975 constitution. Also, in 1975, Greece applied to the European Union as an auxiliary member but did not officially become a member until 1981. During the Karamanlis administration, there was a building boom, fueled primarily by the migration of those from the farms to the cities in search of a better way of life. Karamanlis left office when he was eighty-eight and died at age ninety-one. His nephew, Kostas Karamanlis, served as prime minister from 2004 to 2009, in the same party that his uncle had helped organize, the New Democracy Party.

*Elaine Thomopoulos*

**See also:** Chapter 2: Timeline. Chapter 3: New Democracy.

**Further Reading**

Clogg, Richard. 1987. *Parties and Elections in Greece: The Search for Legitimacy.* Durham, NC: Duke University Press.

Woodhouse, Christopher Montague. 1982. *Karamanlis: The Restorer of Greek Democracy.* Oxford: Oxford University Press.

## Kolokotronis, Theodoros (1770–1843)

Theodoros Kolokotronis, known as the "Old Man of the Morea," was fifty when he became commander in chief of the Morea (Peloponnesus) during the Greek War of Independence. When he was ten, his father and two uncles were killed in the 1877 Orlov Rebellion against the Ottomans, which took place in the Peloponnesus. He subsequently joined a *kleft* (bandit warrior) band and became the leader of his own band at age fifteen. In 1805, he participated in the naval missions of the Russian fleet during the Russian-Turkish War. In 1810, he escaped the Ottomans by going to the island of Zakynthos, where he served in the Duke of York's Greek Light Infantry, being promoted as major. In 1818, he joined the Philiki Etereia, a secret society whose aim was to win Greece's independence from the Ottoman Empire. He showed his mettle as a leader of soldiers in the first year of the War of Independence when insurgents under his command took control of Tripoli from the Ottomans. His troops then went on to defeat the greatly outnumbered forces of the Ottoman general Dramali in the Dervenakia Pass. In 1825, he was jailed by his political enemies in the provisional government under Petrobey Mavromichalis. He was a supporter of Mavromichalis's rival, Ioannis Kapodistrias. However, a few months later, he was released to rejoin the war effort. In 1834, because of his opposition to the government under King Otto, he was tried for treason and given the death sentence. He was pardoned by the king in 1835, when the king came of age, and Greece was no longer under rule of the regents who previously governed. Kolokotronis died at the age of seventy-three in his home in Athens, after celebrating at a party. Being illiterate, he dictated his memoir to

Georgios Tertsetis, which was published in 1851 under the title *A Narration of Events of the Greek Tribe from 1770 to 1836.*

*Elaine Thomopoulos*

**See also:** Chapter 2: Kapodistrias, Count Ioannis.

**Further Reading**

Clogg, Richard. 1976. *The Movement for Greek Independence, 1770–1821: A Collection of Documents.* New York: Barnes & Noble.

Kolokotronis, Theodoros. 1892. *Kolokotrones The Klepht and the Warrior: Sixty Years of Peril and Daring.* Translated by Elizabeth M. Edmonds. London: T. Fisher Unwin.

## Mavrogenous, Manto (c. 1796–1848)

Manto Mavrogenous, a major benefactor of the War of Independence, was born in Trieste, a city in the Austrian Empire (now part of Italy), to a Phanariot family of wealth and nobility. She studied ancient Greek philosophy and history and spoke French, Italian, and Turkish, as well as Greek.

The Mavrogenous family relocated to the Aegean island of Paros, Greece, in 1809. In 1818, following the death of her father, they moved to the island of Tinos. After the War of Independence began, Mavrogenous moved to Mykonos, where her family had originated. She mobilized the islanders of Mykonos to join the War of Independence and repel the Ottomans who had come to attack the island. With the money from her dowry and the sale of her jewelry, she built ships and outfitted men who fought in the war. She participated in the Battle of Karystos in 1822 with a fleet of six ships and an infantry of about eight hundred men. Her men also fought in the battles of Dervenakia, Pelion, Phthiotis, and Livadeia. She also traveled to Paris and other European cities to persuade the women there to support the War of Independence.

Mavrogenous was engaged to the revolutionary war hero Demetrios Ypsilantis, but he broke off their engagement. Although beautiful, she never married. She died poor, having spent her money in the service of independence.

Ioannis Kapodistrias's government honored her by awarding her the title of lieutenant general and gave her a home in Nafplion. Mykonos has named a town square after her, and the house where she lived in Paros stands as a historical monument.

*Elaine Thomopoulos*

**See also:** Chapter 2: Kapodistrias, Count Ioannis. Chapter 7: Sidebar: *Prika* (Dowry) Now Outlawed in Greece.

**Further Reading**

Angelomatis-Tsougarakis, Helen. 2008. "Women in the Greek War of Independence." In *Networks of Power in Modern Greece,* edited by Mark Mazower. New York: Columbia University Press.

Vervenioti, Anastasia. 2006. "Women and the Greek Revolution." In *Women and War: A Historical Encyclopedia from Antiquity to the Present*, edited by Bernard Cook, Vol.2. Westport, CT: Greenwood.

## Metaxas, Ioannis (1871–1941)

Ioannis Metaxas was appointed prime minister of Greece in 1936 and served in that position until his death in 1941. He is best known for standing up to Italy in 1940 by saying "*Ohi*" ("No") to their demand that their troops enter Greece. Within hours of Metaxas's saying "No," the Italians invaded Greece. Although greatly outnumbered, Greek troops repelled the Italians at the Albanian border and advanced into Albania. It was the first land victory of World War II. Ohi Day continues to be celebrated as a national holiday throughout Greece, only one of two national holidays. The other celebrates Greece's declaration of independence from the Ottoman Empire.

Metaxas was born on the island of Kefalonia, Greece, and pursued studies at the Prussian Military Academy. As a career military officer, he first saw action in the Greco-Turkish War of 1897. As a loyal royalist, he supported King Constantine I in his opposition to Greek entry into World War I.

On April 4, 1937, while Metaxas was serving as minister of war, King George II appointed him as interim prime minister, and the position was ratified by the Parliament. On August 4, 1937, using the excuse of widespread labor unrest and fear of a Communist takeover, he called a "state of emergency." His regime is known as the Fourth of August Regime. He took full control by shutting down the Parliament indefinitely and suspending various articles of the constitution and did not allow labor unions or demonstrations. His regime censored the press, burned books such as the works of Heine, Shaw, Freud, and Gorki, banned certain music, and even censored some plays of the ancient Greek theater. His repressive government threw political opponents in jail and went after suspected Communists, using torture to elicit confessions.

Metaxas formed the National Youth Organization (EON), which emphasized nationalism. The youth groups, which met on Wednesdays and Sundays, were supposedly voluntary but lack of attendance at twenty meetings could mean expulsion from school. Some overlook the repressive nature of his regime and remember the good he did for the country. He established a program of public works and a drainage project. He set wages and started a social security program, which is still functioning in Greece. He revamped the military and took pride in the National Youth Movement that he founded to teach children traditional patriotic and religious values. Of upmost importance, he stood up to Italy's demand to invade Greece.

Although Metaxas tried to maintain neutrality during World War II, Greece eventually joined the Allies. The Greek cruiser *Elli*, moored off the coast of Tinos during religious ceremonies celebrating the Assumption of the Virgin Mary, was torpedoed, which resulted in loss of lives. The Italians were believed to be responsible. Yet, Metaxas did not respond. However, within a few months, Greece entered the war on the side of the Allies. In anticipation of war, Metaxas had built up the armed forces. From 1936 to 1939, the budget for defense comprised nearly one-third of total state expenditure. Metaxas constructed fortifications along the border of Bulgaria, but that did not stop the eventual victory of the Axis forces over Greece. He died of an infection in 1941, just before Greece's being occupied by Germany, Italy, and Bulgaria.

*Elaine Thomopoulos*

**See also:** Chapter 12: Modern Greek Architecture.

**Further Reading**

Clogg, Richard. 1987. *Parties and Elections in Greece: The Search for Legitimacy.* Durham, NC: Duke University Press.

Joachim, Joachim G. 2009. *Ioannis Metaxas: The Formative Years 1871–1922.* Mannhein: Bibliopolis.

Petrakis, Marina. 2006. *The Metaxas Myth: Dictatorship and Propaganda in Greece.* London: Tauris Academic Studies.

## Onassis, Aristotle Socrates (1906–1975)

Aristotle Onassis was one of the wealthiest men in the world. From humble beginnings as a refugee, he made a fortune in shipping. He had the largest privately owned shipping fleet and became one of the giants in the industry by shipping petroleum products around the world in supertankers.

Onassis was born in a suburb of Smyrna, Turkey, and was educated at the local Greek high school there. Although he did not have formal education after high school, he spoke four languages: Greek, English, Spanish, and Turkish. He quickly learned survival skills in a world turned topsy-turvy by war. As a teenager, he witnessed the devastation of Smyrna in 1922, following the Turkish victory in the Greco-Turkish War. Turkish soldiers set fire to the Greek and Armenian sections of the city. His three uncles were killed by the Turks, and his aunt, her husband, and their child also lost their lives, burned while trapped in a church. The surviving Onassis family members fled to Greece to save their lives, losing their business and property in Turkey.

In 1923, seventeen-year-old Onassis, seeing better opportunity outside of Greece, went to Argentina. He invested the money he earned as a telephone engineer into trading tobacco. By the time he was in his mid-twenties, he had made a fortune and had been appointed deputy Greek consul in Buenos Aires. By World War II, he had established himself in the shipping industry. A man of boundless energy, he expanded his fleet in the late 1940s by the purchase of Liberty Ships, surplus U.S. war cargo ships. His marriage to seventeen-year-old Athina Mary Livanos in 1947, when he was in his forties, brought two rival shipping families together. Athina was the daughter of shipping magnate Stavros G. Livanos.

After moving to Monaco in 1953, Onassis established a yacht club, hotel, and casino. He competed with rival Prince Rainier for economic control of the city.

Between 1950 and 1956, Onassis made a huge profit in the whaling industry. He purchased Olympic Airlines from the Greek government in 1956 and operated it until 1975, when he sold it to Greece. He was only one of two people (the other being Howard Hughes) who owned a private commercial airline.

While Onassis was still married, he became romantically involved with the beautiful opera diva Maria Callas, following which he and his wife Athina divorced. Although Callas wanted to marry him, he did not marry her. His second marriage, in 1968 at his privately owned Ionian island of Skorpios, was to Jacqueline Bouvier Kennedy, President John F. Kennedy's widow.

Onassis and his wife Athina had two children: Christina and Alexander. His twenty-four-year-old son, Alexander, perished in an airplane crash. Onassis died a broken man, crushed by the death of his son and his suffering from myasthenia gravis. The devastating neuromuscular disease made it necessary in his later years for him to use tape to keep his eyelids open and led to his death by respiratory failure.

His daughter, Christina, and granddaughter Athina Onassis survived Onassis. Christina became the first president of the Alexander S. Onassis Foundation, which had been established by Aristotle Onassis in memory of his son. Onassis directed that nearly half of his estate after his death be used to administer the foundation, which focuses on culture, education, environment, health, and social solidarity.

*Elaine Thomopoulos*

**See also:** Chapter 2: Callas, Maria. Chapter 4: Shipping.

**Further Reading**

Evans, Peter. 1986. *Ari: The Life and Times of Aristotle Onassis.* London: Jonathan Cape.

Frazier, Nicholas, Philip Jacobson, Mark Ottaway, and Lewis Chester. 1979. *Aristotle Onassis.* Philadelphia, PA: J. B. Lippencott Company.

## Otto (Otho), King (1815–1867)

King Otto of the House of Wittelsbach reigned for nearly thirty years, from 1832 to 1862, when he was deposed. He died in exile in Bavaria, the land of his birth. He became the monarch after the 1831 assassination of Ioannis Kapodistrias, the first president of Greece. The Great Powers (England, France, and Russia) chose the king, since Greece was then under their protection. They had forged the treaty with the Ottoman Empire that had given Greece its independence. Because King Otto was only seventeen years old when he came to Greece, three Bavarian regents ruled until he turned twenty. In 1835, when he turned twenty, he took over the leadership and ruled as an absolute monarch until 1843, when the populace revolted and demanded a constitution. The constitution was granted, and the area where the people gathered in

### THE ON-AND-OFF PRESENCE OF THE MONARCHY SINCE 1832

The monarchy was abolished in 1973. It had an off-and-on presence since 1832, when the Great Powers of Britain, France, and Russia appointed King Otto of Bavaria as king of Greece. Because Otto was only seventeen, three Bavarian regents governed the country until 1835. In 1843, Otto granted a constitution and convened a National Assembly. King Otto reigned for thirty years, but he was deposed in 1862 after a military rebellion. The Greek Assembly elected a new king from Denmark, King George I, in 1863. His reign lasted for almost fifty years, until 1913, when he was assassinated. His son, King Constantine, became king until 1917, when he abdicated the throne, fleeing to Switzerland. King Constantine's son Alexander succeeded him, but in 1920, a monkey bit the twenty-seven-year-old king, and he died of an infection. The Greek people, in a rigged plebiscite that showed a majority of 99 percent, voted for the return of King Constantine I. After the loss in the Greek-Turkish War in 1922, however, King Constantine abdicated. His son, King George II, ruled from 1922 to 1924, when the monarchy was abolished. In 1935, the Greek people voted for the return of the monarchy. King George II reigned until his death in 1947. He had spent the years of the World War II Axis occupation, from 1941 to 1944, in exile. He is said to have remarked that "the most important tool for a King of Greece is a suitcase." King Paul I, son of Constantine I, ruled until his death in 1964. King Constantine II, King Paul's son, then assumed the title of king, although he lived much of his rule in exile, from 1967 to 1973, during the military dictatorship. In 1973, a referendum abolished the monarchy, and another referendum held in 1974 confirmed the result of the 1973 referendum.

*Elaine Thomopoulos*

front of the palace to voice their demands was renamed Constitution Square, as it is still called. The king was no longer an absolute monarch. Greek council members now had a voice in the governance of the country. The council members belonged either to the French Party, the English Party, or the Russian Party, depending on the Great Power with which they aligned themselves. King Otto continued as a constitutional monarch until 1862, when he was forced to leave Greece.

King Otto faced many challenges in the thirty years he served as king. During the War of Independence, many of Greece's people had succumbed to bloodshed or had been displaced from their homes. The countryside had been torn up, forests were burned, huge debt payments were due to the Great Powers, and the economy was in shambles. To make things worse, Greece's political parties did not come together to govern the country effectively. Each of the parties had its own agenda, and at the beginning of his reign, they fought each other.

King Otto and the regents decided on Athens as Greece's capital. During his reign, the following buildings were built: the University of Athens (1837), the Old Royal Palace (now the Greek Parliament Building, 1843), the National Gardens of Athens (1840), and the National Library of Greece (1842). Built in the neoclassical style, each building had a view of the Acropolis. During the time that King Otto sat on the throne, Greece established a legal code and a judicial system, as well as a free public educational system that included a university.

*Elaine Thomopoulos*

**See also:** Chapter 12: Neoclassical Architecture.

**Further Reading**

Bower, Leonard, and Gordon Bolitho. 1939. *Otho I, King of Greece: A Biography.* London: Selwyn & Blount.

Kostis, Kostas. 2018. *History's Spoiled Children: The Story of Modern Greece.* Translated by Jacob Moe. New York: Oxford University Press, chapter 4.

## Papadopoulos, Georgios (1919–1999)

Georgios Papadopoulos, along with Brigadier Stylianos Pattakos and Colonel Nikolaos Makarezos, led the military coup d'état of April 21, 1967, that took over the government. From 1967 until 1973, Papadopoulos headed the junta that ruled Greece. His regime squashed thousands who opposed him by arresting them, sometimes torturing them and exiling them to remote Aegean Islands. The country was ruled by martial law. The Greek press was censored and stifled and even musicians, like the popular composer Mikis Theodorakis, were not allowed to perform. Papadopoulos justified his strong-arm policies by believing that this way he could control the Communists lurking in Greece, preventing them from taking over the country. Papadopoulos had supporters, especially in the rural areas. He forgave the debts of the farmers, electricity was brought in, roads were built, and industry, especially the tourist industry, expanded. But the good times did not last. In 1973, the oil crisis loomed, and inflation got out of hand. In May 1973, there was a naval mutiny in protest of the junta, with Commander Nikolaos Pappas refusing to return the *HNS Velos* to Greece after a NATO exercise. In November 1973, students occupied Athens Polytechnic University. This turned into a tragedy after military troops were called in and thirty-four people died.

Papadopoulos was ousted from his position by Brigadier Dimitrios Ioannidis in 1973. The rule of the dictator Ioannidis lasted only eight months, until July 1974, when democracy was once again restored. This followed the abortive attempt of Ioannidis to overthrow the government of Archbishop Makarios of Cyprus, which resulted in the subsequent invasion of Cyprus by Turkey.

Papadopoulos and his fellow conspirators were convicted of treason and torture and sentenced to death. The death sentences were commuted, but he spent the rest of his days in prison.

Papadopoulos, who was born in the village of Elaiohori in southern Greece, graduated from the military academy in Athens. During World War II, he fought the Italians as they entered Greece and was decorated for his service. During the Axis occupation of World War II, he was reported to have been part of the Security Battalions, a brutal unit supported by the collaborationist prime minister Ioannis Rallis of Greece. The Security Battalions supported the occupying forces and attacked Communists who were fighting in the resistance. Papadopoulos went on to fight the Communists during the Greek Civil War between government troops and the Communists. The Civil War took place between 1945 and 1949. In the 1950s, he was sent to the United States for military training. Some believe he worked for the CIA. He did work for the Greek intelligence service, but whether or not he worked for the CIA is still being debated by historians.

*Elaine Thomopoulos*

**See also:** Chapter 13: Art-Popular Music.

**Further Reading**

Clogg, Richard, and George N. Yannopoulos. 1972. *Greece under Military Rule*. New York: Basic Books.

Woodhouse, C. M. 1985. *The Rise and Fall of the Greek Colonels*. New York: Granada.

## Papandreou, Andreas (1919–1996)

In parliamentary elections held in 1981, the Panhellenic Socialist Movement (PASOK), led by Andreas Papandreou, the son of former prime minister George Papandreou, won. He served as prime minister from 1981 to 1989 and again from 1993 to 1996.

Laws passed during his administration, in 1982 and 1983, changed long-standing traditions regarding marriage and the family. These laws included the following: (1) a couple could be married in a civil marriage; (2) the abolishment of the dowry system; (3) a woman could choose to maintain her family name after marriage; (4) a married couple could determine the surname of their children—it did not have to automatically be the surname of the husband; (5) no-fault and mutual consent divorce; (6) the couple could jointly claim property acquired during the marriage; and (7) illegitimate children were granted rights equal to those held by legitimate children.

In 1984, a law was passed that guaranteed women equal pay for equal work. Another law, demonstrating a more liberal agenda, was the one that allowed political refugees (those who had fought with the Greek People's Liberation Army [ELAS]) to return to Greece.

Papandreou, who was born on the island of Chios, started being active in Greek politics as a young man. When he was twenty, he was arrested for political activities against the Metaxas dictatorship. After he was released from prison, he went to the United States, where he received a PhD in economics from Harvard University. He became a professor at Harvard, University of Minnesota, Northwestern University, and the University of California but returned to Greece in 1957. In 1967, he was imprisoned and tortured for his suspected involvement in an organization that was supposedly trying to overthrow the government. He was never convicted, and the government released him after he spent eight months in prison. During the rule of the junta, he lived in exile in Sweden and Canada. When he returned after the fall of the junta in 1974, he organized the PASOK party. He was elected prime minister in 1981 and remained in office until 1989. He divorced his wife Margaret in 1986 and married a former Olympic Airlines stewardess, Dimitra Liani, who was half his age. In 1989, after a scandal regarding the Bank of Greece that implicated Papandreou, the New Democracy Party, under Konstantinos Mitsotakis, took over. In 1992, Papandreou was acquitted of any criminal involvement with the scandal. After Mitsotakis resigned in 1993 because of a lack of parliamentary majority, Papandreou was reelected and served until 1996, when he stepped down Konstantinos because of poor health. He died a short time afterward.

*Elaine Thomopoulos*

**See also:** Chapter 3: Panhellenic Socialist Movement.

**Further Reading**

Clogg, Richard. 1996. "Andreas Papandreou-A Political Profile." *Mediterranean Politics* 1 (3): 382–387.

Kariotis, Theodore C., ed. 1992. *The Greek Socialist Experiment: Papandreou's Greece, 1981-1989.* New York: Pella Publishing Company.

Papandreou, Andreas. 1971. *Democracy at Gunpoint.* Harmondsworth, UK: Penguin.

## Pericles (c. 495–c. 429 BCE)

Pericles supported democracy in Athens and glorified the city with the construction of monumental buildings on the Acropolis of Athens. His father was an Athenian general and statesman, and both his father and mother came from aristocratic families. Pericles studied music and mathematics as a youth and later became interested in philosophy. When he was seventeen, he inherited money that he used to support the arts. He sponsored the staging of Aeschylus's play *The Persians* and the Festival of Dionysus. Pericles entered the political arena in the 460s and carried the title of general for seventeen years, until his death. He was one of ten generals elected yearly by the people. As a general, Pericles could introduce his ideas directly to the Assembly, which consisted of adult male citizens of Athens. People of all classes could serve in the assembly. It was not limited to those of aristocratic heritage. Although Pericles supported a democratic form of government, only a minority of the people of Athens could vote—men who were free and whose fathers were born in Athens. Excluded were women, slaves, and foreigners (which included non-Athenian Greeks). Pericles had introduced the law that limited citizenship to those whose mother and father were both Athenians. This law came back to haunt him when he married a "foreigner," his second wife Aspasia. Pericles had to get the approval of the assembly to enable his wife to become a citizen. Aspasia was known for her intelligence. According to the historian Plutarch, Aspasia's house became a center of learning that attracted the intellectuals of Athens, including Socrates. Pericles introduced legislation to bolster democratic rule and community involvement. The laws included paying citizens who served as jurymen or assemblymen and allowing the poor to watch a play without paying for that privilege. During Pericles's tenure, the Parthenon, the Erechtheum, and the Temple of Athena Nike were constructed. The Parthenon housed a magnificent forty-foot ivory-and-gold statue of the goddess Athena, designed by Phidias. Besides being a gifted civic leader, Pericles was also a soldier. He led the following battles: the recapture of Delphi from the Spartans in 448, the navy's siege on Samos, and the disastrous invasion of Megara in 431, in which Athens was defeated. Pericles died of the plague, which killed not only him but also his two sons and a quarter of the population.

*Elaine Thomopoulos*

**See also:** Chapter 12: Sidebar: The History of the Parthenon.

**Further Reading**

Azoulay, Vincent. 2014. *Pericles of Athens.* Translated by Janet Lloyd. Princeton, NJ: Princeton University Press.

Tracy, Stephen V. 2009. *Pericles: A Sourcebook and Reader.* Oakland: University of California Press.

## Socrates (469–399 BCE)

Socrates, considered the Father of Western Philosophy, is known through the writings of his pupils Plato and Xenophon and the comedies of playwright Aristophanes, which made fun of him. He himself did not believe in communicating his thoughts through writing. Fortunately, *Plato's Dialogues* records Socrates's interaction with his students, his philosophy, as well as the words he spoke at his one-day trial. At the age of seventy, he was condemned to death for corrupting youth by teaching them to doubt the status quo and for impiety by introducing new gods. According to what Plato recorded, Socrates believed that the trial was motivated by politics, such as his perceived association with the pro-Spartan Oligarchy of the Thirty Tyrants. Socrates, refusing the offer of friends to help him escape, died by drinking poisonous hemlock.

Socrates grew up in an aristocratic family in a suburb just outside the city of Athens. His father was a sculptor and his mother a midwife. He became a hoplite (soldier) and fought in three battles of the Peloponnesian War, Socrates participated with valor, saving the life of his pupil Alcibiades in the Battle of Delium. He married Xanthippe, and they had three sons.

Socrates emphasized leading an ethical life and taught his students by asking them a series of questions, forcing them to think critically. The Socratic method of teaching continues to be used even today. Among his words of wisdom are the following:

- "I know one thing, and that is that I know nothing."
- "It is not living that matters but living rightly."
- "Let him that would move the world first move himself."
- "The greatest way to live with honor in this world is to be what we pretend to be."

*Elaine Thomopoulos*

**See also:** Chapter 4: Agriculture.

**Further Reading**

May, Hope. 2000. *On Socrates.* Belmont, CA: Wadsworth.

Taylor, C. C. W. 2001. *Socrates: A Very Short Introduction.* Oxford: Oxford University Press.

## Trikoupis, Harilaos (1832–1896)

Harilaos Trikoupis was born in Nafplion and educated in law and literature in Athens and Paris. He served as prime minister of Greece seven times between 1882 and 1895. To bring Greece into the modern age, he put an emphasis on increasing communication, transportation, manufacturing, and shipping. Trikoupis's administration instituted many improvements in infrastructure. The first railway line, still in use in the Peloponnesus, was built. By 1893, 569 miles of railway had been constructed with another 305 in the process of being constructed. Unfortunately, the railroad was not linked to the rest of Europe until 1916. The communication system was broadened by the laying of 4,000 miles of telegraph line. The Merchant Marine grew because of the introduction of regulations favorable to the industry and the construction of the Corinth Canal, which linked the Aegean Sea to the Ionian Sea. The Corinth Canal also enabled the growth of the port of Piraeus. Manufacturing increased, and by the early 1890s, Greece had seventeen cotton mills and three large woolen mills. The drainage of Lake Copais by a British company added thirty thousand acres of arable land. Trikoupis also restructured and built up the armed forces.

To finance infrastructure, Greece borrowed money. By 1893, more than 50 percent of the annual budget went to service loans. Trikoupis tried to balance the budget by raising taxes and export duties on products such as tobacco and wine, negatively impacting the farmers and merchants. His administration imposed a tithe on produce, as well as on sheep, goats, oxen, and donkeys. Taxes on land holdings were also increased.

Greece relied on its exports for its revenue. Its major export was currants (small black raisins). A 70 percent decrease in export of currants, as well as a worldwide depression and the burden of its loan debt, sent Greece into a tailspin. In December 1893, Trikoupis announced, "Regretfully we are bankrupt."

*Elaine Thomopoulos*

**See also:** Chapter 11: Solomos, Dionysios.

**Further Reading**

Gallant, Thomas W. 2016. *Modern Greece: From the War of Independence to the Present*, 2nd edition. New York: Bloomsbury, 75, 76–77, 78, 156–157, 166.

Gallant, Thomas W. *The Edinburgh History of the Greeks, 1768 to 1913. The Long Nineteenth Century*. 2015. Edinburgh: Edinburgh University Press, chapters 5 and 7.

Kostis, Kostas. 2018. *History's Spoiled Children: The Story of Modern Greece*. Translated by Jacob Moe. New York: Oxford University Press, chapter 6.

Tricha, Lydia. 2009. *Harilaos Trikoupis. A Biographical Journey*. Athens: Ekdoseis Kapon.

## Velouchiotis, Aris (1905–1945)

Athanasios Klaras, his given name, led the ELAS, the military branch of the National Liberation Front (EAM). The EAM became the major resistance organization against the Axis powers that had occupied Greece during World War II. Velouchiotis's nom de guerre came from Ares, the god of war, and Velouchi, a local mountain near his village of Lamia. He is one of the most disputed people of modern Greek history. Some worshipped him (a video on YouTube glorifies him) for fighting the Axis powers during the World War II resistance. Others despised him for supposed atrocities he committed on innocent citizens and for killing Colonel Dimitrios Psarras, another resistance leader.

In his youth, Velouchiotis became a member of the KKE, the Greek Communist party, and during the dictatorship of Ioannis Metaxas, he was arrested and jailed in an Aegean island prison because of his politics. He escaped but was arrested again in 1939 and sent to prison in Corfu where he signed a statement of renouncement of the Communist Party. However, he remained loyal to the Communist Party until his death.

After he was released from prison in 1941, he served as an artillery corporal in the Greek army fighting against the Italian army at the Albanian front. In 1942, he organized partisans to fight the German occupiers and was appointed leader of ELAS, the Communist-controlled resistance army. ELAS not only fought against the Germans who occupied Greece but also other resistance organizations. After the war ended in 1945, he took to the mountains to fight against the royalist army troops in the Greek Civil War. Even though he was ousted from the KKE, he continued fighting in the civil war. He died in 1945, and there is debate about whether he was killed or he committed suicide. After his death, Velouchiotis's decapitated head and that of his second-in-command, Leon Javellas, were displayed in Trikala, hanging from a lamppost in the town square.

*Elaine Thomopoulos*

**See also:** Chapter 2: Overview.

**Further Reading**

Charitopulos, Dionyses. 2012. *Aris: Lord of The Mountains.* Athens: Topos Books.

Farakos, Grigoris. 2011. "Last Letter of Aris Velouhiotis to the Central Committee of the KKE 24 March 1945." Translated by VN Gelis. Accessed March 30. 2019. Marxist Internet Archive, 400–404. https://www.marxists.org/archive/velouchiotis/1945/x01/x01.htm.

## Venizelos, Eleftherios (1864–1936)

Eleftherios Venizelos, one of the most influential statesmen and politicians of twentieth-century Greece, served as prime minister several times from 1909 to 1920 and then again from 1928 to 1933. In his earlier years as prime minister, he guided Greece through the victories of the First and Second Balkan Wars (1912–1913). This resulted in the addition of Epirus, Macedonia, Crete, and some of the other Aegean Islands to Greece's territory, expanding it by 68 percent. During his last term as prime minister, he experienced the heartache of his countrymen's poverty during the Great Depression; in 1932, Greece defaulted on its loans.

Venizelos was born on the Ottoman-controlled island of Crete. His family was forced to flee to the Greek island of Syros when he was two years old, following one of many Cretan rebellions against Ottoman rule. After several years, the family felt safe enough to go back to Crete. Young Venizelos excelled in his studies and became proficient in several languages.

Venizelos earned a law degree from the University of Athens. He returned to Crete where he practiced law and became involved in Cretan politics, working toward gaining autonomy for his beloved island of Crete.

He was initiated into the politics of Greece following the Goudi Rebellion of 1909. The successful rebellion was organized by a group of military men against the government and the king of Greece. They recruited Venizelos to become prime minister. As prime minister, Venizelos ramped up Greece's military machine. A few years later, this effort paid off. Greece and her allies won the Balkan Wars.

Not only did Venizelos bask in the glory of the Balkan Wars during his early years as prime minister, but he took pride in his domestic accomplishments. These included labor reforms such as the creation of a labor relations board, the prohibition of child labor and nightshift work for women, the six-day work week with no work on Sunday, and the prohibition of management-controlled unions that employees had to join. He also instituted

Eleftherios Venizelos was prime minister of Greece sporadically throughout the first three decades of the twentieth century. The prime minister and King Constantine I disagreed over World War I allegiances. Venizelos and his supporters set up a rival government, which was recognized by France and Britain in 1917. The king was forced into exile, and the Venizelos government lent its support to the Allies. (Library of Congress)

the right for the government to confiscate land and property for the national interest. Thus, big estates could be distributed to tenant farmers or small landowners. Venizelos also stressed the importance of educating the populace. His policies to make schooling more accessible seemed to have worked. In 1907, the rate of illiteracy of the populace was 63 percent, with male illiteracy at 43.1 percent and female illiteracy at 82.5 percent. By 1920, the total illiteracy rate was 48.5 percent, with the rate for males being 27.9 percent and the rate for females 68.8 percent. (This was the rate for the old boundaries, i.e., excluding territories added to Greece after the Balkan Wars and World War I.)

For several decades, there was a deep divide between those who supported Venizelos and those who supported King Constantine. What is called "The Great Schism" first started over the disagreement that Venizelos and King Constantine had about Greece's entry into World War I. Venizelos strongly believed that Greece should support the Triple Entente (France, Britain, and the Russian Empire) in its battles against the Central Powers (Austria-Hungary, Germany, and Italy), while the king believed Greece should be neutral. Because of his differences with the king, Venizelos gave up his position of prime minister twice in 1915.

On October 5, 1916, following a coup d'état by Venizelos and his supporters, a rival Greek government, the Government of National Defense, was established under Venizelos.

Venizelos became prime minister of the entire country of Greece in 1917, after the British and French officially recognized his government and forced the king to leave. By July 1917, Greece had declared war on the Central Powers, although it took several months before Greece's armed forces were ready to see action. Greek forces attacked and defeated Bulgarian forces in May 1918 at the Battle of Skra-di-Legen on the

Macedonian front. They continued fighting valiantly in subsequent battles, helping the Entente win the war. As an outcome of the victory, Greece added Western Thrace to its territory.

The Greeks harbored hostility toward Turkey for many reasons, which included the following: (1) Greece had been defeated by Turkey in the Greek-Turkish War, which lasted from 1919 to 1922; (2) Greeks residing in Asia Minor and Pontos had experienced genocide at the hands of the Turks; and (3) more than a million Greeks had to leave Turkey because of the war and the 1923 voluntary exchange of population between the two countries. In spite of the bad will between Greece and new nation of Turkey, Venizelos attempted to strengthen relations between the two countries. He negotiated the Treaty of Ankara, which was put into effect in 1930. The Greek refugees from Turkey strongly objected to the provision of the treaty that specified that they had to give up rights to their properties in Turkey. This dashed their dream of going back to lost homelands or seeking remuneration for lost property.

After the enactment of this treaty, Venizelos lost the support of the refugees. Instead, many turned to the Greek Communist party, which had been formed in 1918. In 1929, Venizelos adopted measures against the Communists by introducing a law that applied to the person "who tries to apply ideas that have as an obvious target the violent overthrow of the current social system, or who acts in propagandizing their application." The law shut down workers' organizations and curtailed strikes.

After Venizelos was defeated in the election of 1933, two unsuccessful military coups led by his supporters followed. After the March 1935 coup, Venizelos fled to Paris, where he died in 1936.

*Elaine Thomopoulos*

**See also:** Chapter 2: Overview.

**Further Reading**

Kitromilides, Paschalis M., ed. 2006. *Eleftherios Venizelos: The Trials of Statesmanship.* Edinburgh: Edinburgh University Press.

Michalopoulos, Dimitris. 2014. *Upheaval in the Balkans: Venizelos and* Politics, 1888–1920. file:///D:/Downloads/Upheaval_in_the_Balkans_Venizelos_and_Po.pdf.

Papadakis, Nikolaos. "Eleftherios K. Venizelos." Accessed May 25, 2018. http://www.venizelos-foundation.gr/en/cretan-european-political-scene/.

## Ypsilantis, Alexander (1792–1828)

Alexander Ypsilantis, one of heroes of the Greek revolution against the Ottoman Turks, led the first battle of the revolution against the Ottomans in 1821. Ypsilantis was born in Constantinople (present-day Istanbul), the eldest of three brothers. His family's roots were Pontian, and they were from the Trabzon area of the Black Sea in present-day Turkey. The Pontic Greeks spoke a dialect of Greek that could not be easily understood by the Greeks of the mainland. Both his grandfather and father became important officials in the Ottoman Empire.

When the Russian-Turkish War broke out in 1805, Ypsilantis's father fled with his family to Russia. Like his grandfather and father, Ypsilantis received an excellent education; he could speak Russian, Romanian, French, German, and Greek.

Ypsilantis rose up the ranks of the Russian army. During the Napoleonic Wars, he fought against France in the battles of Klyastitsy, Polotsk, and Bautzen. His arm was torn off by a shell during the Battle of Dresden. His valor earned him a promotion to major general, although he did not fight in subsequent battles for Russia.

His loss of an arm did not quell his enthusiasm for leading the Philiki Eteria, the secret group that had been formed to plan the revolution of the Greeks, or for commanding the first battle fought to achieve independence. He issued the proclamation "Fight for Faith and Country" after crossing the Prut River from Russia to the principality of Moldavia (present-day Romania). Greek volunteers, many of them students from Italy, Germany, and Russia, joined him. Ypsilantis assembled a battalion of about four hundred young men dressed in long black tunics with headgear that had white plumes. They called themselves the Sacred Band. He had hoped for support from the Serbians or the Russians, but that was not forthcoming. The Sacred Band advanced into Wallachia, but within four months of the campaign, they faced defeat at Drăgășani. The Austrians held Ypsilantis in confinement for several years, and he died shortly after his release. The city of Ypsilanti, Michigan, is named after his brother Demetrios Ypsilantis (1793–1832), who was also a hero of the Greek revolution.

*Elaine Thomopoulos*

**See also**: Chapter 9: Dialects and Minority Languages.

**Further Reading**

Brewer, David. 2001. *The Greek War of Independence: The Struggle for Freedom from Ottoman Oppression and the Birth of the Modern Greek Nation.* Woodstock, NY: Overlook Press.

Dakin, Douglas. 1984. *The Unification of Greece, 1770–1923.* London: Benn.

CHAPTER 3

# GOVERNMENT AND POLITICS

## OVERVIEW

In the first years after the War of Independence from Ottoman Turk rule, Greece, which refers to itself as the Hellenic Republic, was ruled as a monarchy. After a revolt of the populace in 1843, King Otto granted a new constitution, which put in place a parliamentary democracy rather than a constitutional monarchy. Greece has continued as a parliamentary democracy, with the exception of the years when dictators or Axis powers ruled the land.

During the first half of the twentieth century, Greece had a stormy history, including participation in the First and Second Balkan Wars (1912–1913), World War I (1917–1918), the dictatorship of Ioannis Metaxas (1936–1941), the occupation by the Axis powers during World War II (1941–1944), a brutal civil war (1946–1949), and the dictatorial rule of a group of military officers called the Regime of Colonels or the junta (1967–1974). By the 1960s, Greece had started on its way to economic recovery and a restoration of freedoms. When the junta took control of the country in a coup, they curtailed political freedoms. Following the fall of the junta in 1974, Greece entered a path toward democracy and normalcy in what is called *metapolitefsi* (regime change). Work immediately started on a new constitution, which was approved in 1975. This constitution of 1975 was revised three times, in 1986 (after Greece joined the European Union [EU]), in 2001, and again in 2008. The latter is now in force. The 2008 constitution includes rules concerning the structure of the state, the exercise of the power of the executive, legislative, and judicial branches, as well as a list of human rights. The system of governance is based on the principle of separation of powers of the legislative, executive, and judiciary branches.

According to the constitution, the prime minister is the head of government of the Hellenic Republic and the leader of the Greek cabinet and implements government policy within the framework of the constitution and the law. The unicameral Parliament, which consists of three hundred members, enacts the laws, and the judiciary interprets and enforces the laws. The president is essentially a ceremonial position.

Greece's citizens vote every four years for members of Parliament, although special elections can be called before the four years. Citizens over the age of seventeen can vote, and voting is mandatory, except for those over age seventy. Anyone twenty-five years of older can run for parliament.

During the past decade, Greece has faced several challenges. These included:

- the strain of its financial crisis and the austerity measures that followed;
- hundreds of thousands of refugees and migrants from war-torn countries caught in their country after the European countries to the north closed their borders;
- the long-standing problem of corruption;
- the increase of hate crimes against minority groups based on their racial, ethnic, or sexual orientation;
- the long-standing problem of corruption; and
- foreign policy issues involving its neighbor to the north, the new nation that arose out of the breakup of the Soviet Union, the Former Yugoslav Republic of Macedonia (now known as Republic of North Macedonia).

By 2009, the global economic crisis hit Greece hard and took a huge toll on the lower and middle classes. During the summer of 2011, the deepening of the economic crisis led to protests by both the far right and the far left. Street protests during that period, accompanied by extensive rioting, produced spectacular images that were beamed live across the world.

Because of the deepening crisis, the political parties such as the Panhellenic Socialist Movement (PASOK) and New Democracy (ND), which had dominated the political scene since 1975, weakened. Simplistic arguments (e.g., Antonis Samaras of ND declared he could eliminate the debt in one year) and populist politics provided legitimization and publicity to other political actors. SYRIZA, the party of the radical left, and Golden Dawn, an extreme, national-socialist, ultranationalist party led by founder Holocaust-denier Nikos Mihaloliakos, benefited by the people's distrust of PASOK and ND.

In the election of June 2012, PASOK received just 12.3 percent of the votes and joined with ND and the party of the Democratic Left (DIMAR) to form a coalition government. The coalition called an early election in 2015.

With the victory of SYRIZA in the election of January 2015, the hegemony of both PASOK and ND came to an end. SYRIZA came in first, winning 149 seats. However, the seats they won did not constitute a majority of the 300 seats in the Parliament. They joined with ANEL (Independent Greeks), a party with a nationalist right-wing agenda, to form a coalition government. Despite the large ideological party differences between SYRIZA and ANEL, both agreed on not accepting what is known as the Memorandum of Understanding (MoU). This MoU outlined the obligations that were imposed upon Greece by the Troika (the European Commission, the European Central Bank, and the International Monetary Fund) so that Greece could obtain loans to help weather the economic crisis.

Alexis Tsipras (1974–), the leader of SYRIZA, became prime minister. He served his first term of office from January 26, 2015, to August 27, 2015. Tsipras campaigned on promises to ease the tough austerity measures imposed on Greece in the MoUs that had been negotiated by the Troika and the past governments of PASOK and ND.

However, his renegotiation attempts with the Troika after he took office did not bear fruit, since Greece's creditors refused to budge. During the summer of 2015, Tsipras asked the citizens of Greece to decide through a referendum if they wanted Greece to accept conditions of the MoUs, and the people voted against it. Nevertheless, within a month of the referendum, Greece signed the agreement, which included painful government spending cuts and restructuring in return for loans to Greece.

On August 27, 2015, Tsipras stepped down as prime minister so that a snap election to elect delegates to the Parliament could be held. The election was called because intra-party defections resulted in the collapse of the coalition's majority. The election results showed that the SYZIRA was just short of six seats of a majority in Parliament. A coalition government of SYZIRA and ANEL was formed once again. Tsipras was sworn in for his second term on September 21, 2015, a position he held until July 7, 2019.

Tsipras has been in politics since 1999 when he served as the secretary of the Synaspismos Youth, which is the youth organization of the Synaspismos, at one time the largest left-wing political party. It was dissolved in 2013. SYRIZA, which had existed since the early 2000s as a coalition of leftist parties and groups, replaced it. It now constitutes the largest political party of the left.

One of the most important issues Greece has been dealing with for many years is the high rate of corruption in the government, the justice system, law enforcement, health services, education, and business. Corruption in Greece takes many forms, included bribes that are passed on to officials or other recipients to obtain some form of benefit, as for example, in hospitals so that the patient can receive faster and better treatment by the doctors, or to a government employee to expedite service, such as the paperwork needed to establish a business or to get a building permit approved. Another long-standing practice that dates back to the beginning of the country involves promising jobs in exchange for votes. The lack of a civil service test seems to encourage this form of corruption. Widespread tax evasion has been still another way of cheating. This is true of the collection of income taxes, real estate taxes, and sales taxes. Recently, Greece through its National Anti-Corruption Action Plan (NACAP) has been trying to fight corruption.

Other efforts to combat bribery, tax evasion, and money laundering during the past decade included ratifying the OECD Convention, the United Nations Convention against Corruption (UNCAC), the Council of Europe Civil and Criminal Law Conventions on Corruption, and the Additional Protocol to the Criminal Law Convention on Corruption (Law no. 3560/2007, with further amendments in 2008). Furthermore, the government intensified its efforts, while at times provided incentives, in order to collect taxes without, however, the latter being a big burden to the taxpayers. For example, it introduced a new measure by which taxpayers could pay their debts through 120 installments.

The Troika and other European and international institutions have suggested that the economic crisis in the country was caused to a large extent by corruption. Despite laws enacted to curb corruption, it is still evident in the judicial process and among politicians and high-profile individuals. This makes fighting it even more difficult.

Greece makes extensive references to securing individual rights and liberties in its constitution. However, although the constitution and laws enacted guarantee human rights, international organizations such as International Amnesty and Human Rights Watch have recorded hundreds of racist incidents in the past decade alone, along with an increase in hate crimes against minority groups based on racial, ethnic, or sexual orientation. Most recently, thousands of migrants and asylum seekers in northern Greece and some of the islands, most notably in Lesvos, have been subject to appalling reception and detention conditions, with at-risk groups lacking necessary protection.

One of the most pressing foreign policies Greece has had to deal with involved its neighbor to the north, the Republic of North Macedonia, formerly known as the Former Yugoslav Republic of Macedonia (FYROM). Greece and their northern neighbor disagreed on whether or not the newly created nation had the right to use "Macedonia" in its name. This decades-long debate was recently resolved by the SYRIZA-ANEL Greek government and its counterpart in FYROM when they came to an historic agreement on a new name—Republic of North Macedonia—in an attempt to put behind mutual animosity and establish good neighborly relations and economic stability in the region. The country was created in 1991 after the breakup of the former Soviet Union. In 1993, it was admitted to the United Nations, with the provisional name of FYROM. The majority of Greek citizens do not approve of the use of the name "Macedonia" in the new name of the country, even though their parliament approved it, and it became official on February 12, 2019. They believe that the use of the name is indicative of the irredentist desire of the country to take over the province of Macedonia in northern Greece. They also accuse the new nation of falsifying the Greek historical past, saying that the people are Slavs who have no relation to the ancient Macedonians or to their ruler Alexander the Great.

The deal, apart from agreeing on the name of FYROM as "Republic of North Macedonia," as it is now officially called, includes the following:

- Recognition in the United Nations of the Macedonian language. According to Article 7, no. 4, the official language, the Macedonian language, is within the group of South Slavic languages, but the official language and other attributes of North Macedonia are not related to the ancient Hellenic civilization, history, culture, and heritage of the northern region of the First Party.
- The citizenship of the country will be called Macedonian/citizen of the Republic of North Macedonia.
- North Macedonia is to discontinue use of the Vergina Sun, a symbol of Greek history and culture.
- Both counties are to form a committee to review school textbooks and maps in order to remove irredentist content and align them with UNESCO and Council of Europe standards.

Prime Minister Tsipras and his government pointed with pride to the resolution of the Macedonian Question and to the lessening of the economic crisis. Although it enacted extreme austerity and restructuring measures, the sacrifices seem to have paid off. Greece completed the economic programs of the International Monetary Fund in August 2018, enabling it to follow its own economic policies, although EU monitoring still persists.

However, the latest elections on July 7, 2019, gave the ND, with Kyriakos Mitsotakis as its leader, complete majority, and since then, he has replaced Tsipras as prime minister.

*Nikos Christofis*

**See also:** Chapter 2: Overview. Chapter 4: Memoranda of Understanding. Chapter 7: Women in Politics and the Parliament.

**Further Reading**

Beaton, Roderick. 2019. *Greece: Biography of a Modern Nation*. London: Allen Lane.

"Final Agreement for the Settlement of the Differences as Described in the United Nations Security Council Resolution 817 (1993) and 845 (1993), the Termination of the Interim Accord of 1995, and the Establishment of a Strategic Partnership between the Parties." June 17, 2018. Accessed July 1, 2019. morm.gov.mk/wp-content/uploads/2018/08/spogodba-en.pdf.

Gallant, Thomas W. 2016. *Modern Greece: From the War of Independence to the Present*, 2nd edition. London and New York: Bloomsbury Academic.

Kostis, Kostas. 2018. *History's Spoiled Children: The Story of Modern Greece*. London and New York: C. Hurst & Co.

## Constitution

The Constitution of Greece is the fundamental charter of the state. Greece promulgated its first constitution during the War of Independence (1821–1832), which was revised extensively by revolutionary governments in the decade afterward. In 1843, after a revolt of the populace, King Otto granted a new constitution (*syntagma*), which put in place a parliamentary democracy rather than a constitutional monarchy. After the constitution was granted, the area in front of the Parliament building was renamed Syntagma Square. Unlike the other Balkan countries, Greece's experience of representative democracy has been of long standing and a deep parliamentary tradition has evolved, even as the country has undergone political chaos and seen the rise and fall of various constitutional regimes. This became more evident, in particular, after the fall of the colonels' dictatorship in 1974.

Greece's present constitution was enacted in 1975 by the parliamentary assembly that was formed after the collapse of the military regime in 1974. Since then, it has undergone three substantive revisions, the first in 1986 (when Greece joined the European Community) and then again in 2001 and 2008. It includes the main rules concerning the structure of the state, the exercise of the power of the executive, legislative, and judicial branches, as well as a list of human rights.

The Greek Constitution consists of 120 articles and is set out in four parts:

Part I (§1–3) establishes Greece as a parliamentary democracy (or republic—in Greek the word *δημοκρατία (dimocratia)* can be translated both ways). It confirms the prevalence of the Orthodox Church in Greece, but as later specified in Article 13, the people have the right to believe in any religion they choose or not to believe in any religion. The political rights of the people do not depend on the religion they embrace.

Part II (§4–25) outlines individual and social rights. The Greek Constitution respects human rights. It includes the right of assembly; of association; to freedom of religion; to freedom of expression and of the press; to free education; to free art and science, research and teaching; to protection of property; to secrecy of correspondence; to legal protection; to protection of family, marriage, motherhood, and youth; to care for the health of citizens; to work and social security; to the freedom to unionize; to strike; to protection of the environment; to protection and exercise of the fundamental rights.

Part III (§26–105) shows the organization and function of the state. Article 28 formally integrates international laws and conventions into Greek law. Article 102, one of the most important articles, says, "The administration of local affairs shall be exercised by local government agencies, the first level of which comprises municipalities and communities. Other levels shall be specified by law."

Since 2011, Greece has been divided into seven decentralized administrations run by a government-appointed general secretary and assisted by an advisory council drawn from the regional governors and the representatives of the municipalities. They enjoy both administrative and financial autonomy and exercise devolved state powers in urban planning, environmental and energy policy, forestry, migration, and citizenship. Beyond that, they are tasked with supervising the first- and second-level self-governing bodies: the municipalities and regions. There are thirteen administrative regions (peripheries); each one of them has its own head of periphery. In 2011, the government-appointed general secretaries of the regions were replaced with popularly elected regional governors and regional councils. During the 2011 reform, the municipalities were reduced in number from 914 to 325.

Part IV (§106–120) comprises different provisions that provide the constitution with further clarification. According to Article 108, "The State must take care for emigrant Greeks and for the maintenance of their ties with the Fatherland. The State shall also attend to the education, the social and professional advancement of Greeks working outside the State."

*Nikos Christofis*

**See also:** Chapter 5: Overview; Freedom of Religion.

**Further Reading**

Alivizatos, Nikos. 2011. *The Constitution and Its Enemies in Neohellenic History, 1800–2010* (in Greek). Athens: Polis.

Hellenic Parliament. 2008. *The Constitution of Greece* (English version). Translated by Xenophon Paparrigopoulos and Stavroula Vassilouni. Accessed July 1, 2019. https://www.hellenicparliament.gr/UserFiles/f3c70a23-7696-49db-9148-f24dce6a27c8/001-156%20aggliko.pdf.

Hellenic Republic Ministry of Interior, Public Administration and Decentralisation. 2000. *Structure and Operation of Local and Regional Democracy in Greece.* Accessed July 1, 2019. http://unpan1.un.org/intradoc/groups/public/documents/UNTC/UNPAN000205.pdf.

Katrougalos, George. n.d. "The Constitutional History of Greece, in the Balkan Context." Accessed July 1, 2019. http://www.cecl.gr/RigasNetwork/databank/REPORTS/r1/GR_1_Katrougalos.htm#_Toc454518906.

## Corruption

Corruption in Greece is pervasive. It affects the government's accountability, the justice system, health, education, law enforcement, and business. Transparency International concluded in a 2012 report that corruption played a major role in the financial crisis.

A common form of corruption in Greece is known as *fakelaki* (small envelope). This refers to the small envelopes containing bribes that are passed on to officials or other recipients to obtain some favor, as, for example, in hospitals so that the patient can receive faster and better treatment by the doctors, or to a government employee to expedite service, such as the paperwork needed to establish a business or to get a building permit approved.

During election periods, some politicians promise jobs in exchange for votes. The lack of a civil service test seems to encourage corruption of this type.

Widespread tax evasion has been yet another way of cheating. This is true of the collection of income taxes, real estate taxes, and sales taxes, although recently Greece through its NACAP has been trying to remedy this situation.

In comparison to other nations, Greece has not done well according to its score on the 2017 Corruption Perceptions Index as reported by Transparency International. The index ranks countries and territories by perceived levels of public sector corruption, gathering data from entrepreneurs, journalists, and citizens' organizations. It uses a scale of 0–100, with 0 being least corrupt and 100 most corrupt. Greece had a score of 48 points out of 100 and ranked the 59th least corrupt nation out of 180 countries. The most corrupt country in the West is Mexico, followed by Ukraine and the Former Yugoslav Republic of Macedonia (now known as the Republic of North Macedonia). From 1995 to 2017, Greece's corruption index averaged 43.70 on a scale from 0 to 100. It reached an all-time high of 53.50 points in 1997 and a record low of 34.00 points in 2011.

Officials sometimes engaged in corrupt practices with impunity, while indeed, ineffective implementation of existing laws has exacerbated corruption in both the higher and lower echelons of government as "gifts," bribery, and facilitation payments are widespread. This is despite existing provisions that criminalize these acts. Facilitation payment refers to a certain type of payment to a government official in exchange for approval of a business transaction or activity. It is not considered to be bribery according to some states or by the anti-bribery standards of the Organisation for Economic Co-operation and Development (OECD) Convention on Combating Bribery of Foreign Public Officials in International Business Transactions. However, facilitation payments are prohibited directly or indirectly in Greece according to Articles 235 and 236 of the Greek Criminal Code (GCC), and all payments and expenses must be duly justified and relevant documentation must be kept with the tax records of the company; otherwise such payments might be considered questionable (gifts, benefits, etc.).

During the past few years, Greece has made efforts to fight corruption. This included ratifying the OECD Convention, the UNCAC, the Council of Europe Civil and Criminal Law Conventions on Corruption, and the Additional Protocol to the Criminal Law Convention on Corruption (Law no. 3560/2007 with further amendments in 2008).

There have been arrests and conviction of those transgressing the laws, even when the wrongdoing involved politicians. In 2010, Akis Tsochatzopoulos and his wife purchased a house for 1 million euros in one of most prestigious neighborhoods in Athens only a few days before Parliament passed a series of austerity measures aimed at increasing taxes and combating tax evasion. What is more, the purchase took place through an offshore account. In early 2011, following an investigation by a specialized committee of the Hellenic Parliament, evidence emerged that Tsochatzopoulos was also involved in the Siemens bribery scandal. The scandal involved bribes paid by Siemens AG to Greek government officials during the 2004 Summer Olympic Games in Athens, Greece, regarding transactions related to security systems for the Athens Olympics. In 2013, he was found "guilty on all charges." He was imprisoned but was released on July 2, 2018, for health reasons.

More recently, in October 2018, Yiannos Papantoniou and his wife, upon the decision of the prosecuting authorities, were detained and sent to prison pending their trial for grave corruption and money-laundering charges that cost the Greek state an estimated 400 million euros. Papantoniou, before succeeding Akis Tsochatzopoulos as national defense minister in the PASOK government, served as minister of national economy under Kostas Simitis.

The EU is urging Greece to step up anti-corruption efforts as it believes that in large extent, fighting corruption will make the country more viable and healthier economically. Indeed, it seems that, although it needs time to tell, the Greek government's attempts to fight corruption are working to the benefit of the public good and toward a more stabilized economy.

*Nikos Christofis*

**See also:** Chapter 4: Reasons for the Economic Crisis.

**Further Reading**

Anagnostopoulos, Ilias G., and Jerina (Gerasimoula) Zapanti. 2017. "Greece." In *The Anti-Bribery and Anti-Corruption Review*, edited by M. G. Mendelsohn, 128–136. London: Law Business Research.

Council of Europe. 2018. "Group of States against Corruption: Evaluations." Accessed July 1, 2019. https://www.coe.int/en/web/greco/evaluations.

Trading Economics. 2017. "Greece Corruption Index." Accessed July 1, 2019. https://tradingeconomics.com/greece/corruption-index.

# Foreign Policy

Greece's location at the intersection of Southern Europe, the Western Balkans, and the Eastern Mediterranean has made it a crucial geopolitical actor. Greece joined the North Atlantic Treaty Alliance (NATO) in the early 1950s, soon after it was founded. Its NATO allies—in particular the United States and neighboring Italy and, more recently, Bulgaria—have been core partners, as has the European Union. A European Union member since 1986 and also a member of the Union for the Mediterranean, Greece plays a vital role in the Eastern Mediterranean region—with its significant energy reserves and potential for collaboration in exploration and distribution. Greece actively pursues partnerships with other Eastern Mediterranean countries—including Arab countries—in the interests of a stable maritime region. Its Orthodox heritage has also meant strong cultural and diplomatic ties with Russia.

Regarding foreign relations, the government led by SYRIZA from 2015 to 2019 promoted a multidimensional pro-peace policy for Greece, with no involvement in wars or military plans and a policy of independence and friendly peaceful cooperation with all countries, especially the country's neighbors. SYRIZA attaches particular significance to confronting the crucial problems in the broader region (Balkans, Mediterranean, and Middle East) via peaceful dialogue based on international law.

Among the most heated and prominent issues in Greek foreign policy have been disputes regarding the Aegean Sea, Cyprus, and North Macedonia (previously known as the Former Yugoslav Republic of Macedonia).

## AEGEAN SEA

Beginning in 1973 and continuing to the present, the Aegean Sea has been the greatest area of conflict between Greece and Turkey. They have had disagreements over (1) ownership of islands that are claimed by both Greece and Turkey, (2) delimitation of the boundaries of territorial water and airspace, and (3) more recently, the militarization of Greek islands located near Turkey. These conflicts have led to constant diplomatic and military activities and to three major crises, in August 1976, 1987, and 1996, that brought the two countries to the brink of war. During the past few years, and especially since 2016, the relations between the two countries have worsened. They are in the midst of a Cold War.

## CYPRUS

The Cyprus Question remains the main cause of friction between Greece and Turkey. Political developments in Cyprus since the 1950s have always had lasting effects in the "motherlands" of Greece and Turkey. Bicommunal ethnic conflict between the two largest communities of the island, the Greek Cypriots and Turkish Cypriots, erupted during the 1950s. In 1960, after a successful anti-colonial struggle by the Greek Cypriots, Cyprus was declared independent. The peaceful coexistence between the two communities of the island did not last long. A bloody conflict between them during the 1960s ended with the Turkish invasion of the island in 1974. The Greek government, then under the leadership of the dictator Demetrios Ioannidis, orchestrated a coup against the president of the Republic of Cyprus, Archbishop Makarios. This coup led to the Turkish invasion of Cyprus. Since the Turkish invasion, Cyprus has been de facto separated into two parts. The northern 37 percent of the island, which calls itself the Turkish Republic of Northern Cyprus, is governed by the Turkish Cypriots and recognized only by Turkey and the Nakhichevan Autonomous Republic, a landlocked exclave of the Republic of Azerbaijan; less than 350 Greek Cypriots still reside there. The southern part, the Republic of Cyprus, is governed by the Greek Cypriots. The invasion resulted in thousands of displaced, dead, and missing, and nearly 200,000 Greek Cypriots were forced to flee their homes in northern Cyprus.

Ever since, both Greece and Turkey, the so-called motherlands, along with the Turkish community in the north of the island and the Greek community in the south, have been engaged in a poisonous and seemingly endless back and forth to resolve the issue, with little progress having been made in nearly half a century. In 2004, there was a referendum regarding the United Nation's Annan Plan, a plan to find a viable and stable solution to the issue based on a federative system. Loosely based on the Swiss federal model, the plan envisaged two constituent states—one Greek Cypriot and the other Turkish Cypriot—enjoying extensive autonomy but represented externally by a federal state with limited sovereign powers. In the 2004 referendum, however, the majority of Greek Cypriots voted "no," and the plan was abandoned. The central complaint raised by Greek Cypriot voters was that the deal would leave the central government too weak to be effective and also give too much autonomy to the states. More recently, in December 2017 and January 2018, the negotiations revived but again the talks bore no fruit to the issue's resolution.

## REPUBLIC OF NORTH MACEDONIA (PREVIOUSLY KNOWN AS FORMER YUGOSLAV REPUBLIC OF MACEDONIA)

In 2019, the SYRIZA-ANEL Greek government and its counterpart in the FYROM came to an historic agreement. They agreed on a new name, "Republic of

North Macedonia," for what Greece had previously recognized as the FYROM in an attempt to put behind mutual animosity and establish good neighborly relations and economic stability in the region. The country, which lies just north of Greece, was created in 1991 after the breakup of the former Soviet Union. In 1993, it was admitted to the United Nations, with the provisional name of Former Yugoslav Republic of Macedonia. The majority of Greek citizens do not approve of the use of the name "Macedonia" in the new name of the country to the north, even though their parliament approved it and it is now official. They believe that the use of the name is indicative of the irredentist desire of the country to take over the Province of Macedonia in northern Greece. They also accuse the new nation of falsifying the Greek historical past, saying that the people are Slavs who have no relation to the ancient Macedonians or to their ruler Alexander the Great. The ongoing dispute has not prevented the two countries from enjoying close trade links and investment opportunities.

*Nikos Christofis*

**See also:** Chapter 4: Privatization of Transportation. Chapter 5: Leftist Parties of Greece.

**Further Reading**

Christofis, Nikos, Bahar Baser, and Ahmet Erdi Öztürk. 2019. "The View from Next Door: Greek-Turkish Relations after the Coup Attempt in Turkey." *The International Spectator* 54 (2): 67–86.

Christopoulos, Dimitris, and Kostis Karpozilos. 2018. *10+1 Questions and Answers on the Macedonian Question*. Rosa Luxemburg Stiftung. Accessed July 1, 2019. https://www.rosalux.de/fileadmin/rls_uploads/pdfs/engl/MAKEDONIKO_2019_%CE%95%CE%9D.pdf.

Heraclides, Alexis. 2010. *The Greek-Turkish Conflict in the Aegean: Imagined Enemies*. Basingstoke: Palgrave.

## Golden Dawn

The German invasion and the atrocities of the Axis occupying forces during World War II, as well as the military dictatorship in Greece from 1967 to 1974, left a strong imprint on Greek society. Yet, in May 2012, the Golden Dawn Party—which explicitly endorsed an ultranationalist, rabidly anti-immigrant agenda—managed to win the votes of more than four hundred thousand Greeks. Indeed, in the September 2015 national elections, the party finished third (with 6.99 percent of the votes), taking eighteen seats. It managed to retain, at the same time, its support in the 2014 European Parliament elections, receiving 9.38 percent of the vote.

By the election of July 2019, Golden Dawn had lost its power. It failed to win even one seat in Parliament, although another far-right organization, the Greek Solution, won ten seats. Finally, in a five-year trial that concluded on October 6, 2020, Golden Dawn was dealt a death blow—it was ruled a criminal organization.

The Golden Dawn Party was established in 1980 and published its own journal with the same name. The party's main ideological manifesto, "Declaration of Ideological Principles," was issued during the mid-1980s. It was a post–World War II manifesto of neo-Nazism with anti-Marxist and anti-Semitic character. The party's logo was a variation of the Nazi swastika, and its guiding principles were "blood," that is, 100 percent Greek blood, and "honor." The slogan of the Golden Dawn Party was *Aima, Timi, Hrysi Avgi* (blood, honor, golden dawn), and its manifesto hailed national-socialism, although since the 1990s, it stopped any references to national-socialism, replacing it with "nationalism." Golden Dawn presented itself as a successor of ancient Greece. It rejected democracy, called for a "new national-socialist crusade," and praised Adolf Hitler as the hero of European civilization. Throughout its history, party members, including leader Nikos Mihaloliakos, targeted people both because of their ethnic backgrounds and because of their political persuasions. The party has had ties with "brother parties" in many countries, including the United States and the diaspora Greeks there.

Nikos Mihaloliakos, a Holocaust denier, founded the party and became its leader. During the period of the Greek military dictatorship, Mihaloliakos was a member of a Fascist party named "Fourth of August" (K4A). The group's name referred to the beginning of the Ioannis Metaxas dictatorship in 1936 and expressed the same Fascist ideology. After the fall of the military dictatorship in 1974, Mihaloliakos remained loyal to his Fascist activities. Since 1974, he had been arrested four times, with several convictions. The most recent arrest was in 2013 for his alleged involvement in the killing of the left-wing activist and rapper Pavlos Fyssas (aka Killah P) in Athens. He was charged with giving the order to kill Fyssas and forming a criminal organization. After five years of house arrest, he was given a sentence of thirteen years.

In 2013, another Golden Dawn member, Giorgos Roupakias, was arrested for the 2013 murder of Fyssas. Roupakias was released after thirty months because he had served the maximum allowable time in temporary detention. He, like Mihaloliakos, was held in house arrest until the Penal Court of Athens reached its decision.

As new evidence surfaced, other party members were also arrested for (1) Fyssas's murder, (2) the attempted murder and attacks on Egyptian fishermen, and (3) the attempted murder of trade unionists from PAME (Trade Union Front). The victims and their relatives joined together in the three cases. Thus, the Golden Dawn trial, which began on April 20, 2015, included these three cases, as well as the question of whether Golden Dawn was a criminal organization.

The Golden Dawn trial, one of the most important trials in contemporary Greek history, lasted five years. Those arrested included prominent members of Parliament, as well as a number of police officers. During the trial, there were 216 witnesses.

At the end of 2019, the depositions of the witnesses and victims of the Golden Dawn were completed. Since February 2019, both the prosecution and the defense had been presenting their closing arguments. In October 2020, the three-member court ruled that Golden Dawn was a criminal organization and delivered fifty-seven guilty verdicts to party members and associates. Eighteen of those convicted had been members of Parliament. Mihaloliakos was convicted of leading a criminal organization and given a sentence of thirteen years. Roupakias was given a life sentence plus ten for fatally stabbing Fyssas.

The Golden Dawn trial is the most important trial of Nazis since the Nuremberg trials, a series of military tribunals held after World War II by the Allied Powers against prominent members of the political, military, judicial, and economic leadership of Nazi Germany.

*Nikos Christofis*

**See also:** Chapter 2: Overview.

**Further Reading**

Christopoulos, Dimitris. 2018. "The Golden Dawn Trial: A Major Event for Democracy in Greece and Beyond." Accessed July 1, 2019. https://www.opendemocracy.net/en/he-golden-dawn-trial-major-event-for-democracy-in-greece-and-beyond/.

Ellinas, Antonis. 2015. "Neo-Nazism in an Established Democracy: The Persistence of Golden Dawn in Greece." *South European Society and Politics* 20 (1): 1–20.

Vasilopoulou, Sofia, and Daphne Halikiopoulou. 2015. *The Golden Dawn's 'Nationalist Solution': Explaining the Rise of the Far Right in Greece.* Basingstoke: Palgrave Macmillan.

## Human Rights

Human rights, the fundamental individual, social, and political rights and freedoms, are protected in Greece by the Greek Constitution (Articles 4–25). Abuse of human rights is prohibited by law (Article 25.3). The protection of human rights is complemented by the European Convention for the Protection of Human Rights and Fundamental Freedoms of November 4, 1950, which Greece has ratified. Capital punishment was abolished in 2004. The last time the death penalty was used was in 1972.

Greece has been accused of being in violation of basic human rights several times by Amnesty International. Their reports in 2014 and more recently in 2017/18 made extensive references about police abuse of power and maltreatment. Based on the annual report prepared by Reporters without Borders in 2019, Greece was ranked 65th out of 180 countries in their World Press Freedom Index.

From October 2011 to January 2014, Amnesty International recorded over 350 incidents of racist violence. Although there had been a reduction in organized racist attacks on migrants, especially of Albanian descent, there had been an increase in hate crimes against lesbian, gay, bisexual, and transgender (LGBT) and intermarried (people belonging to different races, castes, or religions) individuals in 2014. Between January and June of that year, police and anti-racism bureaus recorded 31 incidents that had a potential racist motive. In early 2018, Human Rights Watch said that Greece has abrogated its responsibility under international law to offer a minimum standard of protection to thousands of migrants and asylum seekers that had sought protection in the wake of conflicts in Syria, Afghanistan, and Iraq. In particular, the report noted, detention facilities in northern Greece were well below acceptable standards and pregnant women, new mothers, and others arriving via the land border with Turkey have been unable to access the basic conditions Greece is required to provide those seeking international protection from violence and political repression.

Public figures have expressed racist and homophobic comments. Metropolitan Anthimos of Thessaloniki expressed his "love" for immigrants and gay individuals but said, "It is a shame that there is not enough space for all of us in Greece" (TheToc 2018). Another leader of the Greek Orthodox Church, Metropolitan Amvrosios of Kalavryta, called upon his flock to spit on all gay men and women anywhere they meet them or to move against the LGBT community even with violent means (Chrysopoulos 2018; Kampouris 2019). He was found guilty of abusing the clerical office and inciting hatred and sentenced to seven months imprisonment (which was suspended) and three years probation.

*Nikos Christofis*

**See also:** Chapter 7: Lesbian, Gay, Bisexual, and Transgendered Acceptance and Legal Protection.

**Further Reading**

Amnesty International Report. 2017/2018. *The State of the World's Human Rights.* Accessed June 22, 2019. https://www.amnesty.org/en/countries/europe-and-central-asia/greece/report-greece/.

"Anthimos: 'Other Gay People in the Church . . .'" (in Greek). *TheToc*, March 15, 2018. Accessed July 1, 2019. https://www.thetoc.gr/koinwnia/article/anthimos-allo-oi-omofulofiloi-tis-ekklisias.

Chrysopoulos, Philip. 2018. "Metropolitan Amvrosios Launches New Attack against Justice Minister." *Greek Reporter*, April 3, 2018. Accessed July 1, 2019. https://greece.greekreporter.com/2018/04/03/metropolitan-amvrosios-launches-new-attack-against-justice-minister/.

Human Rights Watch. 2018. "Greece: Inhumane Conditions at Land Border." July 27, 2018. Accessed July 27, 2019. https://www.hrw.org/news/2018/07/27/greece-inhumane-conditions-land-border.

Kampouris, Nick. 2019. "Greek Bishop Amvrosios Found Guilty of Homophobia and Hatred." *Greek Reporter*, January 28, 2019. Accessed June 22, 2019. https://greece.greekreporter.com/2019/01/28/greek-bishop-amvrosios-found-guilty-of-homophobia-and-hatred/.

Kouzelis, Yerasimos, and Dimitris Christopoulos, eds. 2012. *Idiotita tou Politi. Politikos Logos, Istoria kai Kanones se Sygkritikes Prooptikes* (in Greek). Athens: Patakis.

Reporters without Borders. "Index Details: Data of Press Freedom Ranking 2018." Accessed June 22, 2019. https://rsf.org/en/ranking_table.

Vidali, Sofia. 2012. *Police: Crime Control and Human Rights* (in Greek). Athens: Nomiki Vivliothiki.

Graffiti can be seen throughout Greece and is used to express political views. This slogan was found on Ermou Street in the Plaka, Athens, in 2018. Some of the Greeks see capitalism as the root cause of the maladies of the Greek state, including inequalities and corruption. (Photo by Alexander Fatouros)

## Leftist Parties of Greece

At present, the most prominent party of the left is the SYRIZA, which was formed in 2004. Alexis Tsipras, who is a member of this party, served as prime minister of Greece from January 2015 to July 2019, with a short respite from that role when he called for a snap election in 2015. The SYRIZA party traces its origins to the Communist Party of Greece (KKE), and it split into two separate parties in 1968.

The Greek Communist or Socialist movement was dominated until 1974, to a large extent, by the KKE. Established shortly after the 1917 October Revolution in Russia as the Socialist Workers' Party of Greece (SEKE), it was renamed KKE during the party's Third Extraordinary Congress. The party fully accepted the terms of the Communist International and played a prominent role in strikes, anti-war demonstrations, foundation of trade unions and worker associations, and overthrowing capitalism.

Although the KKE was banned in 1936 by the dictator Ioannis Metaxas and many members of the party were imprisoned or sent to exile, it managed to play a fundamental role in the liberation of Greece from Axis occupying forces (German, Italian, and Bulgarian) during World War II. The KKE led the resistance force, the National

Liberation Front (EAM), a coalition of leftist and republican groups who fought against the Axis. Mainland Greece was liberated in 1944, and the Aegean Islands in 1945.

After World War II ended, a civil war was fought between Greek government troops and the Communist-controlled Democratic Army of Greece (DSE). The government troops defeated the Communists in 1949.

From the end of the civil war until 1975, the KKE was outlawed. Its leadership took refuge abroad so that they would not face imprisonment or death. Many members of the KKE participated and guided the newly established party called United Democratic Left (*Eniaia Dimokratiki Aristera*, EDA), which had the support of the KKE. In 1958, EDA had become the leading opposition party for the first time in Greek political history. Until the military dictatorship took control of Greece in 1967, EDA was the post–civil war representative of the left in Greece.

In 1968, the KKE split into two separate parties: the KKE/Exterior and the Eurocommunists, known in Greece as KKE/Interior. The two parties differed regarding their approach: the KKE/Exterior remained loyal to the Leninist precepts and a rigid Communist ideology, while the KKE/Interior adopted a reformist approach.

After the collapse of the Greek junta in 1974, when the KKE was no longer outlawed, the two parties remained in conflict, but they joined forces for the 1974 elections, receiving nearly 10 percent of the vote. In 1989, they agreed to create a coalition of various Communist parties, called Synaspismos.

In 1991, the coalition was transformed to a unified party, with the subsequent dissolution of the smaller parties that comprised the coalition. Synaspismos as a party represented the convergence of the Eurocommunists (KKK/Interior) and other Communists. Orthodox Communists disagreed with and withdrew from the new political formation.

It was from the Synaspismos party that SYRIZA emerged in 2004. The name the group took, which translates roughly as "Coalition of the Radical Left," reflects its origins as a parliamentary alliance of various factions and splinter groups of the old KKE, and different left-wing currents ranging from Trotskyists to post-Maoists and ecologists, as well as unaffiliated leftists.

The ideological differences between the KKE and SYRIZA continue in the twenty-first century. The main point of difference between them was their political stance vis-à-vis the Memoranda of Understanding (MoUs), which outlined the obligations that were imposed upon Greece by the Troika (the European Commission, the European Central Bank, and the International Monetary Fund) in order to get loans to help them weather the economic crisis. The Troika asked Greece to restructure their economy. This included austerity measures such as extensive salary cuts, reduction in pensions, and massive firings from the public sector. The KKE is staunchly anti-European and supports the country's disengagement from the European Union (EU), while the SYRIZA party is pro-EU. It believes in the European vision as it was originally conceived but not in what it sees as its current neoliberal form, for example, free market capitalism that overlooks a just social policy in order to serve a free market economy.

Ideologically, SYRIZA is a radical leftist, antiestablishment party. Since its formation, it has had ties with the anti-globalization movement, and it is in favor of equality and human rights. In principle, the party is against any military operations regarding foreign policy, seeking peaceful approaches. At the same time, it is against the country's ties with organizations such as NATO, as these are considered to hold the country dependent on foreign powers. Since it came to power, SYRIZA has abandoned its previous hard-left protest voice.

SYRIZA had not played an active political role inside the Greek Parliament until 2009, when it won 4.6 percent of the vote (13 of 300 seats in the Parliament). Two and half years later, in 2012, running on an anti-capitalist, anti-austerity platform, it had jumped to 16.8 percent (52 seats), just 1.7 percent behind the leading conservative ND. Thus, it became the leading opposition for the second time in Greek history.

In the May 2012 elections, no party won an absolute majority, which led to a hung Parliament. The same happened with the new elections in June. SYRIZA came in second, securing 26.9 percent of the vote and 71 members of Parliament (MPs).

Since the 149 seats SYRIZA won in 2015 was not a majority, they had to coalesce with another party. SYRIZA chose the populist right-wing, xenophobic ANEL party, since they were the only party who pledged they were against the Memoranda. SYRIZA made it clear from the very beginning that it would not collaborate with "pro-Memoranda parties," that is, those parties that supported the EU's financial assistance and the austerity measures that accompanied the assistance. Since the KKE rejected any coalition proposal, there remained only two prospective coalition partners: ANEL and To Potami (The River), a political party formed in 2014. Since To Potami's views on the Memorandum were unclear, SYRIZA chose ANEL as a governing partner, despite its xenophobic stand.

SYRIZA's win, despite the frictions the coalition with ANEL created among its voters, brought hope and optimism to the people. It did not take long for the party's leadership to grasp that the commission and leading European governments were in no mood to find a middle ground or to promote Greek restructuring in the context of wider Eurozone reform and that they, rather than the EU, would be expected to do all the compromising.

In June 2015, the Troika offered a final ultimatum to the Greek government. In response, Prime Minister Alexis Tsipras's government held a referendum to decide whether the Greek government should accept the Troika's offer. Sixty-one percent of the people voted no to the Troika's offer. Fearing economic obliteration, the Greek government eventually caved in and accepted a new MoU that included additional austerity measures, often referred to as the Fourth MoU.

*Nikos Christofis*

**See also**: Chapter 4: Memoranda of Understanding. Chapter 7: Women in Politics and the Parliament.

**Further Reading**

Balampanidis, Yiannis. 2018. *Eurocommunism: From the Communist to the Radical European Left*. Basingstoke: Palgrave.

Katsourides, Yiannos. 2016. *Radical Left Parties in Government: The Cases of SYRIZA and AKEL*. Basingstoke: Palgrave.

Ovenden, Kevin. 2015. *Syriza: Inside the Labyrinth*. London: Pluto.

## New Democracy

*Nea Dimokratia* (New Democracy, ND) was founded in the immediate aftermath of the fall of the Greek dictatorship in 1974, and it remains one of the most important political parties. Konstantinos Karamanlis (1907–1998), founder of the party, served as prime minister from 1974 to 1980. He was succeeded by Georgios Rallis (1918–2006) as prime minister when the former was elected to the post of president of the republic. Rallis was prime minister only until 1981, when ND lost the election.

Not until 1990 did ND again assume leadership of Greece, with Konstantinos Mitsotakis (1918–2017) serving as prime minister from 1990 to 1993. Again there was a long lapse before ND regained power, with Konstantinos Karamanlis's nephew, commonly known as Kostas Karamanlis (1956–), holding office from 2004 to 2009. He is now an MP. Antonis Samaras (1951–) of ND served as prime minister from 2012 to 2015, when SYRIZA won the election. However, elections on July 7, 2019, gave ND a complete majority, with Kyriakos Mitsotakis becoming prime minister.

The founder of the party, Konstantinos Karamanlis, had been a predominant political figure on the politics of the right in Greece since the mid-1950s. He had served as prime minister from 1955 to 1963 with the party of National Radical Union (ERE). In 1963, he went into self-exile in France. When Karamanlis returned from France in 1974, following the fall of the military dictatorship, he reconstituted ERE without consulting the then president of the party, Panayiotis Kanellopoulos. All party deputies sided with Karamanlis. The ND adopted a more liberal and conciliatory political program than that of the former ERE. In December 1974, the ND government, following the results of a referendum on whether Greece should have a monarchy, put an end to the monarchy. The constitution of 1975 introduced a presidential/parliamentary democracy as well as other changes, including various clauses on individual and social rights. The Rule of Law was effectively protected. The new constitution also made reference to Greece's participation in international organizations and, albeit indirectly, in the European Economic Community (EEC).

ND supported international organizations, such as NATO. One of its goals was to become a member of the EEC, the precursor of the European Union, in order to accelerate the economic and social development of the country and to secure the country from foreign enemies. The ND's dream came true in May 1979 when Greece was accepted into the EEC.

After ND lost the election of 1981, the party adopted a more conservative agenda. Its tactics of criticizing PASOK on its liberal stance did not work. The latter had since abandoned its Socialist agenda and moved to a more moderate agenda. PASOK dominated Greek politics throughout the 1980s.

The ND party was given a new direction under Mitsotakis, who took over the leadership in the 1980s. The Mitsotakis Manifesto is considered one of the most important ideological manifestos of the party as it reformulated the party's agenda. It included the decrease of state investment activities, reduction in the number of the public servants and public expenditure, and improvement of the quality of services. However, once ND came to power in 1990, not only did it not implement its political program, but it committed itself to further public expenditure and services. In the private sector, ND preferred the previous system instead of liberating the market. Mitsotakis was prime minister from 1990 to 1993.

In 1997, during the Fourth Congress of the party in Athens, Kostas Karamanlis, nephew of Konstantinos Karamanlis, became the leader of the party. He was appointed prime minister of Greece in 2004, and he remained in that post until 2009, winning the elections in 2004 with 45.3 percent of the votes and again in 2007 with 41.84 percent of the votes.

During Karamanlis's terms more than fifty cases of economic scandals, corruption, as well as sex tapes surfaced, implicating the ND government. Some of its members were brought to justice and jailed. Moreover, during his term, in 2008, Alexis Grigoropoulos, a fifteen-year-old boy, was shot dead by a police officer in the center of Athens. The incident sparked an instant reaction among the people and more than two hundred thousand outraged people demonstrated in the streets against the government.

PASOK came back to power in the election of 2009, with Papandreou becoming prime minister. The scandals and the economic crisis that had started in 2008 probably contributed to the election defeat of ND. Karamanlis stepped down from the party leadership in the same year, with Antonis Samaras, who had rejoined the party in 2004, taking over as the new leader.

Amid the economic crisis and the pressure to accept the European Union/International Monetary Fund rescue loan package, PASOK's government was forced to resign and a new national unity government was formed. This was headed by the technocrat Lucas Papademos, an economist, for 187 days.

Failing to elect a majority government in May 2012, ND formed a coalition government with PASOK and DIMAR. It lasted until January 2015, with Samaras as prime minister. During this time, the government introduced a strict immigration policy. The ND party lost creditability when Takis Baltakos, secretary general in the Samaras government, was found to be corresponding, in a series of text messages, with a high-level official of the far-right party Golden Dawn. Baltakos gave instructions on how the latter should vote in Parliament and applauded the hideous language Golden Dawn MPs were using to attack political opponents of the government. In 2018, government officials, including Samaras, were brought to trial for paying bribes to the Swiss drug company Novartis. The charges have now been dropped.

In the January 2015 election, ND was defeated by SYRIZA. As a result of the electoral defeat, Samaras resigned from the leadership of ND and was succeeded by Kyriakos Mitsotakis in January 2016. Mitsotakis is the son of former ND leader Konstantinos Mitsotakis and brother of former foreign minister Dora Bakoyianni. Since Mitsotakis's election to party leadership in January 2016, the ND party has been trying to formulate a neoliberal economic program with strict measures against immigration and extended privatizations. In its attempt to broaden its electoral base, many right-wing nationalists have become members of the party. One such member is the vice president of the party, Adonis Georgiadis. Kyriakos Mitsotakis became the new

Greek prime minister of Greece on July 7, 2019. Although ND's basic principles still stand, it has moved more to the right and has enlisted some right-wing members. It supports a strict immigration policy and has appointed Adonis Georgiadis, known for right-wing nationalist ideas, as the party's vice president. After a little more than a month in power, ND started to legislate a series of anti-liberal measures. In 2020, the party had been criticized by residents of the islands of Lesvos and Chios for the government's plans to build housing for the refugees on their islands. There have been demonstrations on both islands.

*Nikos Christofis*

**See also:** Chapter 2: Karamanlis, Konstantinos. Glossary: European Union.

**Further Reading**

Featherstone, Kevin, and Dimitris Papadimitriou. 2015. *Prime Ministers in Greece: Paradox of Power.* Oxford: Oxford University Press.

Pappas, Takis. 1999. *Making Party Democracy in Greece.* Basingstoke: Palgrave.

Sotiropoulos, Dimitri A. 2010. "A Democracy under Stress: Greece since 2010." *Taiwan Journal of Democracy* 8 (1): 27–49.

# Organization of the State

Greece is governed by civil law (wrongs and quasi-contracts, law of property, rights and duties of persons), in contrast to countries like Britain, Australia, and the United States, which are governed by common law. The system of governance in the Hellenic Republic is based on the principle of separation of powers (Article 26 of the constitution). The state has three branches: the legislative, the executive, and the judiciary.

## THE LEGISLATIVE BRANCH

The legislative branch consists of the *Vouli* (Parliament) and the president of the republic (*próedros t□s ell□nik□s d□mokratias*), who participates in both the executive and the legislative. There is only one parliament.

The president of the republic is elected by parliamentary vote (not direct election by the people) for a maximum of two five-year terms. To be eligible for the office, a candidate must have at least one Greek-born citizen parent and be forty years or older. Greece is a parliamentary system, and the Greek Parliament is sovereign (although it is bound by limits laid down in the Greek Constitution as well as the international treaties and other agreements to which Greece has acceded). As in most parliamentary systems, legislation goes through three readings with a bill (*Nomosxedio*) presented in its parts, then by amendments added, and finally as a unitary statute. In order for a constitutional amendment to pass, a majority of votes is required in the Parliament. Once a bill is passed, it must be ratified by the president of the republic and subsequently published in the *National Gazette* (*Efimerida tis Kyberniseos*) to be deemed a law of the state.

There are 300 members in the Greek Parliament, who normally serve for four-year terms, except if special interim elections (snap elections) are called and they lose. All Greek citizens seventeen and older are eligible to vote and anyone twenty-five years and older can run for election in Parliament. Article 54 of the Greek Constitution authorizes the Parliament to establish rules for the structure of the electoral system overall. Specific rules for the conduct of elections are issued by presidential decree, the last update having been issued in 2007. Traditionally, the electoral system has reflected a form of "reinforced" proportional representation. Out of the 300 MPs, 288 are elected by constituency vote and 12 come from party lists in proportion to the vote-share won by each party. The internal proceedings of Parliament are regulated by law.

The most significant form of delegation is the presidential decree (*proedriko diatagma*) that needs to be ratified by the Parliament to take effect. After the draft is checked by the Council of State, it is also published in the *National Gazette.*

## THE EXECUTIVE BRANCH

The executive branch consists of the government (*kybernisi*) and the president of the republic—generally referred to in English as the "president of Greece." The president also participates in the legislative branch and is the head of state, and since the implementation of a set of reforms to the constitution in 1986, he has assumed a largely ceremonial role. The president is chosen by the Parliament and in turn appoints the prime minister of Greece, depending on the support the latter can muster on the floor of the Parliament.

The government consists of the prime minister (*prothypourgós tis ellinikis dimokratias*) and the various ministers who comprise the cabinet. Each minister heads a particular department. Separate legislation lays down rules for the conduct of the cabinet. According to the constitution, "The Prime Minister shall safeguard the unity of the Government and shall direct the actions of the Government and of the public services in general, for the implementation of Government policy within the framework of the laws." The prime minister acts as the head of cabinet and the Greek government. He appoints the cabinet members. The offices of the prime minister and cabinet are housed in the Maximos Mansion in central Athens.

After elections, the leading party has the right to form a government. If the leading party did not win a qualified majority of votes, it can join together with other parties to form a coalition government.

On many occasions in Greek history, snap elections have taken place. Such an election occurs when the Parliament does not run its full four-year term, typically because the prime minister wishes to decide a pressing issue, such as a major crisis, or believes that such an election will secure a larger parliamentary majority.

The government is politically accountable (i.e., to the Parliament), whereas the Greek president is not.

## THE JUDICIAL BRANCH

The Greek judicial system consists of three divisions: administrative, civil, and criminal. Executive or administrative issues are taken up in the first case by the Court of First Instance (and subsequently the Courts of Appeal) and in the final instance by the superior administrative court, the Council of State (*Symboulio tis Epikrateias*). Within the administrative division, there is also the Legal Council of State (*Nomiko Symboulio tou Kratous*), which has a quasi-judicial function. Article 100 of the Greek Constitution authorizes the council to provide judicial support to any state agency that is subject to a legal claim or dispute. In addition, the council offers legal opinions on controversies concerning the constitutionality of a statute or the designation of rules of international law as they apply to Greece.

Commercial and civil disputes are settled in the civil courts, and all criminal matters are heard in the criminal courts. In Greece, the highest court of appeal for civil and criminal matters is the Court of Cassation (*Areios Pagos*). It, however, is authorized to review only legal or procedural concerns and not the substantive grounds of any particular case.

State finances are also subject to judicial review, in the Court of Auditors (*Elegktiko Synedrio*), typically after a submission of the annual budget or report of state finances to Parliament. The Special Supreme Court (*Anotato Eidiko Dikastirio*) acts as the final court of appeal in matters pertaining to the validity of national elections and referenda, as well as jurisdictional disputes between the courts and administrative commissions or between the various branches of the judiciary—namely, the highest courts of appeal in the respective judicial divisions (the Council of State, the Court of Cassation, or the Court of Auditors).

Articles 87 and 93 of the Greek Constitution authorize all courts in Greece to exercise judicial review (i.e., to assess the constitutionality of laws). Courts, however, may only review the constitutionality of the particular cases that come before them, and—as mentioned earlier—in certain cases only on procedural (not substantive) grounds. The constitutionality of statutes is not examined before their application. Parliamentary rules and guidelines, however, are subject to prior review, as laid down in parliamentary regulations. As early as the late nineteenth century, many years before the current constitutional provisions, the Greek courts had established their authority for judicial review.

*Nikos Christofis*

**See also:** Chapter 5: Freedom of Religion.

**Further Reading**

Alivizatos, Nikos. 2011. *The Constitution and its Enemies in Neohellenic History, 1800–2010* (in Greek). Athens: Polis.

Hellenic Parliament. 2008. *The Constitution of Greece* (English Version). Translated by Xenophon Paparrigopoulos and Stavroula Vassilouni. Accessed June 22, 2019. https://

www.hellenicparliament.gr/UserFiles/f3c70a23-7696-49db-9148-f24dce6a27c8/001-156%20aggliko.pdf.

Venizelos, Evangelos. 2008. *Lessons of Constitutional Law* (in Greek), 2nd edition. Athens: Sakoulas.

## Panhellenic Socialist Movement

*Panellinio Sosialistiko Kinima* (Panhellenic Socialist Movement, PASOK) was founded on September 3, 1974, by Andreas Papandreou after the end of the military junta of 1967–1974. Papandreou was responsible for the party's identity as a democratic Socialist and left-wing nationalist party. He remained the party's chairman until 1996, when he was replaced due to deteriorating health by Costas Simitis.

The party's anti-imperialist and anti-capitalist character, the popularity it gained with the slogan "Change *here and now*," and its championing of the "nonprivileged" against the "privileged" gave the party a landslide victory in the general election of 1981 with a 48.1 percent share of the vote. This also gave the party a secure majority of 172 seats in a 300-seat parliament.

During the 1980s, PASOK initiated a series of important reforms. These included the recognition of civil marriages; the recognition of those who fought in ELAS, the left-wing resistance to the occupied forces during World War II; provision for a state pension to the resistance fighters; and allowing political refugees of the Greek Civil War to return to Greece.

By the end of the 1980s, however, a series of economic and corruption scandals, implicating many PASOK ministers and Papandreou himself, created a crisis within the party, leading a group of ambitious members to compete for the party leadership but to no avail. PASOK's long electoral domination was interrupted just for a short period of three years, from 1990 to 1993. It won again in 1993.

Costas Simitis replaced Papandreou in 1996 due to the latter's prolonged hospitalization and eventual passing. He remained in the PASOK leadership position for two consecutive terms, from 1996 to 2004. During Simitis's term of office, religion was omitted from the country's ID. This caused a huge controversy, especially in the church and among the more traditional segments of Greek society. As a consequence, there were huge demonstrations throughout the country. In addition, during Simitis's two terms, Greece won the right to stage the 2004 Summer Olympic Games, and in 2001, it was confirmed that the country would be included in the Eurozone.

However, because the party had begun adopting free market policies, it lost its traditional appeal to the Greek lower and middle classes. In order to revitalize its chances for the next elections, PASOK decided to replace Simitis with Andreas Papandreou's son, George. However, Papandreou's elections did not bring the expected results. The party's failure to remain in power was due to the people's lack of trust in it, the several scandals that came to the fore, as well as its abandonment of the progressive principles of economic parity on which it was founded.

In the 2007 legislative election, the party suffered a crushing defeat, registering its lowest percentage in almost thirty years. Because of its poor performance, the conflict regarding party leadership returned. In November 2007, during the leadership election, George Papandreou managed to win over the party's informal second in command, Professor Evangelos Venizelos.

The October 2009 election brought PASOK back in power again but only for nearly two years, until 2011. The economic crisis that had started in 2009, the political decisions by the party to adopt free market policies, and George Papandreou's invitation of the International Monetary Fund (IMF) to Greece led to many defections and expulsions. This left the party with only a slim majority of 152 of the Parliament's 300 seats to pass its laws and decisions in 2011.

The PASOK government also had to deal with a series of anti-austerity protests that began in May 2011 in Athens and other major cities and lasted throughout the summer months and early autumn. Sometimes as many as five hundred thousand came out to protest. Among the demands was the resignation of Papandreou's government as it was held responsible, along with ND, for the economic problems Greece was facing. A few months later, in October, Papandreou announced his government's plans to hold a referendum on whether or not Greece should accept the terms of a Eurozone bailout deal, but due to the EU's pressure, he canceled it. Following the turmoil caused by the proclamation, and later cancellation, of the referendum, the opposition party called for early elections. The election results demonstrated the polarization that had been created in Greek society, since none of the two largest parties received the necessary majority to form a government. After that, Papandreou stepped down and following intense negotiations, the two major parties, along with the Popular Orthodox Rally, agreed to form a grand coalition headed by former vice president of the European Central Bank, Lucas Papademos. This government lasted from November 11, 2011, to May 16, 2012.

In the elections of June 2012, PASOK received just 12.3 percent of the votes and agreed with the ND and the DIMAR party to form a coalition government lasting until 2015. In the meantime, several party members who disagreed with the coalition government policies were erased from the party. The disagreements further weakened the party, which in the January elections managed to receive the lowest percentage (4.68) in its history, finishing seventh. What is more, Papandreou, with another seven deputies, left PASOK to form another political party called Movement of Democratic Socialists (KIDISO).

PASOK managed to get a mandate for thirteen seats in the Parliament, since the party received only 4.7 percent in the January 25, 2015, elections. This led PASOK to announce its electoral alliance with DIMAR, dubbed Democratic Coalition, right before the upcoming September snap elections. The Democratic Coalition, however, received only 6.3 percent of the vote in the September legislative election.

Poor performance, loss of electoral base, and the inability to present a fresh program opened the way for replacing party leadership. After a lot of discussions, it was decided to form a broad center-left party that would include politicians and members of other parties. Fofi Gennimata, the daughter of one of the founders of the party and former minister George Gennimatas, was elected as the party chairman with 56 percent of the vote. In the September 2015 legislative elections, PASOK-DIMAR received 6.3 percent of the vote and seventeen seats.

*Nikos Christofis*

**See also:** Chapter 2: Papandreou, Andreas. Glossary: European Union; International Monetary Fund.

**Further Reading**

Draenos, Stan. 2012. *Andreas Papandreou: The Making of a Greek Democrat and Political Maverick*. London and New York: I.B. Tauris.

Featherstone, Kevin, and Dimitris Papadimitriou. 2015. *Prime Ministers in Greece: Paradox of Power*. Oxford: Oxford University Press.

## Synaspismos Leadership

The first leader of the Synaspismos political party was Charilaos Florakis (1914–2005), a historical figure of the left. He served as the KKE's general secretary from 1972 until 1989 when he stepped down from the party's leadership to become the president of the newly founded Synaspismos (Coalition of the Left). He remained in that position until 1991.

Maria Damanaki (1952–) succeeded Florakis in 1991 and served until 1993. Damanaki, the first female party president, had been a member of the Community Youth of Greece and actively involved in the anti-dictatorial struggle. She was the famous voice of "This is Polytechnic" radio broadcast. In November 1973, students occupied the Polytechnic School in Athens as a protest against the military dictatorship. Through the radio broadcast, Damanaki called for the people to resist, thus contributing to the fall of the military junta. She was consistently elected as a member of the Hellenic Parliament from 1977, with the KKE, and from 1991 until 2003, with Synaspismos. Since 2003, she has been a member of PASOK.

The next president of Synaspismos was Nikos Konstantopoulos (1942–), a man who rallied again the dictatorship of the junta. He was arrested, tortured, and sentenced to eight years of imprisonment by the regime in 1970, but he was freed in 1974. He was a charter member of PASOK in 1974 but was expelled a year later because he questioned Andreas Papandreou's leadership. He became a founding and leading member of Synaspismos in 1989. After the failure of Synaspismos to pass the 3 percent threshold in the 1993 general election, Konstantopoulos replaced Damanaki as party leader. He had to resign, however, after the poor performance of Synaspismos in the elections of 2000 and 2004.

The Synaspismos Congress of December 2004 elected Alekos Alavanos (1950–) as the party president. Alavanos had also been active politically since his youth, participating in the student movement against the junta (the colonels' regime). He has been an elective member of the European Parliament in 1981 with the Communist Party, and again in 1989, 1994, and 1999 with Synaspismos, and he was elected as member of the Greek Parliament as leader of SYRIZA in the 2007 legislative elections. SYRIZA more than doubled its parliamentary seats in that election. In February 2008, at Synaspismos's Fifth Party Congress, Alavanos announced that he would not apply for another term as president of Synaspismos.

A few years later, in February 2011, Alavanos attempted to enter the political life of Greece again by forming another party named Front of Solidarity and Overthrow with other former members of the Coalition of the Radical Left. Its aim was to bring development and social justice to the country, but due to political disputes the coalition of several leftist organizations and political formations parted ways in 2012. Alavanos's political life continued in 2013 when he formed a new party, Plan B. The party's main goal was for Greece to exit the Eurozone and thus return to its national currency.

*Nikos Christofis*

**See also:** Chapter 2: Overview.

**Further Reading**

Balampanidis, Yiannis. 2018 (2016). *Eurocommunism: From the Communist to the Radical European Left*. Basingstoke: Palgrave.

March, Luke. 2012. *Radical Left Parties in Europe*. London: Routledge.

Sheenan, Helen, 2016. *SYRIZA Wave: Surging and Crashing with the Greek Left*. New York: Monthly Review Press.

## Tsipras, Alexis (1974–)

In 2015, Alexis Tsipras, the prime minister of Greece, was included by *TIME Magazine* in the list of hundred most influential people. Tsipras was the 185th and current prime minister of Greece, having been sworn in on September 21, 2015; he served until 2019. From the moment he became prime minister, he made an impression. Alexis Tsipras, a secular leftist, is not married, but he and his partner, with whom he has two children, signed a cohabitation pact. Also, for the first time, contrary to what traditionally happens when a new government receives office, he and the rest of his cabinet took a political and not a religious oath.

Alexis Tsipras was born on July 28, 1974, in Athens in a leftist family. He joined the Communist Youth of Greece as early as 1988, while he was still a student. During the 1990s, he participated actively and became the spokesperson of the student movement during the student protests against educational reform plans, which had as a goal, among other things, to stop providing free university textbooks and free room and board. In the year 2000, Tsipras graduated with a degree in civil engineering from the National Technical University of Athens. He pursued postgraduate studies in urban planning and regional development. From 2000 to 2006, Tsipras worked as a professional civil engineer in Athens, primarily in the construction field, during which time he also served as the secretary of Synaspismos Youth (1999–2003). In 2004, he was elected as member of the party's Central Committee of Synaspismos, and he ran as SYRIZA's candidate for mayor of Athens in the 2006 local elections. In those elections, he got 10.5 percent of the vote. In 2008, Tsipras replaced Synaspismos's former leader Alekos Alavanos. Later the same year, during the Fifth Congress of the party, Tsipras was elected party leader with 70.41 percent of the vote. In 2009, he was elected head of SYRIZA and was reelected in May and June 2012, becoming leader of the opposition and appointing his own shadow cabinet. In December 2010, Tsipras was also elected as vice president of the Party of the European Left (EL), and he was endorsed with a resounding majority (84.1 percent) as European Left's European Council candidate in November 2012.

SYRIZA faced various intraparty issues, mainly of ideological nature, about what policies the party would adopt. As a result, many of its members, including those who had been members of KKE/Interior, left the party. The leading figure of this group was Fotis Kouvelis, who along with other members formed the DIMAR. Tsipras's electoral win gave him the opportunity to dissolve Synaspismos and form SYRIZA as a single party in July 2013 and thus lead the anti-austerity front both inside and outside the country.

Tsipras led SYRIZA to victory in the January 2015 snap elections, in which the party took just under half of the seats in the Greek Parliament (149 out of 300). He was appointed prime minister after entering into a governing coalition with the Independent Greeks. This lasted seven months but came apart when intraparty defections saw the coalition's majority collapse. On August 20, Tsipras resigned and called for another snap election, which was held in September. SYRIZA took 145 out of 300 seats, and Tsipras again joined with the Independent Greeks to form a coalition government.

As prime minister, he had simultaneously overseen a range of challenges facing Greece, including negotiations with the Troika over the terms of the Greek bailout, the subsequent bailout referendum, and the European migration crisis, which disproportionately impacted Greece as a primary transit country. His government had come in for heavy criticism both from the opposition parties but also from its governing party itself for the way he had dealt with a series of issues. For example, despite the government's reassurances to the Greek people, the economic crisis deepened or at least remained at a critical point. Neither had he been able to resolve the crisis caused by the massive influx of refugees from Syria and other countries of the Middle East. In addition, the government was accused of continuing the policies of its predecessors, for example, increasing taxation and decreasing government salaries. Many of those who voted no on the referendum considered this "treason" and withdrew their support for Tsipras.

The Greek government under Tsipras accomplished the following:

- For the first time in nearly a decade, new faculty to the universities were appointed; former alternate minister of education Sia Anagnostopoulou managed to secure funds from the 2016–2017 state budget to cover one thousand academic posts.
- The Ministry of Education organized summer schools for the refugees in Greece.

- Significant steps were taken regarding the rights of the LGBT community. This included extending the cohabitation pact that had been instituted in 2008 for gay and straight couples. Also, the law allowed transgendered individuals to choose their gender at the age of fifteen.
- Greece's Parliament agreed to recognize its neighbor to the north as North Macedonia (previously referred to as FYROM). The name is now officially accepted by both Greece and the former FYROM.

The Tsipras government did not resolve the most important issue, the recovery of the economy, although important steps had been made. The most important of these was the country finalizing the economic program of the IMF in August 2018. Symbolically, this meant that the country was free to move forward with the launching of measures that were not dictated by the IMF program. In practice, however, there are still often checks by the IMF officials in order to secure the viability of the Greek debt.

*Nikos Christofis*

**See also:** Chapter 2: Karamanlis, Konstantinos. Chapter 3: Leftist Parties of Greece. Chapter 4: Memoranda of Understanding. Glossary: European Union; International Monetary Fund.

**Further Reading**

Panayiotakis, Michalis. 2015. "The Radical Left in Greece." *Socialism and Democracy* 29 (3): 25–43.

Papadogiannis, Nikolaos. 2015. *Militant around The Clock? Left-Wing Youth Politics, Leisure and Sexuality in Post-Dictatorship Greece, 1974–1981.* New York: Berghahn Books.

CHAPTER 4

# ECONOMY

## OVERVIEW

In 2017, Greece's population was estimated at 10.7 million. Athens, the capital, is the most populous city with around 700,000 inhabitants. Attica, the prefecture in which Athens is located, is home to around 35 percent of the country's population. The largest port of the country is in Piraeus, located only 6.2 miles from the Athens city center. The port of Piraeus is one of the busiest in the Mediterranean and is among the ten largest ports in Europe.

The second most populous city is Thessaloniki, with a population of 350,000. It is located in the prefecture of Central Macedonia, which has a population of around 2 million.

The third and fourth largest cities are Patras and Iraklion (in Crete), respectively. Even though their populations are considerably smaller, they are important transport hubs, with each of them having a large Greek port.

While at the beginning of the 1990s the urban population represented 70 percent of the total population, this has now increased to 80 percent. This shift of the population to urban centers reflects the change in the composition of economic activity. Around 57 percent of the economy's gross value added is produced in urban centers. Gross value added is a measure of the value of goods and services that are produced.

Economic activity has shifted away from agricultural activities to services, while the share of economic activity in the secondary sector (manufacturing, energy, construction) has decreased by much less. In 2017, according to data from the AMECO online macroeconomic database, around 4.5 percent of total value added was generated in the primary sector (industries engaged in agricultural activities or in the extraction of natural resources) compared to around 80 percent in services and 17 percent in the secondary sector (manufacturing and construction). Despite the low contribution of agriculture to total output, employment in this sector represents over 10 percent of total employment.

The composition of economic activity during 2018 and the distribution of employment in the various activities is presented in Table 4.1. Not indicated in the table is the underground economy, which is estimated to be 25–35 percent. The underground economy, a way to avoid paying taxes, has thrived during the economic crisis.

Greece's agricultural output consists mostly of fruits (21.6 percent), vegetable and horticultural products (17.0 percent), olive oil (11 percent), and milk (11 percent) and

**Table 4.1: COMPOSITION OF ECONOMIC ACTIVITY DURING 2018**

| | Output (Gross Value Added) in Million Euros (2010 Prices) | | Total Employment (in '000s) | | Employees (in '000s) | | Self-Employment (in '000s) | |
|---|---|---|---|---|---|---|---|---|
| Total: all activities | 169,783.70 | | 4,216.74 | | 2,843.89 | | 1,372.85 | |
| Agriculture, forestry, and fishing | 7,557.30 | 4.45% | 479.58 | 11.37% | 90.53 | 3.18% | 389.06 | 28.34% |
| Industry (except construction) | 19,956.80 | 11.75% | 390.20 | 9.25% | 329.98 | 11.60% | 60.22 | 4.39% |
| Manufacturing | 14,651.00 | 8.63% | 333.69 | 7.91% | 274.94 | 9.67% | 58.74 | 4.28% |
| Construction | 5,625.80 | 3.31% | 204.30 | 4.84% | 103.09 | 3.62% | 101.21 | 7.37% |
| Wholesale and retail trade, transport, accommodation, and food service activities | 37,970.90 | 22.36% | 1,400.28 | 33.21% | 880.8 | 30.97% | 519.48 | 37.84% |
| Information and communication | 5,159.80 | 3.04% | 95.00 | 2.25% | 80.62 | 2.83% | 14.38 | 1.05% |
| Financial and insurance activities | 6,014.80 | 3.54% | 75.36 | 1.79% | 67.22 | 2.36% | 8.14 | 0.59% |
| Real estate activities | 35,653.80 | 21.00% | 8.74 | 0.21% | 4.95 | 0.17% | 3.79 | 0.28% |
| Professional, scientific, and technical activities; administrative and support service activities | 8,287.20 | 4.88% | 362.80 | 8.60% | 209.32 | 7.36% | 153.49 | 11.18% |
| Public administration, defense, education, human health, and social work activities | 36,442.00 | 21.46% | 915.92 | 21.72% | 847.54 | 29.80% | 68.38 | 4.98% |
| Arts, entertainment, and recreation; other service activities; activities of household and extraterritorial organizations and bodies | 7,115.30 | 4.19% | 284.56 | 6.75% | 229.85 | 8.08% | 54.71 | 3.99% |

Source: ELSTAT

accounts for a little over 4.5 percent of the total agricultural output of the 28 European Union member states (EU-28). It is generated mostly in small units. Over three-quarters of holdings are smaller than 5 hectares (12.4 acres); the corresponding figure for the EU-28 is around two-thirds of holdings. The average utilized agriculture area per holding in Greece is around 6 hectares (14.8 acres) compared to over 16 in the EU-28. A large proportion of farmers are older. Over 31 percent are over sixty-four; this percentage is similar to that in other EU-28 countries. Agricultural products constitute around one-fifth of the country's exports. Because the country also imports a large amount of agricultural products, the trade balance in the sector is negative (by around 1 billion euros in 2017). To a large extent, this deficit is due to the import of commodities (raw material and agricultural products).

Greece, which is rich in minerals, exports many of these products. In 2017, Greece exported marble of a value of around 300 million euros, accounting for around 12 percent of total marble exports globally. It is also one of the largest producers of bauxite—eleventh worldwide.

Tourism is one of Greece's main economic activities, and it has been doing much better now compared to the period before the severe economic slowdown. Tourism contributes to the economy both directly (revenues for enterprises in the hospitality industry) and indirectly (revenues for enterprises involved in retail trade, transport, etc.). For 2017, INSETE, the research institute of the Greek Tourism Confederation (SETE), concluded that the direct contribution of tourism stood at 18.3 billion euros (or 10.3 percent of gross domestic product [GDP]). The total (direct and indirect) contribution of tourism to the economy amounts to at least 2.5 times the above, that is, it is somewhere around 45 billion euros (in other words, around 25 percent of the country's GDP is due to tourism). Around 90 percent of tourism revenues are imported, that is, domestic tourism is not such an important contributor to the economy. In terms of the number of individuals that visited Greece in 2018, it is estimated that over thirty million tourists arrived (or thirty-three million tourists if cruise tourism is also included). Employment in the tourism sector is approximately of the same share as that of the direct impact on GDP, that is, around 10 percent.

Greece, a member of the European Union (EU) since 1981, joined the Euro Area (EA) in 2001 and started using the euro in 2002. The EA consists of members of the EU who use the euro as a common form of currency. Greece believed that they would be more likely to attract investors by adopting a strong currency. Another advantage was that investors would have more confidence, since monetary policy decisions made outside the country would not be affected by short-term political aspirations for electoral gains. The improvement in public finances and inflation, improvements that contributed to Greece's being accepted into the EA, were reversed in the years following entry. Between 1996 and 2007, low interest rates together with an increase in bank lending (credit expansion) contributed to a remarkable increase in Greece's GDP, that is, of the total output produced domestically. The annual average GDP growth rate between 1996 and 2007 stood at 3.9 percent in Greece compared to the EA average of 2.3 percent. GDP growth during this period was mainly driven by an increase in consumption and investment expenditure. These items were financed to a large extent by the inflow of funds from abroad—mainly through interbank lending that provided domestic banks with the ability to lend for consumption and housing purposes—and through the purchase of government bonds by institutional and other investors and government spending on both current expenditure (e.g., expansion of public sector employment, increase in public sector wages and pensions) and to a lesser extent infrastructure expenditure. As a result, the government budget deficit (i.e., the balance between income and expenditure of the government) deteriorated significantly from 5.9 percent of GDP in 2006 to 15.1 percent in 2009. The derailment in public finances was accompanied with a loss in external competitiveness (the ability of the country to compete with its trading partners) as Greek products had become more expensive. The current account deficit (effectively the balance in international trade) deteriorated significantly, from 3.1 percent of GDP in 2006 to 14.0 percent of GDP in 2007.

According to Eurostat figures, the general government deficit as a percentage of GDP stood at 6.7 percent in 2007, 10.2 percent in 2008, and 15.1 percent in 2009. The respective figures for EU-28 were 0.9 percent, 2.5 percent, and 6.6 percent, respectively. The current account deficit as a percentage of GDP stood at 11.5 percent, 15.2 percent, and 15.1 percent in each of the years 2007, 2008, and 2009, respectively. The revelation in October 2009 of the full extent of Greece's fiscal imbalances, together with the reluctance of the new government, which took power at the end of 2009, to take bold measures to correct this imbalance led to the exclusion of Greece from foreign borrowing. Instead, Greece turned to official creditors (the European Commission, the European Central Bank, and the International Monetary Fund [IMF]) for financial support. The three entities were informally called the Troika. Greece has been under supervision since May 2010, and installments of the financial support were released only when Greece met the milestones set for fiscal consolidation, including a reform of the pension system and modernization of its economy. Funding was released from May 2010 until August 2018. The amount of funding and the conditions under which funds were to be released were specified in three different memoranda (May 2010, February 2012, and August 2015). The second memorandum followed the first when it became clear that the financial assistance the first loan provided would not be enough. The third memorandum then followed the second, for the same reason. A country facing serious economic risks is placed by the European Commission on enhanced surveillance status. In other words, the country must provide the European Commission with the data needed for a close monitoring of its economic, fiscal, and financial situation. Since August 2018 and for as long as Greece owes money to its creditors, Greece is under a condition of "enhanced surveillance" by the Troika.

In 2020, the COVID-19 pandemic had an adverse effect on the economy of Greece. In particular, tourism fell drastically.

*Daphne Nicolitsas*

**Further Reading**

Christodoulakis, Nikos. 2012. "Greek Crisis in Perspective: Origins, Effects and Ways-Out." *The New Palgrave Dictionary of Economics*, Online edition. Accessed May 5, 2021. https://link.springer.com/chapter/10.1057/9781137553799_15.

Christodoulakis, Nikos. 2015. "Greek Crisis in Perspective: Causes, Illusions and Failures." *The New Palgrave Dictionary of Economics*, Online edition. Accessed April 20, 2021. https://link.springer.com/referenceworkentry/10.1057%2F978-1-349-95121-5_3020-1.

## Agriculture

The word in Greek for agriculture (*georgia*) comes from *gaia/ge* (earth). Agriculture has defined the Greeks for millennia. Like the Earth, agriculture is sacred.

The most important gods of the Greeks were agricultural gods. Zeus, father of the Olympian gods, was the god of rain. Demeter, sister of Zeus, was goddess of wheat and agrarian civilization. Dionysus, son of Zeus, was the god of wine, grape vine cultivation, and rural culture. Athena, daughter of Zeus, gifted the olive tree to the Athenians. The olive tree and olive oil remain at the center of Greek life and economy to this day.

Pan was the god of flocks. Aristaios was the village god: protecting beekeeping, cheesemaking, shepherding, and olive growing. Artemis was goddess of nature. Her temple in Ephesos, Asia Minor, was one of the Seven Wonders of the World.

The most important Greek festivals were the annual celebrations of Demeter and Dionysus for a prosperous harvest. Rural harvest celebrations are still at the center of Greek life. For example, there is the annual September–October wine celebration at Daphne, near Corinth. This and numerous other festivals have their roots in Greek antiquity.

In sixth century BCE, the Athenian politician, lawgiver, and poet Solon canceled the debts of peasant-farmers and abolished serfdom. His laws sparked a political movement that set the foundations of democracy. *Oikos* (family, household, estate) was at the center of Greek economy. The polis (city-state) was simply the administrative and political center of *Oikoi* (families) making up rural society. Plato, a fifth century BCE moral philosopher, and his student, Aristotle, a fourth century BCE natural philosopher and inventor of science, supported small farms. Xenophon, a fourth century BCE general and historian, praised family farming as the mother of pleasure, military training, patriotism, and civilization.

Greece, in modern times, continues having small farms. The average farming area is about 14.8 acres, and three-quarters of farms are 12.4 acres or less.

Greek farmers lived through the horrors of World War II (1941–1944), with occupying Axis forces destroying villages, executing citizens, and procuring Greek farm animals and produce for their own troops. The Greek Civil War (1946–1949) followed with further devastation. After the wars, poverty in the rural areas led to an exodus of farmers abroad and to big cities like Athens and Thessaloniki. Even though farm areas have decreased, agriculture still plays a role in Greece's economy. Twelve percent of the population works in agriculture and fishing, and this segment of the economy makes up 4.5 percent of the GDP.

Greece entered the European Union (EU) in 1981. EU regulations and agricultural subsidies for industrial crops undermined the viability and tremendous crop variety of small farms. The EU and the Greek government encouraged farmers to produce food for markets and not for self-sufficiency. This meant that the country had to import food. Greece imports hundreds of tons of fruits, vegetables, meats, fish, and even olive oil. The importing of food contributed to the deficit that caused the recent economic crisis. More than ever before, Greece has been at the mercy of foreign lenders.

During the Cold War, the influence of American agribusiness entered Greece on the winds of foreign aid. This included the advertising of chemical and tractor companies and the reports of industry-funded academics. Greek farmers succumbed to these new sirens of modernity and started imitating American farmers in using heavy machinery, confining their cattle in animal farms, consolidating small pieces of land into large ones, and spraying their crops with toxic and carcinogenic pesticides. These policies are having deleterious effects on wildlife, public health, and Greece's rich agricultural biodiversity.

As in other EU countries and the United States, a small number of Greek farmers remain faithful to traditional knowledge and respect for the land and nature and grow food without toxic chemicals. In Europe, these farmers are known as biological farmers, and in the United States, we call them organic farmers.

The crops of Greece include wheat, barley, rice, corn, lentils, olives, potatoes, tomatoes, sugar beets, tobacco, cotton, and peaches, grapes, melons, oranges, apples, figs, dates, almonds, kiwi, pomegranates, and tree nuts. Animals raised in Greece include sheep, goats, cows, pigs, and chickens. Greece produces wine and raisins from the grapes and a variety of cheeses from dairy animals. The EU has awarded protected status to many of Greece's agricultural products. They include at least thirty-three varieties of wines, twenty different cheeses, nineteen varieties of olive oil, twenty-six vegetables, fruits, and pulses, two types of honey, *avgotaracho* (striped grey mullet fish roe that is produced in Messolonghi lagoon), saffron produced in the region of Kozani, and mastic products from Chios Island.

Agricultural statistics give a glimpse of what is happening in the Greek countryside. Greece is 132,049 square kilometers (50,984 square miles) in area; its population in 2011 was 10,816,286. In 2016, the country had 266,209 farms. About 51.9 percent of its farmland raised annual crops. The production of grapes for wine and raisins took 2.3 percent of the land. Olive and fruit trees took about 27 percent. Some 14,699 farms raised 615,123 cattle. And about 86,630 farms raised 8,227,631 sheep. In 2016, there were 652 managers of the large farms of agribusiness firms. Twenty-five percent of Greece's exports are agricultural and include fruit, vegetable and horticultural products, olive oil, and milk products.

Like farmland, forests in ancient Greece were full of gods, trees, and wildlife. There was no separation between them. There were sacred groves of olive trees as well as sacred groves of oak trees.

Some of the forests in Greece, like those on Mt. Olympus, have been set aside for their biodiversity. They are protected parks.

Greece's forests are threatened by fire each summer. In some areas, such as Samothrace, overgrazing by goats has also posed a threat. Although 24 percent of Greece is covered with forests, the forestry industry does not make a significant contribution to the economy; Greece imports timber. An increase in illegal logging has been a result of the recession and the inability of some families to pay for heat.

Next to the land, the seas have always been fields of dreams and livelihood for the Greeks. The country has thousands of islands, which have been landmarks for the exploration of the Mediterranean, the mastering of sea travel, sponge harvesting, and fishing. Homer's wine-dark seas exemplify the supreme role of the seas in the evolution and development of Greek civilization.

Modern Greeks continue making a profitable living in the seas of their ancestors. Their merchant marine is probably the largest in the world. And the small catches of fish in the waters of the Ionian, Aegean, and Mediterranean Seas supplement food from the land. In addition, Greeks farm fish. In 2015, 121,000 tons of sea bream, European bass, and mussel were bred in fisheries on shore and afterward transferred to ocean cages measuring up to four hundred feet in diameter.

*Evaggelos Vallianatos*

**See also:** Chapter 1: Erosion; Pollution of the Water. Chapter 4: Overview. Appendix A: A Day in the Life of a Rural Farmer.

**Further Reading**

"Greece All Time Classics." n.d. Accessed March 1, 2020. http://www.visitgreece.gr/en/gastronomy/traditional_products/select_protected_designation_of_origin_products.

Hellenic Republic, Hellenic Statistical Authority. 2019. *Greece in Figures.* October–December 2019. Athens. Accessed March 20, 2020. https://www.statistics.gr/documents/20181/1515741/GreeceInFigures_2019Q4_EN.pdf.pdf/d0149260-0983-9d80-e5c1-4368dc87fda3.

Illegal logging portal: Greece. n.d. Accessed March 20, 2020. https://www.illegal-logging.info/regions/grprossee.

Lawson, John Cuthbert. 1964. *Modern Greek Folklore and Ancient Greek Religion.* New York: University Books.

Stoyannis, Vangelis, and Paraskevi Dilana. 2001. *The Odyssey of the Greek Agricultural Biodiversity.* Athens: Odyssey Network.

Vallianatos, Evaggelos. 2006. *This Land is Their Land.* Monroe, ME: Common Courage Press.

Vallianatos, Evaggelos. 2011. "The Democratic and Sacred Nature of Agriculture." *Environment, Development and Sustainability* 14 (September): 335–346.

## Art Economy

Artists wanting to convert vacant buildings into studios and exhibition spaces surreptitiously survey the grungy locales of Athens. The cheap rents and industrial setting, which serve as a backdrop, impart a social cachet. Graffiti-laden Exarhia is one of several neighborhoods where an upsurge in creative expression is set in place.

Affordable, artist-friendly quarters contribute to the gentrification of neighborhoods, ultimately stimulating economic growth.

Dubbed the "new Berlin," Athens is becoming an important player in the global art market. Yearning for recognition, young emerging artists take the rein, fully immersed in working out compositions. With the emergence of artist-run spaces come chance meetings with dealers and upper-class art collectors. Private organizations that trade in works of art and museums curators have their eyes peeled, on the lookout for the next superstar virtuoso.

Greece's drawn-out austerity proceedings have become a catalyst for the uptake in artistic production. Greek artists reacting to civil unrest and the social impact of the moment channel their frustrations into extraordinarily impressive showpieces.

The convergence of local and international talent by way of Athenian galleries and museums, such as the Breeder Gallery, the Kappatos Gallery, the Gagosian Gallery, and the National Museum of Contemporary Art, zeros in on cumulative voices vis-à-vis a diverse range of artists. Original drawings, paintings, photography, sculpture, and other works of masterful execution not only foster understanding but also position Athens as a formidable leader in the contemporary art world.

*Alexander Fatouros*

**See also:** Chapter 12: Modern Greek Art. Chapter 15: Bars and Nightlife. Chapter 16: Street Art and Graffiti.

**Further Reading**

Goudouna, Sozita. 2015. "ArtLyst | Art Under Austerity—Contemporary Art Abides Amidst the Greek Economic Crisis." February 9, 2015. Accessed March 28, 2020. https://www.academia.edu/15829436/ArtLyst_Art_Under_Austerity_Contemporary_Art_Abides_Amidst_The_Greek_Economic_Crisis_02-09-2015.

GTP Editing Team. 2020. "Greece's Contemporary Art Museum to Open for Test Run." February 14, 2020. Accessed: March 29, 2020. https://news.gtp.gr/2020/02/14/greeces-contemporary-art-museum-open-test-run/.

Sooke, Alastair. 2017. "Can Athens Become Europe's New Arts Capital?" *BBC*, May 9, 2017. Accessed March 28, 2020. http://www.bbc.com/culture/story/20170509-can-athens-become-europes-new-arts-capital.

## Children and Adolescents in the Workforce

The number of children working reflects the strains placed on families during the economic crisis, as well as the unprecedented number of refugees seeking safe haven in Greece and the number of undocumented immigrants, primarily from Albania. Children are encouraged or forced to work in order to earn money and provide for themselves and their families. Unfortunately, many of these children are placed in danger, work very long hours for minimal pay, or are exploited in some other way. It is expected that as the Greek economy recovers, the number of children in the labor force will decrease.

The type of work children do varies. In Greece, it is common for children in rural areas to work on the family farm, where they can be exposed to dangerous chemicals and pesticides. Others work in fishing, construction, restaurants, or hotels. Children often endure grueling work, long hours, and harsh weather conditions for meager wages and are at increased risk for workplace accidents or injury. Child prostitution, trafficking, and sexual exploitation have also risen in light of the economic and refugee crisis. A sizable number of "streetlight kids" between the ages of three and fifteen can be found washing windshields at street corners, selling small items, or playing musical instruments. Most of these street children are of Roma or Albanian origin; others are native or from refugee families.

In 2012, 11.4 percent of students, or seventy thousand, dropped out of school. It is estimated that 70 percent of those who dropped out did so in order to go to work. Given an environment where nearly five hundred thousand children lived in poverty and nearly half did not have a diet that met basic nutritional guidelines, this was not unexpected.

Moreover, it was estimated that up to 150,000 children worked, as reported by Pemptousia in 2014. The data, which was collected by ARSIS (Association for the Social Support of Youth), in collaboration with the National Centre for Social Studies, the National Statistics Office, and the Democritan and Panteian Universities, also found that of the total number of youth working, only about 30,000 were legally employed.

The Greek government has enacted laws to curb child labor. In 1989, Greek Law 1837/1989 established fifteen as the minimum age of employment. A presidential decree, adopted in 1998, prohibits the employment of children under the legal age in family businesses in the forestry, fishing, livestock, and agricultural sectors. In 2001, a law banned night work for young people working in their family businesses in these sectors.

In 2002, the Greek Parliament unanimously adopted Law no. 3064/2002 on "Measures to Combat Trafficking in Human Beings, Sexual and Economic Exploitation, and Child Pornography." It provides for up to ten years of imprisonment and hefty fines for those who are involved in trafficking of people for labor purposes or sexual exploitation. In 2003, Law no. 3144/2003 further strengthened these laws, including those that applied to the trafficking of children.

Moreover, in 2003, the Greek government banned begging and other forms of street labor such as selling flowers, shining shoes, or wiping windshields. Any person who forces someone under their care to beg faces imprisonment of up to six months. Greece ratified and enacted the standards of the International Convention on the Rights of the Child (UNCRC) on the definition of child labor and Convention 182 of the International Labor Organization on the worst forms of child labor. By most accounts, enforcement is minimal and violations are commonplace. The United Nations and others continue to pressure Greece to aggressively address this matter.

*John Psiharis*

**See also:** Chapter 7: Prostitution and Trafficking.

**Further Reading**

Artemi, Eirini. 2014. "Child Labour in Greece Today." Pemptousia, September 20, 2014. Accessed May 2, 2020. http://pemptousia.com/2014/09/child-labour-in-greece-today/.

Chew, Kristina. 2013. "Is Greece's Child Labor Crisis Getting Out of Hand?" Truthout, July 8, 2013. Accessed February 22, 2018. http://www.truth-out.org/news/item/17448-is-greeces-child-labor-crisis-getting-out-of-hand.

Chrysopoulos, Philip. 2017. "Child Labor in Greece Decreases Despite Crisis." *Greek Reporter*, June 12, 2017. Accessed May 2, 2020. http://greece.greekreporter.com/2017/06/12/child-labor-in-greece-decreases-despite-crisis/.

Hellenic National Committee for UNICEF. 2016. "The State of the Children in Greece Report 2016. Children in Danger." Accessed May 2, 2020. https://www.unicef.gr/uploads/filemanager/PDF/2016/children-in-greece-2016-eng.pdf.

Papademetriou, Theresa. 2007. "Children's Rights: Greece." The Law Library of Congress. September 2007. Accessed May 2, 2020. https://www.loc.gov/law/help/child-rights/greece.php.

Tsimitakis, Matthaios. 2013. "Child Labor a Rising Concern in Crisis-hit Greece." *ekathimerini*, January 7, 2013. Accessed May 2, 2020. http://www.ekathimerini.com/132580/article/ekathimerini/community/child-labor-a-rising-concern-in-crisis-hit-greece.

## Energy

In a formal pledge to appease the Troika—a consortium formed by the International Monetary Fund (IMF), the European Commission (EC), and the European Central Bank (ECB)—Greece was mandated to offer for sale government assets designed to bolster its commercial position. Initiated in 2010 as a means to receive a sequence of loans, Greece was obliged to comply with this directive.

The energy market, once controlled by the public power monopolies, has now broadened to consider initiatives set forth by Greece's ambitious privatization and liberalization programs. As energy consumption increases in 2020 and beyond, Greece is loosening its grip of state-controlled industries in an endeavor to reform the energy sector.

With an eye toward improving energy efficiency and fiscal stability, Greece is expanding power systems. The transition to energy reduction largely relies not only upon environmental constraints but also the policies set forth by the European Union (EU). By the year 2050, Greece's energy system aims to curtail greenhouse gas (GHG) emissions. The two-pronged decarbonization approach will laser focus on the transportation and power sectors, which are to blame for the nation's high levels of GHG.

Despite technological and economic advancements, Greece's push to maximize renewable energy sources (RESs) comes with its challenges. Greece's energy system greatly depends upon oil. As a means to produce electricity, lignite (a coal mined in Greece) had been an important part of Greece's energy consumption. However, with the emphasis on cleaner energy and government policies that will be closing the power plants in Greece, lignite production has now decreased.

Crude oil, which draws substantially upon imports from the Middle East and Russia, is processed at Greece's first oil refinery. Hellenic Petroleum S.A. produces 57 percent of the crude oil processed in Greece; Motor Oil Hellas handles the residual.

Hellenic Petroleum S.A. not only produces petrochemicals and electricity but also operates gas stations all over the Balkan region of Europe and Cyprus. Greece owns a 35.5 percent stake; 21.8 percent is offered to the public through the sale of shares on the Athens Stock Exchange.

With three oil refineries in Greece operated by once government-owned Hellenic Petroleum S.A., crude oil production is small time at best on the world stage. Natural gas—the country's number one fuel source—continues to be sourced offshore, largely from Russia.

In January 2020, an undersea pipeline agreement was struck among Greece, Cyprus, and Israel. Costing nearly 6 billion euros to complete, the "EastMed pipeline" will transport offshore natural gas recently discovered in the Mediterranean Sea to hubs across Europe by 2025, alleviating the EU's reliance on Russia. Moreover, offshore gas and oil projects continue to develop in the Northern Aegean Sea.

Yearning to predominate its position in world trade, the China Ocean Shipping Company (COSCO) has its sights on the industrial town of Aspropyrgos, a critical manufacturing and distribution center known for its petroleum refineries, steelworks, and power plants. China, which owns a majority stake of Piraeus port, aims to connect East Asia with Southeast Europe by rail vis-à-vis infrastructure development and investment initiatives, enabling a streamlined flow of goods from the Mediterranean Sea to Aspropyrgos and on to Prague, Czech Republic, and beyond.

While quite a bit of its energy originates from renewable sources, Greece is rooted in gas distribution networks. Its natural gas transmission operator, DESFA (a division of Public Gas Corporation of Greece, DEPA), was acquired in December 2018 by a guild of energy companies—Italian-based Snam, Spain's Enagás, and Belgium's Fluxys—for 535 million euros in exchange for a 66 percent stake. The Greek state owns 33 percent.

In a strategic move to align energy sources, the Copelouzos Group partnered with ELICA S.A. and PROMETHEUS GAS S.A, overseeing RES activities from wind parks and hydroelectric stations to natural gas and photovoltaic parks. Petroleum refining and trading continue today. Motor Oil Hellas in Corinth, Greece, is Europe's second-largest crude-oil refinery, selling available shares on the stock exchanges of London and Athens in order to keep the gas-producing business viable. Apart from conventional energy sources, Greece has the potential to improve its energy efficiency and security by 2030 as developments unfold around natural gas networks, oil exploration, and the construction of energy projects that highlight renewable energy sources, such as hydro and solar power.

*Alexander Fatouros*

**See also:** Chapter 1: Pollution of the Air. Glossary: European Commission; European Union, International Monetary Fund.

**Further Reading**

Carpenter, Scott. 2020. "New Pipeline Deal Gives Europe Access to Eastern Mediterranean Gas Reserves, Angering Turkey." Accessed March 8, 2020. https://www.forbes.com/sites/scottcarpenter/2020/01/02/new-gas-pipeline-deal-gives-europe-access-to-eastern-mediterranean-reserves-angering-turkey/#71883cea1c69.

Clapp, Alexander. 2017. "Europe's Heart of Darkness." *The Economist 1843*, October 24. 2017. Accessed March 21, 2020. https://www.1843magazine.com/features/europes-heart-of-darkness.

Copelouzos Group. 2020. "Renewable Energy Sources." Accessed March 8, 2020. https://www.copelouzos.gr/en/sector/renewable-energy-sources/.

ICLG. 2020. "Greece: Oil & Gas Regulation 2020." Accessed March 9, 2020. https://iclg.com/practice-areas/oil-and-gas-laws-and-regulations/greece.

MIT Enterprise Forum Greece. 2020. "Startup Competition 2020." Accessed March 9, 2020. https://2020.mitefgreece.org/.

Tigas, Kostas. 2014. "Wide Scale Penetration of Renewable Electricity in the Energy System in View of the European Decarbonization Targets for 2050." Accessed March 7, 2020. https://www.sciencedirect.com/science/article/abs/pii/S1364032114008247.

## Health Care

The health-care system in Greece is available to all Greek citizens through a universal health-care system that is provided by the National Healthcare Service (ESY) and private health-care services. Other EU nationals can also receive free health-care benefits provided they have a European Health Card.

According to the 2015 annual census of the Hellenic Statistical Authority (ELSTAT), there are 283 hospitals in Greece that provide emergency, outpatient, and in-patient care services. Over half (54.8 percent) of the hospitals are private.

Although the standard of precrisis health care overall was considered acceptable when compared to that of other European Union countries, the recent austerity measures and budget cuts of nearly 50 percent brought on several severe changes to health care, social welfare programs, and publicly funded pharmaceutical spending. When combined with the nearly 40 percent reduction of Greek household incomes, a humanitarian crisis erupted with rising mortality rates, an increase of life-threatening infections, and a shortage of staff and medical supplies. ELSTAT noted that the number of hospitals also decreased by 4.0 percent in 2012–2013 and by 2.4 percent in 2013–2014.

In 2015, Greece was facing a double crisis—one caused by the financial crisis and the other by the arrival of nearly a million refugees who were fleeing armed conflicts in the Middle East. Their arrival added to the country's health and social needs. The

Doctors of the World developed several new programs (mobile units and free clinics) to tackle the health crisis. In 2016, the government passed a law that offered free health care and medicine for uninsured and vulnerable people, including undocumented migrants and refugees.

It was not until 1922 that the Greek nation established the Ministry of Hygiene and Social Welfare so that it could deal with the influx of over one million Asia Minor refugees. Until then, only a few public, voluntary, municipal, and communal hospitals existed. Although several state hospitals were created under the new ministry, the level of care was rudimentary when compared to that of other European nations. In 1934, the first Social Security Organization (IKA) was established at a time when Greek society was politically unstable and trying to cope with the influx of refugees, unemployment, and a decline in wages. Its main priority was to provide health and pension coverage to workers. IKA began operating in 1937 in the three largest cities of Athens, Piraeus, and Thessaloniki by providing coverage for large companies. It was eventually extended to other cities and smaller firms. However, farmers and rural laborers were not a part of the scheme. The health-care situation became paralyzed during the devastating World War II (1939–1945) and the Greek Civil War (1946–1949). Temporary public hospitals were established with many remaining thereafter. After these wars, Greece attempted to reconstruct, reform, and decentralize its health-care system. Two decrees were accepted by the Parliament; however, neither was ever implemented.

The 1960s was a period of rapid economic growth. Several financial institutions, such as banks, began offering their own insurance funds, mainly out of employer contributions. Health insurance was also offered for public sector employees and self-employed professionals as well as for farmers and their families. Medical stations were set up in rural areas, and small-scale private hospitals were established in large cities. Despite the rapid economic growth, public health-care expenditure remained low, except for IKA, which developed its own health-care infrastructure for its insured population. The private sector, however, greatly expanded as more physicians started their own private practices and the number of small-scale hospitals increased. Although the seven-year military dictatorship (1967–1974) attempted to organize a comprehensive health-care system, little progress or change was made in the health sector during this era.

After democracy was restored in 1974, a new era began for the Greek welfare system with several needed reforms and legislative acts occurring throughout the 1980s. Until then, the system had remained one of the least developed among the Organisation for Economic Co-operation and Development (OECD) countries with a lacking infrastructure and many inadequacies. In 1983, the National Health System (ESY) was established so that all citizens could be provided with social and health care. One of its main goals was to separate public and private health systems by restricting publicly employed physicians from having private practices. At the same time, the private health-care sector evolved. It now accounts for more than half of health-care expenditure. In the early 1990s, Greece began expanding its investment in the public health sector until it reached the level it is at today.

*Angelyn Balodimas-Bartolomei*

**See also:** Chapter 2: Overview. Chapter 4: Social Security.

**Further Reading**

Athanasiadis, Athanasios, Stella Kostopoulou, and Anastas Philalithis. 2015. "Regional Decentralization in the Greek Health Care System: Rhetoric and Reality." *Global Journal of Health Science* 7, no. 6 (November): 55–67. Published online March 30, 2015. Accessed May 11, 2018. https://www.ncbi.nlm.nih.gov/pmc/articles/PMC4803855/.

Doctors of the World International Network. 2016. "Access to Healthcare for People Facing Multiple Vulnerabilities in 31 Cities in 12 Countries." Accessed May 11, 2018. https://mdmeuroblog.files.wordpress.com/2016/11/observatory-report2016_en-mdm-international.pdf.

Hellenic Statistical Authority. 2018. "Hospital Census, 2015." Accessed May 11, 2018. http://www.statistics.gr/documents/20181/a6584289-355a-4c67-a8bf-0be4e0d7cbdc.

Immergut, Ellen M., Karen Anderson, and Isabelle Schulze. 2007. *The Handbook of West European Pension Politics.* Oxford: Oxford University Press.

Wolper, L. 2004. *Health Care Administration: Planning, Implementing, and Managing Organized Delivery Systems.* Boston: Jones & Bartlett Learning.

World Health Organization. 1996. "Healthcare Systems in Transition. Greece." Regional Office for Europe. Copenhagen. Accessed May 11, 2018. http://www.euro.who.int/__data/assets/pdf_file/0020/120278/E72454.pdf.

## The Labor Market

A period of robust growth that started in the late 1990s continued until 2008. The employment rate (defined as individuals who are working as a percentage of the same age group) increased, and the unemployment rate decreased. The labor force expanded due to the influx of immigrants and upward trend in female participation. However, when the global crisis hit in 2008, things changed. The employment rate decreased, and the unemployment rate increased.

Figure 4.1 demonstrates the changes that occurred in the labor market from 1983 to 2017. Beginning in the early 1990s, the *participation rate* (number of individuals aged fifteen to sixty-four available for work as a percentage of the population aged fifteen to sixty-four in the Greek labor market) increased significantly. This increase during the 1990s was mainly due to increased female participation and the inflow of immigrants—who have a higher participation rate than natives.

From the mid-1990s onward, and accompanying the robust and increasing GDP growth rates, the *employment rate* also started trending upward at a slow but intensifying pace. Employment gains since the mid-1990s were, for the most part, due to the increased employment of women, migrants, and individuals aged between twenty-five and twenty-nine. This development was linked to, among other things, the expansion of the services sector (e.g., tourism, professional services, retail and wholesale distribution), in general, and the wider public sector, in particular, as well as the construction

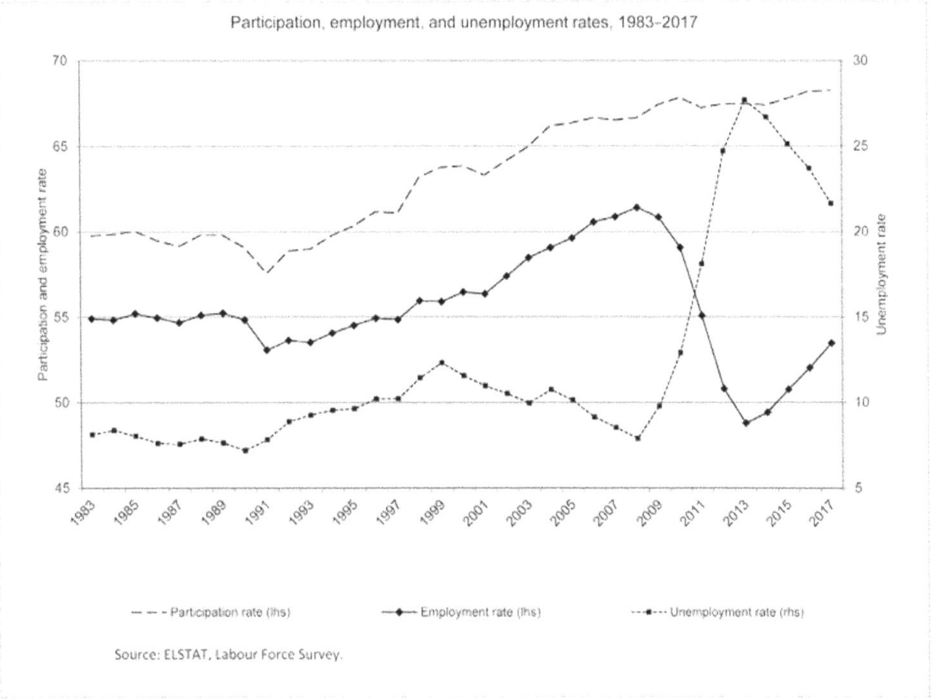


Figure 4.1

sector. In the 1990s, the number of individuals available for work (the so-called active population) increased at a rate that was almost 1.6 times higher that of the number of employed individuals. As a result, the unemployment rate reached 12 percent in 1999 (figure 4.1). Starting in 1999, however, the rate of increase of employment picked up, overtaking the rate of increase of the active population, and thus the unemployment rate decreased to 7.6 percent in 2008.

Developments since 2008 have led to a deteriorating picture in the labor market; the employment rate decreased significantly, and a trough of 48 percent was reached in 2013 (from 61 percent in 2008). The sectors that fared especially badly during the crisis were construction and manufacturing. The two groups of workers that were hurt in particular were immigrants and low-skilled men. By the end of 2017, the employment rate, defined as the percentage of the labor force that is employed, picked up somewhat to 53 percent, still significantly lower than in 2008.

The decline in the employment rate does not reflect the withdrawal of individuals from the labor market, as can be seen from the fact that the participation rate, defined as the number of individuals of working age who are either working or are unemployed over the population of the same age group, remained more or less flat post 2008. In fact, the fall in the employment rate was accompanied by a large increase in the unemployment rate from 8 percent in 2008 to over 27 percent in 2013. Since 2013 there has been a decline in the unemployment rate, which at the end of 2017 stood at 21.6 percent. Notable is the increase in unemployment duration after 2008 as transition rates between unemployment and employment—already low in the case of Greece—deteriorated even further. As a result, over 70 percent of the unemployed in the first three-quarters of 2018 had been unemployed for twelve months or more.

Despite the improvements that had been seen before 2008, there had been some negative indicators during that time. They included significant labor underutilization, which burdened women and youth excessively (see separate entry on "Women in the Workforce"), and low labor productivity (measured as output divided by employment, i.e., the average worker's output). In fact, labor market outcomes (e.g., the unemployment rate, the participation rate) compared unfavorably with those in other EU countries. The overall participation and employment rates were lower, while the unemployment rate has been consistently higher.

The labor market in Greece has been, and continues to be, characterized by:

- Low female and youth participation.
- Large share of employment in the primary sector (industries engaged in agricultural activities or in the extraction of natural resources). Despite having declined over time, the share of the primary sector in total employment still exceeded a tenth of total employment (12.1 percent) in 2017. While the primary sector can act as a buffer in times of turbulence (note that employment in the primary sector decreased by 12.3 percent between 2008 and 2017 while total employment decreased by 17.7 percent), it also implies a low speed of transformation of the Greek economy and low productivity. Further, it impacts negatively on the productivity of the economy overall.
- Significant share of total employment in the wider public sector (public administration and any other activities carried out by the state through, e.g., state-owned enterprises). According to the ELSTAT 2017 Labor Force Survey (LFS) statistics, the wider public sector accounts for 32.3 percent of all employees, while the corresponding figure for public administration is around 15 percent. These figures show a slight decline compared to 2008 when the wider public sector accounted for 34.4 percent of all employees and the public administration accounted for 17.4 percent.
- High share of self-employed in nonprimary employment (around 24 percent in 2017). A high share of self-employed might make the economy flexible—at the cost, however, of foregone synergies and economies of scale. The level and changes in the share of self-employment are important indicators of labor market tightness, since individuals often resort to this form of activity if they cannot find jobs as employees.
- Unpaid family members, which represent around 2.6 percent of nonprimary sector employment.
- High share of small firms (with fewer than ten employees). Before 2018, this reached as high as 50 percent. Recently it has gone down somewhat to 35 percent, suggesting that smaller firms have shut down because of the economic crisis.

- Low mobility between sectors of economic activity (most individuals used to expect to work in the same occupation and in the same sector for life) and across different labor market states (inactivity, employment, unemployment). That is probably due to the labor market reforms undertaken since 2010. However, labor market flexibility has increased as witnessed by the fact that the very low transition rates have risen somewhat.
- Low use of part-time work, although recently this has increased. While in 2008 only 5.8 percent of private sector employees were working part time, in 2017, this rose to 15 percent. The hours of work have been affected by a decrease in the employment rate.
- Long weekly hours of work. Average annual hours of work have been the longest in the EU and much higher than the OECD average (in 2017, on average, Greeks worked 2,111 hours compared to just 1,800 in the countries belonging to the OECD). This is due in part to Greece having a higher share of workers in the type of work where the hours are longer and where there are more self-employed (e.g., tourism-related activities, retail distribution). Recently the hours of work have decreased, perhaps due to the increased use of part-time workers.
- Low labor productivity. This was due to the small size of firms, the focus on trade rather than production, and the low technology readiness of the economy.
- Gap between the labor cost for the employer and the take-home pay for the employee in the private and public sectors. Because of tax obligations, the take-home pay was lower than it would have been without these tax obligations.

The aforementioned features affected labor productivity and determined, to a certain degree, the extent of flexibility and security in the market. They are also, to a large extent, the product of prevailing institutions (e.g., in order to avoid high social security contributions individuals turn to self-employment) and of the composition of economic activity.

Other factors that contributed to the recent economic downturn included:

- Regulations that prevented nominal wages from decreasing even if the firm's financial circumstances deteriorated.
- High pension obligations, for example, a woman under fifty with an underage child could have received a full pension with twenty years of work.
- Minimum wage that varied between types of industries, occupations, and even firms. This changed after 2010 when negotiations between social partners (trade unions and employers' associations) were replaced by a statutory minimum wage set by the government following consultation with the social partners and the advice of research institutes, and a subminimum wage for youth below twenty-five was set.

These factors were addressed through reforms that took place after 2010, when Greece entered into Memoranda of Understanding as outlined by the Troika (the

European Commission, the European National Bank, and the International Monetary Fund) in order to get loans to weather the financial storm.

*Daphne Nicolitsas*

**See also:** Chapter 4: Memoranda of Understanding; Women in the Workforce. Glossary: European Commission; European Central Bank; International Monetary Fund.

**Further Reading**

Christodoulakis, Nikos. 2012. "Greek Crisis in Perspective: Origins, Effects and Ways-Out." *The New Palgrave Dictionary of Economics*, Online edition. Accessed April 20, 2021. https://link.springer.com/chapter/10.1057/9781137553799_15.

Christodoulakis, Nikos. 2015. "Greek Crisis in Perspective: Causes, Illusions and Failures." *The New Palgrave Dictionary of Economics*, Online edition. Accessed April 20, 2021. https://link.springer.com/referenceworkentry/10.1057%2F978-1-349-95121-5_3020-1.

"Greece Tops EU List for Self-employment with 31.9% of Greeks Working for Themselves." 2013. *ekathimerini*, July 6, 2013. Accessed January 2, 2021. http://www.ekathimerini.com/136072/article/ekathimerini/business/greece-tops-eu-list-for-self-employment-with-319-of-greeks-working-for-themselves.

OECD. 2009. *OECD Economic Surveys: Greece 2009.* Paris: OECD Publishing. https://doi.org/10.1787/eco_surveys-grc-2009-en.

## Memoranda of Understanding

In 2010, Greece experienced an economic crisis, and to avoid bankruptcy, the government entered into the first of three Memoranda of Understanding with the Troika (the International Monetary Fund, the European Central Bank, and the European Commission) in order to get loans. Because of its poor credit rating, other banks would not extend loans. Installments of the financial support were released only when Greece met the milestones set for fiscal consolidation, including a reform of the pension system and modernization of its economy. Funding was released from May 2010 until August 2018. The amount of funding and the conditions under which funds were to be released were specified in three different memoranda (May 2010, February 2012, and August 2015). The second memorandum followed the first when it became clear that the financial assistance the first loan provided would not be sufficient. The third memorandum then followed the second. The total amount of the bailout was 330 billion dollars. Greece was placed on enhanced surveillance to make sure the country met the milestones for economic reform as specified in the Memoranda of Understanding, which are described here.

### FIRST MEMORANDUM OF UNDERSTANDING (MAY 2010–MARCH 2012)

Following the revelation by the government that took power in October 2009 that the previous government had underestimated the general government deficit and that the figure for 2009 would stand closer to 15 percent than to 6 percent (OECD 2009), the markets started pricing Greek government bonds (GGBs) continuously lower. Indicative of the declining mistrust in the ability of the Greek economy to deliver growth is the fact that on February 1, 2010, the spread between GGBs and Bunds (German government bonds) stood at 347 basis points (a basis points is one-hundredth of 1 percent) for the two-year bonds and 270 basis points for ten-year bonds. On May 7, the spread reached 1,739 basis points for the two-year bonds and 1,287 basis points for the ten-year bonds. Greece and the Troika reached an agreement on a three-year program of economic and financial policies on May 2, 2010. Greece would receive 110 billion euros of financial assistance (80 billion euros from European Union [EU] countries and 30 billion from the IMF) over the next thirty-six months. The first installment of 20 billion euros (14.5 billion from the EU and 5.5 billion euros from the IMF) was released by May 18, 2010. Subsequent installments were timed quarterly and were subject to quarterly assessments of progress.

The agreement specifies the commitment of the Greek authorities to "frame tight budgets in the coming years with the aim to reduce our deficit significantly below 3 percent of GDP in 2014, achieve a downward trajectory in the public debt-GDP ratio in 2013, safeguard the stability of the financial system, and implement structural reforms to boost the economy's capacity to produce, save, and export." It includes a commitment to a pension reform—strengthening the link between contributions and benefits, prolonging the retirement age in line with life expectancy, and merging pension funds—and ensuring financial sustainability as it was thought that banks would suffer from an increase in nonperforming loans (NPLs) due to the recession. The memorandum also addressed privatization of some government-owned assets as a condition of obtaining the loan. The plans included Agricultural Bank and the Hellenic Post Bank from the banking sector; airports, ports, and the railway operator OSE from the transport sector; water providers EYDAP and EYATH; Public Power Corporation (PPC), gas company DEPA, petroleum company ELPE from the energy sector; OTE from the telecommunications sector; OPAP, casinos, and Horse Racing Organization (ODIE) from the gaming sector; state companies active in real estate as well as real estate owned by the state.

Although the first review of the memorandum was scheduled for the end of the second quarter of 2010, it took place during the summer of 2010. Greece received a positive assessment, which meant that the second installment of 9 billion euros (6.5 billion from the EU and 2.5 billion from the IMF) would be released in September. In its evaluation, the Troika stressed the need to avoid budgetary slippages in the second half of the year and the need for the government to deal with a shortage of liquidity in the economy due to credit restraint. They also addressed conditions that were necessary for stability of the banking sector.

The second review of progress under the memorandum took place in mid-November 2010. The review was successful and the third installment—an amount of 9 billion euros (6.5 billion from the EU and 2.5 billion from the IMF)—was released, but the report noted that policy implementation had become more difficult and assessment had also been delayed. The second review should have taken place closer to the end of the third quarter of 2010 rather than toward the end of the fourth quarter. The third review, which should have taken place in 2010, took place between the end of January and mid-February 2011. Once again, the broad assessment was that the program was on track, but more resolve appeared to be needed as new challenges (in the form increased financial market volatility and the possibility of contagion from other peripheral Euro Area countries that were also experiencing fiscal tightness and contagion from neighboring countries) had emerged. Completion of this review led to the release of a total of 15 billion euros (10.9 billion from the EU and 4.1 from the IMF). The fourth review took place in June 2011. The main concern was the lack of political consensus for the reforms and weakness of institutional capacity. Despite these hesitations, a further installment of 12 billion euros (8.7 billion from the EU and 3.3 billion from the IMF) was released, and it was decided that the European Commission would provide more technical assistance to overcome the lack in institutional capacity. In July 2011 and before the completion of the fifth review, the Euro Area heads of state decided that the loans to be given in the future would be longer in maturity (between fifteen and twenty years compared to around five years up to then) and would be given at much lower interest rates. Furthermore, loans already granted to Greece would have their maturities extended, and thus Greece would not have to start repaying the loans to the EU before 2020. This would give the economy some respite. The fifth review was concluded at the end of September 2011, and the decision was to approve the release of 8 billion euros despite serious concerns on program implementation in the face of much worse than expected macroeconomic performance outcomes. Even though following the fifth review, 73 billion euros out of the 110 billion euros would have been disbursed, talk for the need of a second memorandum started emerging. It was thought that a swift decision on a second program would help reduce economic uncertainty and restore confidence.

## SECOND MEMORANDUM OF UNDERSTANDING (MARCH 2012–JUNE 2015)

The Second Memorandum, agreed in March 2012, involved the disbursement of the undisbursed amounts from the first memorandum and in addition further financial assistance of the order of 130 billion euros for the years 2012–2014. Quarterly reviews of progress under this program were also envisaged as was the case with the first memorandum. The second adjustment program put the structural reforms to restart growth at the forefront and permitted a slower fiscal adjustment than that envisaged in the first adjustment program. It asked for changes involving the labor market as a condition for receiving the loan. These included a change in the way the minimum wage was decided—from it being the outcome of the negotiations of social partners to its being legislated by the government, as well as the introduction of a subminimum wage for youth. Aligning wage developments closer to the financial circumstances of firms was also a target of the changes introduced. The changes implemented included making firm-level agreements easier to sign; until then size restrictions existed as to the firms that could easily sign firm-level agreements. Two other reforms outlined in the memorandum were temporary—only for as long as Greece was under the Troika's financial assistance program. The first did not allow firm-level collective wage agreements to provide wages higher than that of the industry-level collective wage agreements. The second specified that collective wage agreements would not apply to all firms in an industry but only to the firms involved in the bargaining procedure. The goal of privatization of state assets set forth in the first memorandum was carried over, since this was a medium- to long-term target. The first review under this Second Memorandum was not completed until the third quarter of 2012 mainly due to the successive elections that took place in May and June 2012. In the intervening period between March 2012, when the Second Memorandum started and 75.6 billion euros were dispersed, and the completion of the first review in October 2012, the major event was a write down of the debt, the so-called private sector involvement (PSI). The PSI provided for a nominal haircut (reduction of amount to be paid to creditors) on Greek bonds of the order of 53.5 percent. In effect, existing bondholders were asked to voluntarily exchange their GGBs with new GGBs of much lower face value and much longer maturities. Rating agencies considered the event as distressed debt restructuring and decreased Greece's sovereign rating even further making the use of GGBs as collateral for interbank lending even more difficult. The second review under the Second Memorandum was completed by April 2013.

In total under the Second Memorandum, Greece received funding of 141.8 billion euros. The funding was not disbursed in the form of bilateral loans, as in the First Memorandum, but through the European Financial Stability Facility (EFSF).

## THIRD MEMORANDUM OF UNDERSTANDING (AUGUST 2015–AUGUST 2018)

As part of the Third Memorandum of Understanding, Greece received 61.9 billion euros. The funding was distributed after measures were taken to address the NPLs in the banking sector, recapitalize banks, and strengthen governance of banks and their supervisory authorities. In addition, as part of the Third Memorandum, the primarily surplus targets of -0.25 percent, 0.5 percent, 1.75 percent, and 3.5 percent for 2015, 2016, 2017, and 2018, respectively, were adopted. A primary surplus results when a government's current revenue exceeds its current spending, not taking into account the interest paid on debt.

In August 2018, Greece met the terms of the stability program. However, they continue to be under enhanced surveillance—quarterly monitoring by the European Commission.

*Daphne Nicolitsas*

**See also:** Chapter 4: Privatization of Transportation; Reasons for the Economic Crisis. Chapter 16: Overview. Glossary: European Central Bank; European Commission; International Monetary Fund; Memorandum of Understanding.

**Further Reading**

European Commission. 2010a. "The Economic Adjustment Programme for Greece." Occasional Paper 61. Accessed January 20, 2021. http://ec.europa.eu/economy_finance/publications/occasional_paper/2010/pdf/ocp61_en.pdf.

European Commission. 2010b. "The Economic Adjustment Programme for Greece, First Review–Summer 2010." Occasional Paper 68. Accessed January 20, 2021. https://ec.europa.eu/economy_finance/articles/eu_economic_situation/2010-08-20-eap-review-greece_en.htm.

European Commission. 2010c. "The Economic Adjustment Programme for Greece, Second Review–Autumn 2010." Occasional Paper 72. Accessed January 20, 2021. http://ec.europa.eu/economy_finance/publications/occasional_paper/2010/pdf/ocp72_en.pdf.

European Commission. 2011a. "The Economic Adjustment Programme for Greece, Third Review–Winter 2011." Occasional Paper 77. Accessed January 20, 2021. http://ec.europa.eu/economy_finance/publications/occasional_paper/2011/pdf/ocp77_en.pdf.

European Commission. 2011b. "The Economic Adjustment Programme for Greece, Fourth Review–Spring 2011." Occasional Paper 82. Accessed January 20, 2021. http://ec.europa.eu/economy_finance/publications/occasional_paper/2011/pdf/ocp82_en.pdf.

European Commission. 2011b. "The Economic Adjustment Programme for Greece, Fourth Review–October 2011." Occasional Paper 87. Accessed January 20, 2021. http://ec.europa.eu/economy_finance/publications/occasional_paper/2011/pdf/ocp87_en.pdf.

European Commission. 2012a. "The Second Economic Adjustment Programme for Greece, March 2012." Occasional Paper 94. Accessed January 20, 2021. http://ec.europa.eu/economy_finance/publications/occasional_paper/2012/pdf/ocp94_en.pdf.

## Privatization of Transportation

Greece's privatization plan was born out of an attempt to relieve debt as part of a bailout package set forth by the Troika: the European Commission, the European Central Bank, and the International Monetary Fund. As a result, Greece has offered a majority stake to investors in a diversified portfolio of sectors, including telecom, public utilities, gas, refinery, renewable energy, and transportation. The privatized transportation sector embodies railways, seaports, and airports.

China recognized the value of investing in Athens's chief seaport, Piraeus—a hub of geostrategic importance—since it serves as a critical link between East Asia, Europe, and Africa. The privatization agreement Greece reached with China regarding Piraeus port is perhaps Greece's best-known foreign investment transaction.

The Chinese company China Ocean Shipping Company (COSCO) obtained a 51 percent share of the Piraeus Port Authority in 2016 and now manages the port. China views the port as an important distribution hub of its Belt and Road Initiative (BRI).

As a consequence, it continues to invest in the port's infrastructure, boosting its trading capacity.

Utilizing a global infrastructure network of ports, pipelines, and railroads, China's BRI, also known as the "New Silk Road," aims to amplify its trading network. Greece joined the BRI in 2016, one of the few European Union (EU) nations to do so.

As part of this initiative, in 2019, Chinese president Xi Jinping and Greek prime minster Kyriakos Mitsotakis struck a deal to further develop Piraeus port. COSCO is putting forth around 500 million euros (660 million dollars), thereby broadening China's economic and political impact and transforming the strategic spot into what it believes will be Europe's biggest port.

Greece has also privatized the port of Thessaloniki. In March 2018, South Europe Gateway Thessaloniki (SEGT) Limited became Thessaloniki Port Authority's chief owner. Based in Cyprus, SEGT's 67 percent stake in the highly sought-after entrepôt is comprised of investors from Germany, France, and Russia: Deutsche Invest Equity Partners GmbH, Terminal Link SAS, and tycoon Ivan Savvidis, respectively. Private investors make up 26 percent thanks to trading on Athens Stock Exchange (ticker symbol ThPA SA). The Greek government secured 7 percent proprietorship. Privatization efforts on the part of the Greek state significantly expanded the port of Thessaloniki's operational efficiency.

At the regional level in 2020, the Greek government set afloat procedures to develop ten additional ports: Alexandroupolis, Corfu, Elefsis, Heraklion, Kavala, Patras, Igoumenitsa, Rafina, Lavrio, and Volos. The bidding process will be spearheaded by the Hellenic Republic Asset Development Fund (HRADF) and is expected to draw interest from international backers.

Greece has also privatized its railway company. TrainOSE S.A., which operates a robust railway network of passenger and freight trains, was acquired by Ferrovie dello Stato Italiane in 2017 for 45 million euros.

Olympic Airlines (OA), once owned by shipping magnate Aristotle Onassis, was sold to the Greek state in 1975. In an effort to privatize OA, the government began to scout likely investors at the suggestion of the EU in 2005. Government officials sold 100 percent of the enterprise to Greek buyer Marfin Investment Group (MIG) in 2009. In 2012, MIG sold OA to Aegean Airlines, a transaction valued at 72 million euros.

In November 2014, Fraport of Germany partnered with Greek infrastructure investors Copelouzos Group in a deal that would allow the German operator to maintain and further develop eleven island airports and mainland airports in Aktio, Thessaloniki, and Kavala. In April 2017, Fraport paid Greece 1.2 billion euros in exchange for control of fourteen regional airports.

In their quest to amass a 30 percent stake in HRADF-owned Athens International Airport (AIA), nine qualified investors advanced to a second bidding phase in late January 2020.

*Alexander Fatouros*

**See also:** Chapter 4: Memoranda of Understanding.

**Further Reading**

Amaro, Silvia. "China Bought Most of Greece's Main Port and Now It Wants To Make It the Biggest in Europe." CNBC, November 16, 2019. Accessed March 5, 2020. https://www.cnbc.com/2019/11/15/china-wants-to-turn-greece-piraeus-port-into-europe-biggest.html.

Chatzky Andrew, and James McBride. 2020. "China's Massive Belt and Road Initiative." Council on Foreign Relations. Last updated January 28, 2020. Accessed March 8, 2020. https://www.cfr.org/backgrounder/chinas-massive-belt-and-road-initiative.

Kampouris, Nick. 2020. "Greece to Begin Procedures to Privatize Ten Regional Ports." *Greek Reporter,* January 31, 2020. Accessed March 8, 2020. https://greece.greekreporter.com/2020/01/31/greece-to-begin-procedures-to-privatize-ten-regional-ports/.

Stamouli, Nektaria. 2017. "Germany's Fraport Takes Over 14 Greek Airports." April 12, 2017. Accessed March 5, 2020. https://www.marketwatch.com/story/germanys-fraport-takes-over-14-greek-airports-2017-04-12.

Stevens, Charles. 2018. "Along the New Silk Road—Piraeus: China's Gateway into Europe." August 17, 2018. Accessed April 5, 2020. https://geographical.co.uk/people/development/item/2866-silk-road-pir.

Vaggelas, George, and Pallis Thanos. 2018. "Details of a Port Privatisation: Thessaloniki Port." April 17, 2018. Accessed March 20, 2020. http://www.porteconomics.eu/2018/04/17/details-of-a-port-privatisation-thessaloniki-port/.

## Reasons for the Economic Crisis

The economic crisis that Greece faced in late 2009 started about ten years earlier. The records that Greece presented before admission to the Eurozone (officially referred to as the Euro Area) in 2001 did not present the true picture of her economic condition. The Eurozone requires that countries fulfill certain membership criteria, including a budget deficit that does not exceed 3 percent of the GDP and a public debt limited to 60 percent of the GDP. Greece met these criteria but did so by leaving out certain expenses. A short while after Greece was admitted, a derivatives deal that Goldman-Sachs first put in place in 2001 contributed to masking the true nature of Greece's deficit. The bookkeeping tricks that had been used, although not illegal, were deceptive.

Admission to the Eurozone further contributed to Greece's economic woes. Interest rates were low and the government, as well as the general public, took out loans they had difficulty repaying. Because of membership in the Eurozone and the use of the euro instead of the drachma, Greece gave up control of her own currency. When Greece found herself in trouble, she could not print more money or manipulate interest rates to moderate the economic crisis.

When Greek prime minister Georgios Papandreou, who was elected in the fall of 2009, discovered the extent of the deficit that had previously been hidden, he announced it. Several debt-ratings agencies then downgraded Greece's rating to the lowest level in the Eurozone. In May 2010, Papandreou dropped another bomb. He reported that the Greek deficit was 13.6 percent of GDP for 2009, higher than the 12.9 percent originally reported. The members of the Eurozone became very concerned that Greece's economic situation would explode, and they would suffer the fallout. Germany and France were especially vulnerable since Greece had borrowed from their banks, and they worried that Greece would not be able to repay these loans. In May 2010, the Troika (the European Commission, the European Central Bank, and the International Monetary Fund) negotiated the first of three Memoranda of Understanding that specified the amount of loans Greece would receive and the reforms that it would have to make in order to receive the loans. The reforms, which included cutting the wages of government workers, lowering the pensions of retirees, and raising taxes, resulted in recurrent demonstrations and strikes.

Financial experts point out that the worldwide recession of 2008 affected Greece greatly. However, some economists blame part of Greece's bleak economic picture on the underground economy and the use of bribes and patronage. *Fakelakia* (small envelopes) are part of doing business in Greece. These envelopes are slipped to officials to help gain access to medical services, avoid taxes, or obtain building permits or drivers' licenses. Jobs in the government service were given by the politicians to those who supported them. Lack of a civil service exam made it easier to obtain a government job. Patronage jobs contributed to an inflated government service sector.

The ethics of politicians were called into question by Greek citizens. On May 11, 2012, WBEZ, the public radio station based in Chicago, broadcast an interview with a vegetable vendor. Grabbing a potato, she said, "See this potato. If I stole it, I would end up in jail. Yet our politicians steal millions, and nothing happens to them." She continued, "The two main political parties here robbed us blind, but it's our fault. We voted for them."

Tax evasion also contributed to the problem. Tax evasion can include the following:

- Small businesses who do not report true income. This can be done by issuing false receipts or no receipts. This affects the income they report, as well as how much is paid to the government in terms of sales taxes. At present, receipts are mandated.
- Employees who do not report their true income; this can include payment of bribes.
- Smugglers of alcohol, tobacco, fuel, or other commodities.
- Individuals and firms that use tax havens to hide their income.

In a paper published by Theodoris Georgakopoulos in 2016, the scale of tax evasion was estimated to be between 6 and 9 percent of GDP. He reports that personal tax evasion ranges from 1.9 to 4.7 percent of annual GDF, with an additional 3.5 percent of GDP lost to value-added tax fraud. Losses from alcohol, tobacco, and fuel smuggling amount to about 0.5 percent of GDP. For legal entities, revenue lost from tax evasion and tax avoidance is estimated at around 0.15 percent of GDP.

*Elaine Thomopoulos*

**See also:** Chapter 1: Population Decline. Chapter 4: Memoranda of Understanding.

**Further Reading**

Beaton, Roderick. 2019. *Greece: Biography of a Modern Nation.* London: Allen Lane.

Georgakopoulos, Theodoris. 2016. "Tax Evasion in Greece—A Study." Dianeosis Research and Policy Institute. Accessed March 15, 2021. https://www.dianeosis.org/en/2016/06/tax-evasion-in-greece/.

Reinhart, Carmn, and Christoph Trebesch. Fall 2015. "The Pitfalls of External Dependence: Greece, 1829–2015." *Brookings Papers on Economic Activity.* 307–328.

## Shipping

A world leader in shipping, Greece has strategically placed deep-sea terminals that operate a global network of merchant marine fleets and giant container ships. Piraeus and Thessaloniki ports are especially equipped to handle a variety of traffic

A Greek ferry carries passengers and their cars or trucks back and forth from the mainland to the Ionian island of Zakynthos. Situated in the Eastern Mediterranean, Greece is a maritime center whose ships range from huge tankers that transport goods across the oceans, to smaller roll-on/roll-off (Ro-Ro) vessels like this one. In 2019, the Greek-owned ships ranked number one in the world as to the value of its fleet, worth 105.2 billion dollars, besting Japan at number two with 94.7 billion dollars. (Photo by Elaine Thomopoulos)

operations from passenger and cargo vessels to industrial tankers made up of oil and gas. In 2019, maritime business increased by 7 percent from the previous year.

At around 9 billion dollars, 4 percent of Greece's GDP is a result of shipping, according to Greece's Office of Statistics in 2015. Taking into account interconnected maritime trades, the industry's estimation springs to nearly 17 billion dollars, or 7.5 percent of GDP. However, a closer examination of filings and budgetary figures suggests otherwise. A probe set forth by Reuters unveiled that the shipping industry's bestowal is equal to about 1 percent of GDP, if Greece tallied only remittance to Greek companies or persons. Since Greek shipowners include billions of dollars that never pierce Greece's economy in their data calculations, the economic signposts are equivocal.

In an undertaking to promote the Greek shipping industry and maritime services, attractive tax incentives, which serve shipping and chartering businesses, were rolled out in 2020. International lenders have nudged the Greek state to boost its economic position by introducing tariffs on shipowners. However, shipping companies and merchant marine stakeholders asserted their clout, urging the government to avoid curbing generous tax allowances or face an ultimatum of abandonment. Tax revenues had increased in 2013 at the onset of the economic crisis by way of the shipping industry's voluntary commitment to ancillary contributions. However, in 2020 the government reforms have not fully committed to the idea of bridling tax breaks set aside for shipping magnates and the like. Rather, a contribution agreement between the Greek state and the Greek shipping coterie has been established, yielding at least 45 million dollars annually.

In 2017, fourteen Greek shipping tycoons were named among the world's top 100 shipping company owners in a ranking published by Lloyd's List. The eighth-place spot was awarded to billionaire shipping magnate, John Anthony Angelicoussis. Other well-known billionaire fleet owners include Spiro Latsis of Latsco Shipping and Philip Niarchos, son of the late Stavros Niarchos. The illustrious Aristotle Onassis is perhaps Greece's most famous shipping baron.

*Alexander Fatouros*

**See also:** Chapter 2: Onassis, Aristotle Socrates. Chapter 4: Privatization of Transportation.

**Further Reading**

Bergin, Tom. 2015. "How Greek Shipowners Talk Up Their Role, and Why That Costs Athens Millions." Reuters, November 25, 2015. Accessed: March 21, 2020. https://www.reuters.com/investigates/special-report/eurozone-greece-shipping/.

Glass, David. 2020. "Shipping's Contribution to the Greek Economy." *Seatrade Maritime News*, February 5, 2020. Accessed March 22, 2020. https://www.seatrade-maritime.com/finance-insurance/shippings-contribution-greek-economy.

"Lloyd's List Ranks 14 Greek Shipping Tycoons Among World's Top 100." 2017. GTP Publishing Team, December 12, 2017. Accessed March 22, 2020. https://news.gtp.gr/2017/12/18/lloyds-list-ranks-14-greek-shipping-tycoons-among-worlds-top-100/.

## Social Security

On January 1, 2017, the Greek government created the Unified Social Security Body (EFKA) as its new body for main social security. Overseen by the Ministry of Labor, Social Security and Social Solidarity, EFKA operates as a single administrative and financial organization, like the major European Social Security Funds. Until 2017, there were several social security institutions providing coverage for different categories of individuals. These included IKA-ETAM (Social Insurance Institute-Unified Insurance Fund for Employees), ETAP-MME (Institute Fund for Mass Media Employees), ETAA (Insure Fund for Independent Professionals), OAEE (Social Security Organization for Self-Employed), TAYTEKO (Insurance Fund of Bank Employees and Public Utilities Services), ETAT (Unified Insurance Fund for Bank Employees), NAT (Mariners' Insurance Fund), and OGA (Agricultural Insurance Organization). All preexisting funds were integrated into EFKA except for the last two, which have maintained their independent legal status solely for the performance of their noninsurance competencies.

Under the new unified system, the main social security branches are national pension, health care, and auxiliary social security and lump-sum benefits with the same rules applying to all. Those insured under EFKA are subject to new and uniform social security rules and contributions while receiving unified benefits. Due to the social security reform, there has been an increase in contribution and rates and a reduction in the monthly pension payments. All insured persons and pensioners can now find all their data online.

Every individual (employer, employee, pensioner, dependent family member, child) living in Greece needs an AMKA or social security number to receive social security and to obtain a health booklet. Depending on the insured person's personal situation, they may receive benefits and allowances for the following: medical care, hospital care and hospitalization, free preventive dental care and dental treatment, free physiotherapy and rehabilitation, maternity and childbirth, maternity leave, sickness or accident, pensions, and funeral allowance.

There are also several private Greek health insurance companies that comply with the Greek laws and have become popular among the population, especially since the crisis erupted. Private health insurance is compulsory in Greece for anyone not covered by the state system and especially for foreigners living in Greece who when applying for a residence permit are obligated to show proof of health-care coverage. Private health care is recommended for travelers to Greece who intend to stay any length of time in the country. It is also recommended for expatriates who are working in Greece and not receiving full health-care benefits.

*Angelyn Balodimas-Bartolomei*

**See also:** Chapter 4: Health Care.

**Further Reading**

Council of Europe. 2017. "35th Annual Report on the Application of the European Code of Social Security." General Report. Hellenic Republic. Ministry of Labor, Social

Security and Social Solidarity. Application of the European Code of Social Security by Greece. Accessed February 15, 2019. https://rm.coe.int/report-art74-code-greece-submitted-2017/168077c889.

European Commission. 2017. "Your Social Security Rights in Greece." Directorate – General for Employment, Social Affairs and Inclusion. Accessed February15, 2019. http://ec.europa.eu/social/BlobServlet?docId=13767&langId=en.

Imergut, Ellen M., Karen M. Anderson, and Isabelle Schulze. 2007. *The Handbook of West European Pension Politics.* Oxford: Oxford University Press.

## Women in the Workforce

Greek women continue to climb the corporate and educational ladders in Greece, mirroring similar developments throughout Europe and the Western world. This parity was achieved after incremental progress over the course of several decades.

The first concerted efforts to encourage professional education of women began in the late 1800s with a focus on educating women to serve as teachers. One such undertaking was detailed by Dr. Achilles Rose in an address to the Alumni Association of the New York Training School for Nurses in 1901. He described the efforts undertaken by seventy-two men to raise the funds necessary to educate women teachers in 1836. Within fifty years of its founding, the school educated more than two thousand teachers that were based in all areas of Greece. Today, this organization operates a number of schools in Greece that collectively serve more than nine thousand children.

Another early effort encouraged women to pursue nursing education. In 1875, Queen Olga launched the first nursing school in Greece "to educate women nurses according to the rules of science." Named Evangelismos, it was only the third such school in the world at the time. Greece became the first nation in Europe to offer a generalized nursing curriculum.

Today, as throughout the Western world, women are entrenched in most aspects of Greek society, and as such, they are represented in most professional fields and studies. One exception, religion, remains male dominated. In the Greek Orthodox Church, only men can become priests.

As would be expected, women currently occupy the majority of teaching and nursing positions in Greece. Additionally, they are well represented in the fields of engineering, architecture, law, social services, and health care.

An indicator of the level of progress being made is the increasing number of women pursuing higher education degrees. In 2017, the number of women attending colleges and universities in Greece exceeded the number of men. Women account for a majority of the degrees issued within the fields of education, arts and humanities, social sciences, business and law. In 2005, the OECD found that 43 percent of students pursuing doctoral-level degrees in Greece were women. Iceland was at the top of the list with women making up 59 percent of advanced degree students.

Women in the professions encounter challenges similar to those of professional women throughout the Western world. Although equal pay for equal work is the law of the land in Greece, the reality is that women do not earn as much as men. In 2010, women earned 22 percent less than their male counterparts. The European Union average was 16.4. This was a marked improvement from the 1970s when the gap was 35 percent and the 1990s when it decreased to 30 percent.

Another issue that disproportionally impacts working women is the inherent responsibility they have in caring for younger and older members of their family. In Greece, as elsewhere, care of children and elderly is often a task that women bear. These concerns impact the number of women who are able to maintain their employment while also caring for family members. It may also account for a higher number of women in part-time jobs.

The impact of the recent economic crisis in Greece furthered this burden when the austerity measures taken by the government led to significant cuts in social services and health care. Many families that had previously paid migrant women to provide care for children or elderly family members could not afford to pay for this assistance. In 2010, a study of the EU-27 nations revealed that 68.6 percent of the female population in Greece had direct care responsibilities versus an average of 28.3 percent in the EU-27—a striking 40 percent difference. The study referred to the reemergence of the stereotype *nikokira*, the female homemaker who undertakes the burden of the family's care work when financial resources are limited. According to the study, nearly 75 percent of the respondents felt this inequity was a key reason that more women did not enter the political realm.

Professional women were also impacted by the government's austerity measures when drastic reductions in employment, pay, and benefits were enacted. Since a large number of professional women were employed in the health and education sectors (as well as other public sectors) that are government operated, they were disproportionately impacted by these cuts and many lost their jobs.

As Greece begins to recover economically, the number of employed women professionals will increase. Wages and benefits in the government sector are unlikely to increase dramatically in the near term because of the austerity cuts that were made. Women employed in the private sectors are likely to see more growth in wages than their peers in the public sector.

*John Psiharis*

**See also:** Chapter 4: Overview. Chapter 7: Gender Equality; Women in the Armed Forces; Women in Politics and the Parliament.

**Further Reading**

Davaki, Konstantina. 2013. "The Policy on Gender Equality in Greece." European Parliament, Directorate General for Internal Policies, Policy Department C. Citizens' Rights and Constitutional Affairs. Brussels. Accessed December 7, 2017. http://www.europarl.europa.eu/RegData/etudes/note/join/2013/493028/IPOL-FEMM_NT(2013)493028_EN.pdf.

Rose, Achilles. 1901. "The Progress of Women in Modern Greece." *The American Journal of Nursing* 1, no. 11 (August). Accessed December 7. 2017. https://www.jstor.org/stable/3402378?seq=1#page_scan_tab_contents.

Ziogou, Theologia, Aliki Dimitriadou, and Evangelos Fradelos. 2013. "The History of Nursing Education in Modern Greece." *Balkan Military Medical Review* 16, no. 3 (July–September). Accessed December 21, 2017. https://www.researchgate.net/publication/262182738_The_History_of_Nursing_Education_in_Modern_Greece.

CHAPTER 5

# RELIGION AND THOUGHT

## OVERVIEW

Religion is one of the forces that have historically influenced the Greek cultural identity and tradition and one that remains prevalent even today. According to a survey conducted from June 2015 to July 2016 by the Pew Research Center, about 90 percent of Greeks identify religiously with the Greek Orthodox doctrine, one of the major denominations of Eastern Orthodox Christianity that traces its origins to the early Church Fathers, such as Apostle Paul and Disciples Andrew and John.

The same survey concludes that family tradition and national culture constitute integral elements of one's religious identity. For three out of every four Greeks, being Orthodox is a prerequisite to "being truly Greek." Indeed, for most Greeks, Orthodoxy goes beyond being a religious practice. Even those who do not attend church on a regular basis or refrain from observing the church's rites, such as the *Sarakosti* (the seven-week fasting period preceding Easter Sunday), will return to their ancestral villages and join their families and local communities in celebrating the major Orthodox holidays.

The most significant religious observances on the Greek Orthodox calendar include Holy Week and Easter Sunday (whose exact date is determined by reference to the first full moon after the spring equinox), Christmas on December 25, and the Assumption of Virgin Mary into heaven on August 15 (*Dekapentavgoustos*). The common feature of all three is that they are preceded by a period where the faithful are expected to abstain from eating meat and, more generally, engage in prayer, recollection, and penance. The centrality of Lent observance in Greek Orthodoxy has greatly influenced Greek cuisine and culinary culture, inspiring delicacies such as the traditional *lagana* (a type of flatbread), the *taramasalata* (a popular appetizer featuring salted roe), and *magiritsa* (a soup with lamb parts that brings about the end of fasting).

In addition to the aforementioned holidays, the Greek Orthodox tradition is associated with additional festivities. Saints, who are central in the religious doctrine, are celebrated on specific dates. Most Greeks celebrate their name days as fervently as their birthdays, and cities organize large-scale festivities in honor of their patron saints. For example, processions and parades take place in Thessaloniki on October 26, the day dedicated to Saint Demetrios, the protector of the city (*poliouchos*). Likewise, throughout the summer, religious festivals (*panigyria*) are organized across the country, bringing together food, music, dance, and religious observance.

The picturesque monasteries and traditional iconography are also significant aspects of religious life in Greece. More than two hundred monasteries are scattered throughout the country. Each has its own unique history and charm, and many of them are recognized as UNESCO World Heritage Sites. The monastic communities on the Athos peninsula (Holy Mount) are often said to form the "spiritual heart" of Greece. They attract numerous visitors from the Balkan area and beyond. Other iconic Greek monasteries include the Monastery of Saint John the Theologian on the island of Patmos and Meteora (literally translating as "suspended in the air") whose ancient monastic edifices hang on a gigantic rock in the middle of the Thessaly plain.

Iconography in Greek Orthodoxy follows a tradition that dates back to the Byzantine era. As objects of veneration, rather than worship, Orthodox icons are distinctively two-dimensional and abstract. They often appear to be limited to austere facial expression and the reproduction of the same religious scenes. The creation of an icon is, nevertheless, a highly complicated process, and different icons may present substantial variation based on artistic technique, colors selected, and material used. Icons are found not only in churches, monasteries, and other places of religious worship but also in homes, offices, and public buildings, revealing the deep impact that religious tradition continues to maintain over daily life in Greece.

Although Greece is largely secular, the relationship between church and the state has deep roots, which can be traced back to the country's struggle for independence from the Ottoman Empire. The church's financial and spiritual support at the time was a major contributor in the successful outcome of the Greek War of Independence (1821–1929) and the foundation of the modern Greek state in 1832. As a result, in practice, religion continues to determine political outcomes and shape the current affairs agenda.

The Greek Constitution includes several provisions that regulate the interplay between religion and politics, effectively deepening their bond. Article 3 of the constitution notably endorses Greek Orthodoxy as the "prevailing religion" in the country. Even though such designation is not intended to identify Greek Orthodoxy as an official state religion, it does recognize its appeal to a vast majority of the Greek population and its significance in the public sphere.

The constitution additionally includes provisions that safeguard the core values of the Greek Orthodox *dogma* and facilitate its expressions and rituals. For example, Article 3 recognizes the divine inspiration of the original text of the Holy Scripture, which is written in ancient Greek, and states that its content must be maintained unaltered. It thus prohibits its translation into any other "form of language" (including modern Greek) without the prior consent of the church.

In addition, Article 105 of the constitution awards a special, self-governing status to the Athos peninsula and subjects it to the jurisdiction of the Ecumenical Patriarchate. The privileges granted by law to the Holy Mount include the *avaton*, namely the restriction of access of women to the male monastic communities in the area.

Notwithstanding the recognition of the "prevalence" of Greek Orthodoxy, the constitution also recognizes and protects freedom of religion. Article 13 expressly states that the freedom of religious conscience is inviolable: individuals enjoy civil rights and liberties without prejudice to their individual beliefs. In addition, the constitution welcomes the exercise of all known religions. In other words, and subject to very few limitations, individuals who adhere to a religion other than Greek Orthodoxy can freely celebrate their faith or otherwise perform rites of worship.

As Greece's religious composition changes, the aforementioned legal safeguards become increasingly important. The Greek state is often criticized on the lagging implementation of measures intended to facilitate the religious expression of minority religions. A notable example involved the lack of political initiative in establishing a mosque in downtown Athens. The building of the mosque had been part of the city's political agenda for fourteen years before it was opened in November of 2020. Islam is notably the second-largest religion in Greece and maintains a large number of practitioners (estimated to be between two hundred thousand and five hundred thousand) in the large cities. Historically, the majority of Greek Muslims lived in Western Thrace, forming a distinct religious, linguistic, and cultural community (the so-called Muslim minority of Thrace), to whom the Greek state had conferred special status and a series of privileges. In recent years, however, the number of Greek Muslims has been expanding as a result of migratory flows from the greater Balkan area as well as North Africa, the Middle East, and Asia.

The Jews comprise another historically significant religious minority in Greece. However, the number of Judaism practitioners had substantially declined after the Holocaust, and today only about five thousand are estimated to reside in the large metropolitan areas of the country. Finally, Catholics complete Greece's religious demography. Estimated to comprise around fifty thousand practitioners, they are mainly concentrated in Athens, the Cyclades, and the Ionian Islands.

In line with global trends, the number of atheists, agnostics, and otherwise religiously unaffiliated individuals in Greece has been on the rise in the past decades, especially among the younger generations. The general consensus is that censuses and statistical surveys often fail to capture the impact of such change in Greek society and the resulting dynamics.

Among others, the relationship between religious freedom and other civil rights (in particular, the right to free speech) has witnessed significant tensions in recent years. The omission of religious affiliation from identification documents, the introduction of civil oaths, the provision of the option to undergo alternative military service to conscientious objectors, and the abolition of the "blasphemy laws" are examples of administrative practice evidencing that the Greek state is becoming more secular while Greek society is transforming into one that is increasingly tolerant of religious diversity.

*Angeliki Varela*

**Further Reading**

Pew Research Center. 2017. "Religious Belief and National Belonging in Central and Eastern Europe." May 10, 2017. https://www.pewforum.org/2017/05/10/religious-belief-and-national-belonging-in-central-and-eastern-europe/.

## Evil Eye

The ancient Greeks believed in the *mati* (evil eye). As many as 60 percent of modern-day Greeks continue to believe in the power a person can have to harm another person, animal, or even an inanimate object by casting a glance their way. The person causing harm may not even have any ill intent, although it is generally thought that there is admiration and/or jealousy involved. Especially susceptible to the evil eye are brides and babies. Those giving compliments are advised to say "May you not get the evil eye" or "ptu, ptu, ptu," which represents spitting three times. People believe that symptoms of the evil eye include lethargy, headache, aches and pains, illnesses, and even death.

The evil eye can even harm animals or inanimate objects. The author was told the following story about the evil eye's effect: An archaic relic used as a water trough cracked down the middle with a "Bam" the instant an admirer said it was beautiful.

Sophie checks to see if a patron at her restaurant has the *mati* (evil eye) by dropping olive oil into a cup to see what shape it forms. To get rid of the evil eye, she will say silent prayers that she will not reveal to anyone else. A majority of Greeks believe that a jealous person can inadvertently, with just a glance, give someone the evil eye; this can result in malaise, aches and pains, and even death. (Photo by Elaine Thomopoulos)

The belief in the evil eye is prevalent throughout the Middle East and Europe, but what causes it, how to diagnose it, and how to get rid of it varies, even within various regions of Greece. One method of diagnosis is for the "healer," who is usually a woman, to place a drop of olive oil in a cup of water. If the oil dissipates, the person has been *matiasmeni* (evil-eyed); if it floats, there is no problem. Another method is to drop two or three drops of olive oil into a glass of water. If the drops remain separated, the test concludes there is no evil eye, but if they merge into one, the evil eye is present.

The healer, after detemining that the person has the "evil eye," says secret, silent prayers, which she has been taught by an experienced healer, to draw the evil spirits out of the person who is affected.

Greeks use various *philahta* (prophylactics) to guard against the evil eye. Crosses are believed to be one of the best protections.

Glass amulets resembling a blue eye can also be worn to ward off the *mati*. Mothers pin little pillow-like pouches filled with such things as a few drops of holy water, flowers from Good Friday services, and garlic on their children's garments. Another preventative measure is garlic rubbed behind the ear. Some farmers drape amulets on the necks of their goats, sheep, or horses to protect them.

The Greek Orthodox Church does not believe that a lay person has the power to diagnose the evil eye using the aforementioned rituals or get rid of the evil spirits caused by the evil eye. However, the church does believe that a person can be under the influence of evil powers and has special prayers of exorcism written by Saints Chrysostom and Basil that priests can use. The church uses the term *vaskania* for the evil eye.

Rev. Papademetriou explains "Four prayers of exorcism by Saint John Chrysostom and the three of Saint Basil ask in the name of God to deliver the possessed from the captivity of the devil" (Papademetriou 1990).

*Elaine Thomopoulos*

**See also:** Chapter 15: Sidebar: *Komboloi* (Worry Beads) Relieve Tension and Create a Meditative Experience.

**Further Reading**

Cowan, Jane. 1988. "Evil Eye." In *Insights Guide: Greece*, edited by Karen Van Dyck, 277–278. Singapore: APA publication, LTD.

Papademetriou, George. 1990. "Exorcism in the Orthodox Church." September 9, 1990. Accessed April 1l 2021. https://www.goarch.org/-/exorcism-in-the-orthodox-church?__cf_chl_jschl_tk__=e4fd44e3c3624ef550f235e2f1501c4053215383-1620213351-0-AVb6_IgTYAy7XeHybqBeOKOnIYvsswOXvih6PsA0w7LnniWXyW95nYljim1_iwn4VgycDyO8sqL0Yc02L7XUavWH_v8LoTTivC-b6IUJ-bcn4aE88UpkqYOuagcA.

## Freedom of Religion

Freedom of religion is deeply enshrined in the Greek Constitution. Even though it recognizes Greek Orthodoxy as the "prevailing religion" in the country, it also includes a series of provisions safeguarding individuals' religious rights. Specifically, Article 13 of the constitution expressly refers to the freedom of religious conscience and the freedom to worship and engage in religious practices without hindrance, subject to certain limitations.

According to the constitution, the freedom of religious conscience is inviolable. This means that individuals can enjoy civil rights and liberties without prejudice against their individual beliefs. Conversely, an individual cannot be exempt from discharging his obligations to the Greek state or refuse to comply with the laws on religious grounds.

Furthermore, the constitution welcomes the exercise of all "known" religions. Such religions can freely perform rites of worship under the protection of the law, but their ministers are subject to the same treatment, in terms of supervision and obligations vis-à-vis the Greek state, as are Greek Orthodox priests.

There are three important limitations setting the frame for the protection of the freedom of religion. First, the constitutional protection only extends to "known" religions, namely religions that have acquired at least one permit to operate a place of worship. Second, religious practices and rites cannot disturb the Greek public order or good morals. Third, the constitution prohibits proselytism, that is, all actions attempting to convert an individual to another religion.

Although the constitutional framework on the protection of religion in Greek is comprehensive, its implementation has often been the subject of heated debates. Underlying these discussions is the dynamics between the Greek state and the Greek Orthodox Church, as the latter has been historically influential in shaping public affairs and the social agenda. At issue are often the extent to which the state favors administrative practices endorsed by the church and the de facto discrimination of individuals with different religious views.

The construction of a mosque in Athens is a case reflecting lack of political initiative in ascertaining the exercise of religious freedoms by individuals adhering to minority religions. In 2006, the government provided the go-ahead for the construction of an official place of worship for the city's Muslim population; in 2016, the Parliament enacted regulation that would reportedly accelerate the completion of the building; in 2019, it was constructed; and in November 2020, after the appointment of an imam, it opened its doors to the public.

Political reluctance to implement initiatives that could create tension with the Greek Orthodox Church often results in indirect restrictions of the civil rights of Christians as well. Despite strong opposition by the church, which only recognizes the rite of burying the dead in cemeteries, cremation of the dead achieved legal status in 2006. A crematory was finally built in 2019. Before that time, the families of the deceased could only carry out the process abroad, at a high administrative, economic, and emotional cost.

Another field where the freedom of conscience often comes into play is military service. Greece offers conscientious objectors the right to perform alternative community-based service in lieu of the mandatory army conscription. However, conscientious objectors must be verified as such by a special committee of the Greek army. In addition, alternative service (currently set at fifteen months) lasts for a substantially longer duration than military service. In this respect, the provisions on conscientious objector status are often described as punitive.

In recent years, the Greek administration has made progress in safeguarding the right not to disclose religious beliefs in public. In 2000, the government repealed the inscription of the holder's religion on civilian identity cards, claiming that the mandatory revelation of an individual's religious affiliation was contrary to the data protection laws. Likewise, civilians who must formally swear in, to assume an office in the civil service or testify as witnesses in criminal and civil trials, can choose between taking a religious or civilian oath.

Until recently, Greece was one of the few European countries that criminalized blasphemy. Its blasphemy laws punished any "public and malicious blasphemy against

God . . . the Greek Orthodox Church and any other religion tolerable in Greece" with imprisonment for up to two years. In addition, any "public manifestation of a lack of respect for the divinity" could result in jail for up to six months or the payment of a 3,000 euro fine. Opponents of the blasphemy laws viewed them as redundant and as prioritizing religion (particularly the Greek Orthodox faith) over other individual freedoms and criticized their selective enforcement by overly sensitive individuals in "petty" cases. For example, in 1988, Orthodox activist groups protested against Martin Scorsese's film *The Last Temptation of Christ* by demonstrating outside cinemas and eventually initiating legal proceedings. Recognizing religion as a "vector of spiritual civilization," the court granted an injunction and, as a result, the film was banned from public screenings in the country, despite having previously been approved for distribution.

In another notable case, in 2014, a young blogger received a ten-month prison sentence for creating a social media account titled Elder Pastitsios, a wordplay between the name of the revered Athos monk Elder Paisios and the traditional Mediterranean dish *pasticcio*. The court eventually acquitted him of all charges, acknowledging that the intention of the account was to mock the general public's obsession with apocalyptic prophecies and sensational journalism rather than to ridicule religion.

Enforcement of the blasphemy laws had long drawn significant pressure on the government from the national and international communities. The blasphemy law provisions were ultimately repealed on July 1, 2019.

*Angeliki Varela*

**See also:** Chapter 3: Constitution.

**Further Reading**

"Blasphemy Laws: Wrong on So Many Levels." *The Economist*, March 14, 2014. Accessed April 15, 2019. https://www.economist.com/erasmus/2014/03/14/wrong-on-so-many-levels.

Freedom House. 2010. "Policing Belief: The Impact of Blasphemy Laws on Human Rights – Greece." October 21, 2010. Accessed April 15, 2019. https://www.refworld.org/docid/4d5a700bc.html.

Speed, Madeleine. 2019. "The Battle to Build a Mosque in Athens." *FT Magazine*, February 1, 2019. Accessed April 15, 2019. https://www.ft.com/content/ae4fa654-2416-11e9-8ce6-5db4543da632.

U.S. Department of State. 2017. "International Religious Freedom Report for 2017: Greece." Accessed January 5, 2021. http://www.state.gov/j/drl/rls/irf/religiousfreedom/index.htm?year=2017&dlid=280912.

## Greek Orthodox Holidays

The Greek Orthodox Church is not opposed to enjoying life unless doing so separates one from God. Hence church holidays, some of which are also public holidays, often include feasting, dancing, and sometimes parades and fireworks. Additionally, in rural areas select churches celebrate the name day of their patron saints with festivities. Sometimes offices, banks, schools, and businesses are closed not only on feast days but also on the days before and after.

The chief religious holiday, Easter, is preceded by a forty-day Lent during which parishioners are expected to focus on their faith by abstaining from various foods. The first day of Lent, Clean Monday, is a national holiday when Greeks often go on picnics or fly kites. Although festivities are not permitted during Lent, the *Apokries* (carnival) which takes place before Lent can involve up to two weeks of private parties and communal feasting and dancing, if not parades of masqueraders.

On Palm Sunday, which commemorates Jesus's entry into Jerusalem before his crucifixion, parishioners receive crosses made of blessed palm leaves. During the following week, Holy Week, services are held at least once a day. On Good Friday, the day of Jesus's crucifixion, there may be up to three services, and on Easter, Jesus's resurrection is celebrated in candle-lit midnight services, followed by banquets of roast lamb, red Easter eggs, and numerous Greek specialties. After Easter, the major religious holiday is Pentecost. For many Greeks, Pentecost, which commemorates the anointing of Jesus's disciples with the Holy Spirit, is a three-day holiday. Typically, Pentecost occurs about fifty days after Easter. Since the date of Easter is based on the Julian calendar, the date of Pentecost, like that of Easter, is movable and often differs from that of other Christian groups.

In contrast, the date of Epiphany, January 6, is fixed. Epiphany, literally translated as "appearance," celebrates Jesus's baptism in the Jordan River, at which time all three members of the Holy Trinity (God, Jesus, and the Holy Spirit) were present and Jesus was publicly revealed as son of God. During Epiphany, waters are blessed, and parishioners receive bottles of holy water.

The March 25 church holiday of the Annunciation, where Mary learns that she will give birth to a Savior, coincides with Greek Independence Day. Mary's death and her assumption into heaven are commemorated on August 15, the Dormition of the Virgin Mary. People flock in droves to their ancestral villages to light a candle at a local church named after Mary and to enjoy the community festival. Others make pilgrimages to famed churches named after Mary on the islands of Naxos and Tinos.

In recent times, Greeks have adopted the Western custom of exchanging gifts on Christmas, rather than on New Year's. On both holidays, children go from door to door with harmonicas singing *kalanta*, traditional songs about the season. New Year's Day also features the cutting of a special sweet bread containing a coin. The person receiving the piece with the coin is considered to have luck throughout the coming year.

*Aphrodite Matsakis*

**See also:** Chapter 5: Greek Orthodox Regional Celebrations. Chapter 13: Byzantine Ecclesiastical Music. Appendix A: A Day in the Life of a Retired Couple.

**Further Reading**

Tomkinson, John L. 2003. *Festive Greece: A Calendar of Tradition.* Athens: Anagnosis Publications.

## Greek Orthodox Regional Celebrations

*Kathari Deftera* (Clean Monday), a significant public holiday of the year, signals the starting point of Lent, which lasts for approximately forty days before the celebration of Easter. The church prohibits the eating of eggs, dairy, fish, and meat during Lent. Fasting foods such olives and *fasolado* (bean soup) are well established. Made without fermented dough and baked especially for Clean Monday, *lagana*—a crispy flatbread—is a favorite for dipping in *taramasalata*, a pâté created from roe, breadcrumbs, salt, lemon, and olive oil. *Halva* (a popular dessert made with tahini) and *tsipouro* (grape-crush brandy) are traditional household offerings. At coastline vistas and neighborhood squares all over Greece, decorative handcrafted kites blanket the sky. The tradition of flying kites on Clean Monday coincides with other colorful outdoor excursions, such as picnics and circle-dancing hand in hand to traditional folk music.

A unique ritual based in Byzantine mystery occurs at Olympus on the island of Karpathos on the Tuesday before Easter (*Lambri Triti*). Four wooden church icons, each weighing about fifty pounds, are carried on the shoulders of worshippers through rugged terrain for about five miles. The priest accompanies the procession to the first stop, a graveyard, where he says prayers for the deceased.

For the celebration of Easter, churches fill to capacity. At midnight, candles are lit one by one by worshippers, filling the church with light. The priest announces, "Christ has risen," and parishioners respond, "Truly He has risen." The sound of jubilant fireworks and crackling red-dyed eggs charge the air. People compete to see who will break each other's eggshells first. This ritual signals the cessation of the fast. Families and friends get together after the midnight service to eat *magiritsa* (lamb tripe soup) and eggs. This is followed by family gatherings the next day with the main course, usually lamb.

Following the midnight *Anastasis* service on the island of Chios, young people from opposing churches in Vrontados—Agios Markos and Panagia Eridiani—fire twenty-five thousand rockets, which soar through the sky, their target the opposing church. The night brings together parishioners clasping candles aflame, clergy chanting gospel, and youngsters lighting rockets that cloak the sky.

Easter is one of the most important religious holidays. Another is the Assumption of the Virgin Mary into heaven. This religious holiday, celebrated on August 15, brings the pious to churches named after *Panagia* (the Virgin Mary). Some remain in church for an all-night vigil during the night of August 14 and 15. Festive celebrations follow church services on August 15.

One of the largest celebrations honoring *Panagia* occurs on the Aegean island of Tinos, where the icon of the Virgin Mary takes center stage. The miraculous icon was found buried underground in 1823.

The Vitsa, Epirus *Panegyri*, which is celebrated on August 14, 15, and 16, emphasizes the music of the region. The festival in the small village of Vitsa, like many of the other village festivals throughout Greece, reunites Greeks who have immigrated to other places and fills them with a sense of nostalgia. They take comfort in the *parea* of others who come from the same hometown.

Saints' days are also occasions for festivals. Hundreds travel via ferries from the mainland to Zakynthos to celebrate the island's beloved sixteenth-century patron saint, Saint Dionysios, on August 24. On this date, his remains were transferred from the monastery where he died to the city of Zakynthos. Crowds venerate the saint, who is paraded down the streets of the capital in his upright glass-enclosed casket. The parade includes hundreds of clergy, band members, and representatives of the armed forces. Fireworks and dancing, as well as vendors selling trinkets and food, enliven the festivities. Traditional Zakythinean food served includes *fitoures*, a crunchy-crusted delicacy made of deep-fried farina sprinkled with cinnamon and sugar, and *mantolato*, a nougat made from egg whites, almonds, and honey. The community and visitors also celebrate the saint with this type of festival on the date of his death—December 17.

In July, Volissos, Chios, is home to the three-day celebration of Agia Markalla, the island's guardian saint. This fourteenth-century saint was said to have been beheaded by her father.

Originally thought to be a pagan festival, but now honoring Saints Constantine and Helen, the "Anasternaria" is held in both Langada and Agia Eleni in northern Greece. Participants, carrying the icons of Saints Constantine and Helen, dance in a trance-like state on red-hot charcoal embers in a fire-walking ritual.

*Alexander Fatouros*

**See also:** Chapter 10: Holidays. Chapter 13: Overview. Appendix D: Holidays

**Further Reading**

Kolasa-Sikiaridi, Kerry. 2017. "Greece Celebrates with Carnival Events Across the Country." *Greek Reporter*, February 19, 2017. Accessed August 25, 2017. http://greece.greekreporter.com/2017/02/19/greece-celebrates-with-carnival-events-across-the-country/.

Leontis, Artemis. 2009. *Culture and Customs of Greece*. Westport, CT: Greenwood Press.

National Geographic. 2009. "Firewalking." Youtube video, June 30, 2009. Accessed November 17, 2017. https://www.youtube.com/watch?v=aKhbjGKOSIA.

## Greek Orthodoxy

Greek Orthodoxy, also called Eastern Orthodoxy or Orthodox Christianity, is the main religion in Greece. Between 250 and 300 million people of various ethnic groups practice the Eastern Orthodox faith worldwide. Although not all Greeks attend church faithfully, Greece is full of churches, and church holidays are widely celebrated, often with great merriment. Like other Christians, Orthodox Christians believe in the divinity and resurrection of Christ. Yet there are important differences between Orthodoxy, which has preserved much of ancient Christianity, and other Christian groups.

The eleventh-century Greek Orthodox Church of Panagia Kapnikarea stands prominently amid a vibrant shopping thoroughfare, Ermou Street, in central Athens. Built with intricate stones on the ruins of an ancient temple dedicated to a Greek goddess, the Byzantine-styled church offers visitors a sense of calm. By stepping inside the candle-lit church, they can witness the intricate mosaics and fading icons of the Panagia (Virgin Mary), for whom the church was dedicated. (Photo by Alexander Fatouros)

Although Greece has no official state religion, most Greeks consider Orthodoxy part of their Greek identity. Even those who ignore the church's largely vegan fast days proudly note that Orthodoxy can be traced back to the Apostle Paul and two of Jesus's direct disciples, Andrew and John.

These apostles founded churches in Greece, then appointed successors called bishops, who then selected the next generation of bishops, and so forth. Since Orthodoxy maintained this process, its clergy claim a direct connection with Jesus's apostles.

As the early church spread, it was divided into five districts (called patriarchates), each of which was administered by the bishop of a significant city in that district. Beginning in 325 CE, the bishops of these cities (i.e., Constantinople, Rome, Alexandria, Antioch, and Jerusalem) held meetings (ecumenical councils) during which they made decisions regarding church doctrine and regulations for church organization and discipline (canon law).

Based on the belief that Christ is the head of the church and that therefore church issues were best resolved not individually by just one man but by church leaders working together, these decisions represented the consensuses reached by all five bishops, each of whom had equal voting power. Hence, despite certain regional variations and heretical groups, originally all of Christendom adhered to the same basic dogma as today's Greek or Eastern Orthodoxy.

Nevertheless, the patriarchate of Rome became increasingly influenced by Roman law and monarchical views of government. Due to these and other growing cultural and political differences, tensions arose between the Roman patriarchate and the patriarchates east of Rome. Eventually the Roman bishop insisted on being the sole, infallible leader of the church and on changing certain doctrine. The other bishops, however, wanted to continue making decisions collectively and retain the pre-agreed-upon doctrine.

Consequently, in 1054 CE, after some thousand years of relative unity, Christianity was split between Catholicism, headed by the bishop (pope) of Rome, and Orthodoxy. To this day, Orthodoxy has no supreme ruler. Instead it is organized into various self-ruled regional patriarchates. The Church of Greece, for example, is autonomous, save for decisions made jointly during ecumenical councils where, as in the past, each patriarchate has only one vote.

Unlike Catholicism, Orthodoxy allows its priests to marry. Bishops and monastics, however, need to remain celibate. Also, unlike Catholicism (and its offshoot, Protestantism), Orthodoxy rejects the idea of original sin (the belief that everyone is born guilty and condemned due to the sin of Adam). Instead, it holds that everyone is born in the likeness of God and is only responsible for their own sin, not Adam's. Due to Adam, however, humans are attracted to sin, but they need to resist this attraction in order to fulfill the image of God within them from birth.

Orthodoxy also rejects other doctrines that have been cited as contributing to the heightened sin consciousness found in Catholicism and Protestantism. For example, it views as heretical the widespread belief that Christ was crucified primarily as a penalty for sins in order to appease an angry, vengeful God. Although Orthodoxy does not minimize a day of judgment, it focuses on God's love and on how Christ's life, death, and resurrection served to connect God and man and created a pathway to eternal life. Due to these and other doctrinal differences, the heightened sin consciousness frequently found in Catholicism and in certain Protestant denominations is largely absent in Orthodoxy (as practiced in Greece).

Historically, Orthodoxy has rejected any number of other doctrines and practices that it deemed to be inconsistent with those of the apostles. Hence, it has remained largely unchanged for centuries. Literally translated, the term "Orthodoxy" means correct or right belief.

Nevertheless, Orthodoxy is open to metaphorical, as opposed to literal, interpretations of certain biblical passages. It also acknowledges the existence of certain biblical inconsistencies, which it views as reflecting the numerous ways that God spoke to man.

Fundamental to Orthodoxy are the Holy Scriptures (consisting of both the Old and New Testament), the sacraments, the saints, and icons. The central Orthodox worship service is the Divine Liturgy (analogous to Catholic Mass), during which it is believed that the faithful can connect with the Risen Christ by participating in the sacrament of Eucharist (Holy Communion). Other sacraments are confession, baptism, chrismation, matrimony, unction (anointing of the sick), and the holy orders (ordination of clergy). Funerals, the blessing of the waters (Epiphany), and the blessing of homes, rings, gardens, animals, and so on are also considered sacred actions.

Orthodoxy views sacraments as God's way of using ordinary physical matter to strengthen parishioners and help them become more virtuous. An example occurs during the sacrament of communion, when the bread and wine offered by the priest represents the body and blood of Christ. Exactly how this occurs defies human explanation. Hence Orthodoxy refers to sacraments as Holy Mysteries.

Like other Orthodox rites, the Divine Liturgy is rich with incense, singing, Byzantine-style chanting, and pageantry. At one point, the priest, dressed in colorful, embroidered vestments, emerges from a side door holding up the gospels, which are elaborately encased in gold and silver. Accompanying him are altar boys bearing large lit candles or shiny silver and gold banners. As this procession circles the church, parishioners bow their heads and cross themselves.

Another dramatic moment occurs when the priest and altar boys emerge from a side door a second time. The priest holds a glittering gold chalice containing the wine for the Eucharist in one hand and the bread to be used in the other. As this procession passes through the church, the congregation stands in reverent silence.

But the moment the wine and bread are offered up to God, everyone immediately drops to their knees and joins the priest in asking God to consecrate the communion elements. The service culminates with parishioners receiving a spoonful of the Eucharist from the chalice.

Parishioners are expected to prepare for communion by fasting. Technically, they are also to go to confession. During this sacrament, parishioners receive absolution for their sins by confessing them before God and a priest (face-to-face, not in a booth).

Most Greeks, however, skip confession (save in instances of grave sin). Neither do most Greek Orthodox clergy insist on weekly confession (save for monastics). In Orthodox areas outside of Greece, however, sometimes confession is strictly required.

The Divine Liturgy is celebrated every Sunday and on major feast days. Orthodoxy also holds vespers, matins, and other services, especially the week before Easter (Holy Week). In Greece, Easter takes precedence over Christmas and is not commercialized. Typically, Easter, like various other church holidays, is characterized by urban Greeks flooding back to their ancestral villages to attend services and enjoy family and community festivities involving an abundance of food, dancing, and sometimes parades and fireworks.

Feast days are often held to honor a particular saint. Chief among the saints is the Virgin Mary, followed by the apostles and others who risked their lives to uphold the gospel or who helped to lay the foundations of faith. Catholicism requires three miracles for canonization. In Orthodoxy, the only prerequisite is holiness. Yet numerous miracles have been attributed to saints, and saints are often prayed to, but only as intercessors and not as gods.

Among the saints are numerous women. Women played a prominent role in the early church, and in today's Greece, they continue to be a mainstay of Orthodoxy. Although women are not allowed into the priesthood, they can be ordained as deaconesses.

Like saints, icons (paintings of religious figures) are venerated, but not worshipped.

During centuries of Ottoman Muslim rule and numerous other foreign occupations, Greek Orthodox clergy preserved their ancient faith. They also played an active role in Greece's War of Liberation from the Ottomans.

Then, during World War II, unlike official leaders of other Christian groups, the leader of the Greek Orthodox Church in Athens officially denounced Hitler's anti-Semitism and mandated its clergy to protect the Jews. Parishioners were strongly urged to do likewise, despite the risk to their lives. Many Jews were saved, including the entire Jewish population on the island of Zakynthos.

Like their predecessors, today's Greek Orthodox clergy are determined to serve as beacons of Christianity in an increasingly atheistic world.

*Aphrodite Matsakis*

**See also:** Chapter 5: Overview; Greek Orthodox Regional Celebrations; Icons in the Greek Orthodox Church. Chapter 10: Baptism, Chrismation, and Naming Traditions; Funerals; Weddings. Chapter 12: Religious Art and Architecture. Appendix A: A Day in the Life of a Retired Couple.

**Further Reading**

Calivas, Father Alkiviades. "Holy Communion: The Gift of Eternal Life." Accessed December 12, 2018. www.goarch.org/-holy-communion-the=gift-of-eternal-life.

FitzGerald, Kriaki Karidoyones. "Church of Greece Restores Diaconate for Women." Accessed December 10, 2018. https://orthodoxdeaconess.org/contemporary-orthodox-deaconesses/church-of-greece-restores-diaconate-for-women/.

Hughes, V. Antony. "Ancestral versus Original Sin: An Overview with Implications for Psychotherapy." Accessed December 8, 2018. http://stmaryorthodoxchurch.org/orthodoxy/articles/ancestral_versus_original_sin.

Rawlins, Clive. 1997. *Culture Shock! Greece: A Guide to Customs and Etiquette*. Portland, OR: Graphic Arts Center Publishing Company.

"Saint Athanasius and the 'Penal Substitutionary' Atonement Doctrine." Accessed December 4, 2018. http://ww1.antiochian.org/saint-athanasius-and-%E2%80%98penal-substitutionary%E2%80%99-atonement-doctrine.

St. Athanasius Orthodox Academy. 1993. *The Orthodox Study Bible: New Testament and Psalms*. Nashville, TN: Thomas Nelson Publishers.

Thomopoulos, Elaine. 2012. *The History of Greece*: Santa Barbara, CA: Greenwood, an imprint of ABC-CLIO, LLC.

## Icons in the Greek Orthodox Church

Like the saints in the Greek Orthodox Church, icons are to be venerated (deeply respected), not worshipped. In fact, Byzantine icons are not intended to be lifelike or otherwise realistic portrayals of Jesus, the apostles, or the saints. Instead, they attempt to portray their godliness and their God-like love, humility, compassion, devotion to God, or some other virtue.

Icons are also intended to point one to eternity, that is, to a spiritual reality beyond earthly life. Residing in this spiritual realm are the Holy Trinity, angels, and a community of living saints, all of whom are available to support one's Christian journey on earth. Hence in icons, bodies lack musculature and other forms of definition; background scenes, if any, are unrealistically flat and lack any sense of time or season. Instead the focus is on the face, especially the eyes, which, although serious, are to convey a message of comfort and hope.

Icons, such as this one depicting the Virgin Mary and baby Jesus, can be found in every Greek Orthodox church, as well as in homes, sometimes in more than one room, or as part of a spiritual center. Icons depicting people or events from the Bible have been part of the Christian church since its earliest years. The Virgin Mary and the saints depicted in the icons are meant to be venerated, not worshipped. (Photo by Elaine Thomopoulos)

Western religious paintings include a wide variety of individual creative expressions. In contrast, icons are based on church-approved prototypes and can be painted by more than one person. Yet even if only one person is involved, the true creator of an icon is considered to be the Holy Spirit. Hence authentic icons are anonymous and preceded and guided by considerable prayer.

Icons are painted on carefully sanded panels of wood onto which multiple layers of a glue-like substance are applied. After they harden, these layers are covered with a linen cloth, which is then overlaid with gold leaf, onto which paint is applied.

Black, brown, and other dark colors usually symbolize impurity, death, or danger. In general, lighter colors, such as white, blue, and green, represent the heavens, peace, life, or virtue. Although yellow symbolizes sadness, gold, whether in a halo, part of the background, or an area of gold leaf deliberately left unpainted, symbolizes the divine light of Paradise and of Christ.

Icons can be found in every part of a Greek church: the sanctuary, nave, and narthex (entryway). They are also frequently found in homes, sometimes in more than one room, or as part of a spiritual center. In homes, as in churches, icons might be illuminated by a candle floating in a glass container.

In such homes, icons are not decorations but aides to worship and reminders that one is not alone. They are also frequently placed in business establishments, cars, and buses, where they are believed to provide protection from harm.

This abundance of icons and Greece's numerous churches (ranging from majestic cathedrals to one-room chapels) suggest the significance of religion in Greece.

*Aphrodite Matsakis*

**See also:** Chapter 12: Religious Art and Architecture; Modern Greek Art.

**Further Reading**

"The Icon, History, Symbolism, and Meaning." Accessed December 21, 2018. http://www.orthodox.cn/catechesis/iconhistory_en.htm.

## Minority Religions

A survey conducted in 2015 and 2016 by the Pew Research Center showed that 90 percent of the Greek population self-identified with the Greek Orthodox faith. However, despite the country's highly homogenous religious demographic profile, religious minorities have coexisted and thrived in Greece for centuries. Islam is the second-largest religion in the country, while the presence of Jewish, Catholic, and other Christian communities is also significant.

The Pew Research survey showed 2 percent of the Greeks identified with the Muslim religion. Greece's Muslim population is far from homogenous, but it can be broadly divided into two distinct groups. The Muslim minority of Thrace is a religious and linguistic minority comprising Pomak (Bulgarian-speaking), Turkish, and Roma ethnic groups. Under the 1923 Treaty of Lausanne, the Muslim minority enjoys a special status that facilitates the establishment of mosques and waqfs (charitable institutions that administer endowments and real estate property) and the appointment of political and religious leaders, such as muftis and imams. The treaty also confers to members of the Muslim minority a series of privileges, such as quotas for admission to Greek tertiary education and the civil service. Historically, members of the Muslim minority have been entitled to have their family and inheritance matters settled by a mufti in accordance with the Islamic sharia law; however, as affirmed by the European Court of Human Rights in its 2018 decision in *Molla Sali v. Greece*, the application of the sharia law on the Muslim population of Thrace shall be discretionary (not mandatory) and cannot lead to discriminatory outcomes, as compared to the national legal system.

Furthermore, Greece has a substantial active population of Islam practitioners (estimated to be between two hundred thousand and five hundred thousand individuals), which has been increased by recent immigration flows of Muslim populations from North Africa, the Middle East and Asia (Syria, Afghanistan, and Pakistan), and the Balkan area (Albania and North Macedonia). The majority are Sunni practitioners.

Although they do not enjoy the special status and privileges conferred to the Muslim religious minority of Thrace, such practitioners have sizeable and organized communities, mainly in Athens and Thessaloniki. In 2019, a mosque was built in Athens. In November 2020, prayers were held at the mosque for the first time.

The presence of Judaism in Greece dates back to antiquity. Before World War II, the number of Jews in the country was estimated to between sixty thousand and seventy thousand and included both Romaniote and Sephardim populations. The Jewish communities were historically influential in local affairs and played a significant role in the commercial growth and development of Greece's major urban areas. However, as a result of the German occupation of the country during World War II, the vast majority of Greek Jews were deported to concentration camps by the Nazis. After the Holocaust, few of the surviving members returned to Greece. Today, the country's Jewish population is estimated at five thousand. The majority resides in Athens and Thessaloniki.

Catholic Greeks are estimated to be around fifty thousand and are concentrated in Athens, the Cyclades, and the Ionian Islands. The Aegean islands of Syros and Tinos have parishes and villages that are entirely Catholic.

Other Christian denominations with an active presence in Greece include the Ethiopian, Coptic, Armenian Apostolic, and Assyrian Orthodox Churches and Evangelical Church groups. The Jehovah's Witnesses, Seventh-Day Adventists, and Mormons have a small but active population of practitioners in Greece. Buddhism and Hinduism also have small following, mainly in the large cities. As "known religions," they are entitled to operate at least one authorized place of worship. Another notable religious movement is that of Ethnic Hellenism or Hellenic Polytheism. The movement, which achieved "known religion" status in 2017, traces its roots back to mythology and constitutes an attempt to reconstruct the ancient Greek religion and promote a lifestyle based on Hellenic values and virtues.

There is consensus that Greek atheists and agnostics have not been given adequate focus in religious demography studies. With some opinion polls reporting their percentage as high as 14.7 percent, the number of the religiously unaffiliated appears to be rising in recent years, especially among the younger generations.

*Angeliki Varela*

**See also:** Chapter 5: Freedom of Religion. Chapter 6: Jewish Community; Muslim Religious Minority of Western Thrace.

**Further Reading**

Pew Foundation. 2016. "Pew-Templeton Global Religious Projects Future: Greece." Accessed April 22, 2019. http://www.globalreligiousfutures.org/countries/greece#/?affiliations_religion_id=0&affiliations_year=2010&region_name=All%20Countries&restrictions_year=2016.

Pew Foundation. 2017. "Religious Affiliation in Central and Eastern Europe." Accessed April 12, 2021. https://www.pewforum.org/2017/05/10/religious-affiliation/.

Sakellariou, Alexandros. 2017. "Moving from Traditional Religion to Atheism in Greek Society: 'Like a Ship Distancing from the Coast . . .'" April 10, 2017. Accessed April 22,

2019. http://religiongoingpublic.com/archive/2017/moving-from-traditional-religion-to-atheism-in-greek-society-like-a-ship-distancing-from-the-coast.

Tsitselikis, Konstantinos. 2018. "'Old' and 'New' Islam: The Case of Muslims." Accessed April 22, 2019. https://www.sciencespo.fr/ceri/fr/oir/old-and-new-islam-case-muslims.html.

U.S. Department of State. 2017. "International Religious Freedom Report for 2017: Greece." Accessed April 22, 2019. http://www.state.gov/j/drl/rls/irf/religiousfreedom/index.htm?year=2017&dlid=280912.

## Monasteries and Nunneries

Scattered throughout Greece are about two hundred monasteries. Some are on such high cliffs that they seem to be reaching for God. Others are located in or near urban areas. But their goals are the same: to provide spiritual and material support to others and a place of solitude for those who wish to devote themselves to God. Unlike Roman Catholic nuns and monks, Greek monastics do not engage in secular activities. Their days consist of prayer, spiritual counseling, religious services, social welfare, and tasks supporting their monastery, such as farming.

Monasteries also support themselves in one or more of the following ways: by making religious items such as icons, candles, incense, and wood carvings; by teaching traditional arts such as religious painting, Byzantine music, and wine and cheese making; and by making traditional Greek foods, such as jams, breads, and pastries. Some nunneries, such as the Annunciation on the island of Patmos, make and embroider ecclesiastical garments.

### MOUNT ATHOS: OLDEST-SURVIVING MONASTIC COMMUNITY IS HOME TO TWO THOUSAND MONKS

A monastery was established on Mount Athos, referred to as the Holy Mountain, in 961. Seventeen of the twenty Eastern Orthodox monastic communities now located on Mount Athos are Greek; the others are Serbian, Russian, and Bulgarian. There are about two thousand monks. Although the monastery welcomes a limited number of male pilgrims, no females have been allowed there since 1045, although a few have snuck in dressed as males. Mount Athos even bars hens, cows, sheep, nanny goats, mares, and sows. According to the Greek Constitution, Mount Athos is self-governed. In spiritual matters, it is guided by the Ecumenical Patriarchate in Constantinople. Prince Charles of the United Kingdom regularly visits the Vatopedion Monastery on Mount Athos. He and his father, Prince Philip, who was born in Greece but left as an infant, are supporters of the Friends of Mount Athos organization. Prince Philip's grandfather was King George I of Greece.

*Elaine Thomopoulos*

While some monasteries charge for their products and services, others accept donations only. But there are never any charges for spiritual support.

The first monks were hermits who went to deserts, caves, and other isolated areas to pursue a life of contemplation. Over time, however, due to divine inspiration, the desire for greater solitude, or the need to escape marauding invaders, monastic communities were formed in highly inaccessible places.

Hence, during Greece's long periods of invasion, monasteries were able to preserve the Greek language, ancient manuscripts and art, and religious traditions dating back to Byzantine times. Monastics also provided refuge for the needy and played an active role in Greece's War of Independence and in resisting the Nazis during World War II by hiding Jews.

Today monasteries continue to preserve the faith not only by teaching about Orthodoxy but also by respecting the Orthodox belief that human beings are responsible for protecting the earth. Hence monasteries frequently engage in composting, organic gardening, and biological architecture. Biological architecture refers to using materials that are compatible with the environment and designing structures that incorporate the energy-efficient methods of temperature regulation and lighting used by various plants and animals. Some monastics, like the nuns of Holy Monastery of Chrysopigi near Chania, Crete, not only practice biological architecture but also actively promote it. At their Center for Orthodoxy and Conservation, the nuns teach schoolchildren, their teachers, and others various ways of protecting the environment. Additionally, the proceeds from the sale of produce from the nunnery's 130-acre organic farm are used to fund environmental awareness programs both locally and throughout Europe.

Mount Athos, the largest monastic grouping in Greece, is the oldest monastic community in the world. Its twenty monasteries are located on the Halkidiki Peninsula in northeastern Greece. The coastline is so inaccessible and the terrain so rugged that Mount Athos remains one of the most unspoiled parts of Greece. This area is exceptionally beautiful, and its monasteries hold perhaps the richest collection of Christian art, ancient manuscripts, and gold-covered bejeweled Byzantine religious items in Greece. But unlike other monasteries, visitors are restricted to a limited number of select males.

The second-largest cluster of monasteries, the Meteora (which means "suspended in air"), is located on gigantic, vertical rocks in northeast Thessaly. These stone pillars, some over nine meters tall, form a dramatic landscape that draws thousands of tourists. In the past, monks used ropes and nets to descend into the valleys below to grow crops and obtain supplies. Today some steps exist.

In the sixteenth century, Meteora was a thriving community of twenty-four monasteries. However, today only six remain. Some of the monasteries were destroyed due to looting and bombing during the Italian and German occupation during World War II. Two of the six monasteries are nunneries that, as of 2015, housed forty-one nuns, including an Australian woman.

Any number of today's monasteries were built over the ruins of ancient Greek temples or previous monasteries. For example, the Pantokratoros Monastery in Ntaou

Penteli was erected over the remains of an older church that, in turn, was built over an ancient temple. In 1680, pirates looted the monastery and killed all but 2 of its 179 monks. Hence the monastery remained empty until the 1960s, when, with ecclesiastical permission, it was revived by 11 nuns. By 2015, this nunnery housed 40 nuns who ministered to the mentally ill and cared for orphans and provided for their education. Other nunneries, such as the Holy Trinity on the island of Aegina, were also established at the request of a handful of nuns.

Each Greek monastery has its own unique history and charm. But all monasteries are sex segregated and all monastics take vows of celibacy, simplicity, and poverty.

*Aphrodite Matsakis*

**See also:** Chapter 5: Overview; Sidebar: Mount Athos: Oldest-Surviving Monastic Community Is Home to Two Thousand Monks.

**Further Reading**

"Agios Nektarios: Church and Monastery." n.d. Accessed June 10, 2018. https://www.aeginagreece.com/aegina.../aegina.../agios-nektarios-church-monastery/.

"Clifftop Monasteries of Meteora, Greece." n.d. Accessed May 8, 2018. http://www.great-adventures.com/destinations/greece/meteora.html.

Jones, Julia. 2010. "A Spiritual and Ecological Destination." *KPHTH* 2 (April/May): 11—12.

"Nunnery of the Annunciation." n.d. Accessed May 15, 2018. www.patmos-island.com/en/monasteries/info/evangelismos.

Sanidopoulos, John. 2010. "The 179 Martyrs of Ntaou Penteli Monastery." Accessed October 10, 2018. http://www.johnsanidopoulos.com/2010/04/179-holy-martyrs-of-ntaou-penteli-in.html.

Thomopoulos, Elaine. 2012. *The History of Greece*: Santa Barbara, CA: Greenwood, an imprint of ABC/CLIO.

CHAPTER 6

# SOCIAL CLASSES AND ETHNICITY

## OVERVIEW

The composition of the Greek social strata has been drastically transformed throughout the past century and the beginning of this century. After World War II, many Greeks abandoned the agricultural sector and either relocated to the major cities of Greece or settled abroad, resulting in upper social mobility and the expansion of the middle class. Following the fall of the dictatorship in 1974, the composition changed again as new opportunities arose for the Greek citizens and the proportion of educated professionals and family-run businesses increased. Many youths left their villages to study in the free, public universities located in major cities. The education system rapidly developed with enrollment increasing. Since foreign students do not need to take the rigorous entrance examinations, student enrollment became more diverse as more and more immigrants arrived in Greece. In 2009, there were approximately eight thousand students of Albanian, Bulgarian, Romania, Serbian, and Turkish origin studying in Greek universities, technical colleges, professional schools, and private colleges. Additionally, during the same year, there were about twenty-five hundred and three thousand students, mainly Chinese, who were studying in the foreign-language departments of non-Greek-language colleges.

Until the recent economic crisis that started in 2008, it was easier for younger generations, and especially poor rural dwellers, to obtain higher levels of incomes than their parents and to reach the middle class. For decades, the middle class was not only the backbone of the Greek economy and society; it was also considered one of the wealthiest middle classes in the world. Unfortunately, the recent economic crisis has altered this position, with the middle class suffering as a result of decreased incomes, pensions, and property values; increased taxation; and even unemployment. Although the number of billionaires in Greece is low, the country boasts several multimillionaire families who have made their fortune in the shipping, metal, and finance industries.

Throughout most of the twentieth century and still somewhat today, social status in Greece was not based only on economic class but resulted from a combination of other indicators, which included education, occupation, knowledge of foreign languages—especially French and English—and what is known as *philotimo* (love of honor). Therefore, one's sense of social responsibility, community esteem, proper behavior, and public decorum were all determinants of social status. The family, which has always been the most important foundation in Greek society, provided support both financially and emotionally for its members, which often included the extended family. It also played an important role in determining, guiding, and planning each member's career and educational path, even if it meant using the *mesa* (connections) and *rouspheti* (the reciprocal dispensation of favors)—both of which were reinforced during the period of Ottoman rule and are still widely practiced today. Although the role of the family has changed throughout the decades, it continues to be important in Greek society, with elders being highly respected and maintaining specific roles.

Another indicator of social class in Greece has been home ownership with Greeks placing a high value on owning their own urban house or apartment, which is often passed down to the children. As the geographical composition of modern Greece changed and the population became urbanized, more houses and apartments appeared in the major cities. After World War II, many single-family, low-story homes were replaced with blocks of flats, from two stories to ten stories high, so that the urbanized population could purchase apartments at an affordable price. Most of the transformed one-story houses underwent a process called *antiparochi*, which involved a joint venture between the landowner and a builder with the former getting a share of the building rather than being paid in money. The process created what sociologists call a "vertical social differentiation," in which the wealthier, middle-class families lived on the top floors of these apartments with pleasant views of the city while those with lower incomes lived on the first floor or even in the basement. The *antiparochi* process also enabled the owner to provide each daughter with an apartment for her *proika* (dowry), which until 1983 was basically a marriage prerequisite for many young ladies.

In 1821, only 6 percent of the population was urbanized; however, internal migration continued to take place as Greeks moved from the plains and rural areas to urban settlements. This resulted in not only the establishment of several new villages and towns but also the abandonment of others. After World War II, the population became predominately urban with the city of Athens continuing to grow especially during the 1950s and 1960s. The decline of regional areas and the growth of Athens as a primate city were brought on by economic opportunities, international trade, governmental functions, and new educational and health facilities. According to the United Nations estimations, today, 78.7 percent of the population is urban with over three million inhabitants living in Athens. Among the wealthiest areas in the nation's capital are: Ekali, Kifissia, Palio Psychico, and Filothei in Northern Athens; Kolonaki in Central Athens; and Glyfada and Vougliagmeni along the city's Riviera—the coastal area in the southern suburbs of Athens. Despite upward mobility and urbanization, a strong love for one's native village remains, where many Greeks often return to spend their holidays and summer vacations.

The influx of immigrants to Greece has not only changed the composition of the Greek population; it has also led to levels of social and residential segregation among Athenians in the Athens metropolitan area. Immigrant neighborhoods have emerged across the city, in areas such as Patisia, Kipseli, and Sepolia where immigrants find housing in basements or lower floors of degradable, low-rental apartments. Whereas the majority of immigrant and migrant newcomers begin living in Central Athens for a short while upon their arrival, they eventually move into another neighborhood, most often where relatives and other compatriots reside.

One of the first ethnic neighborhoods emerged in the 1970s with a small Pakistani community in Nea Ionia. As more of its members arrived in the 1990s, the community relocated to Agios Ioannis of Renti—a western suburb of Athens. During this time, a Polish neighborhood emerged between Arhanon and the Larissa train station. Another ethnic neighborhood comprised of several immigrant communities from other countries in the former USSR settled in Kallithea, which is located two miles south of the Athens city center. For some, residing near to work was the main priority, with many women from the Philippines and Sri Lanka who worked as babysitters, caretakers, and maids choosing Ambelokipoi. Ethiopians also chose this area.

In addition to the many migrants that have chosen to live in and around Athens, there are also over three thousand unaccompanied migrant and refugee children in Greece. Over one-third have been placed in detention facilities and dirty, crowded police cells in violation of international and Greek law, while the other two-thirds have found safe haven in suitable shelters. Many who are completely homeless have turned to prostitution and/or drug selling to survive and seek to do so in Athens's Omonia and Victoria Squares.

During the 1980s, profound legal policies were introduced that brought forth significant changes, especially for women, in the areas of the Greek family, work, and employment. The reformed "Family Law of 1983" not only modernized the traditional Greek family but also provided for the protection of the human rights and the equality of the sexes. Among several noteworthy measures, the new law instituted civil marriage, abolished the dowry system, facilitated divorce with equal distribution of property, introduced automatic prosecution for the crime of rape, eliminated gender discrimination, decriminalized adultery, allowed women to not take the surname of their husbands, and delimited the dominant position of the father in each family.

The large flow of immigrants, migrants, and asylum seekers arriving in Greece brought forth the requirement for new legislation to address their needs. They faced adverse conditions of work, medical care, and insurance. There is no reliable data on the number of undocumented immigrants in Greece. However, in 1996, the United Nations reported that the media stated that between 80,000 and 110,000 immigrant men and women workers were employed without a work permit.

To work in Greece, one must have a residency permit. In 2015, the Greek Parliament adopted a new law for non–European Union foreign nationals recruited for seasonal employment. The law stipulated that in addition to a fair wage, employers are now obligated to provide them with work contracts, adequate shelter, social security, and the same rights as Greek citizens.

Obtaining Greek citizenship has remained rather difficult for those without Greek origin. In March 2010, the fifty-two-page Citizenship Code was passed specifying eight ways for the acquisition of Greek citizenship, which includes a Greek passport and the Greek national identity card (*taftotita*). Unfortunately, in 2012, the Greek government froze all applications for foreigners of non-Greek origin. The document was revised in 2014, and finally in July 2015, the much-debated Law 4332 was voted in. Until then, Greek citizenship was offered only to individuals who (1) were born to a Greek mother and/or father; (2) claimed Greek origin through an ancestor; (3) were minors under the age of eighteen born out of wedlock, then legally recognized by a Greek national born in Greece; (4) were adopted; or (5) enlisted in Greek armed services. The new law gives the right for citizenship to migrants who were born and/or raised in Greece to acquire citizenship. It includes youth who have completed compulsory education in Greece. Under the new provisions, migrants who have lived in Greece for twelve consecutive years are also eligible. However, they need to take an electronic test of three hundred questions. One year after the law was granted, the number of foreign nationals granted citizenship rose 138 percent compared to the previous year—86 percent were Albanian nationals, 1.5 percent Ukrainians, and 1.2 percent Russians.

The new examinations, called the "Panhellenics," are held twice a year and test the knowledge of Greek citizenship hopefuls—excluding those from the diaspora—in the areas of the Greek language as well as the geography of the nation and its history.

Athanasios Balerbas, Greece's secretary general of citizenship, stated to interviewers from *Ta Nea* that it was of extreme importance to change how individuals acquire Greek citizenship. "When we took over the Ministry," he relates, "we noticed the extremely long delays in the naturalization of foreigners, who have the legal conditions to acquire citizenship, if, of course, they wish to do so."

According to the proposed legislation, foreigners wishing to obtain Greek citizenship must pass the exams with a score of at least 80 percent before they receive a "Certificate of Adequacy of Knowledge for Naturalization," and only then will they be eligible to apply for citizenship.

However, final decisions on exactly who is granted citizenship will rest on the results of an interview with two officials from the General Secretariat for Citizenship, at which time a fee of 550 euros must be paid.

The rapid changes brought on by historical world events, immigration, and the economic crisis have all led to the changing face of the once homogenous and traditional country of Greece. Today in all the major cities of the country, one can find multiethnic neighborhoods comprised of ethnic restaurants, shops, and grocery stores with people speaking an array of languages other than Greek.

*Angelyn Balodimas-Bartolomei*

**Further Reading**

Androulidaki-Dimitriadi, Ismini. 2010. *Family Law in Greece.* Alphen aan den Rijn, The Netherlands: Kluwer Law International.

Clogg, Richard. 1973. *Struggle for Greek Independence: Essays to Mark the 150th Anniversary of the Greek War of Independence.* Hamden, CT: Archon Books.

Clogg, Richard. 2013. *A Concise History of Greece.* Cambridge: Cambridge University Press.

Doukas, Kimon. A. 1945. "Agrarian Reform in Greece." *American Journal of Economics and Sociology* 1, no. 1 (October): 79–92.

Epstein, M. 1932. *The Statesman's Year-Book: Statistical and Historical Annual of the States of the World for the Year 1932*. London: Macmillan.

European Migration Network. Institute of International Relations. 2012. "Immigration of International Students to the EU: Empirical Evidence and Current Policy Practice." Accessed July 13, 2018. http://sro.sussex.ac.uk/id/eprint/55308/.

Kokkinidis, Tasos. 2018. "Recipients of Greek Citizenship up 138 Percent in 2016." *Greek Reporter*, April 9, 2018. Accessed July 13, 2018. http://greece.greekreporter.com/2018/04/09/recipients-of-greek-citizenship-up-138-percent-in-2016/.

Living in Greece. 2007. "Ways to Get Greek Citizenship." March 16, 2007. Accessed July 13, 2018. http://livingingreece.gr/2007/03/16/ways-to-acquire-greek-citizenship/.

Trichopoulos, Dimitrios, and George Papaevangelou. 1974. *The Population of Greece*. Paris: CICRED Series, 202. Accessed June 1, 2018. http://www.cicred.org/Eng/Publications/pdf/c-c19.pdf.

United Nations. 2006. "Consideration of Reports Submitted by States Parties under Article 18 of the Convention on the Elimination of all Forms of Discrimination against Women." Accessed July 14, 2018. http://www.un.org/womenwatch/daw/cedaw/cedaw20/greece.htm.

Worldometers. n.d. "Greece Population." Accessed June 25, 2018. http://www.worldometers.info/world-population/greece-population/.

## ORGANIZATIONS HELPING ETHNIC MINORITIES IN GREECE COMBAT DISCRIMINATION

The officially recognized Muslim group of Western Thrace, as well as the numerous other ethnic minority groups in Greece, often encounters issues of discrimination. In 1993, the Greek Helsinki Monitor (GHM) was founded in support of such groups. According to its website, the GHM frequently monitors, publishes, lobbies, and litigates on human and minority rights and antidiscrimination issues in Greece and the Balkans. It also monitors the media for stereotypes and hate speech; issues press releases; and prepares (usually jointly with other NGOs) detailed annual reports for the public and UN Treaty Bodies on ill-treatment toward ethnonational, ethnolinguistic, religious, and immigrant communities in both Greece and other Balkan countries. GHM operates a website and a Facebook page covering human rights and minority issues in the Balkans. Additional human rights groups that exist in Greece include the Minority Rights Group-Greece (MRG-G); the Coordinated Organizations and Communities for Roma Human Rights in Greece (SOKADRE); and the Humanist Union of Greece (HUG). The groups are particularly concerned about protecting recognized Muslim group and other minority groups in Greece.

*Angelyn Balodimas-Bartolomei*

## Albanians and Arvanites

The largest ethnic minority group to be found in Greece is that of the Albanians. According to the 2011 census, about 480,824 people of those residing in Greece were Albanian citizens. Most of the Albanians arrived after the fall of the Communist government in their country in late 1990 and early 1991. Many were undocumented migrants seeking employment, with some staying on as temporary migrants or seasonal workers. Several of the newcomers changed their names to Greek and even converted from Islam to Orthodoxy in the hope of facing less discrimination while also acquiring Greek citizenship. Among those that immigrated to Greece at this time were Albanians with Greek roots from Northern Epirus (*Vorioeiporotes*). They do not want to be identified as Albanians, but as Greeks.

Very few social services are available for Albanians living in Greece. In 2004, an association of Albanian immigrants established an Albanian complementary school in Thessaloniki—the second-largest city of Greece. This school offers Albanian-language courses for ninety minutes every Sunday morning, which is currently attended by eighty children aged between six and sixteen. The schoolteachers are Albanian-origin immigrants who offer their services on a voluntary basis. As of January 2032, Albanian lessons have also been added to the school curriculum in Aspropirgos, an area of metropolitan Athen where many Albaninas reside. With the ongoing Greek economic crisis, many Albanians have returned home to Albania.

There are very few Cham Albanians (Greek: *Tsamides*), a group who converted to Islam during the rule of the Ottoman Empire and speak a southern Tosk Albanian dialect. In the twentieth century, they migrated and settled in an area of Western Thrace, known among the Albanians as Chameria. After World War II, most of them were forced to flee Greece because they were accused of collaborating with the Italian and German forces. They have not been able to claim Greek citizenship or a return of their lands.

Another group that originated from Albania but identify as Greeks are the Arvanites—Orthodox Christians who immigrated to Greece during the late Middle Ages and were the dominant population of many regions in Attica and the Peloponnesus. It is not clear why they migrated. Some were invited by the Byzantine and Latin rulers of the time. Many were employed as soldiers and fought alongside the Greeks against the Ottomans during the Greek War of Independence. The men have been depicted in historical images and books as wearing kilts or baggy breeches while the women wore heavily embroidered chemise shirts, silk gowns, and thick woolen coats. The Arvanites were organized into clans or *fares*, a word meaning seed in Greek and Albanian. Women were held in high position and had more say in public issues and bore arms. One Arvanite, Laskarina Bouboulina, became a Greek heroine of the 1821 War of Independence for joining the underground resistance, fighting alongside men, and spending all her money in supporting the crew of her ships and feeding the soldiers. She was also the only woman in the world to hold the title of admiral of the Russian Navy.

The Arvanites spoke the Arvanitika language—a variety of the Tosk, Southern Albanian dialect. After the creation of the Albanian state during the twentieth century, the Arvanites in Greece began to dissociate themselves from the Albanians by self-identifying as Greeks. During the next few decades, they were discouraged from speaking Arvanitika, leading to a progressive loss of their spoken traditional language that is today categorized as a severely endangered language. It is estimated that there are currently between 50,000 and 150,000 Arvanites living mostly in Attica and the Peloponnesus—all of whom have fully assimilated into the Greek culture and consider themselves Greek.

*Angelyn Balodimas-Bartolomei*

**See also:** Chapter 2: Bouboulina, Laskarina.

**Further Reading**

Chatzidaki, Aspassia, and Christina Maligkoudi. 2013. "Family Language Policies among Albanian Immigrants in Greece." *International Journal of Bilingual Education and Bilingualism* 16 (6): 675–689.

Gkaintartzi, Anastasia, Angeliki Kiliar, and Roula Tsokalidou. 2016. "Heritage Language Maintenance and Education in the Greek Sociolinguistic Context: Albanian Immigrant Parents' Views." *Cogent Education* 3: 1155259. Accessed May 25, 2018. https://doi.org/10.1080/2331186X.2016.1155259.

"Albanian, Arvanitika: A Language of Greece." 2018. In *Ethnologue: Languages of the World*, 21st edition, edited by Gary F. Simons and Charles D. Fennig. Dallas, TX: SIL International. Online version. http://www.ethnologue.com.

## Immigration and Migration to Greece

From Homeric times to the present, Greeks have been a migratory people. Considered one of the oldest and most significant diaspora groups of Western civilization, the Greeks have established communities and left traces of Hellenism throughout the world. Over the past century, many settled in the United States, United Kingdom, Germany, France, Canada, and Australia during two great waves of emigration—one at the century's start and the other after World War II. With the current crisis, Greece has once again become a country of emigration.

During the past forty years, Greece slowly transitioned from a country of large-scale emigration to that of destination. In the mid-1970s, the government established repatriation incentives for the diaspora Greeks to return to the homeland, as it was concerned about the long-term effects of sustained emigration. Beginning in 1973, the government slowly began allowing leftist political refugees to return to Greece. Every application was examined individually until 1983, when a common ministerial decision was made by the Ministry that allowed the Civil War political refugees to return and take back the Greek citizenship that they had lost. Between 1971 and 1986,

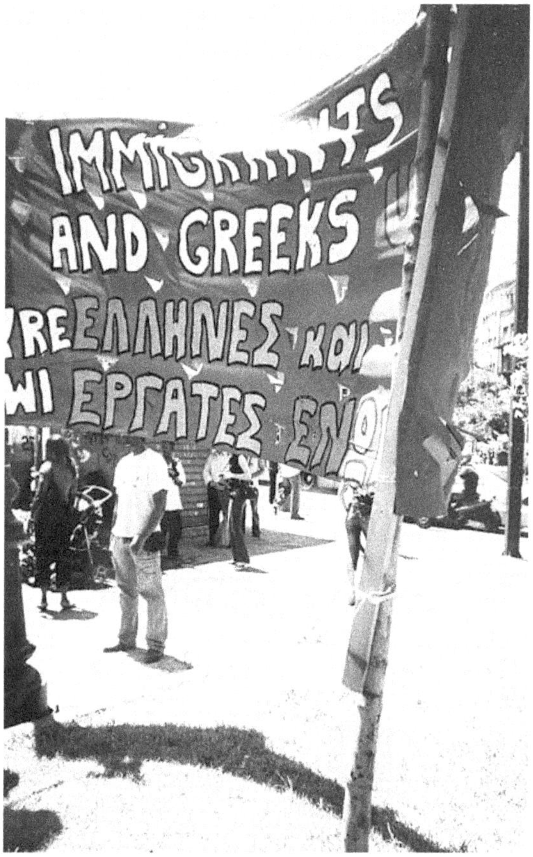


This peaceful demonstration, with children present, took place in the center of Athens in 2006. The sign says "Immigrants and Workers Together." Another sign, which is not shown, states "No, to the Apartheid of the Minister of Commerce," with handwriting at the bottom imploring "What will our children eat?" Immigrants who are not ethnically Greek have found it difficult to get work permits or to settle in Greece. (Photo by Elaine Thomopoulos)

625,000 returned to Greece, settling mainly in Attica, Macedonia, the Peloponnesus, and the Aegean Islands. Immigration to Greece increased slightly during the next decade as Greece became a transit country for Eastern Europeans, Middle Easterners, and Africans. Over 89,000 foreign migrants and refugees resettled mainly in the United States, Canada, Australia, and New Zealand with a small number of Asians, Africans, and Poles staying in Greece and taking on jobs in construction, agriculture, and domestic services.

As the European Union (EU) boundaries opened and the collapse of Communism took place within the Central and Eastern European regimes in 1989, a large flow of immigrants, which included diasporic Greeks, arrived from post-Soviet countries and particularly from Georgia, Russia, and the Czech Republic. The following year brought an influx of immigrants from Albania. Immigration to Greece soon became a massive, uncontrollable phenomenon. Still being one of the less-developed European Union (EU) states, in the 1990s, Greece received the highest percentage of immigrants in relation to its labor force. The once homogeneous country was now faced with challenges on dealing with the newcomers who spoke uncommon languages and maintained different lifestyles.

Many factors account for Greece transforming into a receiving country, including its geographic position, because of which it serves as the eastern gate of the EU; widespread coastlines and easily crossed borders; economic growth from the time it joined the European Economic Community (EEC); higher living standards; and seasonal industries such as tourism, agriculture, and construction.

**GREEKS OF LESVOS EXTEND HEROIC EFFORTS IN RESCUING AND SUPPORTING REFUGEES**

From 2015 to 2018, about five hundred thousand refugees arrived in Lesvos. For their "heroic efforts" in supporting refugees, the Greeks of Lesvos received the inaugural John McCain Prize for Leadership in Public Service. Many of the residents of the island of Lesvos, descendants of refugees who arrived from Asia Minor in 1922, could relate to the difficulties the people who landed on their shores faced. The islanders helped in many ways. Fishermen used their boats to rescue the refugees who were crossing the Aegean Sea from Turkey. They picked them up from rickety dinghies and saved some from drowning. Young Greek scouts arranged for food, built shelters, and organized activities for the children. Old *yiayiades* (grandmothers) cooked food, provided clothing, helped care for the babies, and opened their hearts to the unfortunates who were fleeing violence and poverty. A sad postscript to this story is that the island of Lesvos housed the infamous Moria camp, which, on September 13, 2018, the *Guardian* described as "overcrowded, violent and awash with human sewage." In September 2020, the Moria camp was overcome with fire, leaving thousands homeless.

*Elaine Thomopoulos*

During the summer of 2015, Greece became a gateway to Europe for over one million refugees, asylum seekers, and migrants fleeing their countries of origin due to war, persecution, or violence. More than eight hundred thousand migrants, mainly from Syria, Iraq, Iran, and Afghanistan, were trafficked by sea from Turkey to Greece. They landed on the Greek islands of Lesvos, Chios, Kos, Samos, and Leros and then caught a ship to the mainland. From there, most of the migrants transited through the country, attempting to reach Germany and other northern EU countries where they would seek a new life.

As the influx of refugees increased, reception and identification centers/camps, known as hotspots, were established on the islands. The initial purpose of these camps was to identify, register, and fingerprint incoming migrants and quickly transfer them to the mainland where they would wait for an interview to determine their status. However, two events changed their course of direction. In 2016, the Balkan countries shut their borders resulting in hundreds and thousands of refugees being stranded in Greece. In the same year, the EU-Turkey deal came into force, aiming to cut off the route across the Aegean Sea by sending undocumented refugees back to Turkey. Although both initiatives led to a decrease in newly arrived refugees to Greece, those who had already entered were trapped in the hotspots. They would now have to wait for their asylum applications to be issued—a process that could take over a year. Subsequently, during the second half of 2017, Greece once again experienced a dramatic rise in the number of migrants entering the country.

With the enormous influx of migrants, the centers became inadequate to handle the numbers. For example, the Moria Camp on Lesvos Island, which has a capacity to receive 3,100 people, at one point reached over 9,000. Besides being overcrowded, the center has been internationally criticized for appalling, deplorable, inhumane, and dangerous living conditions. In September of 2020, the camp was burnt down, and another migrant camp was established. Both Greece and the EU partners continue to be criticized for abandoning and ignoring the vulnerable refugees who seek protection in Europe. Today over 60,000–74,000 refugees and migrants are living in Greece. According to UNICEF data, as of June 2018, an estimated 23,500 of the refugees are children, of which 3,448 are unaccompanied; of these, more than 2,313 are still in need of shelter. In response to the dire conditions, the Greek government, EU, and NGOs have established preregistration detention centers, camps, and temporary accommodation facilities within hotels and private apartments on the mainland. Vulnerable individuals, such as sick people, pregnant women, the elderly, and unaccompanied minor children, have been given special priority for accommodation, as well as provision for Greek public health and educational services. Additionally, there is an imperative need for gradually integrating the refugees and migrants, including children, into society. It is critical that the latter group has access to education. As EU commissioner for humanitarian aid and crisis management, Christos Stylianides has stated that the EU has a responsibility to avoid the risk of refugee children growing up without education and becoming a lost generation.

*Angelyn Balodimas-Bartolomei*

**See also:** Chapter 6: Sidebar: Greeks of Lesvos Extend Heroic Efforts in Rescuing and Supporting Refugees. Chapter 8: Immigrant and Refugee Education.

**Further Reading**

Apostolou, Nikolia. "Millions of Child Refugees Do Not Attend School in Adopted Homeland." *USA Today,* October 1, 2018. Accessed March 3, 2019. https://www.usatoday.com/story/news/world/2018/10/01/un-says-millions-children-refugees-not-attending-school/1418231002/.

Cavounidas, Jennifer. 2015. "The Changing Face of Emigration. Harnessing the Potential of the New Greek Diaspora." Transatlantic Council of Migration. Accessed May 20, 2018. https://www.migrationpolicy.org/research/changing-face-emigration-harnessing-potential-new-greek-diaspora.

Doctors without Borders. 2018. "Children Trapped in Greek Island Camps Attempting Suicide and Self-Harm." September 12, 2018. https://www.doctorswithoutborders.org/what-we-do/news-stories/news/children-trapped-greek-island-camps-attempting-suicide-and-self-harm.

IOM. "UN Migration Agency, EU, Greece Help 2,800 Migrant and Refugee Children Go Back to School in 2018." Accessed March 1, 2021. https://www.iom.int/news/un-migration-agency-eu-greece-help-2800-migrant-and-refugee-children-go-back-school-2018.

Kasimis, Charalambos, and Chryssa Kassimi. 2004. "Greece: A History of Migration." *Journal of the Migration Policy Institute* (June 1). Accessed May 20, 2018. https://www.migrationpolicy.org/article/greece-history-migration.

Migration Policy Institute. "Greece. 2001–2018." Accessed May 20, 2018. https://www.migrationpolicy.org/country-resource/greece.

Triandafyllidou, Anna, and Michaela Maroulof. 2009. "Greece: Immigration at the Eve of the 21st Century. A Critical Assessment." Hellenic Foundation for Europe and Foreign Policy (ELIAMEP). Accessed August 2, 2018. http://www.eliamep.gr/wp-content/uploads/en/2009/10/idea_wp4_greece5.pdf.

UNICEF. 2018. "Refugee and Migrant Children in Greece. As of 31 December 2018." Accessed April 13, 2021. https://www.unicef.org/eca/sites/unicef.org.eca/files/2019-01/Refugee%20and%20migrant%20children%20in%20Greece%20Dec%202018.pdf.

Ziomis, Dimitris, Antoinetta Capella, and Danai Constantinidou. "Integrating Refugee & Migrant Children into the Educational System in Greece." European Commission. July 2017. Accessed April 15, 2021. https://ec.europa.eu/social/BlobServlet?docId=18245&langId=en.

## Jewish Community

Today there are roughly five thousand Jews in Greece with nearly three thousand residing in Athens, one thousand in Thessalonica, and about a thousand spread across the six cities of Larissa, Chalkis, Volos, Corfu, Trikala, and Ioannina. Jews have been in Greece since at least the fourth century BCE.

Before World War II, there had been about sixty thousand to seventy thousand Jews living in Greece. After the deportation of Greek Jews to concentration camps by the Nazis during World War II, only ten thousand returned to Greece. Five thousand emigrated, mainly to Palestine and the United States. Despite mixed marriages and an aging population, the existing eight Jewish communities have actively worked at maintaining their schools, synagogues, and organizations, all which fall under KIS—the Central Board of Jewish Communities in Greece. KIS was established by law in 1945 and is the umbrella organization of Greek Jewry in Greece. It is legally recognized by the Greek state and falls under the jurisdiction of the Ministry of Education and Religious Affairs. The organization officially represents the Jewish communities in Greece and coordinates ongoing activities and events.

The Central Board of KIS is administered and situated in Athens. Athens has two synagogues on Melidoni Street, facing each other. The older of the two, Etz Chaim, functions only for High Holidays. Built in 1904 by Romaniote Jews who came from Ioannina, it is often referred to as the Ioannina Synagogue by the elder members. Across the street stands the main synagogue, Beth Shalom Synagogue. This Greek revival–style synagogue, made from Pentelic marble, was founded by the Sephardic Greek community in 1935 and renovated in 1975. The Jewish Museum of Greece, established in 1977, is located in the center of the city, on 39 Nikis Street. The Greek Jewish Lauder Elementary School of Athens, a private school located in the suburb of Paleo Psychiko, has a preschool, kindergarten, and elementary school. The school was recently recognized and awarded by the Greek Ministry of Education for addressing refugee issues and for its best educational efforts for social activism, humanitarian concerns, and pursuit of social justice.

Thessaloniki has three synagogues, a Jewish Museum, a Jewish school, an old people's home, and a cemetery. The city's central synagogue is Monastirioton Synagogue, which is the only one that remains in its pre-Holocaust state. Built between 1925 and 1927, the synagogue served as a religious center for the Jewish refugees of Monastir—known today as Bitola in the Republic of North Macedonia. During World War II, the synagogue was used as a warehouse by the Red Cross and fortunately not destroyed. Immediately after the liberation in 1944, the synagogue was opened for the few remaining Jews of the city that had been saved by Christian friends or returned from the concentration camps. In 1978, a strong earthquake caused serious damage to the synagogue. The Greek government provided the funding for its restoration. Today Monastirioton Synagogue is recognized as one of the historical monuments of Thessaloniki. The Yad Lezikaron Synagogue, inaugurated in 1984, is dedicated to the memory of the Holocaust victims. It was built on the site of the former Burla Synagogue that had been operating since 1921. The small Saul Modiano Synagogue is on the ground floor of the Jewish Old People's Home. It was originally founded from a donation by Saul Modiano, a Jew from Thessaloniki, who died in Trieste in 1924. The home operated until the German occupation when the residents were sent with the other members of the communities to concentration camps. It reopened in 1974 and was remodeled in 1981.

In addition to the two major cities of Greece, traces of Greek Jewry, which include ancient ruins, synagogues, and cemeteries, can be found throughout the country. On the island of Rhodes stands the oldest synagogue of Greece, Kahal Shalom. Before World War II, nearly four thousand Sephardic Jews lived on the island. Only about forty reside in Rhodes today. Thanks to the 2000 World Monuments Fund and generous donations from both Greek Jews in America and the Rhodes Historical Foundation, the synagogue has been beautifully restored and a Jewish museum recently built.

On the island of Crete once lived a thriving Jewish Romaniote community. Today, only the Etz Hayyim Synagogue serves the Jewish community. It is housed in a fine Venetian building that was originally a church. The synagogue, which suffered severe damages during the bombing of Hania in 1944 and then again during the 1995 earthquake, was recently restored. Today it contains a library with over seventeen hundred books and a renovated mikveh (ritual bath) that is fed by underground springs.

Evia is another island that once had a very active Jewish community. In Chalkida, the main town of the island, the Romaniote Jewish Community is the only one in Europe that has been living in the same city for twenty-five hundred years without interruption. The Jewish presence dates to 586 BCE. Mordechai Frizis, a native Jew of Chalkida, was the first Jew to graduate from the Greek officers' school. Known as a brave and popular leader, he was killed during the Albanian campaign of World War II. The synagogue is located at 27 Koutsou St. in Chalkida. The Jewish cemetery on Mesapion Street has graves dating back to the Ottoman Empire. The current Jewish population is approximately one hundred.

A vibrant Jewish community lived for over a millennium on the island of Corfu. By the late eighteenth century, it numbered about five thousand with most of its members being poor wage earners, porters, street vendors, and small shop owners comprised of Romaniote and Southern Italian Jews. Today the Jewish population of Corfu numbers about sixty-five. Their functioning seventeenth-century Scuola Greca or Tempio Greca Synagogue is one of the finest in Greece. It is the only synagogue that survived the destruction of World War II.

At the beginning of the twentieth century, the population of Ioannina, Epirus, numbered about a half million residents, of which five thousand were Romaniote Jews. The Jews lived in two quarters—inside the city's fortress and outside of its wall. During the German occupation, 91 percent of the Ioannina Jews perished. Today the Jewish population totals about sixty people. They attend the Kehila Kedosha Yashan Synagogue, which was built in 1829. There is also a Jewish cemetery.

*Angelyn Balodimas-Bartolomei*

**See also:** Chapter 2: Damaskinos Papandreou, Archbishop.

**Further Reading**

Balodimas-Bartolomei, Angelyn. 2010. "The Inclusion of Invisible Minorities in the EU Member States: The Case of Greek Jews." In *Changing Educational Landscapes*, edited by Dimitris Mattheou, 155–182. New York: B. V. Springer Science and Business Media.

Balodimas-Bartolomei, Angelyn. 2012. "Political & Pedagogical Dimensions in Holocaust Education: A Comparative Analysis among Task Force Member Countries." *Journal of Multiculturalism in Education* 8 (2). Assessed March 1, 2019. https://www.wtamu.edu/journal/volume-8-number-1.aspx#6.

Balodimas-Bartolomei, Angelyn. 2016. "Political and Pedagogical Dimensions in Holocaust Education: Teacher Seminars and Staff Development in Greece." *Diaspora, Indigenous, and Minority Education* 10 (4): 242–254. https://doi.org/10.1080/15595692.2016.1219847.

Ikonomopoulos Haddad, Marcia. 2002. "Remembering the Jews of Corfu." Accessed on July 31, 2018. http://sefarad.org/lm/046/12.html.

KIS, Central Board of Jewish Communities in Greece. 2009. "Historical Background." Accessed May 25, 2018. http://www.kis.gr/en/index.php?option=com_content&view=article&id=411&Itemid=74.

"Kosher Greece." *The Jewish Touring Guide*. Accessed July 15, 2018. http://www.koshergreece.com/templates/articlecco_cdo/aid/66400/jewish/Sites-of-Jewish-interest-in-Greece.htm.

Yad Vashem. 2018. "Ioannina." Accessed July 31, 2018. http://www.yadvashem.org/yv/en/exhibitions/valley/ioannina/italian_occupation.asp.

## Muslim Religious Minority of Western Thrace

Although Greece has become home to numerous minorities, the Greek Constitution recognizes only one minority—the Muslim religious minority of Western Thrace in Northern Greece. They are recognized as citizens of Greece and are protected by the terms of the Treaty of Lausanne of 1923. Under the same treaty, most of the Greek Orthodox in Turkey were sent to Greece and the Muslims in Greece were sent to Turkey under the massive population exchange. The Turks and other Muslims of Western Thrace and the Greeks of Constantinople (Istanbul) and the Aegean islands of Imbros (Gökçeada) and Tenedos (Bozcaada) were exempt from the deportation and thus allowed to remain in their respective countries.

Even though the Muslim minority of Greece, which consists of Turks, Pomaks (Bulgarian Slavic Muslims), and Roma of Western Thrace, is not only religiously diverse from the Greek population but also ethnically and linguistically, its members are officially only recognized as Muslims and not for their ethnicity or linguistic status. Each group speaks fluent Greek in addition to its own language. About 130,000 Muslims currently live in Western Thrace. They are of various ethnicities: 50 percent are of Turkish ethnicity; 35 percent are Pomaks who speak a Bulgarian dialect; and 15 percent are Roma.

The 1923 Treaty of Lausanne (Articles 40 and 41) states that the Muslim minority of Western Thrace shall have equal right to establish, manage, and control at their own expense charitable, religious, and social institutions, schools, and other establishments for instruction and education, so that they may freely use their own language and exercise their own religion. Since the treaty was established, numerous other agreements have been signed, often changing the nature of the schools and even their names, as they were once referred to as Turkish schools but are now referred to as minority schools. The most significant and first legal text signed since the Treaty of Lausanne is the "Council of Europe Framework Convention for the Protection of Minorities" that Greece endorsed in 1997 and ratified in 2010 through Resolution 1704. The document urges Greece to provide high-quality teaching for the Muslim minority in Greece, particularly through the creation of textbooks; to establish upper-secondary schools; and to guarantee that the Special Teacher Training Academy of Thessaloniki (EPATH) will provide high-quality education in both the Greek and Turkish languages for appropriately training future Muslim minority schoolteachers in Thrace. The document also recommends that the Greek government provide funding for Greek-language instruction and support for mutual understanding among the two communities.

Over the past decade, the number of schools that teach the Turkish language serving Muslim students in Western Thrace has dropped from 231 to 115. The students follow a bilingual Greek and Turkish curriculum. They also are permitted to observe both Christian and Muslim religious holidays. At the secondary level, there are only two bilingual minority schools in Xanthi and Komotini and two religious schools (medrese). Both the Turkish community and various human rights organizations have requested improvements in the quality and conditions in Turkish education, which include additional Turkish teachers, updating and improving the schools' infrastructure, additional secondary schools, kindergarten education, dormitories for high school students, compulsory education for minority schools, and open dialogue between the Ministries of Educations of Greece and Turkey.

*Angelyn Balodimas-Bartolomei*

**See also:** Chapter 5: Freedom of Religion.

**Further Reading**

Dragonas, Thalia, and Anna Frangoudaki. 2006. "Educating the Muslim Minority in Western Thrace." *Islam and Christian - Muslim Relations* 17 (1): 21–41.

Greek Ministry of Foreign Affairs. "Muslim Minority in Thrace" (in Greek). Accessed May 19, 2018. http://www.hri.org/MFA/foreign/musmingr.htm.

Hellenic Republic, Ministry of Foreign Affairs. 2010. "Resolution 1704. Freedom of Religion and Other Human-Rights for non-Muslim Minorities in Turkey and for the Muslim Minority in Thrace (Eastern Greece)." Accessed March 1, 2019. https://www.mfa.gr/images/docs/ellinotourkiko/resolution_1704_hunault.pdf.

"Minority Education in Greece. The Case of Western Thrace Turks." 2008. Organization for Security and Co-operation in Europe | OSCE. October 1, 2008. Accessed May 19, 2018. https://www.osce.org/odihr/33832?download=true.

"Treaty of Peace with Turkey Signed at Lausanne, July 24, 1923." 1924. In *The Treaties of Peace 1919–1923, Vol. II.* New York: Carnegie Endowment for International Peace. Accessed April 20, 2021. https://wwi.lib.byu.edu/index.php/Treaty_of_Lausanne.

## Other Minority Groups: Aromanians (Vlachs), Armenians, and Macedonian Slavs

### AROMANIANS (VLACHS)

The Aromanians, also known as Vlachs, are an ethnic group living in the Balkans. Their population in Greece is about two hundred thousand with most Aromanians living in scattered rural communities in Epirus, Macedonia, and Thessaly, mainly around the Pindus, Olympus, and Vermion Mountains and around the Prespa Lakes near the border with Albania and the Republic of North Macedonia. The Vlachs call themselves Aromani; however, in Greek they are called *vlachoi*. The term is almost synonymous with the word "shepherd" because this group consists mostly of such, who in the winter descend from the mountains seeking pasture for their flocks.

The Aromanians appear to be more tolerated than other minority groups in Greece. Throughout time, they have adopted the Greek language, culture, and identity. During the Greek War of Independence, the Aromanians were active participants in the struggle. They have continued to play a prominent role in modern Greek history. The Aromanians speak Aromanian—a language that evolved from Latin and was transmitted from the Romans with additional influences from surrounding languages. Although minority languages in Greece are often overlooked, recently there has been a growing interest in preserving endangered languages (including Aromanian). This has led to numerous cultural festivals taking place in Metsovo. There has also been support outside of Greece. In 1997, the Parliamentary Assembly of the Council of

Europe passed a resolution encouraging the Balkan states to preserve and promote the critical situation of the Aromanian culture and language. Consequently, Konstantinos Stefanopoulos, the former president of Greece, publicly urged Greek Aromanians to teach the ancestral language to their children.

## ARMENIANS

Since Byzantium, there has been an Armenian presence in Greece, especially within the regions of Thessaly, Macedonia, Thrace, and on the islands of Crete and Corfu. Historical testimonies, written genealogical family histories, and villages and towns bearing Armenian names support their existence throughout the country. During the Hamidian Massacre of 1892–1896, more than one thousand Armenians managed to escape the Ottomans, seeking shelter in Greece. Upon their arrival at the harbor of Piraeus, they were warmly received by Prime Minister Theodoros Deligiannis.

A few decades later, Greece welcomed roughly seventy thousand to eighty thousand survivors of the Armenian Genocide from various regions of Asia Minor. Armenian communities sprang up within the cities of Athens, Piraeus, and Salonica.

After the dissolution of the Soviet Union in 1991, more Armenians resettled in Greece. Today the Armenian population of Greece stands at about twenty thousand to thirty-five thousand with the majority living in Attica, Macedonia, Thrace, and Crete.

There are numerous Armenian organizations; Armenian Apostolic, Catholic, and Evangelical churches; and kindergarten/elementary schools in both Athens and Thessaloniki.

## MACEDONIAN SLAVS

Another linguistic minority group that can be found in the northern Greek region of Macedonia is that of the Macedonian Slavs. Slavic tribes began settling in the region during the sixth century CE. After the Balkan Wars, when Greece obtained Macedonian territory from Turkey, many Slavs came under Greek rule. The Macedonian Slavs speak Slavic Macedonian with the majority being Orthodox Christians. The population count of this minority group in Greece is debatable, with numbers ranging anywhere from five thousand to twenty thousand, depending on the various sources.

*Angelyn Balodimas-Bartolomei*

**See also:** Chapter 1: Overview. Chapter 9: Dialects and Minority Languages.

### Further Reading

Badalyan, Arevik. 2010. "Greek Armenian Community: The Struggle Continues." Accessed May 28, 2018. https://arevik.wordpress.com/2010/06/27/greek-armenian-community-the-struggle-continues/.

Kahl, Thede. "Aromanians in Greece: Minority or Vlach-speaking Greeks?" *Society Farsatoul.* Accessed May 28, 2018. http://www.farsarotul.org/nl27_1.htm.

Kahl, Thede. 2002. "The Ethnicity of Aromanians after 1990: the Identity of a Minority that Behaves like a Majority." *Ethnologia Balkanica* 6: 145–169.

Zenian, David. 1999. "The Armenians of Greece: Remembering the Past and Preparing for the Future." *Armenian General Benevolent Society Magazine* (November 1). Accessed July 15, 2018. https://agbu.org/news-item/the-armenians-of-greece-remembering-the-past-and-preparing-for-the-future/.

## Romani (Roma)

The Romani people of Greece are said to have originated from the northwestern Indian state of Rajasthan. They have been in Greece since the fourteenth century and are referred to by several words: *gyftoi* (gypsy—from the Greek word *egiftos* for Egyptians, as it was first believed that they originated from Egypt); *tsiganoi* (from the ancient Greek word *athigganoi*, a sect that gypsies were associated with); and Roma (meaning man in the Romani language). After the Asia Minor Catastrophe in 1922, several Romani from Constantinople and Smyrna arrived and settled in Greece. Most of the Romani that are in Greece today were born there and granted Greek citizenship in 1979.

The Romani speak the Romani language and are either Greek Orthodox or Muslim. Being nomadic in nature, they are scattered all over the country and have no common geographical settlement, although many live in the Athenian suburbs of Agia Varvara and Ano Liosia and other parts of Attika and in Thessaloniki, Thrace, and western Peloponnesus. It is estimated that there are about two hundred thousand to three hundred thousand living in Greece today; however, the number varies according to source and purposes.

The Romani population has faced severe challenges and problems in Greece, including high rates of child labor and abuse, low school attendance, police discrimination, and drug trafficking. One of their most serious problems is housing, since so many of their members still live in tents on properties that they do not own, making them subject to eviction. Within the past decade, wider attention and state funding has been aimed at helping the Roma population. The EU has given Greece a lot of money to improve the situation of the Romani in its country. Human rights groups are constantly striving to support and help the Roma people by documenting key reports on the marginalization of this group. In addition to discrimination, harassment, and victimization, the Roma suffer from dire living conditions, which includes lack of access to water and electricity. In 2008, the European Fundamental Agency reported that the Greek Roma are in the "most disadvantaged position" in the field of education with very few attending school and completing compulsory education. The Roma also have a high rate of unemployment.

*Angelyn Balodimas-Bartolomei*

**See also:** Chapter 6: Sidebar: Organizations Helping Ethnic Minorities in Greece Combat Discrimination. Chapter 9: Dialects and Minority Languages.

**Further Reading**

Clapp, Alexander. 2017. "Europe's Heart of Darkness." *The Economist 1843*, October 24, 2017. Accessed March 2, 2021. https://www.1843magazine.com/features/europes-heart-of-darkness.

"Greece: Status of Minorities." Library of Congress. Last updated June 9, 2015. Accessed May 28, 2018. https://www.loc.gov/law/help/greece-minorities/greece.php.

CHAPTER 7

# GENDER, MARRIAGE, AND SEXUALITY

## OVERVIEW

Greece began to adopt progressive social policies related to gender equality at a slower pace than most of its neighbors. In 1930, women in Greece were granted the right to vote in municipal elections if they were thirty years of age or older and at minimum had completed elementary school. Women did not receive the unconditional right to vote until 1952.

This progress came to an abrupt halt when the military junta assumed control of the Greek government in 1967, and civil rights were suspended. The junta suspended elections and prohibited public assembly. Freedom of the press was nonexistent, and censorship in the media, literature, and the arts was commonplace. The country credited with the founding of democracy was anything but a free nation between 1967 and 1974.

Once a democratically elected government was restored, there was much to be done. Greece had fallen behind its neighbors in advancements in gender equality benchmarks. Long-established women's associations, such as the Greek League for Women and the National Council of Greek Women, were joined by a number of newly formed associations in demanding gender equality and fairness. While most advocated for gender equality, some focused on other facets of the feminist movement, including abortion rights, domestic violence, or maternity and child rearing. In increasing numbers, women stood for election at all levels of government and advocated for gender-related issues as priorities were set and laws were being considered.

The Panhellenic Socialists Movement (PASOK) government led by Andreas Papandreou shared those views, and gender equality became a priority. The Greek Parliament adopted the Family Law Act of 1983, which made gender equality the law of the land, mandated equal pay for equal work, decriminalized adultery, and abolished dowries in a legal sense. Abortion was legalized in 1986. Women have been allowed to enlist in the armed forces since 1977.

Within the family, gender roles are often patriarchal in practice, but these views are dissipating as a growing number of women attain higher levels of education or enter the workforce. By tradition, women are the primary caregivers to children and elderly family members and the keeper of the domicile. They are well represented in most professions, including health care, education, and engineering. In rural Greece, women work in the family farm and may be involved in local tourism or hospitality. Although Greece adopted equal pay for equal work laws, women earned 22 percent less than their male counterparts in 2010. In 2014, the gap lessened and stood at 12.5 percent based on Eurostat statistics. Women have increasingly played a role in politics and government over the years. Among the esteemed positions recently held by women were mayor of Athens, minister of culture, foreign minister, and president of the Hellenic Parliament. In 2015, a woman was appointed to serve as prime minister of Greece on a caretaker basis.

Greece scores in the middle range of European nations in most measures of gender equality, lesbian, gay, bisexual, and transgender (LGBT) rights, and progress in other societal concerns. Basic protections are in place but were often hard-fought and long in coming when compared to other countries. The pace of advancement in some of these areas has been hampered by the conservative Greek Orthodox Church, which has been a vocal opponent to such advances. Those who live in urban areas are more likely to be progressive and open minded, while those in rural areas or residing on the Greek islands tend to have more conservative or traditional beliefs.

Although the majority of citizens supported legal protections for the LGBT community, the Greek Orthodox Church was strongly opposed, and it was not uncommon to see hierarchs and clergy openly condemn the LGBT community and threaten politicians that supported LGBT rights with excommunication from the church. Yet, Greece annually hosts four LGBT pride celebrations, boasts a thriving urban nightlife, and is a worldwide travel destination for LGBT travelers.

The economic crisis greatly affected Greek society at all levels and had a direct impact on all facets of life. Women were disproportionally impacted by the austerity measures that were enacted because many of the government's budget cuts were made in areas related to health care, education, and social services. Incidents of domestic violence increased at an alarming rate and were attributed to the increase in stress and anxiety related to the financial crisis. Many of these incidents went unreported due in part to the difficulties encountered in filing reports. The government and NGOs are working to address these findings.

The current refugee crisis and a large migrant population from neighboring countries contributed to the strains on the fragile economy during this difficult period. Child labor spiked with native children joining the migrant and refugee ranks to earn money. Prostitution, usually a province of migrant women, reached a point where more Greek women were engaged in it than those of other ethnicities. Since it is only legal for women to work in the sex trade, males resort to an underground market. The higher numbers of both males and females involved in the sex trade has contributed to an increase in abuse of sex workers by clients or pimps as well as a spike in HIV and other sexually transmitted diseases (STDs). As economic conditions improve and more are able to find gainful employment, the numbers are expected to return to pre-recession levels.

In modern Greece, progressive values on most societal issues prevail even in some cases with the opposition of the Greek Orthodox Church. In the coming years, as younger generations replace the older populations, it is expected that Greece will continue to pursue further advances in matters related to gender, equality, and LGBT rights.

*John Psiharis*

**Further Reading**

Papademetriou, Theresa. 2007. "Children's Rights: Greece." The Law Library of Congress. Library of Congress. September 2007, Last updated July 2, 2015. Accessed April 18, 2018. https://www.loc.gov/law/help/child-rights/greece.php.

Tsimitakis, Matthaios. 2013. "Child Labor a Rising Concern in Crisis-hit Greece." *ekathimerini*, January 7, 2013. Accessed February 22, 2018. http://www.ekathimerini.com/132580/article/ekathimerini/community/child-labor-a-rising-concern-in-crisis-hit-greece.

## Adolescent Sexuality

Virginity until marriage may be the ideal for some, but there is broad recognition that the loss of one's virginity is a personal decision and that it is not sinful or bad in some way. The Greek Orthodox Church espouses that virginity be maintained until marriage. The influence of the church within Greece is significant, and some adhere to that guidance, but today the stigma associated with loss of virginity before marriage, which was present in earlier generations, is not found. Although they do not encourage it, most parents consider loss of virginity to be a rite of passage and thus are not vocally opposed. Beliefs that an individual should remain a virgin, especially a female, until marriage have faded in recent years. As is the case in many nations, a growing number of children are being born out of wedlock.

The 2005 Global Sex Survey of 317,000 people in forty-one countries found that Greeks were number one in frequency of sex at 138 times, while the global average was 103 times. It was number two in the percentage of people who engaged in unprotected sex at 70.5 percent. Norway was first, and the global average was 47.4 percent. The study detailed the average age of virginity loss in the forty-one countries. Greece ranked twenty-three with an age of 17.5 years, ahead of the United States, which ranked twenty-four with an age of 16.9. India boasted the highest age of 19.8, and Iceland was the lowest at 15.6.

As reported in the chapter entry on Greek youth in the *International Encyclopedia of Adolescence*, the majority of youths engage in sexual intercourse for the first time near the end of their adolescence and the beginning of emerging adulthood. For girls it is usually within a steady relationship and begins between the ages of sixteen and eighteen. Boys begin at a younger age but the mean age for first intercourse has risen for them. Adolescents who dropped out of school began their sexual lives earlier than their peers who remained in school. Adolescent sexual behavior is not related to marriage, which usually occurs after the age of twenty-five.

*John Psiharis*

**See also:** Chapter 7: Sidebar: The Changing Nature of the Family.

**Further Reading**

Efklides, Anastasia, and Despina Moraitou. 2006. "Greece." In *International Encyclopedia of Adolescence*: A-J, index, Vol. 1, edited by Jeffrey Jensen Arnett, 356–357. New York: Taylor & Francis. Accessed February 8, 2018 https://books.google.com/books?id=1A606koL3EQC&pg=PA361&lpg=PA361&dq=virginity+rates+in+greece&source=bl&ots=6D_MafbrB9&sig=UDlBevr95R4_EJH48dNl-_a0ouc&hl=en&sa=X&ved=0ahUKEwjFsJeEzJnZAhVFmuAKHdhWDeI4ChDoAQgoMAA#v=onepage&q=virginity%20rates%20in%20greece&f=false.

Face of Global Sex. 2005 Global Sex Survey Results. 2005 Durex. Accessed February 9, 2018. http://durexnetwork.org/SiteCollectionDocuments/Research%20-%20Face%20Of%20Global%20Sex%202005.pdf.

Haland, Johanne. 2003. "Take, Skamandros My Virginity: Ideas of Water in Connection with Rites of Passage in Greece." National and Kapodistrian University of Athens Department of History and Archeology. Accessed February 10, 2018. http://www.arch.uoa.gr/fileadmin/arch.uoa.gr/uploads/images/evy_johanne_haland/skamandros_brillny_reduced.pdf.

Tsitsika, Artemis, et al. 2014. "Experiencing Sexuality in Youth Living in Greece: Contraceptive Practices, Risk taking, and Psychosocial Status." *Journal of Pediatric and Adolescent Gynecology* 27: 232–239.

# Domestic Violence

Greece has exhibited an alarming rate of domestic violence of late. It is believed the dramatic increase over the past ten years is a direct result of the increased anxiety and stress the nation's economic crisis has caused on the citizenry. Domestic abuse may encompass physical, emotional, psychological, financial, or sexual intimidation or violence.

A 2014 study of European Union (EU) nations revealed that the nation with the highest percentage of women who experienced some sort of physical, sexual, or psychological violence by a current or former partner since the age of fifteen was Sweden at 46 percent followed by the United Kingdom at 44 percent. The EU nations with the lowest percentages were Austria at 20 percent followed by Croatia at 21 percent. Greece ranked thirteenth with 25 percent.

In Greece, police reported a 54 percent increase in domestic violence in 2011 and a further increase of 22 percent in 2012. Ten women were killed as a result of domestic abuse in 2011, and five died in 2012. There were 172 cases of rape or attempted rape in 2011, and 167 reported in 2012.

Between 2013 and 2017, there were 13,700 cases of domestic violence reported to Greek police. Of the total victims, 70 percent were women and 30 percent were men. The offender is often the victim's partner, and one in two women murdered are killed by their partner.

Some victims encountered difficulty reporting domestic abuse. The General Secretariat for Gender Equality estimates that less than 10 percent of abuse victims notify the police. Others found that the police did not take the incident seriously and encouraged the victim to go home and work it out. Those who did not speak Greek or spoke Greek with an accent experienced challenges in communicating with police to file a report.

When cases did make it to the courts, it was noted by professionals in the field of domestic violence that judges were often lenient on the male offenders. Public Law 3500/2006 was enacted in 2006 classifying domestic abuse and spousal rape as crimes and made it easier to prosecute these cases. The law allows for domestic violence charges to proceed without the victim filing charges or being involved in the prosecution. Penalties generally range from two to ten years in prison. Restraining orders are granted when warranted by the court. Efforts were made to educate police and the judiciary about domestic violence, and a national educational campaign was launched to increase awareness and knowledge among the public.

The Greek government is working to address these issues on a number of fronts. It grants funding for a network of sixteen shelters throughout the nation that provide crisis intervention, counseling, and short-term residential shelter. Most of these centers have twenty beds, and women and children can stay there for about two months. Boys over the age of twelve are not permitted. Before enrolling in the shelter, the women are required to file a police report. A twenty-four-hour hotline is available to help callers experiencing domestic violence obtain referrals and counseling.

## *PRIKA* (DOWRY) NOW OUTLAWED IN GREECE

The concept of dowry has long been engrained in the cultural fabric of Greek society. Despite being outlawed in a legal sense, the transferring of personal property or wealth by a bride's family to a groom on the occasion of marriage remains widespread in an informal sense.

This centuries-old tradition began to clash with the growing shift toward gender equality. Women were resolute that this system perpetuated the idea that they were taking part in a business transaction. When the Panhellenic Socialist Movement (PASOK) assumed power in 1981, they instituted sweeping reforms in gender issues and enacted the Family Law Act of 1983, which banned the dowry practice.

Traditionally, the families of the bride and groom would meet prior to announcement of their children's engagement to discuss the marital arrangements. Dowry agreements would specify the money or property that would be given by the father of the bride to the groom or his family. It was not uncommon for middle- and upper-class families to provide homes for their daughters. In some cases, families would begin to save for this purpose when their daughter was born. Many Greeks own a house thanks to this tradition. A 2016 study of Europe found that Greece had a homeownership rate of 73.9 percent. Romania was number one at 96 percent, and Switzerland was last at 42.5 percent.

In modern Greece, although not legally mandated, it is common for the bride's family to pay for the wedding and related costs. The bride's family, sometimes in partnership with the groom's family, will often help with the down payment for the home that the newlyweds will live in. These arrangements remain commonplace in Greece and throughout the diaspora as well.

*John Psiharis*

A number of NGOs, women's associations, and charitable organizations operate shelters or offer other assistance to those who are experiencing domestic violence. These programs provide residential or supportive assistance, job training, counseling, and other services.

*John Psiharis*

**Further Reading**

Daughters of Penelope. 2018. "Fact Sheet: Domestic Violence, Human Trafficking in Greece." Accessed February 19, 2018. http://www.daughtersofpenelope.org/pdfs/FactSheetDomesticViolenceinGreece.pdf.

Immigration and Refugee Board of Canada. 2014. "Greece: Domestic Violence Including Legislation; State Protection and Support Services Available to Victims, Including Non-Citizens." The United Nations Refugee Agency. Accessed February 20, 2018. http://www.refworld.org/docid/53b137394.html.

Papazoglou, Manos. "The Greek Education System. Structure and Recent Reforms." Accessed February 10, 2018 http://adapt.it/adapt-indice-a-z/wp-content/uploads/2014/08/Papazoglou_gre.pdf.

Sedghi, Ami. 2014. "Violence against Women: What the EU-Wide Survey Tells Us." *The Guardian*, March 5, 2014. Accessed February 22, 2018. https://www.theguardian.com/news/datablog/2014/mar/05/violence-against-women-european-union-physical-sexual-abuse.

Smith, John. 2018. "Greece Records 13,700 Cases of Domestic Violence." *Greek Reporter*, January 28, 2018. Accessed February 19, 2018. http://greece.greekreporter.com/2018/01/28/greece-records-13700-cases-of-domestic-violence/.

Svarna, Foteini. 2014. "Financial Crisis and Domestic Violence – The Case of Greece." The Women's International Perspective, May 29, 2014. Accessed February 22, 2018. http://thewip.net/2014/05/29/financial-crisis-and-domestic-violence-the-case-of-greece/.

Zikakou, Ioanna. 2013. "One in Three Women Victim of Domestic Violence." *Greek Reporter*, November 1, 2013. Accessed February 18, 2018. http://greece.greekreporter.com/2013/11/01/one-in-three-women-victim-of-domestic-violence/.

## The Family

Throughout history, the family has been the cornerstone of Greek society. In Greece, a family unit consists of both immediate and extended members and may encompass several generations. In addition to the mother, father, and children, it often will include the maternal and/or paternal grandparents and siblings. In many cases a subset of this group will live under the same roof or in close proximity to each other. Godparents also maintain close ties with the family.

The father is the patriarch of the family. He has authority over the affairs of the family and is usually the primary breadwinner. The mother has primary responsibility for care of the children and home. The children are the center of emotional and financial concern for the nuclear and extended families.

Grandparents are respected for their age and consulted on all major decisions. A *yiayia* (grandmother) and *papou* (grandfather) may step in to care for young children so that a mother may maintain outside employment. If that is not possible, the family may hire a migrant woman to care for the children provided the income the wife generates is sufficient to justify it. Many parents living in metropolitan areas opt to enroll their children in day care centers. Relationships within the families are tightly knit, and they will likely remain close throughout their lives.

In the Greek family, age garners respect, and as such grandparents are revered. Whether or not they live under the same roof, grandparents are generally regarded as the hierarchs of the family and are treated with respect. As an increasing number of

### THE CHANGING NATURE OF THE FAMILY

By 2017, it became apparent that Greece, like other Western nations, was experiencing changes to the traditional family unit. According to Eurostat, the European Union's (EU) office for statistics, there are more single households in Greece (31 percent) than there are married households without children (25.2 percent). Married couples with children could be found in 21.9 percent of households. Unmarried households without children (15.7 percent) make up the balance. The 2017 EU-28 average for single households was 33.6 percent, with the highest numbers found in Sweden (51.4 percent) and Denmark (44.4 percent).

The Hellenic Statistical Authority reported a decline in traditional marriages from 62,195 in 1993 to 50,138 in 2017. In 2017, civil marriages, which are less costly, exceeded religious weddings. An upward trend in divorces has been noted, having risen from 7,725 in 1993 to 13,494 in 2005. After increasing by 30 percent during the financial crisis, the number of divorces fell to 11,013 in 2017.

Out-of-wedlock births increased from 5.1 percent of births in 1993 to 9.4 percent in 2015. In 2019, 6.3 percent of all households were comprised of single-parent families. In 2017, the average family size in Greece was 2.3. In 2005 it was 2.7. The EU average was 2.7 per household in 2017. The largest family units were in Croatia (2.8) and the smallest were in Sweden (1.9). Germany and Denmark were tied for second (both 2).

These changes are attributed to several factors, including the economic crisis, a reduction in the number of children a family has, increased life expectancy, more mothers in the workplace, more same-sex households, and generational and cultural changes.

*John Psiharis*

**Further Reading**

Karaiskaki, Tasoula. 2019. "The Changing Greek Family." *ekathimerini*. February 2, 2019. Accessed June 22, 2019. http://www.ekathimerini.com/237261/article/ekathimerini/community/the-changing-greek-family.

women enter the labor force, the importance of grandparents watching their grandchildren increases. Far from babysitting, this assistance enables the grandchildren and grandparents to forge a lifelong bond.

The family usually showers the first-born child with attention, and even more so if that child is a boy. Although the Greeks value the sanctity of any life, and a child is always cherished, there is a traditional preference for boys, as it is expected that they will carry on the family name into a new generation.

A child's godparents may also be part of the extended family. Becoming a godparent is an esteemed position. In this role, they agree to assume responsibility for the child, along with the grandparents, in the event of death or disability of the parents.

Children will usually live with their parents until they marry, although increasingly in step with the westernized world, some children choose to pursue their independence and move out of the family home, and rural youth may gravitate to the big cities for higher education opportunities. When aging parents need care, they often move in with their adult children. If there are more than one offspring, the primary responsibility often falls to the oldest child. Nursing homes are a last resort for most families and are mainly utilized when the level of care necessary is beyond the capabilities of the family to provide.

Children are usually encouraged by their parents to date and marry a Greek. Mixed marriages may not be frowned upon as much as they were in past decades, but there remains a preference by most parents to have their children marry within the culture and faith. As westernizing cultural influences and generational changes continue, it is less likely that the more traditional views will prevail.

*John Psiharis*

**See also:** Chapter 10: Baptism, Chrismation, and Naming Traditions; Weddings.

### Further Reading

Berberakis, Steylo. 2014. "A Man's Home is Woman's Castle in Greece." Daily Sabah Feature, April 1, 2014. Accessed February 12, 2018. https://www.dailysabah.com/feature/2014/04/01/a-mans-home-is-womans-castle-in-greece.

"Countries and Their Cultures. Greeks – Marriage and Family." Accessed February 12, 2018. http://www.everyculture.com/Europe/Greeks-Marriage-and-Family.html.

Hitton, Shanti. 2018. "Social Culture of Greece. Travel Tips." *USA Today*, February 5, 2018. Accessed February 15, 2018. http://traveltips.usatoday.com/social-culture-greece-17532.html.

"Overview of Greek Marriage Customs." n.d. Greek Boston. Accessed February 12, 2018. http://www.greekboston.com/wedding/marriage-customs/.

Teperoglou, Aphrodite. n.d. "Greece: Role of the Child." Net Industries. Accessed February 15, 2018. http://family.jrank.org/pages/743/Greece-Role-Child.html.

Teperoglou. Aphrodite. n.d. "Greece: The Elderly and the Family." Net Industries. Accessed February 15, 2018. http://family.jrank.org/pages/744/Greece-Elderly-Family.html.

## Gender Equality

The stereotype that men are the providers and decision-makers for their families while women raise the children and tend to the home has diminished in Greece. In response to years of activism from the feminist movement, legal recognition and protections for women are enshrined in law. Although equality is the law of the land, gender roles in Greece are a work in progress. In comparison to other Western countries, it took women a long time to gain basic rights. In 1952, women were granted the right to vote and stand for elections in legislative and municipal elections. They made incremental progress in both voter turnout and running for election until the political upheaval of the junta. During the time of the military dictatorship of the junta (1967–1974), the feminist movement was subverted by the regime, and citizens, including women, experienced restrictions on their rights.

Differences exist between the Greeks of rural Greece, which encompasses many villages spread throughout the nation, including remote mountain areas and 227 inhabited islands, and urban Greece, where two-thirds of the population resides. Those living in the major metropolitan areas, such as Athens and Thessaloniki, are more educated, progressive, and professional than those in rural areas. They enjoy a greater access to higher education, communications, information, culture, and media than their cousins who live on farms or small villages, and the women are more likely to be employed outside the home.

It was not until a democratic government returned to power in 1974 that the women's movement grew in both size and impact. A major outcome of this progress was the enactment of the Family Law Act of 1983. This law recognized equality between men and women, legally banned the dowry tradition, and instituted no-fault and mutual consent divorce. Until that time, the husband was the head of the family and its representative in most legal matters. A husband had rights over his wife's property and the ability to prevent her from working. The law also allowed for women to keep their maiden name after marriage and even pass it on to their children. Parents can choose for the child to have either the mother's or father's surname. The law viewed them as equals in the decision-making process. It also provided for equal pay for equal work.

Further protections for women happened when adultery was decriminalized in the early 1980s. Many viewed adultery laws as disproportionally impacting women. After incremental steps that began in 1970, the conditions for which abortion was permitted were gradually expanded. In 1986, abortion was legalized, and in 1992, Greece complied with European Union (EU) standards and established a maternity leave policy that provided between twelve and sixteen weeks of paid time off. These were major victories for the women's movement and mirrored progress in the United States and Europe.

Despite established laws that are considered to be progressive compared to other European nations' laws related to women's rights and equality, Greece today remains a more androcentric society than many of her peers.

A 2012 study by the European Commission documented gender equality in modern Greece and confirmed that progress has been made. However, the report finds that Greece, when compared to other westernized countries, lags in a number of key measures.

For instance, in 2012, this study found that 45.1 percent of Greek women were in the labor force, significantly lesser than the 58.5 percent average among the EU-27, and 22.8 percent of Greek women had attained university-level education, slightly lesser than the European average of 24.8 percent. However, more women were attending colleges and universities than men (22.8 percent vs. 21.8 percent).

Although Greek women study engineering at a slightly higher level than men (1 percent difference), the majority are studying in areas that are more historically considered to be women's fields such as education, humanities and the arts, and health care and social welfare. A larger percentage of highly educated women reside in urban areas.

Of those women who are working, more than 60 percent are employed in the following five sectors: wholesale and retail; agriculture, forestry, and fishing; education; health care and social work; and the accommodations and food service industries. In contrast the top five fields of employment for men were: wholesale and retail; manufacturing; construction; agriculture, forestry, and fishing; and public administration.

The number of women in management positions has improved. In 2012, 30 percent of women were employed in management positions in large and medium-sized companies within Greece. This was an improvement from 26 percent in 2008 but was lower than the EU-27 average of 33 percent.

Despite legal protections, a pay disparity remains. As noted in the March 8, 2018 issue of *Greek Reporter*, women in Greece were paid an average of 12.5 percent less than men in 2014, the last year for which the country had provided data on the gender pay gap, according to a report by Eurostat. In 2010, the difference was at 15 percent."

In EU countries as a whole, the pay gap was even larger. In 2011 it was 16.8 percent, and in 2016 it was 16.2 percent. The gender pay gap in Europe was only slightly better than in the United States. There women received 20 percent less than their male peers. In 2018, 15 of the European Commission's 28 members published a declaration reaffirming gender equality as one of the EU's keystones.

The gender overall earnings gap is the difference between the average annual earnings of women and men. It takes into account three types of disadvantages women face: lower hourly earnings; working fewer hours in paid jobs; and lower employment rates (e.g., when interrupting a career to take care of children or relatives). The gender overall earnings gap in Greece stands at 41.4 percent (the average gender overall earnings gap in the EU is 39.6 percent). At the heights of the economic crisis, unemployment rates for women who were actively seeking employment reached 27.9 percent. In July 2017, that number had decreased to 25.3 percent. Male unemployment fell from 19.6 percent to 17 percent. Overall, the unemployment rate was 21.5 percent, the lowest jobless numbers since December 2011. The highest was 27.9 percent.

The recent disparity between the unemployment rates of men and women related to the economic crisis was not surprising given that many women were teachers, nurses, social workers, and in other professions where they were employees of the government. The austerity cuts that the Greek government needed to make disproportionally impacted these sectors and resulted in higher numbers of women becoming unemployed. Further, the crisis resulted in fewer people traveling to Greece, and those who did spent less money. As tourism is a major economic engine for Greece, these changes also resulted in major layoffs in the food services and accommodations sectors in which large numbers of women are employed.

*John Psiharis*

**See also:** Chapter 4: Women in the Workforce. Chapter 7: Women in Politics and the Parliament.

**Further Reading**

Kokkinidis, Tasos. 2018. "Greek Women Close the Earnings Gap with Men." *Greek Reporter*, March 8, 2018. Accessed April 20 2021. https://greece.greekreporter.com/2018/03/08/greek-women-close-the-earnings-gap-with-men-graph/#:~:text=Women%20in%20Greece%20were%20paid,difference%20was%20at%2015%20percent.

Sutton, Susan Buck. n.d. "Culture of Greece." Countries and Their Cultures. Accessed October 31, 2017. http://www.everyculture.com/Ge-It/Greece.html.

Trading Economics. 2017. "Greece Unemployment Rates 1998–2017." Accessed March 1, 2020. https://tradingeconomics.com/greece/unemployment-rate.

## Lesbian, Gay, Bisexual, and Transgender Acceptance and Legal Protection

Greece is progressive on matters related to lesbian, gay, bisexual, and transgendered (LGBT) acceptance, equality, and legal protections compared to some of its European, Asian, Middle Eastern, and African counterparts. However, an undercurrent of disapproval still permeates primarily due to the influence of the Greek Orthodox Church and an older generation whose entrenched views against this population remain.

The LGBT population enjoys widespread protections under the law. Same-sex sexual activity for men was decriminalized in 1951 (for women it had not been criminalized), and LGBT antidiscrimination laws in employment were enacted in 2005. LGBT persons have been able to serve openly in the military since 2002. Further antidiscrimination laws, including prohibiting hate speech and violence against LGBT individuals or groups, have been in effect since 2014. The age of consent was equalized in 2015, and same-sex civil unions were recognized in 2015. In October 2017, Greece passed a law that allowed transgendered individuals to affirm their gender identity at the age of fifteen.

As with many societal issues, the government and the conservative Greek Orthodox Church have opposing views. Although these legislative advancements reflected the will of the majority of the citizenry in Greece, they were opposed by the church and conservative elected officials. The church has strongly opposed LGBT advancements at every opportunity. In June 2016, during the Thessaloniki Pride Festival, Orthodox clergy held an all-night prayer vigil and decried the event as a "festival of abnormality and dishonor." In 2014, the bishop of Thessaloniki proclaimed the LGBT community to be a "perversion of human existence." The far-right Golden Dawn party has also fanned flames of anti-LGBT sentiment among its members, which contributed to an increase in homophobic attacks.

Greece was one of the last nations in the EU to recognize same-sex civil unions due to strong opposition from the church. In the days before the parliamentary votes, Bishop Seraphim of Piraeus called sexual acts by gay people "unnatural lewdness," and Bishop Amvrosios of Kalavryta ordered churches in his diocese to sound funeral bells "in mourning" over the bill's expected passage.

In October 2017, as the Greek Parliament voted to approve a gender identity law, the Holy Synod, which governs the Greek Orthodox Church, claimed the measure would "destroy human beings" and was "a satanic deed" that would lead to "the destruction of social cohesion and the spiritual necrosis of man" (Zikakou 2014). Members of Parliament (MPs) were threatened with excommunication from the church. While PASOK and SYRIZA members have been strong supporters of LGBT rights, New Democracy, the Communist Party, and Golden Dawn have been in steady opposition.

A 2013 Pew Research Center report entitled "The Global Divide on Homosexuality: Greater Acceptance in More Secular and Affluent Countries" measured the level of acceptance of gay people in thirty-nine nations. When study participants were asked if society should accept gay men and women, 88 percent of respondents from Spain agreed followed by Germany (87 percent) and Canada and Czech Republic (both 80 percent). The United States was at 60 percent, Greece at 53 percent, Tunisia and Pakistan at 2 percent, and Nigeria had the least acceptance at 1 percent. The study also found that younger people were more likely to be in favor than older generations, more women than men were supportive of LGBT rights, and that acceptance is greater in countries where religion is less central in people's lives. In Greece, 66 percent of those between the ages of eighteen and twenty-nine and 62 percent of those between thirty and forty-nine were in favor of acceptance compared to 40 percent of those over age fifty.

Greece ranked twenty-first in the 2015 Rainbow Europe Map Index Survey sponsored by the International Lesbian, Gay, Bisexual, Trans and Intersex Association (ILGA-Europe). The study looked at forty-eight legal and policy criteria that reflect LGBT legislative priorities and compared each nation's adherence to the criteria. Greece had a rating of 39 percent, placing it in the middle of the study below Ireland and Luxembourg and above Georgia, the Czech Republic, and Estonia. The highest scoring nations were the United Kingdom (86 percent), Belgium (83 percent), Malta (79 percent), and Sweden (72 percent). The lowest scoring nations surveyed were Russia (8 percent) and Azerbaijan (5 percent). Greece, however, achieved the greatest measure of improvement from the previous study than any of the forty-nine countries reviewed.

Despite opposition from religious leaders and conservative politicians, in day-to-day life, the LGBT community continues to become more visible as acceptance by the general populace grows. A preponderance of the LGBT populations is located in the large cities with a majority in Athens. Large numbers also live in Thessaloniki and Patras. The LGBT population is not as widely accepted and thus not as evident in smaller towns and villages where they may experience discrimination or hostility.

A wide array of organizations exists throughout Greece that focus on many facets of the LGBT community, including professional and social networking groups, LGBT sports teams, recreational gatherings, and arts organizations. Other organizations focus on advocating for LGBT equality and acceptance. Some focus on LBGT citizens who are victims of crimes, violence, domestic abuse, or sexual trafficking. The National Committee of Human Rights and the United Nations Refugee Agency in Greece track incidents of homophobic or transphobic attacks. In 2014, Athens-based Colour Youth, a nongovernmental organization run entirely by volunteers between the ages of eighteen and thirty, launched a campaign to educate, raise awareness, and encourage victims of homophobic or transphobic verbal or physical attacks to report the encounter.

Greece hosts annual Gay Pride celebrations in Athens, Thessaloniki, Patras, and Heraklion. An international gay and lesbian film festival is held annually in Athens. A thriving LGBT tourism sector and a vibrant nightlife attract tourists from around the world. Mykonos ranks as a top global vacation destination for LGBT tourists. Athens, Thessaloniki, Crete, Corfu, and Santorini are also popular tourist destinations for LGBT travelers. It is expected that equality and acceptance of the LGBT community will continue to grow in the coming years.

*John Psiharis*

**See also:** Chapter 3: Human Rights; Golden Dawn.

**Further Reading**

Harris, Mary. 2016. "Greek Church Prays for LGBT Abnormality, Ahead of Thessaloniki Pride." *Greek Reporter*, June 24, 2016. Accessed May 8, 2018. http://greece.greekreporter.com/2016/06/24/greek-church-prays-for-lgbt-abnormality-ahead-of-thessaloniki-pride/.

The Pew Research Center Global Attitudes and Trends. 2013. "The Global Divide on Homosexuality Greater Acceptance in More Secular and Affluent Countries." Pew Research Center, June 4, 2013. Accessed May 1, 2018. http://www.pewglobal.org/2013/06/04/the-global-divide-on-homosexuality/.

Popper, Helen. 2015. "Greece Legalizes Same-sex Civil Partnerships. PM Alexis Tsipras Said It Was Long Overdue." Politico-Europe, December 23, 2015. Accessed May 8, 2018. https://www.politico.eu/article/greece-civil-unions-vote-parliament-lgbti-bill/.

Smith, Helena. 2017. "Greece Passes Gender-change Law Opposed by Orthodox Church." *The Guardian*, October 10, 2017. Accessed May 8, 2018. https://www.theguardian.com/world/2017/oct/10/greece-passes-gender-change-law.

Travel by Interest. "Greece Gay Guide." Accessed May 11, 2018. https://www.travelbyinterest.com/destination/1087/gay/guide.

Zikakou, Ioanna. 2014. "Greek Bishop Condemns Gay Pride Parade." *Greek Reporter*, June 19, 2014. Accessed May 11, 2018. http://greece.greekreporter.com/2014/06/19/greek-bishop-condemns-gay-pride-parade/.

Zikakou, Ioanna. 2015. "Greece Ranks 21st on Rainbow Europe Map and Index." *Greek Reporter*, May 14, 2015. Accessed May 6, 2018. http://greece.greekreporter.com/2015/05/14/greece-ranks-21st-on-rainbow-europe-map-and-index/.

## Prostitution and Trafficking

Prostitution in Greece is a complex issue within the fabric of Greek society. It is legal for those who are eighteen years of age or older, but the means by which it is allowed are limited.

Legally, prostitution is only allowed in licensed brothels or studios, often run by older women who are retired sex workers themselves. Since 1999, the government has issued permits for brothels. They cannot be located within 200 meters (656 feet) of public buildings. The brothels provide women with a safer working environment, on-site security, and regular sexual health screenings. Street prostitution is not permitted, and violators are arrested. Those who manage or traffic in underage prostitution are also prosecuted.

Women working as prostitutes legally are required to register and carry a medical card that is updated every two weeks. Laws require that they be at least eighteen years old, have the legal right to live and work in Greece, be free of STDs or other infections, not suffer from drug addiction or mental health issues, and not have been convicted for homicide, pimping, child porn, trafficking, robbery, or blackmail. They must also not be married. In 2015, according to one study, only one thousand of the estimated twenty thousand prostitutes in Greece were legally registered.

Due in large measure to the exclusion of married women, undocumented migrants, and those with mental health issues or drug addiction not being able to legally work in the sex trade, much of the prostitution activity in Greece occurs in an unregulated underground environment. These women have little protection from violence by their customers and are at greater risk of being abused or pimped. Likewise, they do not receive screenings for STDs.

Until the economic crisis, the majority of prostitutes in Greece were undocumented migrants from Albania, Eastern European, or Romas or refugees. As the economy worsened and unemployment reached record levels, Greek women began to take up the vocation as a means of economic survival. A 2015 study of seventeen thousand sex workers revealed that Greek women have replaced Eastern European women as the largest proportion of sex workers in Greece. They account for 80 percent of the total. The average age for those entering prostitution was between seventeen and twenty, and many women drifted in and out of the trade depending on their financial need.

It had been reported that mothers would see clients while their children were at school and doctors would engage in prostitution to compensate for the salary cuts and job losses resulting from the government's austerity program. Women engaged in prostitution for food or drug money or to pay taxes or urgent bills. Due in large measure to the influx of women into the sex trade, costs for a thirty-minute session were among the lowest in Europe. The law of supply and demand prevailed. According to the study, just before the economic crisis, the going rate for thirty minutes with a prostitute in Greece was 53 dollars. By 2015, when the impact of the crisis was at its worse, the average rate fell to 2.12 dollars.

Male prostitution also increased as a result of the economic crisis. Although there are Greek men engaged in prostitution, mainly due to economic necessity, the majority are refugees struggling to survive in Greece.

It is legal for males to enter into prostitution, but the laws that regulate prostitution do not address male sex workers. Male prostitution therefore occurs in the underground market and does not operate in any organized fashion. Male prostitutes frequent public venues or bars, clubs, or saunas to meet their clients. Classified advertisements and the Internet are commonly used. They are typically young and do not consider themselves to be prostitutes. Instead, they see it as a short-term act to make quick money in order to get food or otherwise survive. Many do identify as gay and see it only as work. Another subset of this group involves transgendered prostitutes of which little data is known.

The increased levels of prostitution paralleled a 200 percent increase in the incidence of HIV between the years 2011 and 2015. In 2012, Greek authorities began to release photos of sex workers who had HIV and were working as prostitutes. This further stigmatized women engaged in prostitution and had the end result of significantly reducing the numbers of sex workers who tested for STDs; they feared that they might undergo the same public shaming.

As the economic recovery has begun to take hold and as employment opportunities grow, it is anticipated that the number of natives engaged in prostitution will decline. A decrease in the numbers of sex workers who are undocumented migrants or refugees is a goal as well, but one that may be harder to achieve given the limited options these populations have to earn money.

*John Psiharis*

**See also:** Chapter 6: Immigration and Migration to Greece.

**Further Reading**

Damaskos, Panagiotis. 2014. "Male Prostitutes – An Invisible Group of High Vulnerability." Hellenic Center for Disease Control and Prevention. January 21, 2014. Accessed May 14, 2018. http://www2.keelpno.gr/blog/?p=4934&lang=en.

Damon, Arwa, Barbara Arvanitidis, and Clayton Nagel. 2016. "The Teenage Refugees Selling Sex on Athens Streets." CNN Freedom Project, CNN, November 11, 2016. Accessed May 8, 2018. https://www.cnn.com/2016/11/29/europe/refugees-prostitution-teenagers-athens-greece/index.html.

Deane, Daniela. 2015. "Greek Women Selling Sex for the Price of a Sandwich, New Study Shows." *Washington Post*, November 27, 2015. Accessed May 11, 2018. https://www

.washingtonpost.com/world/young-greek-women-selling-sex-for-the-price-of-a-sandwich-new-study-shows/2015/11/27/c469695e-94d9-11e5-b5e4-279b4501e8a6_story.html?noredirect=on&utm_term=.3c17b1b9fe2c.

Labaree, Aaron. 2016. "Migrant Men in Greece Are Selling Sex to Survive." PRI-Public Radio International, June 2, 2016. Accessed May 11, 2018. https://www.pri.org/stories/2016-06-02/migrant-men-greece-are-selling-sex-survive.

Reid, Rebecca. 2015. "Prostitution: The Hidden Cost of Greece's Economic Crisis." *The Telegraph*, November 13, 2015. Accessed October 6, 2017. https://www.telegraph.co.uk/women/politics/prostitution-the-hidden-cost-of-greeces-economic-crisis/.

## Women in Politics and the Parliament

Women's role in the political life of Greece has paralleled the progress of women throughout the westernized world but at a slower pace than many of its allies and neighbors. Even today, Greece has fewer women in government and politics than most other European Union members.

Greece's first step to legalize voting for women was in 1930, when women were allowed to vote in municipal elections, with two important provisos: They had to be thirty years of age or older, and they had to have attained an elementary school education. In 1930s Greece, the second condition was hard for many women to meet, since only few had achieved that benchmark. In fact, during the 1934 Athens municipal elections, only 439 women voted out of 2,655 who had registered to vote.

Greece is revered for being the birthplace of democracy, but women did not gain the unconditional right to vote or be elected to office until May 28, 1952. This was several decades behind Finland (1906), Norway (1917), Germany (1919), and Britain (1928).

The progress of women in politics and government was incremental. The first vote that women were able to take part in was held in January 1953 and resulted in the election of Eleni Skoura, who filled the term of a deceased member of Parliament (MP).

The first Greek woman to have a leadership role in government was Lina Tsaldari, who became minister of social welfare in 1956 in the government of Konstantinos Karamanlis. She was both the daughter and wife of a prime minister. Her father, Spyridon Lambros, was prime minister from 1916 to 1917, and her husband, Panagis Tsaldaris, was prime minister from 1932 to 1935. In 1956, Maria Desi was elected mayor of the island of Corfu and became the first female mayor in Greece. She would serve in this role for three years.

Between April 21, 1967, until 1974, the era of military rule by the junta in Greece, civil rights were suspended and the Parliament was disbanded. No MP elections were held. The government controlled the media, and many in vocal opposition to the authoritarian rule were tortured or imprisoned. During this period, there were six elections for local government officials and thirteen women were elected. Although many were engaged in anti-junta protests, no women played a prominent role in the national government during this time period.

Emboldened by movements in other nations, particularly the United States and the United Kingdom, as well as the return to a democratic government at home, feminist issues rose to the forefront of the progressive movement and as such became a national cause.

A major achievement of the feminist movement was the adoption of a new family law that established gender equality as the law of the land. Adopted in 1983, the law also guaranteed equal pay for equal work, abolished the dowry, decriminalized adultery, and simplified the process of divorce.

Women have long been active in the political process of Greece and were well represented in party leadership ranks. This in turn had an impact on the platform and policies that the parties adopted. Although involved in many political parties that covered the spectrum of political ideologies, women were more likely to be found in leadership roles in parties that were left of center.

These political pioneers included several well-known women:

Alexandra (Aleka) Papariga (1945–) was a member of the Hellenic Parliament first elected in 1993. She became secretary general of the KKE, the Communist Party of Greece, in 1991 and served through 2013. A leader within the feminist movement since the 1970s, Papariga became the first woman to head a major political party in Greece.

Fofi Gennimata (1964–) was elected president of the PASOK in 2015 winning with 51 percent of the vote in a three-way race. She served as deputy minister of health and welfare during 2010–2011. Her father, a founding member of PASOK, held a number of key ministerial positions in the governments of Andreas Papandreou.

Melina Mercuri (1920–1994) became minister for culture under the PASOK government of Andreas Papandreou that was elected in 1981. She would become the first female cabinet minister since 1956 and continued in that role throughout Papandreou's eight years as premier. A founding member and leader in the PASOK party since its inception, Mercuri lived in exile until the adoption of the new constitution in 1974. She was an internationally acclaimed actress and singer who had been an outspoken critic of the junta. Her grandfather Spyridon Merkouris had been mayor of Athens from 1899 to 1914 and returned to that position between 1929 and 1932.

When the New Democracy party won the 1989 elections, Konstantinos Mitsotakis became premier. Mercuri was elected a member of the Hellenic Parliament and in 1990 launched an unsuccessful campaign for mayor of Athens. When PASOK won the 1993 elections and Papandreou regained the premiership, Mercuri returned to her role as minister for culture and served in that capacity until her death on March 6, 1994. She is credited for her leadership in advocating for the return of the Parthenon Marbles from Britain, establishing cultural exchange programs throughout Europe, and leading Greece's efforts to host the Centennial Olympic Games.

Although an increasing number of women stood for election and some won, the number of women in the Hellenic Parliament was less than 10 percent between 1974 and 2000 when the election of four additional women nudged the percentage slightly above that threshold. In 1995, for example, the general elections saw nineteen women in the Hellenic Parliament, including three university professors, four lawyers, two philologists, one architect, and two other graduates of the Polytechnic, a political scientist, an economist, and an actress.

Subsequent MP elections saw the numbers continue to grow. In October 2009, fifty-two women (17.3 percent) were elected, while another eight entered the Hellenic Parliament because of replacement. In May 2012, fifty-six women (18.6 percent) were elected, and the June 2013 elections resulted in sixty-three women MPs (21 percent). In 2015, there were sixty-eight women elected to Parliament, an all-time record.

Women who achieved ministerial levels were typically responsible for areas that involved culture, welfare, education, or social justice. A notable exception was Vasiliki Papandreou who became the minister of environment, planning and public works in 2000. Before that she had served as alternate minister for industry and as alternate minister of commerce.

Theadora "Dora" Bakoyannis (1954–) was another woman who broke barriers in the world of government and politics. Daughter of former prime minister Konstantinos Mitsotakis, she was first elected to the Hellenic Parliament as an independent in order to complete her late husband's term. Her husband, Pavlos Bakoyannis, a vocal critic of the military dictatorship, was assassinated by members of the 17N (November 17), a radical terrorist group, on September 26, 1989.

Bakoyannis was reelected as a member of her father's New Democracy party and served as minister for culture between 1992 and 1993. She returned to Parliament as a member of the opposition party through 2002 when she became mayor of Athens—the first woman to have been elected to this role in the city's 3,500-year history. Mayor Bakoyannis received more than 60 percent of the vote in a run-off election. During her four years in office, she successfully oversaw the city's arrangements as Athens prepared to host the 2004 Summer Olympic Games.

In February 2006, Bakoyannis left her role as mayor before the completion of her term of office in order to assume the position of minister of foreign affairs in the newly elected cabinet of Constantine Karamanlis. She attained the distinction of being the highest-ranking woman in government up to that point. In September 2006, Bakoyannis, as foreign minister, also assumed the rotating presidency of the United Nations Security Council.

Another achievement for women occurred when Zoe Konstantopoulou was elected president of the Hellenic Parliament in 2015 with 235 of 300 votes, a record. She was the youngest ever to be elected to this position and the second woman to serve in that role after Anna Psarouda-Benaki served between 2004 and 2007. Psarouda-Benaki had also served as both minister for culture and minister for justice.

In the late 1990s and well into the 2000s, the number of women who served as cabinet ministers or in other high-level government positions increased. They included Katerina Batzeli, minister of rural development and food (2009–2010); Tina Birbili, minister for the environment, energy, and climate change (2009–2011); Anna Diamatopoulou, minister for education, lifelong education, and religious affairs (October 2009–?); Tatiana Karapanagioti, minister for culture and tourism (2012); Louka Katseli, minister for labor and social security and minister for the economy, competitiveness, and shipping (2010–2011); Olga Kefalogianni, minister for tourism (2012–2015); Angeliki-Efrosini Kiaou, known as Frosso Kiaou, minister for culture, education, and religious affairs (2012); Elena Kountoura, minister for tourism (2015); Marietta Giannakou-Koutsikou, minister for education and religious affairs (2004–2007) and minister for health (1990–1991); Elisavet Papazoe, minister for culture (1999–2000) and minister for the Aegean (1997–1999); Fani Palli-Petralia, minister for employment and social protection (2007) and minister for tourism (2006–2007); and Mariliza Xenogiannakopoulou, minister for health and social solidarity (2009–2010).

Vassiliki Thanou-Christophilou (1950–), having been appointed president of the Court of Cassation on July 1, 2015, became interim prime minister on August 27 of that year after the abrupt resignation of Alexis Tsipras of the Coalition of the Radical Left (SYRIZA). He had called for new elections to create a mandate for his government to deal with the economic crisis that Greece was experiencing.

According to the Constitution of Greece, the president of the republic was to select and appoint an interim prime minister from one of the three Greek Supreme Court presidents. On August 27, 2015, President Prokopis Pavlopoulos appointed Christophilou to fill that role, and as such she served as the first female prime minister of Greece until September 21, when Tsipras returned to office with what he had hoped would be renewed authority and support from the electorate. Although she held the position in an unelected caretaker role, Christophilou will hold the distinction as the first woman to serve as prime minister of the Hellenic Republic. Katerina Sakellaropoulou was sworn in as president of the Hellenic Republic on March 13, 2020, for a five-year term of office. She was the first woman to serve as president of Greece.

It is worth noting that a number of the women who have thus far attained leadership in the arenas of politics and government in Greece have come from families with significant backgrounds in politics at the highest of levels. In these cases, not unlike other nations, the political pedigree of a family may have provided the opportunity to these women to take part in what many Greeks still perceive to be primarily a male-dominated profession and enabled them to achieve success on their own accord.

*John Psiharis*

**See also:** Chapter 4: Women in the Workforce.

**Further Reading**

Maloutas, M. Pantelidou. 2007. "Women and Politics." About Greece, 397–408. Accessed September 30, 2017. http://docplayer.net/28505527-By-m-pantelidou-maloutas-anna-benaki-psarouda-president-of-the-hellenic-parliament.html.

Nordin, John P. 1999. "Women in Greek Politics." The Plaka, August 25, 1999. Accessed October 21, 2017. http://www.theplaka.com/today/polwomen.htm.

"Women in Greek Politics." 2014. *Greek Reporter*, March 9, 2014. Accessed October 18, 2017. http://www.grreporter.info/en/women_greek_politics/10819.

## Women in the Armed Forces

As with many of the strides Greece has made in the areas of gender equality, Greek women came into the military years later than many of their Western counterparts. After World War II, the need to modernize the Military Nursing Corps became apparent. In February 1946, a law was enacted that provided for the establishment of the Nursing Officers Corps and thus the entrance of women into the Hellenic Armed Forces. In October of the same year, another law established the Military Nursing School. The graduates of this school are commissioned second lieutenants and are assigned to the three services.

Greek women may voluntarily enlist in the military, and those between the ages of twenty and thirty-two are obligated to serve only if they are called upon in the event of war or other large mobilization. Women who are mothers, without family providers or parents, are exempted. The tour of duty for women is fourteen months with the option of a ten-month renewal.

In comparison, Greece has required obligatory military service for males between the ages of nineteen and forty-five. Greek men are conscripted for nine months in the army or for twelve months in the navy or air force. Once discharged from active service, they are placed into the reserves for an additional seventeen months.

Although law provides for widespread equality between male and female service personnel, women may not serve on the front lines. They are also barred from serving on submarines, fast-moving patrol boats, and hovercrafts that are used in landings. Their roles are supportive in nature, freeing the men who occupy those positions for active duty. Typical jobs that women enrollees have are in nursing, finance, and engineering and as medical or legal staffs.

Despite differences in the levels of engagement between the genders within the military, the same rules apply for training, promotion, and discipline. Female officers and noncommissioned officers (NCOs) train and serve alongside their male counterparts. Women are admitted to the military academies upon successful completion of the Panhellenic Examinations. Not more than 10 percent of the students of the military academies can be women at any given time. In 1999, six women (one officer, five NCOs) were chosen to sail upon a naval ship for six months for the first time. Greek women in the military are granted a fifty-six-week paid maternity leave after the sixteenth week of pregnancy, the most generous of all NATO members. In comparison, the United States offers the least, an average of forty-two days.

In 2002, women accounted for 3.75 percent or 6,155 of the total members of the Hellenic Armed Forces. Of that total, 717 were officers while 5,438 (2.6 percent of the army, 8.4 percent of the navy, and 9.6 percent of the air force) were NCOs. Ten years later in 2012, women composed 5.6 percent of the Hellenic Armed Forces. Moreover, 3.1 percent of senior officers and 10.61 percent of junior officers were female. The highest rank to date attained by a woman was brigadier general in the Nursing Corps.

Women are allowed to serve in peacekeeping operations involving the Greek military. In 2002, thirty-seven army women (five officers and thirty-two NCOs) and two air force women (NCOs) were in Kosovo.

It is expected that the influence and roles of women in the Greek military will continue to increase in numbers, ranks, and responsibilities in the coming years and attain parity with its European and Western counterparts.

*John Psiharis*

**See also:** Chapter 7: Gender Equality.

**Further Reading**

Committee on Women in NATO Forces. 2002. "Greece." NATO International Military Staff, March 26, 2002. Accessed October 14, 2017. https://www.nato.int/ims/2001/win/greece.htm.

Obradovic, Lana. 2014. "Gender Integration in NATO Military Forces: Cross-national Analysis." Ashgate Publishing, Ltd. Accessed October 28, 2017. https://books.google.com/books/about/Gender_Integration_in_NATO_Military_Forc.html?id=_qIFBAAAQBAJ&hl=en.

## Women's Education

Education has long been viewed as the key to solving a nation's ills and as a means of empowering its populace. Dating back to the earliest days of ancient Greece, a premium has always been placed on teaching and learning.

In the past, the education of males had been more important than the education of women. The share of female university students grew from about 30 percent in the 1970s to 49 percent in 1995. Parity between male and female students in higher education institutions was achieved in 2000, when 50 percent of students were female. By 2015, the number grew to 53 percent. Women account for a majority of the degrees issued within the fields of education, arts and humanities and social sciences, business, and law.

A 2016 study by the Organisation for Economic Co-operation and Development (OECD) of the thirty-five nations that are members found slightly less of a gender imbalance in education within Greece compared to the others and that a higher proportion of women graduate from engineering, manufacturing, and construction programs than in the other nations. However, discrepancies in employment rates and salaries between men and women are wider in Greece than in most of the other member nations.

A number of the early efforts to encourage advanced education of women focused on teaching and nursing careers. In 1836, seventy-two men gathered to found the Educational Society, which had the goal of establishing "an institution in which girls should be educated to teach in schools throughout Greece, even in the out-of-way villages."

In an April 18, 1901, lecture to the Alumni Association of the New York Training School for Nurses, Dr. Achilles Rose, a noted Philhellene and author of *Christian Greece, Living Greek*, documented the founding of the teacher's college, which would bear the name of a major financial donor, Apostolis Arsakis; it became known as the Arsakeion. According to Rose, more than two thousand women attained teaching degrees during the first fifty years of the school, and they taught in every part of Greece.

That organization, now known as the Society of the Friends of Education, has grown into a network of six private schools located throughout Greece with enrollment of over nine thousand students, including a campus in Albania. A school in Cyprus is in the planning stages. According to the organization's website, in 2014, women made up 64 percent of teaching positions at all levels in Greece.

Efforts to provide nursing education to women began in 1875 when Queen Olga founded Evangelismos, the first school of nursing in Greece and at that time only the third such school in the world. Nine years later, in 1884, the hospital Evangelismos was founded, with one of its purposes being "to educate women nurses according to the rules of science." In the coming years, many efforts were made to provide quality education to nurses, and Greece became the first country in Europe to offer a generalized nursing curriculum, following the lead of the United States and Canada.

*John Psiharis*

**See also:** Chapter 4: Women in the Workforce.

**Further Reading**

The Fulbright Foundation in Greece. 2017. "The Greek Educational System." Accessed December 18, 2017. http://www.fulbright.gr/en/study-in-greece/the-greek-educational-system.

Lancrin, Stephan Vincent. 2015. "The Reversal of Gender Inequalities in Higher Education-an On-going Trend." In *Higher Education to 2030*, Vol. 1: Demography, Chapter 10. Organization for Economic Cooperation and Development. Accessed December 28, 2018. https://www.oecd.org/edu/ceri/41939699.pdf.

Organization for Economic Cooperation and Development. 2016. "Greece." In *Education at a Glance: 2016 OECD Indicators*. Paris: OECD Publishing. Accessed December 5, 2017. http://www.oecd-ilibrary.org/education/education-at-a-glance_19991487.

Rose, Achilles. 1901. "The Progress of Women in Modern Greece." *The American Journal of Nursing* no. 11 (August). Accessed December 7, 2017. https://www.jstor.org/stable/3402378?seq=1#page_scan_tab_contents.

Ziogou, Theologia, Aliki Dimitriadou, and Evangelos Fradelos. 2013. "The History of Nursing Education in Modern Greece." *Balkan Military Medical Review* 16, no. 3 (July–September). Accessed December 21, 2017. https://www.researchgate.net/publication/262182738_The_History_of_Nursing_Education_in_Modern_Greece.

## Women's Associations

Throughout the history of Greece, women have been a powerful and influential force for change, especially in relation to feminist issues. Many efforts in areas such as gender equality, family law, abortion rights, and pay equity were advanced by women's associations in Greece. They represented countless women who shared these values. Through unity of purpose, these groups were integral to achieving landmark progress in these areas. As part of the community of Europe, these Greek organizations often joined forces with organizations from other European nations to advocate for women's issues on a multinational level.

A description of Greek women's associations follows:

- The Greek League for Women's Rights (GLWR) was founded in 1920 in Athens. Early on, their efforts were focused on the rights of women to vote. Their efforts, along with those of allied associations and their supporters from the 1920s and 1950s, were critical to women gaining the right to vote in 1952. The group was forced to suspend their operations during the junta period but quickly resumed their efforts when democracy was restored. The League has also been in the forefront in advocating for repeal of laws that discriminate against women and for progressive measures in family law. The GLWR has published the "Women's Struggle: A Historic Feminist Journal" since 1923 and has been affiliated since 1923 with the International Alliance of Women. A more recent focus of the organization has been on human trafficking and prostitution.
- The National Council of Greek Women, a federation of fifty women's associations from across Greece and Cyprus, represents sixty thousand women. Founded in 1908, it is the oldest women's association in Greece. Located in Athens, it is affiliated with the International Council of Women (ICW) and the European Council of the ICW (ECICW). The mission of the council is "the promotion of the interests and status of women in all sectors of life: family, society, community, and state; the protection of human rights in general and of the rights of women and children in particular; the promotion of peace and cooperation among nations and the healthy upbringing of youth."
- The Movement of Democratic Women (KDG) was formed in 1974 as Greece transitioned into democracy after the junta period. It focused on traditional women's issues, including maternity and child-rearing issues.
- The Movement for the Liberation of Women joined the KDG and other associations in advocating for contraceptives as a means for women to have control of their bodies. The association joined a campaign that demanded the unimpeded right to free abortions. This was enacted into law in 1986.
- The Women's House organized protests condemning sexual harassment, rape, and gender-based violence within and outside of the family.
- The Union of Greek Women, organized in 1976, was affiliated with the PASOK. In 1982, it defined itself as a Socialist feminist organization.
- The Federation of Greek Women (OGE), launched in 1976 during an assembly of forty-four women's associations and clubs, concentrated on women's rights related to employment and social security. It also advocated for the role women play as mothers, as well as for safeguarding peace and opposing nuclear weapons and testing. It is politically linked to the Communist Party of Greece (KKE).

Trade unions and youth associations also established sections or committees focused on the issues related to working women.

As many of the issues that fueled these movements have been addressed and Greece has adopted laws and policies that are on par with its EU neighbors and the United States, the need for massive movements and protests has subsided. In the 1990s, many of the organizations were dissolved and the number of feminist journals and books dwindled. A renewed focus on gender studies and feminism evolved.

Today there are a myriad of women's associations throughout Greece that are organized to bring together women with common purposes or backgrounds. These include organizations such as: League of Women Entrepreneurs and Professionals of Athens, Association of Greek Homemakers, Association of Greek Women in Legal Professions, Progressive Union of Greek Mothers, the League of Women Scholars, and others. In addition to advocating for improvements within their areas of interest, these organizations also provide opportunities for networking, socialization, and enrichment as well as social services to women who encounter domestic violence, rape, prostitution, trafficking, homelessness, and other crisis situations.

*John Psiharis*

**See also:** Chapter 7: Domestic Violence; Gender Equality

**Further Reading**

Couloumbis, Theodore A., Theodore C. Kariotis, and Fotini Bellou. 2003. *Greece in the 20th Century.* London and New York: Psychology Press. Accessed January 20, 2018. https://books.google.com/books?id=1wk1YLdUWjoC&pg=PA280&lpg= &dq=Women%27s+Confederation+Of+Greece&source=bl&ots=ohsLpfbFvs&sig=aWjJVY31YeJSsQqfTXMIDXHNKj8&hl=en&sa=X&ved=0ahUKEwjT0vjyrPTYAhXQlOAKHYIIDlMQ6AEIcjAP#v=onepage&q=Women's%20Confederation%20Of%20Greece&f=false.

"Greek League for Women's Rights." European Institute for Gender Equality, February 20, 2014. Accessed January 11, 2018. http://eige.europa.eu/gender-mainstreaming/structures/greece/greek-league-womens-rights.

Greek League for Women's Rights. National Council of Greek Women. 2012. "Shadow Report on the Compliance of Greece with the CEDAW. Observations on the 7th Greek Report (2005–2008)." January 28, 2012. Accessed January 12, 2018. http://tbinternet.ohchr.org/Treaties/CEDAW/Shared%20Documents/GRC/INT_CEDAW_NGO_GRC_13242_E.pdf.

Greek News Agenda. "Feminism in the Era of Metapolite, 1974–1990: Ideas, Collectives, Claims." Athens. Secretariat General of Information and Communication of the Hellenic Republic. Accessed January 12, 2018. http://www.greeknewsagenda.gr/index.php/topics/politics-polity/6476-feminism-in-the-era-of-metapolitefsi-1974-1990-ideas,-collectives,-claims.

"Movement of Democratic Women." Parliament of Greece. Accessed January 15, 2018. http://foundation.parliament.gr/VoulhFoundation/VoulhFoundationPortal/images/site_content/voulhFoundation/file/Ektheseis/Feminism%20Eng/3/gynaikeies%20organwseis_EN.pdf.

National Council of Greek Women. n.d. "NCGW Profile." Accessed November 28, 2020. http://ncgw.org/%CF%80%CE%BF%CE%B9%CE%BF%CE%AF-%CE%B5%CE%AF%CE%BC%CE%B1%CF%83%CF%84%CE%B5/?lang=en.

CHAPTER 8

# EDUCATION

## OVERVIEW

Education in Greece is a national right. According to the Greek Constitution, "All Greeks have the right to free education at all levels in public educational institutions. The state assists those students who excel as well those who are in financial need or in need of special protection, according to their abilities." The right to a free public education has also been extended to children of immigrants and refugees.

Education is compulsory for children aged five to fifteen. Over 90 percent of schools in Greece are public, and 90 percent of children attend these public schools. The state provides free tuition, textbooks for all students, and transportation for those living far from the local public school.

Education in Greece is divided into primary, secondary, and postsecondary stages. Primary schools consist of kindergarten to sixth grade or ages six to twelve. Secondary schools consist of the *gymnasio* and *lykeio*. The *gymnasio* would be the equivalent of seventh, eighth, and ninth grades, and the *lykeio* the equivalent of tenth, eleventh, and twelfth grades in the United States. In the *lykeio*, students may choose an academic track or a vocational track. There are specialized *gymnasia* and *lykeia*, for example, athletic, musical, art, or experimental, and students must pass certain exams to enter. All schools are coeducational. The language of instruction at all levels has been demotic (Standard Greek).

The school year begins in September and ends in June. There are 5 school days a week for a total of 175 days a year. Students are off for twelve weeks in the summer, two weeks for the Christmas holiday, and two weeks in the spring for the Easter holiday. There are also 7 days off for national or religious holidays.

Students in the primary school spend about five hours per day for about forty-five minutes per subject. The school day runs from 8:15 a.m. to 1:30 p.m. Subjects covered are reading and writing, social studies, science, physical education, mathematics, the arts, and religion.

The length of classes in the *gymnasio* and *lykeio* vary from thirty to forty-five minutes depending on the subject, with the school day running from 8:00 a.m. to 1:30 p.m. The subjects covered consist of history, literature, science, theology, music, art, physical education, and mathematics.

As education in Greece is valued, many students go on to higher education. In June, students wishing to enter a Greek university need to take the Panhellenic

National Examinations. Entrance to a university is very competitive, and only about 20 percent pass these examinations. Many college students who do not pass the exams attend universities in other countries of the European Union (EU). The state does not recognize degrees from private universities in Greece, so those that exist outside the public sector are affiliated with foreign accreditation bodies and universities.

Cram schools (*frondisteria*), which convene after school or on Saturdays, have been popular since the 1960s as a way to help students pass the exams and get into college, as well as to learn a foreign language. Such private schools vary in their size, enrollment, and organization of classes or levels.

Higher education is divided into technological universities, academies, and universities. Most males typically serve in the Greek military before pursuing higher education. Undergraduate students usually complete their studies in four years. Students can major in a variety of subjects, from the liberal arts and sciences, to the humanities and law. Postgraduate education that leads toward a master's degree typically takes one to two years, and doctorate programs between three and six years, depending on the field of study. Medical training is typically six years.

Education expenditure as percent of GDP is lower in Greece than in both the Organisation for Economic Co-operation and Development (OECD) and EU countries. Greece is also among six European countries with no fees for higher education.

The Program for International Student Assessment (PISA), which in 2018 measured fifteen-year-old students' reading, mathematics, and science literacy in 79 countries, indicated that Greek students tested lower than the average.

The Ministry of Education and Religious Affairs exercises centralized control over the state schools, including determining the curriculum, appointing staff, selecting textbooks, and controlling funding for all levels of education. About 6 percent of students attend private schools. Although private schools have more autonomy, they also fall under the mandate of the Ministry. They are required to follow the prescribed national curriculum and textbooks as the public schools; therefore, most lessons are conducted in Greek.

At a regional level, the supervisory role of the Ministry is exercised through Regional and Local Prefecture Directorates of Primary and Secondary Education. The following organizations support the Ministry: (1) the School Buildings Organization (OSK), which is responsible for the construction of school buildings and providing other resources to schools; (2) the School Book Publishing Organization (OEDB), which publishes and distributes all school books; (3) the Pedagogical Institute (PI), which is an advisory body for primary and secondary schools; and (4) the National Council of Education (ESYP), which is an independent advisory body regarding all levels of education.

*Theodore G. Zervas and Angelyn Balodimas-Bartolomei*

**Further Reading**

Gogonas, Nikos. 2010. *Bilingualism and Multiculturalism in Greek Education*. Newcastle, UK. Cambridge Scholars Press.

Kallen, Denis. 1996. *Secondary Education in Greece*. Strasbourg: Council of Europe Press.

Koulaidis, Vasilis, ed. 2003. *The Greek Education System: Facts and Figures.* Athens: Education Research Centre - Ministry of Education and Religious Affairs.

OECD. 2020. "Public Spending on Education." https://doi.org/10.1787/f99b45d0-en.

Zervas, Theodore G. 2012. *The Making of a Modern Greek Identity: Education, Nationalism and the Teaching of a Greek National Past.* New York: Columbia University Press.

Zervas, Theodore G. 2017. *Formal and Informal Education during the Rise of Greek Nationalism: Learning to Be Greek.* New York and London: Palgrave & Macmillan.

## Day Care Centers (*Vrefonipiaki*), Nursery Schools (*Paidikoi Stathmoi*), and Primary Schools (*Dimotiko*)

Early childhood schools are accessible through private, public (state-funded), and municipal (belonging to a municipality) services. These include day care centers (*vrefonipiaki*) for infants and children aged about six months to two and half years and nursery schools (*paidikoi stathmoi*) for children aged two and half years and older. Since the availability is rather limited in Greece, grandparents continue to be the preferred choice of home childcare in a society where family is the core value. Additionally, securing childcare outside the house remains difficult for the following reasons: first, there are few available openings in public childcare centers; second, private day care centers are very expensive; and finally, most centers close early in the afternoon and do not reflect the working parents' schedules.

Primary education is subdivided into kindergarten (*nipiagogeio*), which lasts one or two years, and primary school (*dimotiko*), which spans six years (ages six to twelve). Preprimary schools can be in session either a half day or a full day. Since 2006, attendance has become compulsory for preprimary school children who are five years old. This change aims at helping children become better prepared for entering primary school.

Greek primary school (*dimitiko*) comprises grades first through sixth. The main objective of compulsory primary education is to contribute to the complete, harmonious, and balanced development of the mental and psychophysical abilities of the pupils. Greek classes range in size from fifteen to twenty-five students. Schools usually run from 8:00 a.m. to 2:00 p.m.; however, some schools offer additional optional classes until 4:15 p.m. or 5:00 p.m. The curricula for each grade are developed by the Institute of Educational Policy and then sent to the Ministry for final approval. Once accepted, it is applied in every school unit across the country. All teachers must abide by the official curriculum and can use only Ministry-approved textbooks to teach—all which are based on a cross-thematic approach to knowledge. Textbooks for primary and secondary education are published by the Organization of School Textbooks (OEDB). The primary education curriculum consists of religious education, language, mathematics, history, study of the environment, geography, natural sciences, civics education, arts education (visual arts, music, drama), physical education, ICT (information and communications technology), flexible zone (experiential activities where teachers design, develop, and implement projects using cooperative problem solving, and synergistic methodologies with themes, issues, and problems of everyday life), and foreign languages. The teaching of English begins in first grade, followed by a second foreign language in fifth grade.

*Angelyn Balodimas-Bartolomei and Theodore G. Zervas*

**See also:** Chapter 8: Overview; Secondary Schools (*Gymnasio* and *Lykeio*).

**Further Reading**

Doliopoulou, Elsie. 2006. "System of Early Education/Care and Professionalisation in Greece." Commissioned report for the SEEPRO Project. Accessed May 15, 2018. http://www.ifp.bayern.de/imperia/md/content/stmas/ifp/commissioned_report_greece.pdf.

Efstratiou, Dimitrios, and Nikolaos Sklavenitis. "Structures of Education and Training Systems. Greece, 2009/10 Edition." European Commission. Accessed May 15, 2018. http://daneshnamehicsa.ir/userfiles/file/Resources/18-3)%20Europa/Greece_EN.pdf.

Petrogiannis, Konstantinos. 2013. "Early Childhood Education and Care in Greece: In Search of an Identity." *Nordisk barnehageforskning* 6 (29): 1–9.

UNESCO. 2015. "Education for All 2015 National Review." Accessed May 15, 2018. http://unesdoc.unesco.org/images/0022/002299/229950E.pdf.

## Immigrant and Refugee Education

Article 16 of the 2003 Greek Constitution ensures that every Greek citizen has the right to access all levels of public education. It also mandates education for children aged five to fifteen. Since Greece is bound by international agreements, Article 16 has been ratified to include migrant and child asylum seekers, children of immigrants, and even those whose parents are undocumented, provided that all students are vaccinated before registering for school and that there is no pending enforceable removal measure against the students or their parents.

It was in the 1980s that Greece took its first institutional steps toward addressing multiculturalism in the classroom with the increase of returning Greek migrants from Western Europe, the United States, Canada, and Australia. The numerous initiatives that were taken included schools for expatriate students in Athens and Thessaloniki, newcomer reception classes, and afternoon tutorial classes in mainstream schools. In 1989, the expatriate schools were renamed Schools of Repatriated Greeks to accommodate the influx of Greek-origin students from the former Soviet Union.

The following decade brought a change in demographics with the arrival of migrants from the Balkans, Eastern Europe, Asia, and Africa. Schools were now challenged, as most of the newcomer students had no previous knowledge of the Greek language. The government turned the repatriate schools into intercultural schools, which aimed not only to teach the Greek language but also to socially integrate minority pupils. In 1999, the Ministry of Education mandated that schools had to provide a specialized class if there were at least nine pupils with no or limited Greek-language proficiency. Emphasis was now placed on teaching Greek as a second language along with Greek culture and history. The students could remain in these specialized classes for up to one year before entering a mainstream classroom.

While the numbers have shown a decreasing trend of arrivals since the 2015 Syrian crisis, over 120,000 refugees and other migrants are currently being hosted in Greece. An estimated 42,500 refugee and migrant children were in Greece as of December 31, 2019, up from 27,000 in December 2018, according to statistics released by UNICEF.

Since 2016, the government has placed a high priority on ensuring educational access for these children through the establishment and operation of "Reception/ Preparatory Classes for the Education of Refugees" (DYEP). These classes are part of the mandatory formal educational system (primary and lower secondary education) for all school-age children from four to fifteen. Teachers in these special schools are selected and appointed by the Ministry of Education and Religious Affairs from the list of public school substitute teachers. The educational program aims at facilitating the integration of refugee and migrant children into the educational process and gradually enabling them to enter mainstream classes in Greek schools. It is estimated that in the 2016/17 school year children joined 145 afternoon classes in 111 public schools. Children living in temporary shelters can enroll in afternoon preparatory classes from two to six in neighboring public schools identified by the Ministry. Their transport is organized by the International Organization for Migration (IOM).

Children living in dispersed urban settings (such as relocation accommodations, squats, apartments, hotels, and reception centers for asylum seekers and unaccompanied children) may attend morning classes, alongside Greek children, in Ministry-identified schools near their place of residence. Many Greeks are strongly opposed to integration of refugee and migrant students in Greek schools, with demonstrations constantly occurring throughout the country.

In both school settings, the students are taught Greek as a second language, English language, mathematics, sports, arts, and computer science.

UNICEF estimates that since the beginning of May 2018, 53 percent of all school-age refugee and migrant children (five to seventeen years old) across Greece were enrolled in formal education. Additionally, 56 percent of unaccompanied children aged five to seventeen residing in apartments with their families or in shelters for unaccompanied children are enrolled in Greek schools.

Unfortunately, the right to formal education for children trapped in the hotspot refugee camps, except through occasional volunteer programs and kindergartens, seems to be missing. According to a UNHCR report on refugee children's education, four out of ten children between the ages of five and seventeen were not enrolled in school in Greece. The situation was even worse among sixteen- and seventeen-year-olds with only four out of ten on the mainland and one out of ten on the Greek islands being enrolled.

As refugees are constantly moving to different locations, it is difficult to obtain the exact number of refugee students enrolled in Greek schools, especially since different sources have provided varying figures. According to data from the Ministry, during the 2017–2018 school year, slightly over eight thousand students were enrolled in some or the other type of school program.

*Angelyn Balodimas-Bartolomei*

**See also:** Chapter 6: Immigration and Migration to Greece.

**Further Reading**

Gogonas, Nikos. 2010. *Bilingualism and Multiculturalism in Greek Education.* Newcastle upon Tyne, UK: Cambridge Scholars Publishing.

Greek Council for Refugees. "Access to Education. Greece." Accessed May 5, 2008. http://www.asylumineurope.org/reports/country/greece/reception-conditions/employment-and-education/access-education.

Trouki, Evie. 2012. "The Challenge of Cultural Diversity in Greece: Reflections on Intercultural Education Schools' (IES) strategy for creating inclusive learning environments." *Power and Education* 4 (2).

UNICEF. 2020. "Refugee and Migrant Children in Greece." Accessed April 20, 2021. https://www.unicef.org/eca/emergencies/latest-statistics-and-graphics-refugee-and-migrant-children.

UNICEF. 2020. "Latest Statistics and Graphics on Refugee and Migrant Children." Accessed November 28, 2020. https://www.unicef.org/eca/emergencies/latest-statistics-and-graphics-refugee-and-migrant-children#:~:text=In%202019%2C%20European%20countries12%20recorded,compared%20to%202018%20(20%2C440).

Ziomas, Dimitris, Antoinetta Capella, and Konstantinidou Danai. 2017. "Integrating Refugee and Migrant into the Educational System in Greece." *European Social Policy Network.* ESPN Flash Report 2017/67. Accessed May 5, 2018. Children ec.europa.eu/social/BlobServlet?docId=18245&langId=en.

## Higher Tertiary Education

Greece boasts around one hundred public and private higher tertiary educational institutions that are distributed throughout the country, mainly in urban cities and towns. Most state-accredited universities are public, tuition-free, and nominally autonomous. The Ministry is responsible for their funding, the placement of undergraduate students in the various schools, and providing free-of-charge textbooks.

The tertiary system is divided into two sectors: (1) the university sector, which includes universities (four-year studies), technical universities (five-year studies), and schools of fine arts (five-year studies), and (2) the technological sector, which includes the technological education institutes (TEI—four-year studies) and the school of pedagogical and technological education (ASPETE—four-year studies). All higher

The National Polytechnical University of Athens, one of the oldest higher education institutions in Greece, was established in 1837, a few years after Greece achieved its independence. In 1871, they moved to buildings on Patission Street, where this neoclassical building is located. The university, as is true of all public universities in Greece, is free of charge to Greek students. (Photo by Elaine Thomopoulos)

education institutions in Greece bestow three types of degrees in which postgraduate (MSc level) courses last from one to two years and doctorates (PhD level) from three to six years.

Specialized higher education academies and schools offer four years of continuous studies leading to degrees that are equivalent to those given by any of the Greek universities. The schools include higher ecclesiastical schools, the merchant academy, higher schools of dance and dramatic art, higher schools of tourism education, and higher school of rural police. Some academies offer higher education programs of two years duration for army, navy, air force, police, chief firemen, and tourism personnel. The specialized schools operate under different rules than the universities and are not permitted to run graduate programs on their own.

In 2005, the International Hellenic University was established in Thessaloniki. It is the first state school in Greece to offer postgraduate programs exclusively in English. The university offers degrees in arts and humanities, science and technology, economics, business administration, and executive business. All degrees are recognized internationally and by the EU. The school accepts students from all over the world.

In 1992, the Hellenic Open University (HOU) was founded in the city of Patras. It is a self-administered state university. Modeled on the British Open University, HOU is unique as it is the first and only higher education institution in Greece that provides open and distance learning at the undergraduate, postgraduate, and PhD levels, while also charging a tuition fee for each course. The university is organized into four schools: the School of Humanities, the School of Social Sciences, the School of Science and Technology, and the School of Applied Arts. The latter only offers postgraduate degrees whereas the other three offer both undergraduate and graduate degrees. The institution places great emphasis on research and networks with other academic and research institutes. There are no entrance exams for HOU. Candidates need to apply and are then selected randomly.

Certain groups of students are admitted into the higher education institutions while also being exempt from taking the Panhellenic exams. These include children of Greeks living abroad; children of Greek employees temporarily working abroad; Greek graduates of foreign upper secondary schools; European Union (EU) and non-EU foreign nationals; EU and non-EU foreign nationals holding scholarships; ethnic Greeks from abroad holding scholarships; Muslims from Thrace; pupils distinguished during the Balkan or International Olympiad of Mathematics, Information Technology, Physics, or Chemistry; and pupils suffering from grave illnesses. Foreign students are required to submit their documents plus an entry application to their desired faculty or department. Upon acceptance, the candidates must present a certificate indicating their command of the Greek language or as an alternative, a third-level minimum certificate from the Greek Language Centre of Thessaloniki. Students failing to submit one of the certificates will need to wait until the next admission year, under the condition of then presenting the required document.

In the past two decades, the General Secretariat for Adult Education has created numerous adult education programs throughout the country. They include training centers, second chance schools for those who had dropped out of school, distance learning, teacher-training, and e-learning. These programs are intended for adults and people threatened with social exclusion, such as immigrants, minorities, and refugees. The second chance schools that were created in 1997 were initiated through the European Commission. They fall under the program of lifelong learning and are cofunded by the EU and the state. The two-year schools are tuition free and are designed for adults of any age, gender, and social status who have not completed their basic education. Classes take place during the evenings. The curriculum focuses on English, information technology, as well as basic skills, mathematics, science, and Greek. After successful completion, students are awarded a certificate equivalent to the secondary school diploma.

Article 16 of the constitution does not recognize privately owned education institutions in Greece even though the Greek government is constantly pressured to change its stance. Although there are about twenty-eight private institutions or colleges throughout the country that offer undergraduate and graduate degrees, they run as faculties or franchises of foreign universities or their degrees are validated by foreign accreditation agencies, such as UK NARIC or the New England Association of Schools and Colleges (NEASC) based in Massachusetts. Among these are the American College of Greece, the University of Sheffield International Faculty, CITY College in

Thessaloniki, and the University of Indianapolis's Athens Campus, to name a few. Most of the private colleges offer English-taught courses.

*Angelyn Balodimas-Bartolomei and Theodore G. Zervas*

**See also**: Chapter 7: Women's Education.

**Further Reading**


Efstratiou, Dimitrios, and Nikolaos Sklavenitis. "Structures of Education and Training Systems. Greece, 2009/10 Edition." European Commission. Accessed May 5. 2018. http://daneshnamehicsa.ir/userfiles/file/Resources/18-3)%20Europa/Greece_EN.pdf.

Papazoglou, Manos. 2007. "The Greek Education System. Structure and Recent Reforms." *About Greece*. Athens: Ministry of State/General Secretary for Information, 176–188. http://adapt.it/adapt-indice-a-z/wp-content/uploads/2014/08/Papazoglou_gre.pdf.

Psacharopoulos, George, and Stergios Tassoulas. 2004. "Achievement at the Higher Education Entry Examinations in Greece: A Procrustean Approach." *Higher Education* 47 (2): 241–252.

Sianou-Kyrgiou, Eleni. 2008. "Social Class and Access to Higher Education in Greece: Supportive Preparation Lessons and Success in National Exams." *International Studies in Sociology of Education* 18 (3–4): 173–183.

UNESCO. 2015. "Education for All 2015 National Review." Accessed May 15, 2018. http://unesdoc.unesco.org/images/0022/002299/229950E.pdf.


## Secondary Schools (*Gymnasio* and *Lykeio*)

Secondary education comprises two stages: the three-year *gymnasio* (lower secondary school, i.e., middle or junior high school) and the three-year *lykeio* (upper secondary school, i.e., senior high).

The *gymnasio* constitutes the last period of compulsory education and includes grades *A*, *B*, and *Γ*. A variety of subjects are taught, including modern and ancient Greek language, mathematics, physics, chemistry, geography, history, physical education, religious studies, music and art, and foreign languages. The foreign languages consist of mandatory English as well as another European language selected by the student. The curriculum also incorporates music, art, physical education, computer science, and home economics/health education, which aims to promote the well-being of the students. At the end of the school year, students take exams in all subjects.

There are several types of junior high schools in Greece. Students can attend neighborhood day schools or be admitted to a model experimental school through a lottery. Such schools are known for promoting research and practice in conjunction with teaching departments of higher institutions. Additionally, students can study at evening lower schools; specialized art, music, religious, and athletic schools; special needs schools—many of which offer vocational studies and workshops; minority, refugee, and intercultural schools; and last, the School of European Education in Crete, which is tailored for the children of European Union personnel.

The *lykeio* (senior high school) includes grades *A*, *B*, and *Γ* (equivalent to the tenth, eleventh, and twelfth grades in the United States). Although it is noncompulsory, most Greek young adults, aged fifteen to eighteen, attend senior high school. As in the junior high level, there are several types of specialized senior high schools throughout the country. Class size cannot exceed twenty-seven pupils in public senior high schools. If the enrollment surpasses the limit, students are divided into groups.

In contrast to the primary and lower secondary schools, students can select a course of study according to their interests and skills in one of the three streams—humanities, sciences, and technology/IT. During the final year of senior high school, all students are assessed both orally and through written exams in about thirteen courses. The grades are recorded on the Apolyterio—a diploma of completion or school leaving certificate that serves as evidence for access into higher education.

In June, students wishing to enter a Greek university need to take the dreaded Panhellenic National Examinations. Whereas most universities in America require a personal statement, an essay, letters of recommendation, or lists of extracurricular activities along with test results and grade averages, in Greece, the National Examination results are basically the sole factor for successful admission into a higher education institution. However, even if a student scores high on the examinations, there is no guarantee of acceptance. Due to a limited number of available spots, universities have a 20 percent acceptance rate with usually only the gifted students being admitted into the Greek universities. Thus, the entire process is extremely difficult and competitive.

The Panhellenic Examinations consist of four subject areas with students being testing according to their choice of study. The examinations are centrally designed, organized, and administered nationwide by the state with most of the content based on rote memorization. A great majority of senior high school students seek extra help by attending some type of fee-paying private lessons, which include *frontisteria* (private cram schools after school hours or on Saturdays), tutoring, and sometimes even both. Many students also attend *frontisteria* to help them prepare for the Michigan Language Assessment that leads to a certificate demonstrating their knowledge of English. The ensuing cost of *frontisteria* for families is considerable while adding approximately twenty hours of instruction to the students' regular school week.

*Angelyn Balodimas-Bartolomei and Theodore G. Zervas*

**See also:** Appendix A: A Day in the Life of a High School Student.

**Further Reading**

Apostolou, Nikolia. 2018. "Millions of Child Refugees Do not Attend School in Adopted Homeland." *USA Today*, October 1, 2018. Accessed March 3, 2019. https://www.usatoday.com/story/news/world/2018/10/01/un-says-millions-children-refugees-not-attending-school/1418231002/.

Papazoglou, M. 2007. "The Greek Education System. Structure and Recent Reforms." *About Greece*. Athens: Ministry of State/General Secretary for Information, 176–188. Accessed March 3, 2019. http://adapt.it/adapt-indice-a-z/wp-content/uploads/2014/08/Papazoglou_gre.pdf.

Stylianidou, Fani, George Bagakis, and Dimitris Stamovlasis. 2004. *Country Background Report for Greece: Attracting, Developing and Retraining Effective Teachers*. Country Research Report. OECD. Education Research Centre. Accessed May 25, 2021. https://www.oecd.org/greece/30101431.pdf.

## Special Education

Since 2000, Greek law has mandated that special education be provided for students aged four to twenty-two. The Ministry of Education, Research, and Religious Affairs defines "special needs" as "difficulties in learning and school adjustment due to sensory, intellectual, cognitive, developmental, mental and neuropsychiatric disorders. Pupils who have disabilities in motion, vision and hearing; who suffer from chronic diseases; disorders in speech, attention deficit, and all pervasive developmental disorders are considered as having SEN—special educational needs." SEN students have the right to a free diagnosis, which includes a medical and pedagogical evaluation through KEDDY (Diagnostic Assessment and Support Center), a medical-pedagogical center, or a public hospital. Once officially diagnosed, the SEN student is issued an individual education plan (IEP). The diagnostic centers are staffed by disciplinary teams consisting of school psychologists, social workers, speech pathologists, and regular and special education teachers. Currently only the latter group work as personnel in public schools.

The main objective of special education in Greece is to integrate SEN students into mainstream schools where they receive most of their education through the support of a peripatetic or traveling teacher. Across the country, special programs are established at different educational levels so that SEN students are provided with the appropriate education and vocational training according to their age, abilities, and specific needs. Students who are unable to attend mainstream schools or inclusive settings with non-SEN students can attend special kindergartens and schools. Instruction in hospitals and homes is also available.

Special education teachers who work in primary schools are graduates of university school of education programs. In secondary education, special education teachers are university graduates with a concentration in different subject areas. To become qualified to teach special education, teachers are required to work in mainstream schools for a minimum of five years and then complete a two-year in-service training program in special education. The Ministry of Education and Religious Affairs and various organizations offer several special education training seminars and workshops for primary and secondary teachers working with SEN pupils. Additionally, many teachers earn a postgraduate degree in special education.

*Angelyn Balodimas-Bartolomei*

**See also:** Chapter 8: Overview.

**Further Reading**

Dimakos, I. 2006. "The Attitudes of Greek Teachers and Trainee Teachers towards the Development of School Psychological and Counselling Services." *School Psychology International* 27 (4): 415–425.

European Agency for Special Needs and Inclusive Education. *Greece Overview.* Accessed April 21, 2021. https://www.european-agency.org/country-information/greece/teacher-education-for-inclusive-education.

CHAPTER 9

# LANGUAGE

### HOW TO INTERPRET GESTURES AND BODY LANGUAGE AND WHICH ONES TO AVOID

Greeks, an expressive people, use a variety of gestures and body language. When saying *ohi* (no), they can either nod their head from side to side or more likely lift their heads backwards and upwards and make the "tsk" sound. Sometimes it is just a slight movement and raising of the eyebrows that indicates no. To say yes, Greeks slowly move their head down, with slightly lowered eyelids. That someone is a liar is indicated by stroking an imaginary beard. The *moodza* is the strongest negative gesture one can do in Greece and should be avoided. This gesture involves pushing your open palm, with fingers spread outwards toward the recipient of your curses. Shaking hands is not common in Greece; instead, friends greet with a kiss on both cheeks.

*Kosta Dalageorgas*

## OVERVIEW

The Greek language is the oldest spoken Indo-European language, with a history dating back over three thousand years. Today, between fifteen and twenty-five million people around the world speak a form of Greek, with 99.5 percent of the population of Greece speaking Greek.

The ancient Greek alphabet, which is still in use today throughout the Greek-speaking world, is composed of five vowels and a total of twenty-four letters. The Greek alphabet was adapted and modified from the Phoenician alphabet and consists of the letters α, β, γ, δ, ε, ζ, η, θ, ι, κ, λ, μ, ν, ξ, ο, π, ρ, σ, τ, υ, φ, χ, ψ, and ω. Greek contains both uppercase and lowercase letters. Since the writing reform of 1982, only one accent mark is used.

In regard to pronunciation, modern Greek uses stressed and unstressed vowel sounds. Additionally, modern Greek has diphthongs, which refer to two vowels that are combined in a single syllable, where the sound moves from one sound to another, for example, "join."

Starting during the ancient Hellenistic period, which was from the fourth to sixth century BCE, *Koine* Greek was the common dialect of Greek used and written throughout the Greek-speaking world of the Mediterranean. Important texts written using *Koine* are the Septuagint (the translation of the Hebrew Old Testament), as well as the New Testament, which was originally written in *Koine* Greek. The Greek Orthodox Church continues to use *Koine* in the liturgy today.

The "language question" in Greece has been part of a long and hotly contested debate, going back centuries and is closely intertwined with issues of national identity. One of the earliest language reformers was Adamantios Korais (1748–1833). Korais defended modern Greek against the archaists who wanted the inhabitants of postindependence Greece to use the Ancient Greek dialect. However, he did not completely reject the use of Ancient Greek. He wanted to transpose and graft the grammar of ancient Greek onto the structure and morphology of modern Greek and cleanse the Greek language of foreign elements that had crept into usage. To understand this fiercely contested debate, which has plagued Greece for centuries, it is crucial to understand that throughout its history, modern Greece has been marked by *diglossia*, that is, two different versions of the same language. The common language is *dimotiki* (demotic) language, which has been spoken by the inhabitants of Greece for centuries. The other is called *katharevousa*, which was heavily influenced by ancient Greek, as well as the *Koine* of the church and the New Testament. *Katharevousa* became the language of written discourse for the government, newspapers, and education and was used by the bourgeoisie. In addition, many books were written using *katharevousa*, which required their readers to be highly educated. More liberal members of the populace, including writers, favored *dimotiki*, whereas the Greek Orthodox Church and conservative elements in law, medicine, and the state favored *katharevousa*.

From 1923 to 1967, *dimotiki* was the language favored in lower-level school instruction. In 1967, the military junta banned teaching *dimotiki* in the schools. Since the fall of Greece's military junta in 1974, the use of *katharevousa* went out of favor. The debate was definitively resolved in 1976, with *katharevousa* being eliminated from public schools and government offices. Government offices, the legal profession, and newspapers no longer use *katharevousa*. The language that supplanted *katharevousa* is called Standard Modern Greek, which uses the demotic but has been influenced by *katharevousa*.

There are a variety of dialects and minority languages currently spoken in Greece. Pontian is a language based on ancient Greek that is not easily understood by modern Greeks and is listed as an endangered language. It was spoken by the Pontian Greeks who had originally lived in area called Pontos on the southern coast of the Black Sea. They brought the language, culture, and Greek Orthodox faith with them when they came as refugees from Asia Minor in 1923. In the 1990s, a second wave of Pontians emigrated from Russia and the Ukraine after the breakup of the Soviet Union. Worldwide, it is estimated that there are about 500,000 Pontic speakers, including those Greeks residing in the United States, Russia, and the Ukraine and Greek-speaking Muslims from Turkey. There are about 250,000 or more Pontic-Greek speakers in

East, Central, and West Macedonia in northern Greece, as well as in the region of Attica. In Greece, Pontic Greek is written using the Greek alphabet, whereas in Turkey it is written using Latin, and Cyrillic is used in Russia.

Tsakonian is spoken by about twelve hundred people living in the Tsakonian regions of the Peloponnesus. Tsakonian originates from Attic Greek, which was spoken in the ancient era. Currently, Tsakonian has no official status in Greece. Cappadocian Greek was spoken by members of the Greek Turkish population exchange of the 1920s who were forced to leave their homes in the area of Cappadocia in Turkey. It is facing extinction, as many of its speakers have now shifted to speaking modern Greek. On the island of Crete, the Cretan dialect is spoken by over five hundred thousand people, while in the Maniot region of the Peloponnesus, residents speak the Mani dialect of Greek.

The largest minority language in Greece is Albanian. According to the Greek census of 2011, there were 480,851 Albanians residing in Greece. The Romani language of the Roma is the second most spoken language, with about 160,000 speakers. Turkish is the third most spoken minority language, with over 128,000 speakers, mostly residing in Western Thrace adjacent to Turkey. Other minority languages used in Greece include Armenian, Slavic Macedonian, Bulgarian, Romanian, and Aromanian.

Aromanian is a Latin-based Romance language spoken by about three hundred thousand people in Greece, Albania, Macedonia, Romania, Bulgaria, and Serbia. The exact number of people who speak the language in Greece is not known, but the estimates are as high as one hundred thousand. There is no Aromanian-language newspaper published in Greece. It is similar to Romanian, but Romanian has more influences from Hungarian and various Slavic languages. The speakers of Aromanian are known as *Vlahi* in Greek (or Vlachs in English). It is written using the Latin alphabet.

The Romaniot Greek dialect is spoken by Greece's Romaniot Jewish community, which has had a presence in Greece as far back as 586 BCE. Romaniot Greek is nearly extinct—only fifty speakers remain, and most of them currently reside in Israel. This Greek dialect includes words and phrases from Hebrew, Aramaic, and Turkish.

Ladino is the language used by the Sephardic Jewish community of Spain who were expelled from Spain and Portugal after 1492. The Ottomans welcomed them, and they settled in Istanbul and Thessaloniki. Ladino was written using the Sephardic Hebrew alphabet. Over the centuries, many loan words were added to it from Turkish, Arabic, and Greek. Currently, Ladino is becoming an endangered language due to the destruction of the Jewish community in Thessaloniki during the Holocaust and the subsequent emigration of Sephardic Jews to Israel, the United States, and other countries. It is making a comeback, being spearheaded by educational institutions, colleges, and universities in Israel and the United States. Ladino is also recognized by the Royal Spanish Academy.

Another fast-disappearing minority language is Karamanli. The language contains many Turkic as well as some Greek words and was originally written with the Greek alphabet. Historically, Karamanli had been spoken by Greeks who originated from

A placard is posted on the whitewashed walls outside a bakery just off the horseshoe-port of Hydra, Greece, in August 2018. Patrons parting with pastries in hand are nudged to "Please Don't Feed the Pigeons. Σας παρακαλούμε. Μην ταΐζετε τα περιστέρια. (*Sas parakaloúme. Min taïzete ta peristéria*)." From menus to road signs, visitors to Greece quickly discover that information is offered in both Greek and English. (Photo by Alexander Fatouros)

the Karaman and Cappadocian regions of Anatolia in modern Turkey. Many of the Greek Orthodox Karamanlides had been forced to leave Turkey during the 1923 population exchange between Greece and Turkey. They too, like other refugees from Asia Minor, were discriminated against by the native Greeks when they first came, especially since they used the language of the Turks. Greek slang words like *tourkospori* (Turkish seeds) were used against them.

Another endangered language is Cappadocian Greek, which was spoken in the Cappadocian area of Central Turkey. It is derived and was influenced by Byzantine Greek as well as Turkish. Cappadocian Greek uses Byzantine Greek structure and at the same time Turkish vowel harmony. It is hard for Greeks speaking Standard Modern Greek to understand. The Cappadocian-speaking Greeks, like many other Greeks from Asia Minor, were forced to leave their homes in the population exchange.

One of the more obscure yet fascinating languages is Sfyria, which is a mysterious whistling language used to communicate between villages over long distances. The rare and endangered language is used on the southeast corner of the island of Evia, in the village of Antia. Sfyria, which comes from the Greek word *sfyrizo*, meaning "to whistle," has only six speakers. It is basically a whistled version of modern Greek.

Since Greece is at the crossroads of Europe, foreign languages are an integral part of the Greek educational curriculum. English is first taught in the first grade, followed by a second language in the fifth grade. English, the main language of commerce and business in the country, is spoken by about 60 percent of the Greek population. To accommodate tourists, many of the signs on the highways in Greece are in English. Other frequently spoken foreign languages include German, French, and Italian.

*Kosta Dalageorgas*

**Further Reading**


Baskin, Judith, ed. 2011. *The Cambridge Dictionary of Judaism and Jewish Culture*. Cambridge: Cambridge University Press.

Browning, Robert. 1969. *Medieval and Modern Greek*. London: Hutchinson University Library.

Edwards, Nick, John Fisher, Rebecca Hall, John Malathronas, and Martin Zatko. 2018. *The Rough Guide to Greece*. London: Apa Group.

Gallant, Thomas W. 2016. *Modern Greece: From the War of Independence to the Present*, 2nd edition. New York: Bloomsbury.

Horrocks, Geoffrey. 2010. *Greek: A History of the Language and Its Speakers*. Chichester, UK: Wiley-Blackwell.

Human Rights Watch. 1999. *The Turks of Western Thrace*. January 1999. Accessed January 7, 2019. https://www.hrw.org/reports/1999/greece/.

Mackridge, Peter. 2009. *Language and National Identity in Greece, 1766–1976*. Oxford: Oxford University Press.

Omniglot. n.d. "Aromanian." Accessed January 7, 2019. https://www.omniglot.com/writing/aromanian.htm.

Stein, Eliot. 2017. "Greece's Disappearing Whistled Language." *BBC*. Accessed January 7, 2019. http://www.bbc.com/travel/story/20170731-greeces-disappearing-whistled-language.


### UNIQUE WAYS TO EXPRESS THE GREEK WAY OF LIFE

Greeks use unique words to express themselves. *Opa!*, a declaration of joy, affirms the Greek way of life—one of passion and enthusiasm. It can be used as a compliment to an accomplished dancer or as a shout-out used by waiters in the Greek restaurants of America to accompany the lighting of *saganaki*—a cheese coated in flour, flash fried in olive oil, set aflame with a dash of brandy, and dished up with a squeeze of lemon. Opa is also a way to alert someone to "look out!"

Opa is a word often used when there is a feeling of *kefi* (a time of celebration, high spirits, and joyfulness). *Kefi* is sustaining a zest for life, even when the going gets tough—an outlook of triumph over despair. Zorba the Greek best epitomizes this sensibility in the movie scene when he loses himself in dance.

The concept of *filotimo* (*φιλότιμο*) is inextricably tied to the Greek disposition—one of kindness and a commitment to virtue. People with *filotimo* act honorably, bringing respect to themselves and their families. Another concept akin to *filotimo* is *filoxenia* (*φιλοξενία*)—treating strangers with big-heartedness, generosity, and hospitality.

Greeks are concerned with how they or their families are viewed in the eyes of others. The expression "What will the people say?" (*Ti tha peí o kósmos* [*τι θα πεί ο κόσμος*]) captures this worldview. Greeks strive for perfection, as is typified with the word *Ariston* (*Άριστον*), which means the very best, one of the highest compliments.

*Alexander Fatouros*

## Common Expressions

From pop-culture television shows that emphasize the upside to face-to-face chance encounters with locals engaged in merriment with their *parea* (revered circle of friends), these practical remarks are assembled. Whatever the turn of phrase, Greeks impart earnestness matched with humor. Given here are some commonly used words and quirky phrases Greeks use to express themselves.

### WORDS OF GREETING, ENDEARMENT, AND ENCOURAGEMENT

When Greeks meet, they extend a warm welcome. Among the words of greeting, leave-taking, encouragement, and congratulations are the following:

Hello: *Yia sou/sas* (which means to your health) (*Γειά σου*, singular; *Γειά σας*, plural) or *Herete* (*Χαίρετε*)
Good day: *Kaliméra* (*Καλημέρα*)
Good afternoon: *Kaló apógevma* (*Καλό απόγευμα*)
Good evening: *Kalispéra* (*Καλησπέρα*)
Good night: *Kalinyhta* (*Καληνύχτα*)
Goodbye: *Antio* (*Αντίο*)
Hello/goodbye: *Herete* (*Χαίρετε*)
How are you?: *Ti káneis* (*Τι κάνεις*)
I am well: *Eímai kalá* (*Είμαι καλά*)
Fortunately: *Eftychós* (*Ευτυχώς*)
Friendship: *Filia* (*Φιλιά*)
To the good: *Sto kalo* (*Στο καλό*) (To impart good fortune on someone; a way to say goodbye)
Everything okay?: *Ola kalá* (*Ολα καλά;*)
We are going well/good: *Páme kalá* (*Πάμε καλά*)
Many years: *Hronia Pola* (*Χρόνια Πολλά*) (A general greeting for New Year, birthdays, Christmas, saint's Day or other holidays)
Welcome: *Kalos irthate* (*Καλώς ήρθατε*, plural), *Kalós írthes* (*Καλώς ήρθες*, singular)
Please: *Parakalo* (*Παρακαλώ*) (*Parakalo* can also mean "You are welcome," in response to "thank you")
I love you: *S'agapó* (*Σ'αγαπώ*)
Kisses: *Filía* (*Φιλία*)
Thank you: *Efharisto* (*Ευχαριστώ*)
Very much: *Pára polý* (*Πάρα πολύ*)
Nothing: *Tipota* (*Τίποτα*) (Can be used to answer "nothing"; it can also be used to express "It was nothing"; in response to "Thank you")
You are welcome: *Parakaló* (*Παρακαλώ*) (Can also mean please)
Okay: *Entáxei* (*Εντάξει*)
Me too: *Kai egó* (*Και εγώ*)

**WORDS USED IN EVERYDAY CONVERSATION**

Yes: *Naí* (*Ναί*)
No: *Ohi* (*Οχι*)
Certainly or yes: *Málista* (*Μάλιστα*)
Are you having a good time?: *Pernás kalá;* (*Περνάς καλά;*)
We are having a good time: *Pernáme kala* (*Περνάμε καλά*)
Good luck: *Kalí týhi* (*Καλή τύχη*)
Now: *Tóra* (*Τώρα*)
A moment: *Mia stigmi* (*Μια στιγμή*)
Doesn't matter: *Den peirazei* (*Δεν πειράζει*)
I'm laughing: *Geláo* (*Γελάω*)
Sorry: *Sygnomi* (*Συγνώμη*)
I am: *Eímai* (*Είμαι*)
We are: *Eímaste* (*Είμαστε*)
Enthusiastic: *Enthousiasménos* (*Ενθουσιασμένος*)
I know: *Xéro* (*Ξέρω*)
I understand: *Katalavaíno* (*Καταλαβαίνω*)
I don't understand: *Den katalaveno* (*Δεν καταλαβαίνω*)
That is: *Diladi* (*Δηλαδή*)
We have: *Ehoume* (*Έχουμε*)
I have news: *Ého néa* (*Έχω νέα*)
Good job!: *Kalí douleiá!* (*Καλή δουλειά!*)
In a little while: *Se lígo* (*Σε λίγο*)
Immediately: *Amésos* (*Αμέσως*)
Just a minute: *Miso Lepto* (*Μισο Λεπτό*)
Bon voyage: *Kaló taxídi* (*Καλό ταξίδι*)
Long live/hooray: *Zíto* (*Ζήτω*)
Watch out: *Prósehe* (*Πρόσεχε*)
Beware: *Prosohí* (*Προσοχή*)
Look after: *Prosého* (*Προσέχω*)
How beautiful: *Póso ómorfo* (*Πόσο όμορφο*)
Come here: *Ela edó* (*Ελα εδώ*)
Thank God: *Dóxa to Theó* (*Δόξα τω θεώ*)
I agree: *Symfonó* (*Συμφωνώ*)
For sure: *Sígoura* (*Σίγουρα*)
What do you say?: *Ti les;* (*Τι λες;*)
Exactly: *Akrivós* (*Ακριβώς*)
Perfect: *Téleios* (*Τέλειος*)
I like it very much: *Mou arései pára polý* (*Μου αρέσει πάρα πολύ*)
I don't like it at all: *Den mou arései kathólou* (*Δεν μου αρέσει καθόλου*)
I believe: *Pistévo* (*Πιστεύω*)
In other words: *Me álla lógia* (*Με άλλα λόγια*)
I'm listening: *Akoúo* (*Ακούω*)
Why not?: *Giatí óhi* (*Γιατί όχι;*)

It is not: *Den eínai* (*Δεν είναι*)
I don't know: *Den xéro* (*Δεν ξέρω*)
We will find out: *Tha máthoume* (*Θα μάθουμε*)

## WORDS USED WHEN DINING OUT, AT SOCIAL AFFAIRS, OR WHILE PURCHASING SOMETHING

I am hungry: *Peináo* (*Πεινάω*)
Who is hungry?: *Poios peináei* (*Ποιος πεινάει;*)
I'm thirsty: *Dipsáo* (*Διψάω*)
I have allergies: *Ého allergíes* (*Έχω αλλεργίες*)
I'm a vegetarian: *Eímai hortofágos* (*Είμαι χορτοφάγος*)
To your health/cheers: *Stin ygeía sou* (*Στην υγεία σου*, singular)
I want to order: *Thélo na parangeílo* (*θέλω να παραγγείλω*)
One moment: *Mia stigmi* (*Μια στιγμή*)
One-third: *Ena tríto* (*Ενα τρίτο*)
One-half: *Sto misó* (*Στο μισό*)
Bon appetite: *Kalí órexi* (*Καλή όρεξη*)
Taste it!: *Dokímasé to!* (*Δοκίμασέ το!*)
May I try?: *Boró na dokimáso;* (*Μπορώ να δοκιμάσω;*)
It is: *Eínai* (*Είναι*)
It was: *Itan* (*Ήταν*)
Good: *Kalós* (*Καλός*)
Very good: *Polý kaló* (*Πολύ καλό*)
Moderate/average: *Métrio* (*Μέτριο*)
So-so: *Etsi ki étsi* (*Έτσι κι έτσι*)
The very best: *Ariston* (*Άριστον*)
How much does it cost?: *Póso kostízei;* (*Πόσο κοστίζει;*)
Opens: *Anoígei* (*Ανοίγει*)
Closes: *Kleínei* (*Κλείνει*)
Starts at: *Arhízei stis* (*Αρχίζει στις*)
Finishes at: *Teleiónei sto* (*Τελειώνει στο*)
Let's go: *Páme* (*Πάμε*)
I can show you: *Boró na sou deíxo* (*Μπορώ να σου δείξω*)
How much longer?: *Póso poli* (*Πόσο πολύ*)
You have arrived: *Eheis ftásei* (*Εχεις φτάσει*)
I am playing: *Paízo* (*Παίζω*)
Company: *Parea* (*Παρέα*)
Where can we: *Poú boroúme* (*Πού μπορούμε*)
Where can I: *Pou boró* (*Που μπορώ*)
Where can I eat?: *Poú boró na fáo* (*Πού μπορώ να φάω;*)
I eat: *Tróo* (*Τρώω*)
Dance: *Horós* (*Χορός*)
I dance: *Horévo* (*Χορεύω*)

We dance: *Horévoume* (*Χορεύουμε*)
Where are you?: *Pou eísai* (*Που είσαι;*)
I see you: *Se vlépo* (*Σε βλέπω*)
You have a: *Ehete éna* (*Έχετε ένα*)
Cheerful: *Haroúmenos* (*Χαρούμενος*)

**DIRECTIONS, TIME OF DAY, AND MEASUREMENTS**

Straight ahead: *Olo Eftheía* (*Ευθεία*)
Left: *Aristera* (*Αριστερά*)
Right turn: *Dexiá strofí* (*Δεξιά στροφή*)
Near: *Kontá* (*Κοντά*)
Far: *Makriá* (*Μακριά*)
Here/there: *Edó/Ekeí* (*Εδώ/Εκεί*)
Less/more: *Ligótero/Perissótero* (*Λιγότερο/Περισσότερο*)
Quickly: *Grígora* (*Γρήγορα*)
Slowly: *Sigá* (*Σιγά*)
Entrance: *Eísodos* (*Είσοδος*)
Exit: *Exodos* (*Έξοδος*)
In the morning: *To proí* (*Το πρωί*)
In the afternoon: *To apógevma* (*Το απόγευμα*)
Late: *Argá* (*Αργά*)
At night: *Ti nýhta* (*Τη νύχτα*)

*Alexander Fatouros*

**See also:** Chapter 5: Greek Orthodox Regional Celebrations. Chapter 9: Sidebar: Unique Ways to Express the Greek Way of Life. Chapter 9. Sidebar: How to Interpret Gestures and Body Language and Which Ones to Avoid. Chapter 15: Bars and Nightlife; Beverages: Coffee, Tea, Wine, and Liquor.

**Further Reading**

Callimassia, Markella. 2000. *Greek Phrasebook*, 2nd Edition. Melbourne, Australia: Lonely Planet Publications.

## Dialects and Minority Languages

There are a variety of dialects currently spoken in Greece and quite a few minority languages. On the island of Crete, the Cretan dialect is spoken by over five hundred thousand people. In the Maniot region of the Peloponnesus, residents speak the Mani dialect of Greek. Tsakonian is spoken by about twelve hundred people living in the Tsakonian regions of the Peloponnesus. It originates from Attic Greek, which was spoken in the ancient era. Currently, Tsakonian has no official status in Greece and is facing extinction. Cappadocian Greek, which was spoken by members of the Greek Turkish population exchange of the 1920s, is also facing extinction as many of its speakers have now shifted to speaking modern Greek. Cappadocian Greek, which is derived from and is influenced by Byzantine Greek but uses Turkish vowel harmony, was spoken by Greeks from the Cappadocian area of central Turkey. In Greece, it was spoken by those who came from Asia Minor during the Greek-Turkish War and the subsequent population exchange between Turkey and Greece.

Pontic Greek is spoken in East, Central, and West Macedonia in northern Greece as well as in the region of Attica. In Greece, Pontic Greek is written using the Greek alphabet, whereas in Turkey it is written using Latin, and Cyrillic is used in Russia. There are about seven hundred thousand speakers worldwide, with about two hundred thousand in Greece. Pontian refugees from Asia Minor came to Greece during the Greek-Turkish War and the 1923 population exchange. The language got rejuvenated when Pontic speakers came in the 1990s from countries of the former Soviet Union. However, young people tend to speak modern Greek instead of Pontic Greek, and it has been listed as being in danger of becoming extinct. Pontic Greek is derived from *Koine* Greek but developed separately than the language of those Greeks residing in mainland Greece. It cannot be easily understood by speakers of Modern Standard Greek.

The Romaniot dialect (also called Yevanic) is spoken by a Jewish community that had a presence in Greece as early as 586 BCE. This Greek dialect includes Hebrew and Aramaic words and phrases. The language is nearly extinct, with only fifty remaining speakers; most of them currently reside in Israel.

Arvanitika is a language that was brought to Greece by Albanians who settled in Greece during the late middle ages. The Arvanitis self-identify as Greeks and very few speak Arvanitika.

Karamanli Turkish is an endangered Turkish dialect using Turkic and Greek loan words and the Greek alphabet. It was spoken by the Karamanlides, Greek Orthodox who originated from the Karaman and Cappadocian regions of Turkey. They were forced to leave their homes in Turkey during the Greek-Turkish War and the subsequent 1923 population exchange between Greece and Turkey. It is estimated that about four hundred thousand resided in Greece in 1923. Few continue to speak this dialect, and the written form has fallen out of use.

Ladino is the language used by the Sephardic Jewish community of Spain who were expelled after 1492. The main centers of Ladino became Istanbul and Thessaloniki (Salonika), where Sephardic Jews were given refuge by the Ottoman Empire. Ladino uses the Sephardic Hebrew alphabet. Over the centuries, many Turkish, Arabic, and Greek loanwords were added. Currently, Ladino is becoming an endangered language due to the destruction of the Jewish community in Salonika during the Holocaust and the subsequent emigration of Sephardic Jews outside of Greece. It is making a comeback, being spearheaded by educational institutions, colleges, and universities in Israel and the United States. Ladino is also recognized by the Royal Spanish Academy.

According to the 2011 Greek census, the largest noncitizen residents are Albanians, who number 480,824. They speak the Albanian language. The Romani language of the Roma is the second most spoken minority language, with about 160,000 speakers.

Turkish is the third most spoken minority language, with over 128,000 speakers, mostly residing in Western Thrace adjacent to Turkey. Unfortunately, those of Turkish descent living in Western Thrace, who have been designated by the Greek state as part of the Muslim religious minority of Western Thrace, have been subject to discriminatory actions by the Greek state. The quality of education had been quite poor in many of the schools in Western Thrace that were assigned to teach both Turkish and Greek. Many of the teachers placed by the Greek government had only a rudimentary knowledge of Turkish.

The Pomaks, who are also counted as part of the Muslim religious minority of Western Thrace, speak a Bulgarian dialect. Their number is estimated to be fifty thousand.

*Kosta Dalageorgas*

**See also:** Chapter 6: Muslim Religious Minority of Western Thrace; Other Minority Groups: Aromanians (Vlachs), Armenians, and Macedonian Slavs.

**Further Reading**

Baskin, Judith, ed. 2011. *The Cambridge Dictionary of Judaism and Jewish Culture*. Cambridge: Cambridge University Press.

Browning, Robert. 1969. *Medieval and Modern Greek*. London: Hutchinson University Library. Cambridge: Cambridge University Press.

Edwards, Nick, John Fisher, Rebecca Hall, John Malathronas, and Martin Zatko. 2018. *The Rough Guide to Greece*. London: Apa Group.

Gallant, Thomas W. 2016. *Modern Greece: From the War of Independence to the Present*, 2nd edition. New York: Bloomsbury.

Horrocks, Geoffrey. 2010. *Greek: A History of the Language and Its Speakers*. Chichester, UK: Wiley-Blackwell.

Human Rights Watch. 1999. *The Turks of Western Thrace*. January 1999. Accessed January 7, 2019. https://www.hrw.org/reports/1999/greece/.

Mackridge, Peter. 2009. *Language and National Identity in Greece, 1766–1976*. Oxford: Oxford University Press.

Omniglot. n.d. "Aromanian." Accessed January 7, 2019. https://www.omniglot.com/writing/aromanian.htm.

Stein, Eliot. 2017. "Greece's Disappearing Whistled Language." *BBC*. Accessed January 7, 2019. http://www.bbc.com/travel/story/20170731-greeces-disappearing-whistled-language.

## The Greek Language

Apart for Chinese, Greek is the world's oldest documented living language. Although it has undergone many changes during its more than three-thousand-year history, there is a direct line between the Greek used by the founders of democracy in ancient Athens (fourth and fifth centuries BCE) and today's Standard Modern Greek. The New Testament was first written in Greek, and Greek influenced the development of Latin and the Romance languages. As in the past, Greek permeates the international vocabulary of science, philosophy, and the arts. It is imbedded in English not only in medical and scientific terms (e.g., "dentist," "biology," and "microscope") but also in thousands of everyday words (e.g., "place," "story," "music," and "code") and in hundreds of prefixes and suffixes (e.g., "auto-," "anti-," "pro-," "di-," "tri-," and "mono-").

The first written record of Greek, Linear A (second millennium BCE), remains undecipherable. Linear B or Mycenaean Greek (approximately 1200 BCE), consisting of ninety syllables and used primarily for administrative purposes, coexisted with various other Greek dialects. Around the eighth century BCE, the Greeks added vowels to the Phoenician alphabet (which lacked written vowels), thereby creating the twenty-four-letter Greek alphabet that served as the basis of the Latin alphabet and, consequently, for that of the Romance languages, English, Armenian, and other languages. (The word "alphabet" consists of the first letter of the Greek alphabet, alpha, and the second letter, beta.)

The creation of the alphabet gave rise to written (as opposed to oral) poetry, drama, and other literature and permitted the expression of the philosophical, mathematical, and scientific concepts for which ancient Greece is renowned. Although there were several forms of ancient Greek, Alexander the Great of Macedonia (356–323 BCE) admired and was well versed in the Classical or Attic Greek used by Aristotle and other Athenian intellectuals and wanted to spread it throughout the world.

As Alexander's armies proceeded to conquer Greece (338 BCE), elements of other Greek dialects became incorporated into Attic Greek, leading to the creation of *Koine* (common) or Hellenistic Greek, which would become the lingua franca of Alexander's vast empire (including the Balkans, Middle East, and parts of Northern Africa and East Asia). Later, when the Latin-speaking Romans conquered Greece (146 BCE) and the rest of these territories (as well as parts of today's France, Spain, and Germany), Greek became the unofficial second language of the Roman Empire.

Hence, Latin language came to adopt various words, word roots, and other aspects of *Koine* Greek, especially biblical terms such as angel, demon, apostle, baptize, prophet, and paradise. New words combining Greek and Latin also emerged, leading to a Greco-Latin vocabulary that, to varying extents, was later incorporated into French, Spanish, and other Latin-based languages. After the collapse of the western half of the Roman Empire (Italy and areas to the west of Italy) in 456 CE, Greek continued to be spoken in the eastern half (Greece, the Balkans, Middle East, and parts of Northern Africa), often referred to as the Byzantine Empire (330–1453 CE).

Throughout Greek history, there has always been a gap between the Greek used by officials and other educated elites and that spoken by the vast majority of Greeks or demotic Greek (*demos* meaning "of the people"). As the Byzantine Empire was repeatedly invaded by foreign forces (including French, Italian, and other Crusaders) and then conquered by the Ottoman Turks (1453 CE), this situation of *diglossa* (two languages) only worsened, and demotic Greek came to include French, Turkish, and other foreign words.

Centuries later, when Greece became an independent nation (1830 CE), Adamantios Korais (1748–1833 CE) authored a revised form of Greek (later called *katharevousa*) that was free of foreign influences and whose grammar and form was similar to that of ancient Greek. In 1832 CE, *katharevousa* became the official language of the Greek government.

In an effort to revive Greece's connection to its historic past, Korais had replaced not only foreign words but also many popular demotic Greek words with artificially constructed words composed of various ancient Greek word roots. *Katharevousa* also came to include aspects of ancient Greek grammar that had long fallen into disuse.

Most Greeks, however, lacked sufficient knowledge of ancient Greek grammar and word forms to understand *katharevousa*. Hence, language became both a political and religious issue, leading to language riots (1901, 1904) and heated debates about which form of Greek should be used in government, education, and the church.

Ultimately, in 1976, Standard Modern Greek, which highly favors demotic Greek, was declared the official language of Greece (and Cyprus). Modern Greek is also a recognized minority language in Italy, Albania, and elsewhere and is spoken by the Greek diaspora in the United States, Canada, Australia, and New Zealand. The Greek Orthodox Church, however, continues to use *Koine* Greek for its services and the Bible.

Modern Greek uses the ancient Greek alphabet consisting of twenty-four letters written in both upper and lowercase: Αα, Ββ, Γγ, Δδ, Εε, Ζζ, Ηη, Θθ, Ιι, Κκ, Λλ, Μμ, Νν, Ξξ, Οο, Ππ, Ρρ, Σσ, Ττ, Υυ, Φφ, Χχ, Ψψ, and Ωω. This alphabet includes the five English vowels (*a*, *e*, *i*, *o*, *u*), but there are three forms of the English long e (ι, η, and υ) and two forms of the English o (ο and ω). Greek also has diphthongs where two vowels are combined to form a single syllable. For example, the diphthongs oi (οι) and ei (ει) are pronounced as a long e.

Greek punctuation is the same as that of English, except that semicolons are used as question marks, and the upper dot of a colon is used as a semicolon. Most Greek words are multisyllabic, and an accent mark indicates which syllable needs to be stressed.

Like ancient Greek, modern Greek is a highly inflected language in that suffixes and/or prefixes are added to the root of a word in order to specify the word's exact meaning and grammatical function. Greek nouns are declined based on their gender, number, and grammatical function. Adjectives are declined according to the gender, number, and case of the noun.

There are three cases (nominative, genitive, and accusative), two numbers (singular and plural), and three genders (masculine, feminine, and neutral). Gender is usually determined by the meaning of the word. For example, the word "brother" is masculine; "mother," feminine; and "objects," neuter. But there many exceptions. While the word for river is neuter, ocean is feminine, and waterway is masculine; and some feminine nouns are declined as if they were masculine.

Word order is more flexible in Greek than in English. Noun case is indicated by adding the appropriate suffix and/or prefix to the root of the noun. In contrast, in English, in order to show that a noun is the subject rather than the object of the verb, the noun is placed before the verb. English also uses pronouns ("I," "you," "they," "we," "it," etc.) to indicate the subject of the verb.

In English, auxiliary verbs ("has," "had," "have," "will," etc.) are often used to indicate the tense of a verb. Although modern Greek uses some auxiliary verbs, usually suffixes and/or prefixes are added to verb roots to distinguish the past, past perfect, present, future, future perfect, and other tenses, each of which is declined differently.

In addition, any number of verbs have two voices (active and passive) and/or several moods (subjunctive, imperative, and indicative), with different declensions for each voice and mood as well as tense.

Prepositions can also pose a challenge in that some can only be used with one noun case and others, with two or three cases. Still other prepositions have multiple meanings.

Although Greek grammar can be perplexing, its complexity allows thoughts to be expressed with great clarity and precision. Greek is also a highly expressive language. Its vocabulary is rich with words for the many kinds and degrees of human emotion. Many English psychological terms are of Greek origin, for example, "crisis," "agony," "panic," "trauma," "frenzy," "phobia," "ecstasy," "melancholy," and "paranoia." The word "psychology" is also rooted in Greek, as are most English words spelled with a *ph* pronounced like an f (e.g., "philosophy" and "physics"). Medical terms are also rich with Greek words, as are words in everyday English vocabulary.

Most Greeks love to talk and highly value the musical flow of their language. Every effort is made to avoid words and phrases containing several consonants or vowels in a row. Vowels are usually added before suffixes that start with a consonant; and prepositions ending in a vowel drop the vowel if the next word begins with a vowel. These changes are not intended to alter the meaning of a word or phrase but to effect a smoother, more melodious pronunciation.

In Standard Modern Greek, the intricate grammar of *katharevousa* and ancient Greek has been vastly simplified. Nevertheless (although estimates vary), either in whole, in part, or in some modified form, much of the vocabulary is based on ancient Greek. Indeed, throughout Greek history, ancient Greek has remained highly regarded.

Modern Greek also has English, French, Italian, Turkish, and other foreign words. Some are declined as if they were Greek. But others, especially more recent ones (e.g., "bar," "jeans," and "app"), are not declined because adding the necessary suffixes and/or prefixes would make these words cumbersome or create harsh or unnatural sounding syllables.

Unlike Latin and ancient Sumerian, Greek is a language that never stopped being spoken. Although it is often viewed as a language of historic interest with little contemporary value, Greek is alive in the vocabulary and syntax of many modern languages. Due to its flexibility, expressiveness, and abundance of words, prefixes, and suffixes, Greek (along with Latin) is still being used to create new words in English and in other languages. Even today, *Koine* Greek is studied by clergy and others who seek a more complete and accurate understanding of the New Testament.

*Aphrodite Matsakis*

**See also:** Chapter 9: Common Expressions; Dialects and Minority Languages.

**Further Reading**

Adkins, Lesley, and Roy A. Adkins. 2008. *Handbook to Life in Ancient Greece*, Updated edition. New York: Facts on File, Inc.

Adrados, Francisco R. 2005. *A History of the Greek Language: From Its Origins to the Present.* Boston: Brill Leiden.

Black, David Alan. 1994. *Learn to Read New Testament Greek.* Nashville, TN: Broadman & Holman Publishers.

Newton, B. E. 1960. "Ancient and Modern Greek." *Greece & Rome* 7 (2): 124–127. http://www.jstor.org/stable/641543.

Norris, Mary. 2019. "Greek to Me." *The New Yorker*, January 14, 2019. Accessed May 1, 2019. www.newyorker.com/magazine/2019/01/14/greek-to-me.

Thomopoulos, Elaine. 2012. *The History of Greece*: Santa Barbara, CA: Greenwood, an imprint of ABC-CLIO, LLC.

CHAPTER 10

# ETIQUETTE

## OVERVIEW

Although modern Greeks, like their ancestors, value personal freedom and self-expression, Greek society revolves around family, friendship, and social relationships. Even in urban areas where personal achievement is highly valued, Greeks spend a lot of time socializing.

Greeks tend to distrust written contracts and laws, possibly because of Greece's long history of brutal occupations by foreign powers and betrayal by various groups. They prefer to make decisions based on how much they trust the particular individuals involved. Such trust is developed by getting to know others.

Second, Greeks believe that enjoying life is important and that living without strong emotional bonds and social events would be joyless. For many, a solitary life would seem almost meaningless, for it is in the arena of interpersonal relationships that one can exercise and maintain the core Greek value of *philotimo* (love of honor).

*Philotimo* encompasses numerous virtues, such as civility, loyalty, compassion, and a willingness to sacrifice for a greater good. Although it involves respecting others, it also involves respecting oneself and preserving one's dignity. Hence, in social interactions, Greeks expect to be acknowledged and consider it disrespectful not to be greeted. Avoiding direct eye contact and moving away from someone while talking are also considered offensive.

Greeks are accustomed to a degree of physical closeness while conversing that may be uncomfortable to non-Greeks. Touching is common, as is standing close to one another. Greeks are also accustomed to a degree of openness and emotional expressiveness that may seem excessive to others. For example, they do not consider it impolite to ask others about their income, family, and other personal matters or to comment about another's conduct, dress, or food choices.

Greeks are often willing to talk openly about their lives and show affection verbally and through hugs or kisses on both cheeks. Often they speak with emotional intensity about minor matters as well as urgent ones. Hence, raised voices do not necessarily herald the beginning of a brawl but rather a disagreement about anything from the outcome of a soccer game to the price of an orange.

Certain hand gestures, however, can precipitate major rifts. The *moutza*, the Greek equivalent of "giving someone the finger," which involves making the hand signal for the number five with one's palm turned toward the other, is considered particularly offensive, as is making a fist with one's thumb in between one's middle and index finger.

Such gestures violate the recipient's *philotimo* and, given the importance of family, the *philotimo* of their family. Similarly, if someone displays a lack of *philoxenia* (hospitality), they shame not only themselves but also their relatives.

Despite its ancient origins, the tradition of *philoxenia* continues and involves more than saying "please" and "thank you." Especially in rural areas, guests are to be given food, drink, and the most comfortable seat or bed. In return, guests are expected to reciprocate with gifts and offers of hospitality.

In a family-oriented country like Greece, weddings, baptisms, and funerals are of great importance. Civil marriages are permitted in Greece, but at least half of the couples get married in church. In the first part of the wedding ceremony (the betrothal), the priest blesses the rings, which are then exchanged three times by the best man (*koumparo*) or the maid of honor (*koumpara*). During the second part (the wedding proper), the priest exhorts the couple to respect and love one another and asks God to unite them in sacred union and make them worthy of parenthood.

Decorative wreaths of white flowers and beads are placed on the couple's heads, symbolizing that they are to be king and queen of their household. The *koumparo* or *koumpara* exchanges these crowns three times, and then follows the couple and the priest as they circle around the altar three times as an expression of joy. After the ceremony, guests receive *boubounieres* (favors of white sugar–coated almonds) and typically attend a feast followed by dancing.

Like weddings, baptisms are festive events with a solemn meaning. During baptism, a child is joined to the Greek Orthodox Church and given a name. The godparent carries a large, decorated candle and commits to providing lifelong spiritual support. After the ceremony, guests receive a *martiriko* (a small cross on a ribbon) to wear and sugar-coated almonds wrapped in tulle with a ribbon, symbolizing the wish for the future of the child and the guests to be sweet.

Children are usually baptized as infants. But sometimes baptisms are delayed because one or more family members do not want to the follow the tradition of naming the child after a particular grandparent. Perhaps they want to name the child after a different relative (or a cherished friend or saint) or give the child a nonfamily name. Hence, some families combine the names of several relatives or a family name with a nonfamily name.

Celebrations following baptisms can be either a simple gathering with dessert and coffee or a lavish meal with music and dance. After funerals, however, there are no festivities. Laughter is not permitted, and guests are served hard toasts (symbolic of bones) and fish (a Christian symbol). Like the family, guests wear black or dark colors.

Caskets are often kept open during funerals. Afterward, guests may approach the casket to bid a final farewell. At the gravesite, the priest performs a short service and then throws wine (and perhaps olive oil or water) on the casket. Mourners throw a handful of dirt.

Relatively long periods of mourning are socially acceptable and given expression through forty-day, six-month, one-year, and three-year memorial services. Afterward, there may or may not be a meal. But the family always provides a wheat dish (*koliva*), which symbolizes the circle of life and death, followed by eternal life.

There are considerable regional variations in the social customs surrounding weddings, baptisms, and grieving. These customs have also been influenced by Western practices and technological advances. Greek Orthodox Church services, however, remain unchanged.

Whether attending a wedding, funeral, or any other service, one is expected to dress respectfully, that is, no torn, dirty clothes or low-cut blouses without a jacket. Traditionally, the faithful make the sign of the cross in front of the icons in the narthex. Visitors need not do so but can show respect by lowering their eyes. Those who chose to light a candle are expected to make a small contribution in the designated area. In Greece, some churches still practice the centuries-old custom of men sitting on the right side of the church and women sitting on the left. Many of the churches do not have pews, although there are chair-like structures on the side walls of the church for the infirm or elderly. Congregants are expected to stand.

Few Greeks show up on time for services. However, during certain parts of certain services, for example, when worshippers are kneeling, it may be considered disrespectful to enter the chapel area. Visitors arriving late are advised to ask the attendant in the narthex when it is permissible to enter. The altar area may not be entered at any time without permission, and women are never permitted to enter.

Health permitting, visitors can stand, sit, or kneel as directed by the priest. Instead of kneeling or standing, they can lower their eyes. When others make the sign of the cross, visitors need not do the same. However, when the priest moves up and down the aisles to bless the congregation or as part of a procession, it is considered disrespectful not to turn and look at him.

In sum, Greek etiquette is a mixture of old and new: of traditions going back to the ancient Greeks to the generation growing up with cell phones. Yet even those who have abandoned some of the traditional restrictions regarding premarital sex and courtship know better than to wear red at funerals or show up at weddings without an appropriate gift. Indeed, gift giving is such an integral part of Greek etiquette that most Greeks would not dream of visiting someone for the first time empty handed.

*Aphrodite Matsakis*

**Further Reading**

Rawlins, Clive L. 1998. *Culture Shock! Greece.* Portland, OR: Graphic Arts Center Publishing Company.

Rouvelas, Marilyn. 1993. *A Guide to Greek Traditions and Customs in America.* Bethesda, MD: Attica Press.

## Baptism, Chrismation, and Naming Traditions

Baptisms are festive occasions with a solemn meaning. Baptism joins a child to the Greek Orthodox Church and to a godparent who commits to being a lifelong spiritual support. The church ceremony, during which the child is officially named, is rich with symbolism. The celebration that follows can range from a simple gathering where guests are served dessert and coffee to a lavish banquet that is followed by music and dancing.

Baptism initiates the child into the faith by cleansing the child of original sin and dedicating him or her to God. First the godparent renounces Satan in the church entryway. Then the priest immerses the child (undressed) into a baptismal font containing water and a small amount of olive oil (symbolic of peace) three times (symbolic of Christ's three days in the tomb).

Afterward, the child is wrapped in a white sheet (symbolic of purity) and held by the godparent while the priest asks for the child to be blessed with the Holy Spirit (the sacrament of chrismation). During the chrismation, the priest anoints the child with an oil that has been blessed by the bishop. The child is then dressed in new white clothes and given a cross provided by the godparent. At the conclusion of the ceremony, the priest, the godparent and child, and several children circle the font as an expression of joy.

During the ceremony, the godparent carries a large, decorated candle, and the children participating in the ceremony carry small white ones. Men are expected to wear jackets, and women to refrain from flaunting their sexuality.

Afterward, guests are given a *martiriko* (witness pins—a small cross on a ribbon) to wear and sugar-coated almonds wrapped in tulle with a ribbon. The sugarcoating symbolizes the wish for the future of the child and the guests to be sweet.

The family and the godparent are congratulated with expressions such as "May he or she live for you" or "May he or she live." Appropriate gifts for baptisms include baby clothes, money, or an icon of the child's patron saint or of the Virgin Mary.

Children are usually baptized during infancy. But sometimes baptisms are delayed because of disagreements over the child's name. Traditionally, children were named after grandparents, with the first son named after the paternal grandfather, the second son after the maternal grandfather, first daughter after the paternal grandmother, and the second daughter after the maternal grandmother.

Disputes can arise when one parent comes from a region in Greece where the first daughter is named after the mother's mother (rather than the father's mother) or when one or both parents wish to give their child a nonfamily name, the name of a childless friend or family member, or the name of a favored saint.

Sometimes parents who decide on a nonfamily name for the child's first name may give the child a grandparent's name as a middle name, or find a way to combine their name of choice with a family name, or combine the names of two or more grandparents.

Traditionally, the child was given the father's surname. As of 1983, however, couples can choose to give their child the mother's surname.

*Aphrodite Matsakis*

**See also:** Chapter 5: Greek Orthodoxy.

**Further Reading**

Neos Kosmos. "Naming Rights." Accessed August 4, 2017. neoskosmos.com/news/en/naming-rights.

The Orthodox Church in America. n.d. "Chrismation." Accessed August 4, 2017. https://www.oca.org/orthodoxy/the-orthodox-faith/worship/the-sacraments/chrismation.

Rouvelas, Marilyn. 1993. *A Guide to Greek Traditions and Customs in America*. Bethesda, MD: Attica Press. Accessed August 4, 2017. https://oca.org/orthodoxy/the-orthodox-faith/worship/the-sacraments/chrismation.

## Funerals

Most Greeks are Greek Orthodox and bury their dead in a local cemetery following a wake for the viewing of the deceased and a funeral conducted by the priest at the church. Cremation is not allowed by the Greek Orthodox Church. Cremation was legalized by the state in 2006, but the first crematorium was not built until 2019. The country's first such facility was opened in Ritsona, north of Athens.

Greeks take death seriously. Deep grief is culturally permissible, especially in rural areas. There is considerable regional variation in the intensity of grief expressed at wakes, funerals, or the gravesite. In the past, professional mourners were often hired to sing lamentations, and expressions of grief, such as screaming and collapsing, were more common.

A cemetery in the village of Agios Basilios near the city of Tripoli. The building holds the bones of the deceased, which after three years are exhumed, placed in a box, and stacked inside. Limited space in cemeteries makes this a common practice throughout Greece. (Photo by Elaine Thomopoulos)

At the funeral service, family members wear black. Those in attendance are expected to dress conservatively and in dark colors.

Laughing and talking are not permitted, and during the meal that customarily follows, there is no dancing or music. Nor are there any celebratory sweets, such as baklava. Instead guests are served brandy, hard toasts (symbolic of bones), and fish (a symbol of Christianity).

Traditionally, a small icon is placed in or outside the casket, and during funerals, the casket is left open. Afterward, those in attendance approach the casket to bid the deceased a final farewell. Customarily, they make the sign of the cross and/or kiss the icon.

Before the casket is lowered into the ground, the priest performs a short service, then throws wine (and sometimes olive oil or water) on the casket. Mourners throw a handful of dirt, and in rural areas sometimes shovelfuls of dirt are thrown in the casket.

In big cities, wakes take place at the funeral home. In rural areas, where funeral homes are often nonexistent, viewings usually take place in the home. Also, given the limited amount of space in both rural areas and cities, after three or more years, the deceased's bones are exhumed, washed, and placed in a box in a small building at the edge of the cemetery, taken to the family's home, or placed in a smaller container in a family grave, where containers with bones are placed one on top of the other. In big cities, like Athens, families can rent space. If the family does not pay the rent, the deceased is exhumed and placed in a pit along with others.

Greek women wear black during the mourning period, which usually lasts at least a year. Some Greek women wear black for years, particularly in the villages. Men express their grief by wearing black arm bands, usually for a forty-day period following the death of a family member.

Throughout all of Greece, relatively long periods of mourning are socially acceptable and given expression through forty-day, six-month, one-year, and three-year memorial church services. Additional memorial services can be requested, and the dead can also be honored on Saturdays of Souls. These occur four times a year on a Saturday, the day Christ was placed in the tomb. To announce memorial services, notices are posted at the church and other public places.

During memorial services, the priest prays for the deceased to be granted forgiveness and a peaceful repose. At the end, all may join the priest in singing the refrain: "May his or her memory be eternal." Afterward, the family members sitting in the front pew of the church are offered sympathy by repeating this refrain, along with the expression "Life to you," "May God forgive him," or "*Kalo Paradiso*" (blessed paradise). They also use these refrains at the wake and funeral.

Following memorial services, families may or may not provide a meal or refreshments. But families always provide a boiled wheat dish (*koliva*), usually sweetened with raisins, pomegranates, and powdered sugar, which is blessed during the service and distributed afterward. This wheat dish symbolizes the circle of life and death, followed by eternal life.

During the official forty-day mourning period, the bereaved are expected to refrain from going to social activities. It is customary, however, for others to visit the bereaved during this time period and bring gifts of food or brandy.

Throughout Greece, victims of automobile accidents are memorialized by small shrines set on posts beside the road or highway where the accident took place. They often include a photo of the victim and an icon.

*Aphrodite Matsakis*

**See also:** Chapter 5: Greek Orthodoxy. Chapter 10: Social Interactions.

**Further Reading**

Danforth, Loring M. 1982. *The Death Rituals of Rural Greece.* Princeton, NJ: Princeton University Press.

Leontis, Artemis. 2009. *Culture and Customs of Greece.* Westport, CT: Greenwood Press.

Rouvelas, Marilyn. 1993. *A Guide to Greek Traditions and Customs in America.* Bethesda, MD: Attica Press.

## Holidays

The Greeks believe that enjoying life is important. Hence, their numerous holidays, both national and religious, are often celebrated not only with church services and family dinners but also with private parties, communal feasts, and (sometimes) parades. The Greek Orthodox Church is not opposed to the physical pleasures of earthly life, such as eating and other forms of merrymaking, and only considers these activities to be sinful when they separate one from God. Consequently, except for holidays occurring during Lent, the forty-day period preceding Easter, church holidays often include feasting, dancing, singing, and, in some areas, parades.

Two important national holidays are Greek Independence Day (March 25) and Ohi Day (October 28). Greek Independence Day, which honors the beginning of the 1821 Greek revolt against centuries of Ottoman-Turkish occupation, coincides with the church holiday of the Annunciation, where Mary learns that she will give birth to a Savior. Ohi or "No" Day celebrates the Greeks' refusal to agree to Italy's demand during World War II to surrender without a fight. In the ensuing battles, the Greeks, although outnumbered and ill equipped, drove back the Italian invaders. Ohi Day is also a celebration of how, during the brutal 1941–1945 Nazi occupation, Greeks, young and old, men and women, resisted as fully as possible. This day is also a religious holiday that celebrated the Angel Gabriel telling the Virgin Mary that she would become the mother of Jesus. During national holidays stores and government offices are closed, and there are church services, parades, speeches, and social gatherings. Other commemorative holidays, although not national holidays, include May 1, which honors workers and is an occasion for political demonstrations, and November 17, which commemorates the Polytech uprising against the Greek junta in 1973.

Aside from Christmas, Easter, and New Year's (described in separate entries), major religious holidays include Epiphany (January 6), the Feast of Saint George (April 23), the Day of the Holy Spirit (some fifty days after Easter), and the Assumption of the Virgin Mary (August 15).

*Aphrodite Matsakis*

**See also:** Chapter 5: Greek Orthodox Holidays; Greek Orthodox Regional Celebrations. Appendix D: Holidays.

**Further Reading**

Leontis, Artemis. 2009. *Culture and Customs of Greece.* Westport, CT: Greenwood Press.

## Social Interactions

Greeks put a high value on developing personal ties. They love to talk and feel free to express themselves about everything from the meaning of life to the price of a tomato. It is not considered rude to question the freshness of a grocer's produce or bargain over prices. Nor is it considered impolite to ask new acquaintances about their marital status, political views, or other relatively personal questions or even to comment on their behavior, appearance, or choice of an appetizer.

Greeks are often willing to talk about their lives and show affection not only verbally but also through hugs or a kiss on both cheeks, gift giving, and any number of greetings. They have greetings for everything from national and religious holidays, to childbirth, name days, baptisms, weddings, and funerals, to going to a party or the beach and embarking on a voyage or an educational or business venture.

Saying goodbye can take a while because in addition to "goodbye," there may be wishes for a good week, month, or year and for family members and friends. Not to return a greeting or acknowledge someone at a social gathering is considered offensive, as is avoiding direct eye contact or pulling back while talking. Greeks are accustomed to a degree of physical closeness while conversing that may be uncomfortable to non-Greeks.

While many Greeks value personal achievement, they also put a high value on getting to know others on a personal basis. One reason for this emphasis on socializing is to acquire friends, acquaintances, and business associations whom one can trust.

Greece has been oppressed and betrayed numerous times by foreign powers and by its own government. Hence, Greeks have learned to put their faith in people who they deem trustworthy, rather than in organizations or groups with which they do not have a personal relationship.

In traditional village culture, relationships play a key role not only in terms of self-esteem and social status but also economics. Prices and distribution of limited goods are often influenced by the relationship between buyer and seller; for example, a merchant might refuse to sell to someone who did not bring an appropriate gift to their son's baptism or who failed to adhere to some other cherished tradition.

Today most Greeks live in cities instead of villages. Even in cities, establishing positive relationships is essential. Employment opportunities and business success may depend more on personal contacts than on credentials and expertise. Both cities and small towns are lined with small cafés where people talk for hours, despite the popularity of the media. At night, weather permitting, people often go out to meet with friends.

Emotional expressiveness is part of the Greek character, and Greeks can speak with emotional intensity about everyday matters as well as urgent ones. They love to debate too. Raised voices may not reflect the beginning of a brawl but rather a disagreement about anything from the outcome of an election to the price of a tomato.

*Aphrodite Matsakis*

**See also:** Chapter 9: Sidebar: How to Interpret Gestures and Body Language and Which Ones to Avoid. Chapter 10: Overview.

**Further Reading**

Leontis, Artemis. 2009. *Culture and Customs of Greece*. Westport, CT: Greenwood Press.

Rawlins, C. L. 1998. *Culture Shock! Greece*. Portland, OR: Graphic Arts Center Publishing Company.

## Weddings

In a family-oriented country such as Greece, weddings are of great importance. There are both civil marriages and church marriages. The Hellenic Statistical Authority reported that in 2017 more than half of Greeks got married in a civil ceremony, but these statistics do not include those who also got married in church. The traditional Greek Orthodox Church wedding, followed by a lavish reception, is still popular. Traditionally, marriages were arranged by parents or matchmakers. Today, however, couples usually marry for love. In the past, families were obligated to provide dowries (*prika*) for their daughters. In 1983, however, the government abolished dowries, and civil marriages were legitimized. Most Greeks, however, eagerly anticipate church weddings and the joyous festivities that follow.

The Greek Orthodox Church considers marriage to be a sacrament where a man and woman are not only joined together in a sacred union but also commit to raising a Christian family. Social customs surrounding weddings vary. But the hour-long ceremony has remained unchanged for centuries.

In the first part, the betrothal, the priest blesses the rings. After the rings are placed on the couple's right hands, the rings are exchanged three times by the best man (*koumparo*) or the maid of honor (*koumpara*).

During the second part, the wedding proper, the couple holds hands while the priests asks God to unite them, physically and spiritually, and make them worthy of and bless them with children. Crowns (*stephana*), usually made of small, white flowers and beads and joined together by a ribbon, are then placed on the couple's heads.

These decorative wreaths symbolize that the husband and wife are to be as king and queen of their household and are united. While the *koumparo* or *koumpara* exchange the crowns three times, the priest prays for the couple to be crowned with "honor and glory."

To highlight the fact that marriage involves sharing all aspects of life, the positive as well as the negative, the couple then drinks wine from a common cup. Afterward comes the Dance of Isaiah. Here the priest, followed by the couple (with the *koumparo* or *koumpara* holding the ribbon uniting the couple's crowns), circles around the altar three times as an expression of joy.

During the ceremony, scriptures stressing the importance of mutual respect are read, and the couple holds white candles. The lit candles, symbolizing the light of Christ, reflect the belief that Christ is present, and will remain present, throughout the couple's marriage.

Following the ceremony, guests can expect to receive *boubounieres* (favors of white sugar-coated almonds) and typically enjoy a reception laden with food and Greek pastries and ringing with music and dance. Before eating, however, guests need to wait for the priest to bless the food.

The couple is congratulated with expressions such as "May you live" and family members and the *koumparo* or *koumpara* with "May they live for you" or "May they live for us." Single persons are often greeted with wishes that someday they, too, will marry.

In general, casual attire is considered disrespectful. Formal attire is permissible, if not expected, depending on the couple's preferences. Appropriate gifts for weddings include household items, money, and bottles of expensive liquor.

*Aphrodite Matsakis*

**See also:** Chapter 7: Sidebar: *Prika* (Dowry) Now Outlawed in Greece.

**Further Reading**

Rouvelas, Marilyn. 1993. *A Guide to Greek Traditions and Customs in America*. Bethesda, MD: Attica Press.

CHAPTER 11

# LITERATURE AND DRAMA

## OVERVIEW

Dating back over twenty-eight hundred years, Greek literature is the second-oldest continuous literature tradition in the world (Chinese is the oldest). This long tradition is ordinarily grouped into three broad chronological eras: Ancient, Byzantine, and Modern. As with all historical dating, particularly as related to cultural phenomenon, these periods and the dates ordinarily associated with them are flexible.

The ancient period begins approximately in 800 BCE and continues until the late third century CE. In turn, ancient Greek literature has traditionally been divided into four eras: Preclassical, Classical, Hellenistic, and Roman. The oldest existing pieces of Greek literature are Homer's *The Iliad* and *The Odyssey*, which most scholars date to the ninth century BCE. They are the most famous examples of Preclassical Greek literature. Aside from Homer, the other significant poet of the period is Hesiod. His surviving works are *The Works and Days*, *Theogony*, and (possibly) *Shield of Herakles*. Preclassical literature is almost exclusively poetic in form (particularly the epic) and focuses heavily on mythological and heroic tales. Much is drawn from the preliterary oral tradition, a tradition that Greek-speaking people shared with the Indo-Europeans.

The Classical period of ancient Greek literature, which began around 500 BCE, flourished during the height of ancient Greek political and military power. Unsurprisingly, it is also the period that produced much of what people think of when referring to "ancient Greek literature." Breaking with the monolithic dominance of the epic poetry in the Preclassical period, the Classical period produced lyrical poetry, comedies, tragedies, histories, philosophical treatises, pastorals, odes, and elegies, among other forms. It was during this period that Sappho, Euripides, Herodotos, and Plato all wrote. In no small way, classical literature provided the foundations of what would be thought of thereafter as "Greek" culture, and for much of history in many parts of the world, a conversant knowledge of classical Greek literature became the hallmark of an educated person.

This development may never have happened if the Classical period had not been brought to an end by the armies of Alexander the Great. Alexander conquered the whole of Greece and then turned east, bringing under his control a huge swath of territory reaching as far as modern Afghanistan. With his armies, Alexander carried with him Greek culture; he had been a student of Aristotle after all. When Alexander died without an heir in 323 BCE, his new empire was divided among his most powerful generals, and a new era in Greek, and world, history began: the Hellenistic period. The Hellenistic period was characterized by the blending of classical Greek culture with the local cultures of the conquered territory. Alexandria, the glorious capital city of Hellenistic Egypt, founded by Alexander himself, was the epicenter of Hellenistic literature. The literary production of the period was dominated by long-form poetry, particularly the so-called learned love poetry, which revealed in its own erudition as much, if not more, than any exploration of romantic eros. The most significant writers of this period include Callimachus, Apollonius of Rhodes, and Theocritus, all of whom had connections to the city of Alexandria.

Just as it had begun, the Hellenistic period ended in conquest, as Rome brought the former Hellenistic kingdoms under her sway. The place Greek culture, language, and literature held in the Roman Empire cannot be underestimated. And it is important to note that Greek remained the language of daily life in the eastern half of the Roman Empire and the language of the educated classes in both the East and West. Like the Classical period, the Roman period of Greek literature is characterized by the diversity of the types of literature produced. These included philosophical and scientific treaties, poetry, comedy, drama, and religious texts. The Christian Scriptures, written in the *Koine* dialect, are perhaps the most famous and enduring example of Roman-era Greek literature.

The Christianization of the Roman Empire brought to an end the ancient Greco-Roman world. With the transition of the Roman Empire to Christianity, every aspect of daily life and culture changed radically, including literature. From the late third century CE onward, ancient Greek literature gave way to Byzantine literature, which was produced in five principal genres: histories, encyclopedias, secular poetry, ecclesiastical and theological literature, and popular poetry. Traditionally, modern scholars have given considerably more attention to the ecclesiastical and theological productions of Byzantine literature than to the secular ones. This has left many with the false impression that Byzantium lacked a secular literature, which could not be further from the truth. Furthermore, it is worth noting that Byzantine writers tended to model their work more on Hellenistic literature than the ancient. Byzantine secular authors produced panegyrics, epigrams, didactic poetry, and satires. The Byzantine romance novel is one of the more underappreciated categories of Western literature. Eustathios Makrembolites, Theodore Prodromos, Niketas Eugenianos, and Constantine Manasses, all authors writing in the twelfth century, wrote the Byzantine novels in imitation of the ancient Roman form. Byzantium also produced a great epic in the style of Homer. Like *The Iliad* and *The Odyssey*, *Digenis Akritas* derives from an oral tradition that took its first written form in the tenth or eleventh century CE. It was hugely influential at the time and was among the sources for medieval French ballads, the genre in which modern notions of love and romance first took shape.

Modern Greek literature, the final period of Greek literature, began with the fall of Constantinople in 1453. Ordinarily divided between the Ottoman period and Greek Independence, modern Greek literature is characterized, perhaps more than the literary tradition of any other modern European language, by the ghosts of the past. Much of the modern canon consists of texts that seek to encounter and wrestle with history, exile, and loss. Like most modern Western literature, modern Greek literature takes the novel as its primary form. The most famous and influential Greek novelist of the twentieth century is Nikos Kazantzakis, whose place among the great fiction writers of world literature cannot be questioned. Constantine P. Cavafy occupies a similar place among the pantheon of modern poets. Moreover, two Greek writers have won Nobel Prizes in Literature: Odysseas Elytis in 1979 and Giorgos Seferis in 1963.

Greek literature has not enjoyed the widespread recognition of other literary traditions for two key reasons. First, modern Greek, unlike its ancient predecessor, is not a widely spoken language and so does not enjoy the natural reader base of a language like English or French. This relates to the second problem for modern Greek literature: the relative lack of governmental support for translation of Greece's literary production into more globally spoken languages. This type of support in places such as Norway and the Netherlands has resulted in more global recognition for their literary communities. However, such support has not been forthcoming from the Greek state.

In a repertory of little plays featuring the leading protagonist, Karagiozis (the one with the long arm), these two-dimensional puppets are brought to life on stage in a shadow theater, an art rooted in the nineteenth-century Ottoman Empire. A puppeteer behind an illuminated screen performs the animation and dialogue. Although not as popular as in decades past, audiences continue to relish the slapstick comedic antics of Karagiozis and his ensemble as they perform traditional plays and satires, as well as improvisations with political messages. (Photo by Elaine Thomopoulos)

Finally, when addressing the question of modern Greek literature, one must consider the issue of the Greek diaspora. A significant body of literature has been produced by Greeks living outside of traditionally Greek lands and by those of Greek heritage. Some of this literature has been produced in the modern Greek language and some in other languages. Grappling with the question as to whether this constitutes a part of the Greek canon is an ongoing debate among scholars and practitioners.

*Katherine Kalaidis*

**Further Reading**

Bakker, Egbert J., ed. 2010. *A Companion to the Ancient Greek Language*. Blackwell Companions to the Ancient World. Chichester, UK: Wiley-Blackwell.

Hose, Martin, and David J. Schenker. 2016. *A Companion to Greek Literature*. Blackwell Companions to the Ancient World. Chichester, UK: Wiley Blackwell.

Howatson, M. C., ed. 2011. *The Oxford Companion to Classical Literature*, 3rd edition. Oxford: Oxford University Press.

## Ancient Bards and Dramatists

The ancient Greek bards and dramatists laid the foundation of Western literature and drama. They include the epic poet Homer and the lyric poets Sappho and Pindar. The ancient dramatists include the tragedians Aeschylus, Sophocles, and Euripides and the comic playwright Aristophanes.

Today the Aegean is still a "wine-dark sea," as described by the poet (or poets) named Homer thousands of years ago. Even now, the Aegean is often a dark blue, so deeply hued the waters resemble a bluish-red wine, "wine-dark" as the epithet is traditionally translated into English. Homer frequently uses epithets such as "wine-dark" or "wine-faced" sea. "Wine-faced" is considered the more literal translation, and "wine-dark" the more poetic. An epithet is a set phrase, characteristic of oral poetry, which helps bards tell a story from generation to generation. The Homeric poems were most likely orally transmitted long before they were written down.

Legend has it that Homer was blind, a wandering bard, born near the Asia Minor coast. However, this legend is not supported by definitive historical fact. Some scholars speculate that the Homeric poems were compiled from the oral tradition and written down in the sixth century BCE. Others speculate Homer may have lived earlier than 1000 BCE. He is often dated between 750 and 700 BCE. In any case, two renowned epic poems are attributed to Homer today: *The Iliad* and *The Odyssey*. These long narrative poems are written in dactylic hexameter, a type of poetic meter or rhythm. Both *The Iliad* and *The Odyssey* tell the stories of great heroes.

*The Iliad* is the story of the wrath of the warrior Achilles. It takes place toward the end of the ten-year Trojan War. Hector, son of the Trojan king Priam, kills Achilles's beloved comrade Patroclus. Bereft and furious, Achilles seeks vengeance by killing Hector and then dragging his corpse through the war-torn city of Troy. In one of the most moving scenes in Western literature, Priam begs Achilles for the body of his son in order to give him a proper funeral.

*The Odyssey* is the story of King Odysseus as he journeys home to Ithaca after the fall of Troy. This journey takes ten years. Odysseus has been away from Ithaca for twenty years, and thus his wife, Penelope, and his son, Telemachus, as well as the people of Ithaca, believe he has died. Even so, Penelope has not remarried despite the many suitors who come to woo her. The first part of *The Odyssey* includes Telemachus's search for his father. The second part recounts Odysseus's voyage, homecoming, reunion with his family, and the reclamation of his kingdom.

While Homer is considered the first great epic poet, Sappho and Pindar are among the early great lyric poets. Epic poems are long narratives, and lyric poems are short, expressing emotions. In ancient Greece, lyric poems were often sung, accompanied by a harp-like, stringed musical instrument called the lyre.

Little is known about the life of Sappho, the lyric poet from the island of Lesvos. Scholars think Sappho may have been born around 630 or 620 BCE, and she may have died around 570 BCE.

Most of her poetry has been lost. Among Sappho's remaining poems and fragments are "Hymn (or Ode) to Aphrodite," "Fragment 31," "Brothers Poem," and "Old Age Poem." Sappho most likely composed music to accompany her poetry; she sang her lyrics.

Controversies abound concerning Sappho's sexuality, for she wrote passionately about both women and men. She may have been a wife and mother and may have had at least two brothers. The term "lesbian" derives from Lesvos, the island where Sappho lived. However, scholars are uncertain whether Sappho's poems express her own feelings or whether she spoke with a public or communal voice as she performed her works. Whatever the case, Sappho's poetry, highly regarded in ancient Greece, is widely read and appreciated even today.

More is known about Pindar, perhaps because he was considered the greatest poet among nine lyric poets esteemed in Hellenistic Alexandria. Accordingly, the Ancients may have prioritized the preservation of Pindar's works.

Pindar was born in 522 or 518 BCE in a village near Thebes. He was married and had two daughters and a son. Pindar is thought to have died in Argos, where he was attending an athletic event or a festival, in 443 or 438 BCE. He may have been around eighty years old.

Pindar wrote many choral poems, such as paeans, hymns, and odes. A paean is a song of victory, praise, joy, or gratitude. Many scholars think these works were performed by choruses; some scholars argue for solo performances. Pindar's victory odes often celebrated athletic triumphs, including the feats of athletes in the Olympic Games. Today, Pindar is not as widely read as Homer or Sappho.

The works of the ancient dramatists are not only widely read today, but they are also still performed in modern Greece and elsewhere.

Aeschylus (525–445 BCE) is known as the Father of Tragedy. He was born into a wealthy family in 525 BCE in Eleusis, a small town near Athens. As a young man, Aeschylus was said to have worked in a vineyard until the god Dionysus visited him in a dream and inspired him to write tragedies. Aeschylus was reputed to have been inducted into the Eleusinian Mysteries, the mystical rites for the earth goddess Demeter and her daughter Persephone. Supposedly, while he was acting on stage, Aeschylus's life was threatened because he revealed a secret of these mystical rites. He was married and had two sons.

Of perhaps seventy to ninety plays, only seven of Aeschylus's works remain, including a trilogy of three plays—"Agamemnon," "The Libations," and "The Eumenides"—known altogether as *The Oresteia*. *The Oresteia* concerns the homecoming of King Agamemnon after the fall of Troy and his murder at the hands of his wife, Queen Clytaemnestra; the vengeful murder of Clytaemnestra at the hands of her son, Orestes; and the trial of Orestes.

Sophocles (497/496–406/405 BCE) was born into a wealthy family in the community of Hippeios Colonus, about a kilometer northwest of Athens. He died approximately ninety years later. His son and grandson were also playwrights.

Of over one hundred plays, only seven of Sophocles's complete works remain, the three most famous being the so-called Theban plays: "Oedipus Rex" (or "Oedipus the King"), "Oedipus at Colonus," and "Antigone." Although these three plays are often grouped together today, they were written at different times and were not meant to comprise a trilogy. "Oedipus Rex" concerns the story of King Oedipus who mistakenly kills his father and marries his mother. When he discovers this horrific error, Oedipus blinds himself. In "Oedipus at Colonus," the blind Oedipus, together with his daughter, Antigone, is exiled from Thebes and banished to Colonus. There father and daughter meet King Theseus of Athens. Oedipus dies. Meanwhile, back in Thebes, conflict arises between Oedipus's two sons, Polynices and Eteocles, and they end up killing each other. "Antigone" concerns the struggle of Oedipus's daughter. Although Creon, the new king of Thebes, declares that the dead Polynices should not be buried, Antigone disobeys Creon's order and buries her brother. Creon then imprisons Antigone in a tomb to be buried alive. Although Creon later changes his mind, at the urging of Tiresias, the blind messenger of the gods, Antigone has already committed suicide to escape an agonizing death. Antigone's suicide prompts that of her betrothed, Creon's son Haemon. In turn, Haemon's suicide prompts the suicide of his mother, Creon's wife Eurydice.

Euripides (485/480–406 BCE) was reputed to have been born in Salamis on the exact day of the Greek victory over the Persians at the great Battle of Salamis. He married twice and had a daughter and three sons. Euripides died in Macedonia, and the cause of his death has been attributed to the harsh Macedonian winter or to his being torn apart by hunting dogs.

Eighteen or nineteen of Euripides's more than ninety plays remain mostly intact. The rest are either lost or fragmentary. In his plays, Euripides often sympathized with women and slaves. He frequently engaged in social criticism, thus inciting controversy. Among his best-known plays are "Medea," "The Trojan Women," and "The Bacchae." "Medea" concerns Medea's revenge against her husband Jason for leaving her for another woman. With a poisoned robe, Medea kills the other woman and that woman's father. She also murders her own children in order to punish Jason. The "Trojan Women" depicts the struggles of the women of vanquished Troy: Queen Hecuba, Princess Cassandra, and Hector's widow, Andromache. In "The Bacchae," Euripides casts the god Dionysus as a main character. Here Euripides explores the need for human beings to integrate irrational, sensual experience with rational, civilized order.

Aristophanes (448/446–386 BCE), known as the Father of Comedy, was a comic playwright in ancient Athens. He was thought to be the son of a man named Philippus.

Eleven of Aristophanes's forty plays have survived, mostly intact, as well as numerous fragments of other plays. Among his best-known plays are "The Wasps," "The Birds," and "Lysistrata." In "The Wasps," Aristophanes satirizes the corrupt courts and juries of ancient Athens.

In "The Birds," Aristophanes offers a fantasy where a middle-aged Athenian man convinces the birds to build an avian metropolis in the sky to gain power from the gods over humanity. "Lysistrata," perhaps Aristophanes's greatest work, recounts the efforts of the women of Athens and Sparta to stop the Peloponnesian War between their two city-states. Led by the Athenian Lysistrata, the women withhold sex from their men in order to bring about peace negotiations.

In the *Poetics* (335 BCE), considered the first surviving work of literary criticism, the Greek philosopher Aristotle discusses major elements of epic poetry and drama. The *Poetics* is often studied as a companion to the poems and plays of the ancient Greek bards and dramatists.

*Marianthe Karanikas*

**See also:** Chapter 11: Mythology.

The ancient theatre at Delphi, constructed of limestone from Mount Parnassas, dates back to the fourth century BCE. It continues to host the plays of ancient Greek playwrights, as well as contemporary events. (Photo by Alexander Fatouros)

**Further Reading**

Clay, Jenny Strauss. 1996. *The Wrath of Athena: Gods and Men in the Odyssey.* Lanham, MD.: Rowman & Littlefield Publishers.

Conacher, D. J. 1989. *Aeschylus' Oresteia.* Toronto, ON: University of Toronto Press.

Edwards, Mark. *Homer: Poet of the Iliad.* 1990. Baltimore: Johns Hopkins University Press.

Mastin, Luke. 2009. "Classical Literature: A Basic Level Guide to Some of the Best Known and Loved Works of Prose, Poetry, and Drama from Classical Antiquity." Accessed April 20, 2021. https://www.ancient-literature.com/greece.html.

Nagy, Gregory. 1998. *Best of the Achaeans.* Baltimore: Johns Hopkins University Press.

Rayor, Diane J. 2014. *Sappho: A New Translation of the Complete Works.* Cambridge: Cambridge University Press.

Segal, Charles. 1988. *Sophocles' Tragic World: Divinity, Nature, Society.* Cambridge: Harvard University Press.

## Cavafy, Constantine P. (1863–1933)

Constantine P. Cavafy, one of the most distinguished Greek poets of the twentieth century, was born in 1863 in Alexandria, Egypt. His parents had settled there in the mid-1850s. Cavafy's father's business often took him to England. After the father died in 1870, the family moved to Liverpool, where the older sons assumed control of the family's business operations. In 1877, Cavafy, with his mother and her younger children, moved back to Alexandria. In 1882, the family, because of local unrest, escaped to Constantinople, where they had relatives. Just two weeks after they left, the family home in Alexandria was bombarded by the British. In 1885, Cavafy returned to Alexandria. By this time, he had already written poems and identified as a gay man. In Alexandria, he worked first as a newspaper correspondent and later at the Ministry of Public Works, where he toiled for thirty years. He eventually became its assistant director. In 1933, eleven years after leaving the Ministry, he died of cancer.

During his lifetime, Cavafy wrote in virtual obscurity, published very little, and lived in relative seclusion. In the early 1900s, a short collection of his poetry was privately published. That was the extent of his published poetry, except for those published in newspapers and magazines, until after his death. Due to the highly personal content of his poems, he preferred to make his works available privately among his friends.

Cavafy's language was even and his delivery straightforward, regardless if he wrote about life, death, love, beauty, eroticism, the past, or the present.

Cavafy studied history, particularly ancient civilizations. In many of his poems, life during the Greek and Roman empires is condensed and rendered in an original way.

His best-known poems are "Waiting for the Barbarians" and "Ithaca." In the first poem, leaders in a town in ancient Greece are ready to surrender their land to the barbarians but discover that they do not exist, being only a useful fiction for social and political change. In "Ithaca," the poet conjures up Homer's *Odyssey* and stresses the value is in what is experienced and learned in the journey rather than the destination. Other poems highlight that decadence in a civilization leads to its destruction.

Cavafy explored eroticism in many of his poems. He boldly captured on paper, with a simple but unique collection of words, his raw emotions and sexuality. His erotic poems, as well as his historical works, are all a product of his unique vision and interpretation of the world.

*Beatriz Badikian-Gartler*

**See also:** Chapter 11: Ancient Bards and Dramatists.

**Further Reading**

Cavafy, C. P. 2007. *The Collected Poems.* Translated by Evangelos Sachperoglou. Oxford: Oxford University Press.

Cavafy, C. P. 2008. *The Canon.* Translated by Stratis Haviaras. Cambridge: Harvard University Press.

## Elytis, Olysseas (Odysseus) (1911–1996)

Odysseas (Odysseus) Elytis (née Alepoudhelis) was born in 1911 in Heraklion, Crete. His parents had emigrated from Lesvos to Crete. In 1914, the Alepoudhelis family moved to Athens, where the young poet was educated. His calling as a poet came early in life, a calling so strong he left the University of Athens without finishing his degree. He chose the pen name "Elytis" to distance himself from the family surname, which was associated with soap manufacturing. "Elytis" derives from the Greek words for Hellas, hope, freedom, and Helen, whose beauty could launch a thousand ships, and from the Greek word for citizen. Among Elytis's influences are surrealism, Pindar, and Greek Orthodoxy, as well as the landscapes and seascapes of the Aegean Islands where he often spent his childhood summers.

During World War II, Elytis served as a second lieutenant at the headquarters of the First Army Corps and later in the advanced firing line of the Twenty-Fourth Regiment. During this time and after the liberation of Greece, he wrote many poems and essays. In the mid-1940s and the mid-1950s, Elytis directed the National Greek Radio Foundation. In the late 1940s, early 1950s, late 1950s, and early 1960s, he lived in Paris, attended lectures at the Sorbonne, and met many artists, including Matisse, Picasso, and Chagall. In the late 1940s and early 1960s, he represented Greece at international cultural meetings. In 1960, he won the National Book Award for Poetry. Also, in the 1960s, he accepted official invitations to travel through the United States, the Soviet Union, and Bulgaria.

In 1979, Elytis received the Nobel Prize in Literature, "for his poetry, which, against the Greek tradition, depicts with sensuous strength and intellectual clear-sightedness modern . . . [humanity's] struggle for freedom and creativeness" (The Nobel Foundation). His poetry includes "Orientations" (1940), "Sun the First" (1943), "An Heroic and Funeral Chant for the Lieutenant Lost in Albania" (1946), "The Axion Esti" (1959), "The Sovereign Sun" (1972), and "Maria Nefeli" (1978).

The literary scholar and translator Kimon Friar likens Elytis's poems to Byzantine mosaics and Elytis's "images and words to the bright-colored stones, glass, and pebbles which are the alphabets of these icons" (1974, 8).

Elytis's greatest poem, "The Axion Esti" ("Worthy It Is" or "It Is Truly Meet"), has a complex structure based on the Byzantine Liturgy. Most Greek Orthodox are familiar with the Byzantine Hymn to the Virgin Mary or Theotokos (the God-bearer), "The Axion Esti," which is said to have been revealed by the Archangel Gabriel to a monk on Mount Athos in 980 CE. The angel chanted, "It is truly meet to bless thee, oh Theotokos, ever-blessed and most pure, and the Mother of our God." Elytis's great poem is in three parts: "Genesis," where the poet's life symbolizes the lives of all poets and where the small world of Greece represents the great and vast universe; "The Passions," where Psalms, Odes, and Readings describe the horrors of war and liken Mother Greece to the Theotokos; and the "Gloria," a doxology, or hymn of praises, to the Theotokos-Mother Greece, through symbolic and lyrical images of mythical gods and nature.

"The Axion Esti" was set to music by the composer Mikis Theodorakis and became a beloved anthem of the Greek people. In 1996, at the age of eighty-four, Odysseas Elytis died in Athens.

*Marianthe Karanikas*

**See also:** Chapter 13: Art-Popular Music.

**Further Reading**

Elytis, Odysseus. 1974a. *The Axion Esti.* Translated by Edmund Keeley and George Savidis. Pittsburgh and London: The University of Pittsburgh Press.

Elytis, Odysseus. 1974b. *The Sovereign Sun: Selected Poems.* Translated by Kimon Friar. Philadelphia: Temple University Press.

Elytis, Odysseus. 2005. *Selected Poems: 1940–1979.* Translated by Edmund Keeley, Philip Sherrard, George Savidis, John Strathatos, and Nanos Valaoritis. Manchester, UK: Carcanet Press Ltd.

## Kazantzakis, Nikos (1883–1957)

Nikos Kazantzakis is one of the most controversial figures in modern Greek literature, due primarily to his literary depiction of Christ. A novelist, philosopher, travel writer, playwright, and poet, Kazantzakis was nominated nine times for the Nobel Prize in Literature. His most famous works are *Zorba the Greek* (1946/1952) and *The Last Temptation of Christ* (1952/1955). *Zorba the Greek* and *The Greek Passion*, or *Christ Recrucified* (1950/1953), are considered to be among his best novels. Kazantzakis also wrote philosophical commentary, travel books, various plays, a translation of

Dante's *Divine Comedy* (1932), and an epic poem *The Odyssey: A Modern Sequel* (1938).

Kazantzakis was born in 1883 in Crete, while the island was still under Ottoman rule. He was educated at the University of Athens and the Sorbonne. Kazantzakis was influenced by Friedrich Nietzsche, Henri Bergson, Dante, Greek Orthodox Christianity, Buddhism, and Marxism. His primary philosophical and spiritual aim was to explore how to unite with God and how to transform matter into Spirit. His primary linguistic aim was to champion and to help cultivate a literary, modern (demotic) Greek language.

In 1911, Kazantzakis married Galatea Alexiou, but they divorced in 1926. In 1945, Kazantzakis married Helen (Eleni) Samiou. She devoted her life to her husband, and after his death in 1957, she wrote a biography of him based on his letters (1968).

Throughout many of his works, Nikos Kazantzakis explores the apparent conflict (and possible resolution) of matter and spirit, abstract philosophy and everyday life, the human and the divine.

In *Zorba the Greek*, Kazantzakis contrasts the earthy, passionate, and wise Zorba, a Greek workman, with the rigid, reserved, and intellectual narrator, a half-Greek, half-British writer. Zorba became a world-renowned, fictional character through his film portrayal by the actor Anthony Quinn in the 1964 film *Zorba the Greek*, directed by Michael Cacoyannis.

In *The Greek Passion* (*Christ Recrucified*), Manolis, a humble shepherd, is chosen to play Jesus Christ in a Passion Play, which is performed at Easter. As the novel progresses, Manolis and the other actors begin to change, assuming characteristics of their roles as Christ, the Apostles, and Mary Magdalene. The villagers and the Turkish overlord treat them with misunderstanding and violence reminiscent of the fate that befell Jesus in the Gospels.

In *The Last Temptation of Christ*, Kazantzakis pushed the limit as he explored the apparent conflict between the human striving to unite with God and the human desire to enjoy earthly pleasures. If Kazantzakis had chosen a mortal as a protagonist, he would have not caused religious controversy. However, Kazantzakis chose Jesus Christ as his protagonist. According to Scripture, the Divine Liturgy, and the Greek Orthodox Church, the Lord Jesus Christ is one in essence with God the Father. The Greek Orthodox Church objected to Kazantzakis's fictional portrayal of Jesus as a mortal tempted by the human desire to marry Mary Magdalene.

A campaign to excommunicate Kazantzakis was started. However, he was not excommunicated, because the Greek Orthodox Church recognized that *The Last Temptation of Christ* is not really about the Lord Jesus Christ but instead concerns Kazantzakis's own anguish and struggles. Nevertheless, the novel remained controversial.

Furthermore, the 1988 film based on the novel, *The Last Temptation of Christ*, directed by Martin Scorsese, was denounced as morally offensive by the Roman Catholic Church, the Greek and other Eastern Orthodox Churches, and many Protestant Churches. In 2016, Scorsese and his family met with Pope Francis, almost thirty years after the 1988 controversy and almost sixty years after Kazantzakis's death.

Upon his death from leukemia in 1957, Kazantzakis's body was viewed in the Saint Minas Cathedral in Heraklion, Crete, according to Greek Orthodox Christian custom. Outside the Heraklion city walls, a simple cross stands at his grave. The inscription on Kazantzakis's tombstone reads, "I hope for [expect] nothing; I fear nothing; I am free."

*Marianthe Karanikas*

**See also:** Chapter 2: Overview.

**Further Reading**

Bien, Peter. 1972. *Kazantzakis and the Linguistic Revolution in Greek Literature.* Princeton, NJ: Princeton University Press.

Bien, Peter. 1972. *Nikos Kazantzakis.* New York: Columbia University Press.

Kazantzakis, Helen. 1968. *Nikos Kazantzakis: A Biography Based on His Letters.* Translated by Amy Mims. New York: Simon and Schuster.

Middleton, Darren J. 2005. *Scandalizing Jesus? Kazantzakis' The Last Temptation of Christ Fifty Years On.* New York: Bloomsbury Publishing Continuum.

Sandinopoulos, John. 2014. "The Myth of the Excommunication of Nikos Kazantzakis." Mystagogy Resource Center: An International Orthodox Christian Ministry Headed by John Sanidopoulos, January 31, 2014. Accessed April 18, 2021. https://www.johnsanidopoulos.com/2014/01/the-myth-of-excommunication-of-nikos.html.

## Mythology

Greek mythology likely originated in the oral-poetic tradition of the proto-Indo-European tribes. The earliest evidence of a distinctly "Greek" mythology dates to the Minoan and Mycenaean legends of the eighteenth century BCE. Like in many cultures, Greek mythology was connected to religious practice and contained stories about natural and human phenomenon as well as the origin and activities of the gods. Additionally, the events of the Trojan War and its aftermath became an important subject of the Greek mythological tradition.

While Greek mythology has had a significant influence on Western, and indeed world, literature, there is only one mythographic handbook that survives from antiquity: *Library* by Pseudo-Apollodorus. In antiquity, Homer constituted the most important mythic and literary source. Today only two of the Homeric epics survive: *The Iliad* and *The Odyssey.* These epics recount the events of the Trojan War and their aftermath. It is important to note that while the Homeric corpus does exhibit a magical worldview, there is little theological information conveyed in the extent poems.

The poet Hesiod, however, provides ample information about the gods, creation, and the cosmos. Alongside Homer, Hesiod was the second most important poet of myth in Greek antiquity. Hesiod has left us three surviving works: "Theogony," "Works and Days," and "The Shield of Hercules." Many scholars have, notably, disputed the authenticity of "The Shield of Hercules." "Theogony" is notable for providing the most comprehensive, normative description of the Greek creation myth and of general Greek cosmology.

By the eighth century BCE, largely through the effects of the standardization of the oral-poetic tradition via its commitment to writing, the basic parameters of Greek mythology had taken shape. The Greek pantheon consisted of twelve primary deities who lived on Mt. Olympus, the highest mountain on the Greek peninsula. Their ruler, and father, was called Zeus, the king of the gods. In keeping with other Indo-European mythic traditions, Zeus was a sky god whose own story saw him defeating other previous generations of earth deities. He reigned on Olympus with his wife and sister, the tempestuous and frequently wronged Hera. Along with Zeus and Hera, ten other deities (all children of Zeus, though not necessarily Hera) lived on the mountain. They were joined by a host of minor deities, each with a narrative tradition and cult.

Additionally, Greek mythology included tales of the heroes, and these mortal and semi-mortal figures achieved divinity through great deeds. Odysseus, Herakles, and Achilles are three such figures who have remained significant for later literature and culture. It is likely that the stories of the heroes began as a form of ancestor worship and evolved into their known form over the course of later centuries.

*Katherine Kalaidis*

**See also:** Chapter 9: Overview.

**Further Reading**

Hard, Robin, and H. J. Rose. 2004. *The Routledge Handbook of Greek Mythology.* London: Routledge.

Roman, Luke, and Monica Roman. 2010. *Encyclopedia of Greek and Roman Mythology.* Facts on File Library of Religion and Mythology. New York: Facts on File.

Woodard, Roger D. 2009. *The Cambridge Companion to Greek Mythology.* The Cambridge Companions Complete Collection. Cambridge: Cambridge University Press.

## Papadiamantis, Alexandros (1851–1911)

Alexandros Papadiamantis was a Greek novelist, short-story writer, and poet. Born on March 4, 1851, to a Greek Orthodox priest and his wife on the western Aegean island of Skiathos, Papadiamantis went to Athens as a teenager in order to study. He completed secondary school and enrolled at the University of Athens to read philosophy. However, economic hardship forced him to discontinue his studies before completing his degree. He returned to Skiathos where he would spend the rest of his life.

Papadiamantis supported himself through his writing throughout his life, producing fiction, nonfiction, and poems. Referring to himself as a κοσμοκαλόγερος (*kosmokalogeros*), "a monk in the world," Papadiamantis was famously reclusive. He never married and was seldom seen in public except to chant at his nearby church. He also gained notoriety for turning down fees for his writing that he felt were too high.

Despite growing financial success as a writer, he took little care of his appearance and often appeared dirty and disheveled. Papadiamantis died of pneumonia at the age of forty-nine on January 3, 1911.

In contrast to the simplicity that Papadiamantis sought to maintain in his life, his work is complex, indeed. With narration written largely in the high tones of *καθαρεύουσα* (*katharevousa*), Papadiamantis's repertoire of simple characters from rural Skiathos and the poorest neighborhoods of Athens carry on dialogues in the demotic, the language of the common people. His characters also frequently use local, native forms of Greek. This sharp contrast in language adds a linguistic depth and dexterity to his writing that is almost unique in modern Greek prose of the nineteenth century. The intricacy of his language is one of the reasons that his work has seldom been translated into other languages, despite its importance in the modern Greek canon.

Papadiamantis's stories also reflect his deep religiosity, though they nearly never take up explicitly religious themes. Instead, his Orthodox Christian faith is reflected in the mysticism and "life as sacrament" tenor of the work. His work also displays a deep interest in suffering and the arbitrary way in which it is visited upon human beings, regardless of background, station, or individual morality. His characters present a nuanced understanding of human nature that is both deeply moral and predisposed to sin.

Papadiamantis, a prolific writer, produced numerous works over the course of his life, mainly in the form of short stories. His three longest works were serialized novels: *The Gypsy Girl*, *The Emigrant*, and *The Merchants of Nations*. All of these were adventure stories set around the Mediterranean, complete with pirates, wars, and plagues. By far, Papadiamantis's most critically celebrated work is the novella *The Murderess*. It is the tale of an elderly woman who, after killing her own young daughter, becomes compelled to kill other infant girls as an act of compassion. The tale focuses on the suffering of girls and women, particularly from poor families, in a society in which they had little power and were largely viewed as economic liabilities. An introspective and empathetic story, *The Murderess* deals with the complexities of gender, violence, and poverty in ways that are largely absent from most nineteenth-century Mediterranean literature.

*Katherine Kalaidis*

**See also:** Chapter 9: The Greek Language.

**Further Reading**

Papadiamantis, Alexandros. 1977. *The Murderess*. Translated by George X. Xanthopoulides. London: Doric Publications.

Papadiamantis, Alexandros. 1987. *Tales from a Greek Island*. Translated by Elizabeth Constantinides. Baltimore: John Hopkins University Press.

## Ritsos, Yannis (Yiannis) (1909–1990)

Yannis (Yiannis) Ritsos, one of the most popular, most prolific, and most political modern Greek poets, was born in 1909 in Monemvasia, Southern Greece. His once-wealthy family was tormented by financial ruin and other misfortunes. Both his mother and a brother died from tuberculosis. His father suffered from mental illness and died in an asylum in 1938. His sister, also suffering from mental illness, was committed to the same asylum in 1936.

From age twelve, Ritsos was raised by relatives. He later attended the University of Athens in 1925, but soon left due to his own battle with tuberculosis, which kept him in sanatoria for many of the next fifteen years. When released from the sanatoria, for brief periods of time in Athens, Ritsos slaved at hard, sometimes demoralizing, jobs in order to make a living. He also worked as a dancer and actor. In 1929, while confined to a sanatorium, Ritsos learned Marxist ideas from fellow patients. For Ritsos, as for many others who experienced the harsh, exploitative, and often unforgiving side of capitalism, Marxism offered a vision of hope, a promise of the liberation of working people from the tyranny of their oppressors. He joined the Communist Party of Greece in the mid-1930s. His impassioned and compassionate poems often celebrate the struggles of common men and women.

Ritsos was nominated twice for the Nobel Prize in Literature. In 1977, he received the Lenin Peace Prize from the then Soviet Union. Today Ritsos is considered one of the greatest modern Greek poets. He wrote more than one hundred books, in spite of tuberculosis, and despite punishments imposed upon him due to his leftist politics, which included imprisonment and exile.

Ritsos's first two books of poetry, *Tractors* (1934) and *Pyramids* (1935), are influenced by Marxist philosophy. In 1936, Ritsos saw a newspaper photograph portraying a mother weeping over the dead body of her son as he lay in the snow. Her son was one of over three hundred tobacco workers in Thessaloniki (Salonica) who protested wage controls. The police fired upon these unarmed workers, killing at least twelve (if not thirty) and wounding hundreds. Ritsos, moved by the photo of the grieving mother, wrote one of his most beloved poems, *Epitaphios* (Funeral Lament) (1936).

Ritsos's *Epitaphios* is deeply influenced by the ancient dramatists Sophocles and Euripides, the ancient historian Thucydides, and the Greek Orthodox Christian Lamentations on Good Friday, part of the liturgical reenactment of Christ's burial. Like the Greek Orthodox Christian Liturgy, Ritsos's poem moves from burial to resurrection. The mother, once inconsolable, begins to understand why her son protested. Faced with the horror of his death, she begins to understand his fight for justice in a world that pretends to be Christian but slaughters those people who struggle for equality. She realizes her son lives on in his comrades, and she vows to join their struggle. Ritsos's lament was very popular, selling thousands of copies.

Banned by the Metaxas dictatorship later that year, the last 250 copies of Ritsos's *Epitaphios*, along with other books, were burned at the Temple of Olympian Zeus, 1,640 feet southeast of the Acropolis in Athens. Ritsos was unable to publish freely for many years.

Those were turbulent years. During World War II, Ritsos joined the literary section of the National Liberation Front (EAM), the major resistance movement against the Nazi occupation of Greece. The EAM was sponsored by the Communist Party of Greece, together with smaller Socialist parties. After World War II, Ritsos was imprisoned and exiled for four years. His books were banned until 1954.

In the mid-1950s, Ritsos married the physician Garoufalia Georgiadou. Their daughter, Eleftheria, was born in 1955. From the mid-1950s until the military dictatorship of the late 1960s and early 1970s, Ritsos wrote, wrote, and wrote and enjoyed his family life. A major political poem written during this time, *Romiosini* (1954), likens the EAM resistance movement to the Greek resistance and eventual revolution against the Turkish (Ottoman) occupation.

In 1967, following the Greek colonels' junta, Ritsos was arrested, detained, imprisoned, and then exiled. His works were again banned.

In 1971, a liberated Ritsos returned to Athens and to international recognition. He received a number of honorary doctorates in addition to many literary prizes. From the 1950s on, many of his poems had been set to music. Two musical versions of the *Epitaphios*, one by the composer Manos Hadjidakis and another by the composer Mikis Theodorakis, generated two rival camps of fervent fans. Many more of Ritsos's poems were set to music by Theodorakis, including *Romiosini*. Ritsos also wrote many lyrical, less-political poems, often considered to be his best works. A number of these critically acclaimed poems are suggested in the further reading.

Ritsos died in 1990, at the age of eighty-one, survived by his wife and daughter. The then conservative Greek government announced the renowned, beloved, and leftist poet would be buried with full state honors.

*Marianthe Karanikas*

**See also:** Chapter 13: Art-Popular Music.

**Further Reading**

Ritsos, Yannis. 1977. *Chronicle of Exile*. Translated by Minas Savvas. San Francisco: Wire Press.

Ritsos, Yannis. 1979. *Ritsos in Parenthesis*. Translated by Edmund Keeley. Princeton, NJ: Princeton University Press.

## Seferis, George (1900–1971)

George Seferis (née Seferiadis) was born on February 29, 1900, near Smyrna, now Izmir, Turkey. In 1923, when the Greek calendar changed from the Julian to the Gregorian, Seferis's birthdate disappeared. From then on, he celebrated his birthday every four years.

A diplomat and Nobel Laureate, Seferis was educated in Smyrna, Athens, and at the Sorbonne in Paris. In 1926, a year after his return to Athens, he began his long diplomatic career with the Greek Foreign Ministry. Before World War II, he served in England and Albania. During the war, he went with the Free Greek Government in exile in Crete, Egypt, South Africa, and Italy, and after the war, he returned to Athens when Greece was liberated and the free government reinstated. He continued to serve as a diplomat in Turkey and London. During most of the 1950s, he was a Greek foreign minister in Lebanon, Syria, Jordan, and Iraq. From 1957 to 1961, he served as royal Greek ambassador to the United Kingdom. Subsequently, he retired to Athens.

In 1963, Seferis received the Nobel Prize in Literature, "for his eminent lyrical writing, inspired by a deep feeling for the Hellenic world of culture" (The Nobel Foundation). His early poems appear in *The Turning Point* (1931) and *The Cistern* (1932). His mature poetry includes *Mythistorema* (1935), *Book of Exercises* (1940), *Logbook I* (1940), *Logbook II* (1944), *Thrush* (1947), *Logbook III* (1955), and his book *Three Secret Poems* (1966), which actually consists of twenty-eight lyric poems.

Like Solomos and other poets of the modern revival, Seferis wrote in the demotic language, influenced by traditional Greek song. According to the literary scholars and translators Edmund Keeley and Philip Sherrard, Seferis saw poetic possibilities in demotic Greek, which are not available in *katharevousa*. A wandering diplomat, exiled by the Turks from Smyrna, the place of his birth, and exiled from Greece during World War II, Seferis often explores the themes of exile, as well as the struggle to voyage homeward.

Needless to say, like many modern Greek literary figures, Seferis is also deeply influenced by the ancients. His *Mythistorema* explores thematic variations from *The Odyssey*. "The King of Asine" (in *Logbook I*), perhaps his most critically acclaimed poem, references *The Iliad*. *Mythistorema* is so well known in Greece that one of its most famous stanzas was included in the opening ceremony of the 2004 Athens Olympics.

Seferis died from pneumonia, after a stroke, in 1971, when Greece suffered under a military dictatorship. At his funeral procession in Athens, thousands of people followed his coffin, singing the words of his then banned, rhyming poem "Denial" (from *The Turning Point*), set to music by the composer Mikis Theodorakis.

*Marianthe Karanikas*

**See also:** Chapter 13: Art-Popular Music.

**Further Reading**

Beaton, Roderick. 2003. *George Seferis: Waiting for the Angel, A Biography*. New Haven: Yale University Press.

Seferis, George. 1964. *Poems*. Translated by Rex Warner. Boston: Little Brown and Company.

Seferis, George. 2014. *Collected Poems: 1924–1955*. Translated by Edmund Keeley and Philip Sherrard. Princeton, NJ: Princeton University Press.

## Sikelianos, Angelos (1884–1951)

Angelos Sikelianos, who was nominated for a Nobel Prize several times for his lyric poetry, used references to nature, Greek history, mythology, Christianity, and everyday Greek village life, as is indicated in his poem "The Village Wedding." Using vivid words, he lays bare the emotions experienced by us as we search for the meaning of life and death and explore our connection to the universe and God.

Angelos Sikelianos was born and spent his early childhood on the Ionian island of Lefkada. The rich intellectual tradition of the Ionian Islands (Solomos, Kalvos, et al.) along with his early interests in the literature of ancient Greece (Homer, Pindaros, et al.), modern Greece (Palamas, Katzanzakis, et al.), and Europe (D'Annuncio, Whitman, Hölderlin, et al.) informed his poetry. He published his first collection of poems *Alafroiskiotos (Moonstruck)*, one of his most famous works, in 1909, at the age of twenty-five. Sikelianos published his poems in three volumes under the title *Lyric Life* in 1946 and 1947. In 1965, his entire poetic work was published posthumously in five volumes by the Greek philologist G. P. Savvides.

The renowned poet was also known for his stance against the Nazis. In 1943, when Greece was occupied by the Nazis, he took a risk by giving the eulogy of another renowned Greek poet, Kostis Palamas (1859–1943), who had written the hymn that is used today at the Olympic Games. Sikelianos's words so stirred the crowd of tens of thousands that they spontaneously started singing the National Anthem in defiance of the Nazis. Palamas also put his life on the line by composing a letter, along with Archbishop Damaskinos, protesting the Nazi's persecution of Greek Jews. Prominent leaders of the Greek community cosigned the letter.

Sikelianos married the American Eva Palmer in 1905. Palmer, who appreciated Greek dance, theatre, and music, became his staunch supporter. She and Sikelianos organized the Delphic festivals of 1927 and 1930 with the goal of promoting peace and harmony. The festivals, based on those held during ancient times in the religious sanctuary of Delphi, attracted international artists and intellectuals, as well as Greeks. A variety of programs were presented, including theater, folk music, dance festivities, folk art exhibitions, and athletic contests. A few years later, in 1933, Sikelianos presented his neoclassical play *Dithyram of the Rose* on Philopappos Hill in Athens. Although the couple tried to raise money to continue the Delphic festivals, it was the time of the Great Depression, and they were not successful, and Palmer went back to America to try to raise funds. They divorced, and Sikelianos married Anna Karamani in 1940. He died in 1951. The house on the Ionian island of Lefkada where Sikelianos was born is now a museum.

*Elaine Thomopoulos*

**See also:** Chapter 2: Damaskinos Papandreou, Archbishop.

**Further Reading**

Sherrard, Philip. 1996. "An Approach to the Meaning of Myth in the Poetry of Sikelianos." In *Ancient Greek Myth in Modern Greek Poetry, Essays in memory of C. A. Trypanis*, edited by Peter Mackridge, 45–52. London: Frank Cass.

Sikelianos, Angelos. 1944. *Akritan Songs.* Translated by Paul Nord. New York: The Spap Company.

Sikelianos, Angelos. 1979. *Selected Poems.* Translated by Edmund Keeley and Philip Sherrard. Princeton, NJ: Princeton University Press.

Sikelianos, Angelos. 2009. "Three Poems of Angelos Sikelianos." Translated by Alicia Elsbeth Stallings. *The New Criterion* 27 (10): 28–31. Accessed August 7, 2020. https://www.newcriterion.com/issues/2009/6/frieze.

## Solomos, Dionysios (1798–1857)

Dionysios Solomos, considered the National Poet of Greece, is also often characterized as the "Father of Modern Greek Poetry." Today, the first two verses of Solomos's "Hymn to Liberty" are sung as the Greek National Anthem.

Solomos was born in 1798 on the island of Zakynthos. His father was a count of Cretan descent and his mother a servant. Solomos and his brother, Dimitrios, were born illegitimate, as their father was already married to another woman. The day before his death, Solomos's father married his mother, thereby legitimizing the two brothers.

After his father's death, Solomos was sent to Italy to study. He began his secondary education in Venice and completed it in Cremona. In 1817, Solomos graduated from Pavia University's Faculty of Law. Fluent in Italian, Solomos began writing poems and was soon recognized as a promising poet in Italian. He returned to Zakynthos and eagerly joined literary circles there.

While in Zakynthos, Solomos began to collect songs with lyrics in modern Greek, also called demotic Greek, or *dimotiki*, the language of the people. He also studied various works of Cretan literature, written in modern or demotic Greek.

The Greek War of Independence, which freed many regions of Greece from the rule of the Ottoman Empire, began in 1821. Greece became an independent nation in 1832. The Greek revolution gained much support among members of the Romantic movement, including the great British Romantic poet Lord Byron, who died from a fever while helping the Greek cause in Missolonghi in 1824.

In 1822, influenced by the Greek statesman and diplomat Spyridon Trikoupis, Solomos made the bold decision to begin writing poetry in modern Greek. Why was this decision so courageous? First, Solomos did not know the Greek language very well. Second, in the nineteenth century, as the Greeks sought to reestablish a national language, a bitter dispute raged among proponents of ancient Greek, Modern (demotic) Greek, and an artificial language called *katharevousa*. Proponents of *katharevousa* wished to purify modern Greek from all the Turkish, Slavic, and other foreign words that had entered the language over the centuries. While *katharevousa* became the official language of government documents until 1976, the Greek people continued to speak Modern (demotic) Greek.

Inspired by the war of independence, by the Romantic movement, and by Trikoupis, Solomos wrote the famous "Hymn to Liberty" in 1823. The poem was published a year later and was soon widely known in Greece and elsewhere.

In 1828, perhaps prompted by a conflict with his brother over their inheritance, Solomos left Zakynthos and moved to the island of Corfu. He continued to write poetry and study European Romanticism. In the 1830s, more legal battles distanced Solomos from his mother. Nevertheless, he wrote what many scholars consider to be his best and most mature poems during and after this period: "The Cretan" (1833) and "The Free Besieged" (1845). However, both these poems, like most of Solomos's works, are fragmentary and incomplete. The "Hymn to Liberty" is considered his only complete poem.

Solomos died from a stroke in 1857. He was widely mourned. In 1865, his remains were relocated from Corfu back to Zakynthos.

*Marianthe Karanikas*

**See also:** Chapter 9: The Greek Language.

**Further Reading**

Constantinides, Elizabeth. 1985. "Greek Romanticism." *Journal of Modern Greek Studies* 3: 121–136.

Jenkins, Romilly. 1940. *Dionysios Solomos*. Athens: Reprinted by Denise Harvey, 2000.

Raizis, M. Byron. 1972. *Dionysios Solomos*. New York: Twayne Publishers Inc.

CHAPTER 12

# ART AND ARCHITECTURE

## OVERVIEW

Art and architecture in Greece are continuous since the fourth millennium BCE. Greek sculpture, pottery, metalworking (gold, silver, bronze), and architecture can be traced back to the Bronze Age Cycladic, Minoan, and Mycenaean civilizations of the Fourth Millennium BCE. Greek painting and mosaics were advanced during the Archaic (tenth to sixth century BCE), Classical (fifth to fourth century BCE), Hellenistic (fourth to second century BCE), and Roman (second to third century CE) periods. The Greek Orthodox Church used iconography (religious paintings or mosaics depicting Jesus, the Virgin Mary, the Saints, or biblical themes) during the Eastern Roman or Byzantine Period (third century CE to 1453 CE).

In 1453, the Ottoman Turks invaded the Byzantine Empire and remained in control for four hundred years. Art and architecture continued to develop during that period, although many of artists emigrated to other places in Europe or to locations in Greece, like the islands of the Ionian Sea, which were not in control of the Ottomans.

During Ottoman rule, Greek craftsmen and craftswomen continued to create unique handicrafts with gold, silver, stone, wood, wool, golden thread, and clay, and they continued to produce until the present day. Although most of the artists are anonymous, their work is now respected as part of a long tradition and as a living testament of the colorfulness and multivaried character of Greek culture from antiquity to the present.

After part of Greece gained its independence from Ottoman rule in 1832, it sought to define itself by adopting the art and architecture of classical Greece. Fifth-century Greece is often referred to as the cradle of Western civilization and democracy; Greek literature, drama, poetry, art, and architecture of that period celebrated the scientific and cultural revolutions and sociopolitical changes of the time, which included the rising power of the city-states of Athens, Sparta, and Corinth, as well as the foundation of democratic rule and civic responsibility.

The modern Greek city-state of the nineteenth century sought to model itself on classical Greece. After the selection of Athens as the capital of the newly formed nation-state in 1834, the government modelled its buildings, including the university, in the neoclassical architectural style. Given its influence in the planning of Athens, neoclassical also dominated other nineteenth-century Greek cities such as Aigio, Argos, Athens, Patras, and Pyrgos.

This neoclassical style sought to imitate buildings like those of the classical Greece, and in particular the Parthenon. The architects adopted the geometry and grandeur of classical architecture and imitated structural elements such as pediments and columns at the buildings' entrances. The white-marble buildings included decorative elements, such as ornamental edge tiles, engravings, sculptures, statues, and paintings, that depicted ancient Greek mythical figures. A great majority of the architects of government buildings in modern Greece from the 1830s to the 1860s were foreigners from Bavaria, Prussia, France, and Denmark.

Even though many nineteenth-century Greek artists and architects adopted the belief that archaeology should define modern Greece, others responded differently and asked: Is modern Greece an Eastern or Western country? Is it both? Is it Balkan? What should the characteristics of modern Greek art and architecture be? Should it resemble antiquity, or should it bare its own new features? And what of the art and architecture produced during the centuries of conquest and slavery—was that Greek? From the nineteenth century onward, the answer each artist and architect would give to these questions defined their products.

Greek artists and architects combined their ancient traditions with later influences of the Catalan, Frankish, and Ottoman occupations of Greece (fifteenth to early nineteenth centuries) and with post-nineteenth-century elements. Some combined antiquity with new artistic and architectural forms inspired by other European countries. Others rejected their ancient past altogether and emphasized Byzantine paradigms or folk art or turned to the European avant-garde. This experimentation with style and the consequent more-inclusive responses to the question "How do you define Greekness?" became even more evident from the 1870s onward.

During the past few centuries, Greek artistic styles have varied from the preliberation Cretan School's iconography and the Heptanese School's seventeenth- to early-nineteenth-century experimentation with the dominant European artistic styles, to the twentieth-century artists' use of avant-garde techniques and the incorporation of traditional art.

The following artists are but a few of the many who have enriched European and Greek art with astonishing imagery: Gianoulis Chalepas (1851–1938), Michail Damaskenos (1530/35–1592/93), Nikos Engonopoulos (1907–1985), Dimitris Filippotis (1839–1919), Dimitris Galanis (1879–1966), Nikolaos Gyzis (1842–1902), Nikos Hatjikyriakos-Ghikas (1906–1994), Georgios Iakovidis (1853–1932), Vasso Katraki (1919–1988), Fotis Kontoglou (c. 1895–1965), Ioannis Kossos (1822–1875), Nikolaos Koutouzes (1741–1813), Ioannis Koutsis (1869–1953), Jannis Kounellis (1936–2017), Sophia Laskaridou (1881–1965), Nikiforos Lytras (1832–1904), Nikolaos Lytras (1883–1927), Konstantinos Maleas (1879–1928), Filippos Margaritis (1810–1892), Nellys' (Elli Souyioultzoglou-Seraïdari, 1889–1998), Georgios Oikonomidis (1891–1958), Spyros Papaloukas (1892–1957), Konstantinos Parthenis (1878–1967), Petros Poulidis (1886–1967), Pavlos Prosalentis (1784–1837), Symeon Savvidis (1859–1927), Andreas Ritzos (1421–1492), Doménikos Theotokópoulos (1541–1614), Theodoros Vryzakis (1814–1878), and Nikos Zografos (1881–1967). While some adored ancient myths, others depicted nature or documented the painful and celebratory events of their time. Together, they have all created the wealthy tradition of modern Greek art.

Like the artists, modern Greek architects have had different views on what constituted Greekness and offered us a unique and wide range of buildings. While some built large-scale neoclassical marble monuments that resembled the Parthenon, others designed modernist concrete public buildings or called for a return to traditional architecture. In doing so, they have all helped build the unique character of modern Greece.

Modern Greek architects include: Leonidas Bonis (1896–1963), Ioannis Despotopoulos (1903–1992), Emmanouil Lazaridis (1894–1961), Lysandros Kaftantzoglou (1811–1885), Panagiotis Kalkos (1818–1878), Aris Konstantinidis (1913–1933), Dimitris Pikionis (1887–1968), Thucydides Valentis (1908–1982), Aristotelis Zahos (1871–1939), and Takis Zenetos (1926–1977).

The birth of the nation-state, the establishment and later the official abolition of the monarchy in 1974, the Balkan wars (1912–1913), World War I (1914–1918), the Asia Minor Catastrophe (1919–1922), World War II (1939–1945), the Civil War (1946–1949), the military junta (1967–1974), the Dimitrios Ioannidis' counter-coup (1974-1975), the 1975 restoration of democracy and the 1950s, 1960s, and 1970s urbanization are only some of the events that further forged modern Greece. In turn, these are some of the events documented in the works of artists and architects.

In the twentieth and the twenty-first centuries, artists and architects redefined Greekness itself and questioned both its abuses and the power of aesthetics to hide political debates. Art and architecture often carry implicit or explicit ideological or political connotations. For example, neoclassicism in the 1830s and 1840s emphasized the connection between classical and modern Greece. In the 1930s, neoclassicism and ancient-like rituals such as celebrations on the Acropolis were adopted by the Ioannis Metaxas dictatorship to strengthen beliefs about ethnic superiority. Such nationalism was also nurtured during the military junta (1967–1974). Many modern Greek architects and artists rejected what the dictators saw as "foreign influences" and advocated a combination of antiquity with some forms of traditional art (especially costumes and music). Today, many street artists also represent their social and political views on the facades of buildings.

Much as the history of the country, modern Greek architecture and art narrate a history of experimentation, creativity, contestation, and innovation. Regardless of their different approaches and worldviews, nineteenth-, twentieth-, and twenty-first-century Greek artists and architects have produced extraordinary works.

*Georgia Giannakopoulou*

### Further Reading

Missirli, Nelly, and Olga Mentzafanou-Polyzou, eds. 2003. *Classical Memories in Modern Greek Art.* Athens: National Gallery—Alexandros Soutsos Museum.

Peddley, John Griffiths. 1997. *Greek Art and Archaeology.* London: Laurence King.

## Ancient Greek Art and Architecture

Throughout modern Greece, there are numerous evidence of detailed, well-made, and aesthetically appealing Greek art and architecture in antiquity. Some of the earliest discovered works of Neolithic Greek art are the human-shaped, Cycladic marble figurines (c. 3330–2600 BCE) found in Amorgos, Syros, Paros, Antiparos, Melos, and Pelos. These sculptures often depicted female figures and musicians and are now exhibited in many museums in the country, including the National Archaeological Museum in Athens. Traces of the middle Aegean Bronze Age (2600–1100 BCE) include the surviving Minoan frescoes in Akrotiri (Santorini), as well as the palaces, pottery, and frescoes in Knossos and Phaistos (Crete) that can still be seen on site and the local museums. In most cases, these frescoes depicted festivals, sports, and religious rituals. Finally, Mycenaean gold jewelry, houses, palaces, tombs, and fortifications in Mycenae and Tiryns testify to flourishing Greek art and architecture during the late Bronze Age (c. 1600–1100 BCE). The rise of monumental art (large-scale public structures) occurred during the Archaic period (c. eighth to fifth century BCE).

At that time, sculpture depicted the first realistic representations of human figures and produced the first life-size stone statues known as *kouros* (male) and *kore* (female). With the building of the first stone temples, Archaic architecture celebrated the early stages of the rising, cultural and political power of city-states such as Athens and Sparta, as well as of Greece at large. The now destroyed first temple of Apollo at Delphi and the pediment of the temple of Artemis in Corfu that is exhibited in the Corfu Archaeological Museum are examples of the innovative combination of sculpture and architecture in the Archaic Period.

Notwithstanding its diversified cultural production, the Classical period is the first time when the names of individual artists and architects became known. More than that, many artists of the period were not confined to a single occupation but, rather, combined their knowledge of philosophy and the natural sciences to their art and architecture. Prominent examples of such multitalented individuals include Phidias, the famous sculptor of the classical Acropolis, and Hippodamus whose plan for Miletos is considered by many as the foundation of European urban planning. The sculptors Myron and Praxiteles and the architects Callicrates, Iktinus, Mnesicles, and the younger Polycleitos are few of the most renowned classical artists. The bronze *Heniokhos* (Delphi Archaeological Museum), the now lost Chryselephantine Statues of Zeus (Olympia) and Athena Parthenos (Parthenon), and the marble *Hermes and the Infant Dionysus* (Olympia, Archaeological Museum) are supreme examples of classical sculpture. In turn, among others, architecture of the period has offered us the classical marble structures of the Acropolis, the Delphi Temple and Theatre, the Temple of Theseus (Sounion), the Temple of Hephaestos (also known as Theseion, Athens), the Theatre and Stadium in Epidaurus, the Temple of Zeus in Olympia, and the Temple of Epicurius Apollo (Bassae). Although traces of the colors that were used are sometimes still evident, because of time, most of the red, blue, and green, among others, decorative and symbolic paints on the statues and buildings of the period have faded away. Contemporary restoration work, such as that undertaken by the Acropolis Museum, is discovering more about the use of color in archaic and classical sculpture and architecture.

In following this flourishing of the arts, the Hellenistic period (323–31 BCE) introduced a more naturalistic, realistic style in art and architectural works. The extensive production of mosaics and the constant attention to decorative details are key features of Hellenistic art and architecture. The bronze *Jockey of Artemision* (Athens, National Archaeological Museum) and the marble *Venus de Milo* and *Nike of Samothrace* (Louvre) are some of the most characteristic statues of the period. The Royal Tombs at Vergina and the many findings now exhibited at Vergina, Thessaloniki, and Athens further reveal the rich culture of Hellenistic art and architecture. Finally, with its construction stretching from the sixth to the second century BCE, the Corinthian Temple of Olympian Zeus in Athens is still admired as a masterpiece of ancient Greek art and architecture.

*Georgia Giannakopoulou*

**See also:** Chapter 2: Overview; Pericles.

**Further Reading**

Moon, Warren G., ed. 1983. *Ancient Greek Art and Iconography.* Madison: University of Wisconsin.

Tournikiotis, Panagyiotis, ed. 1994. *The Parthenon and Its Impact in Modern Times.* Athens: Melissa.

Wycherley, Richard Ernest. 1967. *How the Greeks Built Cities.* London: MacMillan.

**THE HISTORY OF THE PARTHENON**

In its list of World Heritage monuments, UNESCO refers to the Acropolis of Athens as "the most striking and complete ancient Greek monumental complex still existing in our times." The Parthenon, built of white Pentelic marble, is the central structure on the Acropolis. The building of the Parthenon began in 447 BCE during the rule of Pericles to celebrate the Greeks' victory over the Persians in 449 BCE. Its symbolic associations with classical Athenian and, later, Western democracy at large have constituted it as one of the prime symbols of Western civilization.

There were other buildings on the site prior to the Parthenon. In 556 BCE, the Athenians erected a temple for the goddess Athena, and in 490 BCE, after the Greeks defeated the Persians at Marathon, the Athenians built the marble "pre-Parthenon." The pre-Parthenon was partially destroyed ten years later during the second and successful Persian invasion. The Parthenon was built over the ruins of the pre-Parthenon.

*Georgia Giannakopoulou*

The ancient citadel of the Acropolis can be seen throughout Athens. This shows the northwest view in the winter of 2020. The Parthenon, under construction as testified by the scaffolding, dominates the landscape to the right. Below the Acropolis, which was constructed in the middle of the fifth century BCE, is the second century CE Herodeion or Odeion of Herodes Atticus. It is one of the oldest and still-functional theaters of Athens. (Photo by John Vlahakis)

## Modern Greek Architecture

Neoclassicism dominated mid- to late-nineteenth-century Greek, and especially Athenian, architecture, but many architects also experimented with eclectic architecture. In general, eclecticism supported the imitation of architectural forms and elements from various historical styles such as Byzantine, neoclassical, and medieval architecture. The latter included styles such as the pre-Romanesque, Romanesque, and Gothic architecture that introduced, among others, the use or vaults, arches, clustered columns, spires, and, with the baroque especially, the extensive use of stained, that is, colored, glass. Even though eclecticism in general was not as widely adopted in late-nineteenth and early-twentieth-century Athens as widely as neoclassicism, there are many eclectic buildings in the Greek capital. The Ophthalmological Hospital, originally designed by Theophilus von Hansen in 1867, and Ernst Ziller's National Theatre (1891–1901) are some examples of nineteenth-century eclectic buildings in

Athens. Panagiotis Zizilas's Hotel Palladion and Hotel Metropol built in the 1910s and Vasilios Tsagris's Athens Theatre (1930–1933) are some of the later eclectic buildings that we can still see in Athens today.

Greek architects of northern Greece experimented with eclecticism on a larger scale. After the late nineteenth and early twentieth century, for example, eclecticism was adopted for a great number of both private and public buildings in Thessaloniki. Early eclectic buildings in Thessaloniki include the "Kapantzis House" (early 1890s), which now houses the Thessaloniki Cultural Center of MIET (the Cultural Center of the National Bank of Greece), and Eli Modiano's "Villa Modiano" (1905–1906), which now houses the Folklife and Ethnological Museum of Macedonia-Thrace. Other significant eclectic buildings in Thessaloniki include the neoclassical and neo-Renaissance Government House (1891), the Bank of Greece (1904) that now houses the Jewish Museum of Thessaloniki, and the neo-Ottoman "Yeni Mosque" (1902) designed by the Sicilian architect Vitaliano Poselli (1838–1918). Along with the many eclectic apartment buildings, other significant eclectic architectural structures of the early-twentieth-century Thessaloniki that survive today include the buildings around Agias Sophia and Aristotelous Squares, and Pietro Arrigoni's "Villa Bianca" (1911–1913) that now houses the Thessaloniki Municipal Art Gallery.

Parallel to the adoption of eclecticism, some Greek architects of the 1920s supported a return to neoclassicism. Architect and Olympic medal winner at shooting Anastasios Metaxas (1862–1937) was one of the prominent advocates of neoclassicism in the early twentieth century. On the other hand, other architects of the 1920s argued that neoclassicism was a foreign style that could not represent modern Greece. The architect and urban planner Aristotelis Zahos (1871–1939) and the architect and academic Dimitris Pikionis (1887–1968) both argued that modern Greek architecture should adopt traditional architectural forms, such as those used for village and island architecture (i.e., small white houses with red ceramic or grey stone roofs). Zahos, who also focused on neo-Byzantine architecture, designed a number of 1930s public buildings and private houses in the city of Ioannina, as well as the temples of Saint Nikolas, Saint Constantine, and Metamorphosis of the Saviour (1927–1928) in Volos. Pikionis, one of the greatest and most influential modern Greek architects, worked on a number of different projects such as private houses, the elementary school of Lycabettus in Athens (1932), the Volos City Hall (1961), and the reconstruction of the archaeological area surrounding the Acropolis and the Hill of Phillopapos in Athens (1954–1957).

By the mid 1930s the Ioannis Metaxas dictatorship supported a return to neoclassical architecture. This time, neoclassicism was used to express the 1930s nationalism and the irredentist "Great Idea" (i.e., the belief that Greece should reclaim the geographical area once occupied by the Byzantine Empire). The question of "Greekness" that was always considered in modern Greek architecture was further emphasized after the Asia Minor Catastrophe (1918–1922) when over a million Greek refugees came to the mainland. During that period, architects were not only concerned with the style of public or government buildings but also with the housing of the increasing urban population. The 1930s search for a modern Greek architecture that satisfied the functional needs of a modern city offered an ideal environment for mid-war (i.e., the period between the two world wars) and postwar modern architecture.

Prominent modern Greek architects of the mid- and postwar periods include the following: Leonidas Bonis (1896–1963), Ioannis Despotopoulos (1903–1992), Basileios Douras (1904–1981), Dimitrios Fotiadis (1884–1974), Patroklos Karantinos (1903–1976), Vasileios Kassandras (1904–1973), Konstantinos Kitsikis (1893–1969), Georgios Kontoleon (1896–1952), Konstantinos Kyriakidis (1881–1942), Emmanouil Lazaridis (1894–1961), Nikolaos Mitsakis (1899–1941), Nikolaos Nikolaidis (1891–1967), Kyriakos Panagiotakos (1902–1982), and Leandros Zoidis (1900–1965).

With the rise of an international modern architecture that focused primarily on the function rather than the aesthetics of buildings, the architects of the postwar period considered Greek folk or traditional architecture. For example, inspired by Pikionis's work, Aris Konstantinidis (1913–1933) and Thucydides Valentis (1908–1982) supported a combination of modern architecture with the simplicity of traditional houses. In contrast to Konstantinidis and Valentis, Takis Zenetos (1926–1977) argued in favor of international architecture. After World War II, the housing necessities of the rapidly growing cities of Greece, and in particular Athens, were satisfied by the extensive building of tenement buildings. Kyprianos Biris (1907–1990), Konstantinos Doxiadis (1913–1975), Pavlos Mylonas (1915–2005), Spyros Stáikos (1913–2012), Nikos Valsamakis (1924–), Prokopis Vasileiadis (1912–1977), and Emmanouil Vourekas (1907–1992) are some of the prominent architects of the 1950s and 1960s.

The Acropolis Museum, designed by Bernard Tschumi with Michael Photiadis, opened to much acclaim in 2009. The stunning building houses a priceless collection of ancient Greek archaeological treasures. The visitor traversing the glass walkway to the museum can look below to view the remains of an ancient Athenian neighborhood that was serendipitously discovered during the excavation. (Photo by Elaine Thomopoulos)

Just like their neoclassical counterparts, significant buildings of modern Greek architecture are now protected by Law 1469/1950 ("On the Protection of a Special Category of Post-1830's

Buildings"), the General Building Regulation that defines the height and all other building regulations established by Laws 1577/1985 and 3028/2002 ("On the Protection of Antiquities and All Cultural Heritage").

In order to record and classify material (photographs, publications, etc.) related to post-1828 Greek architecture, the Benaki Museum has created the Neohellenic Architecture Archives (NAA). Similarly, the National Hellenic Research Foundation has created the "contemporary monuments database" that offer information on preserved postclassical buildings. Modern Athenian architectural monuments include:

- Emmanouil Lazaridis's State General Accounting Office (1928–1934);
- Konstantinos Kitsikis's "OTE," the former Hellenic Telecommunications Organization Branch Building (1930–1931);
- Vasileios Kassandras and Leonidas Bonis's building of the Army Share Fund Building (1927–1929) and the Sikiarideio Building, widely known as "Rex" (1935–1937), that now houses two stages of the National Theatre;
- Alexandros Nikoloudis's "Sarogleio Building" that houses the Armed Forces Club (1924–1932);
- Kyriakos Panagiotakos's "Antonopoulos Apartment Building," also known as the "'Blue' Apartment Building" (1932–1933) because of its blue color painted by the painter Spyros Papaloukas;
- Emmanouil Vourekas, Prokopis Vasileiadis, and Spyros Stáikos's Athens Hilton (1958–1963); and
- Dimitris Pikionis and Konstantinos Doxiadis's National Documentation Centre (1965–1968).

*Georgia Giannakopoulou*

**See also:** Chapter 2: Metaxas, Ioannis. Chapter 6: Overview. Chapter 15: Stavros Niarchos Foundation Cultural Center.

**Further Reading**

Benaki Museum. "Neohellenic Architecture Archives." Accessed June 3, 2018. https://www.benaki.gr/index.php?option=com_collections&view=collection&id=57&Itemid=558&lang=en.

Condaratos, Savas, and Wilfried Wang, eds. 1999. *Greece: 20th-Century Architecture.* New York: Prestel.

EIE. "Archaeology of the City of Athens." Accessed February 13, 2018. http://www.eie.gr/archaeologia/En/arxeio.aspx.

Fessas-Emmanouil, Helen. 2001. *Essays on Neohellenic Architecture.* Athens: J. F. Kostopoulos Foundation.

Filippidis, Dimitris. 1984. *Neohelleniki Arhitektoniki.* Athens: Melissa.

Giakoumatos, Andreas, ed. 2016. *Hellinike Arhitektoniki ston 20° kai 21° Aiona.* Athens: Gutenberg.

## Modern Greek Art (1453 to Present)

Greek art continued even after the fall of Constantinople, the capital of the Byzantine world, to the Ottoman Empire (1453 CE). Ever since then, one of the main questions troubling Greek artists was whether they should continue or reject the art of their ancestors. The first answer to this question came in the fifteenth century with Cretan artists who decided to continue Cretan tradition in iconography as well as to create a new style that differed, for example, from the previous one-dimensional depiction of the figures, and combined Eastern with Western European Renaissance elements. The internationally acclaimed Doménikos Theotokópoulos (1541–1614), widely known as El Greco, is the ideal example of this new approach to modern Greek painting in general. During the last two centuries of Venetian rule (sixteenth to seventeenth centuries CE), this fusion gave rise to the "Cretan School." Michail Damaskenos (1530/35–1592/93), Andreas Pavias (d. between 1504 and 1512), Angelos Pitzamanos (1467–1535), Andreas Ritzos (1421–1492), and Nikolaos Tzafouris (d. c. late fifteenth, early sixteenth century) are some of the leading figures of Cretan iconography. Many post-Byzantine icons are kept in various monasteries in Greece. As with Byzantine icons, many post-Byzantine artifacts are also exhibited at the Byzantine and Christian Museum at Athens, the Thessaloniki Museum of Byzantine Culture, and the Herakleion Historic Museum of Crete. Older icons are now exhibited in museums throughout Greece. Modern Greek churches are also decorated by icons that continue this long iconographic tradition.

During the seventeenth, eighteenth, and early nineteenth centuries, in contrast to the rest of Greece that was mainly under Ottoman occupation, the Ionian Islands (Corfu, Ithaca, Kefalonia, Kythira, Lefkada, Paxi, and Zakynthos) were occupied by the French, the English, and the Venetians. Similarly to the "Cretan School," iconographers—some of whom sought refuge by immigrating to the Ionian Islands after Crete fell to the Ottomans—and local artists had greater access to Western European art than their colleagues in mainland Greece. In contrast to "Cretan School" artists, the "Heptanese School" (School of the Ionian Islands) iconographers mostly rejected Byzantine art. Instead, they focused on Italian and Flemish painting and depicted more secular themes. Panagiotis Doxaras (1662–1729) and his son Nikolaos (1700/1706–1775), Dionysios Kalyvokas (1806–1887), Nikolaos Kantounis (1767–1834), Nikolaos Koutouzes (1741–1813), Pavlos Prosalentis (1784–1837), and Dionysios Tsokos (1820–1862) are some of the most influential painters of the "Heptanese School."

After the official liberation of Greece from the Ottomans, many artists adopted the neoclassical style that was seen as ideal for the modern Greek state; yet there were others who employed techniques associated with European artistic movements such as Romanticism and Realism. This gave rise to the "Greek Academic School," comprised mostly of artists trained at the Munich Royal Academy of Fine Arts and at the Paris French Art Academy. Close to neoclassicism, academic painting portrayed historical and mythic themes, but it also introduced still life, landscapes, portraiture, and genre painting. Genre painting in particular, that is, the depiction of everyday life, was especially important for many Academic painters.

The "Greek Munich School" was composed of influential painters such as Nikolaos Gyzis (1842–1902), Georgios Jakobides (1853–1932), Polychronis Lembesis (1848–1913), Nikiforos Lytras (1832–1904), Georgios Roilos (1867–1928), Nikolaos Vokos (1954–1902), Konstantinos Volanakis (1837–1907), and Theodoros Vryzakis (1814–1878).

The painters who studied at the French Art Academy introduced new themes in painting. For example, Nikolaos Xydias Typaldos (1826–1909) and Iakovos Rizos (1849–1926) became known for their portraiture, and Theodoros Rallis (1852–1909) focused on scenes from the Orthodox Church and on "oriental" genre painting such as scenes from Egyptian everyday life. Many of their works are now displayed at the National Gallery, the National Glyptotheque, and the Municipal Gallery in Athens.

Since women were not initially admitted to the university, female artists were largely excluded from the art schools. More than that, even when they were admitted, women were mostly encouraged to be confined to landscape or still-life painting. However, by the end of the nineteenth century, some, such as Eleni Boukouri-Altamoura (1821–1900), Kleoniki Asprioti (1870–1930), Sophia Laskaridou (1881–1965), Eleni Prosalenti (1870–1910), and Olga Prosalenti (1870–1930), reclaimed their rightful position in the art world.

During the same period, painters tried less strict forms. For example, Ioannis Altamouras (1852–1878), Stylianos Miliadis (1881–1951), and Epaminondas Thomopoulos (1878–1976) used lighter colors and experimented with early impressionism. In the 1880s, Georgios Chatzopoulos (1858–1935), Périclès Pantazis (1849–1884), and Symeon Savvidis (1859–1927) rejected academic art and turned to impressionism. Nikolaos Lytras (1883–1927), the son of Nikiforos Lytras, Konstantinos Maleas (1879–1928), and Konstantinos Parthenis (1878–1967) further cultivated the ground that inspired artists of the twentieth century.

Although some of their colleagues, such as Spyros Vikatos (1878–1960), remained loyal to academic painting, other early-twentieth-century Greek artists challenged older artistic paradigms. Some introduced the European avant-garde styles such ascubism, expressionism, fauvism, and surrealism. Others created a characteristically Greek art that incorporated Byzantine or traditional art. This was the case with Spyros Papaloukas's (1892–1957) and Fotis Kontoglou's (c. 1895–1965) works. Later, Yannis Tsarouchis (1910–1989), who worked under Kontoglou, also incorporated traditional into modern Greek art.

The early-twentieth-century artists' need to discover "Greekness" did not necessarily reflect a move toward nationalism but rather a desire to create art that was related to their experiences of, and responses to, important sociopolitical events such as the Balkan Wars (1912–1913), World War I (1914–1918), and the Asia Minor Catastrophe (1919–1922). For example, Thaleia Flora-Karavia (1871–1960), one of the most distinguished artists of the time, created a series of drawings on the Balkan Wars. The reinterpretation of the artist's role (i.e., the belief that art should express its own time) was best expressed by "the Generation of the '30s." This varied group included unique artists such as Agenor Asteriadis (1898–1977), Georgios Bouzianis (1885–1959),

Georgios Gounaropoulos (1890–1977), and Nikos Nikolaou (1909–1986). Other prominent painters include Diana Antonakatou (1921–2011), Seilia Daskalopoulou (1936–2006), Nikos Engonopoulos (1907–1985), Nikos Hatjikyriakos-Ghikas (1906–1994), Harikleia Hatjisavva-Fotiou (1918–1984), Jannis Kounellis (1936–2017), Giannis Moralis (1916–2009), Eleni Pashalidou-Zoggopoulou (1909–1991) and her sister Alexandra Pashalidou-Moreti (1912–2010), Selest Polychroniadi (1904–1985), Aspa Stasinopoulou (1935–2017), Theodoros Stamos (1922–1997), Panagiotis Tetsis (1925–2016), and Spyros Vasileiou (1903–1985).

The post-nineteenth-century interest in redefining Greek art helped revive techniques, such as engraving, that were previously overshadowed by painting and sculpture. Important nineteenth- and twentieth-century engravers include Charikleia Alexandridou Stefanopoulou (1889–1963), the painter and satirist Dimitris Galanis (1879–1966), Vasso Katraki (1919–1988), Yiannis Kefallinos (1894–1957), Lykourgos Kogevinas (1887–1940), the expressionist Georgios Oikonomidis (1891–1958), Angelos Theodoropoulos (1883–1965), Lela Pashali (1914–1977), Tassos (Anastasios Alevizos, 1914–1985), Nikolaos Ventouras (1899–1990), and Markos Zavitsanos (1884–1923).

The Athens National Museum of Contemporary Art (EMST), the Thessaloniki Macedonian Museum of Contemporary Art, the Rhodes Modern Greek Art Museum, and the Andros Museum of Contemporary Art hold some of the best collections of modern and contemporary Greek and international art works.

Similarly to painters, many modern Greek sculptors rejected neoclassicism as a foreign style and sought an art that would best express their time. Even though they too often worked with historical and mythical themes, they experimented with more realistic representations and later with other styles, including abstract forms.

Leading representatives of Greek sculpture in the late nineteenth and early twentieth centuries were Dimitris Filippotis (1839–1919) and Gianoulis Chalepas (1851–1938). They were both born on the island of Tinos, which has a great marble-sculpting tradition. Their works are displayed around Greece, including Tinos and Athens. Filippotis's "Wood Chopper" (1872) is displayed at Zappeion in Athens, and Chalepas's "sleeping female figure" (1877) decorates the tomb of Sophia Afentaki at the first cemetery of Athens. As tribute to the island's marble sculpture tradition, in 2008, the Piraeus Bank Group Cultural Foundation founded the Tinos Museum of Marble Crafts where visitors can admire the use of marble crafts in both art and architecture. Influential modern sculptors who experimented with various artistic styles include Thanasis Apartis (1899–1972), Georgios Bonanos (1863–1940), Konstantinos Dimitriadis (1881–1943), Memos (Agamemnon) Makris (1913–1993), Thomas Thomopoulos (1873–1937), Lazaros Sochos (1862–1911), Nikolaos Stergiou (1888–1919), the controversial modernist Michalis Tombros (1889–1974) who was criticized as a Nazi sympathizer, Bella Raftopoulou (1902–1992), and Petros Roumbos (1873–1942).

*Georgia Giannakopoulou*

**See also:** Chapter 2: Overview. Chapter 4: Art Economy. Chapter 16: Street Art and Graffiti.

**Further Reading**

Association of Greek Art Historians. 2018. *Art History in Greece – Selected Essays*. Athens: Melissa.

Kambouridis, Haris, and George Levounis. 1999. *Modern Greek Art, the 20th Century: A Comprehensive History of Painting, Engraving, and Sculpture*. Athens: Hellenic Ministry of the Aegean.

Vlachos, Manolis. 2007. *The Emergence of Modern Greek Painting 1830–1930*. Athens: National Bank of Greece.

## Neoclassical Architecture

Although there were many variations across Europe and the United States, in general, neoclassical architecture can be defined as the eighteenth- and nineteenth-century style that imitated classical Greek, Hellenistic, and Roman buildings Among others, neoclassical architecture reappraised and adopted the geometry and grandeur of classical architecture , and especially the Parthenon, and further supported the direct imitation of structural elements such as pediments and columns at the buildings' entrances. Finally, neoclassical architecture supported the extensive use of white marble that was ornamented or complemented by single-color painted surfaces and decorative elements such as ornamental edge tiles, engravings, sculptures, statues, and paintings that depicted ancient Greek mythical figures and stories.

The expansion of neoclassicism in Greece was related to various sociopolitical phenomena, such as the Greek revolution, the creation of the modern Greek state, and the rebuilding of Athens as the new capital. Neoclassicism was first imported to the Ionian Islands in the early nineteenth century by the English and the French. However, even though Ermoupoli, the capital city of the island of Syros, and Nafplion, the city that preceded Athens as the capital of Greece, were largely planned according to neoclassical principles, neoclassicism did not become the official style of Greek architecture until the Bavarian king Otto and the regency moved to Athens. Beginning with the official foundation of Athens as the capital of Greece in 1834, the stylistic affinities between classical and neoclassical architecture served to establish a visual relationship between ancient and modern Greece and dominated the planning of all major Greek cities of the time, such as Patra, Aigio, Pyrgos, and Argos. Similarly, neoclassicism was used for the majority of public buildings, such as municipal offices, libraries, museums, schools, and hospitals. It also predominated in the building of aristocratic and bourgeois mansions and private dwellings.

In the late nineteenth century, with the mass production of cheaper building materials, private houses of the lower middle classes began to incorporate certain neoclassical elements such as pillars and miniature casts of antique-looking figures. The dominance of neoclassicism in the capital, especially, was so extensive that, at first, many of the architects of modern Greece referred to it as "Hellenic architecture."

The rebuilding of Athens as the Greek capital resulted in the demolition of many postclassical monuments. In 1843, the Bavarian administration demolished many abandoned or partially destroyed Byzantine and post-Byzantine churches in order to find materials for the building of the Athens Cathedral (1842–1862). Overall, in rebuilding Athens as a neoclassical capital city from the 1840s to the 1860s, the government demolished seventy-two Byzantine and post-Byzantine churches.

Especially in Athens, the neoclassical architectural style continued to be used until the 1930s. In the 1920s and 1930s, neoclassical forms were connected to various political phenomena such as the irredentist "Great Idea"—that is, the belief that Greece should reclaim the geographical area once occupied by the Byzantine Empire—the rise of far-right politics, and the 1936 dictatorship.

Many neoclassical buildings were demolished during the rebuilding of Athens after World War II. To protect the remaining neoclassical structures, the government enacted a number of provisions: first, Law 1469/1950, "On the Protection of a Special Category of Post-1830 Buildings and Works of Art," and second, the 1979 decree on the "Characterization of the Traditional Sector of Athens." The Greek neoclassical heritage at large is now protected by Law 3028/2002, "On the Protection of Antiquities and Cultural Heritage in General."

The neoclassical buildings now protected by the Greek Law include the Patra Municipal Hospital (Th. Von Hansen, 1857), the Patra Municipal Theatre (Ernst Ziller, 1871), and the Olympia Archaeological Museum (W. Dörpfeld, 1886). In Athens, these include the Piraeus Municipal Theatre (I. Lazarimos), the church of Agia Eirini (L. Kaftantzoglou), the old palace (now the Greek Parliament [F. von Gärtner]), the old Parliament (now the National Historical Museum [F. Boulanger and P. Kalkos]), the National Archaeological Museum (L. Lange, P. Kalkos, A. Vlahos, E. Ziller), the Athens Observatory (Th. Von Hansen), the National Technical University of Athens (L. Kaftantzogou), the Zappeion Exhibition Hall (F. Boulanger, Th. Von Hansen), and the three buildings of the Athenian Trilogy on Panepistimiou Avenue. The neoclassical "Athenian Trilogy" comprises the National University, Academy, and Library. The university (1839–1864) was originally designed by Christian von Hansen (1803–1833) and later supervised by Lysandros Kaftantzoglou, on the site where Hansen's brother Theophil later built the academy. The university is decorated by statues of the patriarch Gregory V (1746–1821); the British prime minister William Ewart Gladstone (1809–1898); Greece's first prime minister, Ioannis Kapodistrias (1776–1831); and prominent figures of the Greek Enlightenment, such as Rigas Velaistinlis (also known as Rigas Feraios [1857–1898]) and Adamantios Korais (1748–1833). Designed by the Bavarian painter Karl Rahl and completed by his Polish colleague Eduard Lebiedzki, the university exterior fresco illustrates the "Renaissance of the Sciences and of the Arts under Otto's Reign"; there, Otto, Greece's first king, is surrounded by figures representing the sciences, such as history, philosophy, and medicine. The academy and library, both designed by Theophilus von Hansen (1813–1891), were decided by the 1859 royal decree "On the Building of Establishments in the Square of the Othonean University." Initially intended for an archaeological museum, the space of the undefined building finally housed the library. The Athens Academy (1859–1885, supervised by E. Ziller) is an Ionic-style building made of white marble. Works for the academy were funded by Baron Simon Sinas (1810–1876). After his death, his wife undertook responsibility for the completion of the academy, which, under Ziller's supervision, was finally opened to the public in 1885. Construction of the building, as it stands today, was completed in 1902. The academy is decorated by Leonidas Drosis's statues of Athena, Apollo, Plato, and Socrates. The National Library (1887–1902), also known as the Vallianos Library after its sponsor Panagi Vallianos, is a white-marble Doric building. The foreground is decorated by a statue of Vallianos made by the prominent late-nineteenth- and early-twentieth-century sculptor Georgios Bonanos (1863–1940).

*Georgia Giannakopoulou*

**See also:** Chapter 2: Overview; Otto (Otho), King. Chapter 8: Photo of the National Polytechnical University of Athens.

**Further Reading**

Birēs, G. Mano, and Marō Kardamitsē-Adamē. 2004. *Neo-Classical Architecture in Greece.* Los Angeles: Getty Publications.

Bires, Konstantinos H. 1999. *Ai Athenai - Apo ton 19on Eis ton 20on Aionan.* Athens: Melissa.

Papageorgiou-Venetas, Alexandros, 1994. *Athens - The Ancient Heritage and the Historic Cityscape in a Modern Metropolis.* Athens: The Archaeological Society at Athens.

## Neoclassical Art

Even though neoclassicism, a dominant mid-eighteenth- to late-nineteenth-century Western European movement that supported the imitation of Classical and Hellenistic art forms and representations, was mostly adopted in architecture, the production of Greek art in this context was no less significant. Moreover, even though neoclassicism was largely imported to Greece and, especially Athens, by the Bavarian monarchy, neoclassical art and architecture can be found before the 1830s, especially in the Ionian Islands that were occupied by the Venetians and other Europeans rather than the Ottomans, and were, therefore, better acquainted with Western culture. For example, Corfu-born sculptor Pavlos Prosalentis (1784–1837), the founder of the first art school in Greece and a student of the famous Italian classicist Antonio Canova, is a prime example of an early-nineteenth-century Greek neoclassical artist.

After the foundation of the modern Greek state, the Bavarian administration imported neoclassicism on a larger scale and established it as the dominant style of official modern Greek art and architecture; both were used as means to visually and symbolically connect classical with modern Greece.

However, even though paintings of the period often adopted neoclassical imagery, they also employed techniques and forms associated with both the Romantic and the Realist movements and gave rise to what became known as Academic Realism in Greece. Foreign artists who were working and teaching in Greece, such as Karl Rahl and Ludwig Thiersch, as well as Greek artists of the Munich School represented this artistic movement. Trained at the Munich Royal Academy of Fine Arts, many Greek academic realists rejected previous post-Byzantine and folk art and, instead, adopted Western European, and especially Bavarian, artistic paradigms. In this context, Greek painters focused largely on mythical and historical themes. Theodoros Vryzakis's (1814–1878) paintings "Grateful Hellas" (National Historical Museum), "Sortie of Messolonghi," and "Exodus of Messolonghi" (Hellenic National Gallery), for example, are dedicated to the Greek revolution and epitomize such historical paintings. Similarly, the painter and photographer Filippos Margaritis (1810–1892), the painter and engraver Nikolaos Gyzis (1842–1901), and the painter Nikiforos Lytras (1832–1904) focused on mythical and historical themes. Lytras trained the second generation of Greek academic realists, including Georgios Iakovidis (1853–1932), Ioannis Koutsis (1869–1953), and Georgios Roilos (1967–1928). Many of their works are now exhibited in the National Gallery in Athens.

Given other later stylistic experimentations of the famous Gianoulis Chalepas (1851–1938) and Dimitris Filippotis (1839–1919), nineteenth-century sculpture was largely neoclassical and usually avoided the often romantic influences of the Munich School painters. Similarly to paintings of the period, historical and mythological motifs were particularly popular in sculpture. White-marble statues and busts of historical figures, such as the fighters of the Greek revolution, as well as of the sponsors of public buildings, wealthy members of the middle class, and the royal families were equally popular themes of sculpture in this context. Led by Ioannis Kossos (1822–1875), Georgios Vroutos (1843–1909), Frangiskos Malakate (c. 1825–1914), Iakovos Malakate (c. 1808–1903), the Fytalis brothers (George Fytalis 1830–1880 and Lazaros Fytalis 1831–1909), and Leonidas Drosis (–1882), neoclassical sculpture defined a great part of modern Greek cityscapes. Indeed, many sculptures of the period, such as Drosis's statues of Apollo, Athena, and Socrates, and the principal pediment of the Academy of Athens are still admired as masterpieces of modern Greek art.

*Georgia Giannakopoulou*

**See also:** Chapter 2: Otto (Otho), King.

**Further Reading**

Giannoudaki, Tonia. 2006. *National Gallery – Permanent Collection.* Athens: National Gallery, Alexandros Soutsos Museum.

Lydakis, Stelios. 2011. *Neo-Hellenic Sculpture. History, Typology.* Athens: Melissa.

## Photography

Photography was introduced in Greece in the 1840s by foreign photographers who visited the country and soon attracted many local artists who wanted to experiment with the potentials of this new art. In general, because of the cost of photography at the time, their clientele were mostly members of the royal court, clerics, politicians, and upper-class families. In contrast to painting and sculpture, these artists were, by definition, using a new medium. However, they, too, had to decide if they would adopt older imageries. Filippos Margaritis (1810–1892), the first Greek photographer, produced popular portraits but also depicted women in local costumes with antiquities in the background. In the 1870s, Xenophon Vathis distanced himself from this dilemma and, instead, produced early photo-reportages. Other prominent nineteenth-century photographers include Konstantinos Athanasiou (1845–1898), Panagiotis Fatseas (1888–1938), Anastasios Gaziadis (1853–1931), Stylianos Kalamatianos, Athanasios Kalfas (1836–?), Eleni Kánta and her sister Kerkyra, Dimitrios Konstantinou, Ioannis Lambakis (1851–1916), Georgios Moraitis, Petros Moraitis (1832–1888), Zoi Papa-Nikolaou, Leonidas Papazoglou (1872–1918), Mary Paraskeva (1882–1951), Evangelia Petyhaki, and Nikolaos Tombazis (1894–1986).

By the mid to late nineteenth century, photographic technology advanced significantly, and the relevant equipment was easier to afford. The growing demand for portraits, particularly, soon popularized photography throughout the country. Nellys' (Elli Souyioultzoglou-Seraïdari, 1889–1998), known for her modern representations of Greek antiquities, became internationally acclaimed. In the late 1920s, she took controversial photographs of the half-naked dancer Nikolska in the Parthenon. Later, her 1930s images of everyday life objects in the Greek countryside, her portraits of prominent Greek artists such as Greek poet Kostis Palamas, and the numerous portraits of people around the country, including the well-known picture of the young shepherds in Ioannina, established her as a pioneer of modern Greek photography.

Given the commercial nature of a great part of their art and the popularity of motifs such as portraits and landscapes, many early to mid-twentieth-century photographers experimented with a wider range of images. Assisted by the ever-growing production of newspapers that reported the social changes and wars of the period, photo-reportage also grew significantly at the time. Petros Poulidis (1886–1967), Aristotelis Romaidis (–1916), and Stefanos Stournaras (1867–1928) documented the Balkan Wars, and Nikos Zografos (1881–1967) was the first to photograph the Greek army in Smyrna before the Asia Minor Catastrophe. Photo-reportage adopted an even more social character during World War II with Voula Papaioannou's (1898–1990) social documentaries and Spyros Meletzis's (1906–2003) photographs of the Greek Resistance movement. From the second half of the twentieth century to today, photography changed in Greece, as in the rest of the world. Many photographers argued that photography should serve as a critique of social reality and that photographers should, therefore, turn the camera to previously non-photographed realities of everyday life, such as poverty, mental and physical illness, migration, and political protest. In the twenty-first century, digital technologies have revolutionized photography and further accentuated these debates. Some of the prominent modern Greek photographers are Pericles Alkidis (1953–), Kostas Antoniadis (1949–), Kostas Balafas (1920–2011), Giannis Dimou (1944–), George Depolas (1947–), Dimitris Harissiadis (1911–1993), Katerina Kalogeraki (1960–), Petros Marifoglou (1954–), Nikos Panagiotopoulos (1945–), Pericles Papachatzidakis (1905–1990), Stefanos Pashos (1948–2017), Platon Rivellis (1945–), and Nikolaos Tombazis (1894–1986).

As well as the various exhibitions and continuous photographic production around the country, there are a number of museums and archives dedicated to modern Greek photography. They include:

- Thessaloniki Museum of Photography,
- Hellenic Centre of Photography based in Athens,
- Benaki Museum—Photographic Archive,
- National and Historical Museum—Photographic Archive,
- Hellenic Literary and Historical Archives (ΕΛΙΑ)—Photographic Archive, and
- I. F. Kostopoulos Foundation—Photographic Archive.

*Georgia Giannakopoulou*

**See also:** Chapter 2: Overview.

**Further Reading**

Xanthakis, Alkis. 1988. *History of Greek Photography, 1839–1960*. Athens: Hellenic Literary and Historical Archives Society.

## Protection of Modern Greek Monuments, Art, and Architecture

Greek legislation on the protection of ancient architecture and works of art is among the first of its kind in Europe. The official protection of Greek art and architecture began in May 1834, when Georg Ludwig von Mauer, a member of the young king Otto's Regency, implemented a law on the protection and preservation of ancient and medieval antiquities. This law was also a first attempt to control the trafficking of works of art that was very common at the time. Similar legislation for the control of trafficking and the protection of more antiquities was further implemented in 1898 and 1932. In 1950, the Greek law included nineteenth-century neoclassical buildings in the list of protected art and architecture.

Other significant legislation implemented to conserve and protect antiquities focused not only on single buildings or works of art but also on entire areas. For example, in 1929, the government decreed the identification and charting of the archaeological sector of Athens, and in 1930, it implemented Law 4512/1930 that defined this sector as the archaeological center of Athens. Subsequent legislation implemented in 1979 defined the historical sector of the Greek capital and included nineteenth-century buildings (1834–1899) in the list of protected architectural monuments (*Government Gazette*, no. 564, October 13, 1979, vol. Δ, 6549–6556).

The latest and most important Greek legislation on the conservation, restoration, and protection of Greek cultural heritage was implemented in 2002 (Law 3028/2002, "On the Protection of Antiquities and Cultural Heritage in General"). In contrast to previous legislation that was focused on specific periods and locations, and especially on classical Athens (fifth century BCE), this new legislation aims at protecting all ancient, traditional, and modern Greek art and architecture.

Similarly to the aforementioned laws on the *protection* of antiquity, Greek legislation on the *restoration* of ancient art and architecture is the first of its kind in Europe. In the early years of the modern Greek state, such legislation focused primarily on Athenian monuments and, especially, the Acropolis. The first restoration of the Acropolis began in 1835 and concluded in 1856. Today, UNESCO has inscribed significant monuments of ancient, Byzantine, and medieval Greek art and architecture to its list of World Heritage Sites, thereby further ensuring their protection. These include the Acropolis of Athens, the Temple of Epicurius Apollo at Basse, the Heraion and Pythogoreion in Samos, the Sanctuary of Asclepius in Epidaurus, as well as the archaeological sites of Delos, Delphi, Mycenae, Olympia, Philipoi, and Vergina. Byzantine and medieval monuments include the fortified Byzantine town of Mystras, fifteen Paleochristian and Byzantine monuments of Thessaloniki, Mount Athos, and the monasteries of Daphni (Attica), Hosios Loukas (Phokida), and Nea Moni of Chios and Metéora. The Historic Centre (Chorá) with the Monastery of Saint-John the Theologian and the Cave of the Apocalypse on Pátmos, the Old Town of Corfu, and the Medieval City of Rhodes are also included as UNESCO sites of world cultural heritage.

Moreover, within the present decade, the Department of Conservation of Antiquities and Works of Arts and St.a.co (Street Art Conservators) have undertaken the documentation and protection of many works of street art, especially graffiti and murals (paintings on walls, ceilings, etc.).

*Georgia Giannakopoulou*

**See also:** Chapter 16: Street Art and Graffiti.

**Further Reading**

UNESCO. "The States Parties." Accessed February 23, 2018. http://whc.unesco.org/en/statesparties/gr.

## Religious Art and Architecture

Ever since antiquity, Greek art and architecture have often been related to religion. Polytheistic figurines made of stone or metals, shrines and sanctuaries made of stone, wood, or marble, and the numerous representations of religious rituals, beliefs, gods, semigods, and mythical figures in ancient frescoes, pottery, and vase painting all testify to a long tradition of religious art and architecture that has been carried through to modern times. In this context, art and architecture of the Byzantine Empire, also known as the Eastern Roman Empire (c. 500–1453 CE), can be defined as both the postclassical religious Greek heritage par excellence and the vessel that first transported this heritage to the West. In its adoption of many ancient forms, Byzantine culture originally kept step with ancient art and architecture. Similarly to the ancient tradition that assigned protector gods to cities—as is the case with the goddess Athena whose name was given to Athens—the Byzantines believed that each city had its protector saint. This tradition continues in Greece today.

Despite the turn from ancient pagan polytheism to Christian monotheism, early Byzantine art and architecture adopted many classical and Hellenistic elements, such as painting, statues, and columns, to celebrate Christianity. Given these affinities with ancient styles, the Byzantine period was itself also highly innovative; among its greatest achievements stand the unique carvings, churches, enamels, frescoes, icons, jewelry, manuscript illuminations, mosaics, murals, paintings, and reliefs. Moreover, in opposing previous monumental forms and representations produced by the Hellenistic and Roman traditions, the Byzantine period introduced two new developments: first, art abandoned realistic for symbolic representations, and, second, architecture rejected large-scale structures; the Hagia Sophia Basilica in Constantinople, now Istanbul in Turkey, is one of the few large-scale Byzantine temples. Byzantine symbolism adopted the proto-Christian fish, peacock, and Chi-Ro (XP) Christogram. Later, mosaics and frescoes further represented scenes from the life of Jesus Christ, the Virgin Mary, and the Christian saints. After the ninth century, there emerged a new flourishing of artistic production, especially in painting and the illuminated manuscripts, that is, text with decorated borders, initials, and small illustrations. Through iconography, architecture, and illuminated manuscripts, Byzantine culture has left its mark in contemporary Greece. Byzantine temples and monasteries, especially, hold a unique place in the history of world architecture and world heritage. The numerous Byzantine churches and monasteries throughout the country are few of the most well-known surviving structures of Byzantine religious architecture. These include the Hagia Sophia in Thessaloniki (ninth century), the temples of Agioi Apostoloi (c. eleventh century), Panagia Gorgoepekoos (twelfth century), Agioi Theodoroi and Kapnikarea in Athens (mid-eleventh century), the Temple of Agia Theodora (twelfth century) in Arta, the Old Metropolis in Veroia (eleventh century), the Byzantine city of Mystras, the Monastery of Porta Panagia in Trikala (1283), and the monasteries in Meteora and Mount Athos.

*Georgia Giannakopoulou*

**See also:** Chapter 5: Icons in the Greek Orthodox Church; Photo of Greek Orthodox Church of Panagia Kapnikarea.

**Further Reading**

Heatherington, Paul. 2008. *Enamels, Crowns, Relics and Icons – Studies on Luxury Arts in Byzantium*. Burlington, VT: Ashgate.

Orlandos, Anastasios. 1999. *Αρχείον των Βυζαντινών Μνημείων της Ελλάδος* [Archive of the Byzantine Monuments of Athens]. 4 Vols. Athens: Archaeological Society.

## Traditional Art

Traditional art, which has its roots in antiquity, includes the Greek handicrafts of stone and wood carving, weaving, embroidery, pottery, and metalworking (including goldsmithing, silversmithing, and jewelry making).

Traditional art of the past century has adopted various decorative patterns from earlier periods, for example, animals, flowers, trees, and geometric designs such as the Greek key, squares, and triangles. It has also reflected local character, depending on the experiences and natural environment of the people of each region. For example, traditional art may include religious symbols such as crosses, as well as images particular to each region, such as the sea, mountains, forests, and people of the region. It has been used to create or decorate objects for the home, such as furniture, fabrics, and kitchenware, as well as objects used in work and public spaces.

In the seventeenth century, stone-carving was initiated in Chios and Tinos to decorate public and private spaces. Materials included any workable stone, such as limestone, available in each area. Later, it developed throughout Greece, and its artistry can be appreciated in public fountains, lintels, dormer windows, church columns, doors, cornices, and various other decorative elements and architectural structures. As most traditional arts, stone carving is still practiced in Greece.

Wood carving, a handicraft still widely used today, developed in the seventeenth and eighteenth centuries. Carvers use wood from walnut, pine, chestnut, and basswood trees. Their work can be observed in church iconostasis (i.e., a wall made of icons marking the nave, the central part of an Orthodox temple), on ship figureheads (usually but not exclusively detailed female figures), or musical instruments. It can also be found on tables, chests, ceilings, and doors, adding beauty to the home. Some herders have become expert woodcarvers, creating fifes and shepherd's crooks. Woodcarvings made at the island of Skyros continue to be popular around the world. Aspropotamos in Thessaly, Athens, Crete, the whole region of Epirus, Kalambaka, Metsovo, Pelion, Trikala, Volos, Serres, and Western Macedonia in general are but few of the places where woodcarving still flourishes.

Up until the massive urbanization of Greece in the 1950s, many women in rural areas had looms and wove in their homes. They created costumes, clothes, furniture covers, blankets, and carpets. With the introduction of machine looms and mass production, traditional handmade domestic weaving declined. However, recently there has been a growing interest in reviving this long tradition.

Traditional embroidery designs depict geometrical patterns, flowers, and animals. Depending on the region, embroidery also represents scenes from everyday life and nature, for example, shepherds, ships, the sea, forests, village bridges, mountains, and the village square. During the nineteenth to the mid-twentieth century, a young girl was trained in embroidery at home as well as at taking embroidery classes if she attended school. At home, her mother, grandmother, an older sister, or an aunt taught her to embroider. Associated with good "housekeeping," such training was seen as a proper pastime for young women and helped her create items for her dowry. She brought her handiwork, such as blankets, tablecloths, and towels, to her new home when she got married. Many young women abandoned embroidery in the mid-twentieth century because of the rise of the feminist movement that questioned the singular identification of women with the private sphere. However, in the twenty-first century, its aesthetic and practical uses have been reappraised, and embroidery is now being revived as an important craft beyond gender divisions.

Embroidery, crocheting, and lacemaking have been used not only to decorate tablecloths, curtains, pillow covers, bookmarks, towels, clothing, and traditional costumes but also to adorn ecclesiastical vestments. The latter has its roots in the Byzantine era, where fabrics embodied with gold were first used for canonicals (the clothes of the high priests of the Orthodox Church). Artisans continue to produce these elaborate vestments as well as church banners that are decorated with gold embroidery.

As with other handicrafts, pottery has a decorative as well as a domestic use. Popular domestic objects include cookware, plates, pots, glasses, and bowls, while popular decorative objects include ornamented vases, figurines, candlesticks, and tiles. Depending on the region, pottery may be single colored or decorated with various images ranging from flowers, animals, fruit, leaves, ships, trees, and houses, to all kinds of geometric and colorful abstract patterns. Pottery remains a widespread handicraft throughout Greece. Aegina, Attica, Evia, Chios, Corfu, Crete, Rhodes, Samos, Sifnos, Skopelos, Skyros, Thessaly, Mytilini, and Macedonia are only some of the places with a significant pottery tradition. Alongside weaving and pottery, metalworking dates back to ancient times. It includes work with the following metals: bronze, copper, iron, steel, gold, and silver. Because of the effort it takes to produce delicate work on hard metal, metalworking, especially goldsmithing, is the most difficult of all the handicrafts. Traditional metalworking includes making objects for ecclesiastical, domestic, and decorative use, as well as for farming implements and weapons. Gold and silver are used for jewelry (e.g., necklaces, rings, bracelets, pins, crowns, chaplets, pendants, earrings) as well as for the construction or decoration of various objects (e.g., belts, buckles, glasses, candlesticks, picture frames, trays, etc.).

Ancient jewelry, including the golden findings from the tombs in Mycenae and Vergina are particularly impressive. During the Byzantine period, metalworkers combined metal with enamel and engraved stones to creating beautiful jewelry. They also used this technique in iconography. Byzantine goldsmithing and silversmithing also created various ecclesiastical objects such as crosses and chalices, which continue to be produced today.

In Byzantine times, gold and silver decorated wealthier people's clothes. During the Ottoman occupation of Greece, the production of more silversmithery allowed more and more people to afford jewelry and silver costume decoration, such as bandoliers, belts, and pins. After the establishment of the modern Greek state in 1828, and

The Eleftheria and Eleftherios Giannakopoulos goldsmith and silversmith jewelry workshop in Skopelos, Greece. In the front of the workshop is the jewelers' workbench, and in the background are the machinery and tools used for the creation of handmade jewelry. With the exception of the use of electric machines, the artists of handmade jewelry still work with traditional tools (e.g., pincers, files, and pliers) used since antiquity. (Photo ©Andreas Theoktistou)

its more "Western" character, many artisans abandoned folk and traditional jewelry and, instead, imitated the jewelry produced in Western and Central Europe. From the 1950s onward, there was a return to traditional jewelry. Many artisans continue to produce exquisite jewelry in their small workshops. There are also wholesale workshops that produce and export gold and silver jewelry around the world.

Since the late twentieth century, there has been a revived interest in traditional arts. Moreover, despite the use of machinery dictated by the commercial need for mass production, there is also a return to the handmade techniques of Greek arts and crafts. The significance and uniqueness of handmade production has also resulted in an attempt to preserve and continue traditional arts. Preservation is being secured at the various departments of the Museum of Greek Folk Art, the Angeliki Hadjimichali Centre for Popular Craft and Tradition, and the Museum of the History of the Greek Costume in Athens, the Folklife and Ethnological Museum of Macedonia-Thrace, the Museum of Rural History and Folk Art at Herakleion, the Metsovo Folk Art Museum, and The Nafplion "V. Papantoniou Museum" of the V. Papantoniou Peloponnesian

Folklore Foundation. The various Byzantine, ecclesiastical, ethnological, folklore, folk art, archaeological, municipal, and historical museums throughout Greece are also dedicated to the preservation of traditional art.

Even though Greek traditional art has customarily been, and still largely remains, family businesses passed on from generation to generation, it is now included in the curriculum of technical higher education. Moreover, many private foundations, associations, and individuals teach the history of traditional arts and offer seminars.

*Georgia Giannakopoulou*

**See also:** Chapter 12: Religious Art and Architecture.

**Further Reading**

Ballian, Anna. 2011. *Relics of the Past. Treasures of the Greek Orthodox Church and the Population Exchange.* Athens: The Benaki Museum.

Delivorias, Angelos. 1999. *Greek Traditional Jewelry.* Athens: Melissa.

Polichroniadi, Eleni. 1980. *Greek Embroideries.* Athens: The Benaki Museum.

CHAPTER 13

# MUSIC AND DANCE

## OVERVIEW

Greece has a highly prized, polymorphous, and vibrant tradition of performing arts that can be traced back to the ancient times. One of the most long-standing and distinctive characteristics of Greek performing arts is the inherent unity between their main forms: singing, music, and dance. One can hardly find any artistic form that excludes one or the other, apart from standard Byzantine music, which serves particular ecclesiastic, cultural, and spiritual functions and consists of music and singing and rejects dance. There are also some types of classical music in Greece that are Western oriented and generally involve "pure" music compositions. Furthermore, there is no overall and unifying music and dance culture in Greece. Instead, there is an assortment of various genres, practices, and symbolisms that, in a considerable number of cases, are blended with each other, thereby creating a fusion of music and dance forms.

The notion of *glendi* is central to understanding music and dance in Greece. *Glendi* is a celebration that occurs either spontaneously or in a prearranged situation such as celebrating a person's name day or birthday or during a saint's feast, which is often called *panigyri*. It takes place either in the closed circle of a family and friends or in the context of a broader community. Most times, *glendi* follows a cyclical course from coolness to excitement and back again. People enjoy themselves by listening to music, singing, dancing, eating, smoking, drinking, and chatting with each other. *Glendi*, thus, becomes an arena where the relationships inside the community are exposed and negotiated. Two more terms are vital for understanding the performance of a Greek *glendi*: *kefi*, indicating high spirits and good mood, and *parea*, meaning "company" as well as "companionship." Subsequently, *kefi* arises as a shared experience within a *parea* and is accomplished through a harmonized blend of music, dance, and verbal expressions combined with consumption of food, cigarettes, and drinks.

In Michael Cacoyannis's (1922–2011) film *Zorba the Greek* (1964), the rough cinematic persona of Alexis Zorbas—dancing passionately to the rhythms of Mikis Theodorakis's (1925–2021) music while teaching his friend Basil—has influenced the public image of Greeks as exuberant entertainers. It is less well known that the particular dance called *syrtaki* is a pretty new folkloric invention and not a traditional form of performance. Although its name refers to the *syrtos*, a group of dances in which the dancers "drag" their feet as opposed to the hopping temperament of *pidichtos*, *syrtaki* incorporates both the slower *hasapiko* and the faster *hasaposerviko* styles. In fact, Zorba's dance has become one of the most spectacular tourist attractions, since it signifies the embodiment of Mediterranean masculinity as well as the ambivalence of contemporary Greek culture and soul that waver between archaicity, tradition, and modernity.

Performing arts (along with philosophy and politics) have always been at the center of worldview in ancient Greece (ninth century BCE to eighth century CE), focusing on the triptych of "*lexis-melos-orchesis*" ("speech-music-dance"). The value of music, in particular, was so immense in ancient Greece that people believed only a musically educated man was actually cultivated. Unfortunately, due to the intangible and ephemeral nature of the performing arts, current knowledge of ancient Greek music and dance is substantially limited and grows out of the physical remains of compositions, musical instruments, and literary sources. Greek folklorists, who support the idea of a unified Greek civilization through the ages, claim that patterns of ancient Greek music and dance have been orally and empirically transmitted to the present from one generation to the next, thus creating a direct link between Classical, Byzantine, and modern Greek culture. There are also some contemporary scholars, artists, and music/dance groups that specialize in reviving ancient Greek music in order to reproduce and present plausible sound and kinetic schemes of Greek antiquity.

During the Byzantine Era (330–1453), another genre of Greek music appeared, which, thereafter, was disseminated under the term "Byzantine music." This type of music was strictly ecclesiastical—although there were also many other forms of secular Greek music in that period—and purely ceremonial. It avoided any connection with dance, entertainment, instruments, and bodily affection. Through the centuries, Byzantine music has developed a unique method of notation, performance, and philosophy under the scrutiny of the Greek Eastern Orthodox Church. Byzantine chant is monodic, except for the vocal drone technique of *isokratima*, it is based on medieval Greek language, and it is performed in relatively free measure in an attempt to singingly illustrate the meaning of the sacred texts. Byzantine music continues to be performed in religious ceremonies throughout the country, mainly as part of the Divine Liturgy sung by male chanters and clerics. Professional-caliber Byzantine choirs also sing in concerts and festivals worldwide. Byzantine music has also influenced Greek folk and popular music genres.

Folk and traditional Greek music share a lot in common with Byzantine hymns, such as the usage of the Greek language, the preference for monophony and heterophony, the predominance of non-Western musical modes (which include microtones) and uneven rhythms, as well as the presence of a joint corpus of textual and musical formulas. All these attributes constitute a distinguishing local *ethos*, associating particular types of music and dance with specific geocultural areas and groups of people engaged in their everyday habits and customs. That is why every single region in Greece has its own styles, forms, and interpretations of music, singing, and dance performances. The two major traditions that dominate rural folk music and dance in Greece are the *dimotika* (tunes of the countryside) and the *nisiotika* (tunes of the islands) songs and their dance counterparts. These practices are rooted back to the early modern period of Greek history, but during the twentieth and twenty-first centuries, novel technology, mass media, and tourism have changed largely the ways through which traditional and folk Greek music and dance link up with local communities and their commonplace rituals.

At the turn of the nineteenth century, a unique genre of urban popular music and dance arose in several Greek underground sites (harbors, hashish dens, coffee shops, and prisons) through an osmosis of Greek folk, Byzantine, classical Ottoman, and Asia Minor music traditions. This is widely known as the *rebetika* songs, a music and dance culture that was at first connected with the subordinate strata of the Greek underworld.

The evolution and renovation of the *rebetika* gave a decisive boost to the long-necked, plucked lute called *bouzouki*. Since then, *bouzouki* has been identified as the key instrument of Greek popular music and dance. It symbolizes Greek mainstream culture and represents modern Greek ethnic identity. Nearly all the subsequent types of Greek popular music and dance have been affected by the *rebetika*. During the postwar era, the music of *rebetika* succeeded in achieving a significant reputation to larger audiences through the transformation of its performance practices. Due to music and dance commercialization via discography, cinema, and the contemporary technologies of sound, this earlier music genre dynamically entered the popular music arena next to the newer *laika* songs.

Western European culture has also been a central factor in the modernization process of Greek performing arts. The Ionian Islands and their deep-rooted links with the European music styles—as a result of the extended period of their Venetian, French, and British Rules (mid-fourteenth century CE until 1864)—played a vital role in the integration of Western music and dance in Greece away from the hegemony of the official Greek Church.

In the Greek capital, Central European music influenced the formation of the Greek National School of Music, in contrast to the earlier Italian music tradition that had inspired the Ionian School of Music. The establishment of systematic music education in Athens, following the German standards, elevated composer Manolis Kalomiris (1883–1962) to a leading position in Greek art music. The Romantic-influenced intention of Kalomiris and his followers was to construct a "national" music scene whose "Greekness" would be emphasized by combining the earlier tradition of Greek folk songs with advanced Western music techniques. Later on, a great number of Greek composers, musicians, and choreographers engaged in creating compound forms of music and dance based on ancient, Byzantine, and/or folk-art traditions mixed together with symphonic European styles.

Besides these music hybrids, after the mid-1940s, a new generation of artists headed by Manos Hadjidakis (1925–1994) and Mikis Theodorakis (1925–2021) rediscovered *rebetika* as a counterbalance to the Greek National School of Music. This process generated the *entechni laiki mousiki* (art-popular music) movement, bringing together aesthetically divergent music forms and styles of the East and the West to produce well-liked compositions that are even nowadays widely acknowledged not only in Greece but also abroad.

A terracotta vessel depicting a female figure playing the *aulos* (double flute) in Attic, Greece (c. 520–510 BCE). The aulos was the most popular wind instrument in ancient Greece. Although it resembles a flute, its sound was much deeper, like that of an oboe or bassoon. (The Metropolitan Museum of Art/ Fletcher Fund, 1924)

During the second half of the twentieth century, Greece underwent noticeable institutional and organizational changes in the field of performing arts. The creation of various orchestras, ensembles, conservatories, artistic associations, dance schools, theatres, radio and television stations, and cultural institutes and venues enhanced music and dance activities in present-day Greece, often acknowledging the expression of styles that had been previously ignored. For instance, the Athens and Epidaurus Festival (established in 1955) is one of the oldest festivals in Europe staging a wide range of music, dance, and theatrical performances every summer. Other major additions were the foundation of the Athens Concert Hall in 1991 as well as the setup of three state university departments of music in Thessaloniki, Athens, and Corfu during the 1980s and the 1990s.

Greek music and dance flourished inside a complex network of heterogeneous cultural settings either in rural or in urban areas of the country. The wide range of folk, popular, and classical music and dance genres reveals the position of Greece as a geographical and ideological crossroads between Europe and Asia. Music, singing, and dance are the main channels for articulating this characteristic cultural style. In recent years, music and dance in Greece constitute a multicolored mosaic of genres. The opening and closing ceremonies of the 2004 Summer Olympics that were held in Athens presented in a postmodern way numerous highlights of these diverse music and dance styles throughout the ages. Most of these older forms continue to exist even today, except perhaps ancient Greek music and dance, which, to a large extent, are considered to comprise a "lost" (i.e., difficult to be actually reproduced and, thus, sustained) tradition. However, novel styles and practices have emerged due to the continuously changing, complex, and highly ecumenical present-day reality. In this context, Greek culture (especially the performing arts like music, singing, and dance) has not become ignored; on the contrary, it has been following the Balkan, the European, and the global trends and motivations. The variety of regional music-making practices shows the traces of specific local histories, places, and identities of the Greeks that, in the present day, try to find new ways of expression and communication inside the sophisticated networks of cultural globalization.

*Nick Poulakis*

**Further Reading**

Kallimopoulou, Eleni. 2009. *Paradosiaká: Music, Meaning and Identity in Modern Greece.* Burlington, VT: Ashgate Publishing.

Rice, Timothy, James Porter, and Chris Goertzen. 2000. *The Garland Encyclopedia of World Music: Volume 8, Europe.* New York and London: Garland Publishing.

Samson, Jim. 2013. *Music in the Balkans.* Leiden and Boston: Brill.

## Ancient Greek Music and Dance

Western art music tradition is considered to be derived from the music of leading antique civilizations, especially from ancient Greek music (twelfth to ninth centuries BCE to sixth century CE), in the same way as many other aspects of ancient Greek art and literature are understood as the roots of modern Western culture. In addition, the widely utilized word "music" has its source in the Greek *mousiki*, which means "the art of the Muses" (female mythological deities). It refers to music and lyrical poetry, thus ascribing a divine origination to music. Ancient Greeks strongly believed that the first music sounds had been created by their gods, such as Apollo (the Olympian deity of harmony, leader of Muses and master of the lyre), Dionysus (the god of ritual dance and ecstatic rhythm who played the aulos), Orpheus (a skillful poet and singer of mystical hymns), and Pan (a pastoral faun who played rustic and improvised music with the syrinx).

The characteristic relation of Apollo and Dionysus to music indicated two archetypical musical and philosophical models (i.e., the Apollonian and the Dionysian) that are also present nowadays. Apollo signified the intellectual, the logical, the meditative, and the highbrow; on the other hand, Dionysus was associated with trance, madness, passion, and energy.

Music played a fundamental role in ancient Greek society and culture, since it often accompanied everyday activities, special rituals, and formal celebrations. It was both a distinct art and an essential means for young people's pedagogy. Ancient Greek philosophers like Plato and Aristotle considered music to be indispensable as a form of entertainment and relaxation, an agent for character development, and a method for mental and aesthetic cultivation. Ancient Greeks rarely performed absolute instrumental music. Most of instrumental music was accompanied by words and movement, thus creating a composite art form of music, song, and dance. Besides that, athletics was inseparably linked to music and dance performance not only because large sports events included musical and dance competitions but also because the athletes in both their training and game required rhythm and synchronization.

In comparison to the numerous and well-retained examples of ancient Greek painting, architecture, sculpture, and primeval inscribed texts, contemporary knowledge of ancient Greek music is based on a few fragments of songs and hymns, a small number of remnants of musical instruments, and also several pottery depictions and literary references stored in various museums in Greece and abroad. Ancient rhythmic and melodic norms were different from our own, but we cannot be sure about what this music sounded like. Its musical notation contained symbols placed over text syllables. The most well-known surviving musical composition of ancient Greece is the famous *Seikilos Epitaph* carved on a tombstone and dated back to the first century CE.

Ancient Greek music, principally monophonic, was based on improvisation. There were three classes of compositions according to the musical mood (elevating, depressing, or soothing). Ancient Greeks used various instruments such as the *lyre* (a kind of small harp), the *kithara* (a two-stringed type of the lyre played by professionals), the *barbiton* (a bass version of the kithara), the *pandoura* (a medium-necked lute), the *aulos* (a double-reed oboe), the *askaules* (a bagpipe), the *syrinx* (a pan flute), the *hydraulis* (an primitive form of pipe organ), the *salpinx* (a brass military trumpet), the *tympanon* (a type of frame drum), the *crotalum* (an equivalent of modern castanets), the *seistron* (a wooden rattle-like object), and the *koudounia* (small metallic bells).

In addition to music, dance (*orchesis*) held a prominent position in ancient Greek culture, especially in theatre. The chorus—a group of masked actors reciting in unison—formed an essential component of the theatrical production, which, besides versification, incorporated gesticulation, singing, and dancing. The famous American dancer Isadora Duncan (1877–1927), inspired by classical Greek forms of movement, costumes, and myths, utilized some of those features (white free-flowing tunics, bare feet, loose hair, natural movement, nonconformity, and improvisation) in her modernist choreographies. In Greece, there have been earlier attempts to revive ancient Greek theatre and dance (such as the Delphic Festivals) or to associate them with Greek folklore and modern tradition in the context of romantic nationalism. Contemporary performances of ancient Greek plays (presented at still existing ancient theatres like the Odeon of Herodes Atticus and the Ancient Theatre of Epidaurus) continue to use the chorus section to point out the collective responses to the drama.

Masterpieces of ancient Greek literature, such as the celebrated Homeric epic poems *The Iliad* and *The Odyssey* and many other tragedies, still exist today because early singers (*aoidos* and *rhapsode*) and musicians (*citharede* and *aulete*) used to present them on a regular basis. Today, there are a lot of modern scholars who accept and promote the concept of the "continuity" of ancient Greek music with the Byzantine and the Greek folk music traditions. Furthermore, several researchers, technicians, and ensembles intensely examine and evaluate ancient Greek music so that they can manufacture "genuine" archaic music instruments, produce music recordings, and recreate their sound through modern performances. Sometimes this process has been heavily questioned as nonscientific.

The Museum of Ancient Greek Musical Instruments and Toys in Peloponnesus contains several reconstructed musical items used in ancient Greece. The exhibits are accompanied by audiovisual data and categorized in thematic units in order to highlight the artistic and technological thought and technique of ancient Greece. Another relevant exhibition is at the Museum of Ancient, Byzantine and Post-Byzantine Musical Instruments in Santorini. The museum hosts the personal collection of Greek composer and scholar Christodoulos Halaris (1946–2019). It includes remade musical instruments that date from the third millennium BCE. The reconstruction and the classification of musical instruments have been carried out with the contribution of the Aristotle University of Thessaloniki. Although ancient Greek instruments are rarely used today, various active ensembles regularly perform concerts worldwide. They present fragments of antique music or other novel compositions that are based on ancient Greek melodies and rhythms. The ensembles include Lyravlos, supervised by Panagiotis Stefos (1955–), and Melos Archaion, directed by Petros Tabouris (1967–).

*Nick Poulakis*

**See also:** Chapter 11: Ancient Bards and Dramatists. Chapter 13: Overview.

**Further Reading**

Mathiesen, Thomas J. 1999. *Apollo's Lyre: Greek Music and Music Theory in Antiquity and the Middle Ages.* Lincoln: University of Nebraska Press.

Michaelides, Solon. 1978. *The Music of Ancient Greece: An Encyclopaedia.* London: Faber & Faber.

Sachs, Curt. 2008. *The Rise of Music in the Ancient World, East and West.* New York: Dover Publications.

## Art-Popular Music

The refinement and modernization of the *rebetiko*, a popular music culture of the urban underworld during the postwar period (after the mid-1940s), gave rise to the *entechni laiki mousiki* (art-popular music). This new-fangled music trend was characterized by an ambivalence, as is shown through the combination of the terms "art" and "popular" in its name. It wove together two opposing music styles—the "Eastern" (folk, traditional, popular) and the "Western" (European, classical, symphonic)—to create likeable music fusions. The art-popular music incorporated an assortment of folk and *rebetiko* music attributes, trying to remain open to musical avant-garde. Typical components of art-popular music include

- the use of modern poetry set to music;
- the unity of melody, rhythm, and verse within the form of the "song cycle" (a collection of songs performed as a unit);

- the inclusion of Greek popular musical instruments such as the *bouzouki*, the santoor, and the Cretan lyre in Western-style symphonic orchestras;
- the use of Greek traditional music elements like particular modes, rhythms, and improvisation techniques; and
- the establishment of outdoor public concerts as a means of shared expression and communication with the people.

The genre of Greek art-popular music is also known as *entechno laiko traghoudi* (art-popular song), for it has mainly been a vocal genre.

Art-popular music and songs were created by composers educated in formal Western music practices and characterized by the absence of dance, the usage of lyrics written by famous poets and songwriters, the political undertones of the songs, and the massive acceptance by the audience. Various figures of Greek musical and cultural life, such as Manos Hadjidakis (1925–1994) and Mikis Theodorakis (1925–2021), got involved. There was an aesthetic divide between Hadjidakis and Theodorakis. More specifically, Hadjidakis's music has been characterized as lyrical, personal, and cosmopolitan, while Theodorakis's music has been identified as epical, communal, and nationalist. Both Hadjidakis and Theodorakis became internationally celebrated due to the widespread distribution of their music and art-popular songs through films like *Never on Sunday* (1960, directed by Jules Dassin, music by Manos Hadjidakis) and *Zorba the Greek* (1964, directed by Michael Cacoyannis, music by Mikis Theodorakis), which formed the musical image of Greece all over the world.

Since the end of the 1940s, Greek popular music had been formed in parallel to the *elafra traghoudia* (light songs), which were based on easy-listening and Western-style melodies. In 1949, having already matured as a composer, Hadjidakis emphasized the creative qualities and cultural significance of the *rebetika* songs in a public lecture. Through his well-known talk, Hadjidakis celebrated a genre that had been a subject of contempt in the recent past by most of the intellectuals as well as for Greek society as a whole. His speech introduced popular songs and dances to the Greek elite audiences, using as example the performances of major figures of the *rebetiko* music, such as Markos Vamvakaris (1905–1972), Vassilis Tsitsanis (1915–1984), Yannis Papaioannou (1914–1972), and Sotiria Bellou (1921–1997).

Influenced by Western art music, which he had studied earlier, along with the *rebetiko* song he was researching, Hadjidakis adapted various polystylistic tendencies to his compositions from the 1950s onward. Having legitimized Greek popular song, he started building up a unique blend of music that soon became his creative path. He would later reveal, "My starting point is the folk song of our homeland in addition to the symphonic music. These two have played a huge role. Somewhere in the middle, I struck the right balance to make the song I have been dreaming about" (Dalianoudi 2009, 11).

*Six Folk Paintings* (1951), initially written for piano solo and later adapted as a folklore ballet choreographed by Rallou Manou (1915–1988), marked Hadjidakis's turn to the "local" (urban folk) essence as a source of motivation and grounding within contemporary Greek actuality. *The Accursed Serpent* (1950), *Lilacs Out of the Dead Land*

(1961), *Gioconda's Smile* (1964), *15 Vespers* (1964), *Liturgical Songs* (1971), *The Cruel April of '45* (1972), *The Great Erotic* (1972), and *The Surroundings* (1974) are his major works of art-popular music. Opera-trained alto Fleury Dantonaki (1937–1998) became best known for her performances of Hadjidakis's songs.

During the second half of the twentieth century, Hadjidakis became one of the most influential personas in the Greek music scene and held several key positions (director of the Athens State Orchestra, the Third Programme of the Hellenic Radio and Television, and organizer of Greek music festivals and ensembles). In 1989, he established the Orchestra of Colors with a vision to create a unique symphonic orchestra that would present original classical and modern music programs.

Mikis Theodorakis with his cycle of songs entitled *Epitaph* (1960) was also involved in the country's cultural transformation. Theodorakis's "metasymphonic" scores employed the rhythms and modes from the underground urban music of *rebetiko* on verses of recognized Greek modernist poets, such as Yannis Ritsos (1909–1990), George Seferis (1900–1971), and Odysseas Elytis (1911–1996). These were groundbreaking symphonic works that go beyond the classical status of typical orchestral compositions, since popular singers were commissioned to interpret them in order to produce a mixture of highbrow and lowbrow (art-popular) performances. During his young adulthood, he had studied classical music theory and composition at the Athens Conservatory and the Conservatoire of Paris. In 1960, after having spent periods with famous composers and music directors and received international praise, he returned to Greece from France. All through the 1960s, Theodorakis wrote dozens of art-popular songs and also composed numerous theater, film, and ancient drama scores. In 1967, the dictatorial government involved in the military coup in Greece forbade his music in reaction to his anti-junta activity. Theodorakis was arrested and kept under surveillance (1967–1968), banished to a mountain village (1968–1969), transferred to a political prison camp (1969–1970), and finally banished to Paris with his family (1970–1974). Outside Greece, Theodorakis continued giving concerts and meeting with world politicians, artists, and intellectuals in order to support the restitution of democracy to Greece, thus becoming the symbol of resistance against the Greek dictatorship.

*Worth of Being* (1964), *State of Siege* (1969), *Arcadia V—Spiritual March* (1970), and *Canto General* (1980) are Theodorakis's most distinguished art-popular pieces written in the form of "popular oratorio"—a "music for the masses" genre. Upon his return to Greece, these compositions, which had a strong political message, were presented in huge live concerts. His early song cycles, such as *Epiphany* (1960), *Prophetic* (1963), *The Little Cyclades* (1963), *Romiosini* (1966), *Mauthausen* (1967), *Sun and Time* (1967), *Popular Songs* (1968), *Songs for Andreas* (1968), *Night of Death* (1968), *Songs of Struggle* (1971), *18 Little Songs of the Bitter Homeland* (1972), *Songs of the Exile* (1975), *Ballads* (1974), and *Lyrical Songs* (1978), are performed worldwide even today. Contralto singer Maria Farantouri (1947–) is considered as the "ideal interpreter" of Theodorakis's songs. Until his death, Theodorakis remained musically active and admired both in his country and abroad, since his work had achieved continued popularity and had been associated with sociocultural national resistance—an aspect that had remained constant throughout his creative career.

Stavros Xarchakos (1939–), Yannis Markopoulos (1939–), and Dionysis Savvopoulos (1944–), three notable Greek composers of the second half of the twentieth century, also took part in the art-popular music debate following the mid-1970s change of polity in Greece and still remain highly active. Xarchakos is best known for his theatrical and cinematic scores that introduced the neo-*rebetiko* music style. Markopoulos is the composer behind the "Return to the Roots" movement in Greek music—a project involving the creation of innovative music anchored in the combination of ethnic elements and contemporary art forms. Finally, Savvopoulos is a singer and songwriter whose music sustains the dialogue with the 1960s Greek rock scene.

The work and attitude of all the aforementioned composers deeply influenced both their epoch and the following generations of musicians. Apart from them, other music creators, such as Thanos Mikroutsikos (1947–2019), Manos Loizos (1937–1982), Nikos Mamangakis (1929–2013), Dimos Moutsis (1938–), and Christos Leontis (1940–), followed a parallel creative path inside the broader genre of art-popular music. Each one had a distinctive, personal aesthetics in music formation and expression (melodies, rhythms, harmonies, and instrumentation), in textual style (lyrics, commentaries, and narration) as well as in their ideological and sociopolitical viewpoint.

The "New Wave" movement (an interrelated Greek music genre) arose out of the blending of Greek art-popular songs with French chansons during the mid-1960s and lasted about a decade. It was characterized by the composition of easy-listening ballads filled up with expressive simplicity and sensitivity. At first, the artists interpreted their songs (usually accompanied only by guitar and piano) in small music bistros. Outstanding Greek artists from this movement include Arleta (1945–2017), Keti Chomata (1946–2010), Kostas Hatzis (1961–), Mariza Koch (1944–), Rena Koumioti (1948–), Notis Mauvroudes (1945–), Yannis Poulopoulos (1941–2020), Yannis Spanos (1943–2019), and Mihalis Violaris (1944–).

Art-popular music is still one of the mainstream categories of music. It is heard both in Greece and abroad and is performed in nightclubs, festivals, concert halls, and live open recitals. The works of Hadjidakis and Theodorakis are still noteworthy and being appreciated. Yet, the term "art-popular" has altered its meanings and functionalities. Nowadays, contemporary art-popular songs do not connect to Greek audiences in the same way they did in the past. They fail to arouse people's excitement, since they hardly ever speak to the heart and are apolitical. This could be, to some extent, comparable to the American blues songs that have lost their initial cultural origins related to the history (slavery, resistance, and liberation) and the religion of the African American community.

*Nick Poulakis*

**See also:** Chapter 13: Popular Music and Dance.

**Further Reading**

Dalianoudi, Renata [Δαλιανούδη, Ρενάτα]. 2009. *Manos Hadjidakis and Popular Music Tradition: From Folk and Rebetiko to "Art-Popular" Song [Μάνος Χατζιδάκις και Λαϊκή*

*Μουσική Παράδοση: Από το Δημοτικό και το Ρεμπέτικο στο "Έντεχνο Λαϊκό" Τραγούδι*]. Athens: Ellinika Prosopa & Empiria Ekdotiki.

Holst-Warhaft, Gail. 1980. *Theodorakis: Myth and Politics in Modern Greek Music.* Amsterdam: Adolf Hakkert.

Papanikolaou, Dimitris. 2007. *Singing Poets: Literature and Popular Music in France and Greece.* London: Modern Humanities Research Association & Maney Publishing.

## Byzantine Ecclesiastical Music

Byzantine music is the oldest form of Greek music that is still in extensive use, fully integrated into the ethics and customs of the everyday life of modern Greeks. Although music in the Byzantine Empire (330–1453) was not only religious but also contained secular folk songs and dances, it is predominantly the ecclesiastical aspect of this period's music that served as the transitional nexus between ancient and modern Greek music. Even after the end of the Byzantine Empire, during Ottoman rule, the Orthodox Church continued its performance of Byzantine music during religious ceremonies and continues to do so in Greek Orthodox churches even today. The continuity of Greek religion, music, and language, from Byzantine times to the present, has contributed to a strong sense of Greek cultural identity.

Byzantine music's mystical character differentiates it from other types of Greek or Western secular music. It conveys the deeper expressions of the Orthodox psyche and aims to upraise the human mind, body, and soul from the sphere of the ordinary (nonspiritual) to that of the exceptional (transcendent); therefore, it must be executed in a reverent, discreet, contrite, and conscientious way. It metaphorically represents a vision of the divine elevation from earth to heaven. Byzantine music calls special attention to the words of the holy texts, hymns, prayers, and doxologies sung by priests, chanters, and the other members of the Orthodox flock, away from melodramatic hyperboles and outbreaks. A representative practice of Byzantine music during its ordinary performance in the church is the "call and response" form. Two groups of chanters—the "right" and the "left," each one with its own leader and soloist—sing one after the other the phrases of the holy hymns concluding with the typical "amen" affirmation. Another important characteristic of Byzantine chanting is the technique of *isokratima*. This is when one or more chanters sing a drone (a single sustained bass note) while, at the same time, the others perform a flourishing melody. Today, clerics and chanters sing Byzantine music in almost every church throughout Greece. Byzantine music is also taught in some conservatories and music schools and performed by numerous amateur or professional choirs and soloists in concert halls.

Byzantine music is monophonic and vocal by its very nature. It is presented as *a cappella* music—an exclusively sung performance in a quasi-recitative style without any kind of accompaniment or dance performance, given that instrumental and entertainment music had always been associated with heterodox or pagan traditions. Although Byzantine music is based upon a concrete notation system, it is performed in a moderate improvisational manner, concerning both its rhythmic patterns and its melodic passages. It follows the system of eight modes (*Octoechos*), which are equivalent to the modes of the Gregorian chant of the Western and Central Europe, yet more complicated, since each one is associated with different melodic and rhythmic types as well as several performance styles. Byzantine modes are divided into four scales: the diatonic, the enharmonic, the hard chromatic, and the soft chromatic. The names of the notes of a Byzantine music scale are Ni, Pa, Vou, Ga, Dhi, Ke, and Zo, which correspond to the seven notes of the Western music scale (C, D, E, F, G, and H). The Byzantine music scale is not divided in twelve semitones as the Western one but in seventy-two micro-intervals (*moria*), thus generating a more flexible and richer-sounding context according to the performer's mood and the requirements of the sacred verses.

Byzantine music from the first to the twelfth centuries CE resulted from the anonymous fusion of Greek holy hymns with the music formulae of ancient Greek, Syrian, and Hebrew traditions. Beginning in the thirteenth century, however, the older repertory had started to be replaced by types of performance that were more creative. Each composer cultivated a personal character and attached his own name to each composition. This novel style of embellished chant the composers used is called *kalofoniko* and reached its greatest artistic prominence by celebrated composers who lived and created around the Fall of Constantinople (1453). They drew on a more elaborate and complex notation with fresh methods of ornamentation that required further technical virtuosity of the performers and added greater significance to the singing than to the lyrics of the chants. Later on, the implementation of the New Method of analytical notation (1814) simplified the transcription of earlier material through a well-structured and commonly understood process. This improvement of music notation facilitated the development of Byzantine music from the eighteenth century to the present.

*Nick Poulakis*

**See also:** Chapter 5: Greek Orthodoxy.

### VANGELIS, THE OSCAR-WINNING COMPOSER

Vangelis (1943–), born as Evangelos Odysseas Papathanassiou, is one of the most famous living Greek composers. Although he never learned to read or write notes, his musical talent and feeling serve as a captivating force for millions of fans all over the world. He was a leading member of the 1960s pop band The Forminx as well as the psychedelic rock group Aphrodite's Child. In the 1970s, Vangelis started working on his solo projects, moving to London and establishing his own studio where he produced most of his famous records and scores for cinema. Vangelis's work has been generally described as electronic, progressive, ambient, jazz, symphonic, new age, or even "space" music. His Oscar-winning synthesized soundtrack to Hugh Hudson's film *Chariots of Fire* (1981) and his celebrated dystopian score for Ridley Scott's movie *Blade Runner* (1982) remain the landmarks of his professional music career.

*Nick Poulakis*

**Further Reading**

Cavarnos, Constantine. 1998. *Byzantine Chant*. Belmont, MA: Institute for Byzantine and Modern Greek Studies.

Conomos, Dimitri E. 1984. *Byzantine Hymnography and Byzantine Chant*. Brookline, MA: Hellenic College Press.

Wellesz, Egon. 1949. *A History of Byzantine Music and Hymnography*. Oxford: Clarendon Press.

## Contemporary Music and Dance

Today, one of the most prevalent Greek music and dance types is known as *moderno laiko* (modern-popular). This genre arose in the mid-1970s as a simplified, mainstream, westernized, and professionalized form of prior *laiko* (popular) style and is, therefore, considered to be a hybrid genre that fused grassroots culture with music and dance of the middle classes and the elites. The role of the recording industry in Greece after the World War II was instrumental in the massive acceptance of this genre. In general, there are six main phases in the evolution of Greek modern-popular music and dance: (1) the conception (1976–1980), (2) the formation (1980–1985), (3) the autonomization (1985–1990), (4) the domination (1990–2000), (5) the universalization (2000–2010), and (6) the attenuation (2010–). Yannis Parios (1946–), Manolis Mitsias (1946–), Christos Nikolopoulos (1947–), Dimitris Mitropanos (1948–2012), Yorgos Dalaras (1949–), Pashalis Terzis (1949–), Haris Alexiou (1950–), Dimitra Galani (1952–), Glykeria (1953–), Alkistis Protopsalti (1954–), Stamatis Kraounakis (1955–), Eleftheria Arvanitaki (1957–), Kostas Makedonas (1967–), Eleni Tsaligopoulou (1963–), and many other artists initially shaped the genre of contemporary popular Greek music by merging earlier (regarded as most "authentic" and "pure") music and dance styles with relatively modern ones. Most of these musicians are still active today both in Greek discography and live performances. They perform in concerts, TV shows, festivals, and recitals in Greece as well as in local communities of Greek diaspora.

Contemporary popular music can be enjoyed in large clubs of major Greek cities, Athens and Thessaloniki in particular. These are nightspots, also named *bouzoukia* (music halls in their earlier and/or more conventional times) or *pistes* (dance floor venues in their modern and/or more stylish phase), especially for young and middle-aged people where they can hear music, have a drink, sing, and dance all together. In recent years, their repertoire is occasionally called *laiko-pop*, since it soundly relies upon Western pop and dance genres; it is generally marketable and fully integrated in modern Greek popular culture.

As depicted in Michael Cacoyannis's (1922–2011) film *Zorba the Greek* (1964), the rough cinematic persona of Alexis Zorbas—dancing passionately to the rhythms of Mikis Theodorakis's (1925–2021) music while teaching his friend Basil—has influenced the public image of Greeks as exuberant entertainers. It is less well known that the particular dance called *syrtaki* is a pretty new folkloric invention and not a traditional form of performance. Although its name refers to the *syrtos*, a group of dances in which the dancers "drag" their feet as opposed to the hopping temperament of *pidichtos*, *syrtaki* incorporates both the slower *hasapiko* and the faster *hasaposerviko* styles. In fact, Zorba's dance has become one of the most spectacular tourist attractions, since it signifies the embodiment of Mediterranean masculinity, as well as the ambivalence of contemporary Greek culture and soul that wavers between archaicity, tradition, and modernity.

Music in Greek nightclubs ranges from earlier traditional *laika* songs to contemporary pop or *laiko-pop* music, kinetically performed as *zeibekiko*, *tsifteteli*, *hasapiko*, or other fashionable kinds of folk dance, although in a more formalized manner and upbeat tempos, sometimes inspired by "exotic" (Arabic and Asian) sounds and rhythms. Noted performers of this genre are, to name but a few: Vassilis Karras (1953–), Angela Dimitriou (1954–), Lefteris Pantazis (1955–), Anna Vissi (1957–), Katy Garbi (1961–), Christos Dantis (1966–), Despina Vandi (1969–), Antonis Remos (1970–), Yannis Ploutarhos (1970–), Sakis Rouvas (1972–), Yorgos Mazonakis (1972–), Thanos Petrelis (1975–), Mihalis Hatzigiannis (1978–), and Elena Paparizou (1982–). The term "*skyladiko*" (doggish) is frequently used for illustrating a decadent aesthetical form, a low-quality show of underground popular Greek music and dance that launched in the early 1980s and is often accompanied by smashing plates, throwing flowers or napkins, and opening several bottles of expensive champagne as a demonstration of conspicuous consumption, easygoing behavior, and second-class entertainment.

Rock has also had a long history in Greek music culture during the second half of the twentieth century till the present. It began as an imitation or adaptation of anglophone rock styles but, later on, acquired more personal and alternative pathways with reference to a mixture of rock forms with Greek lyrics, such as folk rock, blues rock, pop rock, rock and roll, art rock, soft rock, comedy rock, indie rock, progressive rock, and punk rock. Loukianos Kilaidonis (1943–2017), Dimitris Poulikakos (1943–), Lakis Papadopoulos (1948–), Pavlos Sidiropoulos (1948–1990), Nikos Papazoglou (1948–2011), Nikolas Asimos (1949–1988), Kostas Tournas (1949–), Vassilis Papakonstantinou (1950–), Haris and Panos Katsimihas (1952–), Tzimis Panousis (1954–2018), Sakis Boulas (1954–2014), Lavrentis Machairitsas (1956–2019), Sokratis Malamas (1957–), Nikos Portokaloglou (1957–), Yannis Aggelakas (1959–), Thanassis Papakonstantinou (1959–), Filippos Pliatsikas (1967–), Miltos Pashalidis (1969–), and Alkinoos Ioannidis (1969–) are seminal musicians of the Greek rock music scene. At present, one may also find a gamut of minor music and dance genres in Greece like ethnic jazz, electronica, synth pop, teen pop, new age, heavy metal, hip-hop, rap, and low bap music. Staged by either high professional or independent music groups and individuals, these genres are given enthusiastic approval today, aiming not for the general public but predominantly for more sophisticated and targeted audiences inside or outside Greece.

Mention should finally be made of three universally acclaimed Greek music celebrities: famous vocalist Nana Mouskouri (1934–), acknowledged film music composer Eleni Karaindrou (1941–), and widely admired singer Demis Roussos (1946–2015). Mouskouri is best known for her multilingual music shows, Karaindrou for her cinematic collaboration with Cannes-awarded Greek director Theo Angelopoulos (1935–2012), and Roussos for his soaring and warmhearted song performances. All three pursued solo international careers that transcended the borders of the country and reached millions of music enthusiasts all over the world. Their recorded albums, such as Roussos's "Forever and Ever" (1973), Mouskouri's "Qu'il Est Loin l'Amour" (1981), and Karaindrou's "Ulysses' Gaze" (1994), immediately became great hits and firmed them as outstanding Greek artists of the twentieth and twenty-first centuries.

*Nick Poulakis*

**See also:** Chapter 11: Sikelianos, Angelos. Chapter 13: Overview.

**Further reading**

Cowan, Jane K. 1990. *Dance and the Body Politic in Northern Greece*. Princeton, NJ: Princeton University Press.

Pennanen, Risto Pekka. 1999. *Westernisation and Modernisation in Greek Popular Music*. Tampere: University of Tampere.

Tragaki, Dafni, ed. 2009. *Made in Greece: Studies in Popular Music*. New York and London: Routledge.

## Folk and Traditional Music and Dance

The origins of Greek folk and traditional music and dance date back to the oral performance of lengthy narrative poems from the Middle Byzantine years (eighth to ninth centuries CE) until the early nineteenth century CE. There were two main types of epic songs, specifically the *akritika* and the *kleftika*. *Akritika*, the former of the two kinds of songs, praised the heroic acts of the border soldiers of the Byzantine Empire against Arab and Muslim invaders, while *kleftika* referred to the subsequent period of Ottoman rule in Greece until the successful Greek War of Independence (from the mid-fifteenth century CE to 1821) and glorified the fearless Greek rebels that lived in the mountains and fought their oppressors.

In the years that followed, these rural repertoires were transformed to a multifarious milieu of folk and traditional music and dance in Greece. This diversity of music and dance styles brings to light miscellaneous influences from other cultures either from the East or from the West (for instance, Ottomans, Arabs, and Venetians) that came into contact with the Greek natives. In spite of these notable variances that highlight close links with local communities, regional folk and traditional performing arts in Greece also share some common aspects. These key factors of folk and traditional music and dance in Greece are their

- anonymity, given that both the composers and the performers of music and dance remain unnamed, since every member of the group participates in the creation, the performance, and the evaluation of music and dance, and there is no need for ownership;
- (controlled) improvisational character, meaning that every new interpretation maintains a basic structural, aesthetic, and moral formality but has also several novel elements;

- collective, communicative, and symbolic nature that connects their ritualistic procedures with everyday social performance, as songs, music, and dance are functionally integrated into the customs and beliefs of local community; and
- oral intergenerational transmission between the elders and the youth and/or between the teachers and their students that ensures face-to-face dissemination and renewal of mutual music and dance traditions.

Traditional Greek songs and dances are regularly performed in the context of various "rites of passage," which indicate important instances in the indigenous people's real world. Domna Samiou (1928–2012) was an eminent Greek songstress and scholar who performed and documented Greek folk and traditional music.

Today, there are different ways to describe folk and traditional music and dance in Greece. The first involves song and dance performances that follow either the cycle of human life (from childbirth to death, like lullabies and laments) or the annual festive cycle (Christmas, Halloween, etc., such as carols and carnival songs). The second category relates to discrete types of music and dance in accordance with their geocultural region of creation and performance. Mainly, there is a principal distinction between folk and traditional Greek music and dance of coastal areas (Greek islands, Thrace, Asia Minor, and Cyprus) and that of the mainland (Epirus, Thessaly, Peloponnesus or Morea, Central Greece or Roumeli, and Greek Macedonia). Greek folk music and dance of the mainland are labeled *dimotika* while those of islands are called *nisiotika*. The differences between these two types consist of the following attributes:

- Island dances are usually in simple meters of two beats and a rather fast speed, while in mainland Greece one can also find asymmetric rhythms of five and seven beats as well as slower tempos.
- Music of the mainland—unlike music of the islands—is normally created and performed based on anhemitonic modes, which are musical scales without semitones.
- Rhymes (by the use of couplets) and improvisations in melody are quite typical for island music, while in the mainland these components are seldom detected.
- The representative combinations of musical instruments in the Greek mainland was originally the "davul-zurna" and, later on, the "clarinet-davul" pairs, while the groups of "lyre-toubi" or "violin-lute" players dominated the Greek islands.

A unique method of folk song performance in the region of Epirus is a primitive type of polyphonic singing, in contrast with the monophonic traditions of most of the other Greek peripheries. Epirote dances tend to be slow, performed with grave kinesis and absolute solemnity, and accompanied by the melodies played by the clarinet. In Peloponnesus, the principal instruments used are the violin, the clarinet, the lute, and the santur while the most widespread dance is *kalamatianos*, which has been promoted as a Panhellenic dance performed at many social gatherings in the country as well as in the Greek diaspora. Central Greek dances, such as *tsamikos* and *kleftikos*, tend to be moderate and controlled, reflecting the mixture of the local ethnocultural groups of the region. *Dionysiakos* is a special form of dance in Thessaly presented once a year at the Phallus Festival—a modern revival festivity in order to celebrate the ancient Greek god Dionysus. The Macedonian district also covers an area with rich and vivid music and dance multiplicity that is to some extent a result of its geographical adjoining with other countries. Thracian dances are usually bouncy and delicate (*zonaradikos*, *mandilatos*, *sygkathistos*, etc.) and based on intense rhythms and apparently affected by the wider Balkan and Asia Minor music and dance cultures. Pontian dances (of the Greek ethnic group living on the shores of the Black Sea) are performed in a circle mainly by men who follow short steps and the distinctive *tremoulo*, which is a rapid up and down trembling of the dancer's trunk.

Cretan music—also known as *kritika*—is a dominant folk music genre in the largest island of Greece. The duo of the traditional Cretan pear-shaped lyra (or sometimes the violin) accompanied by the lute performs a large number of dances such as *syrtos*, *pentozalis*, and *maleviziotis*. Another frequent type of Cretan music is the *mandinada*. It is an improvised couplet of fifteen-syllable verses, sung by either professional or amateur singers, and composed of lyrics with romantic or social content. The music of the Aegean Islands is a vibrant and cheerful manifestation of insular cultures. Their most common dances are *balos*, *sousta*, *karsilamas*, as well as the renowned and

Following the Greek Orthodox Church liturgy on New Year's Day, the men and women of Neo Monastiri dance the Zonaradikos and sing the song "Nice camels. Nice girls" accompanied by an accordion and *davul* (double-headed drum). Two men, disguised as the camel and its driver, prance in the center of the circle. The camel driver, with a phallus-shaped club, beats the earth to bring on fertility and the dancers to ward off senility. The ritual has its roots in ancient festivals honoring Dionysus, where people in disguise celebrated with ecstatic dances. While this photograph was taken in 1980, the ritual "Camel and its driver" continues today. Although residing in Central Greece, Neo Monastiri residents dance in Thracian rhythms, since most of their ancestors came as refugees from North Thrace, Bulgaria, in the 1920s. (Photo by Irene Loutzaki)

tourist-admired *ikariotikos* (from in the North Aegean island of Ikaria). On the other hand, the music of the Ionian Islands (Heptanese) is heavily based on the Western European music system and, therefore, there is a high presence of guitars and mandolins, while the practice of idyllic serenades (*kantades*) is a very fashionable tradition.

*Nick Poulakis*

**See also:** Chapter 1: Ionian Islands. Chapter 13: Overview.

**Further reading**

Anoyanakis, Fivos. 1979. *Greek Popular Musical Instruments*. Athens: National Bank of Greece.

Hnaraki, Maria. 2007. *Cretan Music: Unraveling Ariadne's Thread*. Athens: Kerkyra Publications.

Hunt, Yvonne M. 1996. *Traditional Dance in Greek Culture*. Athens: Centre for Asia Minor Studies.

## Popular Music and Dance

Apart from their generalized notions, Greek popular music and dance constitute specific genres within modern Greek culture. These genres go back to the Greek Belle Époque (1871–1914) when the urban music of *rebetiko* emerged. Since then, the term "*rebetiko*" has been used to describe the particular Greek music culture as well as the characteristic way of life that was developed both as a personal ideology and as a collective way of expression in subaltern social strata of urban Greek areas from the ends of the nineteenth century CE to the middle of the twentieth century CE. *Rebetiko* flourished inside a complex network of heterogeneous cultural settings, primarily the cosmopolitan culture of Asia Minor Hellenism and, later on, the popular culture of urban underground in the seaports and working-class neighborhoods of Greek cities such as Athens, Piraeus, Thessaloniki, Patra, Volos, and Ermoupoli (Syros). That is why *rebetiko* has also been denoted by some researchers as the "Greek blues." Music, singing, and dance were the main channels for the expression of this idiosyncratic cultural style. It included components of traditional Greek music, Byzantine ecclesiastical music, European music, and earlier Ottoman art and café music. Musical instruments (violin, lyra, oud, qanun, santur, etc.) used in *rebetiko* derived primarily from folk and traditional Greek music. Later on, other instruments such as the *bouzouki*, the baglamas, the guitar, the double bass, the mandolin, and the piano were added. Most songs of the *rebetiko* tradition incorporated Greek folk rhythms, motions, and dances such as *karsilamas* (a nine-beat face-to-face couple dance), *zeibekiko* (a nine-beat solo improvised dance), *hasapiko/hasaposerviko* (a four-beat line or circle group dance), and *tsifteteli* (a type of belly dance).

Most scholars of the *rebetiko* culture agree that there are three distinct periods: (1) First Period or the Smyrna Period (1922–1932), (2) Second Period or the Classical

Period (1932–1942), and (3) Third Period or the Popular Period (1942–1952). *Rebetiko* lyrics usually referred to drug use, hustling, hardship, imprisonment, persecution, and marginalization. A subcultural group of working-class men called *manges* were closely associated with *rebetiko*. They habitually performed and listened to this music. They also liked behaving arrogantly, dressing idiosyncratically (wearing a cap, a jacket, striped-pants, and pointed-shoes, usually armed with a knife strapped in their belt), playing the *komboloi* (worry beads), hanging out at the *tekedes* (underground taverns), and smoking hashish.

Great musicians of the *rebetiko* were, among others, Yorgos Batis (1885–1967), Panagiotis Toundas (1886–1942), Vaggelis Papazoglou (1896–1943), Spyros Peristeris (1900–1966), Stratos Pagioumtzis (1904–1971), Anestis Delias (1912–1944), and the so-called patriarch of the rebetiko Markos Vamvakaris (1905–1972). There were also some prominent women performers of the rebetiko, known as *rebetisses*, namely Roza Eskenazi (c. 1895–1980), Angela Papazoglou (1899–1983), and Rita Abatzi (1914–1969). Since the middle 1970s, there has been a widespread trend of revitalizing *rebetiko* via its reinterpretation by famous modern Greek singers. Today, *rebetadika* clubs survive as nightlife venues where enthusiasts of the *rebetiko* gather around to enjoy themselves by listening and dancing to their favorite songs.

*Elafro traghoudi* (light song) was another popular genre that showed up during the Interwar Period (1918–1940) in Greece and continued until the 1960s. These compositions encompassed less "serious" forms of classical European music combined with Greek lyrics of love and romance with almost no reference to social or political issues. They were tuneful, mellow, and emotional songs of nostalgia and nobility influenced by French ballads, Italian serenades, and operettas, built upon lyrical melodies, simple harmonies, and light orchestrations, usually of small Western ensembles or piano and voice. Although *elafro traghoudi* was usually heard as acoustic, relaxation, and mood music, it also brought together various forms of European and American ballroom dances such as waltz, tango, polka, foxtrot, and quickstep. Nikos Hadjiapostolou (1879–1941), Attik (aka Kleon Triantafyllou, 1885–1944), Kostas Yannidis (aka Yannis Konstandinidis, 1903–1984), Mihalis Souyioul (1906–1958), Christos Cheropoulos (1909–1992), Yannis Spartakos (1914–2001), Takis Morakis (1916–1991), Kostas Kapnisis (1920–2007), Yorgos Mouzakis (1922–2005), and Jacques Iakovidis (1928–2015) had been leading representatives of this trend.

The genre of *laiko traghoudi* (popular song) ensued as a transformation of the *rebetiko*, and it is also a type of urban popular music and dance initiated around the 1950s. Yannis Papaioannou (1913–1972) was the first *rebetis* who used *primo-secondo* (duet) vocals in his songs, but songwriter and music performer Vassilis Tsitsanis (1915–1984) had been the most influential figure of the metamorphosis of the unconventional *rebetiko* style into the fashionable mode of *laiko traghoudi*. Later on, performance expert and composer Manolis Chiotis (1920–1970) contributed to the commercialization of the *bouzouki* by introducing a more harmonic/chordal system of its tuning and by adding Afro-Cuban, Latin, and blues dance rhythms and moods to Greek popular music. Yorgos Zambetas (1925–1992), another *bouzouki* soloist, cooperated with distinguished composers of art-popular song, like Manos Hadjidakis (1925–1994), Mikis

Theodorakis (1925–2021), and Stavros Xarchakos (1939–). He had been best known for his appearances in popular Greek films and theatrical performances. During the 1950s and the 1960s, a massive invasion of popular Hindi films and music in Greece led to the adaptation of a new style called *indoprepes* (Hindi-like). Apostolos Kaldaras (1922–1990), Grigoris Bithikotsis (1922–2005), Panos Gavalas (1926–1988), Stelios Kazantzidis (1931–2001), Akis Panou (1933–2000), Rita Sakellariou (1934–1999), Giota Lydia (1934–), Stratos Dionysiou (1935–1990), and Manolis Angelopoulos (1939–1989) are considered to be some of the most notable personalities of popular song.

Since the 1960s, there have been quite a few Greek composers and singers who developed a fresh aspect of *laiko traghoudi*—often labeled *elafrolaiko traghoudi* (light-popular song)—by fusing Greek popular music with modern idioms of jazz, lounge, Latin, Euromerican pop, and soft rock styles. Mimis Plessas (1924–), Yorgos Katsaros (1934–), Yannis Voyiatzis (1934–), Stamatis Kokotas (1937–), Marinella (1938–), Tzeni Vanou (1939–2014), Tolis Voskopoulos (1940–2021), Yannis Poulopoulos (1941–2020), and Vicky Moscholiou (1943–2005) spotted the period till the mid-1970s. These musicians, along with other artists of various Greek popular music genres, became famous due to the growing impact of the new-fangled star system inaugurated through popular films of the Old Greek Cinema and the Greek record industry of the 1960s. Today *laika* songs are performed at almost every social occasion. They follow a standardized repertoire that encourages live audience participation.

*Nick Poulakis*

**See also:** Chapter 13: Art-Popular Music. Chapter 15: Sidebar: *Komboloi* (Worry Beads) Relieve Tension and Create a Meditative Experience.

**Further Reading**

Holst-Warhaft, Gail. 2006. *Road to Rembetika: Music of a Greek Sub-Culture, Songs of Love, Sorrow and Hashish.* Limni, Evia: Denise Harvey.

Tragaki, Dafni. 2007. *Rebetiko Worlds: Ethnomusicology and Ethnography in the City.* Newcastle upon Tyne: Cambridge Scholars Publishing.

Vamvakaris, Markos. 2015. *Markos Vamvakaris: The Man and the Bouzouki, Autobiography.* Edited and translated by Noonie Minogue. London: Greeklines.

## Western Classical Music

The Ionian Islands (Heptanese) have played a key role in the introduction of Western classical music in Greece. Under the Venetian rule for centuries (1363–1797), their music was shaped by the Italian tradition and other European styles and practices. Nikolaos Mantzaros (1795–1872), a Greek Italian composer who wrote the music of the Greek national anthem for the poem of Dionysios Solomos (1798–1857) "Hymn to Liberty," is considered as the founder of the Ionian School of Music. Today, the "Nikolaos Chalikiopoulos Mantzaros" Music Museum of the Philharmonic Society of Corfu holds numerous collections of music scores of both earlier and modern Ionian composers. Following their tradition, the locals also maintain many wind bands all around the Ionian Islands, where young people study various instruments of Western music by playing together in these large ensembles.

At the turn of the twentieth century CE, systematic efforts have been made by modern Greeks to construct a sense of identity continuity through a constant reflection on the definition of "Greekness" in artistic creation, theoretical discourse, and folklore research. Concerning art music, in particular, the Greek National School of Music developed out of a German influence, along with the integration of regional music features. The school aimed to establish a high-class Greek music identity based on the combination of Western classical and local music elements, following the example of other national music schools in Europe. The foundation of Athens Conservatory and the appearance of Manolis Kalomiris (1883–1962) in the Athenian art music scene led to the advent of a composers' group that espoused neoclassicism, late-romanticism, and impressionism, intermingled with features originated from Byzantine and Greek folk music, poetry, and mythology. These composers broadened their engagement with the development of art music in Greece through music education, music journalism, music research, and harmonization of folk melodies as well as the creation of new melodramatic works (such as large-scale operas) to support their national music idea.

The famous Greek classical composer Manolis Kalomiris was the leader of the art music movement. Having studied music in Vienna, he settled back in Athens where he founded the Hellenic Conservatory (1919) and the National Conservatoire of Athens (1926), two major institutions of Western art music education in Greece that are still in operation today. Kalomiris wrote major symphonic compositions and operas—namely *The Master Builder* (1915), *The Mother's Ring* (1917), *Sunrise* (1945), *The Shadowy Waters* (1950), and *Konstantinos Paleologos* (1961)—chamber music and several songs and piano pieces following the postromantic idiom. On the other side, Dimitri Mitropoulos (1896–1960), an internationally celebrated conductor, pianist, and composer, adopted a distinctive, modern perspective on the concept of national music. He studied in Athens, Brussels, Berlin, and the United States, where he eventually resided and began working. Although he composed a few symphonic and piano works, Mitropoulos rose to international fame as an orchestra director. Along with his friend and collaborator famous opera diva Maria Callas (1923–1977), Mitropoulos has been the most widely recognized Greek persona of Western classical music.

Nikos Skalkottas (1904–1949) was also a modernist Greek composer who studied abroad and adopted early on the twelve-tone and other atonal techniques as a member of the Second Viennese School. However, his masterpiece *36 Greek Dances*

(1931–1936) is a series of compositions on Greek traditional or folk-style themes arranged either for orchestra or, lately, for different ensembles written in tonal language. Iannis Xenakis (1922–2001), a Greek French theorist, composer, and architect, is best known for his pioneering method of employing mathematical and stochastic models in music, his enthusiasm in promoting electronic, electroacoustic, and computer music, as well as his ability to integrate music with architecture and design. He was familiar with incorporating elements from ancient rituals in his music and organizing massive multimedia performances in historical sites in Greece, which he called *polytopa* (polytopes).

Jani Christou (1926–1970) was a Greek composer, philosopher, and mystic whose creations combine metaphysics, spiritualism, theatricality, and liberalism. Christou himself called his compositions "meta-music." *Patterns and Permutations* (1960), *Tongues of Fire* (1964), *Mysterion* (1965), and *The Strychnine Lady* (1967) are some of these works. He also produced *Anaparastaseis*, a cycle of thirty to forty music pieces that refer to the ephemeral nature of performances. In support of his philosophical theories, his work builds a rather ambiguous and psychodramatic impression, since it embodies the world of primitive and magical rituals in coexistence with that of contemporary massiveness and collective hysterias.

Yiannis A. Papaioannou (1910–1989) became recognized for his extensive teaching of young composers and for applying postmodern compositional methods to his works. Most of the notable Greek composers of the second half of the twentieth century were apprenticed to Papaioannou.

Papaioannou's student, Theodoros Antoniou (1935–2018), one of the most prominent and prolific contemporary artists, had a brilliant career as a composer, conductor, and university/conservatory professor both in Greece and in the United States. He founded the Contemporary Music Ensemble in Athens and the Allea Orchestras in Boston and served as a director of the Greek Composers Union. More than 150 of his works have been published in major music houses. Giorgos Koumendakis (1959–), regarded to be among the most important living composers in Greece, was appointed music executive, composer, and author of the music storyline of the opening and closing ceremonies of the 2004 Summer Olympics in Athens and, later on, artistic director of Greek National Opera. Koumendakis has composed a wide range of works in diverse styles for various ensembles giving emphasis to scenic music and the interactions of music with other arts, such as the theatre and the dance. His long-standing collaboration with the stage director, choreographer, and performer Dimitris Papaioannou (1964–) breathed new life into the present Greek artistic sphere. Today, Western art music in Greece is portrayed in a twofold perspective—one side tries to maintain its earlier classical character, while the other searches for pioneering quests and experimentations that produce innovative multimedia forms within a web of artistic universalism.

*Nick Poulakis*

**See also:** Chapter 2: Callas, Maria; Solomos, Dionysios.

**Further Reading**

Mantzourani, Eva. 2011. *The Life and Twelve-Note Music of Nikos Skalkottas.* Aldershot: Ashgate Publishing.

Romanou, Katy, ed. 2009. *Serbian and Greek Art Music: A Patch to Western Music History.* Bristol and Chicago: Intellect Books.

Trotter, William R. 1995. *Priest of Music: The Life of Dimitri Mitropoulos.* Portland, OR: Amadeus Press.

CHAPTER 14

# FOOD

## OVERVIEW

Baked by a brilliant sun, enriched by surrounding salty seas, the food of Greece is among the most vibrant in the Mediterranean. From the dazzling array long gathered from land, sea, and sky, over the millennia the Greeks have spun a cuisine of captivating dishes. Greek cooks marry savory grass-fed meats with just-picked vegetables. They simmer stews laced with robust native herbs gathered from arid hillsides. They rub birds in lemons plucked from their copious citrus orchards and roast them in wood-burning ovens. They simmer lentils thick as pudding, which they top with anchovies, watercress, sun-dried tomatoes, and capers. The Greeks devour more than a hundred varieties of wild greens they forage from streams and meadows. They serve slices of their famous feta cheese—some made from sheep's milk, some from goat's, some from cow's—at every meal. The name "feta" simply means "slice" because it was so popular that even in olden days it was sold like pizza. They crust and fry hard cheese and serve it with fig jam. Many Greek dishes, like *gyros* and *moussaka*, are renowned worldwide, but the true expanse of their culinary repertory is lesser known, inventive, and delectable.

Not a scrap of food is wasted. Greeks mince leftovers into crisp croquettes, stuff tomatoes and peppers with rice and meat or with eggplant, sultana raisins, mint, and cinnamon. They turn mixes of various garden vegetables into robust compotes. They braise rabbits together with tiny onions in a sauce thickened with black-red tomato paste, which they condense from their own dense, plum-sized tomatoes. They smooth soups with beaten egg and zest them with lemon juice. They fold cheese, spinach, leeks, mushrooms, lamb, chicken, and more into pies crusted in layers of paper-thin filo dough. For sweets, they stack nuts, seeds, and sweetened semolina into sheets of dough that they then bathe in syrups of honey, sweet wine, and spiced brandy. They bake cakes and cookies, thicken puddings, fry sesame cheese puffs, and reduce fruit to preserves that are served glistening on spoons to guests.

Olives accompany all these dishes. Greeks grow numerous varieties of their native olives, some ripened black, some still green, some fat, some wrinkled, some colossal, some tiny—the most famous of which comes from a region on the eastern side of the Peloponnesus called Kalamata. They have cured the olives in the oil pressed from the same fruit for millennia. Greek olive trees, the cured fruit, and oils are the oldest known to history. The olive tree is indigenous to the island of Crete. The Minoan forerunners of the Greeks, who occupied the land, learned to cure olives, invented the olive oil press, and thrived on trading olive oil all over the Mediterranean. Some of Greece's olive trees are thousands of years old. Greek olive oils to this day remain essentially family made, instead of being produced by large corporations, and range from the highest first press, gold-medal-winning extra virgin to the last extracted pomace oil used for soap and lamps.

Along with olives, the Greeks collect wild capers from brambly bushes that grow on rocky crags all over the land and brine them, not in vinegar as do others, but by sprinkling sea salt between layers of them. They do the same with the leaves of the plants. As they reduce in reaction to the salt, they make their own briny liquid. They then use both the flower buds and the leaves on salads, fish, and tapenades. They also gather almost all of the many herbs, oregano to thyme, dill, fennel, savory to rue, from their hillsides and still employ the same exotic spices they once received from the ancient spice route.

Many of their food traditions stem from millennia—for example, they invented bread, which in ancient times was called *artos*, the origin of the word "art," and they still bake hundreds of varieties. Nowadays, rather than heading away from their heritage of dishes and products, Greeks have expanded upon their culinary customs and ingredients in a highly contemporary manner. Indeed, after a number of decades of diaspora and urbanization, many Greeks have recently returned to the land to grow their celebrated, and almost entirely organic, produce and expound upon their breads, cheeses, spreads, meats, fish, vegetables, fruits, jams, desserts, and sauces. Greeks everywhere still operate their traditional *tavernas*, serving their renowned dishes like *spanakopita*, village salad, yogurt, and *moussaka*, but now they also operate elegant and modern restaurants everywhere offering inventive compositions based on their culinary legacy. Today's Greek restaurants everywhere garner acclaim and medals. Their traditional ingredients have caused their new offerings to rise to the forefront, especially as the world turns back to fresh, seasonal, and locally sourced foods, a culinary requisite Greeks have practiced forever. In short, modern Greek food is both of the past and the present.

While Greek cuisine has sometimes been thought of as heavy, in reality it is light and healthful. Greeks have the lowest rates of heart disease and cancer in Europe. Their food is always based on what has just come to the market and out of the meadows and sea. At the heart of the cuisine lie vegetables, salads, and fruits. Many meals are entirely vegetarian. Beyond that, the most common main offering is fish. Meat and poultry are eaten only occasionally, although with today's global tastes creeping in, that amount is increasing. Still, many Greek so prefer vegetables they shun meat entirely. The cooking medium and sauce base remain, as of old, health-promoting olive oil and always of the highest quality. Butter is rarely used, and, with the exception of yogurt, which comes so thick it looks like cheesecake, milk is rarely consumed. Countrywide, cow's, sheep's, and goat's milk are turned into regular and regional specialty cheeses. Greeks also employ a wide range of herbs, spices, and other flavorings. Some are well known, some idiosyncratic. They span a range from garlic cloves to geranium leaves, cinnamon to native grown *mastiha* or gum mastic, mountain wild sage to amuck chamomile, potent mint to pine resin.

The ancient Greeks divided their meals into two sections: the *siton* and the *poton*. The *siton* consisted of the filling grains that made up the lion's share of every repast, accompanied by *opson*, bits of flavorful enhancements such as small pieces of vegetables, meats, fish, poultry, or dollops of sauce. The *poton* was the drinking part of the meal that came after the main segment. The *poton*, however, was always squired by snacks. There stood a rule then as now in Greece that one does not drink without eating. Even today when friends get together for the favorite Greek aperitif, anise-flavored *ouzo*, small nibbles like olives, cheese cubes, little fried fish, and certainly bread grace the drinks.

Today's Greeks have two parts to their dining, as well as a very separate third, though the divisions are somewhat different than in earlier times. The main portion of Greek dining, served generally midday, consists of an array of differing plates of food presented all at once. Rather than featuring a single entree, or each person having their own serving, the table may well be topped with a bowl of soup, a platter of fried zucchini, a mound of garlic paste, a toss of radish-cucumber-olive-caper-feta salad, a heap of simmered greens, a red-sauced pasta, rice pilaf, olive-oil fried eggs, a collection of olives, and perhaps a single large grilled fish or roasted chicken for all to share. The various plates cover almost every nutritional element in a balanced diet and at the same time provide a wide span of flavors. Diners pick from each of the dishes as they like. Should the cook feel that the food is not sufficient, a plate of salt-tossed fried potatoes will be added.

Although the meal may be accompanied by wine or beer, it is always accompanied with the Greeks' time-honored water. As with much of the world, Greeks sometimes enjoy a drinking interlude before the evening meal. However, much as in ancient times, socializing and drinking generally occur in the late evening, sometimes before and sometimes after a late dinner, which is smaller than the midday meal. Though not so formal or gender exclusive as the ancient symposium, drinking together is an activity still much enjoyed in Greece both with extended family as in the villages or with what Greeks call *parea*, the company of friends. The foods that go with drinks are not appetizers per se, nor are they the first course of a meal as they now appear in many Greek restaurants, but a separate Greek category of taste treats that act as beverage sops and hunger appeasers. They are called *mezedes* or *oretakia* and are a renowned part of Greek fare. They consist of a far-famed set of spreads such as *tzatziki* (yogurt-cucumber-garlic), fish roe mixed with whipped potato, chopped and mingled or singularly smoothed eggplant, along with rice and pine-nut-stuffed grape leaves, herbed meatballs, toasted cheese cubes, peppers, or sausage slices.

Breakfast is consumed, but it is very casual and individual and not a collective meal. It generally consists of a coffee, some sliced cheese or tomatoes in season, a few olives, and perhaps Greece's twice baked hard toast, called *paximadi*, often dunked in the coffee. The classic dishes, along with all the new, creative takes, still make up the core of the cuisine. They include:

- *tyropita* (cheese pie);
- *spanakopita* (spinach pie);
- globally renowned fried *kalamari* (squid);
- tenderized octopus boiled, herbed, and oiled;
- feta cheese;
- village salad of tomatoes, cucumber, onion, olives, and capers;
- *avgolemono* (lemon-egg) soup;
- braised greens, or *horta*, the same word as in horticulture;
- *gemistes* (tomatoes and peppers stuffed with rice and sometimes rice and meat);
- *paidakia* (little lamb chops);
- *souvlaki* (skewers, or "swords," strung with chunks of meat, sometimes with onions and tomatoes between);
- *gyros*, spinning on stands around the world, is a vertical stack of lamb and herbs, thinly trimmed downward, lined in a pita bread with onion and tomatoes and topped with nippy *tzatziki*;
- spit roasted lamb, an Easter requisite, now served all year; and
- simple grilled fish merely sprinkled with lemon and oregano of which seabass, swordfish, and *barbounia* (Mediterranean red mullet) and other mullets, cod, breams, porgy, shark, grouper, sardines, and anchovies are favorites, along with shrimp, squid, cuttlefish, and octopus.

Beverages include delicate coffee made from powdered coffee grounds and boiled up three times in little-lipped vessels (one's fortunes can be read from the remaining grounds in the cup); *ouzo*, the clear anise- and spice-flavored liqueur that turns milky when ice is added; Metaxa-spiced brandy; and legendary sweet wines, *Vin Santo*, *Mavrodaphne*, *Samos*, and *Komandaria*. Aristotle asked for one as he lay dying.

The ancient Greeks believed that the person who cooked food was no different from the poet, and the Greeks today believe much the same. Greek food is poetry.

*Susanna M. Hoffman*

**Further Reading**

Anthimus. 1996. *On the Observance of Food*. Translated by M. Grant. Totnes, Devon: Prospect.

Archestratus. 1994. *The Life of Luxury*. Edited and translated by J. Wilkins and S. Hill. Totnes, Devon: Prospect.

Dalby, Andrew. 1996. *Siren Feats*. London: Routledge.

Hoffman, Susanna. 2000. "Glories of Greece." *Saveur* 131 (August/September): 60–64.

Hoffman, Susanna. 2004. *The Olive and The Caper: Adventures in Greek Cooking*. New York: Workman Publishers.

Lissarrague, Francois. 1998. *The Aesthetics of the Greek Banquet.* Princeton, NJ: Princeton University Press.

Psilakis, Michael. 2009. *How to Roast a Lamb: New Greek Classic Cooking.* New York: Little Brown.

## Filo Pies

Greek filo pies bask warm and irresistible under the glowing lights of street carts. Inviting towers of them stand in every bread shop window. They are triumphantly ferried through the swinging kitchen doors of bustling Greek *tavernas*. They appear on the dinner tables of every Greek city and village household. They are Greece's renowned savory filo pies, and they well deserve their lionized reputation. The tradition of pie making began early in ancient Greece. Purses of dough were packed with salty cheese, often commingled with honey. Eggs were sometimes added. The famous scribe Philoxenos in his fifth century BCE poem *Banquet* mentions that cheese and milk pies were served with the wine course. Such simple pies were so common, yet so esteemed, they were the only tribute the ever-capricious, hugely popular folk god Pan would accept at his shrines. Pan's pies were fitting, for the shepherds who comprised much of his "flock" had long taken dough pies to dine upon when at their faraway pastures.

On the bottom of each lies four to six to ten or more layers of flaky, tissue-thin filo dough, turned scrumptiously crisp with a brushing of olive oil. An equal number of dough sheets form their golden crown. In between lies an inch or two of zesty cheese, tender chunks of chicken, or bits of succulent lamb. Since time immemorial, the pies have also provided casement to a stunning array of seasonal vegetables: piquant spinach, mushrooms, leeks, fennel, squash, eggplant, onions, potato, even mere herbs like fennel—called *maratho* in Greek and which covered a field in which a famous battle took place ending in a much-copied run. To bring the pies to yet more mouth-watering heights, the fillings are often dotted with olives, capers, pine nuts, walnuts, and raisins; spiced with cinnamon, allspice, cardamom, or nutmeg; and brightened with fresh dill, mint, thyme, savory, marjoram, oregano. The pies are so scrumptious and satisfying, two of them, *tyropita* (cheese pie) and *spanakopita* (spinach pie), have followed Greeks to every corner of the world to become international favorites.

The fabulous pies of today were a development of Greek Byzantine times. Neither the early Greek's animal-driven quern mills nor the Roman's simple water ones could grind flour fine enough for delicate pastry. It was only the clever mechanics of Byzantium, pressed by the needs of a burgeoning population, that invented fully mechanized mills. They even invented a dough-mixing machine. The finer flour led to pastry balls that could be stretched to almost gossamer thinness. And stretch the Byzantine cooks did, until they, in their renowned culinary ingenuity and penchant for layering food in complex arrays, developed the filo pie.

Leeks have been one of the most adored and consumed vegetables in Greece for so long that their name, *prassa*, became the Greek word for the color green, *prasinos*. So commonplace were they in ancient times that the famed historian Herodotus considered them just a snack and not real food. Today they remain beloved, and filo pies filled with leeks are among the most popular dishes. Each district boasts a different version; this one is from lofty, northwest Epirus. (Photo by Susan Goldman)

They would stuff the pies with delightful fillings following a pre-established path. The ancient Greeks loved to mash foods into paste to wrap in leaves or bread. The Romans gloried in the art of stuffing food into food. They would place minced meat in a pigeon, the pigeon in duck, the duck in a pig, and the pig in a cow. The practice carried on to the Byzantine menu. One Byzantine pie recipe reads, "In pastry dough place quails split in half. Add saffron, nutmeg, white cheese, pine nuts, and pieces of fatted pork. Seal with more dough. When the pie is done, pour in muscat wine and bring to a boil." Chefs were so esteemed in the Byzantine realm (they were even released from taxes), they had liberty to fill their newly created pies with whatever they contrived, and they did.

Pies, as with other dishes, vary by region in Greece. The Byzantine habit of putting anything in a pie led to a wide variety of fillings that blossomed in every province, each diverging according to its own special products and produce. Thrace is known for its pork pies. Thracians also make pies of grated winter squash tossed with walnuts. Macedonian lamb pie features almonds, currants, orange, and mint. Thessaly is lauded for its *klostopites* filled with creamy *mizithra* cheese and either grilled eggplant or wild greens. Thessalians also tuck milk and noodles within crusts, thereby constructing crusted pasta pies. In one, ground meat and onions blend with sour noodles, *trahana*, to make the filling and once it is baked, chicken broth is poured over the pie. In Central Greece, cooks make three thick filo coils, one filled with leeks, one with cheese, and one with zucchini, then wind the three around a circular pan so that each cut wedge contains all the flavors. In Corfu, zucchini pies are stacked with tomatoes, hot peppers, and rice. Kefalonia anticipates Lent with pies that offer rice, spicy meat, garlic, lemon, potatoes, tomatoes, cheese, and hard-boiled eggs. As more daily fare, Kefalonians make pies of codfish and ones of feta and artichoke. As on all the other Ionian Islands, their pies always contain rice. The northern Aegean Islands relish leek pies and onion pies, often dressed out with raisins and nutmeg. In Samos, the pumpkin pies feature feta, onions, mint, and bulgur, and pies of spinach and snails are fashioned. Seafood pies are common in the Dodecanese Islands. On the treeless Cyclades, with little kindling available until the arrival of individual kitchen stoves, pies were often fried rather than baked. They continue in that tradition. In the past, when holidays approached, pies were baked communally in one giant oven with each woman bringing an armload of grape twigs to keep the fire going.

The pies of Epirus and Crete, though, are the most storied in all of Greece. Epirus is famous for its beef and veal pies made especially for holidays. These vie with seasonal ones of duck or rabbit ragout. Instead of filo, the people there sometimes top their pies

## BAKED WHITE FISH FILLETS WITH BLOOD ORANGE, SWEET WINE, AND BAY LEAF

This modern version of Greece's beloved fish is adorned with gatherings from the shore. The elements come from both the east and west of the land.

*Serves six.*

2–2½ pounds white fish fillets or steaks, such as swordfish, bass, or halibut, cut into 3- to 4-inch pieces
Fresh lemon juice
Salt
3 tablespoons olive oil
2 medium leeks, white and light green parts trimmed, well rinsed, and cut into 2-inch-long shreds
12 kumquats, sliced into thin rounds
1/3 cup Seville or blood orange juice
½ cup Mavrodaphne or light port wine
1 large or 2 small bay leaves, crumbled
2 tablespoons fresh chives
Freshly ground pepper

1. Place the fish pieces in one layer on a plate and sprinkle them liberally on both sides with lemon juice and salt. Cover and set in the refrigerator for 1–2 hours.
2. Preheat the oven to 450°F and transfer the fish to a large nonreactive baking dish and set aside.
3. Heat the oil in a medium-size nonreactive skillet over medium heat. Add the leeks and kumquats and stir until slightly wilted, 1–2 minutes.
4. Stir in the orange juice, wine, and bay leaf and bring to a boil. Cook over medium heat until the leeks and kumquats are well wilted, 2 minutes. Pour the sauce over the fish, spreading the leeks and kumquats out evenly.
5. Place the dish in the oven and bake until the liquid is bubbling, and the fish flakes easily when pierced with a fork, 15 minutes. Sprinkle the chives and some pepper over the top and serve right away.

*Susanna M. Hoffman*

with cornmeal crusts. The Cretans make a pie that is temptingly packed with liver, sweetbreads, or brain dusted with cinnamon. They pad filo disks with *manouri* cheese, not unlike ricotta salata, and top them with sesame seeds. Other times, they heap little filo boats with boiled egg, ham or sausage, and mushroom. Even more brilliant are their half-moon-shaped *kalitsounia* (calzones). Some are plumped with hard cheese, orange juice, and cinnamon; others are loaded with goat, oregano, and brandy, and served with yogurt; yet others hold shrimp and feta cheese; and some hold black-eye peas and macaroni. At times, bechamel sauce and custard surround the ingredients, and often they are fried as well as baked.

In both Epirus and Crete, as elsewhere in Greece, pies are also filled with what was the forerunner of today's spinach pie, that is, the wild greens gathered since ancient times. That includes dandelion, sorrel, mustard, rocket, endive, chicory, and the like, always intermingled with herbs and sharp cheese. Again, the filling is seasonal. An old Greek proverb says, "Chicken pie in January and duck at threshing time."

*Susanna M. Hoffman*

**See also:** Chapter 14: Regional and Seasonal Variations.

**Further Reading**

Karatassos, Pano. 2018. *Modern Greek Cooking: 100 Recipes for Mezes, Entrees, and Desserts.* New York: Rizzoli.

## Fruits and Desserts

"Every fruit is good to eat," said Xenophon in the fifth century BCE. The fruit of Greece is indescribably divine, enhanced and ripened by the Aegean sun. Even in ancient times, the Greeks knew what a treasure they held in the melons, berries, drupes, citrons, pods, and venerated rosacaea pomes that flourished on their land, and still today they interweave that bounty into their healthful diet and glorious cuisine. Many of the fruits Greeks relish are native to their country or had already migrated to Greece's sunny shores before the earliest Greeks arrived. Wild strawberries, wild grapes, sorbs, and medlar are indigenous to Greece. The Greek name for their native carob fruit, *keras*, gives jewelers their "carat" weight. Melons came early from Egypt, mulberries from the Caucasus, apples from the Tigris-Euphrates. Peaches and apricots traveled along the Silk Route from China. We echo the Greek name for summer early-ripening apricots in classic Greek *praikokion* and modern Greek *verikoko*, meaning "early ripening" in the word "precocious." The Minoans probably introduced quince. Cherries, pears, and figs came from the original Greek homeland west of the Ural Mountains. Plums were found as Greeks explored the Pontos region bordering the Black Sea. The English name for Arabian dates comes from the Greek *daktilos*, meaning "finger," and refers to the way the fruit hangs on the tree. The pomegranate, that rosy jewel of autumn, first grew in Central Asia but spread to the Eastern Mediterranean early on. To the ancient Greeks, it was the fruit of legend and fertility, the fateful nibble Persephone munched on her way back to daylight. To this day Greek grooms and brides smash a pomegranate on the doorstep of their first home. Alexander the Great found citron in India. Later Arabs brought lemons and oranges. Greeks today have added banana, pineapple, kiwi, kumquat, and prickly pear.

Orchards were planted and carefully tended by the Greeks as far back as Homer's day. He describes them as having pomegranate, pear, apple, fig, and grape. The great judge Solon prescribed that a newly married couple should eat a quince together so that their conversation would always be sweet. Fruit remains abundant in Greece; vendors peddle it everywhere from outdoor stands and thread their way through street and village calling out the day's offerings. The fruit of Greece is always tree and vine ripened to full maturity, never plucked early. As the ancients knew exactly which area the best of fruit came from, so do the Greeks today. The finest apples, they say, come from Mount Pelion, the apricots from Naoussa, the figs from Kalamata, the oranges from Missolonghi, and the plums from Skopelos. Yellow, white, cling, and freestone peaches come from the Peloponnesus.

In ancient times, Greeks ended their meal with trays of fruit and nuts served all around. To this day, Greeks always end their repast with a piece of fresh fruit. To leave the table with a taste of nature's own dessert is to praise mother earth for all she provides. Whatever the seasonal fruit, it is washed, pared, and placed upon a plate whole—accompanied by paring knifes or sliced. Even in restaurants, customers order fruit as their finale. At late evening gatherings, fresh fruit is yet again the refreshment, although in Corfu that nocturnal treat might be a mix of black olives and orange slices.

Greeks also cook their copious fruit. Among their most sublime traditional dishes are a stew of quince and pork as well as quince with pot roast or chicken. Whole quince are also stuffed with meats and grains. Meat casseroles and meatballs are paired with prunes. Plump sausage is zested with orange. Lemon is squeezed on fish, baked on chicken, and is one of the two eponymous ingredients in Greece's most famous sauce, *avgolemono*. The ancients also stuffed fruit leaves, in particular fig, mulberry, and grape, as the Greeks do today when preparing dolmades.

With sugar not yet known, next to honey, fruit became the second most common base for sweetening in ancient Greece, reduced into a syrup called *syraion* and *epsima*. The most common fruit reduced was grape, but quince and other fruits were also simmered down to an almost molasses consistency. Greeks still use fruit reductions as sweetener today, now called *petimezi*, and the most usual fruit continues to be grape. The reduction makes a wonderful glaze and sauce for meats, poultry, and even seafood. And of course, Greeks' signature use of fruit appeared—the dulcet preserves called "spoon sweets." Greeks also savor dried fruit. Dried raisins and currants sparkle in stuffings for tomatoes, eggplant, and peppers, are added to rabbit stew, and eaten as snacks. In the villages, they parch figs, whole and also opened up and layered with sesame, in beehive ovens. They spread grapes to sun-dry into

Greece has more beehives than any other nation in Europe, all seated upon one of the richest floral and herb carpets in existence. Like the many olives from Spata, Kalamata, Phthiotis, Crete, Macedonia, and Thrace, each district of Greece produces its own revered variety of honey from its crocus, larkspur, sage, or Hymettus thyme blossoms. The various wines of Greece also have their own unique flavor. Adding pine resin to the retsina wine of Central Greece produces a spectacular, tangy libation. (Photo by Susan Goldman)

raisins on roof tops, then bake them in holiday breads. Fruit is pickled as well, especially quince and watermelon rind. Greeks also sometimes use the fresh or dried peels of fruits as flavoring.

Increasingly, fruit shows up in the exquisite innovations of contemporary Greek cooks in today's stellar Greek restaurants. Chefs top white fish with kumquat, ply duck with *ouzo* and oranges, and simmer pears in chamomile and Samos white wine syrup. Products featuring Greece's incredible fruit, from spoon sweets and on, are available at gourmet markets, and any cook can explore the time-honored fruited dishes of Greece, from salad, to entree, to confection. In ancient Greece, fruit was stored in cool rooms called *oporothikoi*. Today, they are bought in stores called *apothikoi*. From both comes the word "apothecary."

An important part of today's Greek fare, and the third part of Greek dining, is the sweets, or one could say "desserts." The serving of sweets takes place entirely apart from the main meal. It does not follow it. The main meal always ends with fresh fruit. Fruit of all sorts and seasons is idolized by Greeks, and they eat numerous pieces a day. The sweet treats of Greece are eaten as a late afternoon indulgence or sweet-tooth satisfier well into the evening. They include such illustrious Greek classics as *baklava*, *kadaifi*, and fried honey-drizzled dough balls called *loukoumades*, but also rice pudding, ice cream, and a wide variety of cakes made with nuts, semolina, chocolate, and vanilla. They are often accompanied by a tiny cup of Greek coffee and, again, always a glass of sacred water.

Greece's celebrated syrupy preserves of fruit, runnier than jams, are served on spoons accompanied by a glass of water, exclusively as a hospitality offering presented to home visitors. Spoon sweets are made of cherry, apricot, citrus rind, grape, and other foodstuffs. Should the guests be numerous, there are even cut crystal bowls surrounded by silver circlets of spoons from which to serve the sweet. The most famous spoon sweet is made of quince flavored with rose geranium.

*Susanna M. Hoffman*

**See also:** Chapter 15: Bars and Nightlife.

**Further Reading**

Mintz, Sidney. 1985. *Sweetness and Power: The Place of Sugar in Modern History.* New York: Penguin.

## Honey

Far earlier than their olive oil and long before they grew grapes for wine, Greeks fell in love with honey. The love affair has lasted for six thousand years. From ancient times until today, Greeks have produced some of the best honey in the world. To taste Greek honey, whether from Crete, the Peloponnesus, Thassos, Epirus, any of a thousand islands, or from historically the most praised site of all, Mount Hymettos in Attica, is to fall into that same adulation. In modern times, Greek honey continues to enjoy the same high regard as it always has. Try, for example, the honey from pine needles from rocky, mountainous Arcadia.

Honey was the first, and for quite a while the only, sweetener ancient Greeks had in their diet. Even now, it remains the most prestigious one. With its importance from ancient times, honey, along with the olive and the grape, marked the beginning of Greek gastronomy and a cuisine that retains its unique and original aspects even today. Early Greeks very quickly began to lure bees away from logs and crevices in the wild into man-made habitats. With the bee ensnared, they no longer had to forage for honey; they could plunder it at will. The Greeks learned the trick of beekeeping probably from the prior occupants of the land, the Minoans. An intact beehive was found in the Akrotiri ruins and one of the Minoans' most important goddesses was called the "Queen of the Bees." Echoing that, in the later Greek pantheon, Artemis, the goddess most associated with animals, had the bee as her symbol. The first beehives the Greeks manufactured replicated the sort of burrow bees swarm to in nature. Soon, however, they began to make hives of hollowed-out mud and, shortly after, dome-shaped ones of clay. Very early, by about 800 BCE, Greek beekeepers came up with a stunning innovation, one that is essentially still used around the world today: they developed hives that contained removable bars to hold numerous honeycombs. The bars, single combs and their store of golden liquid, could be extracted, leaving others behind for later gleaning. The bars with their separate honeycombs could also be used to start new hives. With this innovation, beekeeping so rapidly proliferated in Greece that regulations had to be enacted to restrict overstocking.

Then as now, Greek honey was produced in such varieties and quality that there were numerous grades of it. Like wine, it was rated by place of origin and specific characteristics, a system that is still used today. Aristotle declared Attica honey the best, followed by that from Salamis. Archestratos, the renowned food writer, waxed lyrical over Attica honey as well, especially over cakes soaked in it. Cheesecakes sweetened with honey are still found all over the Greek islands, especially at Easter. The chefs of Byzantium simmered Greek honey to pour over their famous layered sweets, *baklava*, *galaktoboureko* (semolina custard and filo), *kadaifi*, and the fried doughnutlike puffs, *loukoumades*. All remain savored in today's Greek kitchen. Byzantine cooks also continued the ancient practice of mixing honey with vinegar, the *oximeli* of old, and today such sweet-and-sour flavors are enjoying a resurgence in the

## A NOUVEAU CHICKEN *KAPAMA*

*Serves six to eight*

This is a modern take on a traditional Corfu dish that still uses honey.

3 tablespoons olive oil
1 large frying chicken (about 4–5 pounds), cut up
1 large onion, quartered and thinly sliced
1½ tablespoons tomato paste
1½ cups dry red wine
3 medium (12 ounces) tomatoes, coarsely chopped
3 tablespoons Metaxa or other brandy
1/3 cup strong-brewed Greek or other coffee
3 tablespoons honey
2-inch piece cinnamon stick, broken in half
3 whole cloves
2 bay leaves
1 teaspoon salt
1/2 teaspoon black pepper
1½ cups tender watercress or basil sprigs (optional)

1. Heat the oil in a nonreactive pan until it begins to smoke. Add the chicken pieces and sauté over medium-high heat until browned all around, about 5 minutes. Continue until all the chicken pieces are browned, and transfer chicken to bowl.

2. Add the onions to the pot and stir over medium-high heat until well-coated, about 1 minute. Stir in the tomato paste and wine and bring to a boil. Add the remaining ingredients, along with the chicken and any collected juices, and stir to mix. Bring to a boil, then reduce the heat to a simmer. Cover the pot and cook over medium-low heat for 45 minutes to 1 hour, until the chicken is tender, and the liquid is reduced but not thick.

3. Remove the cover and continue simmering for 35–40 minutes more, until the meat is tender and the liquid thick and glossy. Let rest for 10 minutes before serving.

4. Transfer the chicken to a serving platter. Remove the cinnamon stick, cloves, and bay leaves and pour the sauce over the chicken. Garnish with the watercress and serve.

*Susanna M. Hoffman*

contemporary kitchen. Honey and true, deliciously sour Greek yogurt are all-time classic desserts. In cooking, honey adds flavor in a way other sugars cannot. Along with sweetness, it bequeaths the savor of the original flowers, herbs, and even trees. Greek cooks well recognize this, which is why honey still plays a major role in Greek cuisine. It is utilized not just in desserts but often as an element in classic stews, such as rabbit *stifado* and the intriguing *kapama* from Corfu. In Crete, it is sometimes used as a marinade and tenderizer for lamb and added to various meat stews at the end, simmered until it caramelizes. Contemporary chefs also mix it with raisin vinegar and orange juice and use it as a sauce for everything from seafood to salads.

*Susanna M. Hoffman*

**See also:** Chapter 14: Filo Pies. Glossary: *Baklava*; *Loukoumades*.

**Further Reading**

Archestratus. 1994. *The Life of Luxury.* Edited and translated by J. Wilkins and S. Hill. Totnes, Devon: Prospect.

Brothwell, Don, and Patricia Brothwell. 1969. *Food in Antiquity: A Survey of the Diet of Early Peoples.* Baltimore: The Johns Hopkins University Press.

## *Mezedes* and Wine

There are definite standout and unique features to the Greek cuisine. The first is the famous *meze*, or appetizer/small dish tradition, and with it, beside water, Greece's illustrious beverage, wine. *Mezedes*, which means "little middles" from the Italian, and wine are also the cuisine's celebration and party foods, and no one knows how to throw an hors d' oeuvre and wine party better than the Greeks. They have been doing it for six thousand years. In ancient days when celebrating, the tidbits were called *oretakia*, from *orexi*, meaning appetite, guests reclined on banquet couches and nibbled on roasted chickpeas, fried cheesecakes, shellfish, snails wrapped in leaves, and honey-dipped sorbs. Today's *mezedes* can include spreads such *tzatziki* (yogurt-cucumber-garlic), *taramasalata* (fish roe mixed with whipped potato), *melitzanosalata* (chopped and mingled or singularly smoothed eggplant), and treats such as rice and pine-nut-stuffed grape leaves, herbed meatballs, toasted cheese cubes, peppers, or sausage slices.

To go with each bite, ancient Greeks drank wines that were already so distinguished the casks, or amphora, were labeled, as with today's wine bottles, with place of origin and vintage date. Greek wines remain an object of great pride. Rather overlooked in modern times as other nations' wines gained repute, more recently the truly stellar contemporary wines of Greece have become the talk of wine connoisseurs. Pressed from often indigenous grapes or blended with more recognized international varietals, today's outstanding Greek wines combine age-old cultivation and knowledge with modern techniques and tastes. Greece did not suffer from the devastating grape disease phylloxera as did other European countries, so some of the grape types go back hundreds if not thousands of years. More and more are being unearthed in small, local, long-hidden villages today. They range from the *Agiorgitico* (little Saint George) of Nemea, the *Xinomavro* (sour black) of Macedonia, the grey skinned grape *Moschofilero* from the northeast corner of the Peloponnesus, to the volcanic *Asyrtiko* (meaning from the earth itself), and sweet *Vin Santo* of Santorini to smaller, highly specialized Peloponnesian wines like *Kydonitsa* (quince like), *Malagousia*, *Roditis*, *Savatiano*, *Limniona*, *Liatica*, and *Mandilari* as well as the ambrosial muscats of Samos and Spina.

*Susanna M. Hoffman*

**See also:** Chapter 15: Bars and Nightlife.

**Further Reading**

*Amphora and the Ancient Wine Trade*. 1979. Princeton, NJ: American School of Classical Studies at Athens.

Hoffman, Susanna. 2006. "Making a Meze." *Bon Appetit* 51, no. 6 (June): 113–119.

Hoffman, Susanna. 2008. "Small Plates, Perfect for Entertaining." *Fine Cooking* 93 (June/July): 63–67.

Manessis, Nico. 2000. *The Illustrated Greek Wine Book*. Corfu: Olive Press Publications.

## Regional and Seasonal Variations

Regional variation exists, particularly in the foods and dishes from the stony northern Peloponnesus to those of the breadbasket expanse of Thessaly; the austere, yet sunny Mani to chilly Epirus; the verdant expanse of Macedonia to multifaceted Crete; the Italian-influenced Ionian Islands compared to the Turkish-flirting Dodecanese or Aegean-encircled Cyclades. One of the splendors of Greek cuisine is how each district of the country features foods particular to the area. Rugged Epirus is known for its hearty pies, lamb stews, and river eel. Opulent Macedonia still produces the wines that Alexander tippled, along with spicy broad beans, wild hare, hot peppers, and a distinct syrup cake. As its capitol, Thessaloniki once held the world's largest Jewish population and dishes there reflected Romiotic and Sephardic influence. Cool Thrace, with the Roman highway running through, continues to offer the barley pilafs and the sour milk noodles of the early Greeks.

Thessaly in Central Greece houses magnificent Orthodox monasteries and proffers unique delicacies commemorating numerous saints' days. The Pindos Mountains are known for their steak-size mushrooms. Halkidiki's triple peninsula, with its ancient copper mines, features legendary crops of chestnuts, walnuts, and hazelnuts. In Sterea Ellas, home to Oedipus's cave and Lord Byron's battle camp, everything from periwinkles to the spit-roasted lamb are found. In Attica, fabled with its vibrant metropolis Athens, one can sample the amazing succulent creations of acclaimed contemporary chefs, tanged with Hymettus lavender and honey. The northern Peloponnesus, from the Argolid where the Myceneans flourished and Jason's Argonauts set sail to Arcadia where the god Pan ruled, features roast goat, rustic bread, and incredible honey made from pine needles. The southern half of the Peloponnesus contains celebrated Sparta replete with silvery olive groves and citrus fruit, with the lemons waiting to be used in egg and lemon sauces. The Ionian Islands are the source of Zante currents. Corfu, once British occupied, offers wine-stewed birds as well as kumquats for English-style marmalade. The British brought the kumquats in for landscaping, but the Greeks turned them into jam and a flavoring for fish. Odysseus's wife Penelope on nearby Ithaca served swan. The Northern Aegean and Dodecanese Islands, skirting Turkey and fortress to Crusaders, provide cinnamon chestnuts, unique teardrop mastic, fish stuffed with raisins, and walnut sauce reminiscent of Croesus's neighboring Lydia. Crete, palimpsest of history and eco zones, blossoms with a botany of greens, including purslane, chicory, and dandelion. Its illustrious pies of half-moon shaped snail, meats, and cheese reiterate the shape of the lozenges so enjoyed by Arab conquerors. Every region of Greece turns out ambrosial cheeses that vary from chunky curd to silken.

All Greek cuisine is unfailingly seasonal. No true Greek salad would feature tomatoes in January. In early winter, the main component of the salad toss is radish, then cabbage, then lettuce—which is also turned into lettuce croquettes. Tomatoes do not come into the salad until sun ripened in June. Kazantzakis, the great Greek writer of *Zorba*, would never give a peach to American poet T. S. Eliot before July.

Not only has Greece's regionalism given life to different subsets of Greek cuisine, but it has imbued Greeks with a strong sense of local identity and pride. A Greek met in any part of the globe will tell from exactly which part of country they originate.

*Susanna M. Hoffman*

**See also:** Chapter 5: Greek Orthodox Regional Celebrations. Chapter 14: Filo Pies.

**Further Reading**

Calombaris, George. 2009. *Greek Cookery from the Hellenic Heart.* Sydney: New Holland Publishers

Eden, Esin, and Nikolas Stavroulakis. 1997. *Salonika: A Family Cookbook.* Athens: Talos Press.

Milona, Marianthi, ed. 2008. *Culinaria Greece: Greek Specialties.* Cambridge: Tamden Verlag.

Stavrolakis, Nikolas. 1996. *Cookbook of the Jewish Greeks.* Athens: Lycabettus.

Sutton, David E. 2014. *Secrets from the Greek Kitchen.* Oakland: University of California Press.

CHAPTER 15

# LEISURE AND SPORTS

## OVERVIEW

Modern Greece's pastime happenings range from the celebratory and religious to the competitive and avant-garde. They include world-class sporting traditions, festivals, and carefree leisure activities, such as getting together with a group of friends. Contemporary events draw inspiration from the epic poetry, performance, dance, and sports of ancient Greece.

The Athens and Epidaurus Festival in July revisits Greek tragedies performed by brilliant actors of the day while featuring modern-day musicians, actors, and comedians.

*Apokreas*, one of the major festivals, might have its origins in the ancient festival in honor of the Greek god Dionysus. For three weeks before Greek Orthodox Easter, it is celebrated simultaneously in island and mountain villages, as well as in cities like Patras and in the Plaka area of Athens. The masquerade balls and parades create an exuberant atmosphere comparable to that of Mardi Gras in the United States. At the end of May, the Hadjipetria Festival in Trikala in northwestern Thessaly showcases lectures, national dances, and athletic contests.

Vibrant social affairs, like festivals, impart a feeling of commonality and well-being. But in terms of Greek daily life, *parea* is the most important. Tight-knit groups of confidants, known as *parea*, regularly meet up over coffee and sustenance to explore ideas, catch up on people's lives, and partake in cheerful repartee. Often unmarried and unrelated youths, simulating a second family, find common ground when it comes to a preference for a life of reflection and fun. In the warmer months, Greeks delight in late-night suppers shared with friends and family at outdoor *tavernas* and restaurants.

Serving as quintessential gathering places, *kafenia* (Greek coffeehouses) are designated as "men-only" hubs. These ubiquitous coffeehouses feature Greek coffee, which is boiled in a *briki* (a tapered kettle) and served with fine grounds in demitasse cups. The coffee is prepared either *sketos* (unsweetened) or *glykos* (sweet) and is accompanied by a glass of cold water and cookies. Frappes (a coffee blend of instant coffee, usually Nescafe) are also in demand. Also served are *meze* (light Greek appetizers) such as grilled octopus, *kolokythakia* (fried zucchini), *tiropita* (feta cheese pastry), and *spanakopita* (spinach and feta pastry), to say nothing of *ouzo*, *retsina*, and beer. These social centers are regarded as a cornerstone of village and island life. In the evening,

*Komboloi* (worry beads), on display in the Plaka neighborhood of Athens, are made of a variety of materials, including amber, metal, glass, wood, and semiprecious stone. When set in motion by the thumb and fingers, the *komboloi* relieves tension and creates a pleasurable meditative experience. (Photo by Alexander Fatouros)

men clutch *komboloi* (worry beads), play cards, relax, and catch up on local news.

After guests have enjoyed their Greek coffee, some of them turn their cups upside down to dry. The grounds that remain are read as part of a fortune-telling practice that dates back centuries. The handed-down tradition of interpreting symbols in coffee readings embolden coffee enthusiasts with spiritual guidance and offer reflection for personal growth.

In larger towns and cities, bars and cafeterias supersede the *kafenia* to accommodate both men and women. Most Greeks take a midday siesta; thus, they can party into the wee hours of the night. Greece offers a variety of vivid nightlife venues that spotlight the musical beats of jazz, hip-hop, and *rebetika*.

Games of chance—from card games played at the local *kafenio* to high-stakes poker and roulette at one of Greece's eight casinos—still excite to this day. A "Throw of Aphrodite," or a roll of two sixes, would win today as it did in Greece's ancient past. Equipped with forty tables and over two hundred slot machines, Casino Rio in Patras welcomes players with a penchant for luck and skill from all corners. Vendors promote the lottery on the streets of the big cities, and official lottery retailers offer instant scratch-off tickets and the popular 6/49 Lotto.

While pilgrimages to ancestral homes are common around major holidays, the desire to purchase second homes near seashores is rising in popularity. Greece's 9,333.61 miles of coastline and nearly 10,000 islands and islets make the sea accessible, and Greeks take advantage of a Mediterranean climate that ranges from mild winters to dry, hot summers. Greeks savor sea sport activities. Beach outings complete with salt-water swimming are in vogue among twenty-first-century Greek city dwellers looking for tranquility and quietude within reach. Time-sensitive urbanities in search of a nearby paradise opt for the "Athens Riviera," which follows the coastline from the south of Athens to Cape Sounion. Two popular excursions are the

This *periptero* (kiosk), just off Syntagma Square in Athens, brims with souvenirs, candy, soft drinks, newspapers, magazines, postcards, tobacco, water, and phone cards. These iconic commerce centers can be found throughout Greece, in remote villages as well as seaside resorts, where they add sandbox toys and beach towels to their dizzying array of merchandise. The revered *periptero*, an essential part of the Greek way of life, has been around for more than a hundred years. (Photo by Alexander Fatouros)

ancient ruins of the Temple of Poseidon at Cape Sounion and Athens's sophisticated suburban Asteras and Vouliagmeni Beaches. Other popular excursions for Athenians are to the nearby islands of Aegina, Angistri, Hydra, Poros, Spetses, and Kythnos, which are easily accessed from the port of Piraeus. Near Thessaloniki, the coastlines in Halkidiki offer bathers the opportunity to discover distinct retreats, such as the sandy and family-friendly Epanomi Beach. Family-run *periptera* (kiosks), commerce centers packed with beach buckets, sandbox toys, candy, newspapers, magazines, and cigarettes, dot the seaboard.

Adrenaline-rush aficionados enjoy water polo, yacht sailing, jet skiing, deep-sea scuba and sea-caves diving, kite and wind surfing. Competitive sailors participate in the Cyclades Regatta, International Aegean Sailing Rally, Cretan Cup, or Rhodes Cup. More leisurely pursuits include paddle boarding, fishing, boating, snorkeling, swimming, or just hanging out at the beach.

Leisure sports activities span the four seasons. Downhill skiers and snowboarders can choose from several high-elevation resorts. Located two hours from Athens at an altitude of 7,415 feet or 2,260 meters, Mountain Parnassos is the largest and most popular ski resort boasting thirteen ski and chair lifts and twenty-three ski runs. Named after Greek mythological heroes—Aphrodite, Odysseus, Hermes, and Hera—the ski trails and ski runs range from beginner to difficult. Other well-known snow sanctuaries include Kalmaktsaian Ski Resort, nicknamed "Winter Mykonos," Kalavrita Ski Resort at Mr. Helmos, Mainalo Ski Resort, Pigadia Ski Resort, Vassilitsa Ski Resort, and the Elatochori Ski Centers at Mount Olympus.

Greeks enjoy playing competitive sports and are passionate about their favorite sport, soccer. Sports stadiums are packed, and Greeks congregate at local *tavernas* to watch their favorite teams on television. Fourteen soccer teams compete in the top-division Super League Greece, which was formed in 2006, replacing Alpha Ethniki as the official Greek professional football league system. First National Division Tier Piraeus-based Olympiacos and Athens-based Panathinaikos are Greek Super League teams with the biggest following. Both national division clubs achieved the top thirty of all-time European Cup/UEFA Championships League ranking. Olympiacos holds the most championships with forty-five titles.

Originating in 1908, Panathinaikos F.C. is the most victorious when it comes to European competitions; they made the 1971 European Cup finals. Nationally, the team won twenty Greek Championship titles from 1930 to 2010; eighteen Cups from 1940 to 2014; and four Super Cups from 1970 to 1994 (Football Bible 2014).

Consisting of twelve teams, Super League Greece 2 is part of the second-level professional division. In 2019, the Third National Division emerged. Football League Greece is composed of nineteen clubs, the third highest professional football league. The Greek Football Cup is a soccer competition that brings together teams from various divisions.

With forty-two Greek Championships (1931–2015) and twenty-six Hellenic Cup trophies, Olympiacos F.C. won seven successive league titles from 1996 to 2003. The team plays at Karaiskakis Stadium, which was built in 1895. The arena can accommodate 33,334 fans and houses world-class athletes for many international competitions to this day. The opening and closing ceremonies of the 2004 Athens Olympics took place at the Piraeus port stadium. The renovations were completed at zero hour.

The Greek national football team *Ethniki Ellados* won the UEFA European championship finals in 2004 against Portugal, qualifying for the 2005 FIFA Confederations Cup. The unprecedented victory cemented Greece as a formidable team globally. In 2010, the team wrapped up the FIFA South African World Cup competition with third place.

While soccer is Greece's number one sport in terms of popularity and sheer numbers of fans attending games, basketball comes in as a close second. Greek men's professional basketball clubs, composed of nearly fifty teams, have taken first prize in seventeen European championships, including two World-Cup championships and nine at the first-tier Euro League level. A win by the Greek national team at the 1987 FIBA EuroBasket competition revitalized the Greek national basketball team and brought on dancing and celebration in the host city of Piraeus (port of Athens).

## GIANNIS ANTETOKOUNMPO, WORLD-FAMOUS BASKETBALL SUPERSTAR

Named the National Basketball Association's (NBA) most valuable player in June 2019, Giannis Antetokounmpo is a Greek national sports hero with an international fan base. He stands at six feet eleven and is nicknamed "The Greek Freak." Greek coach Spiros Velliniatis discovered Antetokounmpo when he was thirteen at a playground in Sepolia, the rough-around-edges Athens neighborhood. The Milwaukee Bucks of the NBA drafted nineteen-year-old Giannis in 2013.

Antetokounmpo has four brothers. Older brother Thanasis plays for the Milwaukee Bucks and Kostas for the Los Angeles Lakers. Alex, the youngest, was signed in 2021 by the Sacramento Kings. Soccer player (footballer) Francis is the oldest. The brothers played on teams at an Athens professional basketball club, Filathlitikos, as youths.

The Sepolia Cafe opposite the basketball court where Giannis and his brothers first played is a favorite Antetokounmpo stomping ground. Greek street artist Same84 painted a mega mural of Giannis's likeness in 2017 as part of a project sponsored by Nike. A recent addition to the mural reads, "We can't breathe." It was a response to police violence experienced by blacks in Athens, as well as in other parts of the world. Antetokounmpo is an advocate for the Black Lives Matter (BLM) movement, which was organized in the wake of the unjustified killing of American George Floyd. Using his platform on social media and later though peaceful protests, Antetokounmpo has teamed up with people worldwide calling for the end to systemic racism and police brutality.

*Alexander Fatouros*

The top-ranked Greek Basket League, composed of fourteen teams, is consistently ranked highly in European basketball. Greece has won the gold medal at the FIBA EuroBasket in 2005 and the bronze at FIBA EuroBasket in 2009. It triumphed over the previously undefeated United States at the FIBA world championship semifinals in 2006.

Founded in 1922, Aris Basketball (*Aris Thessaloniki*) is part of multisports club, Athletic Club Aris Thessaloniki. The ancient Greek God of War, Ares, served as inspiration when Athletic Club Aris was founded in 1914. Today, the club sustains professional programs in football, volleyball, water polo, baseball, and ice hockey. Named after Alexander the Great, Alexandro Mellotron Nikos Galis Hall, also known as the Palais des Sports, is the home stadium. Aris Basketball's domestic highlights include ten Greek-Cup victories, eight of which were in a row (1984 through 1991) and ten Greek Basket League wins. It won the 2002–2003 FIBA Euro-Cup Challenge.

Nikos Galis and Panagiotis Giannakis "The Dragon," celebrated figures in Greek basketball, positioned Aris on a winning trajectory during the 1980s and 1990s. Giannis Antetokounmpo, a Greek national of Nigerian descent, played for Greek second-tier basketball league Filathlitikos from 2012 to 2013, before signing on to play for an American team, the Milwaukee Bucks of the National Basketball Association.

*Alexander Fatouros*

**Further Reading**

Football Bible. 2014. "Greek Football." Accessed August 30, 2017. https://www.football-bible.com/soccer-info/greece-football.html.

Hadjidimitriou, Jelly. 1997. *39 Coffee-Houses and One Barber Shop*. Athens: Crete University Press. Accessed November 27, 2017. http://www.explorecrete.com/books/coffee-houses-hadjidimitriou.html.

Leontis, Artemis. 2009. *Culture and Customs of Greece*. Westport, CT: Greenwood Press.

"Olympiacos and Panathinaikos Included in Top 30 of All Time UEFA Champions League Ranking." *Greek City Times*, December 27, 2019. Accessed: January 9, 2021. https://greekcitytimes.com/2019/12/27/olympiacos-and-panathinaikos-included-in-top-30-of-all-time-uefa-champions-league-ranking/.

Van Dyck, Karen, ed. 1988. *Insights Guides: Greece*, 2nd edition. Singapore: APA publication, LTD.

## 2004 Athens Olympic Games and World Championship Games

From August 13 through August 29, the 2004 Summer Olympic Games were held in the capital city of Greece, Athens. More than 10,625 athletes, including 4,329 women and 6,296 men from 200 countries, along with 201 National Olympic Committees (NOCs) descended upon the host city to compete in 301 medal events in 28 distinct sports. Numerous world and Olympic records were broken.

Covering 301 competitive event programs, the 2004 Athens Olympic Games surpassed Sydney 2000 as the most popular; 3.9 billion spectators accessed the Olympic Games by television. Unforgettable moments include Michael Phelps's unprecedented win of eight medals (six gold, two bronze) for the United States in swimming and Gal Fridman's gold medal win in windsurfing for Israel, the country's first-ever gold victory.

Originating in Olympia, Greece, in 776 BCE, the Olympic Games are steeped in mystical reverence and ambitious spirit. Conflicts among city-states would end during this sacred time to allow for safe passage of athletes. A triumphant athlete would be awarded a simple olive-branch wreath. Champions were celebrated at public gatherings with songs performed on the flute and lyre.

The tradition of competitive sport continued in modern Greece. In 1896, Athens held the first modern rebirth of the ancient games, reviving the glory of the event that was held every four years. Participants in the 1896 Marathon ran to Panathenaic Stadium in Athens from Marathon, Greece, at a distance of approximately twenty-six miles. The Greek water carrier Spiridon Lewis brought glory to his country by winning this marathon. The turn-of-the-century revival inspired the formation of the 1902 Tour De Paris Marathon and the 1897 Boston Marathon.

Appropriately titled "Welcome Home," the Athens's motto was also dubbed the "Dream Games" by International Olympic Committee (IOC) president Jacques Rogge. Gianna Angelopoulos-Daskalaki, former Harvard University John F. Kennedy School of Government vice chairperson and former Parliament member, organized and implemented many aspects of the highly successful 2004 Athens Summer Games. She was the first woman to be at the helm of an Olympic organizing committee in over a century.

Preparation for the 2004 Athens Summer Olympic Games began soon after IOC selected Athens in 1997 over Rome, Italy. However, the sports complex was completed at the last possible moment. Spyros Kaprolos, the chief of the Hellenic Olympic Committee, estimated the cost to be around 8 billion euros.

Greece did well in the 2004 Olympics. With an unprecedented medal tally of six gold, six silver, and four bronzes, Greece had broken its all-time record. This feat had not been accomplished since the original 1896 revival games. United States, China, and Russia rounded out the top three.

Men's half middleweight Illias Iliadis brought Greece its first-ever gold medal for judo. Men's heavyweight Alexandros Nikolaidis and women's middleweight Elisavet Mystakidou were each awarded silver medals. The rowing competition for men's lightweight double sculls yielded a bronze medal each for rowers Vasileios Polymeros and Nikolaos Skiathitis. Greece attained a silver medal in men's sailboard in the sailing competition thanks to Nikolaos Kaklamanakis. In the Greco-Roman wrestling arena, Ariom Kiouregkian brought about a bronze for Greece in men's bantamweight. Pyrros Dimas won a bronze medal for men's light heavyweight in weightlifting. In gymnastics, a gold medal was awarded to Dimosthenis Tampakos for men's rings in the Artistic program. Thomas Bimis and Nikolaos Siranidis were awarded the gold prize for men's synchronized three-meter springboard (Olympic Games 2004). The women's water polo team secured the silver medal.

In the women's 400-meter hurdles, Greek Olympian Fani Chalkia not only set an Olympic record of 52.77 seconds in the semifinals but also won Olympic gold in front of her home crowd. "The Greek soul is enough by itself. We don't need anything else. We are born winners," expounded Chalkia to a reporter (CNN 2004). Athanasia Tsoumeleka won a gold medal in the women's 20-kilometer walk road competition. Anastasia Kelesidou brought silver home for women's discus throw. Mirela Manjani won bronze for the women's javelin throw. In sailing, Sofia Bekatorou and Aimilia Tsoulfa took top honors and gold medals in the women's 470 class.

Greece's final medal tally positioned the host country in fifteenth place out of two hundred countries. The Greek public celebrated their athletes, just as they did at the Olympic events thousands of years ago. At the ceremony where Greek athletes were awarded wreaths and medals, roaring fans sang the national anthem, *Ymnos eis tin Eleftherian* (Hymm to Liberty) and shouted "Hellas, Hellas!"

The Athens Olympic Complex consists of five venues and is outfitted with facilities that accommodate public and private events to this day. The Nikos Galis Olympic

Indoor Hall is used for basketball matches, gymnastics, and singing contests. The Athens Olympic Velodrome, located in Marousi, seats 5,250. During the Athens games, 3,330 seats were made available. Made of Afzelia wood, the track is 820 feet (250 meters) long. Water sports teams continue to use the Olympic Aquatic Center. Originally built in 1991 in the Athens suburb of Marousi, the Aquatic Center is now known as Athens Olympic Park. It was renovated by Spanish architect Santiago Calatrava and increased in scope to accommodate the swimming and water polo events. The two outdoor pools can accommodate 11,500 fans. In the run-up to the games, the decision to omit the roof that would shield the swimmers caused controversy. The diving events were held in the indoor pool, accommodating 6,200 spectators.

The triumph of the Greek athletes at the Olympics pressed on at the World Championship Games. In 2005 and 2015, the men's water polo team won two bronze medals at the World Championships. Dual-time World Championship Bronze medal holders Christos Afroudakis and Manolis Mylonakis are perhaps two of Greece's most notable water polo players. When it comes to medal table counts, Greece is one above Germany in the 2017 World Championship standings. Since 1994, Greece has always qualified when participating in World Championships at least at the quarterfinal level.

Although they missed earning a medal in the 2004 Olympic Games, the Greek men's water polo team did well in the following competitions: 2003 World Championship, 1999 European Championship, and the 2016 European Championship. The Greek water polo team is organized and managed by the Hellenic Swimming Federation.

The 2018 European Athletic Championships in Berlin, Germany, brought together competitors from across Europe. Multisport events were held simultaneously in host cities Berlin and Glasgow, kicking off the very first European Championships. The Greek team—formally known as the Hellenic Athletic Federation—walked away with a fifth-place overall ranking, proving to be a remarkable force to reckon with. Thirty-seven Greek nationals participated, resulting in a tally of six medals—three gold, two silver, and one bronze.

Gold medals were awarded to Miltiadis Tentoglou for men's long jump, Katerina Stefanidi for the women's pole vault, and Paraskevi Papahristou for the triple jump. Silver medals were presented to Nikoleta Kyriakopoulou for the women's pole vault and to Maria Belibasaki for the 400 meter. Dimitrios Tsiamis earned the bronze medal for the triple jump.

*Alexander Fatouros*

**Further Reading**

"Halkia Win Sends Athens Crowd Wild." CNN, August 25, 2004. Accessed November 1, 2017. http://edition.cnn.com/2004/SPORT/08/25/olympics.athletics/.

Longman, Jere. 1997. "Athens Wins a Vote for Tradition, and the 2004 Olympics." *New York Times,* September 6, 1997. https://www.nytimes.com/1997/09/06/sports/athens-wins-a-vote-for-tradition-and-the-2004-olympics.html.

Olympic Games. 2004. Accessed October 5, 2017. https://www.olympic.org/athens-2004.

**STEFANOS TSITSIPAS, WORLD-CLASS TENNIS SENSATION**

Born to parents who coached tennis at a summer resort, Greek tennis superstar Stefanos Tsitsipas broke out in the public eye at the age of fourteen in 2013. He is known for his six-foot-four stature, remarkable playing style, and a signature one-handed backhand shot.

Tsitsipas beat world number 1 Novak Djokovic in the Shanghai Masters quarterfinals in October 2019. He qualified for the finals at the Mubadala World Tennis Championship in United Arab Emirates (UAE) in late December 2019 by beating the now ranked number two Djokovic, only to be bested by the world number 1, Rafael Nadal.

Regarding world rankings, Stefanos Tsitsipas's personal best was number 5. In 2019, the twenty-one-year-old was the Association of Tennis Professionals' youngest player to rank in the top ten.

While soccer (football) and basketball remain Greece's most popular sports, the game of tennis is rising in popularity, due in large part to Greek champions Stefanos Tsitsipas and Maria Sakkari.

*Alexander Fatouros*

## Bars and Nightlife

No matter what the season, nightlife activity in Greece invigorates the senses in remarkable and surprising ways. The variety of nighttime pursuits ranges from international hangouts featuring world-renowned DJs to routine social affairs catering to time-honored palettes.

Awakening revitalized from their midday naps (from around two to five), Greeks make their way to their regular nocturnal gathering places or favorite outdoor cafés. The evening meal is usually served between nine and eleven.

Greeks can choose from a variety of eating and drinking establishments where they gather with *parea* (a revered inner circle of friends) or family for an evening of camaraderie and amusement. *Tavernas* are ubiquitous and affordable, ideal for catching up on gossip and life's happenings. Ritzy ones include the high-priced gourmet *estiatorio. Psaro-tavernas* (fish restaurants) and *bouzoukia* (nightclubs playing powerful *bouzouki* music) are other options. The legenday *ouzeri*, a place for drinking, serves *mezedes* (hors d'oeuvres and dips) consumed with *psomi* (bread). A variety of *mezedes* include *tzatziki* (garlic, yogurt, and cucumber dip), *rossikisalata* (eggplant dip), and *kolokithakia* (deep-fried zucchini). Specializing in spit-fired *arni* (lamb), *kotopoulo* (chicken), and *hirino* (pork), *psistaria* (barbeque restaurants) are widespread. The *souvlatzithiko* (spit-roasted eatery) dishes up charred *souvlaki* (chunks of pork or lamb). It is customary for Greeks to walk into the kitchen to inspect the food.

An evening meal can be finished off with a special dessert. The ever-present *zaharoplastio* (patisserie) features desserts like *kataifi* (shredded wheat pastry drizzled with honey), *baklava*, *rizogalo* (rice pudding), and *galaktobouriko* (custard pastry).

Composed of sweet semolina custard wrapped in flaky layers of filo dough, the *bougatsa* is a popular breakfast puff pastry. Regional varieties range from the super-sweet delights dusted with powdered sugar and cinnamon to the savory ones filled with creamy *mizithra*, a cheese made with milk and whey from goats or sheep or a combination of both.

Greek continually strive to redefine fun and experience *kefi*, which is a time of celebration, joy, and passion. Food, wine, and spirits shared with friends, as well as music, combine to create this feeling of utter joyfulness. Music is an important part of Greek nightlife. Classic and modern music concerts are abundant year-round, especially in the bigger cities. The younger generation frequents open air and live music clubs that play jazz and rock or dance clubs and café-bars that feature top-forty music. Older generations of locals prefer establishments that feature live Greek music and family camaraderie.

## ATHENS

Located at the base of the Acropolis, the old-world Plaka district is home to many historic cafés. Crowds emerge on to the narrow streets and illuminated *plateia* (city squares) to dance and throw carnations after a fill from one of their favorite open-air stomping grounds.

Scores of bars and coffeehouses in the Thissio district yield majestic views of the Acropolis. Nearby Monastiráki and Psirri neighborhoods provide a picturesque village-like atmosphere complete with cobbled streets, night bazaars, shops, and alternative bars. Access by automobile is limited and thus makes for an ideal atmosphere for strolling in fresh air.

Exarhia, in downtown Athens, is a rough-around-the edges neighborhood formerly known as Neapolis (New City in Greek), a stopping place for learned Athenians of yesteryear. Today, narrow pathways lead to out-of-sight squares complete with vinyl-record stores, boutiques, *taverna*s, cinemas, alternative bars, and eateries. A labyrinth of courtyards highlights evocative murals, political propaganda, and colorful street art. Protests and live-it-up live performances contribute to a high-octane energy and free-spirited atmosphere. Near at hand are the University of Athens and Technical University of Athens.

DJ events at hotel poolside bars are also in demand. When the moonlight cascades down, social activities take on an entirely different meaning. The Galaxy Restaurant and Bar, located atop the Athens Hilton Hotel, offers lavish cocktails and stunning panoramic views of the city. The Grand Bretagne Hotel rooftop restaurant near Syntagma (the Greek word for constitution) Square imparts an awe-inspiring view of the Parthenon. The Parliament, Acropolis Museum, and National Garden are minutes away. Complete with fine linen-clothed tables, the King George Athens Hotel restaurant is another five-star gourmet dining hotspot.

Athens's downtown cosmopolitan Kolonaki district offers stylish music clubs with impressive contemporary design. Boutiques, such as Gucci and Chanel, can be found amid art galleries, luxury hotel bars, and epicurean delights. The area attracts the well heeled, the well-to-do, and the famous.

Formerly the red-light district in the 1950s and 1960s and characterized by its fabled brothels and cabarets, the area of Trouba near the port of Piraeus puts forward a number of nightlife options. Locals partake in live music concerts at lively watering holes, such as Lola Bar and Troubar. The industrial area once served as a base for the U.S. Navy. Today, Trouba has been refashioned, making it an idyllic setting for the young and carefree.

Popular hip hangouts among the Athenians, Karytsi, and Agia Eirini squares blend the old with the new. The neoclassical buildings, St. George and Agia Eirini churches, the bustle of people on narrow streets, and foodie options give these neighborhoods their remarkable flavor. On the side streets, takeaway food stands offering *kalamboki* (roasted corn on the cob), *spanakopita* (spinach pie), and *tiropita* (cheese pie) are common. Sprinkled-with-sesame *koulouria* and toasted sandwiches are also popular on the go.

Known for its unmistakable lively and jazzy atmosphere, the *pastomageirio*, also known as a *mezedopoleio* (appetizer restaurant), is a one-stop locale, part delicatessen, part tavern. It is filled with a fragrant and colorful array of regional and long-established Greek wines, dried meats, and cheeses. Crowd-pleasing *anthotyros* cheese has a dry variant often topped on salads and spaghetti. Fresh *anthotyros* is creamy and is usually accompanied with fruit and honey.

Diners sit at linen-clothed tables next to deli cases brimming with a seemingly endless exhibition of provisions while delicatessen clerks distribute nibbles of traditional Greek cheese like *saganaki* and cured meats like *pastourma*. Traditional dips like *tzatziki* and *toursi* (pickled vegetables) are also on the bill of fare. *Ta Karamanlidika tou Fani* is perhaps Athens's most popular *pastomageirio*.

While still keeping some of the original machinery and infrastructure, the old gas factory in Technopolis has been transformed into an "Art City," a public space of contemporary design. In addition to a small museum and a children's playground, citizens and international visitors alike partake in cultural events, performances, and exhibitions throughout the year. The Thissio Metro station, which is near at hand, makes Technopolis easily accessible from all parts of Athens. Serving as a haven for artists and musicians, Technopolis—with its changing roster of concerts, festivals, and seminars—reaffirms the city's commitment to preserving culture and exploring new outlets of creative expression. Surrounding Technopolis is the Gazi district.

Serviced by the Kerameikos Metro station, the Gazi district attracts partygoers from all over the city. *Tavernas*, cafés, international galleries, LGBTQ bars and clubs, and venues that feature rock, pop, swing, and retro line the boulevards. Many nightclubs are open until the first light of morning, even during the week.

With over ninety to opt for, outdoor open-air summer cinemas are an alluring entertainment journey's end for many Athenians. Beginning in May and June, moviegoers get a chance to chillax under the stars until September and October. Cine Paris in the Plaka district, Thision Open-Air Cinema, Dexameni Cinema, and Vox rooftop cinema are some of Athens's best-loved attractions. Bar drinks and snacks complement the Greek subtitled moviegoing experience.

Kotzia Square in central Athens features nineteenth-century neoclassical architecture. The National Bank of Greece Cultural Center promotes year-round arts, culture, and leisurely programs. Graffiti-themed rooms painted by emerging artists can be experienced at the chic Grecotel Pallas Athena. With its unmistakable eccentric and quirky vibe, the unique hotel party space allures artists, musicians, and writers from all around the city.

The disheveled, graffiti-laden Kerameikos and Metaxourgeio neighborhoods serve as a cool backdrop to internationally acclaimed galleries like The Breeder, Rebecca Camhi, and Vamiali's. Acclaimed international contemporary art by the likes of Hungarian-born Rita Ackermann, American pop-artist Karen Kilimnik, and British sculptor-painter Clare Woods are showcased and sold to collectors worldwide. With its avant-garde and hip atmosphere, the sister neighborhoods attract the bold—emerging artists, musicians, fashionistas, and image-makers keen on making their mark.

Seaside Vouliagmeni located on the Athens Riviera offers a plethora of high-end hotels, breathtaking views, relaxing hospitality, and restaurants that offer *meze* (small dishes of Greek sustenance). Beachside clubs hosting live rock concerts are also in vogue.

Piraeus, Athens's picturesque port city, offers an abundance of high-end fish restaurants and *psaro-tavernas* where *kalamaria* (squid), *bakaliaros* (cod), and *oktapodi* (octopus) are all the rage. Bon vivants in the mood for sushi, cocktails, and sunset views of the Saronic Gulf head over to Athens's most popular Japanese-fusion restaurant, Matsuhisa, located in Laimos, Vouliagmeni. Athenians have many trendy and foreign-cuisine restaurants to choose from. Featuring vegan pizza, avocado burgers, and a robust vegetarian and vegan menu, "Avocado" on Nikis Street is one of Athens's most popular moderately priced restaurants.

The Keramikos neighborhood is home to "The Funky Gourmet," a Michelin-star eatery known for its innovative flavors. Here the traditional *botargo* (salted-fish roe) is served with white chocolate. Voted "Best Restaurant in Greece" for twelve consecutive years and known for its distinctive French gastronomy, "Spondi" is perhaps the most sought after gourmand restaurant in Athens.

## THESSALONIKI

Situated in the Northeast, Thessaloniki is Greece's second-largest city. Amid historic monuments, Aristotélous Square cultivates bars and cafés for all styles and tastes. The entertainment continues on nearby Nykis Avenue, a waterfront destination brimming with bars, elegant restaurants, and trendy dance clubs. Seascape cafés and fresh-seafood eateries contour the Thermaikos Gulf in the Nea Paralia-Kryni neighborhood.

The romantic and tranquil Kastra area provides a historic castle backdrop ideal for sipping wine under the stars. The city's old market in historic Ladadika hosts numerous street-side entertainers. Located in the city center, Palia Sfayia hosts large-scale nightclubs and *bouzoukia*. Young creative people seeking the unconventional and avant-garde hit the scene in Syggrou-Valaoritou. Fringe bars and high-energy alternative music clubs predominate.

## PATRAS

Music halls, clubs, and bars are widespread in Patras. The cobbled Radinou Street and sophisticated Ayiou Nikolaou Street are favorite stopping places. Packed in the summer months, nightspots Rio and Vrahénika (5.6 miles and 7.4 miles from Patras, respectively) offer fresh seafood and cocktails with views of neoclassical mansions and an illuminated bridge.

Tracing a path to the city center, Riga Feraiou Street boasts a new passageway ideal for walking, shopping, entertainment, and dining. Serving as a panoramic backdrop

As the sun sets, visitors stroll along a pedestrian-only promenade in the seaside village of Nidri on Lefkada Island, a hub of nightlife activity. An invitation to join friends in a lively atmosphere ensues at venues ranging from roadhouse taverns and *psistaria* (grill houses) to upmarket nightclubs and burger bars. The nightspots are set amid the beachfront, pine-forested mountains, olive groves, and an abutting harbor, a port of call for yachts that fly flags of several nations, including France, Germany, Great Britain, and Scandinavia. (Photo by Alexander Fatouros)

to a host of elegant bars and restaurants, Gherokostopoúlou Street is famous for the ancient theatre that inhabits the neighborhood.

### GREEK ISLANDS

Greek islands of the Aegean and Ionian Seas feature a wealth of nighttime entertainment. Guest DJs from around the world make their mark on the cosmopolitan Cyclades Islands in the Aegean Sea. Whether by chartered yacht, Greek ferry network, or hydrofoil, island hoppers embark to the most fashionable destination locales, such as Mykonos, Rhodes, Ios, Milos, and Santorini.

Malia and Hersonissos on the Ionian island of Crete is a favorite destination for all-night party-going youth. Crete dishes up a crispy crunch unlike any other. Made of barley rusk, the traditional *dakos* is a Cretan *meze* composed of a slice of twice-baked bread softened by a crown of vine tomatoes and extra-virgin olive oil. The irresistible blend of *feta* and *mizithra* cheeses, black olives, oregano, and freshly ground pepper make the local favorite a memorable bite.

Popular Ionian Islands destinations among the college youth include Kavos on the southern tip of Corfu and Lagana on Zakynthos. Both are known for their club-culture vibe and attract not only Greeks but other Europeans. Night-owl eateries that feature *keftedes*, meatballs, and *bifteki* (ground-beef patties) nudge partygoers heading home after the night's revels.

*Alexander Fatouros*

**See also:** Chapter 4: Art Economy. Chapter 14: *Mezedes* and Wine.

**Further Reading**

Greece All Time Classic, n.d. "Nightlife in Three Main Cities." Accessed May 9, 2018. http://www.visitgreece.gr/en/leisure/going_out/clubs/nightlife_in_three_main_cities.

Leontis, Artemis. 2009. *Culture and Customs of Greece*. Westport, CT: Greenwood Press.

Van Dyck, Karen, ed. 1988. *Insights Guides: Greece*, 2nd edition. Singapore: APA publication, LTD.

## Beverages: Coffee, Tea, Wine, and Liquor

A typical day in Greece is passed with coffee. Greeks indulge in the time-honored beverage from morning to night. Flavorful and robust *Ellinikos kafes* (Greek coffee) is finely ground coffee, boiled in a *briki*, a narrow pot, and swiftly poured in a demitasse. *Kaimaki*, thick foam, rises to the top, and the fine grounds settle at the bottom. When it comes to coffee and tea, Greeks more often than not add plenty of sugar. An expert in making coffee is called a *kafigis* (coffee maker). Foreigners who prefer no sugar may simply state *horis zahari*, simply translated as "no sugar." When the barista asks how you take your coffee or tea, answering with the term *sketos* accomplishes the same goal. Those who like just a tad of sugar can respond with the term *metrio*. *Me gala* is the Greek phrase for "with milk." The most prevailing way to order is *Ellinikos kafes varyglyos*, heavily sweetened Greek coffee.

The cold, frothy beverage frappe is made from freeze-dried Nescafe instant coffee, sugar, and milk, although a frappe can be made without milk, *horis gala*. Celebrated in the summer months, the frappe ingredients are shaken and served in a tall glass with a *kalamaki* (straw). Widely known as a national drink, the beloved coffee beverage is popular among the youth and middle aged and traces its origin to Thessaloniki where it was invented in 1957. International Coffee Day is celebrated on October 1 during the three-day long Athens Coffee Festival. The event brings together recognized coffee roasters and enthusiasts from all corners.

In 2015, Greeks consumed sixty-six thousand tons of coffee. Estimated to be valued at 990 million euros, the Greek coffee industry continues to thrive. Born in 1993, the freedo espresso and freddo cappuccino, cold coffee brews, are Greece's newest caffeinated inventions. Babycino, a steamed milk drink, is offered at the McDonald's in Athens International Airport.

Teas harvested in Greece and served with lemon or milk are widely known for their health-promoting benefits. They include *tsai tou vounóu* (mountain tea), sage, and *kamomili* (chamomile). Teas grown in Crete are *diktamo* (dittany of Crete), which is known as an aphrodisiac as well as for its healing power, and *tisane*. Hippocrates, Father of Medicine, prescribed *diktamos*. The ancient wild plant, harvested from steep mountains and cliffs, is hard to come by.

Cretan mountain tea is composed of *malotira* or *siderits*, an herb harvested in July. Other herbs used in teas include the widespread *faskomilo* (sage), *mantzourana* (marjoram), *rigani* (oregano), *thymari* (thyme), *menta* (mint), *dafni* (laurel), *dentrolivano* (rosemary), and *tilio* (linden).

Good-humored pleasantries accompanied with goblets filled with *krasi* (wine) are as widespread today in modern Greece as they were in the days of the ancient Greek symposium. Santorini Island is particularly known for its grape and the crisp, sharp-tasting *assyritiko* is its most famous wine. Crete's Heraklion wine region is home to the sweet-scented *vidiano* and *marouvas* (a strong red wine like sherry).

*Tsipouradhika* offer complementary *mezes* to soften the hard-as-nails *tsipouro*, a distillate made from Greek grapes. Eastern Crete's popular pomace brandy, *tsikoudia* or *raki*, is indistinguishable from *tsipouro*.

Made from a brandy and wine blend and traditionally served over ice, *Metaxa* is Greece's most popular spirit. It is an integral element of the "Greek Mojito."

Traditionally served with sustenance, *bira* (beer), *ouzo* (anise-flavored liqueur), *raki*, and *tsipouro* (grape-crush brandies) are noted drinking options. *Krasi* selections are composed of *mávro* (red), *aspro* (white), resin-flavored *retsina*, and *kokkinelli* (rosé). Many brand-name Greek bottled wines from various regions are celebrated. *Hima* (local wine from the barrel) is also on tap.

*Alexander Fatouros*

**See also:** Chapter 14: *Mezedes* and Wine. Appendix A: A Day in the Life.

> ### *KOMBOLOI* (WORRY BEADS) RELIEVE TENSION AND CREATE A MEDITATIVE EXPERIENCE
>
> Although not as popular now as in the years past, many Greek men continue to use *komboloi* (worry beads). As their English name suggests, they are meant to relieve tension and relax. Made of a variety of materials, including amber, metal, glass, wood, semiprecious stone, and plastic, *komboloi* are beads assembled on a string. The beads of the *komboloi* vary in number but are usually set in an odd number. A single fixed crowning bead (sometimes with a tassel attached) is fashioned for holding. The space between the crowning bead and the rest of the set of beads measures approximately the width of four fingers. When set in motion, the *komboloi* is draped and flipped over one's index finger.
>
> The sound, sight, and feel of the clicking beads all work in unison to create a pleasurable and by and by a meditative experience. Some of the *komboloi* include the *kako mati* (evil eye) charm. The *mati*, resembling an eye, is often made using turquoise and obsidian. The light-blue eye charm is thought to guard against negative energy.
>
> The Komboloi Museum in Nafplion is housed in an eighteenth-century mansion. The exhibit features beads that span the globe and include ones from every major religion. Although they look similar to rosaries, Greek *komboloi* do not carry any religious importance.
>
> *Alexander Fatouros*

**Further Reading**

Athens Coffee Festival. n.d. "Preparations Are Underway for the Leading Coffee Festival in Greece." Accessed May 12, 2018. https://www.athenscoffeefestival.gr/en/preparations-are-underway-for-the-leading-coffee-festival-in-greece/.

Leontis, Artemis. 2009. *Culture and Customs of Greece.* Westport, CT: Greenwood Press.

Perfect Daily Grind, n.d. "4 Things You May Not Know About Coffee in Greece." Accessed May 12, 2018. https://www.perfectdailygrind.com/2016/07/4-things-may-not-know-coffee-greece/.

Van Dyck, Karen, ed. 1988. *Insights Guides: Greece*, 2nd edition. Singapore: APA publication, LTD.

## Celebrations and Festivals

Modern Greeks partake in distinct holiday celebrations and public festivals throughout the year. National holidays include Independence Day on March 25, which commemorates Greece's declaration of independence from Ottoman rule, and Ohi Day on October 28, which celebrates Greece's saying *ohi* (no) to Italy's request to enter Greece during World War II. These holidays are celebrated with patriotic parades.

Major religious holidays include Easter, the Assumption of the Virgin Mary (August 15), and Christmas (December 25). Cities and villages throughout Greece also celebrate *panageria* (festivals) dedicated to their patron saint. During the religious holidays, crowds leave the cities to reunite with family and friends. These trips culminate in celebration and gratitude for life's blessings.

Leading up to one of the most important religious holidays, Easter, is a two- to three-week celebration called *Apokreas* (carnival). Carnival is comparable to the Mardi Gras in the United States, with parades with floats, costumed participants, music, food, and drink.

A unique feature of the Carnival of Rethymon, Crete, apart from the colossal parade and music, is a treasure hunt. The Athenian area of Plaka, at the foot of the Acropolis, is another place for the fun and feasting of carnival. The Carnival of Patras commences on the last Sunday before the onset of Lent (*sarakosti*). The western city's floats and parades make for a memorable gathering that ultimately culminates in a feast of village bread, *souvlaki* (pork shish-ka-bob grilled over an open flame seasoned with oregano and lemon), and *baklava* (paper-thin pastries drizzled with walnuts and honey) provided by street vendors.

Carnival terminates with the beginning of *sarakosti*. There are many religious festivals, which are described in the "Greek Orthodox Regional Celebrations" entry in the chapter on religion.

Festivals that focus on history, art, and music are also prominent in Greece. The family-friendly Rhodes Medieval Rose Festival transports people to medieval times. In an effort to share the town's rich history, on the last weekend in May trumpets announce the promenade of nobles, cavalry, and a fitting entourage. The banquets are complete with guests dressed as witches and fairies. The festival takes place in the old city, which was built in the thirteenth and fourteenth centuries by the Order of St. John, a lay Catholic religious order. They ruled Rhodes before the Ottomans took control.

The folkloric festival in Eleusis commences in May. Colorful costumes and performances enrapture audiences that hail from around the world. At the end of May, the Hadjipetria Festival in Trikala in northwestern Thessaly showcases lectures, national dances, and athletic contests.

The music and dance of the Athens and Epidaurus Festival captivate national and international spectators every summer. The Athens Festival showcases productions by world-renowned performers and orchestras. The remarkable views from the Herodian amphitheater at the foot of the Acropolis add another facet to the experience. At Epidavros, near Corinth, contemporary actors breathe life into the comic and tragic characters of ancient playwrights, such as Aristophanes, Aeschylus, Sophocles, and Euripides. They perform in the same fourth century BCE theatre where the plays were originally seen.

On summer solstice day, June 21, European Music Day takes flight. For three days, live shows, which dish up the latest euphonious wonders, pop up all over Greece. In 2017, there were more than 218 venues that featured 20 percussion and dance companies, 24 orchestras, 35 choirs, 95 DJs, and 367 band and music ensembles.

The four-day Beach Street Art Festival, held in Mytilene in July, brings together graffiti artists, DJs, musicians, and poets. Live traditional Cretan music, theatre, and group dancing ensue in late July and early August at the Yakinthia Festival.

A hallmark of the Lefkas International Folklore Festival is its diverse folk-dance groups. Every year from August 20 through August 27, the village squares of this Ionian island are charged with men, women, and children expressing their inventiveness through music and dance.

Mykonos is perhaps the most notable island when it comes to sophisticated jet-set entertainment and high-fashion flair. The Mykonos Summer Festival held throughout the island and Harvest Festival held at the Agricultural Museum in mid-September give rise to mega-million-dollar yachts that line the harbors of this popular hangout of the rich and famous. Inside the after-hours disco, the buzz, glamour, and excitement continue. Superstar models and celebrities bump shoulders with aristocrats, sporting heroes, and image-makers.

The International Film Festivals in Rhodes, Syros, and Thessaloniki attract guests far and wide. From short film and documentary screenings to hobnobbing with image-makers at screening parties, the occasion unites modern film fans with filmmakers and visionaries. Greeks commemorate their food and wine products with special gatherings.

Every other year, in early April, village women from Megara near Athens gather to dance in ancestral attire to the beat of the "Fishermen's Trata." The word "*trata*" refers to a type of fishing boat, and the dance celebrates a successful fishing harvest. At the Agiassos Chestnut Festival, held in early November, guests sample roasted chestnuts grown on the mountains of the island of Lesvos. Wine festivals are held throughout Greece, including the Daphne Wine Festival, just outside of Athens.

There are many celebrations that are unique to a particular region of Greece. On January 8, in the Seres region, the celebratory custom of switching sex roles comes to realization: women relax at the café while the men do the chores at home and tend to the children. In the evening, the families reunite in the village squares to partake in sustenance and merriment.

In July, the village of Pigi in Lesvos hosts the three-day Festival of the Bull where horse races and live music reign supreme. Participants adorn the bull with flowers on the first night. On the second day, there is a parade and a beauty contest for horses. At midnight, the bull is sacrificed. The following morning the village priest blesses the cauldrons of bull's meat that have been boiling, along with lamb and wheat, during the night. The islanders feast on the *kisketsi* and enjoy horse races and live music.

*Alexander Fatouros*

**See also:** Chapter 5: Greek Orthodox Holidays; Greek Orthodox Regional Celebrations

**Further Reading**

Kolasa-Sikiaridi, Kerry. 2017. "Greece Celebrates with Carnival Events Across the Country." *Greek Reporter*, February 19, 2017. Accessed August 25, 2017. http://greece

.greekreporter.com/2017/02/19/greece-celebrates-with-carnival-events-across-the-country/.

Leontis, Artemis. 2009. *Culture and Customs of Greece*. Westport, CT: Greenwood Press.

Petrusichs, Amanda. 2014. "Hunting for the Source of the World's Most Beguiling Folk Music." *New York Times*. Accessed November 17, 2017. https://www.nytimes.com/2014/09/28/magazine/hunting-for-the-source-of-the-worlds-most-beguiling-folk-music.html.

Van Dyck, Karen, ed. 1988. *Insights Guides: Greece*, 2nd edition. Singapore: APA publication, LTD.

## Games of Chance

Mentioned in Homer's epic literature, gambling was one aspect of ancient Greek civilization. It continues to fascinate Greeks of today. The birth of poker has its roots in the Minoan island of Crete. The ancient Greeks entertained themselves with games of luck, including dice games and head or tails. Throwing a double six today would indicate a victory in any parlor game. The origin of this declaration dates back to the ancient civilization when a "throw of Aphrodite" would bestow triumph upon the player.

Greek Pantheon gods Hades, Poseidon, and Zeus amused themselves with the roll of the dice. A mythological legend portrays the gods splitting the universe among themselves in this game of chance. The spirit of risk and the glory of reward live on. *Tavli* (backgammon) games are popular and include two versions: *portes* and *plakoto*. *Billiardho* (billiards), *chartia* (cards), *skaki* (chess), and *podhosferaki* (table soccer) still enchant and amuse as much as *dama* (draughts), *ta zaria* (dice), and dominos do. With the hope of bringing in great luck, Greeks play games of chance, such as card games, at New Year's Eve and New Year's Day.

Youth enjoy playing *koupes*, which is indistinguishable from the game hearts. Similar to the German game 66, and played with thirty-two cards, *mpourloto* and *eksintaeksi* are also popular. *Agonia* with its many variations is the Greek incarnation of crazy eights. Using two decks, *koum-kan* is a rummy game, as is its variant cousin, *thanassis*. During the winter months, the men of Skafia enjoy the game *diloti*, a Cretan fishing game similar to casino.

Greece, which has eight casinos, is one of the few countries in the European Union that is permitted to operate gambling legally. The island of Rhodes boasts the most gaming facilities. Equipped with forty tables and over two hundred slot machines, Casino Rio in Patras welcomes people with a penchant for betting. Thessaloniki's majestic Regency Casino and Loutraki jockey for the number one spot in terms of size. In 2014, Greeks wagered 5.9 billion euros on games of chance (Mandravelis 2015).

In a 2011 decision, the Greek government imparted the rights to manage and operate the Greek Lottery to a private company. Played on Wednesdays and Saturdays, 6/49 Lotto is the most popular. As the name suggests, the top prizewinning ticket will match the players' selected six numbers from a total of forty-nine. Other payouts include prize money for four and five ball matches (Lotto Atlas n.d.).

Instant lottery scratch-off cards, appropriately called "Scratch," are Greece's newest and second most popular game of chance. In 2014, one million cards were sold in the first week, yielding 260,000 cash prizes (ANSAmed 2014).

*Alexander Fatouros*

**Further Reading**

ANSAmed, 2014. "Greece: Games of Chance; OPAP Debuts New Instant Lottery." Accessed November 3, 2017. http://www.ansamed.info/ansamed/en/news/nations/greece/2014/05/08/greece-games-of-chance-opap-debuts-new-instant-lottery_db9d79ba-2da2-4fb3-a7e5-2aa2e77b359c.html.

Black, John. 2013. "Gambling in Ancient Civilizations." Accessed October 7, 2017. http://www.ancient-origins.net/ancient-places-europe/gambling-ancient-civilizations-00931.

Korachai, Maria. 2015. "Voulis Street's Lady Luck." Greece Is Blog, November 2, 2015. Accessed January 31, 2018. http://www.greece-is.com/article/georgia-voulis-streets-lady-luck/.

Lotto Atlas, n.d. "Greek Lottery 6/49 Lotto." Accessed November 12, 2017. http://www.lottoatlas.com/greece-lotto/.

Mandravelis, Vangelis. 2015. "Greeks Bet 5.9 Billion Euros on Games of Chance Last Year." *ekathimerini,* May 5, 2015. Accessed October 26, 2017. http://www.ekathimerini.com/169699/article/ekathimerini/business/greeks-bet-59-billion-euros-on-games-of-chance-last-year.

Pagat. 1995. "Card Games in Greece." Updated May 5, 2020. Maintained by John McLeod. Accessed October 8, 2017. https://www.pagat.com/national/greece.html.

Skafia Crete, n.d. "Diloti Card Game: Sfakia Winter Sports." Accessed October 18, 2017. https://www.sfakia-crete.com/sfakia-crete/diloti.html.

## Stavros Niarchos Foundation Cultural Center

The remarkable Stavros Niarchos Foundation Cultural Center (SNFCC) is situated 4 kilometers (2.48 miles) south of central Athens in Kalithea on a 170,000 square meters (1,829,865 square feet) landscaped park. Completed in 2016 at cost of 566 million euros and designed by architect Renzo Piano, the eco-friendly cultural and education center is home to the Greek National Library, Greek National Opera, and a park. Visitors row, sail, or kayak on a man-made canal, 400 meters (1/4 mile) long and 30 meters (98 feet) wide, that is fed from the water of Faliron Bay.

The architectural elements work in unison to foster a sense of community and family-togetherness. Member events span the arts and include concerts, ballet, experimental performances, festivals, sports and wellness, screenings, shows, and special events for kids and adults, such as computer courses, yoga, and pilates. The SNFCC was nominated for the Royal Institute of British Architects International Prize and served as the backdrop of a speech on the impact of democracy by U.S. president Barack Obama in 2016.

The opera wing, equipped with two lyric theater auditoriums (450 seats and 1400 seats) and assorted art and performance spaces, is home to a variety of activities that preserve culture. With a changing roster of exhibitions, the gallery space designated for art and form comes alive in new and unexpected ways, expanding notions of contemporary Greek culture.

Seminars and workshops run the gamut from arts and crafts, such as "wearable sculpture and jewelry making," to "technology know-how." A library of rare collectibles is open to the public for research and study. The glass-walled library reading room offers incredible views of Athens and the sea and can be easily transformed into a multifunctional space for a variety of exhibitions, including multimedia art projects.

The Agora, a public space within the building, connects people between the library and opera space. Located on the eighth floor, the Faros, a contemporary lighthouse, serves as a lookout. Views of the Faliron Bay can be seen from the top floor of the opera house or from atop the hill, which is on a sloping park facing seaward. With three hundred thousand visitors in 2018, the Great Lawn at Niarchos Park is a favorite summer-time outdoor destination for a variety of happenings—from live musical and sporting events to outdoor theater, bike riding, and skateboarding.

Facing Athens and built on an incline, the park is composed of the Great Lawn and pedestrian paths amid a garden of Mediterranean trees and plants. The foliage and flowers change with each season, making walking along the canal an exhilarating experience.

*Alexander Fatouros*

**See also:** Chapter 1: Athens/Piraeus and Province of Attica.

**Further Reading**

Stavros Niarchos Foundation Cultural Center. 2018. Accessed October 26, 2018. https://www.snfcc.org/en.

CHAPTER 16

# MEDIA AND POPULAR CULTURE

## OVERVIEW

The sector of media in Greece today reflects all the seismic changes that have shaken the country during the years of the financial crisis and have largely transformed many aspects of everyday life, public opinion, and popular culture in the past decade. The media landscape continues to change, as the legal framework for television and radio licenses has not yet been stabilized. Also, new practices, such as the advent of social media, digital press, or digital television platforms, have not yet shown their full dynamics.

The period from the fall of the military junta in 1974 until the Olympic Games of 2004 was considered as a golden era for the development of press and audiovisual media. The number of newspapers and magazines was exceptional, reflecting a vibrating political landscape in the years following the restoration of democracy. Compared to previous years, Greece enjoyed freedom of speech. In 1989, the audiovisual media entered the phase of the so-called deregulation. Before then, only state-owned TV channels and radio stations operated. New legislation opened the way, first for the creation of privately owned radio stations, followed by privately owned television channels. Multiple new television channels emerged on national and local networks. The 1990s can be considered as the golden era of private television in Greece, with the multiplication of new channels on a national and local network. Television in the 1990s dominated the popular culture as they offered a new fashionable entertainment and a more sensational approach toward information. This was in comparison to the previous state-owned monopoly of television channels and radio stations. The latter had a more "serious" attitude, which based its programming on documentaries and art cinema, and were often accused of propagating the opinion of the government. Private channels, radio stations, newspapers, and an impressive number of illustrated magazines proposed a more colorful and glamorous lifestyle. The financing of both audiovisual and press media came almost entirely from advertisement, promoting a consumerist culture that reached its peak at the beginning of the 2000s, especially during the years of the preparation for the Olympic Games of 2004.

The advent of the financial and sociopolitical crisis brought an end to these practices and attitudes, and the established system of mainstream media, including television, radio, press, and cinema, nearly collapsed.

The first signs of a strong discontent of the public with the dominant mediatic and political discourse were displayed in the riots that followed the death by shooting of fifteen-year-old student Alexis Grigoropoulos by a police officer in the district of Exarhia, Athens, in December 2008. The tragic event resulted in massive protests and riots supported by school and university students and in general members of a younger generation. The youth revolted not only against police control and violence, but also against age discrimination, unemployment, and the job precarity that was strongly felt by young professionals starting in 2004. Another target of their discontent was the consumer culture and the mainstream media that promoted it.

This hostile attitude toward mainstream media by the younger generation, who preferred the use of social media and rejected traditional television channels, grew following the debt crisis that began in Greece in 2009, triggered by the global financial recession. After a period of unstable coalition governments and elections, Greece in 2010 officially entered the era of the "memorandum," a program that outlined the conditions, including austerity measures, that were attached to awarding loans to Greece. The forced austerity measures that were imposed by the Troika (the European Commission, the International Monetary Fund, the European Central Bank) led to a rise in unemployment, the impoverishment of the middle class, and even to a humanitarian crisis. For a few years, Greece was in the international media spotlight. In June 2015, the Greek people were asked to vote on whether or not they thought Greece should sign the third Memorandum of Understanding agreement. Although the people voted no, the Greek government agreed to the austerity measures included in the memorandum. The government was concerned that a no vote might lead to a Grexit. One of the most mediatized figures of that period was the minister of finance Yanis Varoufakis, whose provocative interviews and appearances aroused many debates on international and European media, and even inspired the film by Costa-Gavras titled *Adults in the Room* (2019).

During that summer of 2015, many media groups, news journals, and television stations took a clear stance about supporting one or the other side of the debate—either they were for remaining in the Eurozone or not; either they supported a yes vote or a no vote. This controversy was also reflected in very intense debates on social media and digital media at both public and personal levels.

The crisis had a huge effect on Greek media. In the first years of the crisis, most of the mainstream media adopted a pro-Troika discourse, forging a narrative that the Greeks had to pay for years of living above their means. At the same time, there were massive protests by the people who were seriously affected by the austerity measures. These measures instituted by the government and supported by the media triggered a loss of trust and even a rejection of established media groups. As a result, alternative digital media platforms (such as *Pandoras Box*, *TVXS*, and others) emerged. Recent surveys by Reuters show that today most Greeks do not trust traditional media for their information, and they prefer to be informed by social media.

The crisis had a serious financial impact on the media landscape. As revenues from advertisement—its main source of finance—and press circulation declined, many newspapers, television channels, and media groups were shut down. MEGA and Alter, two of the leading television channels of national broadcasting, closed after leaving their personnel unpaid for months. Historic newspapers, such as *Ta Nea* and *To Vima*, which were operated by the Lambrakis Media Group, were auctioned off after the Lambrakis Media Group declared bankruptcy. When the owners of the emblematic newspaper *Eleftherotypia* became bankrupt, the journalists took over the enterprise and circulated an independent newspaper called *The Newspaper of the Euthors* (*Efsyn*). After ten years of the crisis, the hierarchies and practices of the established media were totally transformed, and new players had entered the field.

A critical moment for the Greek media was the sudden decision of the government, in July 2013, to close down ERT (Hellenic Radio Television), the state-owned national broadcaster, without any notice. ERT comprised five TV channels and many radio channels that were broadcast nationally and internationally. When the conservative government made this decision to comply with the austerity measures set forth by the Troika, more than twenty-five hundred employees were fired. When the signals of ERT went "black," this provoked a massive reaction from the population. This occurred despite much of the public being against ERT because they considered it as the mouthpiece of the government. For many months, the employees of ERT continued to broadcast an unofficial program through the European Broadcasting Union, against the will of the government. Among the many reasons for the outcry was that it was the only Greek media that broadcast worldwide and thus reached the Greek diaspora. Also, it supported popular arts and humanities programing. For example, it broadcast the performance of a symphonic orchestra, which had first been established in 1938, and it possessed/owned an orchestra of contemporary music and a chorus that had been created by Manos Chatzidakis in 1977. ERT was also one of the main financial sponsors of Greek cinema, including art-house cinema, documentary, and short films, and a supporter of young creative artists. This halt of ERT had serious impact on films under international coproductions; they were left unfinished for months. Despite the fact that the ratings of the ERT were low compared to television channels, and they had many systemic problems, the general public perceived it as a national institution with the important aim to preserve the country's audiovisual, cultural, and political history. The reaction to the "blackout" of ERT was so strong that one of the leaders of the coalition government resigned. In 2015, the government of SYRIZA and ANEL reopened ERT in its previous form; however, many of its structural problems remain unsolved.

The crisis had a strong effect on all kinds of audiovisual production. Until 2009, the main programming of public and private channels were television serials, soap operas, or dramas. From the beginning of the crisis, the production of serials, as well as other big budget programs, stopped leaving hundreds of professionals of the audiovisual sector, including cinematographers, actors, and technicians, unemployed. The television channels turned to less expensive programs, such as talent shows, games, debates, and infotainment shows. The advent of paid television and platforms such as Netflix made things worse for television channels and audiovisual production. In the same context, the private channels that until 2009 were the main financial source for mainstream cinema and participated as coproducers in popular films also stopped funding

From May to late September, open-air cinemas, like the Cine-Gardinia on the island of Hydra, welcome film aficionados. In the 1950s, Athens alone had more than eight hundred open-air cinemas. By the 1980s, many of them closed and were transformed into parking lots. Today these cinemas are less in number, but their popularity remains. They show not only new releases but also classic films, such as old Hollywood classics and European arthouse films. (Photo by Alexander Fatouros)

cinema production. Nowadays, mainstream films are mostly remakes of emblematic comedies of the "golden era" of popular cinema in the 1950s and the 1960s. In 2018, the most successful productions were spectacles based on old comedies and musicals.

In the first years of the crisis, a number of Greek films such as *Dogtooth* by Lanthimos, *Attenberg* by Tsangari, and *Strella* by Koutras were rewarded in major festivals (Cannes, Berlin, Venice) creating an international interest about Greek cinema. This trend was called "the weird wave" because of the strange humor, absurdism, and performativity of these films, and the combination of a mainstream aesthetics with more obscure themes, cynicism, and irony. Today, more than fifty films have been rewarded in international festivals, confirming this emergence of a cinematic new wave. Because the filmmakers had to deal with the collapse of the state-subsidized system and absence of traditional ways of financing, such as advertisement or television channels, they became more active in European and international coproductions. However, they still face huge difficulties in financing their projects, and most of their productions are low-budget films.

The crisis was not the only factor that contributed to the transformation of the Greek media: the digital revolution and the accessibility of broadband Internet by the majority of the population led to the rise of digital media and social media. Today, most Greeks own a social media account that they use for their information, entertainment, and professional and personal relationships, and they make use of online newspapers, magazines, and lifestyle magazines. Many of these digital sites contrast with the mainstream and established media in terms of practices and content.

*Anna Poupou*

**See also:** Chapter 5: Overview.

**Further Reading**

Papathanassopoulos, Stylianos. 2018. "Greece – Media Landscape." *MediaLanscapes.org*, by European Journalism Center (EJC). Accessed April 14, 2021. https://medialandscapes.org/country/greece.

Veglis, Andreas. 2012. "Journalism and Cross-Media Publishing: The Case of Greece." In *The Handbook of Global Online Journalism*, edited by Eugenia Saperia and Andreas Veglis, 210–223. West Sussex: Wiley-Blackwell.

## Cinema

The first film screenings were presented in Greece at the end of the nineteenth century. However, until the 1950s, film production was sporadic. Following World War II, during the 1950s and 1960s, popular cinema consisted mostly of comedies, melodramas, musicals, and other film genres addressed to a wide audience. Main figures of this "Golden Era" were the producer Filopimin Finos and directors Yorgos Tzavelas, Alekos Sakelarios, and Yannis Dalianidis. These movies were reintroduced during the 2000s by being broadcasted on television channels, and later on by web platforms such as YouTube or greek-movies.com. Although they are not screened in cinema theatres, they remain extremely popular with younger audiences. Some of the older movies were remade with contemporary directors and actors, such as *Ilias of the 16th Department* (Nikos Zapatinas, 2008). Others were restored colorized versions of the original black and white films such as *The Wife Shall be Afraid of the Husband* (Yorgos Tzavelas, 1964), which was distributed in theatres in 2017. The most well-known filmmakers outside Greece were Nikos Koundouros (*The Magic City*, 1953; *The Ogre of Athens*, 1955) and Michalis Cacoyannis (*Stella*, 1955; *Zorba the Greek*, 1964).

At the end of the 1960s and during the military dictatorship, a new example of a political art cinema emerged. Filmmakers such as Theo Angelopoulos, Pantelis Voulgaris, Alexis Damianos, Nikos Panayotopoulos, Nikos Nikolaidis, Tonia Marketaki, and many others represented a new wave that was called New Greek Cinema (NGC). Allegorical forms and elaborated symbolisms were necessary features of the cinematic language of these films, as censorship during the junta was extremely strict and many filmmakers ended up in prison or exile camps. Films such as *Evdokia* (Alexis Damianos, 1971) and *The Travelling Players* (Theo Angelopoulos, 1974) are only a few of the emblematic films of NGC. This generation stayed active after the reestablishment of the democratic regime in 1974, and most of these directors continued to work during the next three decades.

In 1981, the creation of the Greek Film Center and the inauguration of a politics based on state subsidies of film production led to the flourishing of a modernist art cinema. However, because the audience had turned to television and VHS, most of these films failed in commercial terms, and the critics characterized them as elitist, highbrow, and introspective. A few films, however, were successful at the box office. They included *Loafing and Camouflage* (Nikos Perakis, 1984), a comedy that describes the life of soldiers working at the television channel of the army during the dictatorship; *The Stone Years* (Pantelis Voulgaris, 1985), a historical drama based on the true story of a Communist couple who were persecuted from the end of the Greek civil war until the end of the military dictatorship in 1974; and *The Price of Love* (Tonia Marketaki, 1984), a love story set in Corfu at the beginning of the twentieth century. They had a high artistic value and addressed a wider audience.

At the international film festival circuit, Theo Angelopoulos overshadowed other Greek filmmakers. In 1998, he was awarded the Palm d'Or at the Cannes Festival for the film *An Eternity and a Day*, and he remained active until his sudden death in 2012.

In the late 1990s and 2000s, popular comedies or "nostalgia films" were produced to entice the Greek audience to return to the cinema theatres. New multiplex cinema venues were built for the first time in Greece, and television channels became more actively engaged in film production and promotion. Examples of this return to comedy were the films *Safe Sex* (Michalis Reppas and Thanassis Papathanassiou, 1999) and *The Cow's Orgasm* (Olga Malea, 1996). An unusually high number of tickets were sold for both of them. In *Touch of Spice* (Tassos Boulmetis, 2003), a nostalgic film that proved to be a real blockbuster, a Greek family living in Istanbul is obliged to leave Turkey in the 1950s due to the political turmoil. When the boy, the main character, arrives in Athens against his will, he tries to keep his memories of Istanbul alive by obsessive cooking, expressing his feelings through food, spices, and recipes.

During the same period of time, in the 1990s and 2000s, a vein of realist art cinema focusing on the representation of everyday life problems and situations dealt with the theme of emigration (a major issue in Greece after the fall of the Soviet Union) and explored aspects of national, linguistic, class, and gendered identities. Examples of these films include *From the Snow* (Sotiris Goritsas, 1993), *Mirupafshim* (Yorgos Korras and Christos Voupouras, 1997), *From the Edge of the City* (Konstantinos Yannaris, 1998), and *Delivery* (Nikos Panayotopoulos, 2004).

During the time that the international media focused on Greece's financial and political crisis, Greek art films were achieving international renown. In 2009, the film *Dogtooth* by Yorgos Lanthimos was awarded the prize *Un certain regard* at the Cannes Festival. Many other Greek films also won awards at international film festivals. They included *Strella* (Panos Koutras, 2009), *Attenberg* (Athina Rachel Tsangari, 2010), *Homeland* (Syllas Tzourmerkas, 2010), and *Miss Violence* (Alexandros Avranas, 2013). Today, almost ten years after the first signs of this outburst in 2009, we can talk about a Greek New Wave. From 2009 to 2017, more than fifty arthouse films participated in major film festivals.

These film productions took place after state subsidies toward cinema diminished and even completely stopped for a few years due to the politics of austerity. To finance their projects, a young generation of producers and filmmakers turned to establishing partnerships with producers, filmmakers, and actors from other European countries. Another important change was that films targeted a non-Greek audience, rather than addressing only a Greek one. The film *Son of Sofia* (Elina Psykou, 2017) illustrates the transnational process of the production of Greek films: the film had funding from France and Bulgaria, featured Russian and Greek actors, was shot in Athens, used the Russian and Greek languages, and premiered at the Tribeca Film Festival, where it was awarded the Best International Narrative Prize.

These changes in producing, promoting, and financing films resulted as well in more daring narratives than the films of the previous generation. Thematically, most the films of the Greek New Wave dealt directly or indirectly with the crisis and its aftermath at social, sociological, and psychological levels. They criticized the rise of racism, xenophobia, homophobia, and aggressive masculinities. Many of them depicted young heroes in dysfunctional patriarchal families and can be read as allegories of the crisis. They included *Matchbox* (Yannis Economides, 2003), *A Blast* (Syllas Tzoumerkas, 2014), *Wasted Youth* (Argyris Papadimitropoulos, 2011), *Miss Violence* (Alexandros Avranas, 2013), and *Xenia* (Panos Koutras, 2014). In the context of this wave, many directors utilized film genres such as the film noir, the thriller, or the horror movie (*Wednesday 04.45*, Alexis Alexiou, 2014; *Norway*, Yannis Veslemes, 2014; *Stratos*, Yannis Economides, 2014).

*Anna Poupou*

**See also:** Chapter 2: Overview.

**Further Reading**

Andreadakis, Orestis, ed. *Non-Catalogue*. 58th Thessaloniki International Film Festival, Thessaloniki, 88–105.

Karalis, Vrasidas. 2012. *A History of Greek Cinema*. New York: Continuum.

## YORGOS LANTHIMOS AND THE "WEIRD WAVE" OF GREEK CINEMA

The "Weird Wave" of Greek cinema was a label introduced by Steve Rose and Peter Bradshaw, the film critics of the *Guardian*, and adopted by festivals programmers and reviewers worldwide. This label was used originally to describe the films by Yorgos Lanthimos (*Dogtooth*, *Alps*, *The Lobster*, *The Killing of the Sacred Deer*), Athina Rachel Tsangari (*Attenberg*, *The Capsule*, *Chevalier*), and their screenwriter Efthymis Filippou. Later it was used to describe other filmmakers as well. The films of the "weird wave" are characterized by minimalism, performativity, natural lighting, deadpan acting, the combination of humor and violence, cynicism, sarcasm, absurdism, and references to popular culture (pop music, video clips, movies) mainly of the 1980s and 1990s. The two latest films by Lanthimos are considered "weird," but they are not considered Greek films as they are international coproductions with English-speaking stars (Colin Farrell, Rachel Weisz, and Nicole Kidman). These films show the transnational dynamics of Greek cinema as well as the impossibilities of big budget productions in Greece, due mainly to an unstable legal framework and limitations in financing.

*Anna Poupou*

Nikolaidou, Afroditi, and Anna Poupou. 2017. "Post Weird Notes on Contemporary Greek Cinema." In *Non-Catalogue*, edited by Geli Madelmi, 58th Thessaloniki Film Festival, Thessaloniki, pp. 122–131.

Papadimitriou, Lydia, and Yannis Tzoumakis. 2012. *Greek Cinema. Texts, Histories, Identities*. Bristol: Intellect Books.

## Digital Media

The financial recession, the decline of the advertising market, and finally the advent of the broadband Internet, the digitization of the production systems, the popularization of smartphones and tablets, and the expansion of social media led to a rapid descent of the printed editions of newspapers and magazines. By 2010, all newspaper redesigned their web editions and were reoriented into a cross-media convergence (Veglis 2012, 210), following the trends in the global media industry. That means that the news content was created in such a way that it could be used in various formats and for different publication channels. Informative portals such as in.gr (ex-DOL group) or skai.gr (Alafouzos group) are among the most popular cross-media platforms. They are interconnected with television channels, radio stations, and the online editions of the newspapers. With very few exceptions, the online editions of the newspaper and magazines offer free access to their content and are not subscription based.

In recent years, Greece has witnessed a significant increase of digital-born websites and magazines that were originally created in a digital form and are published exclusively online. Some of them were created in the first years of the crisis and position themselves as opposed to mainstream media. They are a result of the strong distrust of Greeks toward established media. New digital websites, such as TVXS, Pandoras Box, Infowar, The Press Project, HotDoc, Protagon, that appeared after 2009 promoted an independent militant journalism based in original research and reporting; they declared their independence from economic and political interests. Some of them were financed by practices of crowdfunding and relied on the contribution of the readers. They were created by well-known journalists who had previously worked in television and other media. For example, TVXS.gr—Television Without Frontiers was created by Stelios Kouloglou as a continuation of his long-running television emission Reportage Without Frontiers, and Pandora's Box was created by militant journalist Kostas Vaxevanis. These websites play an important role as opinion makers in the Greek media landscape. The website Athens.indymedia.org, an important portal for extreme left and anarchist activism, performed a major part in the organization of the riots and demonstrations in the period 2008–2012 and has often been threatened with closure by the Ministry of Citizen Protection.

New digital websites have continued to appear in recent years. They include newsbeast.gr, newsit.gr, cnn.gr, huffingtonpost.gr, as well as thematic portals, such as flix.gr, that focus on cinema (new films, festivals, cinephilia, industry). Today, one of the most influential websites that focuses on popular culture, urban life, arts, fashion, and design is popaganda.gr, an online magazine launched by young independent journalists. During the years of the crisis, it offered an alternative view on the creativity of young artists, designers, and entrepreneurs. The magazine was mentioned in a recent article by the *New York Times* as a sign of the regeneration of the Athenian art scene, urban life, and tourism.

*Anna Poupou*

**See also:** Chapter 16: Newspapers and Magazines.

**Further Reading**

Nikolaidou, Afroditi, and Fani Kountouri. 2016. "The Crisis of Debt as a Public Issue. Controversial Political, Journalistic and Social Discourse." In *Public Issues in the Political* Agenda (in Greek), edited by Fani Kountouri, 203–234. Athens: Kallipos.

Thoreau, Henry David. 2016. "Walking." In *The Making of the American Essay*, edited by John D'Agata, 167–195. Minneapolis: Graywolf Press.

Veglis, Andreas. 2012. "Journalism and Cross-Media Publishing: The Case of Greece." In *The Handbook of Global Online Journalism*, edited by Eugenia Saperia and Andreas Veglis, 210–230. Hoboken, NJ: Wiley-Blackwell.

Wilder, Charly. 2018. "Athens, Rising." *New York Times*, June 18, 2018.

## Newspapers and Magazines

In recent years, no other sector of the Greek media has been so strongly affected as the newspapers. What seemed to be a "golden era" for the newspapers from 1981 to 2004 came to a halt during Greece's economic crisis (Leandros 2013, 32). In 1989, the average circulation of daily newspapers reached a peak of 1.13 million copies. In the beginning of the economic crisis, in 2011, it fell to 216,000 copies. In 2016, Greece published 280 newspapers on a national level, 15 daily newspapers, and 120 magazines. Since the mid-1990s, total sales of the national newspaper sector have dropped, with daily editions suffering the biggest losses (Papathanassopoulos 2018).

The financial and sociopolitical crisis totally reversed the established press practices and hierarchies of the past forty years. The fall of the military dictatorship in 1974 and the restoration of a democratic regime that followed ensured the expression of freedom and abolishment of strict political censorship in the media. After 1974, the newspapers were modernized. It was one of the few moments in modern Greek history that journalists enjoyed full freedom of political speech.

From the end of the 1970s until the end of 2010s, the dual-party system and the competition between the two major parties—PASOK and New Democracy—was covered by the major Greek newspapers. In this period, some of the oldest newspapers such as *To Vima*, *Ta Nea*, *Kathimerini*, *Eleftherotypia*, and *Ethnos* had the highest readership. In the 1990s and early 2000s, due to technological advances, the evolution of the audiovisual sector,

Newspapers and magazines are for sale throughout Greece at newspaper stands, such as this one on Ermou Street in Athens, and in kiosks. Although Greeks today prefer their information from digital media, social media, and websites, the importance of the press and printed newspapers is still visible in public spaces. The press enjoys freedom of speech, as seen in the headline that criticizes Alexis Tsipras, prime minister at the time, comparing him to President Nicolas Maduro of Venezuela. (Photo by Alexander Fatouros)

and the growth of the advertising market, major media groups were restructured, entered the stock exchange, and expanded to include financial activities such as investment in construction. Furthermore, business relations between the media and the political parties became more evident and scandals regarding the media came to light. In these two decades, an extraordinary number of newspapers competed for the advertising market and readership. According to Papathanassopoulos (2018), there was an excess of supply over demand. The web expansion and the development of digital media contributed to this downhill spiral after the crisis, but there were other reasons as well. In the first years of the financial crisis (2010 and 2011), most of the established newspapers and well-known journalists supported the austerity measures that were put forth by the Troika (the International Monetary Fund, the European Commission, and the European Central Bank) as a condition for Greece obtaining loans to pay off its debts. This contrasted with public opinion and the anti-Troika/anti-governmental movement that was growing. Mainstream newspapers remained closely connected with the two major political parties, while new radical political forces from the extreme left to the extreme right were rising. Established media were accused of supporting the elite's interests and not acting as reporters of public opinion (Smyrnaios 2013). Between 2008 and 2012, lack of trust toward established newspapers grew. Anti-journalism and anti-media slogans were frequently repeated in the anti-austerity demonstrations, strikes, and activist events. According to a 2017 Reuter's survey, the percentage of Greeks who trust mainstream media measured only 23 percent, the lowest in Europe.

The lack of trust, together with the financial recession and shrinking of the advertising market, resulted to a reorganization of the major media groups. Some of them changed owners, for example, the group Pegasos, owned by media magnate Yiorgos

Bobolas, was bought by Ivan Savvidis. Others became bankrupt, such as the Journalistic Organism Lambraki (DOL), now owned by Evangelos Marinakis. DOL published two of the oldest leading newspapers, *To Vima* (from 1921) and *Ta Nea* (from 1931): *Ta Nea* ceased its circulation for a few months, and *To Vima* put an end to the daily printed edition and preserved only the Sunday edition on paper. The newspaper *Eleftherotypia*, an emblematic newspaper of the Metapolitefsi era, also ceased publication after the bankruptcy of the owners (Terzopoulos Group) in 2013. The employees of the newspaper, who had remained unpaid for a long period of time, decided to reopen it under a new name, *Newspaper of the Journalists/Efimerida ton Syntakton*. Today it functions as a collective, and all employees have equal wages. It is one of the leading newspapers, with eight thousand copies for the daily edition and twenty thousand for the Sunday edition. *Kathimerini* is one of the few historic newspapers that retained its position in first place based on numbers of circulation, with fifteen thousand copies for the daily paper and sixty-five thousand for the Sunday edition.

These changes created a space for the emergence of new titles that could be characterized as tabloid press. Recently created tabloid newspapers such as *Thema*, *Makeleio*, *Espresso*, and *Starpress*, with sensational front-page headlines and featuring gossip about celebrities, are equally popular as older and established ones. A new trend of the free press appeared in the 2000s with the first free newspapers *Metro* and *City Press*. However, with the first signs of the recession, the papers ceased, since they totally depended on advertising. Today the free weekly editions, *Lifo* and *Athens Voice*, are very popular.

Beginning in the 1990s, there was also an important growth in lifestyle and fashion magazines. This occurred in tandem with the rise of consumerism in Greece. Some of them were extremely influential, for example, the lifestyle magazine *KLIK*, which had a guilt-free attitude toward sex and dealt with night life, clubbing, and youth culture. *KLIK*'s popularity was also quickly followed by other similar magazines. Its chief editor, Petros Kostopoulos, later created his own group named IMAKO, which became bankrupt a few years after its founding. These magazines were accused of promoting an excessive individualistic lifestyle and became the symbol of the moral degradation of the Greek society during the era of the false financial growth. Nowadays, very few of these lifestyle or fashion magazines have survived and some of them are offered for free together with the newspapers' Sunday editions. On the other hand, magazines regarding cooking, well-being, and city guides, as well as specialized magazines, have a modest but stable circulation. Before the crisis there were also a few English-language newspapers; the oldest was *Athens News*, which ceased its circulation in 2013. Today, the major newspapers also have an English language section in their web edition.

*Anna Poupou*

**See also:** Chapter 4: Overview. Chapter 16: Digital Media.

**Further reading**

Kalogeropoulos, Antonis. 2018. *Digital News Report*. Reuters Institute, University of Oxford. Accessed April 14, 2021. http://www.digitalnewsreport.org/survey/2018/greece-2018/.

Leandros, Nikos. 2013. "Media in the Center of the Crisis. The Financial Results of Eight Major Companies." In *Crisis and the Media*, edited by Yiorgos Pleios, 31–37. Athens: Papazissis.

Papathanassopoulos, Stylianos. 2018. "Greece – Media Landscape." *MediaLandscapes.org*, by European Journalism Center (EJC). Accessed April 14, 2021. https://medialandscapes.org/country/greece.

Smyrnaios, Nikos. 2013. "Manufacturing Consent and Legitimizing Austerity. The Greek Media Before and After the Crisis." ESA 11th Conference: Crisis, Critique and Change, Torino, August 2013.

## Radio

In the fluid and fast-changing media landscape during the crisis, radio proved to be a stable preference of the audience. Greeks prefer radio for their information and their entertainment, and it is still an important part of everyday life that not only competes with but works in a complementary fashion with the Internet and social media. The average daily time that Greeks listen to the radio is 3.5 hours according to Focus Bari survey (Papathanassopoulos 2018). As early as 2008, almost all radio stations were also broadcasting live from their websites. Today, Greece has little under one thousand radio stations at the local, regional, and national levels.

Only state radio stations have permission to broadcast on a national level. The Greek Radio and Television (ERT), after a short time of being shut down by the government, started broadcast again in 2015. Now there are five FM radio stations, First Programme (information and politics), Second (culture and entertainment), Third (classical and folk music), ERA Sport and Cosmos (jazz and world music), and AM Voice of Greece, which is addressed to an international audience. All these stations have live web broadcasting at webradio.ert.gr.

Until the 1990s, only state radio stations and a few municipal stations (such as Athena 9.84 inaugurated in 1987) were licensed, and a large number of pirate radio stations were on air. During the so-called deregulation period (from 1987 to the 2000s), the number of nonpirated private radio station multiplied and generated a flourishing of the radio culture, with new popular stations and also famous producers, journalists, and DJs. They were not threatened by the advent of private television during the same period. Today, most of the radio stations are not licenced because of the 2017 legislation regarding the media.

During the years of the crisis, there were a few changes in the radio landscape, with radio stations closing and new ones appearing. However, there was not the radical change experienced by the press and television. The most popular radio stations today are Real FM and SKAI 100,3, both oriented toward information and politics and connected with large media groups. These are followed by music radio stations, Melodia FM, Rythmos FM, Athens Dee Jay, Red and Easy 102,2. There has been an increase in recent years of sports radio stations. According to recent surveys, younger people (ages seventeen to twenty-four) do not listen to the radio and prefer music platforms such as Spotify. On the other hand, audiences aged forty and above listen to radio mostly for information, satirical shows, political debates, and sportscasting, especially when combined with another favorite Greek daily routine, driving.

Unlike in the United States, podcasts are almost nonexistent.

*Anna Poupou*

**See also:** Chapter 16: Overview.

**Further Reading**

Focus Bari. 2018. *Monthly Press Release for Research S.M.A.R.T. Bari: Audience of Radio Stations in Attica (21/5/2018 – 17/6/2018)* (in Greek). Accessed April 14, 2021. https://www.focusbari.gr/images/tips/AKROAMATIKOTHTA_RF_ATTIKHS.pdf.

Papathanassopoulos, Stylianos. 2018. "Greece – Media Landscape." *MediaLanscapes.org*, by European Journalism Center (EJC). Accessed April 14, 2021. https://medialandscapes.org/country/greece.

## Social Media

In the 1990s and 2000s, the use of Internet in everyday practices flourished belatedly in comparison to other European countries, mostly due to the slow advance of technical infrastructure for broadband access and high cost of the Internet services. This situation was reversed at the end of the 2000s, leading to the growth of all activities that related to Internet, including the flourishing of social media. Today, the majority of Greeks use social media such as Facebook, Twitter, Instagram, as well as YouTube on a daily basis. According to the European Committee's 2017 Digital Economy and Society Index (DESI), Greece is only at the twenty-sixth position in regard to the use of digital technologies and communication by citizens, enterprises, state services, and education. However, the utilization of social media by the Internet users is above the European average: more than 65.7 percent, compared to the European Union (EU) average of 63.1 percent.

According to numbers given by Facebook in 2016, almost four million Greeks connect daily to their Facebook accounts, most of them through their smartphone. More than 40 percent of Greeks own an account. However, recent disclosures about the leaks of personal information of the users and the publicity about the influence of the platform on election campaigns worldwide provoked intense debates in Greece. It might generate a decrease in Facebook use. From 2010 to 2017, the use of YouTube on a daily basis for those in the age group of thirteen to twenty-four dramatically increased. In 2010, it was 46 percent; in 2017, it increased to 76 percent, according to a recent survey by Focus Bari.

According to a 2017 Reuters survey, Greeks, compared to other Europeans, have the lowest level of trust in mainstream media journalism, established newspapers, and television news; the rise of the social media seems to fill this gap. During the years of the sociopolitical turmoil in Greece, especially between 2008 and 2012, Twitter and Facebook played an instrumental role in political anti-governmental activism in Athens and other Greek cities—for example, the riots of 2008–2009 that followed the death by shooting of a fifteen-year-old student by a police officer in Exarhia; many of the protestors were school students, teenagers, and young people already adept at using social media. In the following years, riots took a more political anti-austerity orientation, with a more inclusive participation from a wider age range. They also used social media for their information, organization, and safety. Facebook and Twitter were also important in the 2011 organization of the *Aganaktismenoi* movement, a form of protest similar to the Indignados in Spain and Occupy in the United States, and in other forms of political and social activism as well. Another example of the importance of social media to Greek politics is their use by the SYRIZA party. In 2012, since they were a small political party and had the majority of the established media against them, they based their election campaign on social media.

In 2015, with the rise of SYRIZA to the government, the political discussions in social media reached a high point. For example, they included the possibility of a Grexit from the EU: the referendum that asked the people to decide whether Greece should accept the bailout conditions that the European Commission, the International Monetary Fund, and the European Central Bank proposed; and the capital controls (an emergency measure taken by the Greek government beginning in June 2015 that set a limit to the amount of cash that the citizens were allowed to withdraw from their bank accounts each week).

The intensity of the debates and the strong division of the users into either Europhiles or Eurosceptics created an explosive landscape in social media. Many reviewers and media scholars considered this as a sign of a deteriorated journalistic and public discourse. The relation of social media to the political parties and the lies that are broadcast to bolster the parties have generated recent websites such as Ellinikahoaxes.gr that informs about the fake news, hoaxes, and scams on the Greek web.

Greeks rely not only on social media for their information but also use it for entertainment and professional networking. Platforms such as LinkedIn have shown a lot of growth. Commercial enterprises, educational institutions, and cultural organizations use social media in their promotional strategies and in building a community network. Nowadays social media tend to replace older Internet promotional tools, such as the newsletter that arrived in the email inbox of the users or customers. Applications regarding games and utilities such as maps are equally popular, as are communication applications for messaging and sound-camera calling such as Skype, Viber, and WhatsApp. Last but not least, social media that focus on flirting and dating, such as Grindr, OKCupid, and Tinder, continue to show growth with both men and women users. All major television channels promote interaction with the audience via social media, Facebook, Twitter, and Instagram.

Today, a significant number of articles in Greek mainstream media discuss the negative implications of the growing use of social media in the quality of everyday life and point to the problems of emotional fatigue and social media addictions. For example, in 2017, 33 percent of calls processed by Safe Internet help-line.gr, an organization addressed to children, adolescents, and their parents regarding Internet issues, was connected to problems of addiction to social media or cyber-bulling cases.

*Anna Poupou*

**See also:** Chapter 3: Panhellenic Socialist Movement; Leftist Parties of Greece.

**Further Reading**

Afouxenides, Alex. 2014. "Social Media and Political Participation: An Investigation of Small Scale Activism in Greece." *Advances in Applied Sociology* 4: 1–4.

FocusBari.gr. 2018. "Focus on Tech Life. Mobile, Households, Web, Kids." June – December 2020. Accesed April 14, 2021. https://www.focusbari.gr/images/tips/FOCUS_ON_TECH_LIFE_TIPS_-20B.pdf.

Zaroulia, Marilena, and Philip Hager. 2013. "Europhile or Eurosceptic?: Gaps in the Narrative and Performances of Panic." In *Remapping Crisis. A Guide to Athens*, edited by Myrto Tsilimpounidi and Aylwyn Walsh, 226–247. Winchester: Zero Books.

## Street Art and Graffiti

During the past decade, Athens has become one of the most thriving cities for street art and graffiti paintings. The walls of Athens are covered by large-scale murals by famous Greek and international artists. Spray paint graffiti, stencils, and tags (stylized signatures) are today common in the central area of Athens. Districts such as Exarhia, Metaxourgeio, and Psyri are described as open-air permanent galleries and as the new landmarks of the Athenian cityscape. Street art walking tours are today a popular activity for alternative tourism in Athens.

One of the recognizable street artists is INO, whose murals, usually black and white with high contrasts and edgy shadows, compose a narrative related to the financial crisis or make a critical point about the relationship of contemporary Greece to antiquity (e.g., System of a fraud or Access Control). Other known artists are Alexandros Vasmoulakis, Sonke, Woozy, WD, Alex Martinez, and others. Some of the most known works, such as the mural "Praying for Us" near Omonoia Square, which was created by a team from the School of Fine Arts, illustrate articles in international journals, tourist guides, and even academic books about contemporary Greece (e.g., Tziovas 2017).

Before 2000, Greece did not have a strong tradition in street art and graffiti, unlike major European and U.S. cities. However, especially after the fall of the dictatorship in 1974, the building walls on the streets of Athens and other cities were usually covered by political slogans and posters. In the context of the preparations for the Olympic Games of 2004, the municipality of Athens commissioned a number of projects from the School of Fine Arts of the University of Athens. During the years of the crisis, this creative strand was intensified and often enriched with an anti-austerity and political content.

More recently, mainstream media and journals have stressed the negative effects of the expansion of street art. On the one hand, the majority agrees on the high artistic value of many works and murals, but on the other hand, there are complains about graffiti users who paint over artistically recognized graffiti or add tags without any artistic value, destroying public property. Most of the known artists say that they choose to paint on deserted buildings or empty areas in order to respect buildings of architectural interest or private property, proposing an ethics of this unofficial artistic practice.

Street art expanded as a result of the loose or nonexistent enforcement of laws against graffiti. Authorities have been reluctant to intervene in public spaces.

The mediatic debate about the limits of the freedom of artistic expression on monuments culminated in 2015, when the central emblematic building of Athens Polytechnic University was covered by a large-scale mural created in one night by anonymous artists. Although the buildings of the university were already covered by slogans, tags, and posters, this bleak black and white graffiti that covered the whole building aroused negative reactions even from journalists and politicians that in general support freedom of speech and artistic expression, and the dean of the university ordered the rehabilitation of the building, which was done immediately.

*Anna Poupou*

**See also:** Introduction: Photo of Antetokounmpo mural. Chapter 3: Photo of street art about capitalism. Chapter 4: Art Economy. Chapter 12: Protection of Modern Greek Monuments.

**Further Reading**

Henley, Jon. "Greece's Anti-austerity Murals: Street Art Expresses a Nation's Frustration." *The Guardian*, July 4, 2015. Accessed February 20, 2020. https://www.theguardian.com/world/2015/jul/04/greece-street-art-anti-austerity-murals.

Silva, Chantal, and Janice Dickson, "Graffiti City: The Rise of Street Art in Athens." *Independent*, September 15, 2017. Accessed February 20, 2020. https://www.independent.co.uk/arts-entertainment/photography/athens-greece-graffiti-city-street-art-financial-crisis-a7947506.html.

## Television

Television in Greece appeared late in comparison to other European countries, only at the end of the 1960s. A few attempts of experimental broadcasting took place from 1960 until 1966, when two state-owned channels begun official broadcasting. The first was the channel EIR (National Institute of Radiotelevision) and the second was the Channel of the Armed Forces (TED). This double-state monopoly remained solid in the following years despite changes in legislation, technological advances, as well as name changes. During the following forty years, EIR became EIRT, ERT, ET, and ERT1. TED was renamed YENED, ERT2, ET2, NET, and again ERT2.

The military government in the years of the dictatorship (1967–1974) took full advantage of the new medium as it conformed perfectly to the ideology of the regime. They believed it could strengthen family bonds and promote consumerism and Western pop culture, as well as be a vehicle for pro-military and nationalist propaganda. Journalistic and political shows were limited, as the channels operated under strict control of censorship. The basic focus was on entertainment. For example, the programs included:

- U.S. series and soap operas such as *Peyton Place*, *Bonanza*, *I Love Lucy*, and a few years later *Dallas* and *Dynasty*;
- Greek sitcoms and dramas (*Our Neighborhood*, *The Unknown War*);
- pro-military propaganda, with many programs concerning the armed forces; and
- sports shows, especially football (soccer) games.

*Athletic Sunday*, which premiered in 1972, the longest-living show, survives even today.

After the restoration of democracy, strong efforts were made by the government to demilitarize public television. To do this, they hired important personalities such as Manos Chatzidakis, Robert Manthoulis, and Vassilis Vassilikos to administrative posts. As a result, more cultural programming was developed, with shows related to music, cinema, and theatre. These included the prolific show *Monday's Theatre* that broadcast theatrical performances; the *Cinema Night* that presented international arthouse films; and the documentary series *Backstage* by Lakis Papastathis (that lasted from 1976 to 2013), a real laboratory for all genres of documentary. Many of these shows, extremely valuable today for the history of Greek arts and culture, are digitized and can be watched at the open access web platform ERT Archive (archive.ert.gr).

The state monopoly, which consisted of two channels, continued, and after the election of PASOK in 1981, the state added more emphasis to two specific social thematic axes: the development of basic infrastructures of rural areas of the country and the politics of gender equity. The stations produced documentaries about the history and culture of the Greek provinces and villages as well as feminist talk shows. The third national channel, ERT3, broadcasted for the first time from Thessaloniki in 1988.

The year 1989 marked the end of the state monopoly, the creation of private television, and the beginning of the period known as the "deregulation" of the television sector. In 1989, with provisional licenses, two channels started broadcasting, and they soon dominated the audiovisual landscape for the next two decades. MEGA channel was known for its successful sitcoms (*The Three Graces*, *Dolce Vita*, *Retire*, *Two Strangers*) that replaced prime-time foreign fictional shows, while ANT1 was known for its glamorous entertainment shows (*Ciao Antenna*, *Bravo Roula*), its soap operas (*The Glow*, *Goodmorning Life*), and shows of the morning zone (*Morning Coffee*, *Goodmorning Greece*). In the following years, Star Channel, which specialized in entertainment and lifestyle news, and SKY, which focused on news and information, were added. Television news become more focused on specific anchormen and anchorwomen (Nikos Chatzinikolaou, Elli Stai, Liana Kanelli, etc.) and made a turn to infotainment. The 1990s marked the explosion in the audiovisual sector with six channels of nationwide broadcasting and more than a hundred local channels, while spectatorship of the state-owned ET1 and ET2 was low (only 7.3 percent in 1995) in comparison to the private channels. In the 2000s, a shift was made toward political talk shows and reality shows, such as *Big Brother* by Antenna (2001), talent and competition shows, and the production of fictional shows.

The financial and political crisis and intense social climate after 2008 brought serious mutations in the media landscape. The recession, the politics of austerity, and the radical changes in consumer practices had an impact on television. Advertising, which was the main financial source of revenue for private television, continued to shrink rapidly, and as a result, most of the channels faced serious economic problems (for instance, ALTER channel became bankrupt). The production of fictional series and soap operas has stopped, leaving professionals in the audiovisual sector unemployed. Furthermore, Greek serials could not compete with the pirate downloading of international and mainly American series, and as a result spectatorship has fallen, especially in young ages. The programming has turned to low-budget talk shows, talent competitions, and repetitions of older successful sitcoms such as *Crimes* (ANT1) and *Retire* (MEGA). A few satirical shows remained very popular and influential, namely *Ellinofrenia* (SKAI) and the one-man-show *Al Tsadiri News* by comedian Lakis Lazopoulos. In an effort to gain younger audiences, channels launched a more active presence in webTV and social media sites such as Twitter and Instagram. This offered them immediate interaction with their spectators. Two satellite subscription platforms, NOVA and COSMOTE, offer access to international channels and other interactive services.

In the 2000s, the public identified ERT as a slow, bureaucratic organism with an elitist and highbrow programming. Nevertheless, the unexpected closing down of the state radio television network by the government in June 2013, due to austerity politics, provoked massive protests and demonstrations from an extremely wide range of supporters. They included the Greek diaspora (as ERT was broadcasted in many countries), church authorities, political groups, activists, artists, journalists, and so on. This act contributed to the fall of the coalition government a few months later in 2013. In the following years, ERT was restructured, and in 2015 its five channels (ERT1, ERT2, ERT3, ERT HD, and ERT World) started broadcasting again. During the summer of 2016, the government of Greece introduced a new legal framework for the regulation of the audiovisual sector, but a few months later it was canceled.

In the following years, the audiovisual mediascape was unstable, due to the competitions about the official licenses for television broadcasting, new legislations, and the remaining private channels facing serious financial problems as competition with Netflix and other streaming platforms was strong. After 2019, the private channels restarted the production of series, some of them very popular, such as Eteros Ego/The

Other Me (Cosmote TV, 2019) and Agries Melisses/Wild Bees (Ant1 TV, 2019). During the coronavirus lockdown, television viewership increased significantly.

*Anna Poupou*

**See also:** Chapter 3: Panhellenic Socialist Movement.

**Further Reading**

Kaklamanidou, Betty. 2017. "Introduction to the Greek Sitcom. The Case of the 'Three Graces.'" In *Old Games, New Rules: Rethinking Genre in Greek Cinema from 1970 until Today* (in Greek), edited by Afroditi Nikolaidou, Anna Poupou, M. Chalkou. Special Issue of *Filmicon Journal of Greek Film Studies*, No. 5, November 2017. Accessed May 6, 2021. https://filmiconjournal.com/journal/issue/4/2017.

Paschalidis, Grigoris. 2005. "Greek Television." In *Cultural Industries. Procedures, Services, Products* (in Greek), edited by Nikos Vernikos, Sophia Daskalopoulou, Filimon Badimaroudis, Nikos Boubaris, and Dimitris Papageorgiou. Athens: Kritiki.

Valoukos, Stathis. 2008. *History of Greek Television* (in Greek). Athens: Aigokeros.

APPENDIX A

# A DAY IN THE LIFE

*Note:* The following accounts have been fictionalized but are based on the lives of real people.

## A DAY IN THE LIFE OF A HIGH SCHOOL STUDENT

With a yawn, Yiannis, a Greek high school student, wakes up to another sunny spring day in the bedroom he has decorated with soccer posters.

His typical Athenian family lives in a second-floor, two-bedroom, one-bathroom condominium.

Yiannis quickly washes and dresses to prepare for his school day. He must be at school by 8:15 a.m. As he bounds down the stairs, he comes to the flat below where his grandparents live. On the landing, his gray-haired *yiayia* (grandmother) is waiting with a glass of milk and slice of *tsoureki* (sweet bread), encouraging him to eat. Yiayia gives him a loving hug and a wish for the steps of his day to be safe, "*Sto Kalo.*"

During the school day at his public high school, Yiannis carries his jacket and backpack with him, as there are no lockers. Classes are forty-five minutes in length, with five-minute breaks between classes. One fifteen-minute segment will count as a lunch break. Schools usually have no cafeterias; thus, students stream into the school yard to wolf down a snack. Food is not allowed in classrooms, but water bottles are permissible.

The Greek education system is centralized, and the curriculum is dictated by the Greek Ministry of Education. Yiannis will study traditional subjects such as science, mathematics, literature, and history. During the twenty-first century the curriculum and customs have changed due to the influence of the European Union. The time allotted to Greek history and literature has been reduced in order to include more world history and literature. The previously required Greek Orthodox religion class is now a course about religions of the world.

Spring is a particularly stressful time. Progress reports and grades are provided to students every three months. As the time for the June final exams approaches, Yiannis has more intense studying and memorization.

By 2 p.m., the school day will be over for Yiannis, and he will stop with his friends at one of the outdoor coffee shops that offer the popular iced coffees such as frappe and freddo. The jolt of caffeine, along with a *tiropita* (cheese pie), will renew his energy as he continues to one of his private tutoring classes. Because college admission is a priority, his parents budget the 20 euros an hour for tutors.

After the tutoring session, Yiannis will take the bus home and complete his homework. One of his parents will check his homework and quiz him on the answers. Each generation is expected to do better than that of their parents. The student dutifully does his best to meet his parents' expectations. However, in Greece, many graduate, but few find a job. Despite all of his hard work, Yiannis may eventually be forced to emigrate.

*Harriette Condes-Zervakis*

## A DAY IN THE LIFE OF A BANK EMPLOYEE

Greek bank employee Sophia must be an early riser. She is required to be at her desk by 7:45 a.m., and her workday will end at 3:15 p.m. Initially, Sophia had decided to drive to work but the traffic congestion had delayed her arrival at the bank several times. Her electronic punch card revealed she had been late, and she had received a warning letter from the Personnel Office. Since then, Sophia takes the metro train to work. At the Syntagma station, she walks slowly so that she can admire the archeological artifacts that were unearthed when the station was constructed for the 2004 Athens Olympic Games.

During the day, Sophia will take a break or eat lunch when the work seems to slow down. Neither rest breaks nor lunch breaks are mandated. Bank employees will take them whenever possible.

Drinking iced coffee at one's desk is accepted; thirst will not be a problem.

Currently potential bank hires are expected to have a college degree, whether from a Greek or foreign university. However, because Sophia had a relative who was well connected, she was hired, despite the fact that she had not continued her education after high school.

As a new hire, Sophia had twenty days of vacation time, in addition to the official national and religious holidays. Now that she has completed ten years of service, she has twenty-five vacation days, ten of which must be used during the summer.

When Sophia began her career as a teller, more of her tasks required some writing and documenting by hand, especially for foreign currency exchange. Now that she has a position in the business loans department, 98 percent of her work is computerized.

On this day Sophia will not eat lunch. Lines of customers have formed to face the employees and the waiting, coupled with lack of personal space, leads to general frustration and irritability.

Since the beginning of the financial crisis in Greece, bank employees have seen their salaries reduced by approximately 15 percent and their medical insurance and prescription benefits severely limited. However, Sophia, like many others, continues to labor and hope for better days.

*Harriette Condes-Zervakis*

## A DAY IN THE LIFE OF A RETIRED COUPLE

On the balcony of their condominium, the retired couple, Sotiris and Eleftheria, sip Greek coffee from demitasse cups and occasionally dip their *voutimata* (cookies) or *paximadia* (biscotti) into the coffee as they chat. They are planning two trips.

Easter, the most significant holiday of the Greek Orthodox religion, is approaching, and those who have ancestral homes outside of Athens flock to their small towns, villages, or islands, away from the confinement of the condominium, to celebrate the resurrection of Christ.

In Greece, major religious holidays lead to three- to four-day weekends and an exodus of vehicles from Athens. Sotiris must brace himself for he knows he will deal with the aggressive driving of others and traffic congestion on the national road that he must take out of the city. Motorcycle and scooter drivers weaving in and out of lanes, between cars, present a particular challenge. Traffic signs on the national expressways warn drivers that automobile speed limits are monitored by radar, but the couple rarely sees a car pulled over by the police.

Some of their neighbors will be traveling by ferry boats to the dazzling Greek islands, taking their vehicles with them. Drivers wait impatiently to edge into the ferry's limited space. Sometimes they will lean on their car horns in frustration as the process moves slowly. Odors of gasoline and diesel fuel waft into the air. Motorcyclists avoid the line by steering their vehicles between the cars. Holding iced frappes in one hand, the uniformed boat crew members will shout over the sounds of running engines and gesture broadly.

Long weekends are traditionally a consequence of a Christian holiday, such as the Dormition of the Virgin Mary, Christmas, or Epiphany. Yet, Eleftheria complains bitterly; the European Union has forced Greek citizens to legally downplay their religion. Her national identification card no longer includes her religious affiliation, her grandson no longer learns prayers in school, and icons of Jesus and the Virgin Mary have been removed from schools and hospitals.

Meanwhile, following a visit to the doctor regarding pain in the back and legs due to arthritis, Eleftheria has another trip to plan. Her physician has prescribed at least fifty *bania* this summer. Bania are dips into the sea for at least half an hour, which may consist of swimming or any other form of exercise, no matter how mild. The key is to be in salt water.

This is a standard prescription for arthritis. Patients can complete aerobic exercises easily in the salt water, without putting pressure on their joints. Time at the beach allows patients to relax and strengthen their immune system. The warmth of the sun, the soothing sound of the gentle waves, and the time away from obligations are all factors that are considered to be emotionally and physically uplifting and important to treatment. Eleftheria and Sotiris discuss possible locations. Being in Greece means that the sea is never more than sixty miles away.

*Harriette Condes-Zervakis*

## A DAY IN THE LIFE OF A RURAL FARMER

Moshoula lives in a small village on the Greek island of Ikaria, located in the northern Aegean Sea. The island has a permanent population of approximately eight thousand.

Moshoula rises early each morning at approximately six. She drinks a frappe and watches the news on television. Her first task is to feed clover, twigs, and barley to her goats. The goats provide light and tasty goat's milk. After feeding the goats, she drives her pick-up truck a couple kilometers down the mountainous road to a meadow where her bull and two cows are kept. She feeds them hay. One of the cows will provide her with extra cash when she sells it for beef. When she is thinking about having the cow butchered, she will notify the others in the village. They will tell her about how much beef they want, and she will keep a list of orders. Once the local butcher has prepared the meat, Moshoula will weigh the portions of meat herself, deliver the meat to her customers, and collect the euros. She will also keep a large portion of beef to cook for her family.

After the daily routine of feeding the animals, Moshoula collects pieces of wood to take home and save for the fireplace.

Moshoula lives in a comfortable, modern home on the main street of the village. The home is tastefully furnished, and the kitchen has all the modern amenities. She is a meticulous housekeeper and spends some time cleaning the house each day. Moshoula is a *nikokira* (very competent homemaker), and her family appreciates the many delectable treats she makes, from traditional *finikia* (honey cookies) soaked in syrup and covered in ground walnuts, to homemade orangeade.

When it comes time to cook the main meal of the day, Moshoula goes to her garden for ingredients. In April and May, she plants tomatoes, peppers, green beans, and potatoes that she will harvest in July, August, and September. These vegetables are irrigated with water from her well. In the summer, she plants lettuce, cauliflower, cabbage, and onions. In November, she and her husband gather the olives from their olive trees. A large portion of the olives is processed into olive oil, an important staple in the kitchen.

Each afternoon Moshoula takes a nap. After the nap, she prepares two afternoon coffees and discusses current events with her husband, a taxi driver.

Ikaria is famous for its boisterous summer festivals or *panigiria*. However, the most common social interaction is the visit to the homes of friends and family. In the evening, Moshoula and her husband will stroll over to the home of one of their neighbors to share a glass of homemade wine and some local cheese.

Throughout the day, Moshoula chooses the pace at which she wants to complete her responsibilities. She has close ties to her neighbors and to the natural world around her. She may be a prime example of the reason for Ikaria's fame—longevity.

*Harriette Condes-Zervakis*

APPENDIX B

# GLOSSARY OF KEY TERMS

***Antiparochi*:** An agreement between a contractor and a landowner, where the contractor builds on the land and gives the owner one or two flats instead of paying him money for the land.

***Apokreas* (carnival):** Comparable to Mardi Gras in the United States. Celebrations before Lent include parades with floats, costumed participants, music, food, and drink.

**Aromanians, also called Vlachs:** An ethnic group native to the Balkans.

***Baklava*:** Layers of pastry stuffed with honey syrup and walnuts.

***Boubounieres*:** Favors of sugar-coated almonds wrapped in tulle with a ribbon distributed after baptisms and weddings.

***Bougatsa*:** Popular breakfast puff pastry composed of sweet semolina custard wrapped in flaky layers of filo dough.

***Briki*:** Tapered kettle used to make Greek coffee.

**Byzantine art and architecture:** Produced during the period of the Byzantine Empire, also referred to as the Eastern Roman Empire, between the fourth and fifteenth centuries CE.

**Byzantine Empire (330–1453 CE):** The eastern part of the Roman Empire, which survived the collapse of the western part of the Roman Empire in 476 CE. Its territory, which varied throughout its existence, encompassed Greece, the Balkans, the Middle East, and parts of Northern Africa. It came to an end with the conquest of the Ottomans.

**Classical Greek art and architecture:** Produced in Greece between the fourth and the fifth centuries BCE.

**Cretan School:** The fifteenth- to seventeenth-century post-Byzantine school of Greek Orthodox iconography.

***Diglossa* (or two languages):** Two versions of the same language. In Greece, the common people spoke *dimotiki*, and the more educated spoke *katharevousa*.

***Dikos*:** Wild ancient plant that is harvested from steep mountains and cliffs.

***Dimotiki* (demotic) Greek:** The Greek spoken by the common people, as opposed to more formal versions of the Greek language spoken by the educated.

***Dimotiko*:** Primary or elementary schools serving children between the ages of six and twelve and the equivalent of the first through sixth grades in the United States.

**Diphthong:** Syllables consisting of two vowels that are pronounced like one, for example, "join."

**Eclectic architecture:** The post-nineteenth-century architectural fusion of elements from various historical styles.

***Elafro* (light):** Greek urban music genre that emerged during the Interwar Period (1918–1940) and continued until the 1960s, encompassing less "serious" forms of classical European music together with romantic Greek lyrics.

***Elafrolaiko* (light-popular):** Greek urban music and dance genre that developed since the 1960s as a fresh aspect of *laiko* by fusing Greek songs with modern idioms of jazz, lounge, Latin, Euroamerican pop, and soft rock styles.

***Eleniko kafe*:** Flavorful and robust finely ground Greek coffee, boiled in a *briki*, and served in a demitasse.

***Entechni laiki* (art-popular):** Greek urban music genre of the postwar period (after the mid-1940s) characterized by the combination of two opposing styles—the "eastern" (folk, traditional, popular) and the "western" (European, classical, symphonic)—to create likeable music fusions.

**Epic poetry:** Long narrative poems usually involving heroic themes.

**European Central Bank (ECB):** Central bank of the Euro Area (the nineteen European Union countries that have adopted the euro). It administers the Euro Area's monetary policy and participates in the supervision of the banks of countries who have adopted the euro. The main task of the ECB is to maintain price stability in the Euro Area and thereby preserve the purchasing power of the single currency.

**European Commission (EC):** The politically independent executive but subsidiary body of the European Union, which is composed of twenty-seven commissioners, one for each member country. It proposes new European legislation, implements the decisions of the European Parliament and the Council of the European Union, and is responsible for and handles the enforcement of treaties made by the union.

**European Council:** A body of the European Union that is composed of the heads of the governments of European Union member states, as well as the president of the European Council and the president of the European Commission. It defines the European Union's overall political direction and priorities. In most cases, the council decides on legislation together with the European Parliament.

**European Parliament:** The only body of the European Union that is directly elected by citizens of member states. It votes on legislation and the budget.

**European Union (EU):** A unified trade and monetary body of twenty-seven member countries. The EU eliminates all border controls between members, allowing the free flow of goods and people except for random spot checks for crime and drugs. Three bodies run the EU. The EU Council represents national governments. The Parliament is elected by the people and adopts legislation that is usually proposed by the European Commission. The European Commission, the executive body of the EU, makes sure all members act consistently in regional, agricultural, and social policies. The EU's goals can be summarized as follows: promote peace and the well-being of its citizens; offer freedom, security, and justice without internal borders; promote sustainable development based on balanced economic growth and price stability; create a highly competitive market economy with full employment and social progress and environmental protection; combat social exclusion and discrimination; promote scientific and technological progress; enhance economic, social, and territorial cohesion and solidarity among EU countries; respect its rich cultural and linguistic diversity; and establish an economic and monetary union whose currency is the euro. EU values are inclusion, tolerance, justice, solidarity, and nondiscrimination.

**Frappe:** Cold, frothy beverage made from freeze-dried Nescafe instant coffee, sugar, and milk. The frappe ingredients are shaken and served in a tall glass with a *kalamaki* (straw). Widely known as a national drink, a frappe can be made without milk, *horis gala*.

***Frontisterio*:** Private school that offers afterschool or weekend tutoring.

**Golden Dawn:** Far-right political party that is waning in popularity. It lost its seats in Parliament in the 2019 election.

**Greek alphabet:** Composed of five vowels, with a total of twenty-four letters. The Greek alphabet was adapted and modified from the Phoenician alphabet and was the first to use letters for vowels. It consists of the letters α, β, γ, δ, ε, ζ, η, θ, ι, κ, λ, μ, ν, ξ, ο, π, ρ, σ, τ, υ, φ, χ, ψ, ω. Greek contains both uppercase and lowercase letters. Since the writing reform of 1982, only one accent mark is used.

***Gymnasio*:** Junior high school for children between the ages of twelve and fifteen that is equivalent to the seventh, eighth, and ninth grades in the United States.

**Hellenistic period:** The time period of Mediterranean history between the death of Alexander the Great in 323 BCE and the emergence of the Roman Empire after the Battle of Actium in 31 BCE.

**International Monetary Fund (IMF):** An organization of 190 member countries that works to foster global monetary cooperation, secure financial stability, facilitate international trade, promote high employment and sustainable economic growth, and reduce poverty around the world. The IMF, which is based in Washington, DC, is a specialized agency of the United Nations but maintains its own autonomy. Twenty-four executive directors of the IMF exercise voting rights over the strategic direction of the institution. One of these executive directors is from the United States. The largest shareholder in the fund is the United States.

***Kafeneio*:** Greek coffeehouse.

***Kalamboki*:** Roasted corn on the cob.

***Kamomili* (chamomile) tea:** Widely known for health-promoting benefits.

***Katharevousa*:** revised form of the Greek language based on ancient Greek grammar and word forms that was used by the Greek government and for other official purposes from 1832 to 1976 CE.

***Kefi*:** Joy, passion, high spirits, or overpowering emotion.

**KKE:** Communist Party of Greece.

***Koine* Greek (or Hellenistic or Bible Greek):** Fairly uniform form of ancient Greek combining Attic Greek, the Greek spoken in the ancient city-state of Athens, with other ancient Greek dialects. In the fourth century BCE, it was spread by Alexander the Great and his armies throughout the Balkans, the Middle East, and parts of northern Africa and East Asia. Later *Koine* Greek became the unofficial second language of the Roman Empire and was used to write the first New Testament.

***Koliva*:** Wheat dish prepared for funerals and memorial services.

***Komboloi*:** String of beads manipulated to relieve tension, relax, and pass time.

***Koulouria*:** Savory bread, much like a bagel, sprinkled with sesame.

***Koumpara*:** Maid of honor at a wedding.

***Koumparo*:** Best man at a wedding.

**Ladino:** Endangered language used by the Sephardic Jewish community of Spain who were expelled from Spain and Portugal after 1492.

***Laiko* (popular):** Greek urban music and dance genre that ensued around the 1950s as a modernized transformation of the *rebetiko* into a most fashionable style.

***Loukoumades*:** Fried donuts sprinkled with walnuts and drizzled with honey.

***Lykeio*:** Second level of high school that is the U.S. equivalent of tenth, eleventh, and twelfth grades.

***Lyre*:** A harp-like, stringed musical instrument.

**Lyric poetry:** Shorter, personal poems, which express emotions; in ancient Greece, lyric poetry was often accompanied by music played on the lyre.

***Martiriko*:** A small cross on a ribbon distributed after baptisms, which signifies the person who wears the cross had been a witness to the baptism.

***Mati* (evil eye):** The belief that a jealous person can cause harm, even unintentionally, by casting a glance.

**Memorandum of Understanding (MoU or MOU):** A written, formal agreement between two or more parties. In 2010, Greece and the Troika (the European Commission, the European Central Bank, and the International Monetary Fund) signed the first of three MoUs that outlined the conditions, including austerity measures, that were imposed upon Greece by the Troika so that Greece could obtain loans to help weather its economic crisis. The first MoU was followed by a second MoU (2011) and a third (2015).

***Mezedes*:** Appetizers such as hors d'oeuvres and dips.

***Mizithra*:** Cheese made with milk and whey from goats or sheep or a combination of both.

**Modern Standard Greek:** As of 1976, the official language of Greece, which is based primarily on demotic Greek.

***Moderno-laiko* (modern-popular):** Greek urban music and dance genre that arose in the mid-1970s as a simplified, mainstream, westernized, and professionalized form of *laiko.*

***Moutza*:** Greek equivalent of "giving someone the finger," which involves making the hand signal for the number five with one's palm turned toward the other person.

**Munich School:** The art of a group of Greek artists that studied in the Munich Royal Academy of Fine Arts between the mid-nineteenth and the early twentieth centuries.

**Neoclassical architecture:** A post-mid-eighteenth-century style that imitates ancient Greek and Roman architecture, which is also referred to as Greek Revival and Roman Revival architecture.

***Nipiagogeioa*:** Preschool or kindergarten for children under the age of six.

***Opa*:** Declaration of joy, which affirms the Greek way of life—one of passion and enthusiasm.

**Ouzo:** Anise-flavored liqueur.

***Panepistimio*:** University or college.

**Panhellenic Examinations:** Exams in the subject areas of science, humanities, and technology. The exam process is difficult and competitive and intended to ensure that a stream of highly qualified students feed into the colleges and universities.

***Paradosiako* (traditional):** Greek folk music and dance of mainland (*dimotiko*) and island (*nisiotiko*) rural regions, dating back to the early nineteenth century.

***Parea*:** Tight-knit group of friends.

**PASOK:** Panhellenic Socialist Movement, a political party.

***Periptero* (kiosk):** A small cubicle from which refreshments, newspapers, and magazines are sold.

***Philotimo*:** Respecting others and oneself, doing the right thing for the right reason.

***Philoxenia*:** Treating strangers with kindness, generosity, and hospitality.

**Pontians:** Greeks who had originally lived in an area called Pontos on the southern coast of the Black Sea. They came to Greece as refugees in the early part of the twentieth century or as immigrants from Russia and Ukraine in the 1990s after the breakup of the Soviet Union. They speak an endangered language based on ancient Greek that is not easily understood by modern Greeks.

***Prika* (dowry):** The transferring of personal property or wealth by a bride's family to a groom on the occasion of marriage. It was outlawed in Greece in 1983.

**Psistaria:** Barbeque restaurant.

***Rebetiko*:** Greek urban music and dance genre that emerged during the first half of the twentieth century and was connected with lower and working-class populations of the underworld.

***Retsina*:** Resin-flavored liquor.

***Rizogalo*:** Rice pudding.

***Rouspheti*:** The reciprocal dispensation of favors, for example, a politician rewarding a supporter with a government job.

***Sarakosti* (Lent):** The forty days preceding Easter, when devout Orthodox Christians fast.

**Snap election:** Occurs when the Parliament does not run its full four-year term, typically because the prime minister wishes to decide a pressing issue, such as a major crisis, or believes that such an election will secure a larger parliamentary majority.

***Souvlaki*:** Spit-roasted chunks of pork or lamb.

***Spanakopita*:** Spinach and feta pastry.

**SYRIZA (Coalition of the Radical Left):** A leftist political party in which past prime minister Alexis Tsipras plays a leadership role.

***Taramasalata*:** Pâté created from roe, breadcrumbs, salt, lemon, and olive oil.

***Tavernas*:** Affordable casual eating establishments, usually with an outdoor dining option.

***Tiropita*:** Feta cheese pastry.

**Troika:** A group of three working together. The term Troika in Greece refers to the decision group formed by the European Commission, the European Central Bank, and the International Monetary Fund. The usage arose in the context of the "bailouts" of Cyprus, Greece, Ireland, and Portugal necessitated by their prospective insolvency, which was caused by the world financial crisis of 2007–2008.

***Tzatziki*:** Garlic, yogurt, and cucumber dip.

APPENDIX C

# FACTS AND FIGURES

Table 1: GEOGRAPHY

| | |
|---|---|
| **Location** | Greece occupies the southern end of the Balkan Peninsula in southeastern Europe and includes several hundred offshore islands. It is bounded by Albania, Macedonia, and Bulgaria to the north; Turkey to the northeast; the Aegean Sea to the east; the Mediterranean Sea to the south; and the Ionian Sea to the west. |
| **Time Zone** | 7 hours ahead of U.S. Eastern Standard |
| **Land Borders** | 752 miles |
| **Coastline** | 8,498 miles |
| **Capital** | Athens |
| **Area** | 50,929 sq. miles |
| **Climate** | Greece has a Mediterranean climate, with mild, rainy winters and hot, arid summers. Average temperatures in the south range from 40°F during winter months to 90°F in the summer. Temperatures in the north are substantially lower in the winter months, but summer heat and humidity can be high. |
| **Land Use** | 34.88% arable land; 18.16% permanent crops; 25.24% cropland; 22.36% permanent meadows and pastures; 31.69% forest land (2016) |
| **Arable Land** | 34.9% (2016) |
| **Arable Land Per Capita** | 0.22 hectares per person (2015) |

Table 2: POPULATION

| | |
|---|---|
| **Population** | 10,768,000 (estimate) (2017) |
| **World Population Rank** | 85st (2017) |
| **Population Density** | 82.4 people per square kilometer (2017) |
| **Population Distribution** | 79.1% urban (2018) |
| **Age Distribution** | |
| 0–14: | 13.83% |
| 15–24 | 9.67% |
| 25–54 | 42.45% |
| 55–64 | 13.13% |
| 65+: | 20.91 (2017) |
| **Median Age** | 44.5 years (estimate) (2017) |
| **Population Growth Rate** | –.01% per year (estimate) (2018) |
| **Net Migration Rate** | 2.3 (estimate) (2018) |
| **Languages** | Greek |
| **Religious Groups** | Christian (98%) |

Table 3: HEALTH

| | |
|---|---|
| **Average Life Expectancy** | 80.8 years (2018) |
| **Average Life Expectancy, Male** | 78.2 years (2018) |
| **Average Life Expectancy, Female** | 83.6 years (2018) |
| **Crude Birth Rate** | 8.3 per 1,000 people (2018) |
| **Crude Death Rate** | 11.4 per 1,000 people (2018) |
| **Maternal Mortality** | 3 per 100,000 live births (2015) |
| **Infant Mortality** | 4 per 1,000 live births (2017) |
| **Doctors** | 6.3 per 1,000 people (2016) |

Table 4: ENVIRONMENT

| | |
|---|---|
| **$CO_2$ Emissions** | 6.2 metric tons per capita (2014) |
| **Alternative and Nuclear Energy** | 5.3% of total energy use (2014) |
| **Threatened Species** | 374 (2017) |
| **Protected Areas** | 53,574 sq. miles (2016) |
| **Total Renewable $H_2O$ Resources per Year** | 6,129 cubic meters, per person, per year (estimate) (2017) |

Table 5: ENERGY AND NATURAL RESOURCES

| | |
|---|---|
| **Electric Power Generation** | 48,340,000,000 kilowatt hours per year (estimate) (2016) |
| **Electric Power Consumption** | 53,050,000,000 kilowatt hours per year (estimate) (2016) |
| **Nuclear Power Plants** | 0 (2018) |
| **Crude Oil Production** | 3,000 barrels per day (2017) |
| **Crude Oil Consumption** | 304,000 barrels per day (2017) |
| **Natural Gas Production** | 8,000,000 cubic meters per year (estimate) (2017) |
| **Natural Gas Consumption** | 4,927,000,000 cubic meters per year (estimate) (2017) |
| **Natural Resources** | Lignite, petroleum, iron ore, bauxite, lead, zinc, nickel, magnesite, marble, salt, hydropower potential |

Table 6: NATIONAL FINANCES

| | |
|---|---|
| **Currency** | Euro |
| **Total Government Revenues** | $95,360,000,000 (estimate) (2017) |
| **Total Government Expenditures** | $98,080,000,000 (estimate) (2017) |
| **Budget Deficit** | -1.3% of GDP (2017) |
| **GDP Contribution by Sector** | agriculture 4%; industry 16%; services 80% (2017) |
| **External Debt** | $506,600,000,000 (2017) |
| **Economic Aid Extended** | $264,000,000 (2016) |
| **Economic Aid Received** | $0 (2017) |

Table 7: INDUSTRY AND LABOR

| | |
|---|---|
| **Gross Domestic Product (GDP) - official exchange rate** | $218,032,000,000 (estimate) (2018) |
| **GDP per Capita** | $20,572 (estimate) (2019) |
| **GDP - Purchasing Power Parity (PPP)** | $298,678,000,000 (estimate) (2017) |
| **GDP (PPP) per Capita** | $27,737 (estimate) (2017) |
| **Industry Products** | PetrTextiles, plastics, metals, processed food, tobacco products, petroleum products, chemicals, cigarettes, footwear. Greece also has significant tourist and shipping industries. |
| **Agriculture Products** | Sugar beets, wheat, maize, olives, tomatoes, grapes and wine, peaches and nectarines, potatoes, oranges, poultry, goats, sheep |
| **Unemployment** | 23.9% (2016) |
| **Labor Profile** | agriculture 12.6%; industry 15%; services 72.4% (2016) |

Table 8: TRADE

| | |
|---|---|
| **Imported Goods** | Machinery and transportation equipment, basic manufactures, food and live animals, chemicals and related products, petroleum and petroleum products, iron and steel |
| **Total Value of Imports** | $50,230,000,000 (estimate) (2017) |
| **Exported Goods** | Food and live animals, clothing and accessories, fruit and vegetables, textiles, petroleum products, tobacco, beverages |
| **Total Value of Exports** | $29,230,000,000 (estimate) (2017) |
| **Import Partners** | Germany 10.4%, Italy 8.2%, Russia 6.8%, Iraq 6.3%, South Korea 6.1%, China 5.4%, Netherlands 5.3%, France 4.3% (2017) |
| **Export Partners** | Italy 10.6%, Germany 7.1%, Turkey 6.8%, Cyprus 6.5%, Bulgaria 4.9%, Lebanon 4.3% (2017) |
| **Current Account Balance** | $-498,000,000 (estimate) (2017) |
| **Weights and Measures** | The metric system is in use. |

Table 9: EDUCATION

| | |
|---|---|
| **School System** | Greek students begin six years of primary school at the age of six. Early secondary school lasts for three years, followed by three years of upper secondary schooling at an academic upper secondary school or a vocational school. |
| **Mandatory Education** | 9 years, from ages 6 to 15 |
| **Average Years Spent in School for Current Students** | 18 (2016) |
| **Average Years Spent in School for Current Students, Male** | 18 (2016) |
| **Average Years Spent in School for Current Students, Female** | 18 (2016) |
| **Primary School-age Children Enrolled in Primary School** | 643,762 (2016) |
| **Primary School-age Males Enrolled in Primary School** | 331,700 (2016) |
| **Primary School-age Females Enrolled in Primary School** | 312,062 (2016) |
| **Secondary School-age Children Enrolled in Secondary School** | 662,741 (2016) |

| | |
|---|---|
| **Secondary School–age Males Enrolled in Secondary School** | 349,531 (2016) |
| **Secondary School–age Females Enrolled in Secondary School** | 313,210 (2016) |
| **Students Per Teacher, Primary School** | 9.6 (2016) |
| **Students Per Teacher, Secondary School** | 8.7 (2016) |
| **Enrollment in Tertiary Education** | 677,429 (2016) |
| **Enrollment in Tertiary Education, Male** | 347,688 (2016) |
| **Enrollment in Tertiary Education, Female** | 329,741 (2016) |
| **Literacy** | 98 (2016) |

**Table 10:** MILITARY

| | |
|---|---|
| **Defense Spending (% of GDP)** | 2% (2017) |
| **Total Active Armed Forces** | 146,000 (2017) |
| **Annual Military Expenditures** | $4,973,000,000 (2016) |
| **Military Service** | Military service is by selective conscription. Terms of service in both the navy and air force is 21 months and 19 months for the army. (2016) |

**Table 11:** TRANSPORTATION

| | |
|---|---|
| **Airports** | 77 (2013) |
| **Paved Roads** | 35.0% (2016) |
| **Registered Vehicles** | 8,035,423 (2015) |
| **Railroads** | 2,548 miles (2017) |
| **Ports** | Major: 8 (including Piraeus, Patrai, Thessaloniki, Agoiotheodoroi, Irakeion) |

**Table 12: COMMUNICATION**

| | |
|---|---|
| **Facebook Users** | 5,000,000 (estimate) (2017) |
| **Internet Users** | 7,443,016 (2016) |
| **Internet Users (% of Population)** | 69.0% (2016) |
| **Land-based Telephones in Use** | 5,200,950 (2016) |
| **Mobile Telephone Subscribers** | 12,538,927 (2016) |

APPENDIX D

# HOLIDAYS

Public holidays are national holidays. Public offices and schools are closed on these days.

| | | | |
|---|---|---|---|
| New Year's Day | January 1 | Public | Also celebrated ecclesiastically as the feast of St. Basil the Great and of the Circumcision of Jesus Christ. |
| Epiphany or Theophany | January 6 | Public | Celebrates Jesus Christ's baptism in the Jordan River by John the Baptist. Theophany means manifestation of God. |
| Clean Monday | Movable—the beginning of the seventh week before Orthodox Easter | Public | The first day of Lent is celebrated not only by church services but by the flying of kites throughout Greece. |
| Annunciation | March 25 | Public | Celebration of the announcement by the angel Gabriel to the Virgin Mary that she would conceive and become the mother of Jesus Christ. |
| Independence Day | March 25 | Public | Anniversary of the Declaration of Independence from the Ottoman Empire and the beginning of war in 1821. Parades commemorate this day. |
| Good Friday | Movable—Friday before Easter | Public | Commemorates the crucifixion, suffering, and death of Jesus Christ. |
| Easter | Movable | Public | Celebrates the Resurrection of Jesus Christ. The date is based on a decree of the Council of Nicaea held in 325 CE, which decided that Easter must be celebrated on the Sunday following the first full moon of the spring equinox but always after the Hebrew Passover. |
| Easter Monday | Movable—Easter plus one day | Public | Continues the celebration of Resurrection of Christ, when Mary Magdalene found the tomb of Jesus Christ empty. |

| | | | |
|---|---|---|---|
| Labor Day | May 1 | | On this optional holiday, employees may be given time off. May Day is also celebrated by hanging flowers or wreaths on houses and decorating car windshields with flowers. |
| Pentecost Monday or Holy Spirit Monday | Movable—Seventh Sunday after Easter | | Commemorates the descent of the Holy Spirit upon Jesus Christ's disciples. |
| Navy Week | Late June | | Celebrates the country's maritime tradition. Ports, fishing villages, and coastal towns have festivities lasting the week. |
| Restoration of Democracy | July 24 | | Celebrates the restoration of democracy in Greece after the fall of the junta, the military dictatorship that had governed Greece from 1967 to 1974. |
| Dormition and Assumption of the Holy Virgin | August 15 | Public | Celebrates the falling asleep and the assumption of the Virgin Mary into heaven. Festivals are held throughout Greece to commemorate this event. |
| Holy Cross | September 14 | Public | Celebrates the cross that Jesus Christ was crucified on. Saint Helen allegedly found the true Cross of Christ in Palestine. |
| Student Uprising | November 17 | | Anniversary of the student uprising at the Polytechnic University against the junta (military dictatorship) in 1973. |
| Ohi Day | October 28 | Public | Commemorates Prime Minister Metaxas's saying "*ohi*" (no) to Italy's demand that they occupy Greece in 1940. Subsequently Italy invaded Greece. |
| Christmas | December 25 | Public | Celebrates the birth of Jesus Christ. |
| Glorifying Mother of God | December 26 | Public | Day to glorify the Theotokos, the mother of Jesus Christ. |

# Selected Bibliography


Adrados, Francisco R. 2005. *A History of the Greek Language: From Its Origins to the Present.* Boston: Brill Leiden.

Androulidaki-Dimitriadi, Ismini. 2010. *Family Law in Greece.* Alphen aan den Rijn, The Netherlands: Kluwer Law International.

Azoulay, Vincent. 2014. *Pericles of Athens.* Translated by Janet Lloyd. Princeton, NJ: Princeton University Press.

Bakker, Egbert J., ed. 2010. *A Companion to the Ancient Greek Language.* Blackwell Companions to the Ancient World. Chichester, UK: Wiley-Blackwell.

Balampanidis, Yiannis. 2018. *Eurocommunism: From the Communist to the Radical European Left.* Basingstoke: Palgrave.

Baldwin-Edwards, Martin, coordinator. 2008. *Ethnicity and Migration: A Greek Story. Migrance*, No. 31. Accessed May 6, 2021. https://www.scribd.com/document/245726936/Ethnicity-Migration-A-Greek-Story-2008.

Ballian, Anna. 2011. *Relics of the Past. Treasures of the Greek Orthodox Church and the Population Exchange.* Athens: The Benaki Museum.

Beaton, Roderick. 2003. *George Seferis: Waiting for the Angel, A Biography.* New Haven, CT: Yale University Press.

Beaton, Roderick. 2019. *Greece: Biography of a Modern Nation.* Chicago: University of Chicago Press.

Bien, Peter. 1972a. *Kazantzakis and the Linguistic Revolution in Greek Literature.* Princeton, NJ: Princeton University Press.

Bien, Peter. 1972b. *Nikos Kazantzakis.* New York: Columbia University Press.

Birēs, G. Mano, and Marō Kardamitsē-Adamē. 2004. *Neo-Classical Architecture in Greece.* Los Angeles: Getty Publications.

Brewer, David. 2001. *The Greek War of Independence: the Struggle for Freedom from Ottoman Oppression and the Birth of the Modern Greek Nation.* Woodstock, NY: Overlook Press.

Brewer, David. 2003. *The Greek War of Independence.* Woodstock, NY: Overlook Press.

Brothwell, Don, and Patricia Brothwell. 1969. *Food in Antiquity: A Survey of the Diet of Early Peoples.* Baltimore: The Johns Hopkins University Press.

Browning, Robert. 1969. *Medieval and Modern Greek.* London: Hutchinson University Library.

Burns, Margie. "Archbishop Damaskinos." The International Raoul Wallenberg Foundation. Accessed January 24, 2018. http://www.raoulwallenberg.net/es/generales/archbishop-damaskinos/.

Cavafy, C. P. 2007. *The Collected Poems.* Translated by Evangelos Sachperoglou. Oxford: Oxford University Press.

Cavafy, C. P. 2008. *The Canon*. Translated by Stratis Haviaras. Cambridge: Harvard University Press.

Cavallo, Guglielmo, ed. 1997. *The Byzantines.* Chicago: University of Chicago Press.

Cavarnos, Constantine. 1998. *Byzantine Chant.* Belmont, MA: Institute for Byzantine and Modern Greek Studies.

Charitopulos, Dionyses. 2012. *Aris: Lord of The Mountains.* Athens: Topos Books.

Christopoulos, Dimitris, and Kostis Karpozilos. 2018. Translated by Michael Webber. *10+1 Questions and Answers on the Macedonian Question*. Athens: Rosa Luxemburg Stiftung. Accessed March 1, 2021. https://www.rosalux.de/fileadmin/rls_uploads/pdfs/engl/MAKEDONIKO_2019_EN.pdf.

*CIA World Factbook*. 2019–2020. Accessed March 1, 2021. https://www.cia.gov/library/publications/the-world-factbook/geos/gr.html.

Clogg, Richard. 1976. *The Movement for Greek Independence, 1770–1821: A Collection of Documents.* New York: Barnes & Noble.

Clogg, Richard. 1986. *A Short History of Modern Greece*, 2nd edition. Cambridge: University Press.

Clogg, Richard. 1987. *Parties and Elections in Greece: The Search for Legitimacy.* Durham, NC: Duke University Press.

Clogg, Richard. 2013. *A Concise History of Greece*. Cambridge: Cambridge University Press.

Clogg, Richard, and George N. Yannopoulos. 1972. *Greece under Military Rule*. New York: Basic Books.

Conacher, D. J. 1989. *Aeschylus' Oresteia*. Toronto: University of Toronto Press.

Condaratos, Savas, and Wilfried Wang, eds. 1999. *Greece: 20th-Century Architecture.* New York: Prestel.

Conomos, Dimitri E. 1984. *Byzantine Hymnography and Byzantine Chant*. Brookline, MA: Hellenic College Press.

Couloumbis, Theodore A., Theodore C. Kariotis, and Fotini Bellou. 2003. *Greece in the 20th Century.* London and New York: Psychology Press.

Council of Europe. 2018. "Group of States against Corruption: Evaluations." Accessed March 1, 2021. https://www.coe.int/en/web/greco/evaluations.

Cowan, Jane K. 1990. *Dance and the Body Politic in Northern Greece.* Princeton, NJ: Princeton University Press.

Dakin, Douglas. 1984. *The Unification of Greece, 1770–1923.* London: Benn.

Danforth, Loring M. 1982. *The Death Rituals of Rural Greece.* Princeton, NJ: Princeton University Press.

Davaki, Konstantina. 2013. "The Policy on Gender Equality in Greece." European Parliament Directorate General for Internal Policies. Policy Department C. Citizens' Rights and

Constitutional Affairs. Accessed March 1, 2021. http://ekke.gr/ocd/wp-content/uploads/2014/09/IPOL-FEMM_NT2013493028_EN.pdf.

Delivorias, Angelos. 1999. *Greek Traditional Jewelry.* Athens: Melissa.

Doliopoulou, Elsie. 2006. "System of Early Education/Care and Professionalisation in Greece." Commissioned report for the SEEPRO Project. Accessed February 20, 2020. http://www.ifp.bayern.de/imperia/md/content/stmas/ifp/commissioned_report_greece.pdf.

Draenos, Stan. 2012. *Andreas Papandreou: The Making of a Greek Democrat and Political Maverick.* London and New York: I. B. Tauris.

Edwards, Mark. *Homer: Poet of the Iliad.* 1990. Baltimore: Johns Hopkins University Press.

Elytis, Odysseus. 1974a. *The Axion Esti.* Translated by Edmund Keeley and George Savidis. Pittsburgh and London: The University of Pittsburgh Press.

Elytis, Odysseus. 1974b. *The Sovereign Sun: Selected Poems.* Translated by Kimon Friar. Philadelphia: Temple University Press.

Elytis, Odysseus. 2005. *Selected Poems: 1940–1979.* Translated by Edmund Keeley, Philip Sherrard, George Savidis, John Strathatos, and Nanos Valaoritis. Manchester, UK: Carcanet Press Ltd.

Evangelinos, Aris. 1998. *The Komboloi and its History,* 3rd edition. Nafplio, Greece: Komboloi Museum.

Evans, Peter. *1986. Ari: The Life and Times of Aristotle Onassis.* London: Jonathan Cape.

Featherstone, Kevin, and Dimitris Papadimitriou. 2015. *Prime Ministers in Greece: Paradox of Power.* Oxford: Oxford University.

Fessas-Emmanouil, Helen. 2001. *Essays on Neohellenic Architecture.* Athens: J. F. Kostopoulos Foundation.

"Final Agreement for the Settlement of the Differences as Described in the United Nations Security Council Resolution 817 (1993) and 845 (1993), the Termination of the Interim Accord of 1995, and the Establishment of a Strategic Partnership between the Parties." http://s.kathimerini.gr/resources/article-files/symfwnia-aggliko-keimeno.pdf.

Frazier, Nicholas, Philip Jacobson, Mark Ottaway, and Lewis Chester. 1979. *Aristotle Onassis.* Philadelphia: J. B Lippencott Company.

Gallant, Thomas W. 2015. *The Edinburgh History of the Greeks, 1768 to 1913. The Long Nineteenth Century.* Edinburgh: Edinburgh University Press.

Gallant, Thomas W. 2016. *Modern Greece: From the War of Independence to the Present,* 2nd edition. London and New York: Bloomsbury Academic.

Gibbons, Bob. 2003. *Travellers Nature Guides: Greece.* Oxford: Oxford University Press.

Gogonas, Nikos. 2010. *Bilingualism and Multiculturalism in Greek Education.* Newcastle upon Tyne, UK: Cambridge Scholars Publishing.

Gow, Mary. 2005. *Archimedes: Mathematical Genius of the Ancient World.* New York: Enslow Publishers, Inc.

Green, Peter. 2007. *Alexander the Great and the Hellenistic Age.* London: Phoenix.

Hard, Robin, and H. J Rose. 2004. *The Routledge Handbook of Greek Mythology.* London: Routledge.

Harris, Mary. 2016. "Greek Church Prays for LGBT Abnormality, Ahead of Thessaloniki Pride." 2016. *Greek Reporter,* June 24, 2016. Accessed May 8, 2018. http://greece

.greekreporter.com/2016/06/24/greek-church-prays-for-lgbt-abnormality-ahead-of-thessaloniki-pride/.

Heath, T. L. 1897. *The Works of Archimedes.* London: C. J. Clay and Sons.

Heatherington, Paul. 2008. *Enamels, Crowns, Relics and Icons – Studies on Luxury Arts in Byzantium.* Burlington, VT: Ashgate.

Hellenic Parliament. 2008. *The Constitution of Greece* (English version). Translated by Xenophon Paparrigopoulos and Stavroula Vassilouni. Accessed March 2, 2020. https://www.hellenicparliament.gr/UserFiles/f3c70a23-7696-49db-9148-f24dce6a27c8/001-156%20aggliko.pdf.

Hellenic Statistical Authority. "Greece in Figures. October to December 2019." Accessed March 1, 2021. https://www.statistics.gr/documents/20181/1515741/GreeceInFigures_2019Q4_EN.pdf.pdf/d0149260-0983-9d80-e5c1-4368dc87fda3.

Henley, Jon. "Greece's Anti-austerity Murals: Street Art Expresses a Nation's Frustration." *The Guardian*, April 7, 2015. Accessed February 20, 2020. https://www.theguardian.com/world/2015/jul/04/greece-street-art-anti-austerity-murals.

Heraclides, Alexis. 2010. *The Greek-Turkish Conflict in the Aegean: Imagined Enemies.* Basingstoke: Palgrave.

Hoffman, Susanna. 2000. "Glories of Greece." *Saveur* 131 (August/September): 60–64.

Hoffman, Susanna. 2004. *The Olive and The Caper: Adventures in Greek Cooking.* New York: Workman.

Hoffman, Susanna. 2006. "Making a Meze." *Bon Appetit* 51, no. 6 (June): 113–119.

Holst-Warhaft, Gail. 1980. *Theodorakis: Myth and Politics in Modern Greek Music.* Amsterdam: Adolf Hakkert.

Holst-Warhaft, Gail. 2006. *Road to Rembetika: Music of a Greek Sub-Culture, Songs of Love, Sorrow and Hashish.* Limni, Evia: Denise Harvey.

Horrocks, Geoffrey. 2010. *Greek: A History of the Language and Its Speakers.* Chichester, UK: Wiley-Blackwell.

Hose, Martin, and David J. Schenker. 2016. *A Companion to Greek Literature.* BlackwellCompanions to the Ancient World. Chichester, UK: Wiley Blackwell.

Howatson, M. C. 2011. *The Oxford Companion to Classical Literature*, 3rd edition. Oxford: Oxford University Press.

Hunt, Yvonne M. 1996. *Traditional Dance in Greek Culture.* Athens: Centre for Asia Minor Studies.

Jenkins, Romilly. 1940. *Dionysios Solomos.* Athens: Reprinted by Denise Harvey, 2000.

Joachim, Joachim G. 2009. *Ioannis Metaxas: The Formative Years 1871–1922.* Mannhein: Bibliopolis.

Kaklamanidou. Betty. 2017. "Introduction to the Greek Sitcom. The Case of the 'Three Graces.'" In Afroditi Nikolaidou, Anna Poupou, M. Chalkou, eds. *Old Games, New Rules: Rethinking Genre in Greek Cinema from 1970 until Today*, edited by Afroditi Nikolaidou, Anna Poupou, M. Chalkou. Special Issue of *Filmicon Journal of Greek Film Studies*, No. 5, November 2017. Accessed May 6, 2021. https://filmiconjournal.com/journal/issue/4/2017.

Kallimopoulou, Eleni. 2009. *Paradosiaká: Music, Meaning and Identity in Modern Greece.* Burlington, VT: Ashgate Publishing.

Kalogeropoulos, Antonis. 2018. *Digital News Report.* Reuters Institute, University of Oxford. Accessed March 1, 2021. http://www.digitalnewsreport.org/survey/2018/greece-2018/.

Kambouridis, Haris, and George Levounis. 1999. *Modern Greek Art, the 20th Century: A Comprehensive History of Painting, Engraving, and Sculpture.* Athens: Hellenic Ministry of the Aegean.

Karalis, Vrasidas. 2012. *A History of Greek Cinema.* New York: Continuum.

Karatassos, Pano. 2018. *Modern Greek Cooking: 100 Recipes for Mezes, Entrees, and Desserts.* New York: Rizzoli.

Kariotis, Theodore C., ed. 1992. *The Greek Socialist Experiment: Papandreou's Greece, 1981–1989.* New York: Pella Publishing Company.

Katsourides, Yiannos. 2016. *Radical Left Parties in Government: The Cases of SYRIZA and AKEL.* Basingstoke: Palgrave.

Kazantzakis, Helen. 1968. *Nikos Kazantzakis: A Biography Based on His Letters.* Translated by Amy Mims. New York: Simon and Schuster.

Kitromilides, Paschalis, ed. 2008. *The Trials of Statesmenship.* Edingburg: Edingburg University Press.

Kolokotronis, Theodoros. 1892. *Kolokotrones The Klepht and the Warrior: Sixty Years of Peril and Daring.* Translated by Elizabeth M. Edmonds. London: T. Fisher Unwin.

Kostis, Kostas. 2018. *History's Spoiled Children: The Story of Modern Greece.* London and New York: Oxford University Press.

Koulaidis, Vasilis, ed. 2003. *The Greek Education System: Facts and Figures.* Athens: Education Research Centre - Ministry of Education and Religious Affairs.

Leontis, Artemis. 2009. *Culture and Customs of Greece.* Westport, CT: Greenwood Press.

Lydakis, Stelios. 2011. *Neo-Hellenic Sculpture. History, Typology.* Athens: Melissa.

Mackridge, Peter. 2009. *Language and National Identity in Greece, 1766–1976.* Oxford: Oxford University Press.

Manessis, Nico. 2000. *The Illustrated Greek Wine Book.* Corfu: Olive Press Publications.

Mantzourani, Eva. 2011. *The Life and Twelve-Note Music of Nikos Skalkottas.* Aldershot: Ashgate Publishing.

March, Luke. 2012. *Radical Left Parties in Europe.* London: Routledge.

May, Hope. 2000. *On Socrates.* Belmont, CA: Wadsworth.

Mazower, Mark. 2008. *Networks of Power in Modern Greece.* New York: Columbia University Press.

McCarty, Nick. 2004. *Alexander the Great.* Camberwell, VIC: Penguin.

Michaelides, Solon. 1978. *The Music of Ancient Greece: An Encyclopaedia.* London: Faber & Faber.

Middleton, Darren J. 2005. *Scandalizing Jesus? Kazantzakis' The Last Temptation of Christ Fifty Years On.* New York: Bloomsbury Publishing Continuum.

Milona, Marianthi, ed. *2008. Culinaria Greece: Greek Specialties.* Cambridge: Tamden Verlag.

Missirli, Nelly, and Olga Mentzafanou-Polyzou, eds. 2007. *Classical Memories in Modern Greek Art*. Athens: National Gallery – Alexandros Soutsos Museum.

Moon, Warren G., ed. 1983. *Ancient Greek Art and Iconography*. Madison: University of Wisconsin.

Papadiamantis, Alexandros. 1977. *The Murderess*. Translated by George X. Xanthopoulides. London: Doric Publications.

Papadiamantis, Alexandros. 1987. *Tales from a Greek Island*. Translated by Elizabeth Constantinides. Baltimore: John Hopkins University Press.

Papadimitriou, Lydia, and Yannis Tzoumakis. 2012. *Greek Cinema. Texts, Histories, Identities*. Bristol: Intellect Books.

Papadogiannis, Nikolaos. 2015. *Militant around The Clock? Left-Wing Youth Politics, Leisure and Sexuality in Post-Dictatorship Greece, 1974–1981*. New York: Berghahn Books.

Papageorgiou-Venetas, Alexandros, 1994. *Athens – The Ancient Heritage and the Historic Cityscape in a Modern Metropolis*. Athens: The Archaeological Society at Athens.

Papanikolaou, Dimitris. 2007. *Singing Poets: Literature and Popular Music in France and Greece*. London: Modern Humanities Research Association & Maney Publishing.

Pappas, Takis. 1999. *Making Party Democracy in Greece*. Basingstoke: Palgrave.

Peddley, John Griffiths. 1997. *Greek Art and Archaeology*. London: Laurence King.

Pennanen, Risto Pekka. 1999. *Westernisation and Modernisation in Greek Popular Music*. Tampere: University of Tampere.

Petrakis, Marina. 2006. *The Metaxas Myth: Dictatorship and Propaganda in Greece*. London: Tauris Academic Studies.

Petsalis-Diomidis, Nicholas. 2001. *The Unknown Callas: The Greek Years*. Portland, OR: Amadeus Press.

Polichroniadi, Eleni. 1980. *Greek Embroideries*. Athens: The Benaki Museum.

Raizis, M. Byron. 1972. *Dionysios Solomos*. New York: Twayne Publishers Inc.

Rawlins, Clive. 1997. *Culture Shock! Greece: A Guide to Customs and Etiquette*. Portland, OR: Graphic Arts Center Publishing Company.

Rayor, Diane J. 2014. *Sappho: A New Translation of the Complete Works*. Cambridge: Cambridge University Press.

Rice, Timothy, James Porter, and Chris Goertzen. 2000. *The Garland Encyclopedia of World Music: Volume 8, Europe*. New York and London: Garland Publishing.

Ritsos, Yannis. 1977. *Chronicle of Exile*. Translated by Minas Savvas. San Francisco: Wire Press.

Ritsos, Yannis. 1979. *Ritsos in Parenthesis*. Translated by Edmund Keeley. Princeton, NJ: Princeton University Press.

Romanou, Katy, ed. 2009. *Serbian and Greek Art Music: A Patch to Western Music History*. Bristol and Chicago: Intellect Books.

Rouvelas, Marilyn. 1993. *A Guide to Greek Traditions and Customs in America*. Bethesda, MD: Attica Press.

Sachs, Curt. 2008. *The Rise of Music in the Ancient World, East and West*. New York: Dover Publications.

Samson, Jim. 2013. *Music in the Balkans*. Leiden and Boston: Brill.

Seferis, George. 1964. *Poems*. Translated by Rex Warner. Boston: Little Brown and Company.

Seferis, George. 2014. *Collected Poems: 1924–1955*. Translated by Edmund Keeley and Philip Sherrard. Princeton, NJ: Princeton University Press.

Segal, Charles. 1988. *Sophocles' Tragic World: Divinity, Nature, Society*. Cambridge: First Harvard University Press.

Sheenan, Helen, 2016. *SYRIZA Wave: Surging and Crashing with the Greek Left*. New York: Monthly Review Press.

Sikelianos, Angelos. *Selected Poems*. 1979. Translated by Edmund Keeley and Philip Sherrard. Princeton, NJ: Princeton University Press.

Stavrolakis, Nikolas. 1996. *Cookbook of the Jewish Greeks*. Athens: Lycabettus.

Taylor, C. C. W. 2001. *Socrates: A Very Short Introduction*. Oxford: Oxford University Press.

Thomopoulos, Elaine. 2011. *The History of Greece*. Santa Barbara, CA: Greenwood, an imprint of ABC-CLIO.

Tracy, Stephen V. 2009. *Pericles: A Sourcebook and Reader*. Oakland: University of California Press.

Tragaki, Dafni, ed. 2009. *Made in Greece: Studies in Popular Music*. New York and London: Routledge.

Tragaki, Dafni. 2007. *Rebetiko Worlds: Ethnomusicology and Ethnography in the City*. Newcastle upon Tyne: Cambridge Scholars Publishing.

Triandafyllidou, Anna, and Michaela Maroulof. 2009. "Greece: Immigration at the Eve of the 21st Century. A Critical Assessment." Hellenic Foundation for Europe and Foreign Policy (ELIAMEP). Accessed August 2, 2018. http://www.eliamep.gr/wp-content/uploads/en/2009/10/idea_wp4_greece5.pdf.

Tricha, Lydia. 2009. *Harilaos Trikoupis. A Biographical Journey*. Athens: Ekdoseis Kapon.

Trotter, William R. 1995. *Priest of Music: The Life of Dimitri Mitropoulos*. Portland, OR: Amadeus Press.

Vamvakaris, Markos. 2015. *Markos Vamvakaris: The Man and the Bouzouki, Autobiography*. Edited and translated by Noonie Minogue. London: Greeklines.

Van der Kiste, John. 1994. *Kings of the Hellenes*. Stroud, UK: Sutton.

Van Dyck, Karen, ed. 1988. *Insights Guides: Greece*, 2nd edition. Singapore: APA publication, LTD.

Vasilopoulou, Sofia, and Daphne Halikiopoulou. 2015. *The Golden Dawn's 'Nationalist Solution': Explaining the Rise of the Far Right in Greece*. Basingstoke: Palgrave Macmillan.

Wellesz, Egon. 1949. *A History of Byzantine Music and Hymnography*. Oxford: Clarendon Press.

Woodard, Roger D. 2009. *The Cambridge Companion to Greek Mythology*. The Cambridge Companions Complete Collection. Cambridge: Cambridge University Press.

Woodhouse, C. M. 1985. *The Rise and Fall of the Greek Colonels*. New York: Granada.

Woodhouse, Christopher Montague. 1973. *Capodistria: The Founder of Greek Independence*. Oxford: Oxford University Press.

Woodhouse, Christopher Montague. 1982. *Karamanlis: The Restorer of Greek Democracy.* Oxford: Oxford University Press.

Wycherley, Richard Ernest. 1967. *How the Greeks Built Cities.* London: MacMillan.

Zervas, Theodore G. 2012. *The Making of a Modern Greek Identity: Education, Nationalism and the Teaching of a Greek National Past.* New York: Columbia University Press.

Zervas, Theodore G. 2017. *Formal and Informal Education during the Rise of Greek Nationalism: Learning to Be Greek.* New York and London: Palgrave & Macmillan.

# About the Editor and Contributors

## EDITOR

**Elaine Thomopoulos**, PhD, is the author of *The History of Greece* (Greenwood/ABC-CLIO, 2011). She edited *Greek-American Pioneer Women of Illinois* and wrote three books about local Michigan history (Arcadia). Her articles about Greece and the Greek American experience have appeared in newspapers, magazines, and journals. Thomopoulos has served as managing editor and contributor to "Books" and "Greek American Scientists," supplements of the *National Herald*, a Greek American newspaper. She directed the multiyear projects "Greek-American Women of Illinois" and "The Greeks of Berrien County, Michigan," which included research, lectures, and exhibits. She is curator of the Greek Museum of Berrien County in New Buffalo, Michigan.

## CONTRIBUTORS

**Beatriz Badikian-Gartler**, who received her PhD in English from the University of Illinois at Chicago, has taught at Northwestern University, Loyola University, Roosevelt University, University of Illinois, and Columbia College. She is the author of *Old Gloves: A 20th Century Saga* (Fractal Edge Press, Chicago, 2006), *Mapmaker Revisited* (Gladsome Books, Chicago, 1999), and *Akewa Is a Woman* (March/Abrazo Press, 1983).

**Angelyn Balodimas-Bartolomei**, professor in the School of Education at North Park University, Chicago, received a PhD in comparative international education and policy studies, Loyola University, Chicago. Her research areas include Greek and Italian Americans, Southern Italian Griki, Greek Romaniote Jews, the endangered Colognoro dialect of Tuscany, and Greek diaspora communities.

**Alexander Billinis** is a lawyer, author, and historian. He has lived in Greece, Serbia, the United Kingdom, and the United States. Greek history and geography are his lifelong passions.

**Nikos Christofis**, PhD, associate professor at the College of History and Civilization and at the Center for Turkish Studies at Shaanxi Normal University, Xi'an, China, e-publishes extensively in Greek, English, Turkish, and Chinese. His research focuses on comparative historical analysis, comparative politics and ideologies, and foreign policy.

**Harriette Condes-Zervakis**, retired secondary school administrator, has written articles and presented lectures on topics that vary from Greek traditions to school reform. Her master's thesis focused on the use of ethnic media during a crisis in the Greek American community. Condes-Zervakis has served as an officer of several Greek American organizations.

**Kosta Dalageorgas**, MA, University of Chicago, has taught at North Park University in Chicago and at Istanbul Aydin and Kadir Has Universities in Istanbul, Turkey, and is currently teaching in the Washington DC area. He assisted in developing the oral history program at the National Hellenic Museum in Chicago.

**Alexander Fatouros**, an artist, writer, and journalist, covers the arts-music-leisure beat. Fatouros has studied at the School of the Art Institute of Chicago and University of Michigan, Ann Arbor. He has an MS, Columbia University in the City of New York, and an MA in humanities, University of Chicago.

**Georgia Giannakopoulou**, PhD, teaches at Deree—The American College of Greece and is an affiliate researcher with the University of Glasgow, Scotland. Her expertise is on sociological theory and the sociology of architecture. Her dissertation was titled "The Representations of Athens as Antiquity and Modernity: 1834 to the Present."

**Susanna M. Hoffman**, PhD, UC Berkeley, is an internationally recognized anthropologist. She is an expert in disaster, cuisine and nutrition, and Indo-European and Mediterranean culture, and author/coauthor of twelve books, including five on food, over forty articles, and two films. Her books include *The Olive and the Caper: Adventures in Greek Cooking* (Workman Publishing Company, 2004).

**Katherine Kalaidis**, PhD, is visiting assistant professor at Loyola University Chicago and the resident scholar at the National Hellenic Museum in Chicago. She holds a doctorate in classics from the University of London and a BA in classics from the University of California, Berkeley. Her academic interests range the span of Greek history from the Archaic Period to modern Greek American identity.

**Marianthe Karanikas**, PhD, is an associate professor in the English Department at Missouri State University, where she teaches professional writing and creative nonfiction. Her essays have appeared in *Mondo Greco* and her book reviews in the *National Herald*. Her poem "Kyra Despina's Prayer" has been featured on Chicago's *Dial-a-Poem*.

**Aphrodite Matsakis**, PhD, is a licensed counseling psychologist and the author of *Growing Up Greek in St. Louis*, as well as twelve books on a variety of psychological topics. She has also written several book chapters and numerous articles on Greek topics.

**Daphne Nicolitsas** is an assistant professor at the University of Crete. Before that, she worked in economic policy–related jobs and in the financial sector. She has an MPhil from the University of Oxford and a PhD from the University of Manchester.

**Nick Poulakis**, PhD, is an ethnomusicologist at the Department of Music Studies at the National and Kapodistrian University of Athens and an adjunct instructor in the Modern Greek Culture Program at the Hellenic Open University. He is the author of *Musicology and Cinema: Critical Approaches to the Music of Modern Greek Films* (Edition Orpheus, 2015).

**Anna Poupou**, PhD, teaches at the Hellenic Open University and at the Theatre Studies Department of the National & Kapodistrian University of Athens. She has coedited *City and Cinema: Theoretical and Methodological Approaches* (Athens: Nissos, 2011), *Athens: World Film Locations* (Bristol: Intellect, 2014), *The Lost Highway of Greek Cinema 1960–1990* (Athens: Nefeli, 2019), and two academic e-books.

**John Psiharis**, whose articles about Greeks have appeared in numerous publications, cofounded Greek-American Community Services and Greek-American Nursing Home Committee. He is the executive director of the Irving Park Community Food Pantry and co-owner of Big Helpers Services, Inc. in Chicago. He wrote *Ya'sou GACS: How Greek-American Community Services Transformed Chicago's Greek Community.*

**Evaggelos Vallianatos** earned a doctorate in history from the University of Wisconsin and did postdoctoral studies in the history of science at Harvard. He worked on Capitol Hill and the U.S. Environmental Protection Agency. He is the author of six books and hundreds of articles. He has also taught at several universities.

**Angeliki Varela** is a lawyer from Greece. Her areas of interest include industrial organization, public policy, and human rights. She has previously served on the editorial board of legal periodicals *University of Pennsylvania Journal of International Law* and *Applications of Public Law* (University of Athens).

**Theodore G. Zervas**, PhD, is professor of education at North Park University in Chicago.. He wrote *The Making of a Modern Greek Identity: Education, Nationalism, and the Teaching of a Greek National Past* (Columbia, 2012), and *Formal and Informal Education during the Rise of Greek Nationalism* (Palgrave & Macmillan, 2016), and coedited *Educating Greek Americans: Historical Perspectives and Contemporary Pathways* (Palgrave & Macmillan, 2020).

# INDEX

Page numbers in *italics* indicate images. Page numbers followed by *t* and *f* indicate tables and figures.

www.ingramcontent.com/pod-product-compliance
Lightning Source LLC
Chambersburg PA
CBHW080410270326
41929CB00018B/2967
*9798765141106*